Hard Rock Mining

MINERAL RIGHTS ON THE PUBLIC DOMAIN

VOLUME ONE
Hard Rock Mining

VOLUME TWO
Mineral Leasing

Hard Rock Mining

Michael Braunstein
Professor of Law
Ohio State University

MINERAL RIGHTS ON THE PUBLIC DOMAIN VOLUME ONE

Anderson Publishing Co. / Cincinnati, Ohio

MINERAL RIGHTS ON THE PUBLIC DOMAIN VOLUME ONE: Hard Rock Mining

© 1987 by Anderson Publishing Co.

Library of Congress Cataloging in Publication Data

Braunstein, Michael, 1947—
    Mineral rights on the public domain/Michael Braunstein.
       p.   cm.
    Contents: v. 1. Hard rock mining.
    ISBN 0-87084-105-X (v. 1)
    1. Mining law—United States—Cases. 2. Mining leases—United
States—Cases. 3. United States—Public lands—Cases. I. Title.
KF1818.B7 1987
346.7304'685—dc19
[347.3064685]
                                                                                 87-27124
                                                                                    CIP

Anderson Publishing Co. / Cincinnati, Ohio

Jean C. Martin, Executive Editor   William A. Burden, Managing Editor

TO ANNE FORD BRAUNSTEIN

Contents

Preface

This casebook is one of a two-volume series dealing with the acquisition of rights to the mineral resources located on the federal public domain. This volume is devoted to the mining law of 1872. The second volume, by Professor Constance Lundberg, deals primarily with the Mineral Leasing Act. We decided to write two relatively small volumes instead of one comprehensive one because we believed that this approach gave the greatest flexibility to our teaching colleagues in planning their natural resources courses. The two volumes together can be taught comfortably in a three hour course, while either of them alone can be used for a two hour course.

Each volume is designed so that it can be used in a variety of ways. For example, this volume, as noted, can stand alone in a two hour course on the mining law. Here at Ohio State I plan to use the book as part of a three-hour survey course that will be about evenly divided between oil and gas and mining law. I will be able to do this by omitting chapters 5, 7, and 9.

The materials also lend themselves to inclusions as supplementary material in the first year property course. In about ten classes, or twenty percent of the first semester of property, chapters 1, 4 and 8 could be covered. These materials give a student a good understanding of the mining law and also are valuable because they provide a practical illustration of many of the concepts that the students learn in future interests and interests in the land of another, including licenses, defeasible fees, easements and profits.

The mining law of 1872 is an arcane subject, but one of significant current importance. I hope that this text will help to shed some light on a difficult area.

Finally, I am indebted to Professor George Gould for his help in the early stages of this project, to the Rocky Mountain Mineral Law Foundation for a grant that funded a portion of this research, and to Kathy Jackson (Wyoming, 1986), Jamie Swenson (Wyoming, 1986) and Perry Sekus (Ohio State, 1990) for the assistance they provided in researching and proofreading this text.

Michael Braunstein
Columbus, Ohio
August 18, 1987

Table of Cases

The principal cases are in italic type. Cases cited or discussed are in roman type. References are to page numbers.

1 ACQUISITION OF RIGHTS IN THE PUBLIC DOMAIN PRIOR TO DISCOVERY

A. Introduction

The mining law establishes a location system for the mineral resources of the federal public domain. Under this system, the prospector obtains title to the minerals she discovers by "locating" a mining claim. The location system is really just a codification of the rule of "finders keepers." No application to or permit from the government is required in order to locate a claim. Rather, the claim is "located" by performing the acts of location specified by the mining law and applicable state law.

The most important prerequisite to a valid mining claim is the discovery of a valuable mineral deposit. In addition to discovery, there are six acts of location that must be performed to perfect a claim. These acts may be divided into three categories. First, are the acts designed to give actual notice of the claim to other prospectors who might be interested in the same land. They are the dual requirements of staking the boundary of the claim and posting a notice of location on the claim. Second, are the acts designed to give constructive notice of the claim. They are dual requirements of recording a certificate of location in the county where the claim is located and filing an affidavit pursuant to the Federal Land Policy and Management Act of 1976 with the Bureau of Land Management. Third, and finally, are the acts of location designed to demonstrate the prospector's good faith intent to develop the claim for its mineral values.

These include the state law requirement of discovery work and the federal law requirement of assessment work. Most commentators would not include assessment work among the acts of location because technically the requirement comes into existence only after a discovery has been made and the location completed. For reasons that will be developed later, however, it makes more sense analytically to consider assessment work with the acts of location.

When all of these acts of location are completed and a valid discovery has been made, the miner acquires a perfected claim. This claim is a property right, and it carries with it full ownership to all of the minerals present within the claim and equitable ownership to the land embraced by the claim. All these rights are acquired without payment of royalty or rent of any kind to the government. If the miner wishes to obtain legal title to the land, he may obtain a "patent" to it. A patent is a deed from the government. If the miner obtains a patent, she is required to pay the government either $2.50 or $5.00 per acre, depending on the type of claim.

The mining law, like the technology of the nineteenth century miner for whom it was designed, is predicated on the existence of surface outcroppings of valuable minerals and, thus, presumes that discovery will be the initiating act of the mining claim. Indeed, the concept of discovery as the initial act of location was so compelling to the drafters of the mining law that no provision was made for the tenure of the miner on the public domain prior to discovery. Thus, a literal reading of the mining law yields the conclusion that in advance of discovery the prospector has no rights in the public domain, not even the right to exclude others from the spot where he is diligently working toward the discovery of minerals. This conclusion follows from the characterization of the prospector by the courts as a licensee of the United States. A license is not an interest in land, and the common law does not protect it from interference either by the grantor or third parties.

It soon became apparent, however, that such a literal reading would eviscerate the mining law since exploration must usually precede discovery of valuable minerals. In response, the courts developed the doctrine of *pedis possessio*.

Pedis possessio means possession by foothold. A classic formulation of the doctrine is found in *Union Oil Co. of California v. Smith*, 249 U.S. 337, 346-47 (1919).

> Aside from the suggested effect of the act of 1903, it is clear that in order to create valid rights or initiate a title as against the United States a discovery of mineral is essential. * * * Nevertheless, section 2319 extends an express invitation to all qualified persons to explore the lands of the United States for valuable mineral deposits, and this and the following sections hold out to one who succeeds in making discovery the promise of a full reward. Those who, being qualified, proceed in good faith to make such explorations and enter peaceably upon vacant lands of the United States for that purpose are not treated as mere trespassers, but as licensees or tenants at will. For since, as a practical matter, exploration must precede the discovery of minerals, and some occupation of the land ordinarily is

necessary for adequate and systematic exploration, legal recognition of the *pedis possessio* of a bona fide and qualified prospector is universally regarded as a necessity. It is held that upon the public domain a miner may hold the place in which he may be working against all others having no better right, and while he remains in possession, diligently working towards discovery, is entitled—at least for a reasonable time—to be protected against forcible, fraudulent, and clandestine intrusions upon his possession.

As you read the material that follows, you should consider why the doctrine of *pedis possessio* is necessary to the orderly development of the mineral wealth contained on the federal public domain, what rights the doctrine confers, against whom these rights may be enforced, how these rights are acquired, their duration and, perhaps most importantly, the abuses to which the doctrine of *pedis possessio* is subject and how the courts have sought to protect the public domain against these abuses.

B. Pedis Possessio: The Requirements in Time and Space

COLE V. RALPH
252 U.S. 286 (1920)

. . . .

Mr. Justice Van Devanter delivered the opinion of the court.

These suits relate to conflicting mining locations in Nevada and are what are commonly called adverse suits. The locations set up on one side are lode and those on the other placer, the former being designated as Salt Lake No. 3, Midas, and Evening Star and the latter as Guy Davis and Homestake. Joseph Ralph is the lode claimant and the other parties are the placer claimants.

. . . These suits were brought in state court in support of the adverse claims, and Ralph, the sole defendant, caused them to be removed to the federal court, the parties being citizens of different States. . . .

. . . .

As a preliminary to considering other contentions it will be helpful to refer to some features of the mineral land laws, Rev. Stat., sections 2318, *et seq.,* about which there can be no controversy, and also to what actually was in dispute at the trial and what not in dispute.

By those laws public lands containing valuable mineral deposits are opened to exploration, occupation and acquisition for mining purposes; and as an inducement to effective exploration the discoverer is given the right to locate a substantial area embracing his discovery, to hold the same and extract the mineral without payment of rent or royalty, so long as he puts one hundred dollars' worth of labor or improvements—called assessment work—upon the claim each year, and to demand and receive a patent at a small sum per acre after he has put five hundred dollars' worth of labor or improvements upon the claim.

In advance of discovery an explorer in actual occupation and diligently searching for mineral is treated as a licensee or tenant at will, and no right can be initiated or acquired through a forcible, fraudulent or clandestine intrusion upon his possession. But if his occupancy be relaxed, or be merely incidental to something other than a diligent search for mineral, and another enters peaceably, and not fraudulently or clandestinely, and makes a mineral discovery and location, the location so made is valid and must be respected accordingly. *Belk v. Meagher*, 104 U.S. 279, 287; *Union Oil Co. v. Smith*, 249 U.S. 337, 346-348, and cases cited.

A location based upon discovery gives an exclusive right of possession and enjoyment, is property in the fullest sense, is subject to sale and other forms of disposal, and so long as it is kept alive by performance of the required annual assessment work prevents any adverse location of the land. *Gwillim v. Donnellan*, 115 U.S. 45, 49; *Swanson v. Sears*, 224 U.S. 180.

While the two kinds of location—lode and placer—differ in some respects, a discovery within the limits of the claim is equally essential to both. But to sustain a lode location the discovery must be of a vein or lode of rock in place bearing valuable mineral (section 2320), and to sustain a placer location it must be of some other form of valuable mineral deposit (section 2329), one such being scattered particles of gold found in the softer covering of the earth. A placer discovery will not sustain a lode location, nor a lode discovery a placer location. As is said by Mr. Lindley [3d edition], section 323, "Gold occurs in veins of rock in place, and when so found the land containing it must be appropriated under the laws applicable to lodes. It is also found in placers, and when so found the land containing it must be appropriated under the laws applicable to placers"; and again, section 419, "It is the mode of occurrence, whether in place or not in place [meaning in rock in place], which determines the manner in which it should be located."

Location is the act or series of acts whereby the boundaries of the claim are marked, etc., but it confers no right in the absence of discovery, both being essential to a valid claim. *Waskey v. Hammer*, 223 U.S. 85, 90-91; *Beals v. Cone*, 27 Colo. 473, 484, 495; *Round Mountain Mining Co. v. Round Mountain Sphinx Mining Co.*, 36 Nev. 543, 560; *New England & Co. Oil Co. v. Congdon*, 152 Cal., 211, 213. Nor does assessment work take the place of discovery, for the requirement relating to such work is in the nature of a condition subsequent to a perfected and valid claim and has "nothing to do with locating or holding a claim before discovery." *Union Oil Co. v. Smith, supra*, p. 350. In practice discovery usually precedes location, and the statute treats it as the initial act. But in the absence of an intervening right it is no objection that the usual and statutory order is reversed. In such a case the location becomes effective from the date of discovery; but in the presence of an intervening right it must remain of no effect. *Creede & Cripple Creek Mining Co. v. Uinta Tunnel Mining Co.*, 196 U.S. 337, 348-351, and cases cited; *Union Oil Co. v. Smith, supra*, p. 347.

When an application for a patent to mineral land is presented at the local land office and an adverse claim is filed in response to the notice required by the statute (section 2325) further proceedings upon the application must be suspended to await the determination by a court of competent jurisdiction of the question whether either party, and, if so, which, has the exclusive right to the possession arising from a valid and subsisting location. A suit appropriate to the occasion must be brought by the adverse claimant, and in that suit each party is deemed an actor and must show his own title, for the suit is "in aid of the land department." If neither establishes the requisite title the judgment must so declare. Rev. Stats., section 2326; Act March 3, 1881, c. 140, 21 Stat. 505; *Jackson v. Roby*, 109 U.S. 440; *Perego v. Dodge*, 163 U.S. 160, 167; *Brown v. Gurney*, 201 U.S. 184, 190; *Healey v. Rupp*, 37 Colo. 25, 28; *Tonopah Fraction Mining Co. v. Douglass*, 123 Fed. Rep. 936, 941. If final judgment be given in favor of either party—whether the applicant for patent or the adverse claimant—he may file in the land office a certified copy of the judgment and then will be entitled, as respects the area awarded to him, to go forward with the patent proceedings and to have the judgment recognized and respected as a binding adjudication of his exclusive right to the possession. . . .

The situation developed by the evidence presented and admissions made in the course of the trial was as follows: At the outset the land was public and unappropriated, and it remained such save as the locations in question or some of them may have changed its status. The lode locations were made, one in 1897 and the other two in 1907, and the placer locations in September, 1913. . . . The principal controversy was over the presence or absence of essential discoveries within the lode locations, it being denied on one hand and affirmed on the other that a vein or lode of rock in place bearing valuable mineral was discovered in each location before the placer locations were made. It was not controverted, but, on the contrary, conceded, that that point of time was the important one in the inquiry. Thus when the presiding judge indicated his view by saying, "My idea is that you can't take advantage of any discoveries made since the placer locations; and I don't believe there can be any dispute about that," counsel for the defendant responded, "No, your Honor, there is none," and on another occasion counsel said, "We are undoubtedly limited to proving that there was a discovery of mineral in place on each of our lode-claims prior to the location of the placer claims." In all particulars other than discovery the regularity and perfection of the lode locations were conceded. Closely connected with the controversy over lode discoveries was another over the applicability and effect of section 2332 of the Revised Statutes, but it will be passed for the moment and separately considered later. As to the placer claims, it was shown that they were based upon adequate discoveries of placer gold within their limits, and counsel for the defendant announced, "We don't deny this ground is of placer character." Their boundaries were properly marked and the requisite notices were posted and certificates recorded. The only questions respecting their validity that were presented and need present mention were, first, whether at the time the placer locations were made the lode locations had become valid and effective claims, thereby precluding any adverse location of the same ground, and next, if the lode locations had not then become valid and effective, whether the placer locations were initiated and made through wrongful intrusions or tresspasses upon any actual possession of the lode claimant. The defendant, as is admitted in his brief in this court, did not claim that any lode or vein was or should be excepted from the placer claims, but only that they were of no effect for the reasons just indicated.

The evidence bearing upon the presence or absence of lode discoveries was conflicting. That for the plaintiffs tended persuasively to show the absence of any such discovery before the placer claims were located, while that for the defendants tended the other way. Separately considered, some portions of the latter were persuasive, but it was not without noticeable infirmities, among them the following: The defendant testified that no ore was ever mined upon any of the lode claims, and that "there was no mineral exposed to the best of my [his] knowledge which would stand the cost of mining, transportation and reduction at a commercial profit." In the circumstances this tended to discredit the asserted discoveries; and of like tendency was his unexplained statement, referring to the claims grouped in this patent application, that "some of them have not a smell of ore, but they can be located and held on the principle of being contiguous to adjacent claims,"—an obviously mistaken view of the law, —and his further statement, referring to vein material particularly relied upon as a discovery, that he "would hate to try to mine it and ship it."

As respects the initiation and working of the placer claims, the plaintiffs' evidence indicated that the locators entered openly, made placer discoveries, performed the requisite acts of location, excavated several shafts in the "wash" from 35 to 57 feet in depth, ran drifts from the bottom along the bed-rock, and mined a considerable amount of placer gold; and that these acts covered a period between two and three months. None of this was contradicted; and there was no evidence that the locators met with any resistance or resorted to any hostile, fraudulent or deceptive acts. But there was evidence of such ownership of buildings, comparatively recent prospecting, and maintenance of a watchman, on the part of the lode claimant as made it a fair question whether he was in actual possession when the placer locators entered. That he was in possession of the buildings and the ground where they stood was made certain, but that he had any actual possession beyond that was reasonably debatable under the evidence.

The buildings were all on the same claim and covered only a part of it. One was a mill formerly in use but then dismantled and stripped of its machinery. All had been used in connection with mining operations upon other claims, but the operations had then been suspended. The buildings were not disturbed by the placer locators, nor was there any attempt to appropriate them. A watchman was in charge, but so far as appears he made no objection to what was done. Although a witness for the defendant and in his employ, he was not interrogated upon this point. Of course, ownership of the buildings did not in itself give the lode claimant any right in the land or prevent others from entering peaceably and in good faith to avail themselves of privileges accorded by the mineral land laws; but the presence of the buildings and his relation to them did have a bearing upon the question of actual possession—a pronounced bearing as respects the place where the buildings stood and a lesser bearing as respects the other ground.

Even if the lode claimant was in actual possession of all, it still was a disputable question under the evidence whether there had not been such acquiescence in the acts of the placer locators in going upon the ground, making placer discoveries and marking their locations as gave them the status of lawful discoverers and locators rather than wrongful intruders or trespassers, that is to say, the status of explorers entering by permission and then making discoveries. See *Crossman v. Pendery*, 8 Fed. Rep. 693.

The questions of fact to which we have adverted were all submitted to the jury under a charge which was comprehensive, couched in plain terms, and in substantial accord with the legal principles hereinbefore stated. And, while the defendant criticizes some portions of the charge, we think they neither included nor omitted anything of which he rightly can complain. As has been said, the jury returned general verdicts for the plaintiffs, and also special verdicts finding that no lode had been discovered within any of the lode locations before the placer ones were made.

. . . .

What we have said sufficiently disposes of all questions other than that before mentioned respecting the applicability and effect of section 2332 of the Revised Statutes, which provides: "Where such person or association, they and their grantors, have held and worked their claims for a period equal to the time prescribed by the statute of limitations for mining-claims of the State or Territory where the same may be situated, evidence of such possession and working of the claims for such period shall be sufficient to establish a right to a patent thereto under this chapter, in the absence of any adverse claim."

The defendant, conceiving that the section could be invoked in the absence of a mineral discovery, requested the court to instruct the jury that if the lode claimant held and worked the lode claims for a period of two years—the local prescriptive period for adverse possession, Rev. Laws, 1912, section 4951,— before the placer claims were initiated, such holding and working were the full equivalent of all that was essential to the validity of the lode claims, including discovery. That request was refused and others were then presented which differed from it only in that they treated discovery as essential by coupling it with holding and working. These were also refused, but no complaint is made of this,—obviously because the jury were told that under the evidence the lode claims should be regarded as valid, if only the requisite discoveries were made at any time before the placer claims were initiated. The jury, as we have seen, found as matter of fact that there was no such discovery.

The effect which must be given to section 2332 in circumstances such as are here disclosed—whether it substitutes something else in the place of discovery or cures its absence—is the matter we have to consider. That the section is a remedial provision and designed to make proof of holding and working for the prescribed period the legal equivalent of proof of acts of location, recording and transfer, and thereby to relieve against possible loss or destruction of the usual means of establishing such acts, is attested by repeated rulings in the land department and the courts. But those rulings give no warrant for thinking that it disturbs or qualifies important provisions of the mineral land laws, such as deal with the character of the land that may be taken, the discovery upon which a claim must be founded, the area that may be included in a single claim, the citizenship of claimants, the amount that must be expended in labor or improvements to entitle the claimant to a patent, and the purchase price to be paid before the patent can be issued. Indeed, the rulings have been to the contrary.

The view entertained and applied in the land department is shown in the following excerpt from a decision by the Secretary of the Interior: "One purpose of section 2332, ... clearly shown in the history of the proceedings in Congress attending its consideration and passage there, was to lessen the burden of proving the location and transfers of old claims concerning which the possessory right was not controverted but the record title to which had in many instances been destroyed by fire or otherwise lost because of the insecurity and difficulty necessarily attending its preservation during the early days of mining operations. . . .

"The section was not intended as enacted, nor as now found in the Revised Statutes, to be a wholly seperate and independent provision for the patenting of a mining claim. As carried forward into the Revised Statutes it relates to both lode and placer claims, and being in pari materia with the other sections of the Revision concerning such claims is to be construed together with them, and so, if possible, that they may all stand together, forming a harmonious body of mining law." *Barklage v. Russell,* 29 L.D. 401, 405-406.

The views entertained by the courts in the mining regions are shown in *Harris-v. Equator Mining Co.,* 8 Fed. Rep. 863, 866, where the court ruled that holding and working a claim for a long period were the equivalent of necessary acts of location, but added that "this, of course, was subject to proof of a lode in the Ocean Wave ground, of which there was evidence"; in *Humphreys v. Idaho Gold Mines Co.,* 21 Idaho 126, 140, where the section was held to obviate the necessity for proving the posting, etc., of a location notice, but not to dispense with proof of discovery; in *Upton v. Santa Rita Mining Co.,* 14 N. Mex. 96, where the court held that the section should be construed in connection with other provisions of the mineral land laws, and that it did not relieve a claimant coming within its terms from continuing to do the assessment work required by another section; and in *Anthony v. Jillson,* 83 California 296, where the section was held not to change the class who may acquire mineral lands or to dispense with proof of citizenship.

As respects discovery, the section itself indicates that no change was intended. Its words, "have held and worked their claims," presuppose a discovery; for to "work" a mining claim is to do something toward making it productive, such as developing or extracting an ore body after it has been discovered. Certainly it was not intended that a right to a patent could be founded upon nothing more than holding and prospecting, for that would subject non-mineral land to acquisition as a mining claim. Here, as the verdicts show, there was no discovery, so the working relied upon could not have been of the character contemplated by Congress.

The defendant places some reliance upon the decisions of this court in *Belk v. Meagher,* 104 U.S. 279, and *Reavis v. Fianza,* 215 U.S. 16, but neither contains any statement or suggestion that the section dispenses with a mineral discovery or cures its absence. The opinion in the first shows affirmatively that there was a discovery and that in the other shows that the controversy, although of recent origin, related to "gold mines" which had been worked for many years.

The only real divergence of opinion respecting the section has been as to whether it is available in an adverse suit, such as these are, or is addressed merely to the land department. Some of the courts have held it available only in proceedings in the department, *McCowan v. Maclay*, 16 Montana 234, and others in greater number have held it available in adverse suits. *Upton v. Santa Rita Mining Co., supra*, and cases cited. The latter view has received the approval of this court. *Reavis v. Fianza, supra; Belk v. Meagher, supra.*

We conclude that the defendant was not entitled to any instruction whereby he could receive the benefit of section 2332 in the absence of a discovery, and therefore that the District Court rightly refused to give the one in question. The Circuit Court of Appeals held that the instruction should have been given, and in this we think it erred.

Judgments of Circuit Court of Appeals reversed. Judgments of District Court affirmed.

NOTES

1. As the Supreme Court notes in the principal case, the prospector on the public domain prior to discovery is treated as a licensee or tenant at will of the United States. These characterizations are not strictly accurate. A licensee is not protected against interference by the grantor or by third parties. The whole purpose of the doctrine of pedis possessio, however, is to grant the prospector at least a limited protection against rival claimants. Nor is the prospector prior to discovery really a tenant at will. A tenant at will, like any other tenant, has an exclusive right to possession as against the whole world. This right to possession does not depend on the tenant being in actual occupancy of the demised premises. Even while the tenant is away from the demised premises he still has the exclusive right to possess them. Pedis possessio rights, on the other hand, are lost if actual occupancy is relaxed or abandoned.

These characterizations do serve, however, to highlight an important aspect of the doctrine of pedis possessio. It confers no rights on the prospector that are enforceable against the United States. At any time prior to discovery the United States can withdraw the land on which the prospector is searching for minerals and thereby terminate his right to possess that land.

On occasion, Congress has seen fit to grant greater protection to the prospector than is conferred by the judicial doctrine of pedis possessio. Thus, the Pickett Act, 36 Stat. 847, ch 421 (1910) provides:

> . . . the rights of any person who, at the date of any order of withdrawl heretofore or hereafter made, is the bona fide occupant or claimant of oil or gas bearing lands, and who, at such date, is in diligent prosecution of work leading to the discovery of oil or gas, shall not be affected or impaired by such order, so long as such

occupant or claimant shall continue in diligent prosecution of said work.

Provisions such as this substantially enhance the status of the prospector on the public lands prior to discovery. *See United States v. Grass Creek Oil Co.*, 236 F. 481 (8th Cir. 1916); *United States v. Stockton Midway Oil Co.*, 240 F. 1006 (S.D. Cal. 1917). Such provisions, however, are rare.

2. The Forest Reservation Act of 1897, 30 Stat. 36, provided that people owning lands within areas designated as National Forest could exchange their National Forest lands for other vacant unappropriated lands owned by the United States. The purpose of the Act was to eliminate "in holdings" from the National Forest. If someone owning lands within a National Forest desired to exchange them for lands outside of the forest but on which a prospector had previously acquired pedis possessio rights should the prospector or the in-holder prevail? In a case such as this, is the prospector attempting to assert pedis possessio rights against the United States, in which case he must fail, or against the in-holder, in which case he ought to succeed? *See Cosmos Exploration Co. v. Gray Eagle Oil Co.*, 112 F. 4 (9th Cir. 1901).

3. On what specific facts did Ralph (the lode claimant) base his claim to possession? Does the Supreme Court hold as a matter of law that these facts are insufficient to entitle Ralph to the protection of the doctrine of pedis possessio? Since it is admitted that Cole, the junior claimant, entered peacefully, is it possible that Ralph could also have been in actual possession at the time of Cole's entry? Why does the court think it necessary to reach the issue of whether Ralph acquiesced in Cole's entry?

4. When the courts speak of the "actual possession" requirement of pedis possessio, what do they mean? Will anything less than 24 hours a day, 365 days a year presence be required? Based on your answers to the questions contained in note 3 can you articulate an argument against such a literal construction of the "actual possession" requirement?

5. If, as the court concedes, Ralph was in actual possession of a part of the disputed claim, i.e., the part on which his buildings stood, why did Ralph not prevail in the law suit with Cole?

6. How far, in terms of space, does the protection of pedis possessio extend? Should the miner be protected only in the area where he is actually working, or should the protection extend to his whole claim, or to a whole area? What if he has not yet decided exactly where he wants to locate his claim on the ground?

7. What was the gist of Ralph's § 2332 argument? Why did the court reject this argument and what implications would it have had for the mining law if the court had accepted Ralph's interpretation of § 2332?

ADAMS V. BENEDICT
327 P. 2d 308 (N.M. 1958)

PAYNE, District Judge.

This is an appeal from a judgment or decree wherein Russell Benedict, Paul Coupey and the Sombrero Uranium Company were the defendants and were also counter-claimants; and Henry C. Adams and G. R. Kennedy were the plaintiffs and also counter-defendants. Judgment was rendered for the plaintiffs on their complaint and this appeal followed by the defendants. Hence the defendants will be referred to as appellants and the plaintiffs as the appellees.

The case was tried without a jury and findings of fact and conclusions of law were duly filed in the case.

The appellees' complaint was in the nature of a suit to quiet title to twenty-six unpatented lode mining claims in McKinley County and a petition for a restraining order against the appellants, to restrain them from interfering with the asserted possession of the premises involved. The claims consisted of three groups known as the Tomcat, Pool and Bulldog.

The appellants filed an answer and counter-claim in which they asserted a possessory right to a certain unpatented lode mining claim known as the Sombrero No. 1. The Court found the issues in favor of the appellees and quieted the title to the three groups of claims described in the complaint.

This appeal concerns only the mining claim of the appellants, known as the Sombrero No. 1, which conflicts with the appellees' claim known as the Bulldog No. 5. The opinion in this appeal will be limited to the two claims mentioned, since the appellants did not challenge the correctness of the judgment or decree as to the other claims, and since the appellants made no claim to the other property involved in the suit.

In the summer or fall of 1955, the appellees' predecessors in interest staked out their mining claims, which included the Bulldog No. 5, and posted location notices on them; copies were filed in the office of the county clerk of McKinley County. The notices were amended in the fall of 1955, the one covering the Bulldog No. 5 being amended about October 30, 1955. Conveyances were thereafter made to appellees to these purported claims including the Bulldog No. 5. The purported location work consisted of placing four inch by four inch posts at the corner of each claim, posting the notices thereon, and in some instances the digging of discovery holes. The court found that a discovery hole was dug on each claim, including the Bulldog No. 5, by the appellees or their predecessors in interest. This finding was supported by a statement of one witness to the effect that it had been reported to him by an employee that pits were dug on each claim by a bulldozer; but he was unable to verify this or to testify from his own knowledge that there was a pit on Bulldog No. 5. There are the positive statements of at least two witnesses that there were no pits on Bulldog No. 5 up to the date of the filing of the complaint, and we doubt that the findings of the trial court with respect to Bulldog No. 5 were supported by any substantial evidence.

In any event, it was conceded by everyone, on oral argument, before this court, that there was no pit which exposed mineral in place on Bulldog No. 5 at the time of the controversy. The evidence showed that the veins or bodies of uranium were approximately two thousand feet below the surface of the earth, and that no ten foot discovery pit would avail to expose mineral in place.

The pits which were dug on any of the claims, other than the drill holes hereinafter mentioned, were done in the late fall of 1955.

The testimony at the trial was not confined to the two claims in contest, but evidence was introduced concerning activities of the appellees on other claims in the groups described in the complaint in an effort to show that, by an over all plan of action, work was being done looking to the development of all of the claims which would eventually include the Bulldog No. 5.

Whatever the economic reasons may be for following this over all plan of procedure, outlined by the appellees, this court is faced with the application of the existing law to the claim in question. We believe that it is fundamental law that a discovery must be made within the boundaries of the claim in order to make the location valid. We also believe that the statutory provisions requiring a discovery pit on each individual claim is a necessity to perfect the location.

In 30 U.S.C.A. § 23, Congress has provided, among other things:

"but no location of a mining claim shall be made until the discovery of the vein or lode within the limits of the claim located."

The words "vein or lode" mentioned in this sentence refer back to a previous sentence in the section with regard to:

"Veins or lodes of quartz or other rock in place bearing gold, silver, cinnabar, lead, tin, copper, or other valuable deposits."

The appellees entered into working agreements with several other concerns by which several sections of public domain were included in a program for the development of uranium and intended to expend large sums of money over said areas. Tests for uranium had been made with geiger counters, scintillators, and electronic devices, to which tests there were "favorable reactions" or "pretty nice readings" on the surface. This was a general finding and was not confined to any specific claim or locality so far as the record shows. An organized system of drilling was commenced whereby nine holes had already been drilled in various places on appellees' claims. In April 1957, a drilling rig was being operated on appellees' land in the same section in which the Bulldog No. 5 claim was situated, but no drilling had been done on this claim.

Although it is not in the trial court's finding, there is testimony to the effect that sometime immediately prior to the event hereinafter related, the appellees had placed a stake with a red flag on Bulldog No. 5 as an indication of the spot where appellees intended to drill a discovery hole on the claim. The appellants denied that the stake and flag were on the premises when they took possession.

The Sombrero corporation, one of the appellants, obtained a quitclaim deed to twenty-three purported unpatented lode mining claims from a third party, which included, with other property, the same area as the Bulldog No. 5 and appellants' Sombrero No. 1. The location notices were never recorded and there was no evidence to establish what, if anything, was done in connection with these locations. Evidently the appellants do not base their claims on these locations, but rather on possessory rights under the doctrine of *pedis possessio.*

On April 16, 1957, the appellants moved a large drilling rig onto Bulldog No. 4, which joined the Bulldog No. 5. This rig was observed by some of the appellees' employees and pursuant thereto they drove to Grants, New Mexico, the next morning and phoned the attorneys for the appellees. Following this conversation the employees for appellees returned to Bulldog No. 4 sometime before noon of April 17th, and advised Mr. Benedict that the appellees claimed the property in question. At this time there was no machinery belonging to the appellees on the property, and no steps had been taken at that time to do any development work whatsoever, unless it is conceded that a stake with a red flag had been placed on the premises as claimed by appellees which is not in the court's findings and which is a disputed question.

About noon of April 17th, the appellants' drill rig was moved onto Bulldog No. 5, and they started making preparations to drill on the premises. They placed two posts on the northern end of their proposed Sombrero No. 1, but had not yet had time to place the posts at the southern corners.

At about 1:30 in the morning of April 18th, appellees' employees or agents arrived at the scene in a car followed by a bulldozer. They were stopped by appellant Benedict somewhere within the boundaries of appellants' proposed claim. Mr. Benedict protested their entry and stood in front of the bulldozer. The bulldozer was started up and carried Mr. Benedict along for some 25 to 50 yards, when it stopped. Mr. Benedict vigorously protested and resisted the entry of the bulldozer, but he was removed from in front of it and it then went in and prepared a site for the drilling rig of appellees.

Mr. Benedict then departed from the scene of action and left a Mr. Horner in charge of his operations. When the drilling rig, belonging to, or operated by, the appellees came in the next morning, Mr. Horner stood in the way and resisted its entry. The parties in charge of the drilling rig compelled him to move out of the way, although he also protested and resisted. The drilling rig was then driven onto the claim and started drilling the morning of the 18th. The appellants' drill rig also started up on the morning of the 18th, so that both drilling rigs started the same morning. In other words their actual commencement of operations was simultaneous. The appellees completed their drilling before the appellants did, but each of them continued drilling from the time they started until they each discovered uranium ore. In other words each of them actively continued in drilling operations from the morning of the 18th until each of them had completed a discovery hole.

This court must first determine whether or not there was substantial evidence to support a suit to quiet title as to the Bulldog No. 5 claim. Secondly, if we should find that the evidence was insufficient to support a suit to quiet title, it must then be determined which of the parties is entitled to possession of the premises under the doctrine of pedis possessio.

It is fundamental law in New Mexico that in a suit to quiet title the plaintiff must recover on the strength of his own title, and not on the weakness of the title of his adversary.

. . . .

It is our conclusion that the purported location by the appellees was never perfected and the right to quiet title to the claim was not sustained. For that reason it leaves the bare question of who has the right to possession of the mining claim. It seems to us that it is not necessary to decide what constitutes a discovery of uranium in order to decide the question of right to possession. The matter resolves itself into a question of the right of possession under the doctrine of pedis possessio for the reason that the appellants entered before the appellees had completed their discovery work.

There is an expressed invitation in the federal statues to all qualified persons to go upon the land in question to explore for valuable mineral deposits. This exploration work, naturally, precedes the discovery of minerals. This right is explained in *Union Oil Co. v. Smith*, 249 U.S. 337, . . . as follows:

. . . .

> Whatever the nature and extent of a possessory right before discovery, all authorities agree that such possession may be maintained only by continued actual occupancy by a qualified locator or his representative engaged in persistent and diligent prosecution of work looking to the discovery of mineral.
>
> . . . .

It is recognized that no right can be initiated on the public domain by a forcible or fraudulent entry even if the person in possession has an invalid claim. But this rule does not prevent a peaceable entry by a prospector when the first occupant has made a valid location.

This rule is stated in *Thallmann v. Thomas*, 8 Cir., 111 F. 277, 279, as follows:

. . . .

> "But every competent locator has the right to initiate a lawful claim to unappropriated public land by a peaceable adverse entry upon it while it is in the possession of those who have no superior right to acquire the title or to hold the possession."

The case of *Walsh v. Henry*, 38 Colo. 393, 88 P. 449, 450, is an instance where the claim of the first occupant was invalid because of the fact that his discovery cut had not been made and the time for making it had expired. The fact that the second occupant knew of the prior claim and that the land had been surveyed did not matter. The Court said:

> "If defendant's location was invalid because of the absence of a discovery cut, at the time plaintiff made peaceable entry, then the territory within the boundaries of defendant's claim was at the time open to location under the mining laws, and plaintiff could lawfully initiate his location within the boundaries of the Iva C. claim, irrespective of what his belief was as to territory being unoccupied and unappropriated (Lindley on Mines, Vol. 1, § 219); and, if the Iva C. location was invalid for such reason, it was immaterial to the validity of plaintiff's location that plaintiff knew that the claim of defendant had been surveyed for patent, and the boundaries had been marked on the ground, and that situs of the claim was known to him, and that the defendant had posted his patent plats and notices. If the location of

defendant was invalid for the reasons assigned, plaintiff was not a trespasser when he attempted to initiate his location therein."

Although we have not ruled on the question of the validity of the claimed discovery by the appellees, they would be in the same position as one who was in possession without a discovery insofar as intervening rights are concerned. This follows as a result of their failure to perfect their claim. For that reason the statement of the United States Supreme Court in *Cole v. Ralph*, 252 U.S. 286, 40 S.Ct. 321, 325, 64 L.Ed. 567, would be applicable. In that the court said:

> "In advance of discovery an explorer in actual occupation and diligently searching for mineral is treated as a licensee or tenant at will, and no right can be initiated or acquired through a forcible, fraudulent, or clandestine intrusion upon his possession. But if his occupancy be relaxed, or be merely incidental to something other than a diligent search for mineral, and another enters peaceably, and not fraudulently or clandestinely, and makes a mineral discovery and location, the location so made is valid and must be respected accordingly."

In the case at bar the appellees were not and had not been engaged in "persistent and diligent prosecution of work looking to the discovery of mineral" on the Bulldog No. 5 claim. Nor had they been in actual, continued possession of it within the meaning of the rules laid down above. The work done on other claims does not supply the requirement. The law requires a discovery and the requisite location acts on each claim. Likewise, the possession of each claim, where no valid location has been perfected within the statutory time, must be protected by actual occupation of that identical claim and the diligent and persistent exploratory work thereon. If the occupation is relaxed under those circumstances, another may take possession of the claim if he can do so peaceably. The occupation of the second occupant, in that event, will be protected so long as he abides by this same rule.

As hereinabove stated the appellees filed their amended location in the fall of 1955. No work had been done on the claim thereafter until the date of the entry by the appellants with the possible exception of posting a red flag on the claim to mark the site where work was to be done at a later time. The appellants entered peaceably. Any knowledge they had of an overall plan for the development of the area is immaterial. Nor did the knowledge that the claim had been staked out prevent appellants from entering. *Walsh v. Henry, supra.* Even though they were told that someone else claimed the land before the entry, it did not prevent them from taking legal possession. To hold otherwise would allow a person to hold vast amounts of land by merely claiming it without doing the work required by the rules laid down above. It would encourage speculation and would not allow the orderly filing of mining claims anticipated by the law.

Now turning to the entry made by the appellees, we find that it was made forcibly, as above stated. The record shows that Mr. Benedict stood in front of the vehicles being brought onto the premises by the appellees. He vigorously resisted the entry of the vehicles, but to no avail. Later one of the appellants' employees resisted the entry of the well rig, but it went ahead despite his protest and resistance. These entries were forcible and did not establish any rights against the claim made by appellants. It was only when a court order was entered that the appellants relaxed their occupation and allowed the appellees to come upon the premises. This entry was not within the rules laid down above and did not establish any rights on the part of the appellees.

The only question remaining is the extent of the land that can be held by the appellants.

It has been held in some cases that the right of a lode claimant on vacant unappropriated land before the discovery of minerals is confined solely to the land upon which he is conducting his explorations. *Gemmel v. Swain,* 28 Mont. 331, 72 P. 662.

In a number of cases where a placer claim was involved and where the prospector was seeking oil, the courts have arrived at a different conclusion. In those cases several courts have held that the prospector who was actually in possession of a claim and actively and diligently conducting exploratory work, with full intent to make a location if oil was found, would be protected in his possession of the claim he was seeking to locate. It seems that the courts, in those cases, have taken a position that oil is usually located at a great depth below the surface of the earth, and that it is necessary to drill a hole in order to make a discovery. In order to preserve the peace and to provide for the orderly location of such placer claims the courts have, in several instances, taken the position that the prospector was entitled to possession of the full claim he was intending to locate, during the time that he was diligently engaged in an effort to make a discovery of oil. This rule was recognized by the Supreme Court of the United States as being the law in California. In the case of *Union Oil Co. of California v. Smith,* 249 U.S. 337, 39 S.Ct. 308, 310, 63 L.Ed. 635, the Supreme Court stated as follows:

> In the California courts the right of a locator before discovery while in possession of his claim and prosecuting exploration work is recognized as a substantial interest, extending not only as far as the pedis possessio but to the limits of the claim as located; so that if a duly qualified person peaceably and in good faith enters upon vacant lands of the United States prior to discovery but for the purpose of discovering oil or other valuable mineral deposits, there being no valid mineral location upon it, such person has the right to maintain possession as against violent, fraudulent, and surreptitious intrusions so long as he continues to occupy the land to the exclusion of others and diligently and in good faith prosecutes the work of endeavoring to discover mineral theron . . . .

It was conceded by all parties in the case at bar that the uranium was approximately two thousand feet below the surface of the earth, and that the only knowledge of any one were indications that there was uranium which indications were taken from readings on electrical instruments used by uranium miners. The appellees claimed it amounted to a discovery on their part in connection with their Bulldog No. 5 claim. The appellants did not plead a discovery for the reason that their theory of the case was that such indications did not amount to a discovery. We need not pass on this point in the light of what has been said above. We merely point it out to explain that the appellants merely prayed for possession of the premises involved. The pleadings and the proof indicated that the appellants had posted a location notice on the ground and had placed monuments on the north end of the claim at the time of the controversy, but had not yet had time to place their monuments on the south end of the claim. Both appellants and appellees have drilled their holes exposing mineral in place at an approximate depth of two thousand feet.

It is our opinion that the rule which has been applied with regard to the placer claims, where the prospectors were hunting for oil presents a situation very similar to this case, even though it is a lode claim. Whether or not a discovery could be made before the hole was drilled, there is no question that the exposing of mineral in place would require the drilling of the holes as was done by the appellants and appellees. Since the appellants had taken peaceful possession of the premises and since they were actively and diligently working on the claim with bona fide intent to make a location, their right to possession of the claim described in the notice of location and as partly marked on the ground, should be protected. This court is not taking the position that such acts constitute a valid location without a discovery. We merely state that when a person is prospecting for uranium ore which lies at a great depth below the surface of the earth and where he has peacefully taken possession of the premises and is in actual possession, diligently and persistently drilling a hole in an attempt to disclose uranium in place, he should be protected in his possession to the full extent of his proposed claim as against someone with no better right.

It is to be understood that the court does not countenance a prospector taking possession of land in a case such as this without a discovery and holding it indefinitely without going forward with his work. He may hold it only for such time as he is diligently and persistently conducting his operations in good faith with the intent to make a discovery of mineral. . . .

. . . .

Accordingly the judgment of the district court insofar as it affects appellants' claim is reversed with instructions to set aside its judgment or decree and enter a judgment or decree in favor of the appellants, . . .

It is so ordered.

Appellees have filed a motion to dismiss this appeal. We find it without merit and it is denied.

LUJAN, C.J., and McGHEE and COMPTON, JJ., concur.

SADLER, J., not participating.

NOTES

1. On the morning of April 17 Appellees consulted their attorney with reference to the dispute involved in the principal case. If a similar situation arose now and *Adams v. Benedict* was the only relevant authority in your jurisdiction, what advice would you give?

2. "The essential elements of the doctrine [of pedis possessio] which must be satisfied for it to apply to any intended claim were established in older cases, but they have been reaffirmed without diminution by the recent ones. It is necessary that they all be satisfied simultaneously and continuously for a claimant to be afforded the benefits of the concept. The absence of any element terminates the effect of the doctrine upon a claim, and the prospector is reduced to the position of any other competing claimant. While such protection is absent, any party may enter and validly locate a claim, regardless of the vigor with which the first claimant maintains all of the other elements.

There are three of these basic requirements:

(1) Actual physical occupancy of the ground.

(2) Diligent, bona fide work directed toward making a discovery.

(3) Exclusion of others.

It has been indicated that these elements and the resulting status of pedis possessio may exist for only a reasonable period of time [citing *Adams v. Benedict*]. However, there do not appear to be any reported cases in which the reasonableness of the time was an issue."

Fiske, *Pedis Possessio—Modern Use of an Old Concept*, 15 Rocky Mtn. Min. L. Inst. 181, 190-91 (1969) (footnotes omitted).

3. Is the definition of actual occupancy in *Adams v. Benedict* more rigorous than in *Cole v. Ralph*? Does *Adams v. Benedict* require 24 hour per day 365 days per year occupancy? In answering this question consider whether the court would have reached the same result in *Adams v. Benedict* if plaintiff's reentry in that case had not been resisted by Benedict.

4. Should a concept of reasonableness be read into the definition of actual possession? For example, should actual occupancy be required during the winter months when the weather makes productive mining activity impracticable? What if the land is under water or located in a steep ravine, or otherwise situated so as to makes continuous actual occupancy impracticable? *See generally, Ritter v. Lynch,* 123 F. 930, 934 (Nev. Cir. 1903).

5. If it is conceded that the doctrine of pedis possessio ought to be defined in such a way as to minimize the threat of violence on the public domain, then should the emphasis be on diligent exploration, which by definition must involve actual although not necessarily continuous occupation, or should the emphasis be on "exclusion of others?" Which element does *Cole v. Ralph* stress? What about *Adams v. Benedict?* Which view is least likely to lead to violence. Which is most likely to encourage mining companies to patrol large areas of the public domain with "private armies," thereby insuring that no entry can be made by any other party except forcefully?

6. To satisfy the "exclusion of others" requirement of pedis possessio, is it enough to say "get off, or I'll sue," or is physical confrontation or the threat of physical confrontation required? In *Adams v. Benedict,* Plaintiff advised defendant prior to defendant's entry that plaintiff claimed the land in question. Why, in the court's view was this not enough to make the defendant's entry forceful? Should this be enough?

7. What if, while the senior locator is sleeping in his cabin located on his claim, a junior locator jumps the claim? Can the junior locator acquire any rights in the public domain in this manner? What if the senior locator, on discovering the junior locator's entry, does nothing? What if the senior locator, on discovering the junior locator's entry, threatens suit if the junior locator does not leave? What if after threatening suit the senior locator does not actually commence the suit within a reasonable time? *See Sparks v. Mount,* 29 Wyo. 1, 207 P. 1099 (1922).

8. If pedis possessio is viewed as a revocable property right, then it is not surprising that, like other property rights, it may be alienated. "One who thus in good faith makes his location, remains in possession, and with due diligence prosecutes his work toward a discovery, is fully protected against all forms of forcible, fraudulent, surreptitious, or clandestine entries and intrusions upon his possession. They [the locators] have, then, this right of possession, and with it the right to protect their possession against all illegal intrusions, and to work the land for the valuable minerals it is thought to contain. We cannot conceive why these rights may not in good faith be made the subject of a conveyance . . . as well before discovery as after." *Weed v. Snook,* 144 Cal. 439, 77 P. 1023, 1025 (1904). If pedis possessio rights may be sold, as *Weed v. Snook* indicates, does it also follow that they may be leased? *See United Western Minerals Co.. v. Hannsen,* 147 Colo. 272, 363 P. 2d 677 (1961). Is anything more required to transfer pedis possessio rights than to transfer other property rights?

MACGUIRE V. STURGIS
347 F. Supp. 580 (D. Wyo. 1971)

[MacGuire and Sturgis located a series of overlapping uranium claims in Convers County, Wyoming. Although the decision is ambiguous, Sturgis was probably the senior locator. After Sturgis had located his claims, MacGuire entered the land peaceably and not fraudulently. Thereafter, Sturgis repeatedly attempted to reenter the land, but each attempt was rebuffled by MacGuire. In order to end these repeated attempts by Sturgis, MacGuire finally brought suit for a declaratory judgment. At issue were approximately 1800 lode claims (approximately 36,000 acres) claimed by MacGuire. The court found that MacGuire was not in actual occupancy of all the claims and that, although MacGuire did have a "systematic" development plan for the area, neither was he diligently engaged in exploration on all of the claims. Nevertheless, the court found for MacGuire holding as follows:]

. . . . .

CONCLUSIONS OF LAW

8. Plaintiff's entry onto the land covered by the MacGuire claims was peaceable and not fraudulent or clandestine, and plaintiff is presently entitled to the exclusive possession thereof on a group or area basis where, as here, the following exists or was due for his benefit: (a) the geology of the area claimed is similar and the size of the area claimed is reasonable; (b) the discovery (validation) work referred to in Wyo.Stat. § 30-6 (1957) is completed; (c) an

overall work program is in effect for the area claimed; (d) such work program is being diligently pursued, i.e., a significant number of exploratory holes have been systematically drilled; and (e) the nature of the mineral claimed and the cost of development would make it economically impracticable to develop the mineral if the locator is awarded only those claims on which he is actually present and currently working. Plaintiff is entitled to the future exclusive possession thereof so long as he, or his successors in title, remain in possession thereof, working diligently towards a discovery.

NOTES

1. The court cited no authority in *MacGuire v. Sturgis* for its holding that either the Mining Law of 1872 or any of the decisions construing it contemplate that *pedis possessio* may be applied on a group or area basis. Nor does the decision set forth in any detail the competing policy arguments. The best exposition of the policy arguments favoring expansion of *pedis possessio* to a group claim basis is contained in Fiske, *Pedis Possessio—Modern Use of an Old Concept*, 15 Rocky Mtn. Min. L. Inst. 181, 190-91 (1969) (In fact the test adopted by the Wyoming district court in MacGuire is almost identical to that proposed by Fiske in his article.) Evaluate the arguments put forward by Fiske in favor of expanding *pedis possessio* in light of the arguments accepted by the courts in the *Geomet* and *Ranchers* cases, which follow, against expanding the doctrine.

. . .

Pedis Possessio

Reference should again be made to that basic principle of the General Mining Law of encouragement of exploration. Effective exploration for significant deposits of uranium at considerable depth, for example, probably can be conducted only over a wide area during an extended period of time, according to a comprehensive technological plan. The party engaged in such operations must be assured of some protection so that when, and if, the deposit is located by such means, the benefits will be his, wherever within that wide area the deposit may lie, rather than appropriated by others taking advantage of his efforts and interest. Otherwise, that party cannot justify the high pre-discovery expense and commitment of time and skilled personnel. This would be true particularly for areas and deposits of marginal profitability which might otherwise go undeveloped. To require a rigid adherence to outmoded, physical means of satisfaction of pedis possessio could effectively serve to discourage this type of necessary exploration. A requirement now for the type of activity which at one time was appropriate for exploration for other types of minerals could very well prevent exploration for many minerals so much in demand today. Therefore, much more liberal application of pedis possessio may be more in keeping with the fundamental purpose of the General Mining Law than the traditional means of satisfying the doctrine.

Fiske, *Pedis Possessio: Modern Use of an Old Concept,* 15 Rocky Mtn. Min. L. Inst. 181, 210-11 (1969).

2. The continuing debate over the proper scope of the doctrine of pedis possessio is worthy of consideration not just for what it teaches about this area of the mining law, but also for what it teaches about the mining law as a whole. The mining law of 1872, now over a hundred years old is the subject of a procrustean conflict. On the one hand, it is being stretched by the mining industry in an effort to accomodate the law to the reality of contemporary mining practices and contemporary mineral needs. A law designed to regulate the relationships of California 49ers searching for gold with a pick and shovel and pan cannot easily be made to fit the needs and regulate the relationships of modern miners searching for uranium, beryllium and the like, minerals which are often located at great depth, and whose geology, existence and usefulness could not have been imagined in 1872. On the other hand, the mining law is being pinched by enviromentalists and conservationists in order to restrict its applicability. A law enacted in 1872 and reflecting the then prevailing attitude that the natural resources of this country were limitless and not in need of care, does not well allocate resources in times of scarcity. Thus, those who seek to limit the applicability of the mining law reflect a desire to protect the natural beauty of our public lands and to retain those lands in public ownership in an effort to preserve an irreplaceable part of our common national heritage, as well as the conviction that retention of those lands in public ownership is required by principles of sound land management. These attitudes are, in large part, inconsistent with donative statutes like the Mining Law, whose purpose is to provide for the development of the public lands and their ultimate passage into private ownership.

GEOMET EXPLORATION, LTD. V. LUCKY Mc URANIUM CORPORATION
601 P.2d 1339 (Ariz. 1979)

HAYS, Justice.

Geomet appealed from a decision granting exclusive possession of certain unpatented mining claims to Lucky Mc Uranium Corporation. The Court of Appeals affirmed. . . . Geomet petitioned for review and we granted review under A.R.S. § 12-120.24 and Rule 23 of the Rules of Civil Appellate Procedure. We now vacate the opinion of the Court of Appeals.

By use of modern scintillation equipment in September of 1976, plaintiff/appellee, Lucky Mc Uranium Corporation, detected "anomalies" (discontinuities in geologic formations) indicative of possible uranium deposits in the Artillery Peak Mining District in Yuma County, land in the federal public domain. In November, 1976, Lucky proceeded to monument and post 200 claims (4,000 acres), drill a 10-foot hole on each claim, and record notices pursuant to A.R.S. §§ 27-202, 27-203 and 27-204.

Subsequently, defendant/appellant, Geomet, peaceably entered some of the areas claimed by Lucky and began drilling operations. Employees of Geomet were aware of Lucky's claims but considered them invalid because there had been no discovery of minerals in place and Lucky was not in actual occupancy of the areas Geomet entered.

Lucky instituted a possessory action seeking damages, exclusive possession and a permanent injunction against trespass by Geomet or its employees. There was insufficient evidence to establish a valid discovery, but the trial court found that Lucky was entitled to exclusive possession and a permanent injunction. Although Geomet pointed out that, prior to discovery of minerals in place, the doctrine of *pedis possessio* requires a prospector to be in actual occupancy of the claim and diligently pursuing discovery, the court based its reasoning on the economic infeasibility of literal adherence to the element of actual occupancy in view of modern mining techniques and the expense involved in exploring large areas.

Additionally, the court found that Geomet had entered the land in bad faith, knowing that Lucky was claiming it.

We must decide a single issue: Should the actual occupancy requirement of *pedis possessio* be discarded in favor of constructive possession to afford a potential locator protection of contiguous, unoccupied claims as against one who enters peaceably, openly, and remains in possession searching for minerals?

PEDIS POSSESSIO

Mineral deposits in the public domain of the United States are open to all citizens (or those who have expressed an intent to become citizens) who wish to occupy and explore them "under regulations prescribed by law, and according to the local customs or rules of miners in the several mining districts, so far as the same are applicable and not inconsistent with the laws of the United States." 30 U.S.C. § 22 (1970).

The doctrine of *pedis possessio* evolved from customs and usages of miners and has achieved statutory recognition in federal law as the "law of possession," 30 U.S.C. § 53 (1970):

> No possessory action between persons, in any court of the United States , for the recovery of any mining title, or for damages to any such title, shall be affected by the fact that the paramount title to the land in which such mines lie is in the United States; but each case shall be judged by the law of possession.

Regardless of compliance with statutory requisites such as monumenting and notice, one cannot perfect a location, under either federal or state law, without actual discovery of minerals in place. *Best v. Humboldt Placer Mining Co.*, 371 U.S. 334, 83 S.Ct. 379, 9 L.Ed.2d 350 (1963); 30 U.S.C. § 23 (1970); A.R.S. § 27-201. Until discovery, the law of possession determines who has the better right to possession.

The literal meaning of *pedis possessio* is a foothold, actual possession. Black's Law Dictionary 1289 (rev. 4th ed. 1968). This actual occupancy must be distinguished from constructive possession, which is based on color of title and has the effect of enlarging the area actually occupied to the extent of the description in the title. *Id.* at 1325. A succinct exposition of *pedis possessio* is found in *Union Oil Co. v. Smith*, 249 U.S. 337, 346-48, 39 S.Ct. 308, 310-11, 63 L.Ed. 635 (1919):

> Those who, being qualified, proceed in good faith to make such explorations and enter peaceably upon vacant lands of the United States for that purpose are not treated as mere trespassers, but as licensees or tenants at will. For since, as a practical matter, exploration must precede the discovery of minerals, and some occupation of the land ordinarily is necessary for adequate and systematic exploration, legal recognition of the pedis possessio of a bona fide and qualified prospector is universally regarded as a necessity. It is held that upon the public domain a miner may hold the place in which he may be working against all others having no better right, and while he remains in possession, diligently working towards discovery, is entitled—at least for a reasonable time—to be protected against forcible, fraudulent, and clandestine intrusions upon his possession. Whatever the nature and extent of a possessory right before discovery, all authorities agree that *such possession may be maintained only by continued actual occupancy by a qualified locator or his representatives engaged in persistent and diligent prosecution of work looking to the discovery of mineral.* (Emphasis added.)

If the first possessor should relax his occupancy or cease working toward discovery, and another enters peaceably, openly, and diligently searches for mineral, the first party forfeits the right to exclusive possession under the requirements of *pedis possessio. Cole v. Ralph*, 252 U.S. 286, 295, 40 S.Ct. 321, 325, 64 L.Ed. 567 (1920); *Davis v. Nelson*, 329 F.2d 840 (9th Cir. 1964).

Arizona has recognized *pedis possessio* and the concomitant requirement of actual occupancy for a century. *Field v. Grey*, 1 Ariz. 404, 25 p. 793 (1881). In *Bagg v. New Jersey Loan Co.*, 88 Ariz. 182, 188-89, 354 P.2d 40, 44 (1960), we said: "Location is the foundation of the possessory title, and possession thereunder, *as required by law and local rules and customs*, keeps the title alive, . . ." (Emphasis added.) It is perhaps more proper to speak of a possessory right than a title because, until discovery of mineral and issuance of a patent, absolute title in fee simple remains in the United States. *Bagg, supra*, at 192, 354 P.2d 40; *Bowen v. Chemi-Cote Perlite Corp.*, 102 Ariz. 423, 432 P.2d 435 (1967). Since this is a possessory action, the party with the better right is entitled to prevail. *Rundle v. Republic Cement Corp.*, 86 Ariz. 96, 341 P.2d 226 (1959).

Conceding that actual occupancy is necessary under *pedis possessio*, Lucky urges that the requirement be relaxed in deference to the time and expense that would be involved in actually occupying and drilling on each claim until discovery. Moreover, Lucky points out that the total area claimed 4,000 acres is reasonable in size, similar in geological formation, and that an overall work program for the entire area had been developed. Under these circumstances, Lucky contends, actual drilling on some of the claims should suffice to afford protection as to all contiguous claims. Great reliance is placed on *Mac-*

Guire v. Sturgis, 347 F.Supp. 580 (D.C.Wyo. 1971), in which the federal court accepted arguments similar to those advanced here and extended protection on a group or area basis. Geomet counters that *MacGuire, supra,* is an aberration and contrary to three Wyoming Supreme Court cases upholding the requisite of actual occupancy. *Sparks v. Mount,* 29 Wyo. 1, 207 P. 1099 (1922); *Whiting v. Straup,* 17 Wyo. 1, 95 P. 849 (1908); *Phillips v. Brill,* 17 Wyo. 26, 95 P. 856 (1908).

To adopt the premise urged by Lucky eviscerates the actual occupancy requirement of *pedis possessio* and substitutes for it the theory of constructive possession even though there is no color of title. We are persuaded that the sounder approach is to maintain the doctrine intact. In *Union Oil, supra,* the Court considered the precise question of extending protection to contiguous claims and refused to do so:

> It was and is defendant's contention that by virtue of the act of 1903, one who has acquired the possessory rights of locators before discovery in five contiguous claims . . . may preserve and maintain an inchoate right to all of them by means of a continuous actual occupation of one, coupled with diligent prosecution in good faith of a sufficient amount of discovery work thereon, provided such work tends also to determine the oil-bearing character of the other claims.
>
> In our opinion the act shows no purpose to dispense with discovery as an essential of a valid oil location *or to break down in any wise the recognized distinction between the pedis possessio of a prospector doing work for the purpose of discovering oil and the more substantial right of possession of one who has made a discovery. . . . Union Oil,* 249 U.S. at 343, 353, 39 S.Ct. at 309, 312. (Emphasis added.)

We have canvassed the Western mining jurisdictions and found the requirement of actual occupancy to be the majority view. *Davis v. Nelson, supra; United Western Minerals Co. v. Hannsen,* 147 Colo. 272, 363, P.2d 677 (1961); *Adams v. Benedict,* 64 N.M. 234, 327 P.2d 308 (1958); *McLemore v. Express Oil Co.,* 158 Cal. 559, 112 P. 59 (1910).

There are always inherent risks in prospecting. The development of *pedis possessio* from the customs of miners argues forcefully against the proposition that exclusive right to possession should encompass claims neither actually occupied nor being explored. We note that the doctrine does not protect on the basis of occupancy alone; the additional requirement of diligent search for minerals must also be satisfied. The reason for these dual elements—and for the policy of the United States in making public domain available for exploration and mining—is to encourage those prepared to demonstrate their sincerity and tenacity in the pursuit of valuable minerals. If one may, by complying with preliminary formalities of posting and recording notices, secure for himself the exclusive possession of a large area upon only a small portion of which he is actually working, then he may, at his leisure, explore the entire area and exclude all others who stand ready to peaceably and openly enter unoccupied sections for the purpose of discovering minerals. Such a premise is laden with extreme difficulties of determining over how large an area and for how long one might be permitted to exclude others.

We hold that *pedis possessio* protects only those claims actually occupied (provided also that work toward discovery is in progress) and does not extend to contiguous, unoccupied claims on a group or area basis.

Lucky calls our attention to former A.R.S. § 27-203(B), under which a potential locator was allowed 120 days to sink shafts to a specified depth.[1] The contention is that during that period, Lucky should have been granted exclusive possession in order to discover mineral in place, and, since Geomet entered certain claims before the expiration of the 120 days, Lucky did not have the benefit of the full term in which to make discovery.

We point out, however, that the first statute concerning location of claims, A.R.S. § 27-201, reads as follows:

> *Upon discovery of mineral in place* on the public domain of the United States the mineral may be located as a lode mining claim by the discoverer for himself, or for himself and others, or for others. (Emphasis added.)

Discovery is the *sine qua non* that lends validity to other statutory procedures designed to complete a location. A.R.S. §§ 27-202 *et seq.* We have on two occasions held that acts of location confer no right in the absence of discovery. *State v. Tracy*, 76 Ariz. 7, 10, 257 P.2d 860, 862 (1953); *Ponton v. House*, 75 Ariz. 303, 306, 256 P.2d 246, 247 (1953). It is certainly true that, even after discovery, one may be held to have abandoned a location or forfeited his rights for failure to comply with additional statutory requirements. A.R.S. § 27-203(E). But *prior to discovery*, the only right one has to exclude others flows from *pedis possessio* and not from statutory law.

Finally, Lucky asserts that Geomet cannot invoke *pedis possessio* because Geomet, knowing that Lucky claimed the area, entered in bad faith. Lucky relies principally on *Bagg v. New Jersey Loan Co., supra*, and *Woolsey v. Lassen*, 91 Ariz. 229, 371 P.2d 587 (1962). It is true that a potential locator must enter in good faith. *Union Oil Co. v. Smith, supra.*

There is language in our decisions that appears to indicate that mere knowledge of a prior claim constitutes bad faith. Although we are sure that our holdings were sound in the cases Lucky cites, certain statements may have been an inadvertent oversimplification of the issue of good faith and we take this opportunity to clarify the point.

In general terms, good faith may be defined as honesty of purpose and absence of intent to defraud. *People v. Bowman*, 156 Cal.App.2d 784, 320 P.2d 70 (1958); *Thurmond v. Espalin*, 50 N.M. 109, 171 P.2d 325 (1946).

Both *Bagg* and *Woolsey, supra*, dealt with those who had discovered minerals in place and were in actual occupancy when others attempted to usurp their claims. These facts immediately distinguish them from the instant case, in

---

[1] At the time this action was tried, A.R.S. § 27-203(B) read, in pertinent part: The locator of a lode claim shall within one hundred twenty days from the time of the location sink a location shaft on the claim . . . Subsequent amendments by Laws 1978, Ch. 177 § 3, deleted the requirement of sinking a shaft or drilling.

which Lucky had neither made discovery nor was in actual occupancy of the areas Geomet entered.

While acting as agent to oversee claims of the Arizona Mining Company, Mr. Bagg attempted to locate claims himself. An agent is duty-bound not to acquire a private interest antagonistic to that of his employer. See *Mallamo v. Hartman*, 70 Ariz. 294, 219 P.2d 1039 (1950); Restatement (Second) of Agency §§ 387, 393, 395 (1957).

Woolsey concerned a claim against a previous locator who had already discovered mineral and was in actual possession under a lease from the state. Under the circumstances, the challenger simply could not prove a superior right to possession.

In summary, both cases differ significantly from this case in their factual framework and did not depend for their resolution solely upon the element of knowledge. We stand by our conclusions in those cases but wish to emphasize that mere knowledge of a previous claim, in and of itself, does not constitute bad faith. *Columbia Standard Corp. v. Ranchers Exploration & Development, Inc.*, 468 F.2d 547 (10th Cir. 1972); *Adams v. Benedict, supra; Walsh v. Henry*, 38 Colo. 393, 88 P. 449 (1907).

Since Geomet's entry concededly was open and peaceable, we hold that the entry was in good faith.

In conclusion, Lucky was not in actual occupancy of those areas Geomet entered and *pedis possessio* affords Lucky no protection as to those particular claims. Geomet is entitled to the exclusive possession of the disputed claims.

We reverse the trial court, order that the injunction be quashed, and remand for proceedings consistent with this opinion.

NOTES

1. The rule of *MacGuire v. Sturgis* was tacitly approved by the tenth circuit in *Continental Oil Co. v. Natrona Service, Inc.*, 588 F.2d 792 (10th Cir. 1978). If Arizona was within the tenth circuit, would the Arizona Supreme Court have been required to follow the *Continental Oil* precedent in *Geomet*? The Mining Law of 1872 provides that matters of possession are to be determined in accordance with state law. Is the doctrine of *pedis possessio* such a "matter of possession?" Could a state radically expand the scope of the doctrine? Completely eliminate the doctrine?

2. Why did the court in *Geomet* decide not to expand the scope of pedis possessio to cover group claims? In answering this question, consider that the judiciary has traditionally been very sensitive to the fact that the public lands of the United States are held by the federal government in trust for all the people of the United States. In an early public lands case, *Lee v. Munroe*, 11 U.S. (7 Cranch) 366 (1813), the Supreme Court stated that "[i]t is better that an individual should now and then suffer . . . than to introduce a rule against an abuse of which, by improper collusion, it should be very difficult to protect the . . . [public lands]."

Indeed, a common concern running throughout the *pedis possessio* cases, and every area of the mining law, is the fear that the law will be abused in such a manner that valuable public domain will be appropriated to private use and speculation pursuant to the mining law, but for non-mining purposes. This fear is not warranted. "A report from the Department of Agriculture . . . stated that as of January 1, 1952, there were 84,000 unpatented claims, covering more than 2.2 million acres of national forest but only 2% of these mines were producing minerals in commercial quantities . . ." *United States v. Curtis-Nevada Mines, Inc.,* 611 F.2d 1277, 1285 n. 7 (9th Cir. 1980). "In 1974 the GAO reported in a monograph by the Comptroller General entitled Modernization of 1872 Mining Law Needed to Encourage Domestic Production, Protect the Environment and Improve Public Land Management, that in a study of 240 mining claims selected at random only one was being mined and only three had ever been mined." Coggins and Wilkinson, Federal Public Lands.

The reported cases abound with illustrations of the types of abuses to which the mining law is subject. *Coleman v. United States,* page 131, *infra*, is one example. Another egregious example is provided by *Cameron v. United States*, 252 U.S. 450 (1920). In that case a claimant attempted to locate a "mining claim" across the trailhead of the Bright Angel trail, one of the major access routes into the Grand Canyon, in order to collect a toll from tourists.

In the materials that have already been studied and in the materials that follow we will see the courts attempt to balance this justified concern that the Mining Law will be abused by speculators to amass vast tracts of land against the legitimate concern of the mining industry that the miner be permitted to explore for minerals in a manner consistent with the geology of their location and economic necessity (efficiency?).

C. Pedis Possessio: The Requirement of Good Faith

RANCHERS EXPLORATION AND DEVELOPMENT CO.
V. ANACONDA CO.,
248 F. Supp. 708 (D. Ut. 1965) (footnotes omitted)

CHRISTENSEN, District Judge.
The jurisdiction of this court properly has been invoked upon the basis of diversity of citizenship existing between the parties.

Defendants and intervenors are the claimants of numerous lode mining claims spread across an area of more than five square miles of public domain lying on the west flank of Spor Mountain in Juab County, Utah. Over some of these claims plaintiff Ranchers Exploration and Development Co. attempted to locate claims of its own and to make mineral discoveries in support of such relocations. Defendants forcibly prevented the consummation of these attempts. It was then believed, and it since has been confirmed, that a major beryllium field was involved within which numerous claims are highly valuable.

Plaintiff alleged that defendants, having themselves made no valid mineral discoveries, unlawfully interfered with its established rights in particular mining claims on which it had initiated locations and was in the process of making discoveries, and through conspiracy and otherwise violated its right to make further locations and discoveries, for which interference and violations plaintiff sought injunctive, declaratory and legal relief, including that afforded by the Sherman Antitrust Act, 15 U.S.C. 1, 15, and comparable state statutes.

Defendants denied plaintiff's assertions that their claims were not supported by valid mineral discoveries at the time of plaintiff's entries; and defendants alleged that to the extent of any failure in this respect they were entitled to protection in the continued occupation, exploration and perfection of their claims under the doctrine of *pedis possessio.* Defendants asserted that in any event plaintiff was precluded or estopped from questioning or interfering with their rights by reason of conduct on the part of one Ford, with whom plaintiff was associated in the investigation and attempted acquisition of defendants' claims and to whom plaintiff later assigned an interest in any recovery from this lawsuit.

During pre-trial proceedings, in the hope of avoiding unmanageable processing for trial of numerous individual claims, six 'bellwethers' were selected by the parties (three claims by each side) as presenting the major issues of fact and law likely to be encountered in deciding the validity of all of the claims in dispute. Accordingly, the trial upon which the present decision is based was confined to an investigation of these six claims and the rights of the parties concerning them. The position of the hundred or so other claims which could be affected by the ruling and all issues as to antitrust problems and damages, to the extent their consideration may become necessary, have been by agreement reserved for further proceedings.

The wide latitude which the briefs have encompassed has been helpful in permitting us to beat peripheral bushes for obscure conceptual traps. But with that done, the scene of conflict has returned to the broad but variable slopes of established principles. A discussion keyed primarily to the minutia of facts set out in the extended findings proposed by some of the parties or the plethora of comments in the decided cases, would serve only to mask the decisive points. Their solution turns not upon questions of credibility, nor upon nice distinctions in fact or law, but primarily upon the reconciliation or adjustment of competing public policies and foundational legal principles as they met head on, so to speak, during those bleak winter hours of 1963, when the armed guards of the defendants sought out, and with force turned back from the properties in dispute, the plaintiff's scrambling personnel and equipment.

From the maze of factual and legal matters which it is hoped have been adequately, if not from the standpoint of all of the parties satisfactorily, covered by the pre-trial rulings and order and by the findings of fact and the conclusions herein recited, three problems seem to warrant more extended discussion in view of their importance in the mining industry.

The first vital inquiry is whether defendants or their predecessors in interest had made 'mineral discoveries' on or underlying all of the bellwether claims prior to the attempted entries by plaintiff. If so, all issues would have to be resolved in favor of defendants, for even as to its antitrust implications plaintiff concedes that such a finding, if sustainable, would be determinative against it on the whole case. If *discovery* previously had not been accomplished on or underlying all of such claims, defendants would be relegated to their defenses of *pedis possessio* and *estoppel* or *'unclean hands',* thus presenting the second and third major issues to be examined here: Whether defendants at the time of plaintiff's attempted entries were in occupation of and diligently attempting to make discovery on the claims on which mineral discoveries had not been made, within the doctrine of *pedis possessio;* and, if not, whether plaintiff by reason of any unconscionable conduct attributable or imputable to it should be barred from asserting whatever rights it might otherwise have possessed.

. . . .

[The court found that Defendant had not made mineral discoveries on or underlying all of the bellwhether claims prior to the attempted entries by plaintiff.]

The doctrine of *pedis possessio* is succinctly and authoritatively stated in the case of *Union Oil Co. of California v. Smith,* 249 U.S. 337, 39 S.Ct. 308, 63 L.Ed. 635 (1919):

[The quotation from the Union Oil case is omitted;
It is reproduced at page 2, *supra.*]

The contention of the defendants that the doctrine of *pedis possessio* can be applied upon a group or area basis rather than a claim by claim basis must be rejected, since this was the very point upon which the claim of the defendant in *Union Oil Co. of California* was rejected by the Supreme Court in recognition of the doctrine. To say that the doctrine supports this contention is like saying that a blackbird is white, or that a yearling wether is a two-year old buck. Proposals for liberalizing the rule have been considered in the industry and studied by Congress. But even with the press of modern demands and procedures, seemingly it can be agreed upon neither in the industry nor in the Congress. It would be presumptuous, as well as unwarranted, for me to ignore the holding of the Supreme Court, with its expressed limitations. Defendants in effect, although not expressly, say that this, indeed, was done by the Circuit Court of Appeals for this circuit in *Kanab Uranium Corp. v. Consolidated Uranium Mines,* 227 F.2d 434 (9th Cir. 1955). I cannot think so.

Defendants specifically argue that since they are merely resisting plaintiff's attempts to gain initial possession of the areas in question and are not seeking affirmative relief for themselves in this suit, they need show neither mineral discovery upon, nor occupancy of, the bellwether claims, but had the right by force to eject the plaintiff therefrom, and are in a position to defend the suit here, merely by reason of their 'color of title,' i.e., the location notices or their option or leases from purported locators whose mineral discoveries and occupancies similarly are in question.

None of the authorities cited by defendants except *Kanab Uranium* applies the term 'color of title' in the context of our case. I cannot find that the latter case has been followed or cited in any other case, although it has been noted by commentators. Nonetheless, it must here be considered whether *Kanab Uranium* is a controlling decision which precludes the necessity of considering the doctrine of *pedis possessio* in its traditional aspects and forecloses anyone out of possession from entering upon a claim previously located by another notwithstanding the insufficiency of that claim.

The rationale on which *Kanab Uranium* is based is clear enough—that one out of possession seeking affirmative relief by way of possession must rely upon the strength of his own right and not upon the weakness of the title of his opponent. Yet the application of this rule, however common with reference to ordinary property rights has been considered inapplicable as to mining claims. As to them there seems a special situation in which the possessory rights of every private interest are qualified, and the basis of each right is the mining law with its limitations as well as its protections. A recognizable right of entry, unless qualified by some paramount right other than mere possession of another private interest, seems an essential foundation of any orderly and just development of the mineral resources.

In *Kanab* the point upon which the decision ultimately turned was not raised or decided in the lower court, which had based its decision upon a point considered erroneous by the appellate court. There the decision was on a motion to dismiss; here it is upon the merits after the taking of evidence. There it was assumed that the decision was governed by 30 U.S.C.A. § 30 concerning proceedings in connection with applications for patent. Here, no one relies upon that section. There, there was no claim that plaintiff had made discovery or locations upon the disputed property; here locations were established upon at least one claim and discovery was accomplished by plaintiff to the extent, if any, that defendants had accomplished it on some of its claims, further efforts toward discovery having been prevented by defendants by force. Moreover, there was not considered in the *Kanab* case the tort theory advanced by plaintiff here, involving claimed interference with business opportunity and antitrust implications.

While *Kanab Uranium* mentions *Union Oil Co. of California* in somewhat summary fashion, its own statement of the rule qualifies the rights of one in possession with the assumption that he has 'complied with the law.' The court cited in intimated opposition to the *Union Oil Co.* case, *Biglow v. Conradt*, 159 F. 868, 870 (9th Cir. 1908), which itself assumed that the one in possession had 'complied with the law'. Thus the statements in *Kanab Uranium* might be reconciled with the general rule were it not for other statements which on their face tend to render the limitations of *pedis possessio* immaterial by disempowering anyone out of possession of mining claims from questioning the right of those in possession and claiming them under 'color of title' although not in actual occupancy or in diligent pursuit of discovery on any particular claim. Among other cases, *Eilers v. Boatman*, 3 Utah 159, 2 P. 66 (1883), is cited in support of this general position but while dicta in that case recites that constructive possession might be sufficient, the facts showed actual occupancy as well as a prior mineral discovery which was being developed when the adverse entry was attempted. The other cited cases do not seem to support an unqualified rule.

If I am bound to apply defendants' construction of some of the statements in

Kanab Uranium to the present case, there would be little more to be said. Once a claim had been located and transferred, however inadequate the location might be and whatever lack of diligence the efforts toward discovery might appear, the transferees could indefinitely enjoy a monopoly of the entire area, postpone efforts toward discovery to suit its own convenience and exclude by force every other citizen from the entire area of the public domain, however large. Without assuming to question that decision on its own facts, I do not think it can be applied mechanically to the facts of this case without disregarding the dominant meaning and policy of the statutes governing mining claims and the express holding in *Union Oil Co. of California v. Smith, supra.* There the distinction is clearly drawn between rights of locators after a discovery, where constructive possession is sufficient as against other claimants, and rights of locators prior to discovery, where there is protection afforded a claimant only if he is in 'actual occupancy'. The Supreme Court said in *Union Oil Co. of California:*

' * * * Whatever the nature and extent of a possessory right before discovery, all authorities agree that such possession may be maintained only by continued actual occupancy by a qualified locator or his representatives engaged in persistent and diligent prosecution of work looking to the discovery of mineral.
          * * * *

(But) 'Actual and continuous occupation of a valid mining location based upon discovery is not essential to the preservation of the possessory rights. The right is lost only by abandonment, as by nonperformance of the annual labor required * * *.'

The defendants with reference to any of the bellwether claims were not in actual occupancy, nor were they diligently working to make discovery thereon at the time of plaintiff's attempted entries. The possession under the doctrine of *pedis possessio* is not sufficient if only representing an effort to exclude others rather than diligently to discover mineral. There is no doubt that on none of the three claims in question was any discovery or other work being attempted diligently or otherwise, and it seems equally as clear that none was occupied or actually possessed. Manifestly, discovery had been accomplished upon some of the other claims in the general area, and with reference to other claims it could be that there was possession or occupancy with the requisitie diligence in attempting mineral discoveries to support the defense of *pedis possessio.* Even broadly, however, it must be recalled that Anaconda had acquired its interest as late as January 2, 1963, and while it had plans for systematic exploration of the entire area, and later carried them out at the expense of several hundred thousand dollars, it then actually had accomplished little change in the condition which existed previously and which clearly amounted neither to occupancy nor diligent exploration of the area as a whole or any of the bellwether claims.

It may be recognized that modern conditions may make desirable, and governing legal principles may in proper cases be hospitable toward efforts on the part of prospectors to hold possession of substantial areas long enough to lay the foundations of, and to practically accomplish, their diligent exploration, although this may be a congressional and not a judicial problem. It is unnecessary to further explore here the circumstances which might authorize such an accommodation in the interest of practicality and liberality toward prospectors. Suffice it to note that here in my view there would be no basis to hold that up until the acquisition of Anaconda's interest there had been either actual occupancy or diligent discovery efforts as to the three southernmost claims in question, or that in the few weeks following January 2, 1963, Anaconda, without attempting to drill a single hole, or to do any work whatsoever in the general area, merely because of its plans or its use of force against plaintiff, had placed itself in the position of one in actual occupancy of said claims proceeding diligently with efforts to accomplish mineral discoveries. Nor is there anything in the evidence which in this case would authorize a departure from the express holding of *Union Oil Co. of California v. Smith* that *pedis possessio* must be evaluated and maintained on a claim by claim basis.

Defendants maintain that in any event the plaintiff's attempted entries were 'forcible, fraudulent and clandestine' intrusions upon their possession, against which defendants had the right to protect themselves or to enlist the defensive aid of the court. A short answer is that unless claimants can bring themselves within the doctrine of *pedis possessio,* that doctrine in and of itself may not protect them even against forcible, fraudulent or clandestine intrusions. To understand the reasons for this, and in an effort to reconcile and in explanation of the general language in the cases, it seems desirable to analyze this specific part of the doctrine with more particularity than has been attempted heretofore. While the point may or may not alter the ultimate results of this case, it is important that the point be made, I believe, if confusion which seems to exist is not to be perpetuated. I can only hope that I will not add much to the confusion.

To say that one in *pedis possessio* for a reasonable time is to be protected against forcible, fraudulent, and clandestine intrusions upon his possession, is not necessarily to say that he is entitled to the same protection if not in actual possession or if not proceeding diligently in efforts toward discovery. The reason that those in *pedis possessio* are entitled to protection against such acts seems the very confirmation of plaintiff's general position—that in the absence of discovery or *pedis possessio* on the part of the first claimant, another who is in good faith proceeding in accordance with the mining law with efforts toward location and mineral discovery has an equal right to be upon the public domain. Certainly, as here, if the first claimant has made no discovery and has no foothold within the doctrine of *pedis possessio,* his forcible, clandestine or even fraudulent resistance on the public domain to the prospecting of another would be equally as, and perhaps more, unjustifiable than similar action on the part of the second claimant, because in resistance to an otherwise lawful entry the first claimant without authorization might itself be initiating such conduct.

As a matter of fact, here the defendants rather self-righteously protest against the plaintiff's 'forcible and clandestine entries in the nighttime', whereas the nighttime attempts were in order to avoid a clash with defendants' armed guards and the only significant violence employed by anyone was the forcible disablement by defendants' agents of plaintiff's equipment and the physical ejection of plaintiff's agents from this area of the public domain. Under the circumstances, it cannot be accepted that the guns of the defendants could be substitutes for picks, shovels or drills or for proceeding diligently with discovery, or that roving guards patrolling several square miles of desert could be in actual occupancy for the purpose of discovery within the meaning of the doctrine. One seeking to maintain an unlawful possession by force is not entitled to the court's protection on that account.

If a prior locator has perfected his claim by a mineral discovery, no subsequent valid location may be made, for it would be based on trespass, whether clandestine or open. The reasons that one in *pedis possessio* of a mining claim is protected against forcible, clandestine or fraudulent entries of another, or may protect himself therefrom, seem to be these: If there be a peaceable, non-fraudulent and open entry by another, the one in actual possession will in all probability know of it. In such event, if there is consent or even acquiescence, the one first in possession may be deemed to accept such second entry by other as legal and in accordance with law, and both prospectors may proceed lawfully in their efforts to accomplish a mineral discovery, the first to be successful becoming entitled to the exclusive possession of the claim by reason of discovery. But one in *pedis possessio* of a mining claim is protected against forcible, clandestine or fraudulent entries by another, in order that he can maintain his exclusive possession for the purpose of diligently prospecting for minerals if he chooses.

One not in *pedis possessio* properly needs and is entitled to no such protection, for he is merely another prospector before he makes his mineral discovery. This view again rewards diligence and promotes peaceful competition which are keynotes of the mining law. If a mineral discovery has been made, the locator doing the requisite work on his claim is protected from even the peaceable entry of another, which would be, as to him, an unauthorized trespass nonetheless. Absent discovery, if the second entry is attempted clandestinely, fraudulently or forcibly, the locator who has the right to the exclusive possession of the claim within the doctrine of *pedis possessio*, may have no means or opportunity to maintain it even though he might otherwise desire to. If, being in *pedis possessio*, he were not protected against such acts, the doctrine might be rendered meaningless as to him. But if he were granted such protection although not in *pedis possessio*, the doctrine would be extended beyond its purpose and justification to the disruption of the mining law and the related public policy.

To recognize that the defendants have not made out a defense under the doctrine of *pedis possessio*, as we shall presently see, is not fully determinative of related matters. I believe, however, that the key is not the supposed strength of defendants' position under the doctrine of *pedis possessio*, not the supposed weakness of plaintiff's position in view of *Kanab Uranium*, nor the rules governing possessory actions and property rights in general, not even any general requirement of 'clean hands' or any broad remedy of equitable estoppel as urged by defendants, but the inherent limitation of the mining law itself which requires that locators of mining claims proceed in 'good faith'.

III.

Defendants, although they urge an 'analagous' position, concede that the elements of an equitable estoppel probably have not been made out against plaintiff, and I concur. Their contention that plaintiff is foreclosed from equitable relief by application of the doctrine of 'clean hands' is countered by plaintiff's argument that this is not an equitable action; that in any event the facts established by the evidence do not invoke the doctrine relied upon by defendants, and that the 'clean hands' maxim has no force and effect independent of substantive legal and equitable concepts, that is, that it is co-existent with, not independent of, other legal and equitable defenses.

The clean hands doctrine, in its proper application, is not limited to actions purely equitable, nor is the present action limited to legal issues. But in general, as distinguished from application peculiarly relevant to mining locations, it may be doubted whether there was such conduct, attributable or imputable to plaintiff, as to bar consideration by a court of the merits of plaintiff's position. Defendants not being in a position to invoke the protection of *pedis possessio,* an entry accomplished secretly, in the nighttime or even with force in resistance to unwarranted force on the part of defendants, would not tar plaintiff with 'unclean hands', and any conduct in the nature of fraud on plaintiff's part could be deemed hardly so flagrant as to deprive the plaintiff of an opportunity to be heard on the merits in relation to rights less sensitive than mining claims.

But with reference to mining claims, there are at least two related considerations which lead me to believe that the circumstances giving rise to, and attendant upon, plaintiff's attempted entries in January and February, 1963, upon the areas of the bellwether claims, are such as to be determinative, beyond general rules governing the 'clean hands' doctrine: (1) The mining law, the customs of miners and public policy are alike sensitive to the good faith of claimants to mining property, and (2) from this viewpoint the good or bad faith of the plaintiff established, or conditioned and qualified, as the case may be, its right of entry upon the public domain as against others who had already entered in good faith. Thus the 'clean hands doctrine' may be invoked liberally, not as an independent defense but in recognition of substantive legal and equitable concepts relating to the good faith requirement.

I find myself unable to accept here the proposition that citizens acting in good faith to make a mineral discovery upon the public domain upon land open under the law to mineral location, lawfully can be forcibly excluded therefrom by other citizens who are not in actual possession of the area, are not proceeding diligently to make discovery and who have no more than prior constructive possession and the ability and readiness to marshal enough force to preclude entry by the public. As between the parties thus contending, the good faith of one side is no better or worse than the good faith of the other. Each is asserting an exclusive right by force, stealth or otherwise to explore for minerals upon the public domain which both have the right to enjoy. But I have no difficulty in concluding, as I do, that if the subsequent claimant is seeking to obtain possession by questionable means amounting to a demonstration of bad faith, either in the sense that he has unconscionably improved his position at the expense of his

competitor, or unfairly worsened his competitor's position to his own aggran-
dizement, he does not qualify as a locator against such competing interest.

'Good faith' in other contexts has been held to be something more than a
colorable claim, although belief in the propriety of a claim is an element to be
considered. It is axiomatic that a locator must act in good faith, and even though
a prior locator's claim may be invalid, bad faith may render the subsequent claim
ineffectual. It has been said that '[E]ntry must always be peaceable, open, and
above board, and made in good faith, or no rights can be founded upon it', and
while such expressions usually are found when *pedis possessio* is sustained,
they state a more pervasive policy of the law.

Good faith is not specified as a location requirement in the mineral locations laws themselves. It has been inferred by the courts from the purpose of
these laws 'to further the speedy and orderly development of the mineral
resources' of the public lands. Some cases have already broadened the bona fide
doctrine to require a locator to exercise 'good faith' toward prior holders of
defective claims. It has been asserted that these applications are unsound, and
Kanab Uranium Corp. v. Consolidated Uranium Mines, 227 F.2d 434 (10th Cir.
1955), has been cited as a special example in this respect since there was said to
be involved only constructive possession without discovery. But even the writer
entertaining such a view would distinguish cases where there has been a
violation of confidence. It is said:

'This doctrine would permit parties to hold their claims by actual or
constructive possession of any part, without compliance with the specific
location and assessment work requirements of federal and state law. It runs
contrary to the developmental objective of the mining laws and should be
limited to cases where the subsequent party is responsible for infirmities in
prior locations, where an infirmity is of a purely formal nature, or where the
subsequent party enters forcefully or clandestinely upon the actual possession of the prior locator.'

I believe that only in the context of the 'good faith' requirement can *Kanab
Uranium* have continued meaning beyond its own peculiar facts, but that in that
context it is of controlling persuasion here.

Any question of good faith involves primarily the position and activities of
Ford. The evidence showed that he was a consulting geologist, with headquar-
ters at Riverton, Wyoming. He came to the area in question in 1960, and upon
examining the properties which are the subject of this lawsuit, concluded that
they had value. He recognized the ownership of Moody and his predecessors in
the claims and prepared a prospectus in which he represented generally that the
property was worthy of acquisition from Moody. The prospectus was offered to
G.B.C., among other companies. G.B.C. thereupon undertook to acquire the
Rawlinson group from Moody pursuant to the agreement of May 15, 1961. Ford
then secured employment with G.B.C. and assumed control of these properties
on its behalf, expending approximately $250,000 in the maintenance of claim
boundaries, relocating, surveying and mapping, exploration, drilling and assaying. The relocation program, involving the blanketing over the existing claims of
new G.B.C. claims was undertaken after G.B.C. had reported to Moody that the

previous locations were insufficient and that 'substantially all of the claims (were) devoid of apparent mineralization.'

After the July, 1962, default, Moody forfeited G.B.C.'s interest in the claims pursuant to the contract, and commenced a limited drilling program. He employed John Ortman, an employee of Ford, to log the drill holes and to assay samples. The drilling revealed significant beryllium-bearing stuff in some areas. Ortman made available to Ford the information which he had acquired while in the employ of Moody.

During the fall of 1962, Ford attempted to interest a number of companies in acquiring the Moody properties. He furnished a prospectus to Ranchers Exploration and Develoment Corp. 'to provide information regarding beryllium properties of Richard D. Moody as owner and lessor * * * to permit Ranchers * * * to evaluate the property, to determine the extent of its interest and to provide a basis for negotiation.' He indicated therein that he considered all of Moody's claims 'worthy of acquisition'. Ford also contacted other companies in an attempt to interest them in the acquisition of Moody's claims.

Ranchers became interested in the property and was placed in contact with Moody by Ford on several occasions in an attempt to purchase Moody's interest. Anderson, President of Ranchers and another officer, entertained Moody at Las Vegas, and were advised that he was negotiating also with Anaconda and Brush. In November, 1962, Ford recorded a previously executed document giving him a personal royalty interest in anything that G.B.C. owned. Up until that time Moody had no notice that Ford was claiming a personal interest in the Spor Mountain area.

During late December or the first part of January, 1963, Ford and Anderson as President of Ranchers, determined to jump Moody's claims to the extent that discovery had not been accomplished upon them. After this plan was determined upon and while it was undisclosed and unknown to defendants, Ford and Anderson continued to negotiate with Moody and obtained permission to get the results of Moody's prior drilling results from Ortman. At that time Moody did not know that Ford was claiming a personal interest in the area. After plans for staking conflicting claims had been made by Ranchers and Ford, and after Ford was advised on January 8, 1963, that Anaconda was locating certain Filler claims on behalf of Moody, Ford first disclosed to Anaconda and Moody that he asserted a personal interest in that land.

More than a week prior to January 12, 1963, plans had been implemented for relocating Moody's claims, then known to have been acquired by Anaconda, by the mapping of the areas where the new claims were to be located, by the utilization of Moody's drill hole information obtained from Ortman, and other drill hole information available to Ford from his previous employment by G.B.C., in determining the new claims, and by ordering the printing of signs and the procurement of claim stakes.

Ford, acting for and within the scope of his employment by plaintiff, planned each of the three attempted entries by Ranchers, supervised the mapping of the areas where claims should be located in order to cover ore bodies believed by him to exist from information previously obtained as an employee of

G.B.C. and in ostensible negotiations to purchase Moody's claims for Ranchers. Ford personally directed activities during the three attempted entries. Since then, Ford has acquired a personal interest in any rights that may be recognized in Ranchers in the disputed claims and in any damages that may be recovered in this action.

Under these circumstances I have concluded that Ford would not be in the position of one attempting in 'good faith' to locate the particular claims in question in January and February, 1963. I have further concluded that all of his conduct and position is imputable to plaintiff either by reason of authorization or ratification, and that if as to some particular element this does not affirmatively appear in the record, his position and that of the plaintiff Ranchers are so interwoven that it is nonetheless infeasible to separate the bad faith of one from the other by reason of considerations akin to unjust enrichment.

I cannot find that Ford and his principal, Ranchers, were in bad faith in the sense that they did not believe that they had a right to relocate the defendant's claim if no valid discoveries had been made by the latter. But belief in the efficacy of legal technicality is not the only inquiry on the question of good faith. Good faith also necessarily involves an honest intention to abstain from taking any unconscionable advantage of another even through the forms or technicalities of law. Knowledge of an adverse claim does not of itself indicate bad faith and may not even be evidence of it unless accompanied by some improper means to defeat such claim. But here in my judgment the facts transcend these proper situations and require a holding that plaintiff's claims to the bellwethers in question are inferior to the claims of the defendants. The case may be close to the line; and my decision is not in any sense a moral judgment, but a practical application of what I regard to be the proper rule of law that must be applied.

I believe it to be sound doctrine that second entries upon mining claims are rendered insupportable as against those seeking to maintain their prior possession short of mineral discovery or *pedis possessio* only if the subsequent entries are not made in good faith. The law cannot recognize mineral discoveries upon the three bellwether claims specified, nor any rights of the defendants therein under the doctrine of *pedis possessio*. I cannot accede to the theory that citizens acting in good faith can be prevented from entering into, or can be lawfully ejected from, the public domain by other claimants who have not made, or are not working diligently to make, mineral discoveries within the established doctrine of *pedis possessio* merely because they have the physical power to pre-empt large areas of the public domain by force, or because they thereby require the ejected party rather than themselves to seek affirmative relief in court. The public policy against breaches of the peace, monopolization and speculation with respect to mineral rights on the public domain are too compelling to permit any such jockeying for position to be determinative on this point.

For the reasons stated herein, in view of the stipulation of facts on file and the findings herein contained, which are believed adequate to satisfy the requirements of Fed.R.Civ.P. 52(a), relief is hereby denied to the plaintiff on the submitted issues concerning the bellwether claims. I express no opinion concerning the reserved issues nor the effect, if any, of this decision upon them.

In any event, this interlocutory decision involves controlling questions of law as to which there is substantial ground for difference of opinion, and an immediate appeal may materially advance the ultimate termination of the litigation.

NOTES

1. Why does the court refuse to apply *pedis possessio* on a group claim or area basis? Do you agree with the court's reasoning? Does Congress' failure to amend the mining law necessarily imply that Congress is satisfied with things the way they are?

2. If *Adams v. Benedict* were the only relevant authority, do you think *Ranchers* would have been decided as it was? Which decision, *Adams v. Benedict* or *Ranchers,* do you think is most likely to encourage the orderly and peaceful mineral development of the public domain? Why?

3. Why did the court reject the traditional distinction between a quiet title action and a suit for ejectment? What would have been the result in the *Ranchers* case if the court had held that the plaintiff, whose cause of action was for ejectment, had to prove not just a better title than defendant but also had to prove his title "against the world?" Would such a holding encourage peaceful development or would it encourage the use of "private armies"? Would such a holding encourage development and exploration at all, or would it more likely encourage individuals and mining companies to amass vast tracts of the public domain for purposes of speculation?

4. There are at least two aspects to the good faith requirement discussed in the *Ranchers* case. First, one who enters onto the federal public domain must in good faith intend to locate a piece of ground for mining purposes. *See* 30 U.S.C. § 29. *See also, United States v. Coleman,* 390 U.S. 599 (1968). "Therefore, a location made for personal residence purposes, for the purpose of acquiring title to valuable property fronting on water or a highway, or for the purpose of imposing duress upon the prior claimant in order to obtain some economic benefit is void for lack of good faith on the part of the locator." 1 American Law of Mining, § 595, at 914 (1982).

Second, and in addition, the relocator of a mining claim must also be in good faith with respect to his relocation. It was with this second type of good faith that Ford ran afoul in the *Ranchers* case. How does the court in *Ranchers* define good faith? In *Continental Oil Co. v. Natrona Service, Inc.,* 588 F.2d 792 (10th Cir. 1978) the Tenth Circuit defined good faith as follows:

> [A] junior locator lacks good faith when he seeks possession solely on the basis of defects in the senior locator's claims. Mere knowledge . . . of a relocator that a locator claims superior rights does not constitute bad faith when the relocator enters, but that prior location places a duty on the locator to make inquiry to determine the extent of the adverse party's work performed in relation to exploration and development. Presence or absence of good faith on the part of [the relocator] in entering the land

constituted a question of fact for the jury." *Id.* at 797.

5. Definitions similar to the one used by the Tenth Circuit in *Conoco* have been criticized on the ground that, if carried to their logical conclusion they encourage speculation rather than exploration and development. Do you see why this is so? *See* 1 American Law of Mining, § 5.96 at 918-19 (1982). Notice how the court in *Geomet, supra,* limited the holding of *Bagg v. New Jersey Loan Co.,* 354 P. 2d 40 (Ariz. 1960), in order to avoid this problem. *Bagg* had held that "if a subsequent locator enters into possession of a claim knowing that a prior party is in possession of it and has located it, the entry is in bad faith." *Id.* at 45. *See also, Kanab Uranium Corp. v. Consolidated Uranium Mines,* 227 F.2d 434 (10th Cir. 1955), discussed in the principal case.

D. Rights Incident to the Location of a Tunnel Site

ENTERPRISE MIN. CO. V. RICO ASPEN CONSOLIDATED MINING CO.
167 U.S. 108 (1897)

This case involves the construction of Rev. Stat. § 2323, which reads as follows:

> "Where a tunnel is run for the development of a vein or lode, or for the discovery of mines, the owners of such tunnel shall have the right of possession of all veins or lodes within 3,000 feet from the face of such tunnel on the line thereof, not previously known to exist, discovered in such tunnel, to the same extent as if discovered from the surface; and locations on the line of such tunnel of veins or lodes not appearing on the surface, made by other parties after the commencement of the tunnel, and while the same is being prosecuted with reasonable diligence, shall be invalid; but failure to prosecute the work on the tunnel for six months shall be considered as an abandonment of the right to all undiscovered veins on the line of such tunnel."

The facts are these:

The Group tunnel site, under which the Enterprise Mining Company, the defendant and appellant, claims the right to the ores in controversy, was located on July 25, 1887, and the certificate of location was filed in the office of the county clerk and recorder of the county in which the location was made on August 29, 1887.

The Vestal lode mining claim, under which the plaintiffs, the appellees, claim title, is based upon a discovery made on March 23, 1888. The claim was located on April 1, 1888, and the location certificate was filed for record on April 3, 1888.

The situation of the properties is sufficiently disclosed by the following diagram:

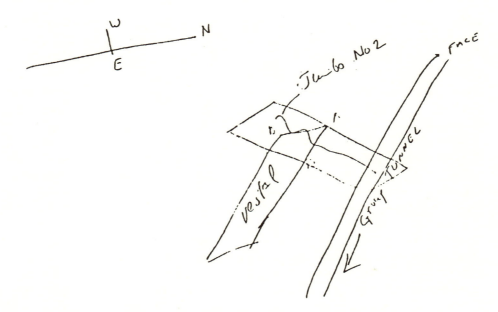

The ore in controversy is within the limits of the tract, A, B, C, D. As to this tract, the two locations, the Vestal and Jumbo No. 2, conflict. The owners of the Vestal claim made application in 1890 for a patent. No adverse proceedings were instituted by the defendant, and a patent for the claim was issued on February 6, 1892. At the time of these proceedings no discovery of a vein in the tunnel had been made. But on June 15, 1892, a vein was discovered 1920 feet from its portal, at the place marked "discovery" on the diagram. Immediately thereafter the defendant caused the boundaries of the claim Jumbo No. 2 to be located upon the surface of the earth, and a certificate of location to be duly recorded, in which it claimed 54 feet along the vein to the northeasterly of the tunnel, and 1446 feet southwesterly. The position of this claim appears sufficiently on the diagram. The portion of this vein within the limits of the Vestal claim is about 750 feet from the line of the tunnel . . . .

Mr. Justice BREWER, after stating the case, delivered the opinion of the court.

It will be observed that so far as the mere location of the two claims, Vestal and Jumbo No. 2, the former was prior in time to the latter, and would, if there were no other facts, give priorty of right to the ore within the limits of the conflicting territory. The tunnel was, however, located some eight or nine months before the discovery and location of the Vestal Claim, and the statute gives to the owners of such tunnel the right to "all veins or lodes within 3000 feet from the face of such tunnel on the line thereof, not previously known to exist." By virtue of this section, therefore, the right of the defendant to this vein was prior to that of the plaintiffs to the mineral in their claim. In this respect the Circuit Court and the Court of Appeals agreed. The matters now in dispute are the extent of that right and the effect of a failure to "adverse" the application for a patent.

The right to this vein discovered in the tunnel is by the statute declared to be "to the same extent as if discovered from the surface." If discovered from the surface, the discoverer might, under Rev. Stat. § 2320, claim "one thousand five hundred feet in length along the vein or lode." The clear import of the language, then, is to give to the tunnel owner, discovering a vein in the tunnel, a right to appropriate fifteen hundred feet in length of that vein. When must he indicate the particular fifteen hundred feet which he desires to claim? Counsel for plaintiffs contend that it should be done when, in the first instance, the tunnel is located, and that if no specification is then made the line of the tunnel is to be taken as dividing the extent of the claim to the vein, so that the tunnel owner would be entitled to only 750 feet on either side of the tunnel; while counsel for defendant insist that he need not do so until the actual discovery of the vein in the tunnel. We think the defendant's counsel are right. In order to make a location, there must be a discovery; . . . The discovery in the tunnel is like a discovery on the surface. Until one is made, there is no right to locate a claim in respect to the vein, and the time to determine where and how it shall be located arises only upon the discovery—whether such discovery be made on the surface or in the tunnel. The case of *Erhardt v. Boaro,* 113 U.S. 527, is not in point, for there the preliminary notice, which was made upon a discovery from the surface, simply claimed "1500 feet on this mineral bearing lode," without further specification as to boundaries or direction; and it was held that that was equivalent to a claim for 750 feet in each direction from the discovery shaft.

It may be true, as counsel claim, that this construction of the statute gives the tunnel excavator some advantages. Surely it is not strange that Congress deemed it wise to offer some inducements for running a tunnel into the side of a mountain. At the same time, it placed specific limitations on the rights which the tunnel owner could acquire. He could acquire no veins which had theretofore been discovered from the surface. His right reached only to blind veins, as they may be called, veins not known to exist, and not discovered from the surface before he commenced his tunnel. . . . Such is the import of the letter to which counsel refer, form Commissioner Drummond, of date September 20, 1872. Land Office Report, 1872, p. 60; 3 Copp's Land Owner 130. It may be also noticed that in this letter the commissioner affirmed the right of location on either side of the tunnel, in these words: "When a lode is struck or discovered for the first time by running a tunnel, the tunnel owners have the option of recording their claim of fifteen hundred feet all on one side of the point of discovery or intersection, or partly on one and partly upon the other side thereof."
. . . .

The remaining question is whether the failure to "adverse" the application for a patent for the Vestal claim destroyed or impaired the rights of the defendant. We think not. . . .

Now, at the time the application for patent to the Vestal claim was presented and the proceedings had thereon, the defendant knew of no vein which would enable it to dispute the right of the owners of the Vestal to a patent. The Vestal claim, it will be perceived, runs parallel to the line of the tunnel, and is distant therefrom some 500 feet. The presumption, of course, would be that the vein ran lengthwise, and not crosswise, of the claim as located, and such a vein would not, unless it radically changed its course, cross the line of the tunnel.

Whether it did or not, or whether any other vein should be found in the tunnel which should cross the territory of the Vestal, was a matter of pure speculation; and there would be no propriety in maintaining a suit to establish defendant's inchoate right, and delay the Vestal claimants in securing a patent on a mere possibility which might never ripen into a fact . . . .

NOTES

1. Why did Congress make special provision and give special protection to prospectors who constructed tunnels in the course of exploring for minerals? Could many of the problems that have been encountered with the doctrine of *pedis possessio* be solved if Congress were to adopt a *pedis possessio* statute analogous in material respects to § 2320 relating to tunnels? What problems would you foresee with such a statute?

2. At the time the Mining Law of 1872 was adapted, tunnels were a viable method for exploring for minerals at depth. Changes in mining technology have made tunnel construction economically impracticable, and it has been largely replaced by drilling. Given this change in mining practice, should § 2320 be read to include drill holes even without further legislation by Congress? If not, why not?

2 THE FORM OF LOCATION

A. Lode or Placer

BOWEN V. SIL-FLO CORP.
451 P.2d 626 (Ariz. 1969)

MOLLOY, Judge.

This is an appeal from a judgment rendered in a declaratory judgment and quiet title action as to unpatented mining claims. The action is, in part, a suit to determine an adverse claim filed in a patent application proceeding. . . .

. . . .

The most significant finding by the trial court in this action was that the areas encompassed by these four lode mining claims contain veins or lodes of perlite ore in place and are of such character that the ground within said lode claims was subject to being located under the lode claim statute. The court made no finding as to whether the areas outside these lode claims and within the placer claims of Bowen are subject to being located as lode or placer, apparently finding that the position of the parties was not adverse on this factual question.

On the basis of its factual findings, the trial court entered judgment which, in effect, quieted the title of Sil-Flo to the two lode mining claims, Elva F. No. 1 and Sandy No. 1, subject to the fee title of the United States of America, and declared that Sil-Flo was the owner of a right to mine and remove perlite ore from Bowen's two lode claims, Superior Perlite No. 1 and David R. No. 1 and from Bowen's two placer claims, Superior Perlite No. 1 Placer and Superior Perlite No. 2 Placer Amended, which right the court declared to be a continuing one for an indefinite term, subject to cancellation only if Sil-Flo defaulted in its obligations under the two written agreements with Bowen. The Court further declared that Bowen's two lode claims were valid and subsisting, that Sil-Flo had not defaulted in its obligations under these agreements, and that, in the event Bowen should acquire title from the United States Government as to any of the subject claims, he would hold such title subject to the paramount rights of Sil-Flo, as established by the decree. Multiple contentions are advanced both attacking and supporting the decisions reached below. We believe that proper appellate disposition is achieved by coping with five questions.

[Only the first of the five questions the court dealt with in its opinion is included here.]

HAS THERE BEEN A DISCOVERY OF A LODE OR VEIN OF PERLITE ORE ON THESE FOUR LODE MINING CLAIMS?

Because of the apparently relentless dichotomy established by judicial interpretation of pertinent mining statutes, there has been a plethora of litigation to determine whether particular ore bodies are locatable as lode or placer. The many judicial decisions have left the distinction as beclouded as when the conundrum was first posed by the 1870 enactment of the second of the two controlling statutes, which, in their evolved form now read in pertinent part:

"Mining claims upon veins or lodes of quartz or other rock in place bearing gold, silver, cinnabar, lead, tin, copper, or other valuable deposits, * * * shall be governed * * *." 30 U.S.C.A. § 23.

"Claims usually called 'placers,' including all forms of deposit, excepting veins of quartz, or other rock in place, shall be subject to entry and patent, under like circumstances and conditions, and upon similar proceedings, as are provided for vein or lode claims; * * *." 30 U.S.C.A. § 35.

Words have been generously included in many judicial opinions in an attempt to remove the latent ambiguity inherent in this statutory language which results from the infinite variety of forms in which mineral wealth is found deposited in the earth's crust. Among the more quoted explanations of this elusive distinction is:

"What constitutes a lode or vein of mineral matter has been no easy thing to define. In this court no clear definition has been given. On the circuit it has been often attempted. Mr. Justice FIELD, in the Eureka Case, 4 Sawy. 302, shows that the word is not always used in the same sense by scientific works on geology and mineralogy, and by those engaged in the actual working of mines. After discussing these sources of information, he says: 'It is difficult to give any definition of this term, as understood and used in the acts of congress, which will not be subject to criticism. A fissure in the earth's crust, an opening in its rocks and strata made by some force of nature, in which the mineral is deposited, would seem to be essential to a lode in the judgment of geologists. But to the practical miner the fissure and its walls are only of importance as indicating the boundaries within which he may look for and reasonably expect to find the ore he seeks. A continuous body of mineralized rock lying within any other well-defined boundaries on the earth's surface, and under it, would equally constitute, in his eyes, a lode. We are of opinion therefore, that the term as used in the acts of congress is applicable to any zone or belt of mineralized rock lying within boundaries clearly separating it from the neighboring rock."

"This definition has received repeated commendation in other cases, especially in Stevens v. Williams, 1 McCrary, 488, where a shorter definition by Judge HALLETT, of the Colorado circuit court, is also approved, to-wit: 'In general it may be said that a lode or vein is a body of mineral, or a mineral body of rock, within defined boundaries, in the general mass of the mountain.' " Iron Silver Min. Co. v. Cheesman, 116 U.S. 529, 6 S.Ct. 481, 483, 29 L.Ed 712 (1886).

In our view, there is substantial evidence in this record to support the trial court's finding that this perlite ore is in the form of a lode or vein. Three contentions are advanced as to why this deposit of perlite should not be regarded as a lode. Before considering these, it will clear the air to consider attacks that are *not* made here.

There is no contention made that, because this body of ore lies in a blanket or 'pancake' shape, it is not subject to the lode mining statute. As to this, *see* Iron Silver Min. Co. v. Mike & Starr Gold & Silver Min. Co., 143 U.S. 394, 12 S.Ct. 543, 36 L.Ed. 201 (1892); San Francisco Chemical Co. v. Duffield, 201 F. 830 (8th Cir. 1912); Iron Silver Min. Co. v. Campbell, 17 Colo. 267, 29 P. 513 (1892); Duggan v. Davey, 4 Dak. 110, 26 N.W. 887 (1886); and 1 American Law of Mining § 5.20, at 763.

Nor is there any contention made that this perlite does *not* lay in a blanket-like shape. The appellant's expert witness, Robert Wilson, described this perlite as a "* * * blanket deposit * * *." All of the geological evidence indicates that, in order to form perlite, the flow of lava from which it originates must cool at a relatively rapid rate in comparison with other rhyolite rock and that, if it were covered deeply, it would crystalize to form a harder rhyolite with no known commercial use. Two diamond drill holes in the pit on the Elva F. No. 1 claim showed that the perlite turned abruptly to rhyolite at a depth of approximately 40 feet, this level being, in turn, approximately 100 feet below the top of the pit.

Nor is there any contention that this perlite is of the 'softer' material, *see* Reynolds v. Iron Silver Min. Co., 116 U.S. 687, 6 S.Ct. 601, 605, 29 L.Ed. 774 (1866), or in a 'loose state,' *see* United States v. Iron Silver Min. Co., 128 U.S. 673, 9 S.Ct. 195, 197, 32 L.Ed. 571 (1888), so as to be placer. All of the evidence is to the effect that this perlite is hard rock and must be detached from its position in the earth by blasting methods customary to those used in open pits of hard rock ore.

Of the three attacks made, the principal one is that perlite does not satisfy the requirements of 30 U.S.C.A. § 23, because, though it is admittedly mineral in nature, it is not in lode form because it is not "* * * rock in place *bearing* gold, silver * * * or other valuable deposits * * *." (Emphasis added.) The argument is made that the perlite found in these beds is a valuable rock in itself but that it does not *contain* or *bear* valuable minerals. Bowen relies upon two authorities to support this view: Henderson v. Fulton, 35 L.D. 652 (1907); and 2 Lindley, Mines § 421 (3d ed. 1914). While the authority cited is pertinent, it is our view that there are more authoritative declarations that it is not disqualifying that a lode consists of nonmetallic minerals of such a nature that the entire body of ore has commercial value.

Decisions which are persuasive to this court are: San Francisco Chemical Co. v. Duffield, 201 F. 830 (8th Cir. 1912); Webb v. American Asphaltum Mining Co., 157 F. 203 (8th Cir. 1907); Duffield v. San Francisco Chemical Co., 205 F. 480 (9th Cir. 1913), reversing District Court decision at 198 F. 942 (1912). The impact of these decisions is summarized in the following statement:

> "The idea that nonmetallic minerals were excluded from lode locations because only metallic minerals were mentioned by name in the statute was laid to rest in Webb v. American Asphaltum Mining Co. 157 F. 203 (8th cir. 1907), where gilsonite, a petroleum type of mineral, was held to be locatable as a lode, if the lode characteristics were present. Thereafter, deposits of calcium phosphate in Wyoming and Idaho were held to be lodes were [*sic*] circumscribed within the general mass of the mountain." 1 American Law of Mining § 5.10, at 741.

The second contention advanced as to why this perlite cannot be a lode is that it lies on the surface of the ground. Unquestionably, in the area of three of these lode claims (David R. No. 1, Superior Perlite No. 1 and Elva F. No. 1), there is exposed on the surface an irregularly shaped area of perlite ore, approximately 3,000 feet, in a north-south direction, by 1,000 feet in an east-west direction. In places within the area, the ore is covered by rhyolite or obsidian breccia, or by a thin pumiceous skin of waste material. This exposed, or nearly exposed area is in a depression between hills and has been subject to erosion for a substantial period of geologic time. Sil-Flo's Sandy No. 1 claim, to the east, has only a small area of exposed perlite, most of its deposit being covered by a layer of a rock called 'Gila conglomerate.' Whether the ore there discovered is a projection of the same ore body exposed in the western claims is not conclusively shown by the evidence and there is no finding of fact on this point. A geologic study made at Sil-Flo's behest indicates that, to the west, the exposed body of ore disappears under a bluff of noncommercial rhyolite rock, and, on the east, projects under the same layer of Gila conglomerate that covers the Sandy No. 1. To the north of this main body of ore, the perlite grades into obsidian breccia, a rock with a similar chemical constituency to perlite but without its valuable physical properties. To the south, the geologic study does not indicate the reason for the termination of the exposed ore (the study being limited to the area of these claims), but Bowen's patent application and testimony at trial indicate that the north-south dimension of the exposed ore is 2000-3000 feet.

There is reputable authority holding that, in order for a mineral deposit to be a vein or lode, it cannot lie "merely on the surface." Quote from Ricketts, American Mining Law § 158, at 131 (4th ed.). Among the cases cited by Ricketts, to support his position and principally relied upon by the appellant here, are: Stevens v. Gill, Case No. 13,398, 23 Fed.Cas. 12 (D.C.Colo. 1879); Tabor v. Dexler, Case No. 13,723, 23 Fed.Cas. 615 (D.C.Colo. 1878); and Leadville Co. v. Fitzgerald, Case No. 8,158, 15 Fed.Cas. No. 98 (D.C.Colo. 1879). Each of these federal decisions was authored by Judge Hallett, a trial judge of early renown in mining jurisprudence. In each of this trilogy, the concern was with whether there were extralateral rights, *not* whether the lode claim was valid. That Judge Hallett considered that surface ore might be validly located as a lode is indicated by the following:

> "For the decision of this motion it is enough to say, that where the mass overlying the ore is a mere drift, or a loose deposit, the ore is not 'in place,' within the meaning of the act. *Upon principles recently explained, a location on such a deposit of ore may be sufficient to hold all that lies within the lines;* but it can not give a right to ore in other territory, although the ore body may extend beyond the lines." (Emphasis added.) Tabor v. Dexler, 23 Fed.Cas. at 615.

No case has been cited which fits the facts here. In its findings, the trial court found that this perlite has "*** a clearly defined hanging wall, readily apparent to visual inspection * * *." The physical evidence would suggest that the "hanging wall," now existing to the west and east, at one time covered the exposed ore in the area of these claims. No authority has been called to our attention which would hold that, because a substantial portion of a vein or lode has been exposed by erosion, that it no longer has the characteristic of a lode. We see no purpose in creating new law which would thus metamorphose a lode into a placer and thus defeat bona fide efforts to satisfy these ambiguous statutes. This ore body is certainly fixed "in place" from a layman's view. If a lode cannot exist without a "hanging wall," and we do not find the law to be clear on this, we find a sufficient one here.

If our decision needs reinforcement, we find it in the fact that at the time this lode claim was initiated it was a custom in this mining district to locate similar ore under the lode statute. We agree with the following:

> "A locator who makes a good faith location in reliance upon past practice should be protected regardless of the court's view as to what might have been the most appropriate form of location." 1 American Law of Mining § 5.20, at 764.

The third attack upon lode status is that perlite is locatable as building stone under 30 U.S.C.A. § 161, and therefore cannot be a lode. 30 U.S.C.A. § 161 reads, in part, as follows:

"Any person authorized to enter lands under the mining laws of the United States *may* enter lands that are chiefly valuable for building stone under the provisions of the law in relation to placer-mineral claims." (Emphasis added.)

By its very terms, this statute is permissive ("may"), and the appellant has cited no authority holding that, because a mineral deposit might be locatable under this section of the code, it necessarily could not be located as a lode. Again, this court sees no reason to create new law in this direction. The purpose of these statutes is to encourage development of the public domain by bona fide miners. Bagg v. New Jersey Loan Company, 88 Ariz. 182, 190, 354 P.2d 40, 45 (1960); Rummell v. Bailey, 7 Utah 2d 137, 320 P.2d 653 (1958). We see no reason to create a new trap for the unwary. Moreover, the only authority coming to our attention would indicate that perlite, being a building *material,* rather than building *stone,* does not come within the above-quoted "Stone Act." Dunbar Lime Co. v. Utah-Idaho Sugar Co., 17 F.2d 351 (8th Cir. 1926).

Finding that this perlite ore in the area of these four lode claims is a lode formation, it necessarily follows from the undisputed facts of this case that the judgment of the court quieting Sil-Flo's title to the Elva F. No. 1 and the Sandy No. 1 must be sustained.***

NOTES

1. The mining law (30 U.S.C. § 22) speaks of the manner of locating "veins or lodes." Although the courts often use the terms synonymously, they do have distinct meanings.

Originally the word "vein" was narrow in its significance, defining a single clearly marked seam or fissure-filling in the country rock. The word "lode" was a broader term, applied not only to ore-bearing veins in a narrow sense, but to various more complicated forms of ore-deposits as well.

Under the influence of the mining acts of congress, it has gradually become more and more customary to use the two terms synonymously, and to give to the word "vein" the broad definition that would formerly have been regarded as more properly applicable to the word "lode." Still the custom is not rigid, and the miner, as a rule, continues to make certain distinctions in the use of the terms. For example, when his deposit contains separate parallel seams, or sheets, of ore, and he regards the whole as a unit, he may call it either a "lode" or a "vein," but the separate sheets he designates as distinct veins within the limits of his lode. He calls the entire mass vein-matter, and his conception is, that the word "vein" refers either to the entire mass or to narrow streaks within the mass, while the word "lode" always refers to the entire mass.

In a very general way a lode may be described as a mass of mineralized rock in place, the word "mineral" referring only to commercially valuable constituents. The form is usually more or less tabular or sheet-like, but occasionally too irregular to fit such descriptions.

Referring to ores of the more valuable metals, such as gold, silver, quicksilver, copper, lead, etc., the lodes in which they are found are generally formed by fissuring of the country rock and subsequent introduction of mineralizing solutions depositing ore-bearing material in the fissures and occasionally mineralizing portions of the wall-rocks by processes of pre-existing cavities, such as occur in limestone.

The lode as it commonly occurs may then be defined as the ore-bearing filling of a single fissure or of a system of interconnected fissures and pre-existing cavities in the country rock, together with occasional mineralized masses of the wall-rocks.

Lindley on Mines, § 290A, at 649-50 (3d ed. 1914)

2. "The whole subject of the classification of mineral deposits [is] . . . one in which the interests of the miner have entirely overridden the reasoning of the chemists and geologists. 'The miners . . . made the definition first. As used by miners, before being defined by any authority, the term lode simply meant that formation by which the miner could be led or guided. It is an alteration of the verb 'lead', and whatever the miner could follow, expecting to find ore was his lode. Some formation within which he could expect to find ore, and out of which he could not expect to find ore, was his lode." *Eureka Consolidated Mining Co. v. Richmond Mining Co.,* 8 Fed. Cas. 819, 822-23 (D. Nev. 1877).

GLOBE MINING CO. V. ANDERSON
318 P.2d 373 (Wyo. 1957)

[The following excerpt is taken from footnote 4 of the Globe Mining Co. decision:)

4. Uncertainty presently exists regarding the type of claim by which a disseminated uranium deposit of epigenetic origin should be located. Divergent viewpoints on this subject seem well illustrated in the following statements:

"* * * Normally * * * a discovery [of uranium] at depth would be classified as a *lode* or *vein,* though an exception to this rule arises in the case of buried channels of ancient rivers which, historically, have been classified as *placers.* * * *" (Emphasis supplied.)

101 Cong.Rec., p. 9196, 81st answer (being a portion of the questions and answers developed during the panel discussions of the Wyoming Stock Growers Association, June 9, 1955, and the Wyoming Natural Resources Board, June 10, 1955, and later reported to Congress by Senator Barrett).

"* * * the locatable mineral [uranium] should be classified as lode or placer. A 'lode' is a vein or 'aggregation of metal embedded in quartz or other rock in place,' while a 'placer' is a location of minerals 'found loose in sand or gravel and not in the vein or in place.' Though the distinction is essential there is uncertainty, and the Utah court has stated that 'lode' is a pratical, nonexacting miner's term. The test is the character of the deposit

("rock in place") rather than the type of mineral involved. Whether to locate uranium as a lode or placer is in doubt since uranium minerals have been found in every formation in the Colorado Plateau and in no definite pattern. While some vertical deposits of uranium in fractures are now being mined the predominant formation is horizontal, being 'flat-bedded' and 'isolated' as are the host rock sediments. Since uranium deposits found in fractures should clearly be located as lodes, and most other uranium deposits are produced from ores which 'interfinger with mudstones or silt stones' so that they are generally considered by the mining industry to be lodes, it is herein assumed that uranium mining claims should properly be so located."
4 Utah L.Rev. 239, 244, 245.

"*** the deposits of uranium in the shinarump sands were epigenetic. That is to say, carried into the formation by some solution after the host rock was laid. While the decisions of courts which have dealt with the problem do not make the epigenetic feature a necessary characteristic of a lode formation, it is important in this case in that it indicates in some degree that the formations above and below the shinarump sands were less penetrable by the solution carrying the uranium ores and therefore became boundaries to the zone of mineralization. What I have stated is not to be interpreted as a conclusion on my part that in all cases the boundaries of a lode deposit must consist of country rock so different from the host rock that it does not or cannot contain in some degree mineralization like that of the host rock. In other words, I find and believe from what I have heard in this case and in the investigation I have made bearing upon the issues involved that the boundary of a lode deposit may be fixed by the impoverishment of the mass beyond the limits of profitable extraction."
Ula Uranium, Inc., v. Allen (an unappealed case from the District Court of San Juan County, Utah, the foregoing being an excerpt from Judge F. W. Keller's Memorandum Decision, dated October 6, 1956).

Ambiguity in legal interpretations regarding the location of mining claims for this apparently vital mineral may be more than merely frustrating and expensive to well-intentioned prospectors. It may seriously retard a crucial industry by undue litigation, ultimately forcing a new method of mining development to be adopted by legislative action—such as the withdrawal of public land from mineral entry and the reservation of same for acquisition by lease, as is presently done with petroleum. Whether or not this might be desirable is not for judicial decision but is a matter for legislative determination. Meanwhile, there could be irreparable loss, both public and private. Accordingly, we would perhaps be remiss if we did not express our views on the subject.

A commonly used definition of a lode is "a body of mineral, or mineral-bearing rock, within defined boundaries in the general mass of the mountain." 1 Lindley on Mines, 3d ed., p. 656. This definition has been most often applied to discussions of primary deposits of minerals. It is significant that at the time of the enactment of R.S. § 2320 (1878) those minerals in which this Nation was most interested often occurred in fissures and along weak lines in rock. For that reason, many decisions have emphasized the fact that a vein or lode must have "well defined boundaries." Some courts recognized that many ore deposits possessed all the essential attributes of lodes even though they did not have well defined boundaries in the original sense. However, the words "well defined boundaries" became so firmly ensconced in the legal vocabulary that they often haunted the decisions. Today, the economic necessity of modern civilization has created a need for minerals which by geologic chance frequently occur in ill defined or formless masses. Many of these were deposited epigenetically, i.e., by mineral in solution (a) permeating between grains and crystals of the country rock, (b) replacing certain existing formations, and (c) filling cracks, crevices, and pore spaces—*after* the surrounding rock had been laid down. See Page, Stocking, and Smith, Contributions to the Geology of Uranium and Thorium, International Conference, 1955—Geological Survey Professional Paper 300, pp. 41 and 97; Nininger, Minerals for Atomic Energy, 2d ed., p. 21 ff. Therefore, even though *placer, vein,* and *lode* are primarily miners' terms, evolved for practical rather than technical meaning, the scientific definitions of these words as used by geologists become important in legal considerations.

Such definitions by various authors writing on geological subjects vary to some extent but in general are remarkably uniform, and we think may be fairly summarized as: A *placer* is a deposit of heavy minerals concentrated mechanically; a *vein* is a deposit of minerals formed in weaknesses in the earth's crust either by injection of molten rock or by water solution moving through openings and depositing minerals in and along such openings or in replacement of materials already there; a *lode* is a portion of the earth containing several veins spaced closely enough together so that all of them together with the intervening rock can be mined as a unit. See generally Longwell and Flint, Introduction to Physical Geology, 1955, p. 382; Emmons, Thiel, Stauffer, and Allison, Geology: Principles and Processes; 4th ed., p. 597; and Longwell, Knopf, and Flint, Physical Geology, 3d ed., p. 531.

These geological definitions indicate that the basic characteristic of a vein is the origin of the deposit contained therein. However, the earlier decisions usually dealt with minerals which by nature tended to form largely in cracks and crevices so that courts and administrative agencies found no occasion to consider the origin of the mineral as important but instead relied entirely on its form as being confined within narrow, definite boundaries. They often used such rigid definitions of lode as "mineral lying within well defined seams or fissures in the surrounding rock," 36 Am.Jur., Mines and Minerals § 70, or "any zone or belt of mineralized rock lying within boundaries clearly separating it from the neighboring rock," 58 C.J.S. Mines and Minerals § 3, at p. 31—sometimes saying, "The critical test is the manner in which the deposit occurs rather than the origin of the deposit," U.S. Gypsum Co., 60 I.D. 24, 25. Fortunately, there has been some much-needed recognition of the fact that such rigid definitions cannot be of universal application but rather must be tempered by scientific findings as to the nature of the deposits under consideration. For instance in the case of Moulton Mining Co. v. Anaconda Copper Mining Co., 9 Cir., 23 F.2d 811, 814, the court said:

"* * * while the existence or nonexistence of a vein is often dependent upon mixed questions of law and fact, in this instance the evidence of mineral showing and of the physical characteristics of a vein are so strong that as a matter of law the only conclusion that could properly be reached was that it was a vein. Fundamentally, of course, we are guided by the well-recognized knowledge that in the complexities of lodes, with indefinite and irregular walls, while the mineral association of rock in place is an essential element in the definition, the nature of the material, the form of the deposit, and the character of the boundaries are often variant (Lindley on Mines, § 294, p. 265; Iron Silver Co. v. Cheesman, 116 U.S. 529, 6 S.Ct. 481, 29 L.Ed. 712; Star Mining Co. v. Federal Mining & Smelting Co., 9 Cir., 265 F. 881), and that it is not necessary for the formation of a disseminated lode that there should be any walls or any sheering. 'It simply requires a more or less porous rock through which the solutions may pass. * * * They may have indefinite boundaries.' [This quote is a portion of the illuminating views of Winchell, a mining engineer who testified in the Star case, *supra,* at pages 891, 892, and apparently fully convinced the court of appeals.] Thus, while what are spoken of as structural boundaries are not always necessary to constitute a vein or lode, there must be ore bodies coming from the same source, impressed with the same form, and appearing to have been created by the same processes."

The views thus expressed would seem to apply to disseminated, epigenetic deposits of uranium. Under this interpretation, except as specifically provided by State or Federal laws, various portions of a mineral-bearing area coming from the same general source and found to have been created by the same processes of deposit *from solution* constitute a *lode* (rock in place) for the purpose of locating mining claims even though they may be formless and are not enclosed by definite boundaries.

* * *

NOTES

1. In some mining areas hundreds of fissures bearing valuable minerals may occur in close proximity to each other. In such an area, does each fissure have to be located as a separate lode claim, or can all of the fissures collectively be located as one claim? The answer to this question has important practical consequences. The increased expense of locating many claims instead of one is obvious. In addition, depending on the physical relationship of the fissures to the claim (that is, if any of the fissures cross the sidelines of the claim) valuable extralateral rights may be lost (see chapter 9 *infra*). The most widely accepted test for determining whether a particular area contains one lode or many was originally formulated in *Eureka Consolidated Mining Co. v. Richmond Mining Co.,* 8 Fed. Cas. 819, 823 (D. Nev. 1877) as follows:

We are of the opinion, therefore, that the term [lode] as used in the acts of congress is applicable to any zone of mineralized rock lying within boundaries clearly separating it from the neighboring rock. It includes, to use the language cited by counsel, all deposits of mineral matter found through a mineralized zone or belt coming from the same source, impressed with the same forms, and appearing to have been created by the same processes.

2. In the excerpted portion of the *Globe* opinion, did the Court conclude that all uranium deposits should be located as lodes, only that epigenetic uranium deposits should be located as lodes, or merely that the uranium deposit under consideration should be located as a lode? If the latter, couldn't the Court have eliminated much of the "uncertainty" about how uranium claims should be located by holding at least that all epigenetic deposits are lodes? What would be the disadvantages of such a holding? Could these disadvantages be eliminated or reduced if the Court made its holding prospective only?

3. A lode must have distinct boundaries although, as the principal case illustrates, not necessarily structural ones. Does the Court in *Globe* hold that if the ore bodies within the lode come "from the same source, [are] impressed with the same form, and appear to have been created by the processes" then the distinct boundaries requirement is satisfied? In what sense are these characteristics substitutes for distinct boundaries?

TITANIUM ACTYNITE INDUSTRIES V. McLENNAN
272 F. 2d 667 (10th Cir. 1960) (footnotes omitted)

Before MURRAH, Chief Judge, and PHILLIPS and PICKETT, Circuit Judges.
PICKETT, Circuit Judge.

In 1936 and 1938 defendant and his predecessors in interest located three placer claims in the White Earth Mining District, Gunnison County, Colorado. Shortly thereafter the plaintiffs located 34 lode mining claims covering approximately the same surface area included within the placer claims. In 1952 defendant applied for a patent to his claims and plaintiffs filed an adverse claim and brought this action as required by 30 U.S.C.A. § 30, to determine the right of possession. Although the adverse suit raised several issues, the parties agreed to a trial on the "sole question of whether or not the nature of the mineral deposits lying in and under the ground in question are such that the surface area was subject to mineral location as placer or as lode claims."

Expert testimony, and that of practical miners, was introduced by both parties to describe the several kinds of minerals and their arrangement within the disputed area. The trial court, after hearing the testimony and making a personal inspection of the premises, found for the placer claimant. That decision is challenged as being contrary to the established facts and to applicable principles of law.

The trial court found that the exterior boundaries of the contested area lie within the 8 to 10 square mile surface dimensions of a mass of pyroxenite, and igneous rock containing several different minerals; that listed according to average percentage by volume, these minerals are pyroxene (60%), biotite (15%), magnetite (10%), perovskite (10%), and lesser amounts of apatite and ilmenite; that the minerals are distributed unevenly throughout the pyroxenite so that there are a great number of relatively high mineral segregations arranged in a generally haphazard fashion; that in the discovery pits highly mineralized zones are visible, but they are irregular in shape and have little continuity; that there are no contacts between mineral bearing material and country rock free of mineralization; rather, any particular zone composed of relatively large amounts of mineral is bounded by rock containing lesser quantities of that same mineral; and that the whole surface of the pyroxenite mass has been weathered and some alluvium has been transported in from surrounding areas. On these facts, the trial judge, a distinguished jurist in the field of mining law, concluded that there were no individual veins or lodes of mineral-bearing rock in place within the area, so as to make lode locations appropriate. This conclusion must be upheld unless the findings were clearly erroneous or unless the legal concept of a vein or lode applied to those facts was wrong as a matter of law. See Iron Silver Mining Co. v. Cheesman, 116 U.S. 529, 6 S.Ct. 481, 29 L.Ed. 712.

The findings of fact have complete support from the testimony of the defendant's experts, and in reality, they are not too much at variance from that part of plaintiffs' evidence directed to actual description of the physical characteristics of the contested area. But the experts did disagree in their opinions as to whether the mineral deposit was subject to lode or placer locations. The question must be resolved from the form and character of the mineral deposit as disclosed by the facts.

The general mining laws of the United States provide two methods of locating and acquiring unappropriated mineral lands. Lode mining claims are required by 30 U.S.C.A. § 23 to be made upon "* * * veins or lodes of quartz or other rock in place bearing * * * other valuable deposits * * *." Placer claims may be located upon other "forms of deposit, excepting veins of quartz, or other rock in place * * *." 30 U.S.C.A. § 35. In a discussion of the application of these statutes for the exploration and acquisition of unappropriated mineral lands, the court, in Webb v. American Asphaltum Mining Co., 8 Cir., 157 F. 203, 205-206, said:

"Section 2318 provides that all 'lands valuable for minerals' shall be reserved from sale, except as otherwise expressly directed. Section 2319 declares that 'all mineral deposits in lands' belonging to the United States shall be open to exploration and purchase. Section 2320 specifies the method by which 'veins or lodes of quartz or other rock in place bearing gold, silver, cinnabar, lead, tin, copper or other valuable deposits' may be secured, and section 2329 provides that 'claims for placers including all forms of deposit, excepting veins of quartz or other rock in place may be entered and patented.' The 'mineral deposits' treated in this legislation include nonmetalliferous deposits, alum, asphaltum, borax, guano, diamonds, gypsum, resin, marble, mica, slate, amber, petroleum, limestone, and building stone, as well as deposits bearing gold, silver, and other metals, and the term 'lands valuable for minerals' in the law means all lands chiefly valuable for any of these mineral deposits rather than for agricultural purposes. Northern Pacific Ry. Co. v. Soderberg, 188 U.S. 526, 534-537, 23 S.Ct. 365, 47 L.Ed. 575; Pacific Coast Marble Co. v. Northern Pacific R.R. Co., 25 Land Dec.Dept.Int. 233, 240. Thus it clearly appears that the plan of this legislation was to provide two general methods of purchasing mineral deposits from the United States—one by lode mining claims where the valuable deposits sought were in lodes or veins in rock in place, and the other by placer mining claims where the deposits were not in veins or lodes in rock in place, but were loose, scattered, or disseminated upon or under the surface of the land. The test which Congress provided by this legislation to be applied to determine how these deposits should be secured was the form and character of the deposits. If they are in veins or lodes in rock in place, they may be located and purchased under this legislation by means of lode mining claims; if they are not in fissures in rock in place but are loose or scattered on or through the land they may be located and bought by the use of placer mining claims. Reynolds v. Iron Silver Mining Co., 116 U.S. 687, 695, 6 S.Ct. 601, 29 L.Ed. 774; Clipper Mining Co. v. Eli Mining & Land Co., 194 U.S. 220, 228, 24 S.Ct. 632, 48 L.Ed. 944."

There can be no unyielding rule of thumb definition of a vein or lode; each case must be decided with reference to its own peculiar facts. Lindley on Mines, Vol. 1, 3d Ed., § 289. It is often said that the mineral-bearing rock, to constitute a lode, must be fixed in the enclosing mass of the surrounding country (Meydenbauer v. Stevens, D.C. Alaska, 78 F. 787; Book v. Justice Min. Co., C.C.Nev., 58 F. 106; Lindley on Mines, Vol. 1, 3d Ed., §§ 293, 294), it must have fairly well-defined boundaries separating it from the country rock. Iron Silver Mining Co. v. Cheesman, *supra* (116 U.S. 529, 6 S.Ct. 483); McMullin v. Magnuson, 102 Colo. 230, 78 P.2d 964; San Francisco Chemical Co. v. Duffield, 8 Cir., 201 F. 830, certiorari denied 229 U.S. 609, 33 S.Ct. 464, 57 L.Ed. 1350. In McMullin v. Magnuson, *supra*, this language was quoted with approval:

> "Thus the two essential elements of a lode are (a) the mineral-bearing rock, which must be in place and have reasonable trend and continuity, and (b) the reasonably distinct boundaries on each side of the same." (102 Colo. 230, 78 P.2d 968.)

However, the boundaries or walls do not have to be visually discernible, but instead can be established by assay analysis. Hyman v. Wheeler, C.C.Colo., 29 F. 347; Beals v. Cone, 27 Color. 473, 62 P. 948; Lindley on Mines, Vol. 1, 3d Ed.§ 294. The country rock need not be totally barren of minerals, but the mineral content of a lode must be appreciably greater than that of the surrounding rock. Grand Central Min. Co. v. Mammoth Min. Co., 29 Utah 490, 83 P. 648. A lode usually is said to exist where the body of mineral-bearing rock has such continuity and apartness that it can be traced in the general enclosing mass. Hyman v. Wheeler, *supra*; Eureka Consolidated Min. Co. v. Richmond Min. Co., C.C.Nev., Fed.Cas.No. 4,548, affirmed 103 U.S. 839, 26 L.Ed. 557. In Globe Mining Co. v. Anderson, Wyo., 318 P.2d 373, Justice Parker of the Wyoming Supreme Court presents a thorough analysis of what has been said by writers and the courts about the difficulties not only of the courts, but of practical miners, in attempting miners, in attempting to define veins, lodes and rock in place. See note 4, 318 P.2d 377.

The three placer claims were located for the mineral vermiculite, a form of altered mica, and a good grade of vermiculite was tested and developed in nearby mills.

It is quite evident here that plaintiffs' claim covered no well-defined veins or lodes as those terms are ordinarily used, unless it can be said that the entire area was a single lode. The record discloses that we are dealing with a large, shapeless coarsely grained mass of ore which, with the possible exception of the disintegrated top portion, is 'in place' in the sense that it is in a fixed position. However, the mass extends over several miles of country and has no known dimensions or boundaries and none of the ordinary lode characteristics, not even as to the method of recovering the minerals. The theory that the entire mass is a lode in place with undetermined boundaries would create a single lode covering somewhere between 8 to 12 square miles.

The import of the testimony of plaintiffs' witness Griffith, who made some of the locations for the plaintiffs on deposits of black iron, was that the whole area was the same. When asked if he found a vein on one of the claims, he answered: "We found black iron all through there on all those claims." Another of plaintiffs' witnesses, Ziegler, an oldtime miner also employed by plaintiff to make locations, in answer to an inquiry about the existence of lode formations, testified: "I would say that this black iron is similar all the way through the extent of the deposit over there." The witness further testified: "It is what I would call, from a prospector's viewpoint, a tremendous deposit of 'black iron', with no 'hanging wall' or footwall or anything else." The witness Thompson, a geologist and metallurgical engineer who had made an extensive examination of the property over a period of years, performing drilling as well as surface work, testified that the mineral segregations lacked continuity and depth; that they were not bounded or defined by footwalls or hanging walls, but the entire deposit was "ore from the grassroots." He also testified that the entire surface area was covered by alluvial and eluvial pyroxenite material to unknown depths; that this was brought about by weathering and erosion and that he had never found a place where a bulldozer could not cut a trench through the pyroxenite. It was the opinion of this witness that "you cannot have a lode where the walls are more of the same thing," and that from a practical point of view the claims were properly classified as placer.

There is no need for us to attempt a precise definition of a lode or vein. It is enough if the legal principles, when applied to the court's findings, indicate that there were no lodes within the area. While it is true that the higher mineral segregations were fixed in place in the pyroxenite, the evidence discloses that even assay tests could indicate no ascertainable boundaries setting them apart from the general mass. The bodies of higher mineral content were irregular in shape and lacked continuity so that extreme difficulty would be encountered in attempting to trace them, even if selective mining methods were advisable. The evidence is without conflict that the minerals can best be mined by traditional placer methods. The area was generally considered to be placer territory, in spite of three very old lode claims which had gone to patent without contest. In an adverse proceeding, a Colorado court had upheld a placer claim within the same deposit. Black Mica Mines, Inc. v. Vernon and Swank, Civil Action No. 3076, Dist.Ct. of Gunnison County, Colo. Under these circumstances, the trial court's findings that there were no veins or lodes in the area in question were not clearly erroneous and "the theory that the whole mass can be called a lode or a vein and be located as a lode mining claim on that basis" is not tenable under the facts of this case.

Concern is expressed that, in effect, the trial court's findings and conclusions establish the broad principle that mineral-bearing rock in place may never be located as a lode unless there is a conventional vein formation, and that they permit a placer location on mineral-bearing rock in place. We think the decision goes no further than to find that there were no lodes or veins in the mineralized mass and that the entire mass of pyroxenite was not shown to be a single lode or vein.

There is no merit in plaintiffs' contention that the trial court erred in striking the testimony of the witness Koch or in giving consideration to the placer patent issued on ground within the same area and in refusing to consider three nearby patented lode claims.

Koch, an employee of the Bureau of Land Management, testified on the issue of whether the ground was locatable as placer or as lode. The court struck the testimony when the witness refused on cross-examination to produce a report which he had made following his examination of the premises and had submitted to the Bureau. We need not consider the court's action in striking this testimony, because if there was error, it was not prejudicial, as the testimony was merely cumulative of other evidence and added nothing new to plaintiffs' case. Grand Valley Water Users' Ass'n v. Zumbrunn, 8 Cir., 272 F. 943; in re Livingston's Estate, 102 Colo. 148, 77 P.2d 649; Inyo Marble Co. v. Loundagin, 120 Cal.App. 298, 7 P.2d 1067.

Complaint also is made of the court's action in largely disregarding evidence admitted to show that lode locations had been made within the disputed area. The weight to be given that evidence was for the trial court, whose determination in that regard did not constitute error. Nor did the trial court commit error by considering a Colorado District Court decision which held that a nearby area was placer, for, while not conclusive, it could be considered the same as any other case involving similar facts.

Affirmed.

NOTES

1. As a general proposition, in any contest between rival private mining claimants in which the issue of technical compliance with the formalities of the mining law or with state regulations promulgated pursuant to the mining law, the courts will show a definite preference for upholding the good faith claim of the senior locator. Thus, even though a miner may not have technically complied with the mining law, and may, for example have located a placer deposit as a lode, the courts, at least to the extent the miner has acted reasonably, will strain to validate his claim. The preference accorded to the senior locator is recognized in *Iron Silver Mining Co. v. Mike & Starr Gold & Silver Mining Co.,* 143 U.S. 394 (1892). In that case the Supreme Court held that title to a "blanket vein" could "be acquired under the sections concerning veins, lodes, etc.," notwithstanding that location of the blanket vein as a placer would probably have been technically more correct. The court's expressed rationale was:

> The fact that so many patents (involving veins similar to the blanket vein in question) have been obtained under these (the lode) sections, and that so many applications for patent are still pending, is a strong reason against a new and contrary ruling. That which has been accepted as law and acted upon by the mining community for such a length of time should not be adjudged wholly a mistake and put entirely aside because of difficulties in the application of some minor provisions to the peculiarities of this vein or deposit.

Iron Silver Mining Co. v. Mike & Starr Gold & Silver Mining Co., 143 U.S. 394 (1892).

2. Does the lode/placer distinction serve any useful purpose, or is it merely an unnecessary complication of the mining law and trap for the unwary miner (and perhaps the unwary mining lawyer)? In formulating your answer to this question consider not only the preceding materials, but also that no similar distinction is made in the Mineral Leasing Act of 1920, and no one seems the worse as a result of that omission. Consider further that "(t)he troublesome legal distinction between lode and placer deposits stems more from historical accident than from any need or desire on the part of Congress to so classify deposits of minerals on the public lands. The lode law of 1866 was designed to protect the appropriations of vein and lode deposits made on the public domain by trespassing miners under the aegis of local custom and mining district regulations, . . . It did not grant specific tracts of surface land, and consequently made no provision for the exploitation of deposits not found in the form of veins or lodes. The omission was remedied by the Placer Act of 1870 which permitted the location of deposits not found in the form of a vein or lode. The Mineral Location Law of 1872 retained the distinction between lode and placer claims which had been created by the earlier legislation. 1 American Law of Mining § 5.9A at 738-39 (1982).

3. Does the general savings clause contained in the mining law, 30 U.S.C. § 38, protect the mining claimant who improperly locates a lode as a placer or vice versa? In *United States v. Guzzman,* 81 I. D. 685 (1974) the Board held that section 38 did apply and, if the section was otherwise applicable, would cure the failure to properly locate a claim. "An examination of the history of the provision suggests that, indeed, one of its purposes was to regularize the possession of placer deposits by claimants who had entered, located, held and worked such deposits under the law relating to lode claims before the enactment of the statute which authorized placer locations." *Id.* For a general discussion of 30 U.S.C. § 38 and the requirements for its applicability, see *United States v. Haskins,* page 179, *infra.*

B. Lodes in Placers

NOYES V. MANTLE
127 U.S. 348 (1888)

Mr. Justice Field delivered the opinion of the court:

This is a suit in equity to determine the adverse claims of the defendant below, appellant here, to a certain quartz lode mining claim, known as the Pay Streak lode in Summit Valley Mining District, in the County of Silver Bow, in the Territory of Montana. The plaintiffs below assert title to the claim as grantees of Daniel Zinn and John O. McEwan, who discovered and located it on the 23rd of April, 1878, under the provisions of the Act of Congress of May 10, 1872, which are re-enacted in the Revised Statutes, Title 32, c. 6.

The defendant below asserts title to the lode claim under a patent of the United States issued to him on the 23rd of April, 1880, for a placer mining claim, which includes that lode within its boundaries. The application for the patent was made December 14, 1878.

Several interrogatories touching matters in issue were submitted to a jury called by the court, though sitting in the exercise of its equity jurisdiction. Their findings in answer to the interrogatories were, with one exception, adopted by the court. The excepted finding gave an erroneous date to the application of the defendant for the patent, and was therefore set aside. The court thereupon found the fact as to the date as it appeared from the evidence. Upon the facts thus established the court rendered its decree. They were substantially these: That on and prior to December 14, 1878, a vein or lode of quartz, bearing gold and silver was known to exist in the ground in controversy; that its existence could have been readily ascertained by any person examining the ground with an honest purpose to inform himself of the fact; that in the month of April, 1878, Zinn and McEwan, the grantors and predecessors in interest of the plaintiffs, discovered in the ground a vein or lode of quartz-bearing gold and silver, and they posted a notice claiming the ground, and the vein or lode which it included; that at the same time they marked off the ground by stakes so that its boundaries could be readily traced; that they named the claim in their notice of location as the Pay Streak lode, and within twenty days after its discovery filed in the proper office of the county a notice of their claim, and of its location, such as was usual where lode claims were located in that mining district; that in July, 1881, they conveyed to the plaintiffs all their interest in the claim; that in August, 1881, before the commencement of this suit, the plaintiffs caused a survey of the claim to be made, and its boundaries marked so as to be readily traced; that they then relocated the claim, of which notice within twenty days thereafter was filed in the recorder's office of the county; and that they were in its possession at the commencement of this suit.

The jury did not find that the existence of a vein or lode in the ground in controversy was known to the defendant at the time of his application for a patent; and reported that they were unable to agree on this point. The District Court, in which the suit was brought, did not consider that this want of a finding on the question of knowledge by the defendant affected the position of the plaintiffs, and it rendered a decree adjudging that the right of possession to the lode claim was in them, and that the defendant had no title, estate, or interest therein, and that he be enjoined from asserting or claiming any as against them. The Supreme Court of the Territory affirmed the decree, holding that the title to the lode mining claim had passed to the grantors of the plaintiffs by their discovery and location under the statute, and that the subsequent patent to the defendant of a placer claim did not affect their title to the lode claim, for that title was not then subject to the disposition of the government. The court also held that the lode claim was known to exist within the meaning of the statute when it had been located pursuant to its requirements, whether knowledge of its existence was possessed or not by the defendant at the time he made his application for a patent. These rulings constitute the only matters meriting consideration in this court.

Section 2322 of the Revised Statutes, reenacting provisions of the Act of Congress of May 10, 1872 (17 Stat. 91), declares that the locators of mining locations previously made or which should thereafter be made, on any mineral vein, lode, or ledge on the public domain, their heirs and assigns, where no adverse claim existed on the 10th of May, 1872, shall have the exclusive right of possession and enjoyment of all the surface included within the lines of their locations, so long as they comply with the laws of the United States, and with state, territorial, and local regulations, not in conflict with those laws governing their possessory title. There is no pretence in this case that the original locators did not comply with all the requirements of the law in making the location of the Pay Streak lode mining claim, or that the claim was ever abandoned or forfeited. They were the discoverers of the claim. They marked its boundaries by stakes, so that they could be readily traced. They posted the required notice, which was duly recorded in compliance with the regulations of the district. They had thus done all that was necessary under the law for the acquisition of an exclusive right to the possession and enjoyment of the ground. The claim was thenceforth their property. They needed only a patent of the United States to render their title perfect, and that they could obtain at any time upon proof of what they had done in locating the claim, and of subsequent expenditures to a specified amount in developing it. Until the patent issued the government held the title in trust for the locators or their vendees. The ground itself was not afterwards open to sale. The location having been completed in April, 1878, antedates by some months the application of the defendant for a patent for his placer claim. That patent was subject to the conditions of § 2333 of the Revised Statutes, which is as follows:

"Where the same person, association, or corporation is in possession of a placer claim, and also a vein or lode included within the boundaries thereof, application shall be made for a patent for the placer claim, with the statement that it includes such vein or lode, and in such case a patent shall issue for the placer claim, subject to the provisions of this chapter, including such vein or lode, upon the payment of five dollars per acre for such vein or lode claim and twenty-five feet of surface on each side thereof. The remainder of the placer claim, or any placer claim not embracing any vein or lode claim, shall be paid for at the rate of two dollars and fifty cents per acre, together with all costs of proceedings; and where a vein or lode, such as is described in section twenty three hundred and twenty, is known to exist within the boundaries of a placer claim, and application for a patent for such placer claim which does not include an application of the vein or lode claim shall be construed as a conclusive declaration that the claimant of the placer claim has no right of possession of the vein or lode claim; but where the existence of a vein or lode in a placer claim is not known, a patent for the placer claim shall convey all valuable mineral and other deposits within the boundaries thereof."

This section was before us for consideration in *Reynolds v. Iron Silver Mining Company,* at October Term, 1885, 116 U.S. 687; and also at the present term, 124 U.S. 374. As stated by the court at both times, it makes provision for three classes of cases:

1. When one applies for a placer patent, who is at the time in the possession of a vein or lode included within the boundaries, he must state the fact, and then, on payment of the sum required for a vein claim and twenty-five feet on each side of it at $5 an acre, and $2.50 for an acre for the placer claim, a patent will issue to him covering both claim and lode.

2. Where a vein lode, such as described in a previous section, is known to exist at the time within the boundaries of the placer claim, the application for a patent therefor, which does not also include an application for the vein or lode, will be construed as a conclusive declaration that the claimant of the placer claim has no right of possession to the vein or lode.

3. Where the existence of a vein or lode in a placer claim is not known at the time of the application for a patent, that instrument will convey all valuable mineral and other deposits within its boundaries.

The section can have no application to lodes or veins within the boundaries of a placer claim which have been previously located under the laws of the United States, and are in possession of the locators or their assigns; for, as already said, such locations when perfected under the law are the property of the locators, or parties to whom the locators have conveyed their interest. As said in *Belk v. Meagher,* 104 U.S. 279, 283: "A mining claim perfected under the law is property in the highest sense of that term, which may be bought, sold, and conveyed, and will pass by descent." It is not therefore subject to disposal of the government. The section can apply only to lodes or veins not taken up and located so as to become the property of others. If any are not thus owned, and are known to exist, the applicant for the patent must include them in his application, or he will be deemed to have declared that he had no right to them. *Sullivan v. Iron Silver Min. Co.,* 109 U.S. 550, 554.

When can it be said that a vein or lode is "known to exist" within the meaning of the section? In *Reynolds v. Iron Silver Mining Company,* when first here, the court said that it might not be easy to define the words "known to exist," and as it was not necessary to determine whether the knowledge must be traced to the applicant for the patent, or whether it was sufficient that it was generally known, and what kind of evidence was necessary to prove this knowledge, it was better that the questions should be decided as they arise. When the case was here a second time the court said that the language of the section appeared to be sufficiently intelligible in a general sense, and yet it became difficult of interpretation, when applied to the determination of rights asserted to such veins or lodes, from the possession or absence of knowledge at the time application is made for a patent; and that if a general knowledge of their existence were held sufficient, the inquiry would follow as to what would constitute such knowledge, so as to create an exception to the grant, notwithstanding the ignorance of the patentee. These suggestions indicated the difficulties of some of the questions which might arise in the application of the statute; but in the present case we think that difficulty does not exist. Where a location of a vein or lode has been made under the law, and its boundaries have been specifically marked on the surface, so as to be readily traced, and notice of the location is recorded in the usual books of record within the district, we think it may safely be said that the vein or lode is known to exist, although personal knowledge of the fact may not be possessed by the applicant for a patent of a placer claim. The information which the law requires the locator to give to the public must be deemed sufficient to acquaint the applicant with the existence of the vein or lode.

A copy of the patent is not in the record, so we cannot speak positively as to its contents; but it will be presumed to contain reservations of all veins or lodes known to exist, pursuant to the statute. At any rate, as already stated, it could not convey property which had already passed to others. A patent of the government cannot, any more than a deed of an individual, transfer what the grantor does not possess.

Judgment affirmed.

<hr />

NOTES

1. The United States has an important interest in the stability of the patents that it issues. Consequently in cases involving known lodes within placers it is held that "all presumptions favor the validity of the placer patent; that the patentee had fully complied with the law in all respects; that at the time of his application the . . . vein was not a know vein; and that, unless the [proponents of the known lode] overcome these presumptions by clear and convincing proof, the [placer patentee] must prevail". Montana Cent. Ry. Co. v. Migeon, 68 Fed. 811 (Mont.) *aff'd* 77 Fed. 249 (1895).

2. Does the fact that lode claims were previously located on ground now claimed to be valuable for placer deposits, and for which application for a placer patent has been made, establish the existence of known lodes? In *Thomas v. South Butte Mining Co.,* 211 Fed. 105, 107 (9th Cir. 1914), the court held that " . . . the mere fact that mineral lode locations were made is not proof that the ground on which they were located contained a vein or lode within the meaning of section 2333 of the Revised Statutes. . . . A mine location of an alleged vein or lode is not sufficient to prove that a vein or lode was known to exist. . . . The lode or vein which is known to exist so as to be excluded from the patent must be one that contains mineral of such extent and value as to justify expenditures for the purpose of extracting it."

INYO MARBLE CO. V. LOUNDAGIN
7 P.2d 1067 (Cal. 1932)

. . . .
MARKS, J.

Appellant, Inyo Marble Company, is a California corporation and the patentee of three placer mines containing about 480 acres within their exterior boundaries, to which they received the patent from the United States on August 26, 1921. The claims were first located in January, 1915, and the application for the patent was made on December 6, 1919. The patent contained the folowing provision: "That should any vein or lode of quartz or other rock in place bearing gold, silver, cinnabar, lead, tin, copper, or other valuable deposits, be claimed or known to exist within the above-described premises at said last-name date (Dec. 6, 1919), the same is expressly excepted and excluded from these presents."

The respondents claimed portions of the property described in the patent, and also adjoining property by reason of discoveries and locations of mineral lode or vein claims made by J. D. Leary and J. A. Loundagin in the latter part of 1925 and early in 1926. These locators went into possession of their claims, did assessment and development work thereon, shipped ore therefrom to smelters, and received pay therefor.

Appellant sought to quiet title to all the land in its placer mine, to recover the value of the ore sold by respondents, and damages, and to enjoin respondents from further work upon the property described in its patent. The court found in favor of appellant's title to its placer mine with the exception of one lode or vein claim lying entirely within the placer mine, and those portions of two of such claims lying partly within the boundaries of the placer mine, title to which lode or vein claims was found to be in respondents. Leary No. 6 was entirely within the boundaries of the patented placer mine and the two others, Leary and Calamine Queen, were partly within and partly without such boundaries. The court held against respondents as to seven other lode or vein claims located by Leary and Loundagin, some of which were also partly without the boundaries of the patented ground.

The trial court further found that upon the three above-named claims of respondents there were, on December 6, 1919, and prior thereto, known veins or lodes in place containing valuable minerals and metals which were not conveyed to appellant by the government patent but were expressly reserved from the grant by the terms of the patent and by section 37, title 30, page 306, U.S. Code, Annotated, . . .

. . . .

Appellant assails this finding as not supported by the evidence, and that it is contrary to it. We have gone over the record carefully and cannot agree with appellant. In fact, the great weight of the evidence supports the finding. Kenneth K. Ash, who was employed by appellant as its superintendent in 1913 and 1914 and from the latter part of 1919 to early in 1921, testified that he knew of these valuable mineral and metal bearing lodes and ledges in 1913; that after midnight on January 1, 1920, he had two employees of appellant make quartz mining locations of the lode and veins for the company. . . .

. . . .

The evidence further shows that in April, 1918, James Wiggington located lode and vein claims in the placer property. He mined and kept possession of his claims and shipped and sold ore therefrom until they were "jumped" by the two employees of appellant on January 1, 1920.

There is other and ample evidence in the record which, with that already summarized, is sufficient to satisfy us that on December 6, 1919, there were lodes and veins in place carrying valuable deposits of minerals and metals which were clearly visible from the surface of the ground and from the shafts, cuts, and tunnels upon it, and which were then known to appellant and to many others in the mining district. The evidence to the contrary is meager.

As these lodes and veins were known at the time appellant applied for its patent, and as it did not follow the legal procedure to acquire title to them, they were not granted to it, but were reserved by the patent and by operation of law, and remained part of the public domain subject to entry by others. As is said in the case of Mutchmor v. McCarty, 149 Cal. 603, at page 611, 87 P. 85, 88: "The decisions of the Supreme Court of the United States and of other courts of high authority, both state and federal, have settled the construction of this provision of the Revised Statutes, and of these reservations in placer patents as applied to a great variety of cases, and especially as they apply to this case. A vein known to exist within the boundaries of a placer claim at the date of the application, may be located by an adverse claimant after the issuance of the patent, and a vein is known to exist within the meaning of the statute (1) when it is known to the placer claimant; (2) when its existence is generally known; (3) when any examination of the ground sufficient to enable the placer claimant to make oath that it is subject to location, as such would necessarily disclose the existence of the vein. Iron S. M. Co. v. Mike & Starr Co., 143 U.S. 403, 12 S. Ct. 543, 36 L. Ed. 201, Lindley on Mines § 781, and cases cited."

This also disposes of appellant's contention that the placer claims were in its possession and that a lode location could not be made thereon and a right thereby initiated by a trespasser. Clipper Mining Co. v. Eli Mining & L. Co., 194 U.S. 220, 24 S. Ct. 632, 636, 48 L. Ed. 944; Mt. Rosa M., M. & L. Co. v. Palmer, 26 Colo. 56, 56 P. 176, 180, 50 L. R. A. 289, 77 Am. St. Rep. 245. Since the lode and vein claims were not owned by appellant but were a part of the public domain, entry upon them for the purpose of location was not a trespass. `

. . . .

Appellant complains of the rulings of the trial court in admitting evidence of the appearance of outcroppings and of mineralized rock in the workings of the lodes and veins and of the value of the ore taken therefrom after December 6, 1919. It contends that since under the law, in order to defeat its title, knowledge of the lodes and veins must have existed on the date of its application for its patent, all evidence of such condition and of the value of the mineralized structures should have been limited to the knowledge obtained by witnesses prior to that date. While the premise of appellant is correct, we cannot agree with its conclusion. The mountain structures were rock and the outcroppings of the lodes and veins could not have materially changed between the date of appellant's application for a patent and the time of the trial of this case. The question of the value of the deposits in the known lodes and veins is always important and often a controlling factor in determining the legality of a quartz location. Mutchmor v. McCarthy, *supra*. Evidence of the values of the deposits need not be limited to what is known of these values at the time of the application for the placer patent, but may include knowledge gained by subsequent workings of the property. Noyes v. Clifford, 37 Mont. 138, 94 P. 842, and cases cited. The evidence of these values, obtained after the application, is obviously evidence of a condition existing at that time which in the very nature of things had not changed during the lapse of a few years.

. . . .

The final assignment of error which we must consider is full of difficulties. Appellant urges that the extent of each of the lode or vein locations which the trial court could award to respondents is limited by federal statute to an extreme length of fifteen hundred feet and an extreme width of 25 feet on each side of the center line of each known vein or lode. In support of this contention it cites the cases of Clipper Mining Co. v. Eli, etc., Co., supra; Mt. Rosa, etc., Co. v. Palmer, supra; Noyes v. Clifford, *supra;* and Puett v. Harvey, 51 Nev. 40, 268 P. 41, 42.

In the Clipper Mining Company Case the Supreme Court of the United States used the following language: "For if the claim of the lode locator be sustained it carries, under §§ 2320 and 2333 [30 USCA §§ 23, 37], at least 25 feet of the surface on each side of the middle of the vein." Counsel for appellant attempts to construe this language as a direct holding that the surface ground to which the lode locator would be entitled must be limited to 25 feet on each side of the middle of the vein. We think no such construction must be placed on this language in view of the fact that the question was not an issue in the case before the trial court, and further, in view of the federal statute in which the language used is, in substance, 25 feet on each side of the lode or vein.

In the Mt. Rosa Mining Case the Supreme Court of Colorado used the expression "twenty-five feet on each side of the center of the vein" several times in discussing the extent of a quartz or other rock claim upon a known lode or vein within a placer location. In using this language the court seemed to have overlooked the provisions of the federal statute that the 25 feet shall be on each side of the lode or vein and not on each side of its center. These expressions become unimportant in view of the final conclusion of the Colorado court which is as follows: "It follows that the court below erred in adjudging to appellee surface ground in excess of 25 feet *on each side of the lodes* in question."

. . . .

In the case of Reynolds v. Iron Silver Mining Co., 116 U.S. 687, 6 S. Ct. 601, 607, 29 L. Ed. 774, it was said: "We are of opinion that congress meant that lodes and veins known to exist when the patent was asked for should be excluded from the grant as much as if they were described in clear terms. It was not intended to remit the question of their title to be raised by some one who had or might get a better title, but to assert that no title passed by the patent in such case from the United States. It remains in the United States at the time of the issuing of the patent, and in such case it does not pass to the patentee. He takes his surface land, and his placer mine, and such lodes or veins of mineral matter within it as were unknown, but to such as *were known* to exist he gets by that patent no right whatever. The title remaining in his grantor, the United States, to this vein, the existence of which was known, he has no such interest in it as authorizes him to disturb any one else in the peaceable possession and mining of that vein. When it is once shown that the vein was *known to exist* at the time he acquired title to the placer, it is shown that he acquired no title or interest in that vein by his patent."

It is evident that appellant, under its patent from the United States, received title to the 480 acres described therein, excepting therefrom the known lodes and veins and 25 feet of the surface on each side thereof. This left open for location the known lodes and veins and 25 feet of the surface on each of their sides, within the exterior boundaries of the placer mine. We think it the plain intention of the law to limit the known lode or vein locations within patented place ground to these dimensions. The lode or vein locator could not claim or receive more ground within the placer mine than that reserved in the patent.

. . . .

The dimensions of the claims which the trial court set aside to respondents are as follows: Leary, 1,500 feet in length by 541.9 feet in width; Leary No. 6 and Calamine Queen, each 1,500 feet in length by 600 feet in width. The trial court did not find, and the evidence does not disclose, the dimensions of the known lodes or veins which form the foundation of the rights of respondents. From the record it seems apparent that the dimensions of these lodes and veins are not sufficient to support setting aside to respondents all of the surface of the three claims as described in the judgment. From the evidence now before us it appears that some portion of the surface of the three claims extends beyond the lodes or veins and the area 25 feet laterally on each side thereof. It is therefore necessary to remand this case to the trial court for further proceedings. With the exception of the size of the three claims given to respondents, the judgment should not be disturbed.

The judgment is reversed, with directions to the trial court to take evidence on the dimensions of the lodes or veins known to be in the quartz or other rock claims, known as Leary, Leary No. 6, and Calamine Queen, on December 6, 1919, make additional findings upon such new evidence taken and render judgment in accordance with the findings and with the views herein expressed.

NOTES

1. What is the purpose of the "known lode" provision of § 37? In *Duffield v. San Francisco Chemical Co.,* 205 F. 480 (9th Cir. 1913) the court held that § 37 was designed to prevent a fraud on the government. Since valid lode claims may be acquired from the government for $5.00 per acre while placer claims may be acquired for half that price, the government is vulnerable to being defrauded of a portion of the sales price of lode claims. Hence, the exclusion of known lodes.

2. Clearly, after a placer claimant has applied for a patent, a lode locator has the right to enter the placer location for the purpose of claiming lodes that were known to exist at the time the application for the placer patent was made. Does the lode claimant also have the right to enter the placer location for the purpose of locating known lodes prior to the time the application for the placer patent is made?

3. If a claimant locates a known lode within a patented placer location, what size claim is he entitled to make?

4. When is a lode a known lode? *Noyes v. Mantle* makes clear that actual knowledge is not required for the existence of a lode to be known. Certainly, the constructive notice imparted by the public records ought to be sufficient to establish that a lode is "known" to exist. In addition, a lode will be deemed to be a "known lode" if it was "known to the applicant for the placer patent, or known to the community generally, or else disclosed by workings, and obvious to anyone making a reasonable and fair inspection of the premises for the purpose of obtaining title from the government." *Iron Silver Mining Co. v. Mike & Starr Gold & Silver Co.,*143 U.S. 394 (1892).

5. If it is agreed that the lode/placer distinction no longer has much to recommend it, if it ever did, should the body of law concerning lodes in placers have any continued validity? Does this body of law represent merely a trap for the unwary, or are there larger policy issues involved? See *Iron Silver Mining Co. v. Mike & Starr Gold & Silver Co.,* 143 U.S. 394 (1892) (Field, J., dissenting).

6. In order for a lode to be a known lode, not only must a locator know or be charged with knowledge of its existence, he must also know or be charged with knowledge of its value, for it is only valuable known lodes that are covered by 30 U.S.C. § 37. . . . "And the reason is that lodes exist throughout the mining country. Not one in hundreds justifies development and proves of value. No reason exists to except the valueless from placer patents or grants, and such patents issued or grants made without excluding them prima facie [establishes] lodes of value did not exist. The issue is determined now by conditions as they were when the placer patent was applied for, even as though tried and determined then. Subsequent developments and results, however marvelous, are immaterial. * * * The sanctity of a solemn grant of lands by the United States and the definiteness and certainty that should attach thereto and the stability of titles evidenced thereby, can only thus be preserved." *Crofoot v. Hill,* 326 P. 2d 417 (Nev. 1958).

7. Section 37 is implemented by the following language contained in placer patents issued by the United States:

> FIRST. That the grant hereby made is restricted in its exterior limits to the boundaries of the said mining premises, and to any veins or lodes of quartz or other rock in place bearing gold, silver, cinnabar, lead, tin, copper, or other valuable deposits, which may have been discovered within the said limits subsequent to and which were not known to exist on [here insert the date of the patent].

> SECOND. That should any vein or lode of quartz or other rock in place bearing gold, silver, cinnabar, lead, tin, copper, or other valuable deposits be claimed or known to exist within the above described premises on [here insert the date of the patent] the same is expressly excepted and excluded from the patent. 30 U.S.C. § 37.

8. Assume that your client has discovered a valuable deposit of a valuable mineral, but because of the geology of the deposit is unsure whether to locate it as lode or placer. What would be the safest course of action for your client to take in such circumstances? *See* Knutson and Morris, *Coping with the General Mining Law of 1872 in the 1980's,* 16 Land and Water L. Rev. 411 (1981).

BOWEN V. CHEMI-COTE PERLITE CORPORATION
432 P.2d 435 (Az. 1967)

UDALL, Justice:

This case was commenced in the Superior Court for the County of Pinal by the appellee, Chemi-Cote Perlite Corporation, against the appellant, Arthur C. W. Bowen. An amended declaratory judgment was entered in Chemi-Cote's favor and Bowen appealed to this Court. The case was transferred to the Court of Appeals, Division Two, for decision and that court, in its opinion, affirmed the judgment of the superior court. Thereafter, an amicus curiae brief and reply was filed by the United States and by Chemi-Cote respectively. The case is here on a petition for review pursuant to Rule 47(b), Rules of the Supreme Court, 17 A.R.S.

Chemi-Cote is the successor in interest to two lode claims of twenty acres each located on the public domain in 1944. The required discovery and location work to perfect the claims was performed and all annual assessment work or any alternative notices to hold mining claims without assessment work were filed for each year to the present time. Chemi-Cote and its predecessors in interest have been in continuous possession of said lode mining claims since their location and perlite ore has been mined therefrom since 1945.

Bowen is the successor to locators of two placer claims of one hundred sixty acres each, one of which was located in 1950 and the other in 1954. They include within their boundaries Chemi-Cote's lode claims and are based on the same perlite ore. All of the required discovery and location work was done to give the claims validity and the assessment work was done thereafter.

Prior to the commencement of this action, Bowen filed with the United States Bureau of Land Management of the Department of Interior an application for patent and conformed to the federal mining laws as to notice by posting, publication, etc. Chemi-Cote did not file an adverse claim within the sixty-day period prescribed by federal law, but after expiration of the period it did file a protest with the land department against issuance of a patent to Bowen. Departmental proceedings culminated in a decision dismissing the protest based on Chemi-Cote's failure to file an adverse claim. Chemi-Cote Perlite Corp. v. Arthur C. W. Bowen, 72 I.D. 403 (1965). Chemi-Cote thereafter filed its complaint in this action to quiet title to the two lode claims situated within the boundaries of Bowen's placer claims. Bowen answered and counterclaimed to quiet title to his placer claims and for damages for wrongful removal of perlite from his claims. The trial court asserted jurisdiction of the case and received testimony on the question of whether the mineral in question should be located as a lode or as a placer under applicable federal law. Finding that Chemi-Cote's lode claims were validly located with the knowledge of Bowen, that Chemi-Cote and its predecessors had been in continuous possession and performed necessary annual assessment work on its lode mining claims, that the cause of action was possessory and the court had jurisdiction over the parties and the subject matter, and that the right of possession of Chemi-Cote to its mining claims was superior to that of Bowen, the court entered judgment for Chemi-Cote and against Bowen.

The first question raised on appeal was whether the trial court had jurisdiction of the subject matter of the suit. The Court of Appeals, in concluding that the issue of temporary possession was triable by the state court, determined that the validity of Chemi-Cote's lode claims was not at issue before the Land Department because section 37, 30 U.S.C.A. operated to exclude the lode claims from Bowen's patent application. It reasoned that since a perfected mining claim is property in the highest sense, it is not subject to disposal by the United States, and that once a property right is acquired, it would be violative of basic due process concepts to conduct a hearing on its validity without reasonable notice and an opportunity to be heard.

Individual rights in public mineral lands can be acquired and held, and an absolute title obtained through the land office, only upon the terms and conditions prescribed by the mining laws of Congress. Lily Mining Co. v. Kellogg, 27 Utah 111, 74 P. 518 (1903); see also, Old Dominion, etc., Smelting Co. v. Haverly, 11 Ariz. 241, 90 P. 333 (1907). The procedure for obtaining title to mineral land by way of a patent application is set forth in section 29, 30 U.S.C.A. and section 30, 30 U.S.C.A. They read in part:
30 U.S.C.A. § 29:

'* * * The register of the land office, upon the filing of * * * (an application for patent to a mining claim) * * * shall publish a notice that such application has been made, for the period of sixty days, in a newspaper to be by him designated as published nearest to such claim; * * * If no adverse claim shall have been filed with the register of the proper land office at the expiration of sixty days of publication, it shall be assumed that the applicant is entitled to a patent, * * * and that no adverse claim exists; and thereafter no objection from third parties to the issuance of a patent shall be heard, except it be shown that the applicant has failed to comply with the terms of this chapter. * * * '

30 U.S.C.A. § 30:

"Where an adverse claim is filed during the period of publication, * * * all proceedings, except the publication of notice making and filing of the affidavit thereof, shall be stayed until the controversy shall have been settled or decided by a court of competent jurisdiction, or the adverse claim waived. It shall be the duty of the adverse claimant, within thirty days after filing his claim, to commence proceedings in a court of competent jurisdiction, to determine the question of the right of possession, and prosecute the same with reasonable diligence to final judgment; and a failure so to do shall be a waiver of his adverse claim. * * * "

Congress has not given the Interior Department jurisdiction to resolve disputes as to the right of possession. When a patent to mineral lands is applied for, however, the jurisdiction of the Department becomes exclusive, and can be stayed only by the filing of an adverse claim as provided by section 30. This Court in Warnekros v. Cowan, 13 Ariz. 42, 108 P. 239 (1910), said:

"Upon the filing of an application for patent to public mineral land, the jurisdiction of the Land Office becomes exclusive as to all questions affecting the title to the lands therein applied for, and so remains until the final determination of the application. The excercise of its jurisdiction may be stayed only by the filing of an adverse claim as provided by section 2326 of the Revised Statutes (30 U.S.C.A. § 30) of the United States * * *. Without the filing of such adverse claim, neither the state nor federal courts will exercise jurisdiction in actions affecting the title to lands included within the application." 13 Ariz. at 45, 108 P. at 239.

In an adverse proceeding, the court may make one of the three determinations: That the plaintiff is entitled to possession of the claim; that the defendant-applicant is entitled to possession of the claim; that neither are entitled to possession. The judgment of the court is conclusive as between the rights of the competing mining claimants, but such decision does not preclude the Department of Interior from refusing to issue a patent. Clipper Mining Co. v. Eli Mining & Land Co., 194 U.S. 220, 24 S.Ct. 632, 48 L.Ed. 944 (1904).

It is so well established as to be axiomatic that a failure to file an adverse claim within the prescribed period operates as a waiver of all rights which were the proper subject of such a claim. See Turner v. Sawyer, 150 U.S. 578, 14 S.Ct. 192, 37 L.Ed. 1189 (1893); Healy v. Rupp, 37 Colo. 25, 86 P. 1015 (1906); South End Min. Co. v. Tinney, 22 Nev. 19, 35 P. 89 (1894). The following language of the Utah Supreme Court in Lily Mining Co. v. Kellogg, supra, is typical of the case law to this effect:

"It follows that in such statutory actions an allegation by the plaintiff that an adverse claim, in due time and form, showing its nature, boundaries, and extent, was filed in the land office, is traversable and necessary to confer jurisdiction upon the court to decide the controversy * * * 'and that an action brought in support of such adverse claim must be based upon the right asserted in such claim, for the reason that it must be conclusively assumed that no adverse claim exists, except such as has been filed' (Marshal Silver Min. Co. v. Kirtley, 12 Colo. 410-415, 21 P. 492). * * * Under section 2325, Rev.St.U.S. (U.S.Comp.St.1901, p. 1429), when no adverse claim within the time therein prescribed is filed, it must be assumed that the applicant is entitled to a patent, and that no adverse claim exists. In Lavagnino v. Uhling, 26 Utah 1, 71 P. 1046, this court held that the expression in the mining law, 'It shall be assumed,' must be construed to mean 'conclusively assumed.' " 74 P. at 519.

In discussing what is the proper subject of an adverse claim contemplated by sections 29 and 30, the United States Supreme Court in Iron Silver Min. Co. v. Campbell, 135 U.S. 286, 10 S.Ct. 765, 34 L.Ed. 155 (1890) said:

"It is true that there are no very distinctive words declaring what kind of adverse claim is required to be set up as a defense against the party making publication; but throughout the whole of these sections, and the original statute from which they are transferred to the Revised Statutes, the words 'claim' and 'claimant' are used. These words are, in all legislation of congress on the subject, used in regard to a claim not yet perfected by a title from the government by way of a patent; and the purpose of the statute seems to be that, where there are two claimants to the same mine, neither of whom has yet acquired the title from the government, they shall bring their respective claims to the same property, in the manner prescribed in the statute, before some judicial tribunal located in the neighborhood where the property is, and that the result of this judicial investigation shall govern the action of the officers of the land department in determining which of these claimants shall have the patent—the final evidence of title— from the government." 10 S.Ct. at 769.

In quoting with approval from the Eureka Min. Co. v. Richmond Mining Co., 8 Fed.Cas. p. 819, No. 4548, 4 Sawy. 302, the Utah Supreme Court in Lavagnino v. Uhlig, 26 Utah 1, 71 P. 1046 (1903), affirmed 198 U.S. 443, 25 S.Ct. 716, 49 L.Ed. 1119 (1905), in different words indicated the type of adverse claim intended by the statute. It said:

"(U)nder the mining act of 1872, where one is seeking a patent for his mining location, and gives the prescribed notice, any other claimant of an unpatented location objecting to the patent on account of extent or form, or because of asserted prior location, must come forward with his objections and present them, or he will be afterwards precluded from objecting to the issue of the patent." 71 P. at 1049.

The Supreme Court of Montana in O'Hanlon v. Ruby Gulch Mining Co., 48 Mont. 65, 135 P. 913 (1913) said:

"* * * (T)he statute was intended to apply only to those cases in which there are adverse claims arising out of conflicting locations, or where the adverse claimants derive title from different sources." 135 P. at 919.

It is apparent that sections 29 and 30 have been interpreted to require the filing of all adverse claims not yet perfected by a title from the government by way of a patent or be precluded from objecting to the issue of a patent. Until such an adverse claim is filed, the jurisdiction of the Land Department is exclusive, and upon failure to file such a claim within the required time, the state courts are without jurisdiction to hear matters which should have been so raised.

If Chemi-Cote's claim in the instant case is "adverse" to Bowen's patent application, we can see no reason to except it from the provisions.

The Court of Appeals takes the position that section 37, 30 U.S.C.A. creates an exception to the requirement of sections 29 and 30, and that Chemi-Cote falls within this exception. This section provides a procedure whereby the owner of an unpatented placer claim can acquire title to lode claims within the boundaries of his placer claim. It reads as follows:

30 U.S.C.A. § 37:

"Where the same person, association, or corporation is in possession of a placer claim, and also a vein or lode included within the boundaries thereof, application shall be made for a patent for the placer claim, with the statement that it includes such vein or lode, and in such case a patent shall issue for the placer claim, subject to the provisions of sections 21-24, 26-30, 33-48, 50-52, 71-76 of this title, including such vein or lode, upon the payment of $5 per acre for such vein or lode claim, and twenty-five feet of surface on each side thereof. The remainder of the placer claim, or any placer claim not embracing any vein or lode claim, shall be paid for at the rate of $2.50 per acre, together with all costs of proceedings; and where a vein or lode, such as is described in section 23 of this title, is known to exist within the boundaries of a placer claim, an application for a patent for such placer claim which does not include an application for the vein or lode claim shall be construed as a conclusive declaration that the claimant of the placer claim has no right of possession of the vein or lode claim, but where the existence of a vein or lode in a placer claim is not known, a patent for the placer claim shall convey all valuable mineral and other deposits within the boundaries thereof."

Undoubtedly it is the law that a claimant to a "known lode or vein" within a placer need not adverse a placer patent application where the lode claimant bases its claims upon a mineral deposit other than that which is the basis of the placer patent application. Clipper Mining Co. v. Eli Mining & Land Co., supra; Sullivan v. Iron Silver Min. Co., 145 U.S. 431, 12 S.Ct. 555, 36 L.Ed. 214 (1892); Iron Silver Min. Co. v. Mike & Starr Gold and Silver Co., 143 U.S. 394, 12 S.Ct. 543, 36 L.Ed. 201 (1892). Section 30 is inapplicable since there is no "question of the right of possession" upon which a state court suit could be brought. Rather than create an exception to the requirement of sections 29 and 30 requiring the filing of adverse claims section 37 is merely a recognition that in this situation no adverse claim exists, for if the lode claim is known and the placer applicant does not claim it in his application, there is no adverse claim and no need to adverse.

It cannot be said, however, that an adverse claim does not exist and that consequently there is no need to adverse when, as in this case, the claimed lode is the identical deposit as that supporting the placer patent application. A lode-placer dispute or a dispute over whether certain material is properly located as placer or lode is the proper subject matter of an adverse suit. Duffield v. San Francisco Chemical Co., 205 F. 480 (9 Cir. 1913). In this instance, the two claims cannot coexist and the issue to be decided is whether the mineral deposit, which is claimed by both parties, may be secured as a lode or a placer claim. The ruling of the Land Department, to which the Court of Appeals took issue, that "* * * a lode claimant asserting a right to the same deposit as a placer claimant cannot rely upon the 'known vein or lode' provisions * * *" is a recognition of this principle. Indeed, if such a distinction were not made, in the instant case Bowen's failure to include Chemi-Cote's lode claim in his patent application would act as a disclaimer to any right of possession of the vein or lode claim, but if he did include the lode claim in his application, it would be equivalent to a recognition on his part that the deposit should be located as a lode claim.

The Court of Appeals notes that the issuance of a placer patent does not foreclose the rights of known lode claimants. It argues, therefore, that since the filing of an application for a placer patent does not in and of itself put in issue the question of whether there are known lodes within the area covered by the placer patent application, the claims of a known lode claimant cannot be categorized as 'adverse' to a placer patent application. Interestingly enough, this argument impliedly admits that if the two claims were adverse, the lode claimant would necessarily have to file an adverse claim notwithstanding the language of section 37. Furthermore, the weight of the argument is lost because it is based on the situation where the lode claim is based on a deposit different than that supporting the placer claim. Where the same deposit is used to support both a lode and a placer claim, as in the instant case, the placer patent application puts in issue whether there is a 'known lode' because the same deposit cannot be located both as a placer and a lode claim. By its very definition there could be no "known lode" if the perlite deposit should have been located as a placer location.

Were we to accept the construction placed upon section 37 by the Court of Appeals, the rights of the parties would be unsettled in the absence of further litigation. As the matter stood pending this decision, the action of the Superior Court giving Chemi-Cote a possessory title to the land in question superior to that of Bowen was not a bar to the adjudication of Bowen's patent application. The judicial determination of the possessory rights of conflicting mining claimants is not necessarily binding upon the Land Department in determining to whom a patent should be issued, and the pendency of such proceedings, having been commenced after expiration of the statutory period for initiating such action, does not bar the issuance of a patent. Madison Placer Claim, 35 L.D. 551 (1907); Nettie Lode v. Texas Lode, 14 L.D. 180 (1892). For these reasons, we are persuaded that the Court of Appeals erred in holding that a lode claimant asserting a right to the same deposit as a placer patent applicant can rely upon the 'known vein or lode' provisions of section 37.

It is argued that Chemi-Cote's lode claims are not within the land included in Bowen's patent application for the reason that at the time of the patent application the lode mining claims were the property of Chemi-Cote and not subject to disposal by the United States. The basis for this argument is the language often stated by the courts that a perfected unpatented mining claim is property—freely transferable, inheritable, taxable, and otherwise carrying with it many of the incidents of real property in general. See e.g. Belk v. Meagher, 104 U.S. 279, 26 L.Ed. 735 (1881). The title to an unpatented mining claim is not an absolute title, but merely a possessory title subject to a paramount title in the United States. As against third parties, the locator or his assignees have exclusive right to use the surface of the land for mining purposes, but as against the United States, his right is conditional and inchoate. United States v. Etcheverry, 230 F.2d 193 (10 Cir. 1956). Contrary to Chemi-Cote's argument, a location embracing a prior valid and subsisting location is not *ipso facto* void and ineffectual, but if unopposed, may properly become the subject of mineral patent. Thus, a valid and subsisting location will in no case avail to defeat a junior location, as to which patent proceedings are regularly prosecuted, except upon the invocation of judicial intervention. The Clipper Mining Co. v. The Eli Mining and Land Co., 34 L.D. 401 (1906). Having failed to assert its claim, Chemi-Cote lost its title against the United States and it cannot now defeat Bowen's patent application.

The case of Dahl v. Raunheim, 132 U.S. 260, 10 S.Ct. 74, 33 L.Ed. 324 (1889) requires this same conclusion. There the plaintiff brought action to quiet title to certain placer mining ground. The defendant asserted title to a portion of the ground as a lode claim made subsequently to the location of the premises as placer mining ground and subsequently to the application by the plaintiff for a patent therefor. To this application, no adverse claim to any portion of the ground was filed by the defendant. The court said:

"It is earnestly objected to the title of the plaintiff that he did not present any proof that the mining ground claimed by him was placer ground. * * * That it was placer ground is conclusively established, in this controversy, against the defendant, by the fact that no adverse claim was asserted by him to the plaintiff's application for a patent of the premises as such ground. That question is not now open to litigation by private parties seeking to avoid the effect of the plaintiff's proceedings." 10 S.Ct. at 75.

From the court's holding in the Dahl case, it follows that Chemi-Cote's failure to adverse conclusively established, as between the two litigants, that Bowen's claim was properly located as a placer deposit. Since a placer discovery will not sustain a lode location, Cole v. Ralph, 252 U.S. 286, 40 S.Ct. 321, 64 L.Ed. 567 (1920), Chemi-Cote's location was thus defeated and its possessory title lost.

It is suggested that it would be "violative of basic due process concepts" to read sections 29 and 30, 30 U.S.C.A. as requiring Chemi-Cote to adverse Bowen's patent application. The argument is made that Adams v. Witmer, 271 F.2d 29 (9 Cir. 1958) requires that Chemi-Cote have a remedy through jurisdiction of the state courts to test the loss of its mining claim. We do not think such a conclusion is warranted. The court held that the decision of the Bureau of Land Management in a contest proceeding denying an application for a patent to mining claims was subject to the Administrative Procedure Act. As if distinguishing between that situation and the situation here involving adverse claims, the court said, "Thus § 30 of Title 30 U.S.C.A. provides an elaborate manner for court trial of adverse claims to mining claims as a part of the procedure provided for issuing patents under § 29." Whatever property rights Chemi-Cote acquired in the mining claims involved in this case were not lost because of a non-reviewable decision of an administrative official, but because of its failure to comply with the applicable statutory requirements regulating distribution of the public domain. No allegation is made by Chemi-Cote that Bowen did not satisfy the statutory requirements of notice.

Bowen, in his pleadings, counterclaimed for damages for wrongful removal of perlite from his claim. The trial court dismissed the counterclaim and entered judgment for Chemi-Cote, which judgment was affirmed by the Court of Appeals. Having concluded that it was error to quiet title to the right of possession of the two lode claims in Chemi-Cote, the question remains whether Bowen is entitled to damages on his counterclaim.

A claim for wrongful removal of ore must be characterized as a "possessory action" as distinguished from an "adverse suit." The judgment in a possessory action affects only the title to the ground as between the litigating parties, and the rule to be applied is not that respecting the strength of plaintiff's title, but the rule that the better title prevails. Location is the foundation of the possessory title, and possession thereunder as required by law and local rules and customs keeps the title alive, and the government holds the superior title in trust for the person thus holding the possessory title. Bagg v. New Jersey Loan Company, 88 Ariz. 182, 354 P.2d 40 (1960). The court's determination on the question of right of possession as between the litigating parties is not of binding force and effect as against the United States since the government is not a party to the suit and a right thus effective depends finally upon the character of the land involved. Perego v. Dodge, 163 U.S. 160, 16 S.Ct. 971, 41 L.Ed. 113 (1896).

The Bureau of Land Management has the exclusive jurisdiction, insofar as the parties to this action are concerned, to make a determination as to whether or not perlite is subject to location as lode or placer. The jurisdiction of the state court to rule upon the the question of right to possession is not withdrawn, however, because such a determination is not a question "affecting title" to the land embraced by the patent application. See Warnekos v. Cowan, supra. The court below found that the mining claims of Chemi-Cote were located prior to the time Bowen's claims were located and that Chemi-Cote or its predecessors were in continuous possession and performed the necessary annual assessment work since the date of the original location of the two claims. Without determining whether perlite is subject to location as lode or placer, Chemi-Cote had a better right of possession to the area encompassed by the two lode claims in question because of its prior possession than did Bowen. That possessory title was lost, however, by reason of its failure to file an adverse claim to Bowen's patent application within the prescribed period of time.

We hold that Bowen is entitled to damages for ore removed by Chemi-Cote subsequent to the date of Bowen's patent application. See Dahl v. Raunheim, supra. . . .

NOTES

1. *Noyes v. Mantle,* the first case in this section, and *Bowen v. Chemi-Cote Corp.* are factually similar. In both cases the lode claimant was first in time, in both cases a placer patent was applied for by the junior locator and in both cases the lode claimant failed to file an adverse claim in the patent proceeding. Yet in *Noyes v. Mantle* the lode claimant won and in *Bowen v. Chemi-Cote Corp.* the lode claimant lost. Can you reconcile the two cases?

2. Patent procedures are introduced at this point only by way of introduction and to give you some insight into the procedural setting of mining claim disputes. These procedures are covered in greater detail in the materials that follow.

C. Mill Sites

UTAH INTERNATIONAL, INC.
36 IBLA 219 (1978)

. . . .

Utah International, Inc. (Utah), appeals from decisions of the Wyoming State Office, Bureau of Land Management (BLM), dated February 24, 1977, rejecting, in part, application for millsite patent W-30586 and rejecting in its entirety application for millsite patent W-36502, each filed pursuant to 30 U.S.C. § 42 (1970).

The rejections were based on the fact that BLM interpreted 30 U.S.C. § 42 as giving the Government discretion as to whether a patent should issue, and in its assumed discretion it found that Utah's use of the lands was temporary and did not warrant a patent.

The applicable part of 30 U.S.C. § 42 (1970) reads as follows:

(a) Where nonmineral land not contiguous to the vein or lode is used or occupied by the proprietor of such vein or lode for mining or milling purposes, such nonadjacent surface ground may be embraced and included in an application for a patent for such vein or lode, and the same may be patented therewith * * *.

. . . .

Two mineral reports were filed in this case.[1] The first was submitted by mining engineer W. C. Ackerman in 1972. On pages 38 and 39 of this report, Ackerman summarized his findings as follows:

On the basis of the field examination conducted during the week of August 1, 1972, examination of technical literature, maps and data submitted by the applicant, it is the opinion of the examiner that the applicant has shown good faith and has perfected the subject lands as mill sites in accordance with R.S. 2337 (30 U.S.C. 42).

---

[1]   In addition to the applications in issue, W-30586 and W-36502, the mineral reports also included an examination of claims in Utah's patent applications W-29048, W-31660. A total of 314 claims are involved in the 4 patent applications.

Utah International has demonstrated that the area underlain by the mill sites is nonmineral in character. They have demonstrated that the 314 mill sites under four patent applications are properly utilized for the purpose of processing and milling of uranium bearing ores from the properties in close proximity to their mill.

. . . .

The Environmental Protection Agency (EPA) has addressed the Bureau of Land Management by letter * * * with some concern of patenting mill site claims with tailings ponds which contain radioactive material having a half life of 1016 years. Their concern is that after a pond is abandoned, it dries, and the material may be used for other purposes such as land fill. This particular hazard was brought to light in land fill programs at Grand Junction, Colorado and Riverton, Wyoming. Normally, as stated above, a mill site invariably proceeds to patent if the criteria is met. That is (1) the land is nonmineral in character and (2) the land is occupied for mining and milling purposes. It is the opinion of the EPA that these lands should be retained under Federal ownership in order that they may be under surveillance, that is (1) beyond the life of the operation and (2) beyond the life of the applicant receiving the patent.

. . . .

A second report dated May 11, 1976, was prepared by Alan J. Ver Ploeg. Ver Ploeg's report differed from Ackerman's on the question of mineralization. Ver Pleog reported at page 45 that examination of radiometric logs indicated a few shows of mineralization, but that only one (claims 78, 127, and 128 within application W-30586) was considered to be of sufficient quality and quantity to be classified as mineral-in-character. Regarding use and occupancy, Ver Ploeg concluded that except for areas which are planned for future use, the land in question was being used for the purpose of processing and milling of uranium-bearing ores from the properties in close proximity to the mill.

Ver Ploeg's recommendation for the applications reads as follows at pages 46-47:

On the basis of the field examination conducted during the week of November 3, 1975 and data supplied by the applicant, it is the opinion of the examiner that * * * portions of application W-30586 be contested * * * for failure to comply with the requirements set forth in R.S. 2337 (30 U.S.C. 42). The remainder of the claims in application W-30586 (excluding those encompassing the mill, office, and maintenance facilities) and all of W-36502 should be contested also. Although the company is utilizing these lands (W-36502 and remainder of W-30586) for mining purposes including primarily stockpiling overburden and tailings ponds; these uses are considered temporary in nature after which the land is reclaimed as required by Wyoming State law. This temporary use of the land does not warrant the issuance of patent to these claims. In addition, EPA has requested these lands be retained in Federal ownership to allow for monitoring the radioactive materials and chemical waste * * *. Only those claims encompassing the mill, office, and maintenance facilities are recommended to proceed to patent.

. . . .

In its decisions dated February 24, 1977, the State Office rejected application W-36502 in its entirety and application W-30586 [in part].

. . . .

The State Office said that unlike a locator of a lode or placer mining claim, a millsite claimant's rights do not "vest" at the time he fulfills the requirements for perfecting his claim. *Reed v. Bowron,* 32 L.D. 383, 386 (1904). Furthermore, the State Office interpreted the language of the statute "may be patented" as being directory or permissive as distinguished from "shall be patented" which is mandatory or imperative. Based on this construction, the State Office concluded that while the statute permits occupancy of nonmineral lands for millsite purposes which occupancy must be respected by the Government, the statute does not require the issuance of a patent for such claims. The State Office noted that the lands are being used primarily for stockpiling, overburdens and tailings ponds, and concluded that since these uses are temporary they do not warrant the issuance of a patent. It commented that appellant would be required to reclaim these lands in accordance with Wyoming law.

The State Office referred to a letter dated May 4, 1973, addressed to the Director, Denver Service Center, Bureau of Land Management (BLM), in which the EPA recommended that ownership of land on which radioactive tailings are stored be retained by the Federal Government in order that the lands may be under constant surveillance beyond the life of the operation and beyond the life of the applicant receiving the patent. In light of that recommendation, the State Office rejected that part of the application for patent in issue without prejudice to the applicant's right to continue to make legal mining and/or milling uses of the lands embraced within the subject millsite claims.

In its Statement of Reasons, appellant asserts that it has complied with all the requirements of 30 U.S.C. § 42 in that the lands in question are nonmineral, not contiguous to a vein or lode, and are used or occupied by Utah for mining or milling purposes.

Appellant makes reference to the fact that the Government's only argument as to the criteria of the statute not being met is that stockpiling and tailings pond use is temporary in nature and does not warrant the issuance of a patent. In response to the argument appellant points to *Charles Lennig,* 5 L.D. 190 (1886), a case in which it was held in dicta that if the land is used for depositing tailings or storing areas, it would be used for mining or milling purposes.

In support of its assertion that it has met the requirements of the law, appellant quotes from pages 38 and 39 of Ackerman's report (set forth, *supra,* in this decision) concerning his findings from the field examination and his recommendation that patent should issue.

Appellant further contends that compliance with the statute vests in it an absolute right to a patent and the Government's refusal to issue a patent in this case is arbitrary, capricious, without Congressional sanction, an abuse of discretion and therefore unconstitutional.

Appellant's argument focuses on the Government's interpretation of "may be patented" in 30 U.S.C. § 42 as meaning that the Government has discretion whether or not to issue a patent even if the statutory requirements have been met.

Based on this interpretation BLM refused to issue the patent because, in its discretion, it considered the "millsite" use as only temporary and thus, on the recommendation of EPA, it decided that title should remain in the Government. Appellant contends that EPA cannot empower the BLM to do what it has no statutory authority to do, *i.e.*, deny a patent to a millsite once the statutory prerequisites are met. Appellant asserts that "may be patented" as used in 30 U.S.C. § 42 does not vest the BLM with discretion to refuse to issue a patent.

Appellant comments that an Environmental Impact Statement (EIS), which included potential radiation effects on the environment with respect to the claims in issue has been filed with the EPA. This report was approved in 1974 simultaneously with the issuance of an operating license for the uranium mill by the Atomic Energy Commission (AEC) the governmental body having jurisdiction at that time. The EIS was subsequent to both the patent application and Ackerman's report. Appellant notes that Ackerman anticipated the effects of radioactivity on the environment and still recommended patent.

Appellant claims that approval by the EPA, AEC, and BLM with awareness of possible adverse environmental effects constitutes a waiver by the Government of all objections to such adverse effects and is an estoppel in pais of both EPA and BLM to raise this objection.

The crux of the argument in this case is whether or not the phrase "may be patented" as used in 30 U.S.C. § 42 (1970) is correctly interpreted to mean that the Government has discretion whether or not to issue a patent to a millsite when the requirements of the law have been met.

The history of cases in this area of the law shows that patents for millsites are denied, or millsite claims are contested because the applicant has not fulfilled the requirements of the law. Commonly, the Government charges in a contest complaint that the claimant has not used or occupied the lands embraced within the claim for mining or milling purposes. *United States v. Rukke,* 32 IBLA 155, 160, (1977); *United States v. Dietemann,* 26 IBLA 356, 364-365 (1976).

It often happens that the claimant can show past use of the claim for mining or milling purposes or plans to use the claim in the future for such purposes, but these assertions have been held to be insufficient to meet the requirements of the law, and the claim is declared null and void. *United States v. Dietemann, supra; United States v. Cuneo,* 15 IBLA 304, 81 I.D. 262 (1974). Claims have also been declared null and void when the requirements of the law have not been met as of the time the lands embraced by the claim are withdrawn from location. *United States v. Almgren,* 17 IBLA 295 (1974); *United States v. Cuneo, supra.*

The body of law in millsite cases does not reveal any cases in which the requirements of the law have been fulfilled but the Government refuses to issue patent for other reasons. Ackerman aptly summarized the usual BLM procedure in these cases when he said on page 39 of his report: "Normally, * * * a mill site invariably proceeds to patent if the criteria is [sic] met, that is (1) the land is nonmineral in character and (2) the land is occupied for mining and milling purposes."

In its decision the State Office says that a patent is not warranted in this case because the lands are being used for stockpiling, overburden and tailing ponds and such uses are temporary. In commenting on the word "use" as it appears in the statute, Secretary Lamar, in the case of *Charles Lennig,* 5 L.D. 190, 192 (1886), said that if a claimant used the land for depositing tailings or storing ores, he thought it was clear that the claimant would be using it for mining or milling purposes. Moreover, this Board expressly ruled in *United States v. Swanson,* 14 IBLA 158, 81 I.D. 14 (1974), that storage of ore was a validating use under the millsite provisions of the mining laws. *See United States v. Swanson, supra,* 166-83, 81 I.D. at 17-26. We surmise, however, that the real thrust behind the rejection is BLM's concern, prompted by EPA's letter, that these uses may cause adverse environmental effects.

If Utah receives a patent for these lands, its mining operations will come under the scrutiny of the State of Wyoming. In reviewing that State's environmental protection statute (Wyoming Stat., 1975 Cum, Supplement §§ 35-502.1 to 35-502.56) we find that there are detailed and forceful provisions regarding mining operations and subsequent reclamation. Specific standards for backfilling, recontouring, and revegetation are coupled with strict requirements for the disposal of toxic or radioactive waste to make the statute more exacting than any comparable Federal control. We note, moreover, that the civil and criminal penalties for noncompliance appear to be drafted so as to assure a maximum amount of protection for the environment.

In conclusion, we find that appellant has met all the applicable requirements of 30 U.S.C. § 42, *supra,* and a patent must therefore issue. The concerns expressed by EPA regarding radioactive waste on the sites seem to be addressed more than adequately by Wyoming's environmental statute and the EPA recommendation should thus constitute no bar to appellant's application. In light of these determinations it is unnecessary for us to reach the question of the authority of the Department to refuse to issue a patent for a millsite where all of the conditions of the millsite law have been met.

Accordingly, pursuant to the authority delegated to the Board of Land Appeals by the Secretary of the Interior, 43 CFR 4.1, the State Office's decision rejecting application of W-36502 is reversed and its decision partially rejecting W-30586 is reversed as to those parts of the application which were rejected.

NOTES

1. 30 U.S.C. § 42 provides that only "nonmineral" land may be embraced within a mill site. What constitutes nonmineral lands was the subject of litigation in *Cleary v. Skiffich,* 65 P. 59 (Colo. 1901). There, the court held that land occupied by a mill site does not lose its status as nonmineral even though, in fact, it does contain some minerals. The test for determining the mineral character of the land was enunciated by that court as follows: "Unless the premises in dispute did in fact contain mineral deposits of a value and quantity which, under the conditions existing at the time when the rights of the original owners of the mill-site premises attached, could have been extracted at a fair mining profit, they were nonmineral in character, and the jury should have been instructed accordingly." *Id.* at 62.

2. 30 U.S.C. § 42 (1970) further provides that the mill site must not be contiguous to the vein or lode. In *Montana-Illinois Copper Mining Co.,* 42 L.D. 434 (1913) the issue was whether a mill site that was contiguous to a lode claim, but not to the lode itself, was permissible under section 42. The Department held that such a mill site could be validly located. The Department reasoned that the purpose of the "non-contiguity" provision of section 42 was to provide additional assurance that the land claimed for the mill site was nonmineral in character. Such a provision was necessary "in the light of the previously existing practice, to prevent the appropriation within any such [mill site] area of a further segment of the actual vein or lode upon which the mining claim itself was predicated." *Id.* at 436. Reasoning from the purpose of the statute, the Department concluded that a mill site could be contiguous to a claim "provided it be clearly shown that the lode or vein along which the mining location is laid either terminates before the end abutting upon the millsite claim would otherwise be reached or that it departs from the sideline of the mining claim and the ground embraced in such adjoining millsite claim is nonmineral in character." *Id.* at 436 -37.

3. Even assuming that all the requirements of section 42 are met including that the millsite is being used for "mining or milling purposes," the locator of the mill site is not necessarily entitled to the full five acres allowed by the statute. "[T]he law requires a claimant, when challenged by the government, to demonstrate use or occupation of all the area claimed within a millsite location before he will be granted a patent for the full amount requested. That area which is not proved to be needed for milling and mining purposes may not go to patent." *United States v. Swanson,* 14 I.B.L.A. 158, 174 (1974).

D. Tunnel Sites

See Enterprise Mining Co. v. Rico Aspen, page 39, *supra.*

NOTES

1. There is nothing in the mining law of 1872 which permits a tunnel site to be patented. This is for the reason that a tunnel site is not a mining claim. Rather, it is designed to serve only an exploratory function, and when that function is complete, the law contemplates that if valuable minerals are discovered, a lode or placer claim will be made on the surface.

2. Tunnel sites are no longer of much importance, however. This is for the reason that exploratory work for minerals located at depth can now be accomplished more cheaply by drilling than by tunnelling.

3. Notwithstanding that a tunnel site is not technically a mining claim, it is subject to the same recording requirements under FLPMA as lode or placer claims.

3   QUALIFIED LOCATORS

Thompson v. Spray
Hugh MacCallum Woodworth

THOMPSON V. SPRAY
72 Cal. 528 (1887)

   HAYNE, C.   The action is in relation to a placer mining claim in Amador County, and was brought by Alex. Thompson, Sr., and his five children mentioned below. At the trial a notice of location was introduced in evidence, dated January 20, 1882, and signed with the names Alex. Thompson, James Thompson, Alex. Thompson, Jr., and Matilda Thompson. The plaintiffs then offered what they styled an "amended" notice, which bore the same date, and contained a fuller description of the property, and was signed with the names Alex. Thompson, Matilda Thompson, Margaret Thompson, and Bedelia Thompson. It will be observed that the second notice omits two of the names on the first, and inserts two new names in their place. The defendant objected to the introduction of the second notice, on the ground that it was not an "amended" notice, inasmuch as the names were not the same, and that no abandonment of the first notice had been shown. The court sustained the objection, and excluded the evidence.
   We think this was error. There does not appear to be any statute of this state providing for amending notices of location, as is the case in Colorado. But we see no reason why, if locators have any apprehension as to the sufficiency of their notice, they may not put up another one. Whether the second notice is to be treated as an original notice, or whether it relates back to the posting of the first one, is a question as to its effect which it is not material to consider. In the present case the rights of James Thompson and Alex. Thompson, Jr., whose names were on the first notice, but not on the second, could not be affected by the posting of the second notice. (*Morton* v. *Solambo Co.,* 26 Cal. 527; *Gore* v. *McBrayer,* 18 Cal. 588.) Margaret and Bedelia Thompson had nothing to do with the first notice. Their rights rested on the second, which, as to them, was an original notice; and they were certainly entitled to have it introduced in evidence. With respect to the two who were on both notices, we think that they also were entitled to have the second introduced in evidence. The second would not operate as an abandonment of the first. *Weill* v. *Lucerne Co.,* 11 Nev. 212, 213. But it was not necessary to show

such abandonment to render the second notice admissible. The question as to the rights of the plaintiffs, as between themselves, does not arise in this action.

Upon the close of the plaintiffs' evidence several motions for nonsuit were made and granted. The first motion was as to Margaret and Bedelia Thompson. Their notice of location having been excluded, the motion was granted; but, as above shown, the exclusion of the notice was erroneous. The defendant then moved for a nonsuit as to James, Matilda, and Alex. Thompson, Jr. This motion was denied as to Matilda, and granted as to the others. It was upon four grounds, viz.: That they were not citizens of the United States; that they were minors at the time of the location: that the use of their names was unauthorized; and that the notice was recorded before it was posted.

Were the plaintiffs citizens of the United States at the time the location was made? We think the evidence shows that they were. The father testified as follows: "I and each of my co-locators were, at the time of location of said mining claim, citizens of the United States. My children were born in the state of California." The testimony that all the locators were "citizens" would perhaps have been excluded, as being a conclusion of the witness, if it had been objected to. But, it having been allowed to go in without objection, we think it was of itself sufficient to prevent a nonsuit upon this ground. With reference to the children, the matter was put beyond cavil by the statement that they were born in California. The provision of the statute is that "all persons born in the United States, and not subject to any foreign power, excluding Indians not taxed, are declared to be citizens of the United States." Rev. St. § 1992. Here citizenship from birth is the rule. Subjection to a foreign power is the exception. A case will not be presumed to fall within the exception. Hence proof of birth within the United States is sufficient, in the absence of a showing of subjection to a foreign power. See *Golden Fleece Co.* v. *Cable Con. Co.,* 12 Nev. 325, 326. The testimony of the father was good evidence of the place of birth. The provision for proof of citizenship by affidavit, if it applies, (Rev. St. U.S. § 2321,) is not exclusive of other modes of proof.

Does the fact that these plaintiffs were minors at the time of the location invalidate the notice as to them? We have not been referred to any decision which holds that it does. The provision of the statute is that mineral deposits in public lands are open to "citizens of the United States, and those who have declared their intention," etc. Section 2319. No requirement that the citizen shall be of any particular age is expressed; and, unless we are prepared to affirm that minors are not citizens, we do not see how we can say that they are not entitled to the benefit of the act. This conclusion is strengthened by the circumstance that in some instances the statute expressly requires that the citizen shall be of age. Thus, in reference to coal lands, the provision is that "every person above the age of twenty-one years who is a citizen of the United States," etc. Section 2347. So with reference to homesteads the provision is that "every person * * * over the age of twenty-one years, and a citizen," etc. Section 2259. The expression of a requirement as to age in some instances, and the omission of it in others, is significant. Nor is there any reason in the nature of things why a minor may not make a valid location. After the preliminary steps are taken, all that is required is that a certain amount of work shall be done. If the minor can do it, or can get any one to do it for him, the condition imposed by the statute is fulfilled. If he cannot, his claim lapses, and the mine is open to location by others. It may be added that, so far as we know, it is the practice, in many mining communities, for minors to locate claims.

Did the father's want of authority from his children invalidate the notice as to them? He testified as follows: "I had no power of attorney to sign the notice for my children, nor to authorize Mr. Price to sign their names. None of them gave me or him authority to sign their names. * * * I acted for them, but without their knowledge, until after their names were signed, notice recorded and posted." Unless there is an implication from the foregoing that he acted with their knowledge after their names were signed, etc., it does not appear that there was any ratification by all the children, except the bringing of the suit.

It cannot be doubted that the location of a mining claim may be made by agent, (*Gore* v. *McBrayer,* 18 Cal. 587;) and wherever there is a local custom to that effect, it is not necessary that the person in whose name a location is made should be aware that it has been made, (*Morton* v. *Solambo Co.,* 26 Cal. 534.) In the absence of evidence of such a custom, we think that there must be either authority in the first instance or a ratification. Whether a ratification will be presumed, in accordance with what is said in *Gore* v. *McBrayer,* above cited, and whether, if presumed or proven, it will relate back to the posting, so as to cut off intervening rights, (compare *Hibberd* v. *Smith,* 67 Cal. 547, 4 Pac. Rep. 473, 8 Pac. Rep. 46,) need not be decided; for the bringing of the suit, which must be taken to have been by authority, is a sufficient ratification; and, as far as the record goes, we cannot know that there were any intervening rights,—the assertions in the answer being denied by force of the statute, and the defendant not having introduced any evidence.

Does the fact that the notice was recorded before it was posted render it invalid? We think not. No record is necessary in the absence of a custom requiring it. *Golden Fleece Co.* v. *Cable Con. Co.,* 12 Nev. 323; *Southern Cross Co.* v. *Europa Co.,* 15 Nev. 384; *Jupiter Co.* v. *Bodie Co.,* 7 Sawy. 114, 11 Fed. Rep. 666. No such custom was proved in this case; and it is clear that the doing of an unnecessary act cannot vitiate the notice. But, if such a custom were shown, we do not think the mere order in which the acts are done of sufficient importance to render them of no effect. See, generally, *North Noonday Co.* v. *Orient Co.,* 6 Sawy. 313, 1 Fed. Rep. 522.

This motion, therefore, was improperly granted. After it had been granted, the defendant moved for a nonsuit as to the two remaining plaintiffs, viz., Matilda and Alex. Thompson, Sr., partly upon grounds already considered, and partly upon the ground that the dismissal of the action as to the other plaintiffs left these two claiming more than they were entitled by law to hold. But in such case the location is good for as much as the party is entitled to hold, and void for the excess only. *Richmond Co.* v. *Rose,* 114 U.S. 576, 5 Sup. Ct. Rep. 1055.

It results that the nonsuit as to Matilda and Alex. Thompson, Sr., was improperly granted.

The respondent, however, seeks to uphold the judgment on the ground that the action is under section 2326 of the United States Revised Statutes, and that, so treating it, the complaint is defective in that it does not aver that the plaintiffs are citizens. But there is nothing in the complaint to lead any one to suppose that it was brought under the provision mentioned. It is sufficient as a complaint to quiet title to a mining claim. See *Pralus* v. *Jefferson Co.,* 34 Cal. 559; *Pralus* v. *Pacific Co.,* 35 Cal. 34. The plaintiff's motive in bringing the action, or the use which he may be able to make of the judgment, should he obtain one, cannot affect the question of the sufficiency of the complaint.

In the case of *Lee Doon* v. *Tesh,* 68 Cal. 44, 6 Pac Rep. 97, and 8 Pac. Rep. 621, the complaint itself showed that it was brought under section 2326, and the question whether it could not have been upheld as a complaint in an ordinary action to quiet title was not made or considered. The court did not hold that, in all actions in relation to mining claims, the complaint must aver the citizenship of the plaintiffs. It guarded its decision from any such inference by saying: "We must not be understood as holding that in all actions in relation to mining claims, it is necessary for plaintiffs to aver citizenship." And we think that in ordinary actions in relation to mining claims the general allegation that the plaintiff is "the owner," etc., covers all the essential elements of ownership.

We therefore advise that the judgment be reversed, and the cause remanded for a new trial.

We concur: BELCHER, C. C.; FOOTE, C.

BY THE COURT. For the reasons given in the foregoing opinion the judgment is reversed, and cause remanded for a new trial.

NOTES

1. As the principal case illustrates, the benefits of the mining law are available only to citizens and those who have declared their intention to become citizens. The Senate debates on this point reveal that at least part of the reason for the inclusion of this requirement was racially motivated. Consider the following excerpt from Gates, The History of Public Land Law Development at 712-13 (1968) (footnotes omitted):

Senator Seward of New York felt that any person expressing an intention to become a citizen should be eligible for a permit [to mine]. Undoubtedly aware of the California legislation already taxing foreigners at exorbitant rates for the privilege of mining, the California Senators immediately aligned themselves with those from Georgia, Mississippi and Ohio, and all went on record to the effect that this would encourage Mexicans (an inferior caste) to cross over the American borders and rob us of the fortune that "belonged" to the American people (presumably as the spoils of the conquest of California). It was only the Senator from Wisconsin who was heard to sympathize with the thousands of people of foreign birth who had migrated to the California mines from Wisconsin alone. The Iowa Senator also thought the Mexicans were a miserable lot and should be excluded from the mines, but he did not think it would be possible to exclude

Europeans. Senator Foote of Mississippi suggested, apparently seriously, that eligibility should be limited to Europeans who could produce "testimonials of good character." The Senate finally adopted a . . . bill making English and Europeans who had not been convicted of crimes eligible for permits. How this was to be administered in the gold fields no one quite seemed to know for sure.

The debate summarized above was with reference to an early version of the mining law, and one, fortunately, that was not enacted.

2. 30 U.S.C. § 22 opens the public lands not just to citizens, but, in addition to aliens who have "declared their intention to become" citizens. "The filing of a declaration was made optional by the Immigration and Nationality Act of 1952, but the fact that it has been made optional does not affect the requirement of the mining law that an alien, in order to locate, must have declared his intention to become a citizen. The right of an alien to locate a mining claim may be lost by his abandonment of his intention to become a citizen." 1 American Law of Mining § 31.04[2] (2d ed. 1984)(footnotes omitted).

3. Not all citizens are qualified to locate mining claims. George Schultz married Diana Webb on February 16, 1979. At the time Diana Webb was employed by the Moab District Office, BLM. Diana Webb's jobs did not involve her with the management of mining claims nor with mining claim records. The BLM nevertheless contended that certain claims located by Schultz while he was married to Diana were void pursuant to 43 U.S.C. § 11 (1982), which provides that "officers, clerks and employees in the Bureau of Land Management are prohibited from directly or indirectly purchasing or becoming interested in the purchase of public lands; and any person who violates this section shall forthwith be removed from his office."

Schultz argued that Utah, the state in which the claims were located, was not a community property state, and therefore that his wife had no legal interest in any of his claims. The Board rejected this argument, stating that:

This is not conclusive . . . of whether Diana Webb is "indirectly purchasing or becoming interested in the purchase of any of the public land." There are, of course, numerous legal or business arrangements under which Webb could be or become indirectly interested in the lands involved. We do not know, for example, whether any will or trust of Schultz's creates in her any legal interests in the claims or any eventual patents emanating from them [Footnote omitted]. Nor do we know about her role, if any, in Chinle Associates, of which Shultz is president, which is named as "operator" of the claims. Either of these routes could bring her within the ambit of the statutory prohibition.

Schultz, gentleman that he was, argued that even if Diana Webb had an interest in the claims, the "proper sanction is to dismiss his wife from the employ of the BLM, not to declare his mining claims void." Id. at 84. The Board concluded that the BLM had the authority under 43 U.S.C. § 11 to declare the claims void and to take "remedial action" against Diana Webb.

HUGH MacCALLUM WOODWORTH
72 Interior Dec. 233 (1965)

APPEAL FROM THE BUREAU OF LAND MANAGEMENT

Hugh MacCallum Woodworth has appealed to the Secretary of the Interior from a decision by the Division of Appeals, Bureau of Land Management, dated February 20, 1964, affirming a Spokane land office decision rejecting his verified statement filed after notice to him of proceedings initiated by the United States Forest Service under section 5(a) of the act of July 23, 1955, 69 Stat. 369, 30 U.S.C. § 613 (1958), on the ground that the verified statement did not contain the dates of location of the mining claims listed in the statement as required by the act. The land office had also stated another ground for rejection, that the claimant is not a citizen of the United States. The Division of Appeals, however, stated that the question of the claimant's citizenship is pertinent to patenting the claims and did not need to be determined in this proceeding.

A notice requiring mining claimants to file verified statements in accordance with section 5(a), of the act of July 23, 1955, *supra,* was first published on May 8, 1957, at the request of the Forest Service. Appellant's affidavit was timely filed on July 31, 1957, setting forth a portion of the required information. The information held to be lacking was data setting forth the dates of location of the claims and recording information. Appellant in his affidavit as to the date of location and book and page of recordation of the notice or certificate of location simply stated:

Unknown, as records were destroyed by a fire at Ellensburg (then County Seat) about 1889.

Appellant in his present appeal refers to this statement and asserts that it "at least places the dates as 'prior to 1889'." He contends that the "act of God which removed the official records from all human access" should excuse him from supplying them more precisely.

The act of July 23, 1955, requires a verified statement to set forth the date of the mining location and the book and page of recordation of the notice or certificate of location, together with other information. The argument implied in appellant's statement on appeal regarding the information given in his verified statement is that he furnished all the information available to him because of the impossibility of furnishing the explicit information due to the destruction of the records.

Although it is likely that the appellant could have given more information than he chose to, even assuming that literal compliance with the requirements of the statute and notice was not possible, it is not necessary to decide the appeal on this ground because the decision below must be affirmed for another reason. This reason is the second ground given by the land office, the appellant's lack of citizenship. The appellant has not denied his lack of citizenship in the United States but indeed has affirmatively stated in a letter to the land office that he is a citizen of Canada and has not declared his intention of becoming a citizen of the

United States. He contended in his appeal from the land office decision that the absence of citizenship could not be a defect in his statement because United States citizenship was never stated as a requirement. He also stated that the State of Washington recognizes possessory title to mining claims by aliens and that he has not been informed of any "overruling of this" by the Federal Government.

The Division of Appeals suggested that the issue of citizenship need not be raised as to a verified statement because it is pertinent only to the patenting of claims. This suggestion overlooks the fact that the proceedings brought under the 1955 act raise a question of superior right and title in mining claims, so far as surface uses of the claims are concerned, as between the claimant or claimants and the United States. The 1955 act provides a means whereby the usage of surface resources on mining claims can be limited solely to that necessary for mining purposes by permitting the owner of a mining claim to waive any rights to surface resources, either expressly, or by failing to file timely the required verified statement. If the statement is filed a hearing is held to determine the validity and effectiveness of any right or title to, or interest in or under, the mining claim contrary to rights of the United States to manage and dispose of surface resources other than mineral deposits subject to location under the mining laws. See the discussion regarding the necessity of proving a discovery in order for a claimant to prevail at such a hearing. *United States* v. *Clarence E. Payne,* 68 I.D. 250 (1961).

The mining law, particularly Rev. Stat. § 2319 (1875), 30 U.S.C. § 22 (1958), provides that lands having valuable mineral deposits shall be free "and open to occupation and purchase by citizens of the United States and those who have declared their intention to become such." See also Rev. Stat. § 2321 (1875), 30 U.S.C. § 24 (1958). Patent may be issued to any person authorized to locate a claim under that provision. Rev. Stat. § 2325 (1875), 30 U.S.C. § 29 (1958). In cases applying these provisions where there have been questions of alienage, the general rule that has been followed is that the incapacity of a person to take and hold a mining claim by reason of his lack of citizenship is open to question by the government only and not by others except in behalf of the government. See *Manuel* v. *Wulff,* 152 U.S. 505 (1894). In that case the naturalization of a Canadian alien was held to have a retroactive effect giving validity to his mining location "so as to be deemed a waiver of all liability to forfeiture and a confirmation of title." Id. at 511.

As stated in another case, the meaning of *Manuel* v. *Wulff* is that the "location by an alien and all the rights following from such location are voidable, not void, and are free from attack by anyone except the government." *McKinley Mining Co.* v. *Alaska Mining Co.,* 183 U.S. 563, 572 (1902); see also *Billings* v. *Aspen Mining & Smelting Co.,* 51 Fed. 338. (8th Cir. 1892), *rehearing denied,* 52 Fed. 250, *appeal dismissed, Aspen Mining & Smelting Co.* v. *Billings,* 150 U.S. 31 (1893), and other cases listed under the notes on citizenship in 30 U.S.C.A. following sec. 22. These cases generally involve disputes among private claimants and not a dispute between an alien and the United States. In the cases, there is the recognition that, although the possessory title of an alien may not be subject to collateral attack because of his alienage by citizens, it is defeasible by the sovereign, the United States.

Thus, although the appellant as an alien may have a possessory interest in the mining claims which would be recognized in any disputes between him and other claimants, he is here attempting to assert a possessory right and title superior to the United States. The fact that he acquired his interest in the claim from his father who acquired it through a sheriff's sale, which was recognized in the Washington courts, does not matter here. The essential factor is that by filing the verified statement under the 1955 act, although it is not a request for a patent, nevertheless, the appellant is asserting rights superior to those of the United States as to the surface resources of the claim. Because appellant has admitted his lack of citizenship and also that he has not filed a declaration of intent to become a citizen, there are no essential facts in dispute which require a hearing to resolve.

The question then remains: what rights, if any, does the appellant, as an alien, have against the United States with respect to this mining claim? As mentioned previously, the mining laws declare that public lands are open to "occupancy and purchase" by citizens and those who have declared their intent to become citizens. The appellant, not falling into either of those categories, thus is not qualified to purchase a claim from the United States nor can he hold a claim under possession or occupancy against the United States. This being the case his verified statement cannot be accepted as giving him a right superior to the United States to the use and management of the surface resources on the claims.

Accordingly, pursuant to the authority delegated to the Solicitor by the Secretary of the Interior (210 DM 2.2A (4) (a); 24 F.R. 1348), the decision is affirmed as to the rejection of the verified statement but for the reasons above given.

NOTES

1. Smith locates a mining claim supported by a valid discovery. Thereafter, Smith sells his claim to Swenson, who is not a United States citizen and has not declared his intention to become one. In *Manuel* v. *Wulff,* 152 U.S. 505 (1894) the Supreme Court held on similar facts that the title acquired by the grantee Swenson, was voidable at the instance of the government. It was not void for all purposes, however, and could not be challenged by a rival locator.

2. Assume in the preceding note that after receiving the conveyance from Smith, but prior to any challenge by the United States, Swenson became a citizen or declared his intention to do so. Would that cure the defect in his title? "Where an alien who has located a mining claim on public lands subsequently becomes a citizen or declares his intention to become such, before any rights have intervened, such declaration operates back to the date of location and renders the claim valid from that time; upon such declaration he is entitled to the benefit of work previously done and of a record previously made by him in locating the claim." *Herrington* v. *Martinez,* 45 F. Supp. 543, 546-47 (S.D. Cal. 1942).

3. Would it be proper under the principles set forth above for a rival claimant to raise alienage in an adverse suit? *See O'Reilly* v. *Campbell,* 116 U.S. 418 (1886).

4. PCM Corporation applied for a patent to certain mining claims that it located in Alaska. One issue in a suit brought to protest the issuance of the patent was whether PCM was a qualified locator. Consider the following excerpt from the decision in *In Re Pacific Coast Molybdenum,* 90 Interior Dec. 352, 364-65 (1983).

> The last issue pressed in the appeal is whether PCM is qualified to receive patent for these claims. Section 1 of the Mining Law of 1872 states that "[e]xcept as otherwise provided, all valuable mineral deposits in lands belonging to the United States * * * shall be free and open to exploration and purchase, and the lands in which they are found to occupation and purchase, by citizens of the United States." Act of May 10, 1872, 17 Stat. 91, 30 U.S.C. § 22 (1976). Section 7 of the 1872 Act further provides that "[p]roof of citizenship * * * may consist * * * in the case of a corporation organized under the laws of the United States, or any State or Territory thereof, by the filing of a certified copy of their charter or certificate of incorporation." Act of May 10, 1872, 17 Stat. 94, 30 U.S.C. § 24 (1976).

> Appellants argue that, while PCM is a corporation organized under the laws of the State of Nevada, it is, in point of fact, a wholly owned subsidiary, through a web of corporate holdings, of Rio Tinto-Zinc Corp., Limited, a United Kingdom corporation, *See* note 2, *infra.* Both PCM and the Solicitor's Office contend that proof of incorporation under the laws of a state gives rise to a conclusive presumption of citizenship in that state.

> The question of the authority of a corporation to locate mining claims was first examined in *McKinley* v. *Wheeler,* 130 U.S. 630 (1889). Justice Field, speaking for a unanimous court, stated that the provisions of section 1 of the Mining Law of 1872 "must be held not to preclude a private corporation formed under the laws of a State, *whose members are citizens of the United States,* from locating a mining claim on the public lands of the United States." (Italics supplied.) *Id.* at 636. While the underlined language in this decision might be read as an implicit holding that all of the members of a corporation must, themselves, be citizens of the United States, it actually was merely a restatement of the averments of the appellant therein, that all of the stockholders of the corporation were, in fact, citizens of the United States.

> The first case to directly examine the question of the subsidiary citizenship requirements of stockholders of a domestic corporation was *Doe* v. *Waterloo Mining Co.,* 70 F. 455 (9th Cir. 1895). That case involved the question whether, having alleged domestic incorporation, it was also necessary to allege that the stockholders were citizens of the United States.

The Court's response was guided by two factors. First, it noted that section 7 of the Mining Law of 1872 provided that proof of citizenship could be established for a corporation by the filing of a certificate of incorporation. As the Court noted:

> The question might arise, why would the certificate of incorporation establish the citizenship of the stockholders? In considering the question of jurisdiction in the federal courts, it is an established rule that, when a corporation organized under state laws is a party, it is conclusively presumed that the stockholders thereof are all citizens of that state. Muller v. Dows, 94 U.S. 445. Congress was familiar with this rule, and it seems probable it intended to establish a similar rule under the mineral land act of 1872.

70 F. at 463.

The Court's second line of analysis proceeded from the actual practice of the Department of the Interior. Thus, the decision stated:

> The practice in the United States land office has been, I think, universal, not to require of a corporation seeking to patent mining ground proof of the citizenship of its stockholders, other than by the production of a certified copy of articles of incorporation. * * * The practice in the land department of the United States under this statute should have great weight in construing it. Hahn v. U.S., 107 U.S. 402, 2 Sup. Ct. 494; U.S. v Moore, 95 U.S. 760, Brown v. U.S., 113 U.S. 568, 5 Sup. Ct. 648. Considering the statute and the practice thereunder, I think the citizenship of the stockholders of the Waterloo Mining Company was sufficiently established. It was not necessary to allege in the answer what was conclusively presumed from the facts alleged.

Id.

Practice in the Department was, indeed, as indicated by the Court. Thus, Secretary Hitchcock stated "a corporation organized under the laws of the United States or of any State or Territory thereof may * * * occupy and purchase mining claims from the government, irrespective of the ownership of stock therein by persons, corporations or associations not citizens of the United States." *Opinion,* 28 L.D. 178, 180, (1899). This was reiterated in the *Instructions* published at 51 L.D. 62 (1925) relating to the right of United States Borax Co., having been acquired by Borax Consolidated, Ltd., to hold and patent mining claims. This interpretation has continued to the present day. *See* 43 CFR 3862.2-1; *Alien Ownership of Shares in a Corporate Mining Location,* M-36738 (July 16, 1968). Appellants have failed to show why this consistent interpretation, stretching over nearly a century of adjudication, should be abandoned at this late date. *See State of Wyoming,* 27 IBLA 137, 83 I.D. 364 (1976), *aff'd sub nom. Wyoming* v. *Andrus,* 602 F.2d 1379 (10th Cir. 1979). We decline to alter the rule that proof of incorporation in a state is conclusive proof of citizenship by the stockholders.

4 THE ACTS OF LOCATION: DISCOVERY

A. **Discovery of a locatable mineral**
     Layman v. Ellis
     United States v. Toole
B. **Common varieties**
     United States v. Henderson
     United States v. McClarty
     Andrus v. Charlestone Stone Products Co., Inc.
C. **Leasing act minerals**
     Applicability of the Mineral Leasing Act to Deposits of Bentonite
D. **Discovery of a marketable mineral**
     Castle v. Womble
     Foster v. Seaton
     Marketability Rule
     Coleman v. United States
     Barton v. Morton
     Roberts v. Morton
     United States v. Denison
     Andrus v. Shell Oil Co.
     Berto v. Wilson
E. **Proving the Discovery**
     Globe Mining Co. v. Anderson
     Dallas v. Fitzsimmons
     United States v. Kosanke Sand Corporation

In order to have a valid and perfected location that will withstand attack by both the United States and rival claimants, all of the acts of location specified in the Mining Law of 1872, the Federal Land Policy and Management Act and applicable state law must be either complied with or excused.

These acts of location are as follows:
1. Discovery of a valuable mineral deposit;
2. Posting a notice of location;
3. Discovery workings;
4. Marking the boundaries of the location;
5. Recording the instruments required by both state law and the Federal Land Policy and Management Act.

Of these acts, discovery is by far the most important and difficult, and it will be dealt with in this chapter. All of the other acts of location will be dealt with in chapter 5.

Discovery is the *sine qua non* of a valid, perfected mining location. 30 U.S.C. § 22 provides that "all valuable mineral deposits . . . shall be free and open to exploration and purchase . . ." Further, 30 U.S.C. §§ 23 and 35 provide that no location shall be made until mineral has been discovered within the confines of the claim. Once a valid discovery has been made, the locator acquires a vested right in his claim, a right which the courts describe as property in the fullest sense of the term. *Cole v. Ralph,* Chapter 1, *supra.* Thus, rights acquired under the mining law are within the ambit of protection provided by the property clause of the Fifth Amendment.

It is the policy and requirement of law that, except as otherwise provided, all valuable mineral deposits in lands belonging to the United States shall be open to exploration under regulations prescribed by law, and to the extent consistent therewith according to local customs or rules of miners in the several mining districts. A prospector has a statutory right to enter upon unoccupied public land in good faith to search for minerals unless the land is held by another with superior rights. A mineral discovery upon a claim is the *sine qua non* for its validity; and although location of boundaries and monuments upon the ground may precede discovery or discovery may precede such location so long as intervening rights are not affected, it is essential to validate it that a mineral discovery be within the limits of the claim located. Discovery of mineral upon one claim in and of itself will not support rights to another claim or group of claims, even though contiguous. To constitute a mineral discovery, something more than conjecture, hope or even indication of mineralization is essential; there must be for a lode claim discovery within rock in place of mineral having actual or potential value or of such a character that a person of ordinary prudence would be justified in the further expenditure of his labor and means on the particular claim, with a reasonable prospect of success in developing a valuable mine. And while liberality in applying these rules will be indulged in determining superiority of rights as between private claimants, and there may be taken into account the geological indications and other discoveries in adjacent areas, as well as utilization made of developing technological aids, these of themselves may not be substituted for discovery of minerals within the exterior boundaries of the claim in question, as that discovery may be so aided. Otherwise, established public policy for the promotion of mineral resources through recognition of diligence as distinguished from speculation or monopoly could be frittered away and an express statutory requirement nullified without the comprehensive congressional re-evaluation and redirection that seem especially requisite in this field for any such basic change.

Ranchers Exploration and Development Co. v. Anaconda Co., 248 F. Supp. 708, 714-715, (Utah 1965) (footnotes omitted).

The task of the present chapter is to determine the precise meaning of the phrase "all valuable mineral deposits" as used in 30 U.S.C. § 22. To accomplish this task two distinct but interrelated questions must be answered: first, what is a valuable *mineral,* and, second, what is a valuable *deposit* of that mineral. This inquiry will be simplified somewhat if it is kept in mind that the word "valuable" in 30 U.S.C. § 22 modifies both the word "mineral" and the word "deposit."

Although the courts do not always distinguish between these two aspects of the discovery question as carefully as they might, it is essential for a proper analysis of the decisions that this distinction be carefully observed. Consequently, throughout this chapter different terminology will be used to indicate the aspect of the discovery question with which we are concerned. When the question is whether a valuable mineral has been discovered, we will speak in terms of locatability, i.e., is the particular mineral involved a locatable one. When the question is whether a valuable deposit of that mineral has been discovered, we will speak in terms of marketabilty or profitability, i.e., is the particular deposit involved rich enough that mineral can be removed from it and sold at a profit. It is important to remember that to have a valid discovery both of these questions must be answered in the affirmative.

Three separate acts, which are really amendments to the Mining Law of 1872, are closely interrelated with this aspect of the Mining Law. They are:

1) The Building Materials Act of 1892, 30 U.S.C. § 161 which provides:

Entry of Building-Stone Lands; Previous Law Unaffected

Any person authorized to enter lands under the mining laws of the United States may enter lands that are chiefly valuable for building stone under the provisions of the law in relation to placer mineral claims: Provided, that lands reserved for the benefit of the public schools or donated to any State shall not be subject to entry under this act [this section]. Nothing in this act [this section] shall be construed to repeal section twenty-four of the act entitled "An act to repeal timber-culture laws, and for other purposes," approved March third, eighteen hundred and ninety-one [16 U.S.C.S Section 471].

2) The Materials Act of 1947, 30 U.S.C. § 601 which provides:

Rules and Regulations Governing Disposal of Materials; Payment; Removal Without Charge; Lands Excluded

The Secretary, under such rules and regulations as he may prescribe, may dispose of mineral materials (including but not limited to common varieties of the following: sand, stone, gravel, pumicite, cinders, and clay) and vegetative materials (including but not limited to yucca, manzanita, mesquite, cactus, and timber or other forest products) on public lands of the United States, including, for the purposes of this Act, 30 U.S.C.S. land described in the Acts of August 28, 1937 (Stat. 874) [43 U.S.C.S. Sections 1181a et seq.], and of June 24, 1954 (68 Stat. 270) [43 U.S.C.S. Sections 1181f et seq.], if the disposal of such mineral or vegetative materials (1) is not otherwise expressly authorized by laws, including, but not limited to, the Act of June 28, 1934 (48 Stat. 1269), as amended, and the United States mining laws, and (2) is not expressly prohibited by laws of the United States, and (3) would not be detrimental to the public interest. Such materials may be disposed of only in accordance with the provisions of this Act and upon the payment of adequate compensation therefore, to be determined by the Secretary: Provided, however, That, to the extent not otherwise authorized by law, the Secretary is authorized in his discretion to permit any Federal, State, or Territorial agency, unit or subdivision, including municipalities, or any association or corporation not organized for profit, to take and remove, without charge, materials and resources subject to this act, for use other than for commercial or industrial purposes or resale. Where the lands have been withdrawn in aid of a function of a Federal department or agency other than the department headed by the Secretary or of a State, Territory, county, municipality, water district or other local governmental subdivision or agency, the Secretary may make disposals under this Act only with the consent of such other Federal department or agency or of such State, Territory, or local governmental unit. Nothing in this Act shall be construed to apply to lands in any national park, or national monument or to any Indian lands, or lands set aside or held for the use or benefit of Indians, including land over which jurisdiction has been transferred to the Department of the Interior by Executive order for the use of Indians. As used in this Act, the word "Secretary" means the Secretary of the Interior except that it means the Secretary of Agriculture where the lands involved are administered by him for national forest purposes or for the purpose of title III of the Bankhead-Jones Farm Tenant Act or where withdrawn for the purpose of any other function of the Department of Agriculture.

3) The Common Varieties Act of 1955, 30 U.S.C. § 611, et seq., which provides:

Section 611. Common varieties of sand, stone, gravel, pumice, pumicite, or cinders, and petrified wood.

No deposit of common varieties of sand, stone, gravel, pumice, pumicite, or cinders and no deposit of petrified wood shall be deemed a valuable mineral deposit within the meaning of the mining laws of the United States so as to give effective validity to any mining claim hereafter located under such mining laws: *provided, however,* That nothing herein shall affect the validity of any mining location based upon discovery of some other mineral occurring in or in association with such a deposit. "Common varieties" as used in this Act does not include deposits of such materials which are valuable because the deposit has some property giving it distinct and special value and does not include so-called "block pumice" which occurs in nature in pieces having one dimension of two inches or more. "Petrified wood,"* or any material formed by the replacement of wood by silica or other matter.

As we review the cases that follow, two complimentary trends will emerge. First we will see the Congress acting to remove certain materials from the list of locatable minerals. Second, we will see the courts acting to make the test of what constitutes a valuable deposit of a locatable mineral more stringent. While the courts have probably moved faster in this area than has the Congress, the combined effect of their actions has been to significantly increase the difficulty of perfecting a mining location and bringing it to patent.

A. Discovery of a Locatable Mineral

LAYMAN V. ELLIS
52 I.D. 714 (1929)

Edwards, Assistant Secretary:

Joseph Thomas Ellis has appealed from a decision of the Commissioner of the General Land Office, dated April 13, 1929, holding for cancellation [of] his homestead entry. . . .

On April 29, 1928, Gertrude B. Layman and Dallas E. Layman instituted a contest against the entry, alleging prior possessory rights to the land by virtue of two certain mining locations made November 30, 1925, for valuable deposits of gravel; that the locations were valid and existent at the date of said homestead entry; that by reason of the mineral character of the land and also their actual and continued possession thereof, the land was not subject to entry under the homestead law.

Upon evidence adduced at a hearing of the contest the register found that the land was valuable for its gravel deposits, the commissioner found that at least one-half of it was so valuable, but in view of the rule in *Zimmerman v. Brunson* (39 L. D. 310), both officers considered that they were bound to hold that lands valuable on account of sand and gravel deposits were not subject to entry under the mining laws and not excluded by reason thereof from entry under the homestead law. The register, however, held that as the land within the Gertrude B. Layman claim was actually occupied and used in good faith under color of title, at the date of the entry of Ellis, the entry to the extent of its conflict with such claim should be canceled. The commissioner's action was based upon the finding that the entry was made for the purpose of speculating on the value of the gravel deposits.

The material facts disclosed by the record appear to be as follows: Copies of the location notices show that the mining claims were located as veins or lodes and according to the dimensions permissible for lode claims, and not in conformity with legal subdivisions of the township wherein the land lies. Maps filed show the locations adjoin on the end lines, the Gertrude B. Layman claim being the northernmost and the Dallas E. Layman claim the southernmost, and that, roughly speaking, they together cover the east half of the homestead entry and fractions of adjacent tracts to the east. The gravel deposits had been utilized before the locations in question were made, and since their location the Laymans have extracted, sold, and delivered about 40,000 cubic yards of gravel of the value of $20,000 from the Gertrude B. Layman claim for use in road and building construction on the State highway system and have installed facilities to the value of $5,000 on that claim to elevate, screen, and segregate the gravel. . . . No gravel has been mined or removed by the Laymans from the other claim, but the testimony is uncontradicted that deposits of gravel were discovered in the post holes dug thereon. The record clearly established that the entryman at the time he made his entry had full knowledge of the nature and extent of the locations, of the Laymans' claims of title and of the actual possession and development of the Laymans but was of the opinion they were without right or color of title. . . .

. . . .

[While the homestead entry was, therefore, not in bad faith] . . . the question arises whether the entry or any part thereof was invalid because of the existence of gravel deposits thereon admittedly valuable. The question is not new. In *Zimmerman v. Brunson, supra,* it was held (syllabus) that—

> Deposits of gravel and sand, suitable for mixing with cement for concrete construction, but having no peculiar property or characteristics giving them special value, and deriving their chief value from proximity to a town, do not render the land within which they are found mineral in character within the meaning of the mining laws, or bar entry under the homestead laws, notwithstanding the land may be more valuable on account of such deposits than for agricultural purposes.

Although the commissioner held that he was governed by the rule in *Zimmerman v. Brunson, supra,* he was of the opinion that valuable deposits of gravel should be held subject to appropriation under the mining law for the reason that they are valuable mineral deposits, and that the rule in that case should be modified.

Data are presented contained in publications of the Geological Survey, entitled "Mineral Resources of the United States," as evidence of the marked increase in production, use, and price of this commodity since 1909, when the decision in the *Zimmerman* case was rendered. . . . In these publications gravel and sand have uniformly been classed as a mineral resource. They are also included in the list of useful minerals and mineral supplies [Citations omitted].

From what has been stated there can be no question that gravel deposits are definitely classified as a mineral product in trade and commerce and have a pronounced and widespread economic value because of the demand therefor in trade, manufacture, or in the mechanical arts.

The *Zimmerman* case quotes the rule in *Pacific Coast Marble Co. v. Northern Pacific R.R. Co. et al.* (25 L. D. 233), frequently since applied as a test of the mineral character of land, reading as follows (p. 244):

> Whatever is recognized as a mineral by the standard authorities on the subject, whether of metallic or other substances, when the same is found in the public lands in quantity and quality sufficient to render the land more valuable on account thereof than for agricultural purposes, should be treated as coming within the purview of the mining laws.

But it was nevertheless attempted to take the deposit under consideration from under the rule, *first,* because the standard authorities have failed to classify sand and gravel as mineral, and *second,* because the deposit had no special property or characteristic giving it special value, and *third,* its chief value arose from industrial conditions peculiar to the locality where the deposit was found.

The deposit here is characterized as beach gravel. . . . As gravel is not composed always of the same mineral substances, it would not be expected that gravel would appear in a strict mineralogical classification based on definite chemical composition, but examination of the decisions of the department and the courts disclose that questions whether a given substance is locatable or enterable under the mining law are not resolved solely by the test of whether the substance considered has a definite chemical composition expressible in a chemical formula. Such a criterion would exclude a number of mineral substances of heterogeneous composition that have been declared to be subject to disposition under the placer mining law, for example, guano, granite, sandstone, valuable clays other than brick clay, which may be made up of a number of minerals and not always the same minerals.

In Lindley on Mines, section 98, after review of the adjudicated cases and rulings of the department, deductions, which seem warranted, are made as to when the mineral character of public land is established. It is stated:

The mineral character of the land is established when it is shown to have upon or within it such a substance as—

(a) Is recognized as mineral, according to its chemical composition, by the standard authorities on the subject; or—

(b) Is classified as a mineral product in trade or commerce; or—

(c) Such a substance (other than the mere surface which may be used for agricultural purposes) as possesses economic value for use in trade, manufacture, the sciences, or in the mechanical or ornamental arts;—

And it is demonstrated that such substance exists therein or thereon in such quantities [sic] as render the land more valuable for the purpose of removing and marketing the substance than for any other purpose, and the removing and marketing of which will yield a profit; or it is established that such substance exists in the lands in such quantities as would justify a prudent man in expending labor and capital in the effort to obtain it.

That valuable gravel deposits fall within categories (*b*) and (*c*) of Mr. Lindley's text can not be disputed.

Good reason also exists for questioning the statement that gravel has no special properties or characteristics giving it special value. While the distinguishing special characteristics of gravel are purely physical, notably, small bulk, rounded surfaces, hardness, these characteristics render gravel readily distinguishable by any one from other rock and fragments of rock and are the very characteristics or properties that long have been recognized as imparting to it utility and value in its natural state.

As to the third ground for exclusion in the *Zimmerman* case it has not been shown that the gravel deposits in this case derive their value from the proximity between place of production and use, and as heretofore indicated gravel is generally recognized as having special characteristics that render it valuable generally in the mechanical arts. The conclusion, hardly justified when the decision in the *Zimmerman* case was rendered, that the value shown was one arising chiefly from exceptional and peculiar conditions in the locality where the deposit in question was found, is not warranted under present conditions.

In *Northern Pacific Railway Co. v. Soderberg* (188 U.S. 526, 534) it was held that the overwhelming weight of authority was to the effect that mineral lands include not merely metalliferous minerals, but all such as are chiefly valuable for their deposits of a mineral character which are useful in the arts or valuable for purposes of manufacture, and the opinion quotes with approval certain observations in *Midland Railway v. Checkley* (L. R. 4 Eq. 19), reading:

> Stone is, in my opinion, clearly a mineral; and in fact everything except the mere surface, which is used for agricultural purposes; anything beyond that which is useful for any purpose whatever, whether it is *gravel,* marble, fire clay, or the like, comes within the word "mineral" when there is a reservation of the mines and minerals from a grant of land. (Italics supplied.)

. . . .

. . . . There is no logical reason in view of the latest expressions of the department why, in the administration of the Federal mining laws, any discrimination should be made between gravel and stones of other kinds, which are used for practically the same or similar purposes, where the former as well as the latter can be extracted, removed and marketed at a profit. The rule in *Zimmerman v. Brunson* will therefore no longer be followed but is overruled.

The evidence in the case warrants the classification of the east half of the entry, to wit, east half of lots 2, 11 and 13, as mineral in character, valuable for deposits of gravel. The entry to that extent was therefore invalid and should be cancelled.

Although the land last described was mineral in character, no valid right to possession was aquired by the Laymans by attempted location of them as lodes or veins. The deposits are loose, scattered deposits, not rock in place. It is well settled that a placer discovery will not sustain a lode location. *Cole v. Ralph* (252 U.S. 286, 295). The lode claimants had no rights that would prevent others entering peaceably and in good faith to avail themselves of the privileges accorded by the mining laws, *Cole v. Ralph, supra,* p. 300, but the east half of the entry being mineral in character, the entryman could acquire no right under the homestead law to such half, no matter if his entry was peaceable and with the acquiescence of the mineral claimant.

. . . .

The entry will be held intact as to west half thereof; as to the east half it should be cancelled.

As modified the commissioner's decision is affirmed.

NOTES

1. The specific holding of *Layman v. Ellis* that gravel is locatable has been legislatively overruled by the Common Varieties Act, quoted *supra.* Is the *Layman v. Ellis* definition of mineral still good law? Compare it with the definition contained in 43 C.F.R. § 3812.1 (1982) which provides as follows:

Mineral Subject to Location

Whatever is recognized as a mineral by the standard authorities, whether metallic or other substance, when found in public lands in quantity and quality sufficient to render the lands valuable on account thereof, is treated as coming within the purview of the mining laws. . . . The so-called "common variety" mineral materials and petrified wood on the public lands may be acquired under the Materials Act, as amended. . . .

2. Not all lands containing minerals are subject to location and appropriation under the mining law. As a preliminary matter, it must be shown that the land itself is mineral in character.

> . . . [F]rom an early date the determination of the character of land as mineral or nonmineral was made by a comparison of its relative value for each purpose. Thus, in a controversy between a mineral claimant and an agricultural claimant, where the land had been classified as agricultural, the mineral claimant was required to show not only that the land was not clearly agricultural, and that the land was valuable for minerals, but also that the land was more valuable for mining than for agricultural purposes, for "when the statutes provide for mineral entries upon land valuable for minerals, and for agricultural entries upon land clearly agricultural, there arises of necessity a comparison of their respective values whenever these two classes of claims come in conflict." [Quoting *Caledonia Min. Co. v. Rowen,* 2 L. D. 714, 717-18 (1883).] In some cases the agricultural value of the land was determined from the actual production of crops from the land, which suggests that the rule requiring actual production of minerals was merely a corollary of the comparative value rule.

Reeves, *The Origin and Development of the Rules of Discovery,* VIII Land and Water L. Rev. 1, 23-24 (1973) (footnotes omitted).

3. Proving the mineral character of the land is much easier than proving that mineral has been discovered on that land. "The most obvious difference between the two tests then is that a determination that land is mineral in character does not depend upon an actual discovery or exposure of mineral upon the land. The existence of the mineral, its quality and quantity, may be determined by geologic inference or by less conclusive evidence than is required to establish the existence of a discovery under the mining laws. Thus, a determination that land is mineral in character may not be inconsistent with a finding that a valuable mineral deposit has not been found on that land. However, whether the question is one of a discovery under the mining laws or the mineral character of land under a nonmineral land law, the end inquiry is essentially the same, namely, whether or not exploitation of the minerals is believed to be economically feasible." *California v. Rodeffer,* 75 I.D. 176, 181 (1968).

4. Does not the comparison of values referred to in the Reeves selection and the "end inquiry" referred to in *Rodeffer* indicate that, at least in some cases, evidence that land could be mined profitably has traditionally been required to establish the validity of a mining entry?

5. The Board in *Layman v. Ellis* quoted approvingly from *Midland Railway v. Checkley* that "everything except the mere surface, which is used for agricultural purposes. . . " is a mineral. The court in *Midland* was concerned with a mineral reservation. Do you think it follows that just because something is a mineral for purposes of construing a reservation in a patent that it must also be a mineral within the meaning of the Mining Law?

30 U.S.C. § 23 provides that deposits of "gold, silver, cinnabar, lead, tin,

copper [and] other valuable minerals" are locatable. Since all of the minerals listed in the statute are metallic, the question early arose whether non-metallic minerals, such as diamonds, were also locatable under the Mining Law. If that question had been answered in the negative, this chapter would probably be quite a bit shorter, and many thorny issues could have been avoided. The question was answered in the affirmative, however:

> Diamonds, then, are clearly "valuable mineral deposits," and the provisions of said act are as applicable to lands containing them, as to lands containing gold or other precious metals. Comprehensive words, no doubt, were used to include as well what might afterward be discovered, as what might be overlooked as an enumeration of minerals in the statute.
>
> . . . .
>
> I think these acts ought to be most liberally construed, so as to faciliate the sale of such lands; for in that way and not otherwise, can they be made to contribute something to the revenues of the Government, and controversy and litigation in mining localities, to a great extent, be prevented.

Reeves, *supra,* at 6. (Quoting from 14 Op. Att'y Gen. 115, 116 (1872)).

Subsequent rulings of the Commissioner of the General Land Office "uniformly held that nonmetallic minerals were subject to location under the mining law." *Id.* at 6.

6. Note that the attorney general's rationale for "liberally construing" the Mining Law was to increase the salability of public lands. As you study the remaining materials in this chapter, you might consider to what extent the observed difficulties in applying the discovery requirement flow from the Mining Law itself, and to what extent these difficulties result from a fundamental change in public policy that no longer favors disposal, whether by sale or otherwise, of public lands, but, rather, strongly favors retention of these lands in public ownership.

UNITED STATES V. TOOLE
224 F.Supp. 440 (D.Mont. 1963)

[footnotes omitted]

JAMESON, District Judge.

This is a civil action brought by the United States to cancel mining claims located on land belonging to the United States, to quiet the title of the United States, and to recover damages for alleged trespass and conversion of materials from the land. The land is located within the Lewis and Clark National Forest, in Judith Basin and Meagher Counties, Montana, and contains approximately 160 acres described as the Northeast Quarter of Section 28, Township 11 North, Range 10 East, Montana Principal Meridan. Jurisdiction is derived from 28 U.S.C.A. § 1345 and is not in dispute.

The defendants' claim is based upon certain placer mining locations, and the validity of their claim depends upon whether they have discovered material locatable under the mining laws of the United States.

The land contains a meadow area known as Clyde Park. It is a semi-bog area covered with a peaty muck material varying in depth from approximately six to twelve inches. In 1956, Lee Salsbury, a greenhouse owner and operator of Billings, Montana, who was interested in extracting the peat material, took samples and corresponded with Forest Service officials about the possibility of obtaining a lease to remove the material. Eventually he was informed that the Forest Service would not permit any excavation or removal of the peat, although apparently the officials were mistaken as to the area in which Salsbury was interested. James W. Toole, one of the defendants, first learned of the peat material on Clyde Park from Salsbury. Toole was interested in the nursery business, and in 1959 accompanied Salsbury to Clyde Park to examine the material. Samples were taken, and subsequently Toole visited the Billings Office of the Bureau of Land Management, Department of the Interior, to obtain information on mining claim procedures.

In the latter part of 1959, Toole filed five certificates of location of lode mining claims. Counsel for the defendants stipulated that the lode claims are invalid, and no right or interest is predicated upon these claims.

On April 11, 1960, the individual defendants, James W. Toole, Peter G. Milohov, Susan C. Milohov, Leonora E. Toole, Adele O. Milohov, Lillian E. Toole, E. W. Boegler, and Nicolo Ottolino filed a certificate of location of a placer mining claim called the J-W-T Placer Mining Claim. By two quitclaim deeds, executed October 21, 1960, the individual defendants conveyed their interest to the defendant Tracana Enterprises, Inc.

Tracana Enterprises, Inc. was incorporated under the laws of Montana on January 21, 1960, for the purpose of severing, processing and selling materials of the type found on the placer claim.

Sometime prior to March 30, 1960, stripping and removal operations were commenced on the J-W-T placer claim. Two types of materials have been severed and removed—the peaty muck material, described above, and the soil which lies immediately below the muck.

Tracana Enterprises, Inc. operates a plant and warehouse at Harlowton, Montana, and loading and hauling equipment as well as a small hammer mill at the claimsite. The peaty muck material is dried, shredded or hammered, bagged, and sold by Tracana as horticultural "Peat Moss." The soil beneath is crushed or hammered until it is quite fine, then bagged and sold as Tracana "Soluble Mineral," claimed by defendants to be a source of "trace elements" or "micro nutrients" beneficial to the development of plant and animal life. The defendants claim that each type of material is "mineral," within the meaning of the mining laws of the United States, and subject to location.

. . . .

Two elements are essential in a valid mining location—first, a "location" by staking the claim, posting notice, and recording in accordance with state laws; and second, a proper discovery of valuable mineral. United States v. Lillibridge, S.D.Calif.1932, 4 F.Supp. 204; see also 1955 U.S.Code, Cong. & Adm. News, p. 2474 et seq. We are concerned in this case with the second element, i.e., whether defendants have discovered a "valuable mineral deposit" rendering the lands open to mineral location and entry.

. . . .

For purposes of the mining laws, it is generally held that a "mineral" is "whatever is recognized as mineral by the standard authorities on the subject." But only *valuable mineral* is locatable and only lands containing *valuable mineral deposits* are subject to mineral entry. 30 U.S.C.A. §§ 21 and 22, *supra*.

Courts have held mineral deposits to be locatable when they occur on lands "chiefly valuable" for mining or other than agricultural purposes. But the test most often utilized and best supported in reason is the so-called "prudent investor" test. See Best v. Humboldt Placer Mining Co., *supra*, and cases there cited. This test requires the mineral to exist in such quantity and quality as to enhance the value of the lands and invite the expenditure of time and labor for their development by a person of ordinary prudence, not necessarily a skilled miner, with a reasonable expectation of success. Chrisman v. Miller, 1905, 197 U.S. 313, 25 S.Ct. 468, 49 L.Ed. 770; United States v. Lillibridge, *supra*; Cataract Gold Mining Co., et al., 1914, 43 L.D. 248.

Mining works have combined the various rules of what constitutes mineral and valuable mineral into an able and workable definition of "valuable mineral deposit" locatable under the United States Mining Laws. It is said:

> The mineral character of the land is established when it is shown to have upon it or within it such a substance as: (a) Is recognized as a mineral, according to its chemical composition, by the standard authorities on the subject, or (b) Is classified as a mineral product in trade or commerce, or (c) Such a substance (other than mere surface which may be used for agricultural purposes) as possesses economic value for use in trade, manufacture, the sciences, or in the mechanical or ornamental arts, * * * and it is demonstrated * * * that such substance exists in the lands in such quantity as would justify a prudent man in expending labor and capital in the effort to obtain it. 1 Lindley, Mines, 3rd ed. 1914, 174-175, § 98, as restated in 2 Amer. Law of Mining 171, § 2.4.

Aside from these rules of inclusion, the Materials Act of July 31, 1947, and its amendments, now 30 U.S.C.A. § 601 et seq., operates to exclude common materials from the operation of the mining laws. Section 601 provides that, "The Secretary (of Agriculture), under such rules and regulations as he may prescribe, may dispose of mineral materials (including *but not limited to* common varieties of the following: sand, stone, gravel, pumice, pumicite, cinders, and clay) and vegetative materials * * * on public lands of the United States * * *." (Emphasis added.) By § 611 (added by amendment of July 23, 1955) it is provided [that common varieties are not subject to location].

. . . .

The defendants have the burden of proving that the materials in question are valuable mineral deposits. When the Government contests a mining claim it bears only the burden of going forward with sufficient evidence to establish a prima facie case. The burden then "shifts to the claimant to show by a preponderance of the evidence that his claim is valid." Foster v. Seaton, 1959, 106

U.S.App.D.C. 253, 271, F.2d 836, 838. The court continued: "One who has located a claim upon the public domain has, prior to the discovery of valuable minerals, only 'taken the initial steps in seeking a gratuity from the Government,' Ickes v. Underwood, 78 U.S.App.D.C. 396, 399, 141, F.2d 546, 549, certiorari denied 1944, 323 U.S. 713, 65 S.Ct. 39, 89 L.Ed. 574; Rev.Stat. § 2319 (1875), 30 U.S.C.A. § 23. Until he has fully met the statutory requirements, title to the land remains in the United States."

Have the defendants sustained their burden of showing that (1) the peat or peat moss and (2) the trace minerals are valuable mineral deposits subject to location and entry?

The peaty material may be classified as a "sedge" or "sedge reed" peat. It derives its name from the sedge grasses which cover it in place and which make up a substantial portion of its composition. From the evidence it may be said that peat is high in organic matter and is a form of vegetation below that of higher plants. Estimates of the organic content of the peat from the J-W-T Placer Claim varied greatly among the various witnesses, as did their estimates of its value as a soil conditioner.

The nature of peat moss was considered in Premier Peat Moss Corporation v. United States, S.D.N.Y. 1956, 147 F. Supp. 169. In holding that peat moss was an agricultural commodity exempted from the permit requirements of 49 U.S.C.A. § 309 by § 303(b)(6), the court said:

"Indubitably peat moss is of vegetative origin. 'It is produced by nature from what was once vegetation, and chemically it is substantially the same as the vegetation from whence it is derived. In fact, its chief characteristic results from the fact that nature itself has arrested any substantial change which without the protection of water would otherwise have taken place. Its principal uses, too, are either agricultural or horticultural.'

"The defendants urge that peat moss is unlike any commodity produced on a farm and is more in the nature of coal. But in the case of coal, although in origin derived from vegetation, the processes of nature have converted it into a mineral. Not so in the case of peat moss. There the processes of decay have not progressed far enough to cause any substantial change in its original chemical content." 147 F. Supp. at 174.

It is true, as defendants contend, that this case in no way involved the interpretation of the mining laws. . . .

Both parties rely upon the Materials Act of 1947, supra, amendments thereto in 1950 and 1955, and the legislative history of the Act and amendments in support of their respective contentions. Defendants argue that while the Materials Act of 1947 removed from the purview of the mining laws certain materials which had theretofore been locatable minerals, peat was not included among these materials. Plaintiff contends that it was unnecessary to exclude peat from the mining laws since peat is a vegetative matter and was never within the purview of the mining laws.

The Materials Act was amended in 1950 to provide that moneys recovered from the disposition of materials from school lands in Alaska should be paid into the territorial school fund (30 U.S.C.A. § 603). The amendment further provided (§ 604) that the Secretary of the Interior "may dispose of sand, stone, gravel, and vegetative materials located below high water mark of navigable waters * * *". When this section was titled for official publication, it was headed "Disposal of sand, peat moss, etc. in Alaska; contracts". This title presently appears in § 604. This is the only specific reference to "peat moss" in the Materials Act or the amendments thereto. While not conclusive, it is some evidence of a congressional intent to equate peat moss with vegetative material. Moreover, even prior to the amendment to the Materials Act of 1947, Alaska was receiving moneys derived from the disposition of minerals and timber lands under the Act of March 4, 1915, 48 U.S.C.A. § 353, relating to public lands in Alaska. The 1950 amendment to the Materials Act was designed to extend these provisions to other materials, including peat moss.

Defendants contend that the subsequent amendment of July 23, 1955, and particularly the addition of section 611, *supra*, manifests a contrary congressional intent, in that peat was not included among the materials listed in section 611. The purpose of the 1955 amendment was to curb nonmining activities and similar abuses causing waste of surface resources in national forests under color of the mining laws and to give the Secretary of Agriculture the same authority as to land under his jurisdiction as the Secretary of the Interior possessed as to lands under his jurisdiction in the disposition of mining and vegetative materials. This amendment does not militate against the conclusion that peat was considered by Congress to be a vegetative material within the meaning of the Materials Act.

Defendants also rely upon 30 U.S.C.A. § 3, prescribing the duties of the Bureau of Mines. This section provides that it shall be the province and duty of the Bureau of Mines "to conduct inquiries and scientific and technologic investigations concerning mining, and the preparation, treatment, and utilization of mineral substances with a view to improving health conditions, and increasing safety, efficiency, economic development, and conserving resources through the prevention of waste in the mining, quarrying, metallurgical, and other mineral industries; * * * to investigate explosives and peat; * * *." It will be noted that the duty "to investigate explosives and peat" is set apart from the Bureau's duties with respect to "mining", "mineral substances", and "mineral industries". The mere fact that the Bureau of Mines has the duty to investigate explosives and peat does not in itself justify a conclusion that they should be classified as mineral. On the contrary, the fact that they are treated separately in prescribing the duties of the Bureau leads to the conclusion that Congress did not consider them as mineral substances.

Defendants also refer to numerous government publications relating to mineral resources which discuss peat. It is true, as defendants contend, that in many of these articles the discussion was not confined to the use of peat in the fuel industry, but also included its use in agriculture and horticulture. The mere fact that peat has been included in these government publications relating to mining and mineral resources is not sufficient to show that peat is a locatable mineral. . . .

Based on the evidence in this case, the statutes and legislative history, and the decided cases, I must conclude that the peat or peat moss in question is not of the character subject to location and purchase under the provisions of the mining laws of the United States.

We turn now to the question of whether the material called "Tracana Soluble Mineral" is a valuable mineral locatable under the mining laws, as defendants contend, or a common variety of soil having no property giving it a distinct or special value, as plaintiff contends. Defendants rely upon the presence of "trace elements" in the material, many of which are alleged to be beneficial to plant and animal life. The reports of spectrographic analyses show the constituents of the material to be silicon and aluminum with intermediate trace amounts of the following: calcium, iron, sodium, potassium, magnesium, titanium, barium, strontium, manganese, zirconium, boron, vanadium, copper, chromium, lead, gallium, and sometimes nickel and cobalt. Obviously, those substances would be termed mineral by standard authorities. Whether the material is a "locatable" mineral turns upon the factual question of whether trace elements, available and beneficial to plant and animal life, exist in such quantities and in such form as to render the deposit "valuable" within the meaning of the United States mining laws.

[The court's detailed review of the testimony presented concerning the presence and value of "trace elements" is omitted.]

I can see no useful purpose in setting forth further testimony. The well qualified expert witnesses called by the plaintiff were all definitely of the opinion that the material has no value as a plant nutrient and is incapable of enriching an agricultural soil. On the other hand, many reputable, experienced and disinterested users were honestly and firmly of the opinion that the application of Tracana had been beneficial and resulted in increased productivity.

Assuming, without deciding, that the use of Tracana benefited the soils to which it was applied, there is no substantial evidence to show what produced the beneficial results. Defendants produced no witnesses who had analyzed the product and could say what elements were present in the material which would enrich an agricultural soil or produce beneficial results when fed to animals. In the light of the testimony of the expert witnesses, I must conclude that defendants have failed to sustain their burden of proving that the trace elements in the material constituted "valuable minerals" within the meaning of the mining laws.

Plaintiff seeks substantial damages, contending that defendants were willful trespassers and converters and accordingly liable for the full value to defendants of the material taken, without deduction for any values added by their labor and capital.

I am convinced from the evidence as a whole that the defendants asserted and operated their claim in good faith. The land was open to mineral entry, and the defendants determined that to be the fact. The material beneath the peat contained many "trace materials". The trace materials listed in the Smith Emery Company reports which defendants received, seemed to compare, to the untrained eye, with mineral nutrient products on the market, as far as could be ascertained from their labels. They had been advised by Mr. Welsh that the subsoil material was valuable as a fertilizer by reason of the "abundance of mineral feed". The defendants' own growing tests appeared to them successful. Later there were many satisfied customers to back defendants' belief in the worth of their product. Their attorney advised them that the claim was valid.

. . . .

This is not a case where the lands had been withdrawn from the provisions of the mining laws or were acquired National Forest Lands not subject to mineral development, as in Thompson v. United States, 9 Cir.1962, 308 F.2d 628. Nor is it a case of controversy over ownership or mineral rights in private land wherein defendants conducted their exploration, examination and location of the property under a clouded or colorable title. Cf., Reickhoff v. Consolidated Gas Co., 1950, 123 Mont. 555, 217 P.2d 1076. It is not a case in which the material was taken by knowing and wilful trespassers. Cf., Pine River Logging & Improvement Co. v. United States, 1902, 186 U.S. 279, 22 S.Ct. 920, 46 L.Ed. 1164; Bolles Wooden Ware Co. v. United States, 1882, 106 U.S. 432, 1 S.Ct. 398, 27 L.Ed. 230.

The fact that the claimants received advice of reputable counsel that their claims were valid may be considered in determining the question of their good faith. And this was not a mere mistake of law for which there is no excuse. In determining the validity of defendants' claim the court has found it necessary to rely upon evidence supplied by experts in the fields of animal and plant nutrition, soil science, geology, mineral engineering, chemistry, agronomy and horticulture, as well as conduct considerable research into the applicable law with the aid of able and exhaustive briefs on both sides.

I find that the defendants asserted and operated the J-W-T Placer Claim in good faith and were not willful trespassers and/or converters of the materials located thereon.

In such case the measure of damages is the value of the material in place before it was disturbed. Bolles Wooden Ware Co. v. United States, supra. According to plaintiff's witnesses, the peat muck material is common and similar to that found covering approximately 80 million acres in the United States and is so low in organic matter it may not be classified as better than muck and is an inferior grade of peat below standards set by the Federal Trade Commission regulations (see 16 CFR 185.2); and the subsoil material is of no commercial value. Plaintiff's witnesses testified that it would cost $767 to restore the premises to their original condition.

30 U.S.C.A. § 612 provides that rights under mining claims of the United States shall be subject to the right of the United States to manage and dispose of the vegetative surface resources. 43 CFR § 185.122 regulates surface use of mining claims pursuant to that statute. Some 1605.3 cubic yards of peat material were disturbed and 1192.43 cubic yards of that removed. The going price for Government peat was $2 per cubic yard, although, as noted supra, the Government witnesses testified that this is an inferior peat. The peat was in fact removed, however, and the Government will be allowed $2 per cubic yard for the 1192.43 yards removed, together with the sum of $767 to cover the cost of restoring the premises.

. . . .

Defendants have requested permission to restore the premises in lieu of payment of the estimated cost thereof. I assume that the parties will reach an agreement for this method of restoration.

NOTES

1. Does *Toole* provide a workable test for determining when the conversion from vegetable to mineral has occurred, or does the decision, in Learned Hand's phrase, leave us "to step from tuft to tuft across the morass?"

2. The issue of what is a mineral for purposes of the mining law appears deceptively simple. One might think that a chemical examination of the substance under consideration ought to be sufficient to resolve it. This is not the case, however. The determination of whether a substance is a mineral is not a question of fact, but a conclusion of law. Consequently, whether something is properly classified as a mineral depends on the purpose of the intended classification. In the context of the mining law, calling something a mineral means that it is subject to being located under that law. For a court to make this determination, it must first decide that the transfer of the substance and the lands containing it from public to private ownership under the mining law is appropriate in light of contemporary concerns and policies. Indeed, the question of whether a substance is a mineral is almost entirely a question of policy and only incidentally a question of chemistry.

B. Common Varieties
(Refer to 30 U.S.C. § 611 set forth in full in the introduction to this chapter)

UNITED STATES V. HENDERSON
68 I.D. 26 (1961)

[footnotes omitted]

. . . .

J.R. Henderson has appealed to the Secretary of the Interior from a decision of the Acting Director of the Bureau of Land Management. . . declaring null and void his placer mining claims, the Dickie, Big Hall, Sandy and Teddie, all in Clark County, about 2 miles south southwest of Whitney, Nevada.

The claims were located on public land of the United States on April 4, 1957, and quitclaimed by the locators to the appellant on June 28, 1957. On May 6, 1959, the United States contested the validity of the claims by filing charges that minerals have not been found within the limits of the claims in sufficient quantity or quality to constitute a valid discovery and that the minerals found within the limits of the claims are not valuable mineral deposits under section 3 of the act of July 23, 1955 (30 U.S.C., 1958 ed., sec. 611). The appellant denied the charges and a hearing was held on September 15, 1959.

. . . .

The appellant does not rely upon some other mineral in or in association with sand and gravel; his case rests upon an alleged discovery of sand and gravel on the claims which he contends have characteristics giving them distinct and special value.

His evidence shows that the deposits on the claims contain hard sand and gravel free from blow sand and caliche of the proper size and gradation in size and mixed in proportions very close to the perfect percentage for construction use so that it is possible to use or sell pit run material which meets construction specifications for concrete aggregate and, because of the sharpness of the grains, to sell the sand for mortar and plaster. The area wherein such deposits are found is about 3½ miles wide and 7 miles in length but the claims are adjacent or near to the appellant's patented land where the processing plant and the well which furnishes water for washing are located so that it is economically advantageous for him to work them from the existing plant. There is a ready market for ready mix concrete and plaster and mortar sand in the vicinity.

The appellant's evidence also showed that concrete made from aggregate produced on the claims can be ground and polished to produce an attractive stone of various muted shades of cream, coral, brown, purple, gray and black in irregular shapes and surrounded by the light gray of the concrete mix. The result is an acceptable substitute for terrazzo, the marble for which is normally shipped in from Italy or Georgia. This so-called poor man's terrazzo has been used in the rotunda area and entrance walkways of the Clark County convention hall, in the hospital at Henderson and several of the Las Vegas schools. The appellant submitted a sample as his exhibit A at the hearing which he explained was the polished product obtained by sawing a slice from a concrete test cylinder made from the aggregate. Other aggregate not of volcanic origin used in this manner would present only a contrast between the light gray of the concrete and the darker gray of the cross sections of the aggregate.

The conclusions to be drawn from the appellant's evidence are that the sand and gravel found on the contested claims are of good quality and suitable in every way for concrete aggregate as extracted from the pit or with some blending of materials taken from deep and shallow pits. The value of these materials to the appellant is derived from their good quality as building materials without expensive processing, their location close to his processing plant and the lack of caliche. Their use in the terrazzo substitute is not a demonstration of special and distinct value since it is limited in amount and restricted to local use. The predominant use of the sand and gravel is for ordinary construction purposes. The appellant did not even suggest that he contemplates shipping aggregate out of the area for widespread use. The distinct and special value for which he contends consists only of the factors which make the materials suitable for his particular local business and cause his processing costs to be low and thus give the materials more value to him than like materials in the area.

The Senate report on a companion bill (S. 1713) under consideration at the same time as the bill which became the act of July 23, 1955, declares that—

The proviso in this section reading—

* * * nothing herein contained shall affect the validity of any mining location based upon discovery of some other mineral occurring in or in association with such a deposit—

has been incorporated in the bill to make clear the committee intent to not preclude mining locations based on discovery of some mineral other than a common variety of sand, stone, etc., occurring in such materials, such as, for example, a mining location based on a discovery of gold in sand or gravel.

The last sentence of this section declares that—

"Common varieties" as used in this act does not include deposits of such materials which are valuable because the deposit has some property giving it distinct and special value * * *.

This language is intended to exclude from disposal under the Materials Act materials that are commercially valuable because of "distinct and special" properties, such as, for example, limestone suitable for use in the production of cement, metallurgical or chemical-grade limestone, gypsum, and the like. (Sen. Rept. No. 554, 84th Cong., 1st Sess., pp. 7-8.)

The House report on the bill which became the act of July 23, 1955 (H.R. 589), also notes that the language of the bill excludes "material such as limestone, gypsum, etc., commercially valuable because of 'distinct and special' properties." (House Rept. No. 730, 84th Cong., 1st Sess., p. 9.)

The pertinent regulation provides:

"Common varieties" as defined by decision of the Department and of the courts include deposits which, although they may have value for use in trade, manufacture, the sciences, or in the mechanical or ornamental arts do not possess a distinct, special economic value for such use over and above the normal uses of the general run of such deposits. Section 3 of the law has no application where the mineral for which a location is made is carried in or borne by one of such common varieties.

These observations do not lend support to the appellant's contention that he has a discovery of sand and gravel possessing special and distinct value. They indicate, rather, that there was no contemplation that sand and gravel suitable for construction purposes would be regarded as anything but common varieties of these materials.

The fact that these sand and gravel deposits may have characteristics superior to those of other sand and gravel deposits does not make them an uncommon variety of sand and gravel so long as they are used only for the same purposes as other deposits which are widely and readily available. See *United States v. Duvall & Russell,* 65 I.D. 458, 462 (1958).

Therefore, pursuant to the authority delegated to the Solicitor by the Secretary of the Interior, the decision of the Acting Director of the Bureau of

Land Management is affirmed.

NOTES

1. The legislative history quoted by the court in *Henderson* indicates that materials "such as, for example, limestone suitable for use in the production of cement" were not to be deemed "common varieties." Since the sand involved in *Henderson* was used for making cement, why wasn't it a material "such as" limestone? Should the nature of the material govern or the purpose for which it is used? In fact, no reported decision has found that any material not expressly excluded from the common varieties act is nevertheless excluded by virtue of the "such as" clause. Thus, notwithstanding the existence of that clause, it may well be that the list of "common varieties" excluded from the operation of the common varieties act is exclusive rather than illustrative.

2. Why was the "poor man's terrazzo" not locatable? The court seems to indicate that the material is not locatable because it is not used much. If that is the case, how much end use of a product is required before it is locatable? Is it possible that a mineral could be so rare, i.e., so little of it exists that it can't be used much, as to be non-locatable?

3. Frank Melluzzo located two lode claims. The claims contained mostly ordinary quartz, which, although useful in construction, is one of the most abundant minerals on earth. When the Secretary of the Interior challenged the claims based on the Common Varieties Act, Melluzzo responded that notwithstanding the commonness of most of the quartz, his claim also contained small, widely scattered deposits of rose quartz, useful in making jewelry, and that rose quartz was not a common variety. What result would you expect? See *United States v. Frank Melluzzo,* 70 I.D. 184 (1963). In cases like *Melluzzo* and *Henderson,* would it be appropriate for a court to consider the total value of the "rare" mineral as compared to the value of the land being claimed? Is there authority in the mining law for a court to do so?

4. The ores of many minerals appear in combination with common varieties of rock. Thus, some milling process is usually required to separate the ore from the host rock. When is a miner mining a common variety of "host" rock, and when is he mining the valuable mineral embedded within the rock? The Interior Department addressed this issue in *United States v. Melluzzo,* 85 I.D. 441, 461-62 (1978) as follows:

> Melluzzo asserts both below and on appeal, that his sale of decorative stone from El rame claims constitutes "copper mining." Judge Koutras refused to accept this contention and counsel for contestees refers to the judge's logic as creating "a reverse Midas touch." While we agree that Melluzzo has been successfully selling stone from the El rame group, and this stone contains a certain amount of copper coloration, this does not, without more, support Melluzzo's characterization of the rock as "copper ore." Melluzzo defines "ore" as "any material that a prudent man could make a

profit off of" (Tr. 357) and points out that his records refer to material from the El rame claims as "copper" or "copper stone." Melluzzo thus appears to reason that, since he is selling stone from the El rame claims at a profit, the stones are "ore," and since the stones are "ore," he is mining copper. We disagree.

In the first place, no showing has been made of the actual copper content of this building stone. Melluzzo protests that he cannot be forced to sell the stone to a smelter when he profits more by selling it to builders. He neglects to prove, however, that the stone would be in any way useful to a smelter. The fact that Melluzzo calls the rock "copper" does not make it so, and Dr. Fair's observation, *supra,* that a small amount of copper can produce a striking coloration effect leads us to believe that Melluzzo's decorative building stone may have been low in actual copper content. We do not wonder that Melluzzo's records show only the removal of "copper" as opposed to "building stone" from the El rame since, as Melluzzo undoubtedly knows, common varieties of building stone were excluded from the coverage of the mining laws by the Act of July 23, 1955, *as amended,* 30 U.S.C. § 611 (1976), commonly called "The Multiple Use Act." While "uncommon varieties" of building or decorative stone remain locatable under the Act of Aug. 4, 1892, 30 U.S.C. § 161 (1976), such location must be supported by a showing that the deposit in question has a unique property giving it a special value reflected by the fact that the material commands a higher price in the marketplace than "common varieties" of the same material. *United States v. Chartrand,* 11 IBLA 194, 80 I.D. 408 (1973). Locations of such claims, moreover, must be made as placer locations, and a lode claim location, such as the claims here at issue, cannot support a building stone placer claim under the Act of Aug. 4, 1892, *supra. U.S. v. Chartrand, supra; United States v. Edwards,* 9 IBLA 197 (1973). We therefore hold that Melluzzo's removal of building stone from the claims cannot be considered as evidence of a discovery of a valuable mineral deposit on the El rame claims. *See also Cole v. Ralph,* 252 U.S. 286, 295 (1920), holding that a placer discovery will not support a lode location nor a lode discovery a placer location.

Accordingly, pursuant to the authority delegated to the Board of Land Appeals by the Secretary of the Interior, 43 CFR 4.1, the decision appealed from is affirmed.

UNITED STATES V. McCLARTY
81 I.D. 472 (1974)

[footnotes omitted]

. . . .

Kenneth McClarty has filed briefs in opposition to the recommended decision of the Administrative Law Judge dated September 23, 1971, in which the Judge recommended that McClarty's Snoqueen placer claim be declared null and void because the andesite found on the claim is a common variety of building stone and therefore not locatable after July 23, 1955, under the Act of July 23, 1955, 69 Stat. 367, 30 U.S.C. §§ 601-615 (1970).

. . . .

The Snoqueen placer claim, situated in the Snoqualmie National Forest, Yakima County, Washington, was located on August 1, 1960, for andesite, a building stone. This stone sells under the trade name Heatherstone and is used in both commercial and residential construction. It is used for veneer walls, patios, fireplaces, planters and other purposes.

Common varieties of stone have not been locatable under the mining laws since the enactment of the Act of July 23, 1955, *supra*. 30 U.S.C. § 611 (1970). . . .

. . . .

The enact [sic] of 30 U.S.C. § 611 affected only common varieties but left the Act of August 4, 1892, 27 Stat. 348, 30 U.S.C. § 161 (1970) entirely effective as to building stone that has some property giving it distinct and special value. See *United States v. Coleman*, 390 U.S. 599 (1968). . . . Therefore, in order for Heatherstone to be locatable under the Act of August 4, 1892, appellant must prove that the stone from the Snoqueen claim is valuable because the deposit has some uncommon property giving it such distinct and special value as to distinguish it from the so-called common varieties.

. . . .

The main issue for determination by this Board is whether Heatherstone possesses unique properties giving it a special and distinct value, thereby making it locatable under the Act of August 4, 1892.

According to the evidence in this case, the most unusual and notable characteristics of Heatherstone are its natural fracturing and flat surface cross sectioning. [The Board's detailed recitation of McClarty's evidence is omitted.]

. . . .

In *McClarty v. Secretary of Interior*, [408 F.2d 907 (9th Cir. 1969)], the Court of Appeals reviewed the criteria established by the Department in *United States v. U.S. Minerals Development Corporation*, 75 I.D. 127 (1968), for determining the difference between a common and uncommon variety of stone. These guidelines, as discussed at 908, are as follows:

*** (1) there must be a comparison of the mineral deposit in question with other deposits of such materials generally; (2) the mineral deposit in question must have a unique property; (3) the unique property must give the deposit a distinct and special value; (4) if the special value is for uses to which ordinary varieties of the mineral are put, the deposit must have some distinct and special value for such use; and (5) the distinct and special value must be reflected by the higher price which the material commands in the market place.

The Court of Appeals, however, in its review of this case, explained "value" by indicating that price cannot be the exclusive way of proving that a deposit has a distinct and special economic value attributable to the unique property of the deposit. The Court discussed other possibilities for determining value at 909:

*** [I]n the *McClarty* case, where the unique properties of the stone are the natural fracturing into regular shapes and forms suitable for laying without further fabrication, the distinct and special economic value of the stone may or may not be measurable by the retail market price in comparison with the price of other building stones. It is quite possible that the special economic value of the stone would be reflected by reduced costs or overhead so that the profit to the producer would be substantially more while the retail market price would remain competitive with other building stone. * * *

In applying these guidelines to the facts in the present case, the Court found the Snoqueen deposit to be unique. We agree. Our determination of uniqueness is based on the testimony of Hupp and Meyers [expert witnesses who testified on behalf of McClarty] that they did not know of any other stone having the same inherent properties as Heatherstone which enable it to be readily usable for construction. . . . No other example of stone possessing the properties of natural fracturing and flat surface cross sections was offered into evidence.

. . . .

The only facet of the guidelines enumerated in *U.S. Minerals Development Corporation, supra,* that remained unsettled was the question of value, and the Court therefore remanded the case to the Department for further evidence on this issue.

. . . .

From the facts presented we find that while the price per ton of Heatherstone is not significantly higher than other stone used for the same purposes, its unique qualities do impart definite economic advantages over other competitive types of stone. Heatherstone is cheaper by half to quarry and prepare for market, resulting in significantly higher profits to the quarry operator. It yields a greater volume of usable stone per ton and the same volume of usable Heatherstone covers a broader area, which means that fewer tons of Heatherstone are required for a given job, thereby effecting a significant saving to the builder. A mason can lay a substantially broader area of Heatherstone in a day's work, which affords a definite economic advantage to the masonry contractor. Where the wall exceeds five feet in height this advantage is further enhanced.

The finding that Heatherstone's unique properties impart special economic advantages does not hinge on the advantages in quarrying alone, but also on the economic advantages in installation that may be appreciated by the contractor, stonemason and customer.

The dissenting opinion questions whether a special and distinct value which accrues to the user of the stone is within the ambit of the Court's guidelines. Regardless of whether it is or is not, our finding of special value to the builder, contractor or subcontractor is not essential to the conclusion. There is an established special value to the producer, reflected by reduced costs of overhead so that the producer's profit is substantially increased, and this is attributable to the uncommon physical properties of the stone. This, of itself, is sufficient to meet the Court's criterion for determining whether the stone has a special economic value.

. . . .

Accordingly, pursuant to the authority delegated to the Board of Land Appeals by the Secretary of the Interior, 43 CFR 4.1, the recommended decision of the Administrative Law Judge is not adopted and the contest is dismissed.

NOTES

1. Is *McClarty* consistent with *Henderson*? Which test is more favorable to the locator? The Interior Department has promulgated regulations setting forth its interpretation of the proper test for determining whether a particular mineral is an uncommon variety or a common variety. Those regulations provide that "common varieties includes deposits which, although they may have value for use in trade, manufacture, the sciences, or in the mechanical or ornamental arts, do not possess a distinct, special economic value for such use over and above the normal uses of the general run of such deposits. Mineral materials which occur commonly shall not be deemed to be 'common varieties' if a particular deposit has distinct and special properties making it commercially valuable for use in manufacturing, industrial, or processing operations." 43 C.F.R. § 3711.1(b) (1983). Are the Interior Department regulations consistent with *McClarty*? Which test is more favorable to the locator?

2. In determining whether a common variety has unique characteristics or properties, should the scarcity of the material within a particular geographic area be considered a characteristic of the mineral? For example, if deposits of sand and gravel only very rarely occur in certain areas of the country, should such deposits as exist in those areas be deemed to have a unique characteristic simply because of their geographic location? In *U.S. v. Stewart,* 79 I.D. 27 (1972) the Department held that while scarcity in a particular area might give a deposit "special value," it could not be considered a unique characteristic of the mineral itself.

3. One of the key issues in determining whether a particular mineral is possessed of unique characteristics is a determination of what the mineral in issue will be compared to. Thus, gravel might have unique characteristics when compared to stone in general, but not when compared to other gravel. What test does *McClarty* adopt with respect to this determination? Do you think it is a workable test? See *United States v. Kaycee Bentonite Corp.,* 64 I.B.L.A. 183 (1982).

4. In the third paragraph from the end of the McClarty case, the Board states that "The finding that Heatherstone's unique qualities impart special value does not hinge on the advantages in quarrying alone, *but also on the economic advantages in installation that may be appreciated by the contractor, stonemason and customer.* Can this statement be reconciled with the Board's statement in the penultimate paragraph of the decision that "our finding of special value to the builder, contractor or subcontractor is not essential to our conclusion"?

ANDRUS V. CHARLESTONE STONE PRODUCTS CO., INC.
436 U.S. 604 (1978)

Mr. Justice MARSHALL delivered the opinion of the Court.

Under the basic federal mining statute, which derives from an 1872 law [footnote omitted], "all valuable mineral deposits in lands belonging to the United States" are declared "free and open to exploration and purchase." 30 U.S.C. § 22 [footnote omitted]. The question presented is whether water is a "valuable mineral" as those words are used in the mining law.

I

A claim to federal land containing "valuable mineral deposits" may be "located" by complying with certain procedural requisites; one who locates a claim thereby gains the exclusive right to possession of the land, as well as the right to extract minerals from it. See generally 30 U.S.C. §§ 21-54; 1 American Law of Mining § 1.17 (1974). The claim at issue in this case, known as Claim 22, is one of a group of 23 claims near Las Vegas, Nev., that were located in 1942. In 1962, after respondent had purchased these claims, it discovered water on Claim 22 by drilling a well thereon. This water was used to prepare for commercial sale the sand and gravel removed from some of the 23 claims.

In 1965, the Secretary of the Interior filed a complaint with the Bureau of Land Management, seeking to have all of these claims declared invalid on the ground that the only minerals discovered on them were "common varieties" of sand and gravel, which had been expressly excluded from the definition of "valuable minerals" by a 1955 statute, § 3, 69 Stat. 368, 30 U.S.C. § 611 [footnote omitted]. At the administrative hearing on the Secretary's complaint, the principal issue was whether the sand and gravel deposits were "valuable" prior to the effective date of the 1955 legislation, in which case the claims would be valid.[1] The Administrative Law Judge concluded after hearing the evidence that respondent had established pre-1955 value only as to Claim 10. On appeals taken by both respondent and the Government, the Interior Board of Land Appeals (IBLA) affirmed the Administrative Law Judge in all respects here relevant. 9 I.B.L.A. 94 (1973) [footnote omitted].

Respondent sought review in the United States District Court for the District of Nevada [footnote omitted]. The court concluded that the decisions of the Administrative Law Judge and the IBLA were not supported by the evidence and that "at least" Claims 1 through 16 were valid. App. to Pet. for Cert. 26a. The court further held "that access to Claim No. 22 must be permitted so that the water produced from the well on that claim may be made available to the

---

[1] The question of value has traditionally been resolved by application of "complement[ary]" tests relating to whether "'a person of ordinary prudence'" would have expended "'his labor and means'" developing the claim at issue and whether the minerals thereon could have been "'extracted, removed and marketed at a profit.'" *United States v. Coleman*, 390 U.S. 599, 600, 602 (1968), quoting decisions of the Secretary of the Interior in *Coleman* and in *Castle v. Womble*, 19 L.D. 455, 457 (1894).

operations on the valid claims." *Ibid.* The IBLA's decision was accordingly vacated, and the case remanded to the Department of the Interior.

On the Government's appeal, the United States Court of Appeals for the Ninth Circuit affirmed. 553 F.2d 1209 (1977). It agreed with the District Court as to Claims 1 through 16 and also agreed that respondent was entitled to access to the water on Claim 22. It grounded the latter conclusion, however, "upon a rationale other than that relied upon by the District Court," *id.,* at 1215, a rationale that had not been briefed or argued in either the District Court or the Court of Appeals. Noting that "[s]ince early times, water has been regarded as a mineral," *ibid.,* the appellate court stated that it could not assume "that Congress was not aware of the necessary glove of water for the hand of mining and [that] Congress impliedly intended to reserve water from those minerals allowed to be located and recovered," *id.,* at 1216. Since the water at Claim 22 "has an intrinsic value in the desert area" and has additional value at the particular site "as a washing agent for . . . sand and gravel," the court ruled that respondent's "claim for the extraction of [Claim 22's] water is valid." *Ibid.*[2]

The difference between the District Court's and the Court of Appeals' rationales for allowing access to Claim 22 is a significant one. The District Court held only that respondent is entitled to use the water on the claim; the Court of Appeals, by contrast, held that the claim itself is valid. If the claim is indeed valid, respondent is not merely entitled to access to the water thereon, but also has exclusive possessory rights to the land and may keep others from making any use of it. By complying with certain procedures, moreover, respondent could secure a "patent" from the Government conveying fee simple title to the land. See 30 U.S.C. §§ 29, 37; 1 American Law of Mining, § 1.23 (1973). See generally *Union Oil Co. v. Smith,* 249 U.S. 337, 348-349 (1919). In view of the significance of the determination that a mining claim to federal land is valid, the Government sought review here of the Court of Appeals' *sua sponte* holding regarding Claim 22's validity. The single question presented in the petition is "[w]hether water is locatable mineral under the mining law of 1872." Pet. for Cert. 2.

We granted certiorari, 434 U.S. 964 (1977), and we now reverse.

II

We may assume for purposes of this decision that the Court of Appeals was correct in concluding that water is a "mineral," in the broadest sense of that word, and that it is "valuable." Both of these facts are necessary to a holding that a claimant has located a "valuable mineral deposit" under the 1872 law, 30 U.S.C. § 22, but they are hardly sufficient.

This Court long ago recognized that the word "mineral," when used in an Act of Congress, cannot be given its broadest definition. In construing an Act granting certain public lands, except "mineral lands," to be railroad, the Court wrote:

---

[2] In reaching this conclusion, the court correctly noted, 553 F.2d, at 1216, that water is not listed among the "common varieties" of minerals withdrawn from location by 30 U.S.C. § 611. Hence the fact that respondent did not discover water on Claim 22 until after 1955 is irrelevant to the question of the validity of the claim. See *supra,* at 606-607, and n. 3. See also *infra,* at 617.

"The word 'mineral' is used in so many senses, dependent upon the context, that the ordinary definitions of the dictionary throw but little light upon its signification in a given case. Thus, the scientific division of all matter into the animal, vegetable, or mineral kingdom would be absurd as applied to a grant of lands, since all lands belong to the mineral kingdom. . . . Equally subversive of the grant would be the definition of minerals found in the Century Dictionary; as 'any constituent of the earth's crust'. . . ." *Northern Pacific R. Co. v. Soderberg,* 188 U.S. 526, 530 (1903).

In the context of the 1872 mining law, similar conclusions must be drawn. As one court observed, if the term "mineral" in the statute were construed to encompass all substances that are conceivably mineral, "there would be justification for making mine locations on virtually every part of the earth's surface," since "a very high proportion of the substances of the earth are in that sense 'mineral.' " *Rummell v. Bailey,* 7 Utah 2d 137, 140, 320 P.2d 653, 655 (1958). See also *Robert L. Beery,* 25 I.B.L.A. 287, 294-296 (1976) (noting that "common dirt," while literally a mineral, cannot be considered locatable under the mining law); *Holman v. Utah,* 41 L.D. 314, 315 (1912); 1 American Law of Mining, *supra,* § 2.4, at 168.

The fact that water may be valuable or marketable similarly is not enough to support a mining claim's validity based on the presence of water. Many substances present on the land may be of value, and indeed it seems likely that land itself especially land located just 15 miles from dowtown Las Vegas, see 553 F.2d, at 1211—has, in the Court of Appeals' words, "an intrinsic value," *id.,* at 1216. Yet the federal mining law surely was not intended to be a general real estate law; as one commentator has written, "the Congressional mandate did not sanction the disposal of federal lands under the mining laws for purposes unrelated to mining." 1 American Law of Mining, *supra,* § 1.18, p. 56; cf. *Holman v. Utah, supra* (distinguishing mining law from homestead and other agricultural entry laws). In order for a claim to be valid, the substance discovered must not only be a "valuable mineral" within the dictionary definition of those words, but must also be the type of valuable mineral that the 1872 Congress intended to make the basis of a valid claim.[3]

III

The 1872 law incorporates two provisions involving water rights that derive from earlier mining acts. See 17 Stat. 94-95. In 1866, in Congress' first major effort to regulate mining on federal lands, it provided for the protection of the "vested rights" of "possessors and owners" "to the use of water for mining, agricultural, manufacturing or other purposes," to the extent that these rights derive from "priority of possession" and "are recognized and acknowledged by

---

[3] By referring to the intent of the 1872 Congress, we do not mean to imply that the only minerals locatable are those that were known to exist in 1872. But Congress' general conception of what a "valuable mineral" was for purposes of mining claim location is of obvious relevance in construing the 1872 law.

the local customs, laws, and the decisions of courts." 30 U.S.C. § 51.[4] In 1870, Congress again emphasized its view that water rights derive from "local" law, not federal law, making "[a]ll patents granted . . . subject to any vested and accrued water rights . . . as may have been acquired under or recognized by [the 1866 provision]." 30 U.S.C. § 52.[5]

In discussing these mining law provisions on the subject of water rights, this Court has often taken note of the history of mining in the arid Western States. In 1879 Mr. Justice Field of California, writing for the Court, described in vivid terms the influx of miners that had shaped the water rights law of his State and its neighbors:

> "The lands in which the precious metals were found belonged to the United States, and were unsurveyed. . . . Into these mountains the emigrants in vast numbers penetrated, occupying the ravines, gulches and canons, and probing the earth in all directions for the precious metals.- . . . But the mines could not be worked without water. Without water the gold would remain forever buried in the earth or rock. . . . The doctrines of the common law respecting the rights of riparian owners were not considered as applicable . . . to the condition of miners in the mountains. . . . Numerous regulations were adopted, or assumed to exist, from their obvious justness, for the security of . . . ditches and flumes, and the protection of rights to water. . . ." *Jennison v. Kirk,* 98 U.S. 453, 457-458 (1879).

See also *Basey v. Gallagher,* 20 Wall. 670, 681-684 (1875) (Field, J.); *Atchison v. Peterson,* 20 Wall. 507, 510-515 (1874) (Field, J.). Over a half century later, Mr. Justice Sutherland set out this same history in *California Oregon Power Co. v. Beaver Portland Cement Co.,* 295 U.S. 142, 154-155 (1935). He then explained that the water rights provisions of the 1866 and 1870 laws were intended to

> "approve and confirm the policy of appropriation for a beneficial use, as recognized by local rules and customs, and the legislation and judicial decisions of the arid-land states, as the test and measure of private rights in and to the non-navigable waters on the public domain." *Id.,* at 155.

Our opinions thus recognize that, although mining law and water law developed together in the West prior to 1866, with respect to federal lands Congress chose to subject only mining to comprehensive federal regulation. When it passed the 1866 and 1870 mining laws, Congress clearly intended to preserve *"pre-existing* [water] *right[s]."* *Broder v. Natoma Water & Mining Co.,*

---

[4] Title 30 U.S.C. § 51 provides in full: "Whenever, by priority of possession, rights to the use of water for mining, agricultural, manufacturing, or other purposes have vested and accrued, and the same are recognized and acknowledged by the local customs, laws, and the decisions of courts, the possessors and owners of such vested rights shall be maintained and protected in the same; and the right-of-way for the construction of ditches and canals for the purposes herein specified is acknowledged and confirmed; but whenever any person, in the construction of any ditch or canal, injures or damages the possession of any settler on the public domain, the party committing such injury or damage shall be liable to the party injured for such injury or damage."

[5] Title 30 U.S.C. § 52 provides in full: "All patents granted, or homesteads allowed, shall be subject to any vested and accrued water rights, or rights to ditches and reservoirs used in connection with such water rights, as may have been acquired under or reorganized by section 51 of this title."

101 U.S. 274, 276 (1879). Less than 15 years after passage of the 1872 law, the Secretary of the Interior in two decisions ruled that water is not a locatable mineral under the law and that private water rights on federal lands are instead "governed by local customs and laws," pursuant to the 1866 and 1870 provisions. *Charles Lennig,* 5 L.D. 190, 191 (1886); see *William A. Chessman,* 2 L.D. 774, 775 (1883). The Interior Department which is charged with principal responsibility for "regulating the acquisition of rights in the public lands," *Cameron v. United States,* 252 U.S. 450, 460 (1920), has recently reaffirmed this interpretation. *Robert L. Beery, supra.*

In ruling to the contrary, the Court of Appeals did not refer to 30 U.S.C. §§ 51 and 52, which embody the 1866 and 1870 provisions; to our opinions construing these provisions; or to the consistent course of administrative rulings on this question. Instead, without benefit of briefing, the court below decided that "it would be incongruous . . . to hazard that Congress was not aware of the necessary glove of water for the hand of mining." 553 F.2d, at 1216. Congress was indeed aware of this, so much aware that it expressly provided a water rights policy in the mining laws. But the policy adopted is a "passive" one, 2 Waters and Water Rights § 102.1, p. 53 (R. Clark ed. 1967); Congress three times (in 1866, 1870, and 1872) affirmed the view that private water rights on federal lands were to be governed by state and local law and custom. It defies common sense to assume that Congress, when it adopted this policy, meant at the same time to establish a parallel federal system for acquiring private water rights, and that it did so *sub silentio* through laws designed to regulate mining. In light of the 1866 and 1870 provisions, the history out of which they arose, and the decisions construing them in the context of the 1872 law, the notion that water is a "valuable mineral" under that law is simply untenable.

IV

The conclusion that Congress did not intend water to be locatable under the federal mining law is reinforced by consideration of the practical consequences that could be expected to flow from a holding to the contrary.

A

Many problems would undoubtedly arise simply from the fact of having two overlapping systems for acquisition of private water rights. Under the appropriation doctrine prevailing in most of the Western States, the mere fact that a person controls land adjacent to a body of water means relatively little; instead, water rights belong to "[t]he first appropriator of water for a beneficial use," but only "to the extent of his actual use," *California Oregon Power Co. v. Beaver Portland Cement Co., supra,* at 154; see *Jennison v. Kirk, supra,* at 458; W. Hutchins, Selected Problems in the Law of Water Rights in the West 30-32, 389-403 (1942); McGowen, The Development of Political Institutions on the Public Domain, 11 Wyo. L.J. 1, 14 (1957). Failure to use the water to which one is entitled for a certain period of time generally causes one's rights in that water to be deemed abandoned. See generally 2 W. Hutchins, Water Rights Laws in the Nineteen Western States 256-328 (1974).

With regard to minerals located under federal law, an entirely different theory prevails. The holder of a federal mining claim, by investing $100 annually in the claim, becomes entitled to possession of the land and may make any use, or no use, of the minerals involved. See 30 U.S.C. § 28. Once fee title by patent is obtained, see *supra,* at 609 even the $100 requirement is eliminated.

One can readily imagine the legal conflicts that might arise from these differing approaches if ordinary water were treated as a federally cognizable "mineral." A federal claimant could, for example, utilize all of the water extracted from a well like respondent's, without regard for the settled prior appropriation rights of another user of the same water.[6] Or he might not use the water at all and yet prevent another from using it, thereby defeating the necessary Western policy in favor of "actual use" of scarce water resources. *California Oregon Power Co. v. Beaver Portland Cement Co., supra,* 295 U.S., at 154. As one respected commentator has written, allowing water to be the basis of a valid mining claim "could revive long abandoned common law rules of ground water ownership and capture, and . . . could raise horrendous problems of priority and extralateral rights."[7] We decline to effect so major an alteration in established legal relationships based on nothing more than an overly literal reading of a statute, without any regard for its context or history.

B

A final indication that water should not be held to be a locatable mineral derives from Congress' 1955 decision to remove "common varieties" of certain minerals from the coverage of the mining law. 30 U.S.C. § 611; see *supra* at 606-607, and n. 5. This decision was made in large part because of "abuses under the general mining laws by . . . persons who locate[d] mining claims on public lands for purposes other than that of legitimate mining activity." H.R. Rep. No. 730, 84th Cong., 1st Sess. 5 (1955); see S. Rep. No. 554, 84th Cong. 1st Sess., 4-5 (1955); U.S. Code Cong. & Admin. News 1955, p. 2478. Apparently, locating a claim and obtaining a patent to federal land was so inexpensive that many "use[d] the guise of mining locations for nonmining purposes," including the establishment of "filling stations, curio shops, cafes, . . . residence[s] [and] summer camp[s]." H.R. Rep. No. 730, p. 6; see S. Rep. No. 554, at 5.

Water, of course, is among the most common of the earth's elements. While it may not be as common in the federal lands subject to the mining law as it is elsewhere, it is nevertheless common enough to raise the possibility of abuse by those less interested in extracting mineral resources than in obtaining title to

---

[6] The holder of a valid mining claim is generally understood to have an unlimited right to extract minerals from the claim, "even to exhaustion." *Union Oil Co. v. Smith,* 249 U.S. 337, 349 (1919). Respondent suggests that this right could be limited in the context of a mining-law claim to water, if the law were construed to require the claimant to respect water rights previously vested under state law. Brief for Respondent 31 n. 8; see *id.,* at 25-26.

[7] Trelease, Federal-State Problems in Packaging Water Rights, in Water Acquisition for Mineral Development Institute, Paper 9, pp. 9-17 n. 47 (Rocky Mt. Min. L. Fdn., 1978).

valuable land.[8] See *Robert L. Berry,* 25 I. B. L. A., at 296-297. Given the unprecedented nature of the Court of Appeals' decision, it is hardly surprising that the 1955 Congress did not include water on its list of "common varieties" of minerals that cannot confer validity on a mining claim. But the concerns that Congress addressed in the 1955 legislation indicate that water, like the listed minerals, should not be considered a locatable mineral under the 1872 mining law.

V

It has long been established that, when grants to federal land are at issue, any doubts "are resolved for the Government, not against it." *United States v. Union Pacific R. Co.,* 353 U.S. 112, 116 (1957). *A fortiori,* the Government must prevail in a case such as this, when the relevant statutory provisions, their historical context, consistent administrative and judicial decisions, and the practical problems with a contrary holding all weigh in its favor. Accordingly, the judgment of the Court of Appeals is
  Reversed.

---

[8] The Court of Appeals' suggestion that a claim to water might be validated simply because of the "intrinsic value" of water "in the desert area," 553 F.2d, at 1216, makes abuse particularly likely, since the "intrinsic value" theory would substantially lessen a claimant's burden of showing the "valuable" nature of his claim. See n. 4, *supra.*

NOTES

1. The list of common varieties in the Common Varieties Act appears to be exclusive, but, as *Charlestone Products* makes clear, it is not. Apparently we must await a case by case determination to find out what other minerals are nonlocatable common varieties.

2. Does the court in *Charlestone Products* hold that water is a common variety? If so, should that be the end of the inquiry?

3. Why was it necessary for the lower court to consider whether the claims in question had "pre-1955" value?

4. Since both the lower court and the court of appeals found that the locator had the right to use the water on Claim 22, what was so significant about the difference in the rationales employed by the court to reach their respective conclusions?

5. When the United States issued patents pursuant to the Stock Raising Homestead Act, it reserved to itself all the subsurface minerals contained in the patented lands. *Charlestone Stone Products* stands for the proposition that water is not a mineral for purposes of the Mining Law of 1872. Does it follow, therefore, that geothermal steam is not a "mineral" for purposes of the Stock Raising Homestead Act? See *United States v. Union Oil Company of California,* 549 F.2d 1271 (9th Cir. 1977). Cf. *United States v. Western Nuclear Corporation,* 103 S. Ct. 2218 (1983).

C. Leasing Act Minerals

APPLICABILITY OF THE MINERAL LEASING ACT
TO DEPOSITS OF BENTONITE
79 I.D. 642 (1972)

. . . .

The question of whether bentonite is a mineral subject to the Mineral Leasing Act of February 25, 1920, *as amended* and supplemented (30 U.S.C. secs. 181-287), has been before this office for a considerable period. No one has suggested that all bentonite is leasable under the existing statute, but it has been suggested that bentonites may be divided into calcium bentonites and sodium bentonites. Sections 23 and 24 of the Mineral Leasing Act, *as amended* (30 U.S.C. secs. 261-262), provide for the issuance of prospecting permits and leases for "chlorides, sulphates, carbonates, borates, silicates, or nitrates of sodium." The question before this office has revolved around the possibility that some bentonite may be a silicate of sodium. Whether or not any bentonite is a silicate of sodium is a technical question and outside the scope of this office's competence. If the technical experts of the Geological Survey determine that bentonite of an identifiable type is a silicate of sodium, the legal question could be easily solved. Such bentonite would be leasable.

However, there has not been such a determination by the Geological Survey. . . . It would be highly inappropriate for this office to essay the role of mineralogists and to attempt to determine whether some bentonite is a silicate of sodium. . . .

The history of the nation's mineral laws may be succinctly stated. All minerals (*i.e.,* all substances popularly recognized as minerals, but not such substances as water which, although technically a mineral, is not popularly recognized as one) were originally subject to the general mining law of 1872 (30 U.S.C. secs. 21-54). From time to time various minerals have been removed from the scope of that statute and put under other statutes. A major excision from the mining law was the Mineral Leasing Act of February 25, 1920, which removed coal, phosphate, oil, gas, oil shale, and sodium from the mining law. Whether a mineral has been removed from the mining law depends upon the terms of the amendatory statute, and it is my opinion that the Department is required to treat any mineral as subject to the mining law until it has been determined to have been excluded from the scope of the statute and placed under some other statute. Following that principle, I conclude that bentonite must still be regarded as not subject to disposition under the Mineral Leasing Act. If at some future time technical experts in the Department determine that bentonite (or some type of bentonite) is a silicate of sodium, a different legal conclusion will probably be reached. Meanwhile bentonite should continue to be subject to disposition under the same laws as in the past.

A mining claim, which is validly located for bentonite at a time when that mineral is locatable, would continue to be valid as long as the mining claimant maintained it in compliance with the law. Having been property in the highest sense of the word, an existing claim should not be nullified because of a new interpretation of law by the Department. See *Franco Western Oil Company, et al.* (Supp.), 65 I.D. 427 (1958), and the cases cited in that decision.

However, although mining claims located for bentonite at any time before a new departmental interpretation is issued would be protected, it would be appropriate to encourage bentonite claimants to seek patents in order to remove all doubt as to their claims' validity.

NOTES

1. 43 C.F.R. § 3812.1 (1982) provides:

. . . Deposits of oil, gas, coal, potassium, sodium, phosphate, oil shale, native asphalt, solid and semisolid bitumen, and bituminous rock including oil-impregnated rock or sands from which oil is recoverable only by special treatment after the deposit is mined or quarried, the deposits of sulphur in Louisiana and New Mexico belonging to the United States can be acquired under the mineral leasing laws (see § 3100.0-3(a) (1)), and are not subject to location and purchase under the United States mining laws. . . .

2. Dawsonite is a compound of sodium, and sodium compounds are subject to disposition only pursuant to the Mineral Leasing Act. Aluminum, however, is a constituent element of dawsonite, and aluminum is subject to disposition only pursuant to the general mining law. Is dawsonite a locatable or leasable mineral? *Wolf Joint Venture,* 75 I.D. 137 (1968), holds that dawsonite is not locatable. What if the aluminum, instead of being a chemical constitutent of the dawsonite just occurred as part of the same ore body that contained the dawsonite. Would the aluminum then be locatable independent of the dawsonite? See *Solicitor's Opinion,* 75 I.D. 397 (1968).

3. In *United States v. Union Carbide Corp.,* 84 I.D. 309 (1977) the Board held that the determination of whether a particular compound was subject to the leasing act or the mining law was to be determined pursuant to a two-pronged test. First, it must be determined that the compound in question contains some leasing act mineral "in sufficient quantity to be commercially recoverable", and, second, it must be further determined that the presence of the leasing act mineral "is essential to the existence of the" compound in question. Is *Union Carbide* inconsistent with the Solicitor's opinion?

D.   Discovery of a Marketable Mineral

1. Introduction

CASTLE V. WOMBLE
19 L.D. 455 (1894)

. . . .

April 15, 1892, Womble filed notice of intention to submit final proof June 13, 1892, and Walter Castle filed protest, alleging in substance that, March 15, 1890, he, with others located the Empire Quartz mining claim, embracing a portion of lots 10 and 11, and the NW. 1/4 of the SE. 1/4 of said section thirty; that said mining claim contains a lode of quartz rock in place, carrying gold in paying quantities; that said land is more valuable for mineral, than for agricultural, grazing, or other purposes.

On this protest a hearing was had before the register and receiver, testimony taken, and a decision rendered by them, finding the land to contain gold sufficient to justify further development, and that Womble's declaratory statement having expired by limitation of law, and the Empire Quartz mining claim having attached to the land by location, Womble should be required to procure, at his own expense, a segregation of the Empire Quartz mining claim, before he be permitted to enter the remainder of the land embraced by his declaratory statement.

Womble appealed, and your office held that the part of the land embraced within the limits of the Empire Quartz mine contains sufficient mineral to justify the belief that it will develop into a paying mine, and affirmed the judgment of the local officers. Womble appealed to the Department.

The law is emphatic in declaring that "no location of a mining claim shall be made until the discovery of the vein or lode within the limits of the claim located." (Revised Statutes, 2320.) And this Department said in the Cayuga Lode (S.L.D., 703), 5—"This is a prerequisite to the location, and, of course, entry of any mining claim. Without compliance with this essential requirement of the law no location will be recognized, no entry allowed. Has such discovery been made in this case?

. . . .

In this case the presence of mineral is not based upon probabilities, belief and speculation alone, but upon facts, which, in the judgment of the register and receiver and your office, show that with further work, a paying and valuable mine, so far as human foresight can determine, will be developed.

After a careful consideration of the subject, it is my opinion that where minerals have been found and the evidence is of such a character that a person of ordinary prudence would be justified in the further expenditure of his labor and means, with a reasonable prospect of success, in developing a valuable mine, the requirements of the statute have been met. To hold otherwise would tend to make of little avail, if not entirely nugatory, that provision of the law whereby "all valuable mineral deposits in lands belonging to the United States .-

. . are . . . declared to be free and open to exploration and purchase." For, if as soon as minerals are shown to exist, and at any time during exploration, before the returns become remunerative, the lands are to be subject to other disposition, few would be found willing to risk time and capital in the attempt to bring to light and make available the mineral wealth, which lies concealed in the bowels of the earth, as Congress obviously must have intended the explorers should have proper opportunity to do.

Entertaining these views, your judgment is affirmed.

NOTES

1. "The prudent man rule has two separate requirements. The first requirement is that valuable minerals, whether in a vein or lode, or in a placer deposit, be found within the limits of the claim. The second requirement is that the evidence be of such character that a person of ordinary prudence would be justified in the further expenditure of his labor and means, with a reasonable prospect of success, in developing a valuable mine. The first requirement is not related to the facts as they exist at the time in question. The second requirement is related to the effect these facts would have upon the conduct of a reasonable man." Reeves, *The Origin and Development of the Rule of Discovery,* VIII Land and Water Law Review, 35 (1953).

2. The word "develop" as used in *Castle v. Womble* is susceptible to at least two meanings. On the one hand it could mean all the steps leading toward the accomplishment of an ultimate goal. Thus, if initial exploration indicated that a particular claim might have value, further exploration directed toward confirming that value and its extent could be characterized as development. On the other hand, "develop" has a more limited technical meaning, namely those steps between the conclusion of exploration and the commencement of marketing activities. Most cases have accepted the more restrictive meaning.

2. A Discovery Good Against the United States

FOSTER V. SEATON
271 F.2d 836 (D.C. Cir. 1959)

[footnotes omitted]

Before PRETTYMAN, Chief Judge, and BAZELON and BURGER, Circuit Judges.

PER CURIAM.

This case relates to appellants' claims under provisions of the mining laws which authorize "occupation and purchase" of Government lands containing "valuable mineral deposits." Rev.Stat. §§ 2319, 2325, 2329 (1875), 30 U.S.C.A. §§ 22, 29, 35. The Department of the Interior instituted proceedings contesting the claims on the ground that the allegedly "valuable mineral deposits" of sand

and gravel, located thirteen miles from the center of Las Vegas, Nevada, were insufficient, *inter alia,* in quantity, quality and accessibility to a market to constitute a valid discovery. The hearing officer rendered a decision favorable to appellants, but it was reversed by the Director of the Bureau of Land Management upon an appeal by rival claimants who had intervened to assert an interest in the land under the Small Tract Act, 68 Stat. 239 (1954), 43 U.S.C.A. § 682a *et seq.* The Secretary of the Interior sustained the Director's ruling. Appellants then instituted this suit in the District Court under the Administrative Procedure Act to review the Secretary's decision. On cross motions, the District Court granted a summary judgment in favor of appellee and this appeal followed.

Appellants have raised a number of points relating to errors of procedure and statutory interpretation allegedly committed throughout the administrative process. We have examined them carefully and find no merit in the contentions. We discuss them briefly.

Appellants claim that they were prejudiced because intervenors were improperly admitted to the hearing, and that, without such intervention, the ruling of the initial hearing examiner in favor of appellants would never have been appealed and hence never reversed. It is clear, however, that the intervenors as rival claimants for the land under the Small Tract Act, allowing the Secretary to lease or sell vacant Government lands for certain residential and commercial uses, were interested parties. We find no basis for disturbing the administrative action with respect to this intervention.

Appellants also contend that the hearing examiner erroneously denied their request to examine a confidential document from which a Government witness was testifying. The record shows that upon the witness' claim of a governmental privilege appellants' counsel withdrew his request for disclosure. Thereafter the hearing officer expressly stated that he would, if again requested, rule in appellants' favor. Since the objection was not revived, the point is plainly not now available to appellants.

Appellants' third allegation of error is that the Secretary failed to hold the Government to the standard of proof required by the Administrative Procedure Act, which states that "the proponent of a rule or order shall have the burden of proof." 60 Stat. 241 (1946), 5 U.S.C.A. § 1006. The Secretary ruled that, when the Government contests a mining claim, it bears only the burden of going forward with sufficient evidence to establish a prima facie case, and that the burden then shifts to the claimant to show by a preponderance of the evidence that his claim is valid. The short answer to appellants' objection is that they, and not the Government, are the true proponents of a rule or order; namely, a ruling that they have complied with the applicable mining laws. One who has located a claim upon the public domain has, prior to the discovery of valuable minerals, only "taken the initial steps in seeking a gratuity from the Government." Ickes v. Underwood, 78 U.S.App.D.C. 396, 399, 141 F.2d 546, 549, certiorari denied 1944, 323 U.S. 713, 65 S.Ct. 39, 89 L.Ed. 574; Rev.Stat. § 2319 (1875), 30 U.S.C.A. § 23. Until he has fully met the statutory requirements, title to the land remains in the United States. Teller v. United States, 8 Cir., 1901, 113 F. 273, 281. Were the rule otherwise, anyone could enter upon the public domain and ultimately obtain title unless the Government undertook the affirmative burden of proving that no valuable deposit existed. We do not think that Congress intended to place this burden on the Secretary.

Appellants' principal assignment of error is that the Secretary misinterpreted the statute by requiring a demonstration of present value. They earnestly contend that their claim can also be sustained on the basis of prospective market value.

The statute says simply that the mineral deposit must be "valuable." Rev. Stat. § 2319, 30 U.S.C.A. § 22. Where the mineral in question is of limited occurrence, the Department, with judicial approval, has long adhered to the definition of value laid down in *Castle v. Womble,* 19 L.D. 455, 457 (1894):

> "[W]here minerals have been found and the evidence is of such a character that a person of ordinary prudence would be justified in the further expenditure of his labor and means, with a reasonable prospect of success, in developing a valuable mine, the requirements of the statute have been met."

With respect to widespread non-metallic minerals such as sand and gravel, however, the Department has stressed the additional requirement of present marketability in order to prevent the misappropriation of lands containing these materials by persons seeking to acquire such lands for purposes other than mining. Thus, such a "mineral locator or applicant, to justify his possession, must show that by reason of accessibility, *bona fides* in development, proximity to market, *existence of present demand,* and other factors, the deposit is of such value that it can be mined, removed and disposed of at a profit." Layman v. Ellis, 54 I.D. 294, 296 (1933), emphasis supplied. See also Estate of Victor E. Hanny, 63 I.D. 369, 370-72 (1956). Particularly in view of the circumstances of this case, we find no basis for disturbing the Secretary's ruling. The Government's expert witness testified that Las Vegas valley is almost entirely composed of sand and gravel of similar grade and quality. To allow such land to be removed from the public domain because unforeseeable developments might some day make the deposit commercially feasible can hardly implement the congressional purpose in encouraging mineral development.

Thus the case really comes down to a question whether the Secretary's finding was supported by substantial evidence on the record as a whole. We think it was. There may have been substantial evidence the other way also, but we do not weigh the evidence. The testimony of Shafer and his colleagues in support of the Government was clearly substantial and most certainly was not destroyed. He was an experienced man, knew sand and gravel, knew the Las Vegas area, and his testimony was clear, succinct and convincing.

Affirmed.

NOTES

1. What is the difference between the rule in *Foster v. Seaton* and the rule in *Castle v. Womble?*

2. Does the discovery test enunciated in *Foster v. Seaton* apply to all minerals or just to mineral of widespread occurrence? Is there authority in the Mining Law of 1872 for such a distinction? Much of the confusion concerning what constitutes a discovery has its roots, at least indirectly, in the conviction of the courts that the Mining Law of 1872 contemplates only one rule of discovery no matter what mineral is involved.

3. The citation in the principal case to *Layman v. Ellis* is actually not to that decision, but to an opinion of the solicitor that quoted from and purported to affirm *Layman v. Ellis.* Do you think that the case of *Layman v. Ellis, supra,* is authority for the proposition for which it is cited in *Foster v. Seaton?*

MARKETABILITY RULE
69 I.D. 145 (1962)

Your memorandum to the Secretary requesting a review of this rule has been referred to this office for reply.

After giving careful consideration to this subject, it is our conclusion that there is no basis for making any change in the test which the Department applies to mining claims in determining whether there has been a valid discovery. However, we believe that, since our decisions may have been misunderstood and an undue rigidity may have been ascribed to them, we should explain the position taken.

The test which we apply, the prudent man test, is based upon the provision in R.S. 2319 (30 U.S.C. sec.22) that only "valuable mineral deposits" may be located. A valuable mineral deposit, it has been held, is one the discovery of which would justify a man of ordinary prudence in the further expenditure of time and money with a reasonable prospect of success in the effort to develop a paying mine. *Castle v. Womble,* 19 L.D. 455 (1894); *Chrisman v. Miller,* 197 U.S. 313 (1905).

The marketability rule about which you have particularly asked our views is merely one aspect of this test. The Department and the courts have, we believe, rightly held that a prudent man would not be justified in developing a mineral deposit if the extracted minerals were not marketable. This marketability test is in reality applied to all minerals, although it is often mistakenly said to be applied solely to nonmetallic minerals of wide occurrence. Many minerals are deemed intrinsically valuable.

An intrinsically valuable mineral by its very nature is deemed marketable, and therefore merely showing the nature of the mineral usually meets the test of marketability. On the other hand, where we are concerned with a nonmetalic [sic] mineral found in a great many places, application of the prudent man test requires that a market for the mineral be shown by the locator. The extreme example is probably sand and gravel, which are found in every State. There is a demand for sand and gravel, but in many areas the available deposits far exceed the market. In such cases we must insist that the locator show that there is a market actually existing for his minerals. To validate any sand and gravel claim proof of present marketability must be clearly shown.

Other cases fall between the two extremes of the intrinsically valuable mineral on the one hand and sand and gravel on the other hand. Each case must be judged on its own merits. When a nonmetallic mineral is not of extremely wide occurrence and when a general demand for that mineral exists, it may be enough, instead of showing an actually existing market for the products of that particular mine, to show that a general market for the substance exists of a type which a reasonably prudent man would be justified in regarding as one in which he could dispose of those products.

There are two points which we wish to stress. The first is that the marketability test is only one aspect of the prudent man test, albeit a very important aspect since in the absence of marketability no prudent man would seem justified in the expenditure of time and money. The second is that each case must be judged on its own facts. Too rigid application of rules mistakenly interpreted from departmental decisions could lead to incorrect decisions in the field.

NOTES

1. When Solicitor Barry refers to a mineral as being marketable, does he mean that the mineral can be sold, i.e., that there is a market for it, or does he mean that it can be sold at a profit? Does any specific language in the opinion compel a conclusion one way or the other?

2. Assuming that by marketable all the Solicitor means is saleable, is it correct to say that all intrinsically valuable minerals are saleable? Most minerals in nature occur in a form that requires processing before they are useful. The ore of the mineral may naturally occur in an oxidized form or be combined with a host rock from which it must be separated. Obviously, even an "intrinsically valuable" mineral, such as copper, may not be saleable if the ore in which it is found on a particular claim is so poor that the cost of extracting the copper would be greater than the price for which it could be sold. Should the inquiry focus on the mineral in its refined state or on the ore in which that mineral is found on a particular claim?

COLEMAN V. UNITED STATES
390 U.S. 599 (1968)

Mr. Justice BLACK delivered the opinion of the Court.

In 1956 respondent Coleman applied to the Department of the Interior for a patent to certain public lands based on his entry onto and exploration of these lands and his discovery there of a variety of stone called quartzite, one of the most common of all solid materials. It was, and still is, respondent Coleman's contention that the quartzite deposits qualify as "valuable mineral deposits" under 30 U.S.C. § 22[1] and make the land "chiefly valuable for building stone" under 30 U.S.C. § 161.[2] The Secretary of the Interior held that to qualify as "valuable mineral deposits" under 30 U.S.C. § 22 it must be shown that the mineral can be "extracted, removed and marketed at a profit"—the so-called "marketability test." Based on the largely undisputed evidence in the record, the Secretary concluded that the deposits claimed by respondent Coleman did not meet that criterion. As to the alternative "chiefly valuable for building stone" claim, the Secretary held that respondent Coleman's quartzite deposits were a "common variet[y]" of stone within the meaning of 30 U.S.C. § 611[3] and thus they could not serve as the basis for a valid mining claim under the mining laws. The Secretary denied the patent application, but respondent Coleman remained on the land, forcing the Government to bring its present action in ejectment in the District Court against respondent Coleman and his lessee, respondent McClennan. The respondents filed a counterclaim seeking to have the District Court direct the Secretary to issue a patent to them. The District Court, agreeing with the Secretary, rendered summary judgment for the Government. On appeal the Court of Appeals for the Ninth Circuit reversed, holding specifically that the test of profitable marketability was not a proper standard for determining whether discovery of "valuable mineral deposits" under 30 U.S.C. § 22 had been made and that building stone could not be deemed a "common variet[y]" of stone under 30 U.S.C. § 611. We granted the Government's petition for certiorari because of the importance of the decision to the utilization of the public lands. 389 U.S. 970.

We cannot agree with the Court of Appeals and believe that the rulings of the Secretary of the Interior were proper. The Secretary's determination that the quartzite deposits did not qualify as valuable mineral deposits because the stone could not be marketed at a profit does no violence to the statute. Indeed, the marketability test is an admirable effort to identify with greater precision and objectivity the factors relevant to a determination that a mineral deposit is

---

[1] The cornerstone of federal legislation dealing with mineral lands is the Act of May 10, 1872, 17 Stat. 91, 30 U.S.C. § 22, which provides in § 1 that citizens may enter and explore the public domain and, if they find "valuable mineral deposits," may obtain title to the land on which such deposits are located by application to the Department of the Interior. The Secretary of the Interior is "charged with seeing . . . that valid claims . . . [are] recognized, invalid ones eliminated, and the rights of the public preserved." *Cameron v. United States,* 252 U.S. 450, 460.

[2] The 1872 Act, *supra,* was supplemented in 1892 by the passage of the Act of August 4, 1892, 27 Stat. 348, 30 U.S.C. § 161, which provides in § 1 in pertinent part: "That any person authorized to enter lands under the mining laws of the United States may enter lands that are chiefly valuable for building stone under the provisions of the law in relation to placer mineral claims. . . ."

[3] Section 3 of the Act of July 23, 1955, 69 Stat. 368, 30 U.S.C. § 611, provides in pertinent part as follows: "A deposit of common varieties of sand, stone, gravel, pumice, pumicite, or cinders shall not be deemed a valuable mineral deposit within the meaning of the mining laws of the United States so as to give effective validity to any mining claim hereafter located under such mining laws. . . . 'Common varieties' as used in this Act does not include deposits of such materials which are valuable because the deposit has some property giving it distinct and special value. . . ."

"valuable." It is a logical complement to the "prudent-man test" which the Secretary has been using to interpret the mining laws since 1894. Under this "prudent-man test" in order to qualify as "valuable mineral deposits," the discovered deposits must be of such a character that "a person of ordinary prudence would be justified in the further expenditure of his labor and means, with a reasonable prospect of success, in developing a valuable mine. . . ." *Castle v. Womble,* 19 L.D. 455, 457 (1894). This court has approved the prudent-man formulation and interpretation on numerous occasions. See, for example, *Chrisman v. Miller,* 197 U.S. 313, 322; *Cameron v. United States,* 252 U.S. 450, 459; *Best v. Humboldt Placer Mining Co.,* 371 U.S. 334, 335-336. Under the mining laws Congress has made public lands available to people for the purpose of mining valuable mineral deposits and not for other purposes.[4] The obvious intent was to reward and encourage the discovery of minerals that are valuable in an economic sense. Minerals which no prudent man will extract because there is no demand for them at a price higher than the costs of extraction and transportation are hardly economically valuable. Thus profitability is an important consideration in applying the prudent-man test, and the marketability test which the Secretary has used here merely recognizes this fact.

The marketability test also has the advantage of throwing light on a claimant's intention, a matter which is inextricably bound together with valuableness. For evidence that a mineral deposit is not of economic value and cannot in all likelihood be operated at a profit may well suggest that a claimant seeks the land for other purposes. Indeed, as the Government points out, the facts of this case—the thousands of dollars and hours spent building a home on 720 acres in a highly scenic national forest located two hours from Los Angeles, the lack of an economically feasible market for the stone, and the immense quantities of identical stone found in the area outside the claims—might well be thought to raise a substantial question as to respondent Coleman's real intention.

Finally, we think that the Court of Appeals' objection to the marketability test on the ground that it involves the imposition of a different and more onerous standard on claims for minerals of widespread occurrence than for rarer minerals which have generally been dealt with under the prudent-man test is unwarranted. As we have pointed out above, the prudent-man test and the marketability test are not distinct standards, but are complementary in that the latter is a refinement of the former. While it is true that the marketability test is usually the critical factor in cases involving nonmetallic minerals of widespread occurrence, this is accounted for by the perfectly natural reason that precious metals which are in small supply and for which there is a great demand, sell at a price so high as to leave little room for doubt that they can be extracted and marketed at a profit.

We believe that the Secretary of the Interior was also correct in ruling that

---

4 17 Stat. 92, 30 U.S.C. § 29, provides in pertinent part as follows: "A patent for any land claimed and located for valuable deposits may be obtained in the following manner: Any person . . . having claimed and located a piece of land *for such purposes* . . . may file, . . ." (Emphasis added.)

"[i]n view of the immense quantities of identical stone found in the area outside the claims, the quartzite stone must be considered a 'common variety' and thus must fall within the exclusionary language of § 3 of the 1955 Act, 69 Stat. 368, 30 U.S.C. § 611, which declares that [a] deposit of common varieties of . . . stone . . . shall not be deemed a valuable mineral deposit within the meaning of the mining laws. . . .'" Respondents rely on the earlier 1892 Act, 30 U.S.C. § 161, which makes the mining laws applicable to "lands that are chiefly valuable for building stone" and contend that the 1955 Act has no application to building stone, since, according to respondents, "[s]tone which is chiefly valuable as building stone is, by that very fact, not a common variety of stone." This was also the reasoning of the Court of Appeals. But this argument completely fails to take into account the reason why Congress felt compelled to pass the 1955 Act with its modification of the mining laws. The legislative history makes clear that this Act (30 U.S.C. § 611) was intended to remove common types of sand, gravel, and stone from the coverage of the mining laws, under which they served as a basis for claims to land patents, and to place the disposition of such materials under the Materials Act of 1947, 61 Stat. 681, 30 U.S.C. § 601, which provides for the sale of such materials without disposing of the land on which they are found. For example, the Chairman of the House Committee on Interior and Insular Affairs explained the 1955 Act as follows:

"The reason we have done that is because sand, stone, gravel . . . are really *building materials,* and are not the type of material contemplated to be handled under the mining laws, and that is precisely where we have had so much abuse of the mining laws. . . ." 101 Cong. Rec. 8743. (Emphasis added.)

Similarly, the Senate Committee Report stated that the bill was intended to:

"Provide that deposits of common varieties of sand, *building stone,* gravel, pumice, pumicite, and cinders on the public lands, where they are found in widespread abundance, shall be disposed of under the Materials Act of 1947 (61 Stat. 681), rather than under the mining law of 1872." S. Rep. No. 554, 84th Cong., 1st Sess., 2. (Emphasis added.)

Thus we read 30 U.S.C. § 611, passed in 1955, as removing from the coverage of the mining laws "common varieties" of building stone, but leaving 30 U.S.C. § 161, the 1892 Act, entirely effective as to building stone that has "some property giving it distinct and special value" (expressly excluded under § 611).

For these reasons we hold that the United States is entitled to eject respondents from the land and that respondents' counterclaim for a patent must fail. The case is reversed and remanded to the Court of Appeals for the Ninth Circuit for further proceedings to carry out this decision.

It is so ordered.

Mr. Justice MARSHALL took no part in the consideration or decision of this case.

NOTES

1. What is the difference between the marketability enunciated in *Coleman* and the prudent man rule of *Castle v. Womble?* Is it true, as the Court says, that the marketability rule is a refinement of the prudent man rule, or does it really overrule it? Consider the following:

> The verbal formulation introduced by *Coleman* is unworkable because it treats the prudent man rule and the marketability rule as logical compliments when, in fact, they are irreconcilable. Thus, notwithstanding the Court's assertion to the contrary, *Coleman* represents a departure from and not a refinement of *Castle v. Womble.* The marketability rule requires proof of profitability as a *present* fact, the prudent man rule requires only proof of a reasonable prospect of success *in the future. Castle v. Womble* contemplated the transfer of entitlements for claims on which valuable deposits do not actually exist. *Coleman* requires that the transfer await proof of the existence of a commercially exploitable deposit. The marketability rule is thus much more conservative than the prudent man rule.

Braunstein, "Natural Environments and Natural Resources: An Economic Analysis and New Interpretation of the General Mining Law," 36 U.C.L.A. L. Rev. 301, 341 (1985).

2. Reconsider note 2 (the *Reeves* selection) following *Layman v. Ellis.*

3. Does the marketability rule require a showing that the mineral in question *can* be sold at a profit or that it *has* been sold at a profit? The reported decisions consistently iterate that actual sales are not required to establish marketability. The following language from *United States v. Barrows,* 76 I.D. 299 (1969) is fairly typical:

> The Department has, in fact, repeatedly stated that it "has never held that proof that minerals from a mining claim have actually been sold is an indispensable element in establishing their marketability" [citations omitted]. It has, however, recognized the difficulty of proving marketability without showing any sales, pointing out in numerous cases that, while the fact that no sale had been made at the critical time is not controlling in itself, the fact that nothing is done toward the development of a claim after its location may raise a presumption that the market value of the minerals found therein was not sufficient to justify the expenditure required to extract and market them. At 305-6.

4. Is the presumption referred to in *Barrows* a rebuttable or irrebuttable one? In theory? In practice? Would you advise a client who had not yet sold any of the mineral from her claim to try to get a patent? Would it make any difference to your advice what kind of mineral had been discovered?

5. After *Coleman,* does the Building Materials Act have any continued vitality, or, for that matter, any life at all?

6. Ideal Basic Industries, Inc. applied for patents on 45 limestone mining claims which it had located in Alaska. Ideal did not sell the limestone which it mined, but used it in its own operations in making cement. Ideal claimed that since the cement which is sold could be marketed at a profit, and since the cement which it sold contained the limestone which it mined, that by definition the limestone could be removed and marketed at a profit. The Ninth Circuit disagreed with Ideal's logic on the ground that Ideal might actually be losing money on the limestone, but nevertheless showing an overall profit because of "large profits it derives from either the manufacuring or selling processes, or both. Profits derived from sources other than the limestone itself cannot be imputed to the material for the purpose of satisfying the marketability rule." *Ideal Basic Industries, Inc. v. Morton*, 542 F. 2d 1364 (9th Cir. 1976).

7. In *Baker v. United States*, 613 F. 2d 224 (9th Cir. 1980) the claimant appealed from the Interior Board of Land Appeals' decision that two of his four claims for cinder cones were invalid. The IBLA decision was based on the ground that the claims contained mineral far in excess of the reasonably anticipated market demand for cinder cones (the excess reserves or "too much" rule). The Ninth Circuit held that Baker was entitled to patent all four of his claims and the IBLA's adoption of the "too much rule" was an abuse of discretion. "The 'too much' rule limits the overall amount of mineral and land an individual can claim under the mining laws. Although the mining laws limit the size of the claims, they have never set a limit on the number of claims an individual may stake and work. The validity of a claim has always been determined by an inquiry into that particular claim, not by an examination of the individual's other claims. The 'too much' rule changes the focus of the relevant inquiry. Although Congress has addressed various abuses under the mining law, it has never attempted to either limit the amount of mineral or the overall number of claims which can be patented by an individual." *Id.* at 228-29.

Is the Ninth Circuit's holding consistent with *Coleman*? If Baker's claims contained mineral far in excess of the market demand, could he sell mineral from all of the claims at all, much less sell it at a profit?

8. In order to satisfy the marketability rule, the claim must be capable of not only yielding a profit, but of yielding a reasonable profit. The profit must be such as would prove attractive to the prudent man. *Melluzzo v. Morton*, 534 F.2d 860 (1976). In determining what is a reasonable profit, should the speculative nature of the mining industry be considered?

9. "If the profitability of the market for such [newly discovered] material is realistically to be ascertained by setting the factor of demand opposite that of supply, the new material must be included with that from all other known potentially competitive sources in calculating the factor of supply. If supply so calculated amounts to a superabundance and so overwhelms the existing demand as to reduce the value or profit increment to a level below that which would prove attractive to a prudent man, the material cannot be said to be marketable at a profit. *Id.*, at 864.

10. "It is not enough that a claimant demonstrate that merely a profit or a prospect of a profit be present to validate a "common variety" claim. As here, for example, where there is every indication that appellant spent little or even

nothing, other than the time required for location, to improve a claim, a sale, of $1.00 would in fact be a "profit" for a claimant. It is unconscionable to think that the intent of the mining laws was to authorize the issuance of a patent for fee title to land to anyone who derived or foresaw a profit no matter how small from minerals on the claim, particularly where no effort was expended to explore for and extract the minerals. The Department has long held that the sale of minor quantities of a mineral at a profit or the disposal of substantial quantities at no profit, does not demonstrate the existence of a market for the material found . . . which would induce a man of ordinary prudence to expend his labor and means in attempt to develop a valuable mine. . . ." *United States v. Penrose,* 10 I.B.L.A. 332, 334 (1973).

   11. In *In Re Pacific Coast Molybdenum Co.,* 90 I.D. 353 (1983) the Board of Land Appeals held that:

> As a conceptual matter, the theory that the situs of the land alters the nature of the test applied is untenable. Where the mining laws apply, they necessarily apply with equal force and effect, regardless of the characteristics of the land involved. The test of discovery is the same whether the land be unreserved public domain, land in a national forest, or even land in a national park. *Id.* at 363.

Do you agree that one ought to be able to locate mining claims in, say, Yosemite National Park with the same ease as one might locate claims in the deserts of Nevada? Does the mining law require this result? *In Re Pacific Coast Molybdenum Co.* is criticised in Braunstein, Natural Environments and Natural Resources: An Economic Analysis and New Interpretation of the General Mining Law, 32 *U.C.L.A. L. Rev.* 301 (1985).

BARTON V. MORTON
498 F.2d 288 (9th Cir. 1974)

Before CHAMBERS, BROWNING and ELY, Circuit Judges.
OPINION

BROWNING, Circuit Judge:

   Appellant and another applied to the Department of the Interior for patents to two lode mining claims. The applications were denied and the claims held void on the ground that applicants had not shown discovery of a valuable mineral deposit as required by the applicable statutes. 30 U.S.C. §§ 22, 23, 29, 35. Appellant filed this action to obtain judicial review of the Department's ruling. The district court gave judgment for the Government. We affirm.

   The general legal standards to be applied are well established. "[T]he only statutory standard has been and still is the 'discovery' of 'veins or lodes' containing 'valuable deposits' of the named metals or others." Converse v. Udall, 399 F.2d 616, 619 (9th Cir. 1968). Appellant relies upon recognized glosses upon this statutory standard. Thus, the cases have held that whether a valuable deposit has been discovered is a factual question to be resolved by asking whether "a person of ordinary prudence would be justified in the further expenditure of his labor and means, with a reasonable prospect of success, in developing a valuable mine . . . ." Castle v. Womble, 19 Interior Dec. 455, 457 (1894), approved in Chrisman v. Miller, 197 U.S. 313, 322, 25 S.Ct. 468, 49 L.Ed. 770 (1905).[1] Appellant emphasizes that under this "prudent man" test, "proved ability to mine the deposit at a profit need not be shown." Adams v. United States, 318 F.2d 861, 870 (9th Cir. 1963). The question is not "whether assured profits were presently demonstrated, but whether, under the circumstances, a person of ordinary prudence would expend substantial sums in the expectation that a profitable mine might be developed." *Id. See also* Barrows v. Hickel, 447 F.2d 80, 82 (9th Cir. 1971).

There is no dispute as to the material facts. Veins have been exposed on both of the claims at issue. They contain some gold and silver, together with base metals. The mineralization is spotty and uneven. The vein material thus far exposed is not of sufficient value to be mined economically. However, along some veins of this kind on nearby claims, shoots or pockets have been found containing ore of sufficient quality and quantity to be profitably mined. Expert witnesses testified that a prudent man would be justified in tunneling into or along the veins on the claims in search of similar shoots or pockets. This testimony was not controverted.

Appellant contends that this showing precisely meets the "prudent man" test. As appellant puts it, he and his predecessors "have exposed veins which carry so much mineral values that all parties agree that further work is justified and should be carried on to pursue further these same veins with a reasonable expectation that a profitably mineable quantity of such ore will be reached. The basis for the reasonable expectation is that similar veins in nearby mines have yielded profitable ore shoots under comparable geologic conditions."

The Department's position is that appellant has not yet discovered a mineral deposit, but is only searching for one, albeit with good prospects for success. No matter how bright those prospects may be, the Department argues, they are not a substitute for actual discovery of the deposit itself. In the Department's view, the "prudent man" test comes into play only after a mineral deposit has been discovered, not before; and it is then applied to determine whether the discovered deposit is "valuable."[2]

The Department held that while the evidence shows that further expenditures are justified in exploration for a mineral deposit, what is required is discovery of a mineral deposit of such quality and quantity that further expenditures are

---

[1] This "prudent man" test is complemented by a "marketability test," requiring that it "be shown that the mineral can be 'extracted, removed and marketed at a profit. . . .'" United States v. Coleman, 390 U.S. 599, 600, 88 S.Ct. 1327, 1329, 20 L.Ed.2d 170 (1968).

[2] The Hearing Examiner wrote: The prudent man rule is not an alternative to the substantive provision of the mining laws requiring the discovery of a valuable mineral deposit. The rule is applicable only in the determination of whether a particular deposit is valuable. In this case, the further expenditure of labor and means would not be directed toward the development of a deposit which has been found but would be directed toward the finding of a deposit which the evidence indicates might be found and could be developed.

justified in the development of a profitable mine.[3]

We drew the same distinction in Henault Mining Co. v. Tysk, 419 F.2d 766 (9th Cir. 1969). In that case the claim was adjacent to property on which the Homestake formation had been extensively mined for gold. The Homestake formation dipped toward the claim for which a patent was sought, and out-cropped beyond it. Dikes containing some mineral values surfaced within the boundaries of the claim. These dikes were thought to have originated below the Homestake formation and to have penetrated that formation, carrying minerals from the formation to the surface. Valuable ore was expected to be found where the dikes intersected the Homestake formation. Experts testified that the presence of valuable mineral deposits at these points was so probable that in excess of $150,000 should be spent in drilling shafts to reach them. The claimant in *Henault* contended that this uncontradicted testimony satisfied the "prudent man" test. We rejected the argument (419 F.2d at 768-769):

> No vein or lode containing valuable mineral deposits has yet been disco-vered. The dikes that have been discovered through outcroppings simply constitute an indication that a vein or lode, yet unexposed, may exist at depth. A reasonable prediction that valuable minerals exist at depth will not suffice as a "discovery" where the existence of these minerals has not been physically established.
>
> . . . .
>
> The further exploration by drilling as recommended by Henault's expert is not then in the nature of development of a discovered lode. It is a search for values not yet discovered, the discovery of which would justify development.
>
> Henault's "prudent man," then, is not a prudent mine developer but a prudent prospector.[4]

Appellant seeks to distinguish *Henault* on the ground that while no veins had been discovered in *Henault*, veins have been discovered here. Appellant contends that these veins, admittedly containing some gold and silver, constitute the required mineral deposit. Appellant argues that he is now "searching for ore shoots, zones of enrichment, within the mineral deposits (veins) which have already been discovered," whereas in *Henault*, "the target was not [a] deeper enriched zone in an already exposed structure but a different . . . mineral deposit altogether, which had not yet been

---

[3] On appeal the Assistant Solicitor wrote: The most that can be said from this evidence, and all that the appellants have asserted, is, as observed by the hearing examiner, that the values of the minerals which have been found are sufficient to induce further exploration. Thus, when appellants assert that "a prudent man would be justified in expending further time and effort with a reasonable prospect to develop a paying mine," it is clear that they mean that a prudent man would be justified in expending further time and effort in exploring for minerals with a reasonable prospect of finding a mineral deposit which could be expected to lead to the development of a paying mine. Appellant points out that the Department's finding is misstated in a concluding paragraph of the district court's opinion. It is evident from the opinion as a whole, however, that the district court understood the distinction drawn by the Department and approved it.

[4] *See also* Chrisman v. Miller, 197 U.S. 313, 320, 323, 25 S.Ct. 468, 49 L.Ed. 770 (1905); Converse v. Udall, 399 F.2d 616, 623 (9th Cir. 1968).

physically encountered on the claims." Appellant contends that tunneling or sinking into the veins on these claims, as uniformly recommended by the witnesses, would not be "exploration" to "discover" a "valuable mineral deposit," but would be "development" of an already discovered deposit into a paying mine.

But a mineralized vein is not the equivalent of a deposit of mineable ore. Such a vein may not contain material of substantial value. In this case, as the Department pointed out, "[i]t is nowhere suggested that any quantity of material of the quality of the vein matter thus far disclosed would constitute a mineable body of ore. The evidence does not, in fact, establish any mineral quality of any consistent extent. Although appellants have found ore *samples* with indicated values exceeding $70 per ton, the record does not support a finding that they have found a *deposit* yielding ore or that quality, or of any other quality, the exploitation of which may be contemplated. The evidence of record indicates that the values thus far found are spotty, and appellants do not argue otherwise" (emphasis in original).

The Department held, and we agree, that there is "no difference between the showing of isolated mineral values, not occurring in a vein, which only suggests the existence of a valuable mineral deposit within the limits of the claim and the showing of isolated values occurring in a vein which only suggests the possible existence of a valuable mineral deposit in the course of the vein. That which is called for in either case is further exploration to find the deposit supposed to exist." *See also* Converse v. Udall, *supra,* 399 F.2d at 619, 622.

Appellant argues that in practical effect this approach nullifies the "reasonable anticipation" aspect of the "prudent man" test, and is inconsistent with the rule that "proved ability to mine the deposit at a profit need not be shown." Adams v. United States, *supra,* 318 F.2d at 870. We do not agree. Room remains after discovery of the mineral deposit for application of the principle that the claimant need only show a reasonable prospect that a profitable mine will be developed. The margin between a valuable mineral deposit and a profitable mine may be substantial. As the Department said, "Where ore has been found, the likelihood that ore of the quality found, or of any mineable quality, will continue remains a matter for speculation, and, until a mineral deposit has been exploited through actual mining operations, its true value will remain a matter of uncertainty."[5]

---

[5]   The Assistant Solicitor continued: Thus, the opinions of experts, based upon knowledge of the geology of the area, the successful development of similar deposits on adjacent mining claims, deductions from established facts—in short, all of the factors which the Department has refused to accept singly or in combination as constituting the equivalent of a discovery—may be, and as a practical matter must be, accepted in determining whether or not a prudent man would be justified in the expenditure of his means with a reasonable anticipation of developing a valuable mine. However, while inference may be relied upon to establish the *extent* of a particular mineral deposit, it may not be relied upon to establish the *existence* of that deposit. The showing thus far made with respect to the claims in question, allowing maximum credibility to appellants' factual allegations, would require reliance upon inference to establish the existence of an ore body as well as its quantity and quality, and all that appellants have shown is a possibility that valuable mineral deposits may exist within the limits of the claims (emphasis in original).

The reason for accepting less than demonstrated profitability as a condition to patentability is to encourage the investment of capital in the development of mineral resources.[6] No doubt it would further that purpose to offer the incentive of patentability to "prudent" prospectors as well as "prudent" mine developers. But there are other considerations. A patent passes ownership of public lands into private hands. So irrevocable a diminution of the public domain should be attended by substantial assurance that there will be a compensating public gain in the form of an increased supply of available mineral resources. The requirement that actual discovery of a valuable mineral deposit be demonstrated gives weight to this consideration.

Denial of a patent does not bar a claimant from continuing the search for a valuable mineral deposit; it only withholds passage of title until that discovery is made.[7]

Affirmed.

---

[6] As stated in Castle v. Womble, 19 Interior Dec. 455, 457 (1894): to hold otherwise would tend to make of little avail, if not entirely nugatory, that provision of the law whereby "all valuable mineral deposits in lands belonging to the United States . . . are . . . declared to be free and open to exploration and purchase." For, if as soon as minerals are shown to exist, and at any time during exploration, before the returns become remunerative, the lands are to be subject to other disposition, few would be found willing to risk time and capital in the attempt to bring to light and make available the mineral wealth, which lies concealed in the bowels of the earth, as Congress obviously must have intended the explorers should have proper opportunity to do.

[7] In closing the opinion for the Department on appeal, the Assistant Solicitor stated: One other point merits some comment. Since the decision in United States v. Kenneth F. and George A. Carlile, 67 I.D. 417 (1960), the Department has consistently held that the rejection of an application for patent to a mining claim is necessarily a determination that the claim is invalid. This does not necessarily limit a mining claimant in his right to continue to explore for minerals. If the land is still open to mining entry, as it appears to be here, the claimant is free to relocate his claims and proceed with his efforts to find a valuable mineral deposit. The determination that appellants' claims are invalid is simply a finding that no rights have been initiated against the United States by virtue of the appellants' location of the claims and that, if any rights are to be obtained, they must be obtained through a discovery made subsequent to the determination that the existing claims are not valid. Such rights, of course, must be initiated in accordance with the terms and limitations now governing the location of mining claims.

NOTES

1. Why does the court in *Barton* only discuss the *Castle v. Womble* prudent man rule and not the marketability rule? Is the marketability rule useful when the issue is the existence of mineralization within a claim rather than the value and extent of that mineralization?

2. What sort of evidence should a mining claimant and his attorney be prepared to introduce to establish that a discovery has been made? In *Thomas v. Morton,* 408 F. Supp. 1361 (D. Ariz. 1976) the claimant's expert witness, when asked whether a prudent person would be justified in expending time and money with the reasonable expectation of developing a paying mine, testified "Oh, I would think there is definitely enough value shown there to justify a man who is in the business to spend time and money and effort *in further exploration, yes.*" Not surprisingly, the claimant lost his case.

3. The decision in the principal case turned on the distinction between exploration and development. In *Santa Fe R.R. Co. v. United States,* 378 F. 2d 72 (7th Cir. 1962), the issue was whether certain expenses incurred by Santa Fe were for "exploration" or "development" within the meaning of the Internal Revenue Code. The court defined the terms as follows:

> [T]he development of a mine or deposit is commonly understood by author-ities in the mining field to mean activity necessary to make a deposit accessible to mining. . . . The techniques employed in development—strip-ping the overburden and constructing means for its removal (in the case of open pit mining), or sinking shafts and installing raises, tracks, pumps, et cetera (in the case of underground mining)—are all designed to prepare the deposit for extraction or exploitation. The development of a mine or deposit is to be distinguished from exploration, which the mining industry generally defines as the activity undertaken to ascertain the existence, location, extent or quality of a mineral deposit. The techniques employed in exploration— drilling, trenching, pitting, sampling, assaying, et cetera—are calculated to achieve these objectives.

Is the distinction drawn between development and exploration in the principal case consistent with *Santa Fe R.R. Co.?* Is the distinction drawn between development and exploration in *Santa Fe R.R. Co.* a workable one?

ROBERTS V. MORTON
549 F.2d 158 (10th Cir. 1976)

Before HOLLOWAY, McWILLIAMS and DOYLE, Circuit Judges.
HOLLOWAY, Circuit Judge.

This appeal is taken from a decision of the district court, 389 F.Supp. 87, which sustained the ruling of the Interior Board of Land Appeals, 11 IBLA 53, affirming the administrative law judge's decision that 2,910 unpatented placer mining claims of the plaintiffs-appellants are null and void. *United States v. Zweifel,* Colorado Contest No. 441 (C.C. No. 441). We agree with the district court's conclusions, and affirm.

The decisions cited above amply state the facts. We will only outline the background briefly as a premise for treating the appellate contentions before us.

These proceedings began when the United States filed a complaint in 1968 contesting the validity of these 2,910 unpatented placer mining claims covering portions of the Green River Formation in Rio Blanco, Garfield and Moffat Counties of Western Colorado. Most of these claims lie within the Piceance Creek Basin which contains vast deposits of oil shale. Oil shale has not been locatable under the mining laws since the passage of the Mineral Leasing Act of 1920.

The claims were filed between May, 1966 and February 1967 (C.C. No. 441, p. 2) for the dawsonite and other alumina-bearing compounds. Alumina is the source compound for aluminum. The dawsonite and other alumina-bearing compounds are commingled with the oil shale host rock. (C.C. No. 441, p. 32).

The administrative law judge found that certain of the claims were void *ab initio* since they had been filed on lands withdrawn for reclamation purposes by Public Land Order 2632, 25 Fed. Reg. 2572 (March 17, 1962) (Tr. 53-54). He also dismissed the complaint as to other claims previously patented by the United States without mineral reservation. (Tr. 53).

In addition, the administrative law judge concluded that all the remaining mining claims were null and void based on findings: (1) that the claimants failed to locate their claims in accordance with the applicable mining laws and regulations, 30 U.S.C. §§ 22 and 28; 43 C.F.R. § 3401.1 (now § 3831.1); Colorado Revised Statutes (C.R.S.) § 92-22-12 (1963), [now C.R.S. § 34-43-112 (1973)]; and (2) that the claimants did not sustain their burden of showing the discovery of a valuable mineral deposit within the limits of each claim within the meaning of the mining laws. 30 U.S.C. §§ 22 and 23. The claimants appealed this decision to the Interior Board of Land Appeals. The Board reviewed the record and upheld the decision of the administrative law judge. The instant suit was then brought in the district court seeking declaratory and injunctive relief and to set aside the final administrative order.

Defendants moved for summary judgment and dismissal on the pleadings. Plaintiffs also moved for summary judgment, with a supporting affidavit. The court considered the propriety of summary judgment on review of an administrative record in light of *Nickol v. United States*, 501 F.2d 1389 (10th Cir.). With the pleadings, motions, briefs and the administrative record before it, the district court concluded that the case was "ripe for final disposition upon the entry of appropriate findings of fact and conclusions of law by this Court." *Roberts v. Morton, supra,* 389 F. Supp. at 90.

Those findings and conclusions followed in the court's written opinion, order and judgment which sustained the agency's rulings and dismissed this action with prejudice. This appeal now challenges both the procedure followed by the court and its rulings sustaining the two conclusions on which the claims were held void.

. . . .

Third, plaintiffs challenge the findings that they did not discover a valuable mineral in compliance with the mining laws. They argue that their claims in Piceance Creek Basin consist of valuable minerals—dawsonite, nachcolite, dolomite, ferroan; that the claims contain other alumina bearing compounds such as gibbsite, analcite and nordstrandite; that marketability is not required to be shown as to intrinsically valuable minerals such as gold, silver, alumina, uranium, etc.; and that it is sufficient as to them to show a general market, which was done for alumina (Reply Brief for Appellants, 12-16, 23).

The statute making mineral deposits in Government lands open to exploration and purchase refers only to "all valuable mineral deposits." 30 U.S.C.A. § 22. In interpreting the mining laws the Secretary has used a "prudent-man test" formulated in *Castle v. Womble*, 19 L.D. 455, 457 (1894):

Where minerals have been found and the evidence is of such a character that a person of ordinary prudence would be justified in the further expenditure of his labor and means, with a reasonable prospect of success, in developing a valuable mine, the requirements of the statute are met.

The Supreme Court has approved the test for some time. See *United States v. Coleman*, 390 U.S. 599, 602, 88 S.Ct. 1327, 20 L.Ed.2d 170, and cases there cited.

In the *Coleman* case the Court sustained a determination by the Secretary that quartzite deposits did not qualify under the statute because the stone could not be marketed at a profit. This refinement, the marketability test, was commended. And the Court said that ". . . profitability is an important consideration in applying the prudent-man test. . . ." *Ibid.*

Plaintiffs argue that they have shown the presence of alumina, an intrinsically valuable mineral, and that *Coleman* recognizes that this showing satisfied the statute. Reliance is placed on this statement in *Coleman, supra* at 603, 88 S.Ct. at 1331:

While it is true that the marketablity test is usually the critical factor in cases involving non-metallic minerals of widespread occurrence, this is accounted for by the perfectly natural reason that precious metals which are in small supply and for which there is a great demand, sell at a price so high as to leave little room for doubt that they can be extracted and marketed at a profit.

We agree, however, with the district court's view that marketability at a profit remains an essential consideration in this case. We are persuaded that the Court's statement in *Coleman*, cited above, does not mean that marketability has no relevance where a discovery even of a precious metal is involved. See *Converse v. Udall*, 399 F.2d 616, 621 (9th Cir.). It is still proper here that the Secretary "take into account the economics of the situation." *Id.* at 622.

We are persuaded that the findings against plaintiffs are amply supported. There was expert Government testimony from Messrs. Jinks and Smith that alumina could not be profitably extracted at the time from deposits in the oil shale in the Basin (Tr. 499-507; 591-92; 628-29). Mr. Smith believed that a commercially feasible method can be developed in the future for extracting alumina from the compounds found in the shale, but he was not sure when such a process could be developed (Tr. 637-39, 694). And the plaintiffs' witness, Dr. Stevenson, testified that while alumina had been extracted from dawsonite in laboratory experiments, it was beyond his field whether one of the processes could be used commercially (Tr. 819-820).

Data cited by plaintiffs in publications after the hearings are similarly unpersuasive. They were based on studies and economic conditions several years after the location of these claims (See Plaintiffs' Ex. 3, Appendix). The required showing by a claimant, however, is that at the time of discovery there is a market sufficiently profitable to attract the efforts of a person of ordinary prudence. *Barrows v. Hickel*, 447 F.2d 80, 83 (9th Cir.).

Again considering the record as a whole we are satisfied that the findings against plaintiffs are supported by substantial evidence in the administrative record. We sustain the ruling that the claims were void for failure to establish discovery of minerals satisfying the marketability test.

Last, we will treat several remaining claims of error unrelated to the major issues we have covered:

Plaintiffs argue that the contest proceeding brought by the Government was barred by the doctrine of laches (Brief for Appellants, 4). It was argued to the Interior Board of Land Appeals that the Government should have acted by earlier proceedings when it learned that vast numbers of location notices were being filed in the Basin and that failure to do so precluded the later proceedings. The argument was rejected by the Board (11 IBLA at 97-98).

No further particulars are shown going to lack of diligence by the Government nor of any prejudice to plaintiffs resulting from delay in commencement of the contest proceeding. The administrative record shows that the claims in question were filed beginning in May, 1966 and extending until February, 1967, and that the contest proceeding was not commenced until issuance of a complaint dated August 7, 1968 (C.C.No. 441, 1-2).

We start with the general rule that ". . . the United States is not bound by state statutes of limitation or subject to the defense of laches in enforcing its rights." *United States v. Summerlin,* 310 U.S. 414, 416, 60 S.Ct. 1019, 1020, 84 L.Ed. 1283; *Board of Commissioners v. United States,* 308 U.S. 343, 351, 60 S.Ct. 285, 84 L.Ed. 313. But even assuming some relaxation of these strict rules might be developing, there are no circumstances shown here to support the defense of laches. It is an affirmative defense requiring a showing of lack of diligence by a plaintiff and prejudice to the defendant. *Costello v. United States,* 365 U.S. 265, 282, 81 S.Ct. 534, 5 L.Ed.2d 551; *Bradley v. Laird,* 449 F.2d 898, 902 (10th Cir.). We cannot say the Government was precluded from asserting its rights here. See *United States v. California,* 332 U.S. 19, 39-40, 67 S.Ct. 1658, 91 L.Ed. 1889.

. . . .

Additional arguments of administrative error seem insubstantial to us and require no further discussion. We agree with the decision of the district court upholding the administrative rulings and the judgment is

AFFIRMED.

NOTES

1. In the principal case the Board holds that present marketability must be shown even for intrinsically valuable minerals. The Board apparently concluded that possible technological advances that might reduce the cost of extracting aluminum from oil shale deposits were too speculative to consider. Would the possibility of future changes in the price of aluminum also be too speculative to consider in applying the marketability rule? Keep in mind that mineral prices are subject to wide and volatile price swings.

2. "'Present Marketability' has never encompassed the examination of either cost or price factors as of a specific, finite moment of time, without reference to other economic factors. Rather, the question of whether something is 'presently marketable at a profit' simply means that a mining claimant must show that, as a present fact, considering historic cost and price factors and assuming that they will continue, there is a reasonable likelihood of success that a paying mine can be developed. For example, if a claimant has located a deposit of gold which can be mined at a profit, if the price of gold is $500 an ounce, and the evidence is such that there is a reasonable likelihood of sufficient quantity and quality to justify development, that claim can be deemed valid despite the fact that on any specific day gold may be selling for $420 an ounce. This is so because a selling price of $500 an ounce for gold is both within the historic range and expectations of it reaching that level again can be justified as a present matter." *In Re Pacific Coast Molybdenum*, 90 I.D. 352, 360 (1983).

UNITED STATES V. DENISON
71 I.D. 144 (1964)

[footnotes omitted]

. . . .

Separate contest proceedings initiated by the United States Forest Service, Department of Agriculture, were brought against certain lode mining claims located in Coconino County, Arizona, within either the Coconino or Sitgreaves National Forests, following the filing of mineral patent applications for the claims by the locators or their successors in interest. In all the proceedings, the Forest Service charged basically that the claims were invalid because no valid discovery, within the meaning of the mining laws, existed on the claims, and because the lands were nonmineral in character. . . .

. . . .

All of the claims in these proceedings were located for, and the claimants allege them all to be valuable for, manganese. The Shoup, Smith, and Beecroft claims lie in adjoining townships and the Denison claims are about 40 miles distant. In all of these cases, the Forest Service has raised a central issue as to what criteria should be applied to determine whether therer has been a valid discovery. It contends that the Bureau improperly failed to consider present economic conditions in determining whether the mineral deposits on the claims are "valuable" within the meaning of the mining laws and that the Bureau improperly relied only on past economic conditions and hypothetical possibilities in the future. It contends that there is no general market in this country for magnanese of the quality and quantity that may be found on these claims, that market conditions are depressed due to the availability of imported magnanese of a much higher quality at cheaper prices and the termination of the United States Government's stockpiling program in manganese, with manganese currently being declared in excess quantities in the stockpiles.

The mining claimants object to these contentions. Generally, the claimants allege that manganese is a mineral having intrinsic value and that therefore marketability need not be shown, citing a Solicitor's opinion of September 20, 1962 (69 I.D. 145), and that the test of discovery as enunciated in the leading case of *Castle v. Womble,* 19 L.D. 455, 457 (1894), requires only that a prudent man have a reasonable prospect of success in developing a "valuable" mine and not a "profitable" mine, as contended by the Forest Service.

Although in these cases there does appear to be a diversity in the quality and quantity of manganese present on the claims, which may to a certain extent account for the differences in the rulings of the hearing examiners and the Assistant Director in these cases, there also appears to be some inconsistency in the application of the prudent man test to these cases. Because of the importance of the central issue raised by the Forest Service and similarities in these cases as to the nature of the minerals involved, their deposition, and their commercial usage and marketability, and because several of the witnesses testified in two or more of the hearings, these cases have been consolidated for consideration of the appeals.

The prudent man test, [was] originally stated in *Castle v. Womble, . . .*

This test has been quoted or cited with approval by the United States Supreme Court in *Chrisman v. Miller,* 197 U.S. 313, 322 (1905), and other cases, most recently in *Best v. Homboldt Placer Mining Co.,* 371 U.S. 334, 335 (1963).

After establishment of the basic rule on discovery, the Department was confronted with situations in which applications for mineral patent were filed for claims which might previously have been valuable for gold but which were not shown to be valuable for gold at the time of the applications for patent. In *United States v. Margherita Logomarcini,* 60 I.D. 371 (1949), the Department held that before a patent can be issued it must be shown as a present fact that the claim is valuable for minerals. The department held to the same effect in *United States v. Lem A. and Elizabeth D. Houston,* 66 I.D. 161 (1959), pointing out that although a mining claimant need not apply for a patent to his claim he exposes himself to chance that at some time the conditions on his claim will no longer support the issuance of a patent. Both the *Logomarcini* and the *Houston* decisions were cited for these propositions by the Supreme Court in *Best v. Homboldt Placer Mining Co., supra* at 336.

In the *Houston* case, the Department cited as precedent not only the *Logomarcini* case but also the cases of *United States v. Pumice Sales Corporation,* A-27578 (July 28, 1958), and *United States v. Alonzo A. Adams,* A-27364 (July 1, 1957). The *Pumice* case, unlike the others, involved mining claims located for a mineral of widespread occurrence, pumice. The validity of such claims depends upon an affirmative showing of a present demand or market for the mineral. *Foster v. Seaton,* 271 F.2d 836 (D.C. Cir. 1959). In the *Pumice* case it was shown that pumice from one of the claims had been sold and used for commercial purposes in the past but that operations were then shut down and no present demand existed for the pumice. The Department held that although the claims may have been valid in the past they had become invalid for lack of a discovery. The *Pumice* case did not involve applications for patent.

The *Adams* case involved applications for patent to gold placer claims. The Department held the claims to be null and void for the reason that the evidence showed that the gold values on the claims were so low in comparison to the cost of operations required to recover the gold that a prudent man would not be justified in the further expenditure of labor and means with a reasonable prospect of developing a valuable mine. The Department rejected the claimant's contention that more weight should have been given to the evidence of values recovered in the past, saying that it was not sufficient that a valuable discovery may have been made in the past, citing the *Logomarcini* case.

The *Adams* decision was challenged in court but sustained in *Alonzo A. Adams v. United States,* 318 F.2d 861 (9th Cir. 1963). The court expressly affirmed the ruling in the *Logomarcini* case.

More recently the same court has rendered another decision which appears to be decisive of the central issue presented in the appeals under consideration. In *Mulken v. Hammitt,* 326 F.2d 896 (1964), the court sustained a decision of the Department holding two mining claims null and void for lack of a valid discovery of gypsum or silica. . . . The claims, which were located on December 23, 1922, were contested in 1944 and a hearing was held in 1957. The issue was whether during the period from December 23, 1922, to May 15, 1926, or between August 31, 1928, and May 3, 1929, there had been a valid discovery on the claims. The two periods of time were the only times in which the land in the claims was open to mining location. The evidence at the hearing was largely to the effect that at the time of the hearing there was no market for the minerals in the claims. There was only slight evidence as to marketability prior to May 3, 1929. The Department held the claims to be null and void for lack of a showing of marketability during the two periods of time when the land was open to location.

In the ensuing litigation, the claimant contended that conditions in the 1957 period, when the hearing was held, had no bearing on the issue of discovery; that the testimony as to such conditions was irrelevant; and that the only question was whether, in 1922 and the years immediately thereafter, the situation satisfied the *Castle v. Womble* test. The court rejected the contention, saying—

> The appellant's contention is erroneous. This court, in the recent case of *Adams v. United States,* 318 F.2d 861, dealt with this very question, and held that even though the mining claim there in litigation would, at one time, have satisfied the test, nevertheless the Government rightfully denied a patent to the claimant since, *because of changed economic conditions,* the claim did not *presently* satisfy the test. The fact that in *Adams* the attack was upon the Government's refusal to issue a patent, while in the instant case the Government was seeking to nullify the appellant's claim as to which he had never requested or received a patent, does not distinguish the *Adams* case from the instant one. The problem in both cases is whether the public lands of the United States should be perpetually incumbered and occupied by a private occupant just because, at one time, he had there a valuable mine which has now been completely worked out; or because he had on his location a mineral which, in the then practice of the building industry, had a market, but which, on account of a change in building practice, *no longer has a market or a reasonable prospect of a future market;* or because, at the time of his discovery, transportation facilities were

available which made exploitation feasible, which facilities are no longer available. (P.898; italics added.)

The *Mulken* case, then, is clear authority for the proposition that although a mining claim may once have been valid because it contained a valuable deposit of mineral the claim will become invalid if the mineral deposit loses its value because of changes in economic conditions, such as the loss of a market or transportation facilities. That the ruling is not confined to instances involving minerals of common occurrence, such as pumice, is plain from the court's statement that the *Adams* case decided the same question. That case, of course, dealt with gold.

In the *Adams* case, also, the court ruled that in applying the prudent man rule "evidence as to the cost of extracting the mineral is relevant" and that the Department properly considered evidence on that point with respect to the Adams claims. 318 F.2d at 870. And, years earlier, the Supreme Court had indicated that "the cost of mining, transportation and reduction" was relevant to determining whether a valid discovery had been made. *Cole v. Ralph,* 252 U.S. 286, 299 (1920). That case, too, concerned claims located for gold.

Thus, the economic conditions which may be considered in determining whether a valuable mineral deposit has been discovered include such factors as the cost of mining, transporting, and processing the mineral and the existence of a market for the mineral, whether it be deemed one of intrinsic value, such as gold, or one of common occurrence, such as pumice.

In this connection, note should be taken of references by the parties to the Solicitor's opinion of September 20, 1962, *supra* on the "Marketability Rule" as applied to the law of discovery. The claimants purport to find comfort in the statement in the opinion that

An intrinsically valuable mineral by its very nature is deemed marketable, and therefore merely showing the nature of the mineral usually meets the test of marketability. 69 I.D. at 146.

Claimants state that manganese is an intrinsically valuable mineral and therefore is marketable. This overlooks the fact, however, that the opinion carefully states that showing the mineral discovered to be an intrinsically valuable one only *"usually* meets the test of marketability" (italics added). The opinion otherwise makes it amply clear that the marketability test

. . . is in reality applied to all minerals, although it is often mistakenly said to be applied solely to nonmetallic minerals of wide occurrence. *Id.*

Thus, it is entirely proper to require the holder of a claim containing a low grade of an intrinsically valuable mineral to show that there is a market or demand for the mineral in the claim.

What does the application of these rules to the four cases under consideration show?

First, the evidence developed at the respective hearings seems to show that deposits of manganese exist on the claims in question and that some of the manganese is of a grade that was mined and sold in the past from patented manganese claims in the same area and from some of the contested claims themselves. The quantity of such manganese in each claim is not clearly established and it is questionable to what extent minable deposits exist on the claims.

Second, the evidence establishes that, except possibly in the case of the Beecroft claim, all sales of manganese were made during World War II and the post-war period to August 5, 1959, when a Government carlot buying program was in effect. Upon termination of the Government program on August 5, 1959, sales of manganese in the area of the claims, and indeed, of practically all domestically produced manganese, ceased. This apparently was caused by a break in the price of manganese from around $90 per ton to $40—$50 per ton.

Third, up to the time of the respective hearings (the last one being held on March 1, 1963, in the Beecroft case), no further sales of domestic manganese had been made, except possibly in the case of some captive mines owned by steel companies, because no profit could be realized from sales. The market for manganese has been supplied by imported manganese of the same or higher grade.

Fourth, the claims are being held in reserve with the hope and expectation that some day the market will return. However, little basis has been given for this hope or expectation.

. . . .

Considering the evidence as a whole, it seems inescapable that what sales of manganese have been made from some of the claims and from other patented claims in the area were made during a period of national emergency and of a Government price support program which ended, on August 5, 1959, and that the manganese on the claims has had no market since that date because of a 50 percent reduction in the market price which makes it unprofitable to mine and sell domestic manganese today. Outside of some speculation about development of new processes for utilizing low grade manganese economically, there is no evidentiary basis for any reasonable expectation that in the reasonably near future high price levels will return which will make it economic to mine the claims. The fact is that manganese has not been sold from the area in recent years and there is no evidence that sales may reasonably be expected in the future.

In the circumstances, the ruling in the *Mulkern* case is clearly applicable and it must be concluded that the contested claims are null and void for lack of a present discovery of valuable mineral deposits due to changed economic conditions.

. . . .

NOTES

1. The principal case was overruled in *Denison v. Udall,* 248 F.Supp. 942 (D. Ariz. 1965). The district court found for the mining claimants on the grounds that (1) "[t]here was little or no proof adduced that a reasonable man might *not* expect the market to return, and a substantial amount to indicate that he could" (at 944), and (2) that the marketability rule did not apply to intrinsically valuable minerals. In light of *Coleman* and its progeny, do you think the *Denison* decision in the Interior Department or in the District Court contains the more accurate expression of the law?

2. Some minerals, gold for example, are characterized by widely fluctuating market prices. Assume that all of the costs associated with extracting and marketing gold from a particular claim total $425. Does *Coleman* require the conclusion that a locator would have a valid discovery when gold is selling for $600 per ounce, would lose his discovery a month later if the price fell to $400 per ounce, and would regain his discovery if the price of gold subsequently jumped to $800? Would adoption of a rule that compelled such a result be good public policy?

3. The United States is dependent on foreign sources for some essential minerals. Should the possibility of a disruption of supply be taken into account in determining whether the marketability test has been satisfied as to those minerals? Would it make any difference to your answer if the government of the source country were unstable and subject to being ousted by a government that once in power would likely be hostile to the United States? Are the courts well suited to making the kinds of determinations that would be required if these kinds of factors were taken into account?

4. Should an otherwise profitable claim be deemed to fail the marketability test only because a temporary disruption, for example, the use of higher cost alternative transportation during a railroad strike, has the effect of increasing costs above sales price?

ANDRUS V. SHELL OIL CO.
446 U.S. 657 (1980)

Mr. CHIEF JUSTICE BURGER delivered the opinion of the Court.

The general mining law of 1872, 47 Stat. 437, as amended, 30 U.S.C. §§ 22 *et seq.,* provides that citizens may enter and explore the public domain, and search for minerals; if they discover "valuable mineral deposits," they may obtain title to the land on which such deposits are located.[1] In 1920 Congress altered this program with the enactment of the Mineral Leasing Act. 30 U.S.C. § 181 *et seq.* The Act withdrew oil shale and several other minerals from the general mining law and provided that thereafter these minerals would be subject

---

[1] Discovery of a "valuable mineral" is not the only prerequisite of patentability. The mining law also provides that until a patent is issued a claimant must perform $100 worth of labor or make $100 of improvements on his claim during each year and that a patent may issue only on a showing that the claimant has expended a total of $500 on the claim. 30 U.S.C. §§ 28,29. See *Hickel v. Oil Shale Corp.,* 400 U.S. 48 (1970). In addition, a claim "must be distinctly marked on the ground so that its boundaries can be readily traced." 30 U.S.C. § 28; *Kendall v. San Juan Silver Mining Co.,* 144 U.S. 658 (1982). If the requirements of the mining law are satisfied, the land may be patented for $2.50 per acre. 30 U.S.C. § 37. There is no deadline within which a locator must file for patent, though to satisfy the discovery requirement the claimant must show the existence of "valuable mineral deposits" both at the time of location and at the time of the determination. *Barrows v. Hickel,* 447 F.2d 80, 82 (CA9 1971).

to disposition only through leases. A savings clause, however, preserved "valid claims existent at date of the passage of this Act and thereafter maintained in compliance with the laws under which initiated, which claims may be perfected under such laws, including discovery."[2]

The question presented is whether oil shale deposits located prior to the 1920 Act are "valuable mineral deposits" patentable under the savings clause of the Act.

I

The action involves two groups of oil shale claims located by claimants on public lands in Garfield County, Colo., prior to the enactment of the Mineral Leasing Act.[3] The first group of claims, designated Mountain Boys Nos. 6 and 7, was located in 1918. In 1920 a business trust purchased the claims for $25,000, and in 1924 an application for patent was filed with the Department of the Interior. Some 20 years later, after extended investigative and adjudicatory proceedings, the patent was rejected "without prejudice" on the ground that it was not then vigorously pursued. In 1958 Frank W. Winegar acquired the claims and filed a new patent application. In 1964, Winegar conveyed his interests in the claims to respondent Shell Oil Company.

The second group of claims, known as Harold Shoup Nos. 1-4, was located in 1917. In 1923, the claims were acquired by Karl C. Schuyler who in 1933 bequeathed them to his surviving spouse. In 1960, Mrs. Schuyler incorporated respondent D. A. Shale, Inc., and transferred title to the claims to the corporation. Three months later, the corporation filed patent applications.

In 1964, the Department issued administrative complaints alleging that the Mountain Boys claims and the Shoup claims were invalid. The complaints alleged, *inter alia,* that oil shale was not a "valuable mineral" prior to the enactment of the 1920 Mineral Leasing Act.

The complaints were consolidated and tried to a hearing examiner who in 1970 ruled the claims valid. The hearing examiner observed that under established case law the test for determining a "valuable mineral deposit" was whether the deposit was one justifying present expenditures with a reasonable prospect of developing a profitable mine. See *United States v. Coleman,* 390 U.S. 599 (1968); *Castle v. Womble,* 19 L.D. 455 (1894).[4] He then reviewed the

---

[2] The savings clause is contained in § 37 of the Act, 30 U.S.C. § 193, which provides in full: "The deposits of coal, phosphate, sodium, oil, oil shale, and gas, herein referred to, in lands valuable for such minerals, including lands and deposits in Lander, Wyoming, coal entries numbered 18 to 49, inclusive, shall be subject to disposition only in the form and manner provided in this chapter, except as to valid claims existent on February 25, 1920, and thereafter maintained in compliance with the laws under which initiated, which claims may be perfected under such laws, including discovery."

[3] Oil shale is a sedimentary rock containing an organic material called kerogen which, upon destructive distillation, produces a substantial amount of oil.

[4] In *Chrisman v. Miller,* 197 U.S. 313 (1905), this Court approved the Department of Interior's "prudent-man test" under which discovery of a "valuable mineral deposit" requires proof of a deposit of such character that "a person of ordinary prudence would be justified in the further expenditure of his labor and means, with a reasonable prospect of success, in developing a valuable mine." *Castle v. Womble,* 19 L.D. at 457. Accord, *Best v. Humboldt Placer Mining Co.,* 371 U.S. 334, 335-336 (1963); *Cameron v. United States,* 252 U.S. 450, 459 (1920). In *United*

history of oil shale operations in this country and found that every attempted operation had failed to show profitable production. On the basis of this finding and other evidence showing commerical infeasibility, the hearing examiner reasoned that "[i]f this were a case of first impression," oil shale would fail the "valuable mineral deposit" test. However, he deemed himself bound by the Department's contrary decision in *Freeman v. Summers,* 52 L.D. 201 (1927). There, the Secretary had written:

> "While at the present time there has been no considerable production of oil shales, due to the fact that abundant quantities of oil have been pro-duced more cheaply from wells, *there is no possible doubt of its value and of the fact that it constitutes an enormously valuable resource for future use by the American people.*
>
> "It is not necessary, in order to constitute a valid discovery under the general mining laws sufficient to support an application for patent, that the mineral *in its present situation* can be immediately disposed of at a profit."
>
> *Id.,* at 206. (Emphasis added.)

The hearing examiner ruled that *Freeman v. Summers* compelled the conclusion that oil shale is a valuable mineral subject to appropriation under the mining laws, and he upheld the Mountain Boys and Shoup claims as valid and patentable.

The Board of Land Appeals reversed. Adopting the findings of the hearing examiner, the Board concluded that oil shale claims located prior to 1920 failed the test of value because at the time of location there did not appear "as a *present* fact . . . a reasonable prospect of success in developing an operating mine that would yield a reasonable profit." (Emphasis in original.) The Board recognized that this conclusion was at odds with prior departmental precedent, and particu-larly with *Freeman v. Summers;* but it rejected that precedent as inconsistent with the general mining law and therefore unsound. The Board then considered whether its newly enunciated interpretation should be given only prospective effect. It found that respondents' reliance on prior rulings was minimal and that the Department's responsibility as trustee of public lands required it to correct a plainly erroneous decision.[5] Accordingly, it ruled that its new interpretation applied to the Mountain Boys and Shoup claims, and that those claims were invalid.

Respondents appealed the Board's ruling to the United States District Court for the District of Colorado. The District Court agreed with the Board that by not requiring proof of "present marketability" the decision in *Freeman v. Summers* had liberalized the traditional valuable mineral test. But it found that Congress in

---

States v. Coleman, the Court approved the Department's marketability test whether a mineral can be "extracted, removed and marketed at a profit"—deeming it a logical complement of the prudent-man standard.

5 The Board observed that "[a]lthough Shell . . . expended some $18,780 in perfecting title to and preparing patent application for the Mountain Boy claims before 1964, it did not purchase [the claims] from Frank Winegar for $30,000 [until] after initiation of the contest proceedings." And it found no evidence that D. A. Shale, Inc., or its predecessors had invested "more than a minimal amount" in the purchase of the Shoup claims in reliance on the *Freeman* decision.

1931 and again in 1956 had considered the patentability of oil shale and had implicity "ratified" that liberalized rule. Alternatively, the District Court concluded that the Department was estopped now for departing from the *Freeman* standard which investors had "relied upon . . . for the past half-century." *Shell Oil v. Kleppe,* 426 F.Supp. 894, 907 (1977). On these grounds, it reversed the Board's ruling and held that the claims at issue were valid.

The Court of Appeals for the Tenth Circuit affirmed. 591 F.2d 597 (1979). It agreed with the District Court that the "different treatment afforded all oil shale claims as to the 'valuable mineral deposit' element of a location became a part of the general mining laws by reason of its adoption and approval by both Houses of Congress" in the years after 1920. *Id.,* at 604. And it held that the Department now must adhere to the *Freeman* rule. We granted certiorari because of the importance of the question to the management of the public lands. 444 U.S. 822 (1979). We affirm.

II

The legislative history of the 1920 Mineral Leasing Act shows that Congress did not consider "present marketability" a prerequiste to the patentability of oil shale.[6] In the extensive hearings and debates that preceded the passage of the 1920 Act, there is no intimation that Congress contemplated such a requirement; indeed, the contrary appears. During the 1919 floor debates in the House of Representatives, an amendment was proposed which would have substituted the phrase "deposits in paying quantities" for "valuable mineral." That amendment, however, was promptly withdrawn after Mr. Sinott, the House floor manager, voiced his objection to the change:

"Mr. SINOTT. That language was put in with a great deal of consideration and we would not like to change from 'valuable' to 'paying.' *There is quite a distinction.* We are in line with the decisions of the courts as to what is a discovery, and I think that it would be a very dangerous matter to experiment with this language at this time." 58 Cong.Rec. 7537 (1919) (emphasis added).

An examination of the relevant decisions at the time underscores the point. Those decisions are clear in rejecting a requirement that a miner must "demonstrat[e] that the vein . . . would pay all the expenses of removing, extracting, crushing, and reducing the ore and leave a profit to the owner," *Book v. Justice Mining Co.,* 58 F. 106, 124 (CC Nev. 1893), and in holding that "it is enough if the vein or deposit 'has a present *or prospective* commercial value.' " *Madison v. Octave Oil Co.,* 154 Cal. 768, 772, 99 P. 176, 178 (1908) (emphasis added).

---

[6] Congress was aware that there was then no commercially feasible method for extracting oil from oil shale. The 1918 report of the House Committee on the Public Lands, for example, had emphasized that "no commercial quantity or any appreciable amount of shale oil has ever been produced in this country, nor any standardized process of production has yet been evolved or recommended or agreed upon in this country by the Bureau of Mines or anyone else, and it has not yet been demonstrated that the oil-shale industry can be made commercially profitable. . . ." H.R.Rep.No. 563, 65th Cong., 2d Sess., 18 (1918). See also 58 Cong.Rec. 4271, 4279 (1919) (remarks of Sen. Smoot); Hearings on H.R. 3232 and S. 2812 before the House Committee on the Public Lands, 65th Cong., 2d Sess., 811, 890, 1257 (1918) (hereafter Hearings).

Accord, *Cascaden v. Bartolis,* 146 F. 739 (CA9 1906); *United States v. Ohio Oil Co.,* 240 F. 996, 998 (Wyo.1916); *Montana Cent. R. Co. v. Migeon,* 68 F. 811, 814 (CC Mont.1895); *East Tintic Consolidated Mining Co.,* 43 L.D. 79, 81 (1914); 2 C. Lindley, American Law Relating to Mines and Mineral Lands § 336, pp. 768-769 (3 ed. 1914). See generally, Reeves, The Origin and Development of the Rules of Discovery, 8 Land & Water L. Rev. 1 (1973).

To be sure, prior to the passage of the 1920 Act, there existed considerable uncertainty as to whether oil shale was patentable.[7] That uncertainty, however, related to whether oil shale was a "mineral" under the mining law, and not to its "value." Similar doubts had arisen in the late 19th century in regard petroleum. Indeed, in 1896 the Secretary of Interior had held that petroleum claims were not subject to location under the mining laws, concluding that only lands "containing the more precious metals . . . gold, silver, cinnabar etc." were open to entry. *Union Oil Co.,* 23 L.D. 222, 227. The Secretary's decision was short-lived. In 1897, Congress enacted the Oil Placer Act authorization entry under the mining laws to public lands "containing petroleum or other mineral oils." Ch. 216, 29 Stat. 526. This legislation put to rest any doubt about oil as a mineral. But because oil shale, strictly speaking, contained kerogen and not oil, see n. 3, *supra,* its status remained problematic. See Reidy, Do Unpatented Oil Shale Claims Exist? 43 Denver L. J. 9, 12 (1966).

That this was the nature of the uncertainty surrounding the patentability of oil shale claims is evident from remarks made throughout the hearings and debates on the 1920 Act. In the 1918 hearings, Congressman Barnett, for example, explained:

"Mr. BARNETT. . . . If the department should contend that shale lands come within the meaning of the term 'oil lands' they must perforce, by the same argument, admit that they are placer lands within the meaning of the act of 1897.

"The Chairman. And patentable?

"Mr. BARNETT. And patentable under that act."

Hearings, at 918.

The enactment of the 1920 Mineral Leasing Act put an end to these doubts. By withdrawing "oil shale . . . in lands valuable for such minerals" from disposition under the general mining law, the Congress recognized—at least implicitly—that oil shale *had been* a locatable mineral. In effect, the 1920 Act did for oil shale what the 1897 Oil Placer Act had done for oil. And, as Congressman Barnett's ready answer demonstrates, once it was settled that oil shale was a mineral subject to location, and once a savings clause was in place preserving pre-

---

[7] Mr. John Fry, one of the Committee witnesses who represented the oil shale interests before Congress, was candid on that point:

"Mr. TAYLOR. There is a large amount of this shale land that has been located and is now held under the placer law. But none of it has yet gone to patent.

"The Chairman. Has one acre of this land withdrawn in Colorado been patented?

"Mr. FRY. No.

"The Chairman. So you do not know what the holding of the department will be?

"Mr. FRY. We do not." Hearings, at 912. See also *id.,* at 626, 873, 913, 918, 1240, 1256-1257.

existing claims, it was fully expected that such claims would be patentable. The fact that oil shale then had no commercial value simply was not perceived as an obstacle to that end.

III

Our conclusion that Congress in enacting the 1920 Mineral Leasing Act contemplated that pre-existing oil shale claims could satisfy the discovery requirement of the mining law is confirmed by actions taken in subsequent years by the Interior Department and the Congress.[8]

A

On May 10, 1920, less than three months after the Mineral Leasing Act became law, the Interior Department issued "Instructions" to its General Land Office authorizing that Office to begin adjudicating applications for patents for pre-1920 oil shale claims. The Instructions advised as follows:

> "Oil shale having been thus recognized by the Deparment and *by Congress* as a *mineral* deposit and a source of petroleum . . . lands valuable on account thereof *must be held to have been subject to valid location and appropriation under the placer mining laws,* to the same extent and subject to the same provisions and conditions as if valuable on account of oil and gas." 47 L.D. 548, 551 (1920) (emphasis added).

The first such patent was issued immediately thereafter. Five years later, the Department ruled that patentability was dependent upon the "character, extent, and mode of occurrence of the oil-shale deposits." *Dennis v. Utah,* 51 L.D. 229, 232 (1925). Present profitability was not mentioned as a relevant, let alone a critical, consideration.

In 1927, the Department decided *Freeman v. Summers,* 52 L.D. 201. The case arose out of a dispute between an oil shale claimant and an applicant for a homestead patent, and involved two distinct issues: (1) whether a finding of lean surface deposits warranted the geological inference that the claim contained rich "valuable" deposits below; and (2) whether present profitability was a prerequisite to patentability. Both issues were decided in favor of the oil-shale claimant: the geological inference was deemed sound and the fact that there was "no possible doubt . . . that [oil shale] constitutes an enormously valuable resource for future use by an American people" was ruled sufficient proof of "value." *Id.,* at 206.

For the next 33 years, *Freeman* was applied without deviation.[9] It was said

---

[8] This Court has observed that "the views of a subsequent Congress form a hazardous basis for inferring the intent of an earlier one." *United States v. Price,* 361 U.S. 304, 313 (1960). This sound admonition has guided several of our recent decisions. See, *e.g., TVA v. Hill,* 437 U.S. 153, 189-193 (1978); *SEC v. Sloan,* 436 U.S. 103, 119-122 (1978). Yet we cannot fail to note Chief Justice Marshall's dictum that "[w]here the mind labours to discover the design of the legislature, it seizes everything from which aid can be derived." *United States v. Fisher,* 2 Cranch 358, 386 (1805). In consequence, while arguments predicated upon subsequent congressional actions must be weighed with extreme care, they should not be rejected out of hand as a source that a court may consider in the search for legislative intent. See, e.g., *Seatrain Shipbuilding Co. v. Shell Oil Co.,* 444 U.S. 572, 596 (1980); *Red Lion Broadcasting Co. v. FCC,* 395 U.S. 367, 380-381 (1969); *NRLB v. Bell Aerospace Co.,* 416 U.S. 267, 274-275 (1974).

[9] See, *e.g., John M. Debevoise,* 67 I.D. 177, 180 (1960); *United States v. Strauss,* 59 I.D. 129,

that its application ensured that "valid rights [would] be protected and permitted to be perfected." Dept. of Interior Ann. Rep. 30 (1927). In all, 523 patents for 2,236 claims covering 349,088 acres were issued under the *Freeman* rule. This administrative practice, begun immediately upon the passage of the 1920 Act, "has peculiar weight [because] it involves a contemporaneous construction of [the] statute by the men charged wtih the responsibility of setting its machinery in motion," *Norwegian Nitrogen Co. v. United States,* 288 U.S. 294, 315 (1933). Accord, *e.g. United States v. National Assn. of Securities Dealers,* 422 U.S. 694, 719 (1975); *Udall v. Tallman,* 380 U.S. 1, 16 (1965). It provides strong support for the conclusion that Congress did not intend to impose a present marketability requirement on oil shale claims.

B

In 1930 and 1931 congressional committees revisited the 1920 Mineral Leasing Act and re-examined the patentability of oil-shale claims. Congressional interest in the subject was sparked in large measure by a series of newspaper articles charging that oil-shale lands had been "improvidently, erroneously and unlawfully, if not corruptly, transferred to individuals and private corporations." 74 Cong.Rec. 1079 (1930) (S. Res. 379). The articles were based upon accusations leveled at the Interior Department by Ralph S. Kelly, then the General Land Office Division Inspector in Denver. Kelly's criticism centered on the *Freeman v. Summers* decision. Fearing another "Teapot Dome" scandal, the Senate authorized the Committee on Public Lands to "inquire into . . . the alienation of oil shale lands."

The Senate Committee held seven days of hearings focusing almost exclusively on "the so-called Freeman-Summers case." Hearings on S. Res. 379 before the Senate Committee on Public Lands and Surveys, 71st Cong., 3d Sess., 2 (1931). At the outset of the hearings, the Committee was advised by E. C. Finney, Solicitor, Department of Interior, that 124 oil shale patents had been issued covering 175,000 acres of land and that 63 more patent applications were pending. Finney's statement prompted this interchange:

"Senator PITTMAN: Well, were the shales in those patented lands of commercial value?

"Mr. FINNEY: If you mean by that whether they could have been mined and disposed of at a profit at the time of the patent, or now, the answer is no.

. . . .

"Senator PITTMAN: So the Government has disposed of 175,000 acres in patents on lands which in your opinion there was no valid claim to in the locator?

Mr. FINNEY: No; that was not my opinion. I have not held in the world, that I know of, that you had to have an actual commercial discovery of any commodity that you could take out *and market at a profit.* On the contrary, the department has held that that is not the case. . . ." *Id.,* at 25 (emphasis added).

140-142 (1945); *Location of Oil Shale Placer Claims,* 52 L.D. 631 (1929); *Assessment Work on Oil-Shale Claims,* 52 L.D. 334 (1928); *Standard Shales Products Co.,* 52 L.D. 522 (1928); *James W. Bell,* 52 L.D. 197 (1927).

Later in the hearings Senator Walsh expressed his understanding of the impact of the *Freeman* decision:

"Senator WALSH: [It means] . . . that the prospector having found at the surface the layer containing any quantity of the mineral, that is of oil bearing shale or kerogen, that that would be a discovery in view of the beds down below of richer character.

"Mr. FINNEY: In this formation, yes sir; that is correct." *Id.,* at 138.

See also *id.,* at 22-23, 26, 163. The Senate Committee did not produce a report. But one month after the hearings were completed, Senator Nye, the Chairman of the Committee, wrote the Secretary of the Interior that he had " 'conferred with Senator Walsh and beg[ged] to advise that there is no reason why your Department should not proceed to final disposition of the pending applications for patents to oil shale lands in conformity with the law.' " App. 103. The patenting of oil shale lands under the standards enunciated in *Freeman* was at once resumed.

At virtually the same time, the House of Representatives commenced its own investigation into problems relating to oil shale patents. The House Committee, however, focused primarily on the question of assessment work—whether an oil shale claimant was required to perform $100 dollars work per year or forfeit his claim—and not on discovery. But the impact of the Freeman rule was not lost on the Committee:

"Mr. SWING. In furtherance of the policy of conservation, Mr. Secretary, in view of the fact that there has not been discovered, as I understand it, any practical economical method of extracting oil from the shale in competition with oil wells . . . would it not be proper public policy to withdraw all shale lands from private acquisition, since we are compelled to recognize, perforce, economic and fiscal conditions, that no one is going to make any beneficial use of the oil shale in the immediate future, but is simply putting it in cold storage as a speculative proposition?

"Secretary WILBUR: As a matter of conservation, what you say is true, but what we have to meet here is the fact that in the leasing act there was a clause to the effect that valid existing claims were not included, and so we are dealing with claims that are thought to be valid, and the question—

"Mr. SWING (interposing). I realize that, and I undertand the feeling of Congress, and I think generally the country, that in drawing the law we do not want to cut the ground from under the person who has initiated a right." Consolidated Hearings on Applications for Patent on Oil Shale Lands before the House Committee on Public Lands, 71 Cong., 3d Sess., 100 (1931).[10]

Congressman Swing's statement of the "feeling of Congress" comports

---

[10] At the conclusion of its hearings, the Committee recommended legislation placing a deadline on the filing of patent applications for oil shale claims and permitting an oil shale claimant to pay $100 a year to the Land Office in lieu of $100 in annual assessment work. Other aspects of the oil-shale patentability — including the question of discovery — were not addressed in the proposed legislation. H. R. Rep. No. 2537, 71st Cong., 3d Sess. (1931). The proposal was not enacted by the Congress.

with our reading of the 1920 statute and of congressional intent. To hold now that *Freeman* was wrongly decided would be wholly inconsistent with that intent. Moreover, it would require us to conclude that the Congress in 1930-131 closed its eyes to a major perversion of the mining laws. We reject any such conclusion.

C

In 1956 Congress again turned its attention to the patentability of oil shale. That year it amended the mining laws by eliminating the requirement that locators must obtain and convey to the United States existing homestead surface-land patents in order to qualify for a mining patent on minerals withdrawn under the 1920 Mineral Leasing Act. See Pub.L. 743, 70 Stat. 592. Where a surface owner refused to cooperate with the mining claimant and sell his estate, this requirement prevented the mining claimant from patenting his claim. See *James W. Bell,* 52 L.D. 197 (1927). In hearings on the amendment, it was emphasized that oil-shale claimants would be principal beneficiaries of the amendment:

> "Mr. ASPINALL. This [bill] does not have to do with any other minerals except the leaseable minerals to which no one can get a patent since 1920. . . . As far as I know there are only just a few cases that are involved and most of those cases are in the oil shale lands of eastern Utah and western Colorado. That is all this bill refers to." Hearings on H.R. 6501 before the House Committee on Interior and Insular Affairs, 3-4 (1965).

See also Hearings on H.R. 6501 before the Subcommittee on Mines and Mining of the House Committee on Interior and Insular Affairs, 4, 13-14, 16 (1956). The Reports of both Houses also evince a clear understanding that oil shale claimants stood to gain by the amendment:

> "Under the Department of the Interior decision in the case of James W. Bell . . . the owner of a valid mining claim located before February 25, 1920, on lands covered by the 1914 act, in order to obtain a patent to the minerals, is required to acquire the outstanding interest of the surface owner and thereafter to execute a deed of reconveyance to the United States. . . . From 1946 to 1955, inclusive, 71 mining claims, *including 67 oil shale claims,* were issued under this procedure. The committee is informed that in a few cases mining claimants have been unable to obtain the cooperation of the owners of the surface estate and have been pre-vented thereby from obtaining patent to the mineral estate." S.Rep. No. 2524, 84th Cong., 2d Sess., 2 (1956); H.R. Rep. No. 2198, 84th Cong., 2d Sess., 2 (1956), (emphasis added).

The bill was enacted into law without floor debate. Were we to hold today that oil shale is a nonvaluable mineral we would virtually nullify this 1956 action of Congress.

IV

The position of the Government in this case is not without a certain irony. Its challenge to respondents' pre-1920 oil shale claims as a "nonvaluable" comes at a time when the value of such claims has increased sharply as the Nation searches for alternative energy sources to meet its pressing needs. If the

Government were to succeed in invalidating old claims and in leasing the lands at public auction, the Treasury, no doubt, would be substantially enriched. However, the history of the 1920 Mineral Leasing Act and developments subsequent to that Act persuade us that the Government cannot achieve that end by imposing a present marketability requirement on oil shale claims.[11] We conclude that the original position of the Department of Interior, enunciated in the 1920 Instructions and in *Freeman v. Summers,* is the correct view of the Mineral Leasing Act as it applies to the patentability of those claims.[12]

The judgment of the Court of Appeals is

Affirmed.

Mr. Justice STEWART, with whom Mr. Justice BRENNAN and Mr. Justice MARSHALL join, dissenting.

[The dissenting opinion is omitted]

---

[11] This history indicates only that a present marketability standard does not apply to oil shale. It does not affect our conclusion in *United States v. Coleman* that for other minerals the Interior Department's profitability test is a permissible interpretation of the "valuable mineral" requirement. See n. 4, *supra.*

[12] The dissent overlooks the abundant evidence that Congress since 1920 has consistently viewed oil shale as a "valuable mineral" under the general mining law. The dissent dismisses the 1931 hearings and the 1956 Act as irrelevancies: as for the 1931 hearings, the dissent states that "not a single remark by a Senator or Representative" approved the *Freeman* standard; as for the 1956 Act, we are informed that Congress "dealt with [a] totally unrelated problem." *Post,* at 676. Neither of these observations is correct. The 1931 Senate hearing was called specifically to review the *Freeman* case for fear that another "Teapot Dome" scandal was brewing. Rarely has an administrative law decision received such exhaustive Congressional scrutiny. And following that scrutiny, no action was taken to disturb the settled administrative practice; rather Senator Nye advised the Interior Department to continue patenting oil shale claims. Similarly, to characterize the 1956 Act as "totally unrelated" is to blink at reality. The patentability of oil shale land was an essential predicate to that legislation; if oil shale land was nonpatentable then Congress performed a useless act.

The dissent also overlooks that beginning in 1920 and continuing for four decades, the Interior Department treated oil shale as a "valuable mineral." In paying deference to the doctrine that a "contemporaneous [administrative] construction . . . is entitled to substantial weight," *post,* at 676, the dissent ignores this contemporaneous administrative practice. The best evidence of the 1920 standard of patentability is the 1920 Interior Department practice on the matter. The suggestion of the dissent that "future events (such) as market changes" were not meaningful data under the *Castle v. Womble* test, *post,* at 678, is inaccurate. As a leading treatise has observed "[t]he future value concept of *Freeman v. Summers* is nothing more than the 'reasonable prospect of success' of *Castle v. Womble,* and the reference to 'present facts' in *Castle v. Womble* . . . relates to the existence of a vein or lode and not to its value." 1 Rocky Mountain Mineral Law Foundation, The American Law of Mining, § 4.76 p. 697, n. 2 (1979).

NOTES

1. Can *Shell Oil* be reconciled with *Coleman?* Do the same arguments which the Supreme Court finds so persuasive in *Shell Oil* with respect to *Freeman v. Summers* apply with equal force to *Castle v. Womble?* If so, should Congress' long acquiescence in the rule of *Castle v. Womble* not preclude the courts from appending the marketability rule to the prudent man rule?

2. As the Court indicates in the principal case, the United States is immune from equitable estoppel. Traditionally, three reasons are given in justification of this immunity. First, "[i]t is better that an individual should now and then suffer . . . than to introduce a rule [of equitable estoppel against the United States] against an abuse of which, by improper collusions, it would be very difficult for the public to protect itself." *Lee v. Munroe*, 11 U.S. (7 Cranch) 366, 369-370 (1813). Second, were the United States subject to equitable estoppel, "officers who have no authority at all to dispose of Government property [could] by their conduct cause the Government to lose its valuable rights. . . ." *United States v. California*, 332 U.S. 19, 40 (1947). Third, the United States is not subject to equitable estoppel because, were it otherwise, the constitutional doctrine of separation of powers would be violated. The argument, simply stated, is that the executive branch should not be permitted to negate through carelessness and neglect that which the legislature has mandated. A fourth reason, although not one of the traditional ones, for the rule that the government is not subject to equitable estoppel is that an opposite rule would lead to a "drying up" of government provided information. *See generally*, Braunstein, *In Defense of Traditional Immunity: Toward an Economic Rationale for Not Estopping the Government*, 14 RUTGERS L. REV. 1, 27-39 (1982).

---

3. Discovery Good Against Rival Claimants

BERTO V. WILSON
324 P.2d 843 (1958)

. . . .

MERRILL, Justice.

This is an action to quiet title to mining property. Mining claims located by the respective parties overlap and to that extent are in dispute. Judgment was entered by the trial court, sitting without jury, quieting title in the respondents to the property claimed by them. From that judgment this appeal is taken. The sole question involved is whether the record supports the determination of the trial court that respondents were senior in the posting of their claims and in the discovery of mineral in place and thus were senior in location of the disputed area.

The problem is an old one in modern setting. The rush to a new strike and the scramble for the most desirable locations set the stage for a drama well-known to the west. Today the magic word is "uranium"; the scintillation counter and the mineral-light lamp have taken their places as prospectors' tools; the airplane and the 4-wheel-drive truck have reduced the factors of time and distance. The plot of the drama, however, remains essentailly the same: the rush, the locations, the overlapping of claims, the discovery of value, the dispute. And in the orderly resolution of the dispute the principles of law remain substantially unchanged from the days of the mother lode and the Comstock.

Appellants' first contention is that the record fails to support the trial court's findings that respondents were the first in the posting of their claims. There is no merit to this contention. The record amply supports the findings. Appellants are in the position of contending that the trial court chose to believe the wrong witnesses, a proposition which this court rejects. [Citations omitted].

The record presents a tale worth the telling, however.

In October, 1955 the Atomic Energy Commission was engaged in a series of aerial explorations seeking by airborne scintillation counters to locate radio-active anomalies: areas in which scintillation indicates the presence of greater radioactivity than is normally found as natural background. Notice was given that an anomaly map would be posted on the morning of October 17, at the post office bulletin board in Tonopah, Nevada. Uranium prospectors, thus alerted, were on hand ready for a race to the announced anomaly.

Respondents, while engaged in other mining activities, had observed the commission airplane in its explorations and judged that the anomaly would be located in southern Lander or northern Nye Counties. They gambled in support of their judgment and respondent Wilson was posted at Carver's Station in Smoky Valley, halfway between Tonopah and Austin, to await a telephone call from respondent Woods in Tonopah as soon as the map was posted. The call came at about 11 o'clock a.m. and Wilson was directed to a point a few miles south-east of Austin near the Blackbird ranch. He was off in a jeep at 75 miles an hour with a substantial lead over all competitors. He reached the anomaly area about noon, first on the ground, and commenced his search for the anomaly by aid of scintillator. By 1:15 he was satisfied that he had found it. By 2 o'clock, when Woods arrived to join him, Wilson had posted two claims. The two men completed posting two additional claims, concluding at about 2:30. Location notices were immediately recorded at Austin.

Meanwhile, back at the Tonopah post office, appellants had prepared themselves with a plane stationed at the Tonopah airport and rented a pick-up truck. In their assault upon the anomaly it was to be Woolever by land and Berto by air. They ran into time-consuming difficulties, however. The truck broke down about halfway to Austin. The mishap was discovered by Berto who landed on the highway and took Woolever aboard with him. They returned to Tonopah to radio a request that arrangements be made for a truck to meet them at the Austin airport. En route back to Austin they detoured to fly over the anomaly area in an air reconnaissance. They observed several motor vehicles already there. By the time they had landed at Austin, had been driven to the anomaly area and had hiked into the ground itself, several two-man parties were already at work posting claims. Several witnesses, including both respondents, testified to having seen the plane on its reconnaissance at about 2 o'clock. While appellants deny this and fix a much earlier time, we shall not question the manner in which the trial court apparently resolved this dispute.

We conclude that respondents have been properly established as senior in the posting of their claims.

Appellants next contend that the record discloses that respondents had not made any discovery of mineral in place on October 17 and that their locations for that reason cannot be recognized as of that date.

The right to location of a mining claim presupposes the discovery of a lode or vein, for that which is claimed is the lode which has been discovered. N.R.S. 517.10. The location of a mining claim, therefore, cannot rest upon the conjectural or imaginary existence of a vein or lode. King v. Amy & Silversmith Consol. Min. Co., 152 U.S. 222, 14 S.Ct. 510, 38 L.Ed. 419. In Cole v. Ralph, 252 U.S. 286, 40 S.Ct. 321, 326, 64 L.Ed. 567, involving conflicting mining claims in the state of Nevada the court stated, "To sustain a lode location the discovery must be of a vein or lode of rock in place bearing valuable mineral.*** In practice discovery usually precedes location, and the statute treats it as the initial act. But in the absence of an intervening right it is no objection that the usual and statutory order is reversed. In such a case the location becomes effective from the date of discovery; but in the presence of an intervening right it must remain of no effect."

Appellants, having posted their claims on the 17th, returned to the property the following two days for further prospecting and location work and the staking of corners. Several shallow pits were dug and a deposit of radio-active mineral-bearing ore was uncovered. Samples were taken which proved to be autunite, a commercially valuable uranium-bearing ore.

Respondents, on the other hand after posting their claims and recording location notices on the 17th, were required to return to Tonopah that same day due to the illness of respondent Woods. They did not return to their property for six days. On their return they came prepared for active mining. A shaft was dug at their original point of discovery and considerable additional work was done in the development of their discovery and in the improvement of their claims. No question is raised as to the sufficiency of their development work or the survey of their claims or the location certificates ultimately filed. The question is as to the sufficiency of their original discovery on the 17th to give them a prior location over appellants.

Appellants read the record as demonstrating that respondents' original location was based solely upon the indications of radio-activity produced by their scintillator. They contend that this is no more than an indication of the possible presence of commercially valuable ore and that in the absence of the discovery of the source of the radiation it cannot be said to constitute a discovery of mineral in place; citing Rummel v. Bailey, 7 Utah 2d 137, 320 P.2d 653; Globe Min. Co. v. Anderson, Wyo. 318 P.2d 373. Appellants emphasize that scintillation may have many other causes than uranium-bearing ore, a fact which is not disputed. Berto testified that in the anomaly area there was no mineralized rock in place exposed without digging; that without pick-and-shovel prospecting a discovery of mineral in place could not have been made. Appellants concede that under these circumstances their own locations must date from their discovery the day following posting (the 18th). They contend, however, that this was five days before any discovery was made by respondents.

Testimony of both appellants and respondents may be said to be sketchy as to the details of discovery. It would appear that both sides were primarily concerned with an attempt to establish priority of posting and that the nature of their discoveries and the particulars thereof upon each individual claim were secondary considerations at the time of trial. A study of the record, however, convinces us that there is sufficient [sic] to support a determination that, at the time of posting, mineral in place had been discovered by respondents to the extent required by law.

In determining whether a sufficient discovery of mineral has been made, the courts make a distinction between two classes of cases: (1) those (such as the one before us) where the dispute is between two locators upon the same lode as to which is the prior locator; (2) those where the issue is whether that which is claimed is a true lode of value and the land truly mineral in character.

In cases of the first type the court is not primarily concerned with the nature of the discovery or the extent of the mineral value which it has demonstrated. The question is as to which of two contestants is entitled to possession of that which each independently has found. Each is claiming possession of the same thing for the same values, whatever they may be. An examination of values, therefore, is of little if any consequence.

Accordingly, what may constitute a sufficient discovery in such a case may be wholly insufficient in cases involving issuance of patent or establishment of an apex; or where the ground is claimed as placer or under agricultural or townsite entry. Golden v. Murphy, 31 Nev. 395, 103 P. 394, 105 P. 99; Fox v. Myers, 29 Nev. 169, 86 P. 793; See V. 2, Lindley on Mines, sec. 336.

The test here is whether the discovery is such as to justify a reasonable miner in expending his time and money in prospecting and developing the claim. Fox v. Myers, supra. This court in that case quoted Shoshone Min. Co. v. Rutter, 9 Cir., 87 F. 801, to the following effect, (29 Nev. at page 184, 86 P. at page 797) "The purpose of the statute, in requiring that 'no location of a mining claim shall be made until the discovery of a vein or lode within the limits of the claim located,' was to prevent frauds upon the government by persons attempting to acquire patents to land not mineral in character. But as was said in Bonner v. Meikle, C.C., 82 F.697: 'It was never intended that the court should weigh scales to determine the value of mineral found, as between a prior and subsequent locator of a mining claim on the same lode.' "

In Nevada-Pacific Development Corp. v. Gustin, 9 Cir., 226 F.2d 286, 287, dealing with a dispute between prior and subsequent locators of a tungsten lode near Gabbs, Nevada, the court stated that in such a dispute "no more than a slight showing by a prior locator of discovery of a mineral bearing vein or lode is needed to satisfy the legal requirements requisite to a valid location."

In the case at bar the conflicts are between appellants' Linda group of five claims on the one hand; and, on the other, respondents' Lowboy group of four claims and two of the Nura group located by others and conveyed to respondents.

The testimony of respondent Wilson and his witnesses is to the effect that at his first discovery monument on Lowboy a vein had been observed in surface outcropping, appearing to strike east and west and extending through Lowboy No. 1 in one direction and into the Nura group in the other. It was a solid formation protruding from the surface. On each of the Lowboy and Nura claims outcroppings similar to this vein gave indication of vein or lode material. Radio-activity was apparent on all claims and was highest at the original point of discovery. A sample was broken by Wilson from the vein outcropping at the original point of discovery and appeared to him to be autunite. His prospecting prior to location involved not only visual observation in the light of his prior mining experience, but use of a scintillator and mineral-light lamp. In the opinion of one witness, a man of many years experience in mining and prospecting, the appearance of the outcropping at the point of discovery was not only that of a lode but of the apex of the lode.

While foresight rather than hindsight is the gauge of the reasonable miner's expectations, in this case subsequent events lend weight to the proposition that Wilson's expectations were justified and reasonable. Development work clearly demonstrated that the discovery was genuine. The shaft was dug at the very point of discovery. Along one side it exposed a vein of autunite. Samples from seven different points throughout the claims demonstated that what Wilson and his witnesses had judged to be outcroppings of mineral-bearing ore or vein matter were such in fact.

We conclude that a sufficient discovery was made by respondents.

Affirmed.

E. Proving the Discovery

1. Proving the Existence of Mineral within the Claim

GLOBE MINING CO. V. ANDERSON
318 P.2d 373 (Wyo. 1957)

[footnotes omitted]

Mr. Justice PARKER delivered the opinion of the court.

Plaintiff, Globe Mining Company, successor in interest to the partnership of H. D. Hand and Page T. Jenkins, brought a suit in Fremont County to quiet title on ten lode mining claims, Phil Nos. 3-12. Plaintiff alleged that, as relating to said land, beginning October 2, 1953, it had complied with Federal and Wyoming mining laws pertaining to location of lode claims but in defiance of plaintiff's interest defendants had entered upon said claims May 5, 1955, overtaking same and attempting to initiate rights therein. On May 12, 1955, the court issued a temporary restraining order against defendants who thereafter filed an answer and cross-petition, denying any rights of plaintiff, alleging themselves to be the legal owners of a substantial portion of said lands by virtue of compliance with the Federal and Wyoming mining laws on their five lode claims, Andria and Andria No.s 1-4, and praying that title be quieted in them.

The trial court in "findings of fact," expressing views on the law as well as the facts, decided against plaintiff and in favor of defendants, entering judgment accordingly. . . .

. . . .

The trial court indicated that there must be a discovery of valuable mineral "in a lead, lode, ledge or vein or rock in place," using each of these terms synonymously; and no question has been raised by the parties as to this interpretation. Accordingly, we need not pursue any detailed definition of the word lode but instead shall look to the evidence of the parties and the findings of the court.

In the "findings of fact," the court said that plaintiff took:

"*** three samples from the area within the boundaries of what was later staked as Phil Claims numbered 6 and 8 and at a point on the boundary line between Phil Claims 5 and 6. The evidence does not disclose that these samples were taken from a vein or rock in place. When assayed they showed the presence of uranium."

This positive finding of the discovery of uranium on these three claims, which finding is borne out by the evidence and is unquestioned by the defendants, presents a situation requiring a review of the evidence as to the nature of the *place* from which these assay samples were taken.

On this point Hand testified that on October 6, 1953, from Pit A on what later became Phil No. 6, he took a sample, chiseling a channel down the side of the pit through yellow mineralization "in place"; from Pit A-2 on what later became a midway point in the center end line between Phil Nos. 5 and 6, he took a sample from "mineralization in place"; and from Pit A-3 on what later became Phil No. 8, he took a sample from "rock in place" and stated that this was sampled "in the same manner as the other two." The assays of these samples by the Brown Laboratory were admitted in evidence as Exhibit 6 without objection and showed quantities of U_3O_8 as well as V_2O_5, on which analyses the court apparently relied in finding that the samples "showed the presen of uranium." The above-mentioned evidence standing uncontradicted as it does must be taken as conclusive proof of plaintiff's discovery of secondary uranium in a *vein* or *rock in place.*

The trial court found that with the exception of the discoveries on Phil Nos. 5, 6, and 8 Hand took no samples or assays from the other Phil claims; that Newman and Hewitt in 1954 collected samples from a pit on Phil No. 8, which when assayed showed uranium; that Grant in 1954 obtained some mixed samples, the assays of which showed uranium; and indicates that no further assays were taken. The evidence disclosed by the record substantiates this latter finding. A report of assay (Exhibit 27) disclosed uranium in samples taken from various of these claims, but there was nothing to show that this was from *rock in place.* There was an attempt made to introduce evidence of the assays of samples taken from drilling by the A. E. C. on Phil Nos. 4, 5, and 6 (Exhibit 28); but this evidence was correctly rejected by the court for lack of proper foundation after plaintiff's witness, Jenkins, had stated:

"All I can say is that we send very few samples to the Atomic Energy Commission for assay, and this would be a case where just by deductive reasoning I am sure that these are samples that we took from the Phil 4, 5 and 6 claims and sent to the Atomic Energy Commission. *** I can't positively say that these samples passed from my hands to the Atomic Energy Commission."

Thus, there was no evidence of a sampling and assaying of a vein, lode, or rock in place in Phil Nos. 3, 4, 7, 9, 10, 11, and 12 and, therefore, no discovery on these claims—unless we recognize the readings of electrical instruments such as scintillation and Geiger counters as sufficient to support discovery. This we are reluctant to do, since such counters while helpful in prospecting for uranium cannot be relied upon as the *only* test.

. . . .

DALLAS V. FITZSIMMONS
323 P.2d 274 (Colo. 1958)

[The facts of the case are adequately set forth in the excerpt that follows]

. . . .

The Second Question to be Determined is:

"If mineral lode locations are made on state lands in compliance with the state laws relating to discovery, posting, notice and other applicable provisions, do such claims take priority and precedence over a subsequent mineral lease issued by the duly authorized state leasing body?"

This question is answered in the affirmative. The applicable Colorado Statutes read:

"C.R.S. '53, 112-3-41 "Mineral locations—assessment—lease.—Locations of mineral claims not exceeding three hundred feet wide and fifteen hundred feet long each, or of three ten-acre subdivisions or mineral lots, may be made upon *unleased mineral lands belonging to the state.* The discoverer of a body of mineral, in either a lead, lode, ledge, deposit, vein or contract shall immediately post conspicuously a notice declaring that he has made such discovery on the date attached to the notice. The locator shall be allowed ninety days from such date in which to perform assessment work by shaft or tunnel, which assessment work shall not be at a less cost than one hundred dollars in each year, and to survey and set the corner posts of said claim and to file a certificate of location with the register of the state board of land commissioners, which certificate shall be recorded in said office, and an entry made upon the plat and tract books of such location. This procedure shall empower the locator to retain possession of and operate the claim for a period of one year, at the end of which time he shall be required to take a lease upon such terms as may be agreed upon by the state board of land commissioners." (Emphasis supplied.)

C.R.S. '53, 112-3-13—"Leases—rental—mineral lands.—The state board of land commissioners may lease any portion of the land of the state at a rental to be determined by it, except * * *."

"* * * If stone, coal, oil, gas, or other mineral not herein mentioned be found upon the state land, such land may be leased* * *."

On April 15, 1955, there became effective an amended C.R.S. '53, 112-3-41 which altered in some respects the law applicable to future cases of this type. However, it is not material here for it cannot retroactively affect prior vested rights.

Plaintiffs state that they proved their lease was issued pursuant to the statute. They rely solely thereon for their title, and allege that defendants as claim locators are trespassers.

The record discloses that Dallas, in December 1954 or January 1955, with one Vernon Chandler went to Fitzsimmons' ranch. Chandler asked for and was granted permission to prospect for uranium on Fitzsimmons' deeded land. The record does not disclose any discovery or claim locations by either Dallas or Chandler as a result thereof.

On February 27, 1955, Fitzsimmons with his six co-defendants, while prospecting in the area with a Geiger counter, found a count of "four to five times" the background count. They at first believed the discovery to be on federal lands possibly joined with some state land and some of Fitzsimmons' deeded lands. On that same day they prepared location notices and proceeded to post them on the original three claims involved here. The uncontradicted testimony of Fitzsimmons was that he had made a note that he believed they had 60 days from their discovery date in which to file their notices and through some error that date was first placed on the notices, but when the mistake was discovered that same day, it was forthwith corrected to the day of discovery and actual posting; i.e., February 27, 1955.

The original discovery pits were dug by defendants where the original location notices were posted and the original discoveries made, even though Geiger counter readings were gotten elsewhere on the claims. Fitzsimmons on direct examination testified with reference to the discovery by Geiger counter and then:

"Q. And after discovery was made what next was done?
A. We proceeded to prospect some ore and then get our notices and get them up."

On April 2, 1955, Dallas and some friends visited Fitzsimmons' ranch and the next day, which was a Sunday, they were shown the located claims. By this time it was realized that the claims were on state land. Dallas was told this and that the area was already taken and posted. Fitzsimmons testified that at that time Dallas wanted to lease the claims from the discoverers but was refused. Effective at noon on April 4, 1955, Dallas secured mining lease No. 778 Book 16, from the Board to the East half of Section 27, Township 7 South, Range 73 West of the 6th P.M., Park County, Colorado, which area includes the claims here in quesiton, and on the same date beginning at 4:55 p.m. defendants recorded their location certificates in Park County. In the "middle of April" Fitzsimmons received a letter from the Board advising that defendants were trespassers on the land covered by their recorded claims.

It appears that defendants first posted location notices on their then three claims in accordance with the federal law providing for lode claims 1,500 feet in length and 600 feet in width being 300 feet on each side of the discovery lode; that defendants later made up amended location certificates dividing these into four claims known as Redskin Mining Claims No. 1-A, No. 1-B, No. 2-A and No. 2-B; and on May 25, 1955, attempted to file these four separate location certificates with the Board in order to comply with the state law. The Board refused to accept the filings and Fitzsimmons then left them on the registrar's desk at the Board's office.

Assessment work, as required by the statute, was done on the various claims in April and May, 1955. There is evidence that uranium was found on each claim by use of the Geiger counter. Assays of the claim samples from one of the discovery pits showed chemical results of up to 1.24% uranium and 0.4% vanadium according to testimony objected to but not ruled on below.

Much of the material evidence was disputed; however there is adequate support in the record for the findings in defendants' favor by the trial court. Whether a vein or lode has been discovered or exists within the limits of the location in controversy, and as to the continuity of ore and mineral matter constituting the length, width and extent of any particular vein or lode, is always a question of fact to be determined by a jury, or by the court if the case is tried without a jury. Book v. Justice Mining Co., C.C. Nev. 1893, 58 F. 106. We need not again cite Colorado cases stating the rule that findings and conclusions of the trial court, when supported by competent evidence, will not be disturbed on review.

We are constrained to comment on one phase of the fact situation in this case; viz., the methods of determining proper discovery of radioactive minerals as occured here.

The record and briefs carefully and ably detail the lengthy history of just how defendants made their discoveries with a Geiger counter and later had samples from one of the claims chemically assayed. The assays proved what the Geiger counter indicated on the ground; i. e., mineralization sufficient to constitute a "discovery" within the meaning of our statute. Mineral in the statutory discovery sense means valuable rock in place subject to definable boundaries. The discoveries here fall within this definition. See Nevada Sierra Oil Co. v. Home Oil Co., C.C.Cal. 1899, 98 F. 673. The assayed samples were not mere indications of mineral, radiometrically or by float; they established mineralization. Mineral location statutes should be liberally construed in behalf of bona fide locators with due regard for a fair application of the statutory requirements. As is said in Nevada Sierra Oil Co. v. Home Oil Co., supra, 98 F. at page 676:

"Indications of the existence of a thing is not the thing itself. It is entirely true that the statute, requiring as a condition to a valid location the discovery of mineral within the limits of the claim, should, as between conflicting claimants to mineral lands, receive a broad and liberal construction, and so as to protect bona fide locators who have really made a discovery of mineral, whether it be under the statute providing for the location of vein or lode claims or placer claims. As was well said by Judge Hawley in Book v. Justice Mining Co., C.C., 58 F. 106, 120, in speaking of vein and lode claims: 'When the locator finds rock in place containing mineral, he has made a discovery, within the meaning of the statute, whether the rock or earth is rich or poor, whether it assays high or low. It is the finding of the mineral in the rock in place, as distinguished from float rock, that constitutes the discovery, and warrants the prospector in making a location of a mining claim.' "

Where as here the assay samples come from at least one of the claims, and all the claims are contiguous, and where the trial court could and did conclude from the evidence that the nonassayed claims lie in similar ground, it is not unrealistic to hold that competent radiometric reactions supported by a chemical assay as to a part of the claims, clearly show the presence of uranium on the adjacent claimed locations showing the same or similar radiometric readings. The latter are then valid "discoveries" under our statute as much as are outcrops visible to the naked eye. Such other "discoveries" however must be capable of competent radiometric delineation in similar rock in place or along the same vein or lode. See *Smaller v. Leach,* 136 Colo. 297, 316 P.2d 1030, for a discussion of radiometric discoveries; and compare Rummell v. Bailey, 1958, 7 Utah 2d 137, 320 P.2d 653, and *Globe Mining Company v. Anderson*, Wyo., 318 P.2d 373.

Keeping in mind that technical prospecting methods, such as the use of counters and scintillators, are only exploration tools and not complete exploration and discovery systems, we hold that here the radiometric results coupled with the other evidence, such as the assay and type of rock in place show an overall fair compliance with the statute requiring discovery.

We also hold that the leasing powers of the Board under C.R.S. '53, 112-3-13, are subject to the implied limitation that it cannot lease state land already properly in the physical possession of others under the mining laws. Defendants' claims, under the facts presented, have priority and must be accepted by the Board which must then in due course permit mineral leasing of the same under C.R.S. '53, 112-3-41. This is not to say, however, that plaintiffs' lease is invalid as to lands not included within the limits of defendants' claims. We are not called upon to, nor do we, rule on that point.

The judgment is affirmed.

NOTES

1. The term float rock is used by "miners and geologists for pieces of ore or rock which have fallen from veins or strata, or have been separated from the parent vein or strata by weathering agencies." U.S. Department of the Interior, A Dictionary of Mining and Mining Related Terms (Thrush ed.) Float is distinguished from rock in place by the fact that float is "rock lying detached from, or resting upon the earth's surface without any walls." *Id.*

2. Would you expect that evidence which established the existence of a discovery in the principal case would have been sufficient to establish a discovery if federal lands were involved and the United States were a party? Why not?

3. Does the principal case hold that radiometric readings alone are sufficient to establish a discovery? Note the court's use of the phrase "radiometric discoveries."

4. In *Western Standard Uranium v. Thurston,* 355 P.2d 377 (Wyo. 1960), the Wyoming Supreme Court held that radiometric readings alone were insufficient to establish a discovery between rival private claimants. The court went on to find, however, that such readings combined with visual examination of samples, the general geology of the area, and discoveries on adjoining and adjacent claims was sufficient to establish a discovery as between miners.

5. In a suit between rival claimants should evidence of assays taken after the institution of the suit be admitted for the purpose of proving that a discovery had been made prior to the commencement of the suit? In *Western Standard Uranium v. Thurston,* 355 P. 2d 377 (Wyo. 1960) the court held that such evidence was admissible "if for no other purpose than in corroboration of the facts claimed by plaintiff as constituting his discovery."

6. In the principal case the court held that assays of ore taken from only one of the claims in question could be used to establish discoveries on all of the claims at issue. Is this holding consistent with *Globe Mining v. Anderson?* What other evidence did the court rely on in determining that Fitzsimmons had made a discovery? Why were the assay results even relevant, since they were taken after Dallas had obtained his lease?

2. Proving the Ability to Mine the Claim as a Profit

UNITED STATES V. KOSANKE SAND CORPORATION
80 I.D. 538 (1973)

. . . .

Contestant next argues that the evidence adduced at the original hearing does not support a finding of discovery on each claim. Upon re-examination of the record, we conclude that the evidence is insufficient to make a final determination as to the validity of the claims. Therefore, all parties are afforded a further opportunity to produce evidence on those issues which were insufficiently covered at the first hearing.

Upon rehearing, in order to establish a discovery on each claim in issue, evidence should be further developed on the following points:

1. Significant variations in value occured between the samples taken by contestant and contestee. Therefore, further sampling is necessary to demonstrate clearly the quality and quantity of silica sand on each claim. In the analysis of the samples care should be taken to avoid combining samples from different claims. As this Board stated in *United States v. Bunkowski,* 5 IBLA 102, 79 I.D. 43, 51-52 (1972):

> [T]here must be a discovery on each claim. The appellants must show *as to each claim* that they have found a mineral deposit which satisfies the prudent man rule as complemented by the marketability test.

In order to avoid further problems in connection with sampling, we recommend that joint sampling be conducted on each claim.

2. The quantity of sand on the claims should be considered in connection with the existing and foreseeable market; *i.e.,* evidence should be presented on the presence of sufficient reserves within the limits of each claim. The record contains no such evidence. Should the validity of one or more of the claims be established, the issue of possible excess reserves must be considered. *See*

United States v. Anderson, supra.

3. Different grades of silica sand produce different types of glass. Thus, the critical issue in establishing marketability is the nature and extent of the market for each grade of glass sand and the approximate amount of each grade on each claim.

4. The milling and flotation process described by contestee in the original hearing needs further clarification in order to determine whether the costs of beneficiation permit the silica sand to be marketed at a profit. In developing this evidence, to the extent it is reasonably possible, similar costs of other producers should also be presented.

Contestant contended, and the Judge so held, that absent an actual pilot testing of the proposed process, it cannot be determined whether the process can be worked at a profit. We reject such a position. Certainly, the existence of a successful pilot plant would greatly increase contestee's ability to demonsrate the costs of producing its silica sand and the feasibility of its process. When the contestee's case rests on a proposed flotation process which has yet to be tested, expert corroborative evidence would be helpful and might be essential in determining the potentiality of success. The Government, of course, may rebut such evidence.

5. Evidence relating to the costs of transportation should be further developed on rehearing. The subject claims are closer to the existing markets than the deposits of present suppliers. It does not necessarily follow, however, that contestee's costs of transportation will be lower. While distance is an important factor in determining transportation costs, it is not necessarily the only factor. Transportation costs may vary depending upon whether sand is shipped by road, rail, or water. Costs may also vary depending upon the difficulty presented by the geographic conditions of the route, as well as other factors.

Contestee argues that silica sand is shipped "f.o.b. plant at $4.25 per ton" and that transportation costs under these terms are incurred by the glass producers rather than the sand suppliers. We recognize that where a glass producer quotes a price for sand and incurs the transportation costs, the producer, in all likelihood, reflects this cost in the price per ton he is willing to pay a particular supplier for silica sand. However, we cannot determine from the present record whether glass producers would quote the same terms to contestee as they apparently have quoted to existing sand suppliers.

It may be that, because of geographic conditions or the mode of transportation, glass producers will offer better terms to contestee than they apparently have made to existing suppliers. On the other hand, because of geographic conditions or the mode of transportation, glass producers may not want to incur the expense of transportation, and therefore may offer contestee a price for its sand which does not reflect transportation as a cost. In the latter instance contestee would have to produce evidence to establish its cost of transporting sand from its claims to the glass producers. Whatever the situation might be, evidence should be developed on transportation costs so that an informed determination can be made with regard to this issue in applying the marketability test.

5 THE ACTS OF LOCATION: PROCEDURES UNDER STATE LAW AND THE FEDERAL LAND POLICY AND MANAGEMENT ACT

A. **The relationship between state and federal law**
 Roberts v. Morton
 Barton v. DeRousse
 United States v. Haskins
B. **Posting the notice of location**
 Anaconda Co. v. Whittaker
C. **Discovery workings**
 Globe Mining Co. v. Anderson
D. **Marking the claim on the ground**
 Parker v. Jones
E. **Filing the location certificate**
 Lombardo Turquoise Milling & Mining v. Hemanes
 Atherley v. Bullion Monarch Uranium Co.
 Henry D. Friedman
F. **Special considerations in the location of placer claims**
 Snow Flake Fraction Placer
 United States, ex rel. United States Borak Co. v. Ickes

A. The Relationship Between State and Federal Law

ROBERTS V. MORTON
549 F.2d 158 (10th Cir. 1976)

[The facts of this case are set forth at page 142, *supra.*]

Second, plaintiffs challenge the administrative ruling that their claims were void due to plaintiffs' failure to locate their claims in accordance with the mining laws.

The federal mining laws provide generally that valuable mineral deposits in Government lands shall be free and open to exploration and purchase, and the lands in which they are found to occupation and purchase, by citizens "under regulations prescribed by law, and according to the local customs or rules of miners in the several mining districts, so far as the same are applicable and not inconsistent with the laws of the United States." 30 U.S.C.A. § 22. The statute requires that the location must be distinctly marked on the ground so that its boundaries can be readily traced. See 30 U.S.C.A. § 28.

Plaintiffs' mining claims were located by Merle I. Zweifel. At the time he located the claims the federal regulation concerning the manner in which rights are initiated by location provided that a "location is made by staking the corners of the claim, posting notice of location thereon and complying with the State laws, regarding the recording of the location in the county recorder's office, discovery work, etc." 43 C.F.R. § 3401.1 (1969).[1] And the Colorado statute, C.R.S. 92-22-12(2) (1963), now C.R.S. 34-43-112 (1973), which should be observed in the location of placer mining claims provided:

(a) Before filing [the] location certificate the discoverer shall locate his claim;

(b) By posting upon such claim a plain sign or notice, containing the name of the claim, the name of the locator, the date of discovery and the number of acres or feet claimed;

(c) By marking the surface boundaries with substantial posts, sunk into the ground, one at each angle of the claim.

Plaintiffs argue that State law location requirements do not apply in contest proceedings initiated by the United States, citing *Reins v. Murray,* 22 L.D. 409 (1896). It is true that the Secretary in *Reins* said the public surveys are permanent and fixed and that it is the statute's [30 U.S.C. § 28] intent that location of placer claims by legal subdivision makes marking of boundaries an idle ceremony not contemplated by the law. See also Location of Oil Shale Placer Claims, Instructions, 52 L.D. 631 (1929). Nevertheless, as a result of 43 C.F.R. § 3401.1 the State location requirements did apply when Mr. Zweifel located these claims. In view of the federal regulation and the Colorado statute we cannot agree with the plaintiffs that the marking of the surface boundaries at each angle of the claim was not required to effect a valid location.

As the district court pointed out, 389 F.Supp. at 93-94, the Department has not required strict compliance with State location laws in every case, citing *Reins v. Murray,* supra. But substantial or colorable compliance with State location requirements has been enforced even in controversies between the Government and private claimants. *United States v. Zweifel,* 508 F.2d 1150, 1153-54 (10th Cir.).

The administrative law judge found that it was obvious from Zweifel's testimony and pictures that his efforts in addition to filing claim notices at the courthouse, were basically directed at posting notices or identification markers on groups of claims, not on individual claims. He found that Zweifel made no effort to establish individual claim corner monuments nor to ascertain whether

---

[1] The present regulation relaxes the requirement on staking by providing that a "location is made (a) by staking the corners of the claim except placer claims ... *where State law permits* location without marking the boundaries of the claim on the ground ..." Colorado law does not so permit (Emphasis added).

the individual claims were in fact monumented by the public land surveys, that in fact simple arithmetic would reveal the impossibility of a person's being able to set foot and post a notice on each of the numerous claims within the time limits of Zweifel's activities, and that the finding was inescapable that Zweifel did not and could not post a notice on each and every claim. He thus concluded that the plaintiffs (contestees) did not establish possession over the claims as required by the general mining laws and that the claims are invalid (C.C.No. 441, 27).

The Board of Land Appeals affirmed, concluding that although Zweifel could have properly staked, posted notice on and located some claims, the burden rests on plaintiffs to establish which claims were properly located, which burden they had not met; and that plaintiffs failed to comply with the federal law in location of their 2,910 claims and the claims are invalid (11 IBLA at 88).

In attacking the findings against them on the location procedures of Zweifel, plaintiffs make no persuasive argument on the record. In proceedings where the validity of mining claims on Government land is at issue the Government bears the burden of establishing prima facie the invalidity of the claims and then the burden shifts to the claimant to prove that his claims are valid. See *United States v. Zweifel,* supra, 508 F.2d at 1157. Here there was Government proof that the area resource managers never saw any of the notices Zweifel posted, although they could have been there (Tr. 328-29; 346-48; 351-54; 454-57; 465-68). This, coupled with admissions from Zweifel (Tr. 215-22), made a prima facie case of invalidity.

Arguing that validity of the claims was established, plaintiffs point to proof that Zweifel used several men in locating the claims and that by use of Y stakes each claim would be staked, and flags and location notices were posted on each claim (Tr. 864, *et seq.*). And they argue that in any event where a claim is challenged by the Government, compliance with State law is not required (Reply Brief for Appellants, 25-31).

We cannot agree. State requirements have been held by us to apply in such controversies between the Government and mining claimants. See *United States v. Zweifel,* supra, 508 F.2d at 1153-54. Those requirements included the marking of surface boundaries at each angle of the claim. While at one point Zweifel asserted he did this (Tr. 188), he later testified that he had not posted the four corners of each claim (Tr. 215-22). We are satisfied that the record as a whole amply sustains the findings that the claims were not properly located.

In sum, we agree with the district court's view that the administrative findings of invalidity of the claims for lack of proper location are supported by substantial evidence.

. . . .

BARTON V. DeROUSSE
535 P. 2d 1289 (Nev. 1975)
OPINION

ZENOFF, Justice:

The Nevada State Legislature in 1971 amended the provisions of Chapter 517, Nevada Revised Statutes, so that as of July 1, 1971, it became incumbent upon the establishing of new mining claims and for already existing mining claims under the provisions of Chapter 517 that maps of the location of these claims be filed with the county recorder of the county in which such claims are situated. NRS 517.030(2), NRS 517.050(1)(e), NRS 517.080, NRS 517.100 and NRS 517.230(3).

The respondents are holders of certain unpatented lode and placer claims in Mineral and Nye Counties. They successfully challenged in the trial court the constitutionality of Chapter 517 on the grounds that the mapping requirements are in conflict with federal law in that they are inconsistent with the federal discovery requirements of 30 U.S.C.A. § 23 and the federal recordation requirement of 30 U.S.C.A. § 28 that any record of the location of a claim contain ". . . such a description of the claim or claims located by reference to some natural object or permanent monument as will identify the claim," and that the Nevada statutes violate due process because they cannot be enforced.

1. As regards the mapping requirements of Chapter 517 relating to the location and recordation of location of mining claims, they are not inconsistent with the federal requirement of discovery and are not a substitute for the federal requirement of discovery. Section 28 of Title 30, U.S.C.A., does not preclude state laws presenting the manner of locating mining claims and recording them so long as they are not inconsistent with the laws of the United States. Butte City Water Company v. Baker, 196 U.S. 119, 25 S.Ct. 211, 49 L.Ed. 409 (1905); Gustin v. Nevada-Pacific Development Corp., 125 F.Supp. 811 (D.Nev. 1954), cert. denied, 351 U.S. 930, 76 S.Ct. 787, 100 L.Ed. 1459 (1956). Thus, a state legislature, as is the case here, may impose additional burdens on the locator of a mining claim either as a requirement that the work shall be made as an incident to the location or as a condition to the subsistence of the mining claim, and can add further requirements as to the recordation of notices of location without being in conflict with federal law. Northmore v. Simmons, 97 F. 386 (9th Cir. 1899); Gustin v. Nevada-Pacific Development Corp., supra; Sisson v. Sommers, 24 Nev. 379, 55 P. 829 (1899). The mapping requirement here is not inconsistent with any provision of federal mining law and is merely an additional burden within the state's prerogative.

2. As to the trial court's determination that Chapter 517 is in violation of the federal recordation requirement that any record of the location of a claim contain ". . . such a description of the claim or claims located by reference to some natural object or permanent monument as will identify the claim," 30 U.S.C.A. § 28, a reading of NRS 517.030(2) and NRS 517.100 in conjunction with the other requirements for recordation of a certificate of location as set out in NRS 517.050(1) and NRS 517.110, reflects that the mapping requirement is in addition to the other requirements of recordation listed therein and is a graphic representation of the federal requirement of reference to some natural object or permanent monument. The maps' required contents must provide connections to an official corner of the public survey or to a claim marker if the land has not been surveyed or the official corner can't be located. Official United States surveys have been held to be permanent monuments under the federal requirement, McNulty v. Kelly, 141 Colo. 23, 346 P.2d 585 (1959), and the claim

marker, as defined in NRS 517.030, appears to qualify as a permanent monument or natural object under the federal requirement. North Noonday Mining Co. v. Orient Mining Co., 1 F. 522, 534 (C.C.Cal. 1880); Book v. Justice Min. Co., 58 F. 106, 113 (C.C.D.Nev. 1893); Southern Cross Co. v. Europa Co., 15 Nev. 383 (1880); Bismark Mountain Gold M. Co. v. North Sunbeam Gold Co., 14 Idaho 516, 95 P. 14 (1908). When considered together the Nevada statutes are in compliance with the recordation requirement of 30 U.S.C.A. § 28. If anything, the mapping requirement assures better accuracy in the recordation of mining claims.

3. The trial court's final determination that NRS 517.030(2), NRS 517.100 and NRS 517.230(3) violate due process of law for lack of definiteness and certainty is without merit. Men of common intelligence are not called upon to guess at the statutes' meaning and differ as to its application. Connally v. General Constr. Co., 269 U.S. 385, 391, 46 S.Ct. 126, 70 L.Ed. 322 (1926); In re Laiolo, 83 Nev. 186, 426 P.2d 726 (1967).

NRS 517.030(2), NRS 517.100 and NRS 517.230(3) are explicit as to what the map shall contain. The express requirement is that the map must set forth the boundaries and location of the mining claim. The fact that under NRS 517.030(2) and NRS 517.230(3) the map may vary as to the ability of the locator to draw these requirements does not render the fact indefinite and uncertain. Further, the burden of showing the unacceptability of a map rests with the county recorder who can only refuse to accept a map submitted if he can ". . . affirmatively show that the map submitted does not accurately reflect the location of all the claims." NRS 517.040(2).

. . . .

Reversed.

NOTES

1. "State regulation and the regulation of the mining districts preceded the enactment of the general mining law. Gold was discovered in California in 1848, and by 1849 the gold rush had started in earnest. During the almost two decades between the discovery of gold and the enactment of the first mining law, the miners formed themselves into mining districts and made provision for their own governance. A romantic account of this period appears in [Jennison v. Kirk, 98 U.S. 453, 457, (1879)]:

> The discovery of gold in California was followed, as is well known, by an immense immigration into the State, which increased its population within three or four years from a few thousand to several hundred thousand. The lands in which the precious metals were found belonged to the United States, and were unsurveyed and not open, by law, to occupation and settlement. Little was known of them further than that they were situated in the Sierra Nevada mountains. Into these mountains the emigrants in vast numbers penetrate, occupying the ravines, gulches and cañons, probing the earth in all directions for the

precious metals. Wherever they went, they carried with them the love of order and system and fair dealing which are the prominent characteristics of our people. In every district which they occupied they framed certain rules for their government, by which the extent of ground they could severally hold for mining was designated, their possessory right to such ground secured and enforced, and contests between them either avoided or determined.

"The mining law not only ratified the regulations of these districts and the states, it also recognized their prospective effectiveness insofar as they were compatible with the policies and basic requirements of the mining law. The mining law thus delegated authority to the states to supplement its procedural requirements." Braunstein, Natural Environments and Natural Resources: An Economic Analysis and New Interpretation of the General Mining Law, 32 U.C.L.A. L. Rev. 133, 1140-41 (1985).

2. The relationship between federal and state mining laws was explained by the Supreme Court in *Butte City Water Co. v. Baker,* 196 U.S. 119 (1905). That case involved a challenge to certain Montana statutes regulating the location of mining claims. "What," the Court asked, "is the ground upon which the validity of these supplemental regulations prescribed by a state is challenged? It is insisted that the disposal of public lands is an act of legislative power, and that it is not within the competency of a legislature to delegate to another body the exercise of that power; that Congress alone has the right to dispose of the public lands, and cannot transfer its authority to any state legislature or other body. The authority of Congress over the public lands is granted by § 3, article 4, of the Constitution, which provides that 'the Congress shall have the power to dispose of and make all needful rules and regulations respecting the territory or other property belonging to the United States.' In other words, Congress is the body which is given the power to determine the conditions upon which the public lands shall be disposed of. The nation is an owner, and has made Congress the principal agent to dispose of its property. Is it inconceivable that Congress, having regard to the interests of this owner, shall, after prescribing the main and substantial conditions of disposal, believe that those interests will be subserved if minor and subordinate regulations are intrusted to the inhabitants of the mining districts or state in which the particular lands are situated? While the disposition of these lands is provided for by congressional legislation, such legislation savors somewhat of mere rules prescribed by an owner of property for its disposal. It is not of a legislative character in the highest sense of the term, and, as an owner may delegate to his principal agent the right to employ subordinates, giving to them a limited discretion, so it would seem that Congress might rightfully intrust to the local legislature the determination of minor matters respecting the disposal of these lands."

3. Assessment work is a requirement of federal law. The mining law provides that each year $100 worth of labor or improvements must be performed on unpatented mining claims. The period during which the work must be done runs from 12 noon of September 1st of one year to 12 noon of September 1st of the next. 30 U.S.C. § 28 (1982). Could a state, without changing the substantive requirement of the law, change the assessment work year, so that, for example, the period ran from July 1 to July 1. In *Norris v. United Mineral Products,* 158 P.2d 679 (Wyo. 1945), the Wyoming Supreme Court held that federal and not state law controlled. " 'State statutes in reference to mining rights upon the public domain must . . . be construed in subordination to the laws of Congress, as they are more in the nature of regulations under these laws than independent legislation.' " Id. at 689, *quoting* 1 Lindley on Mines § 249 at 544 (3rd ed. 1914).

UNITED STATES V. HASKINS
505 F.2d 246 (9th Cir. 1974)

Before HUFSTEDLER and WRIGHT, Circuit Judges, and THOMPSON, District Judge.

OPINION

BRUCE R. THOMPSON, District Judge.

This is an action in ejectment brought by the United States to enforce its right to possession of an area in the Angeles National Forest near Los Angeles, California, described as Section 28, T. 3 N., R. 14 W., San Bernardino B & M.

The Complaint alleges that defendant, Richard P. Haskins, claims the right to possess the property by virtue of four invalidated mining claims denominated as Lone Jack, Lap Wing, Roger Williams and Lady Helen, and two invalidated millsites called Lap Wing Millsite and Lady Helen Millsite. The claims in question were located as lode mining claims and encompass approximately 85.1 acres. The Complaint alleges that after appropriate administrative proceedings, the claims in question were declared null and void by final decision of the Interior Board of Land Appeals on July 30, 1971.

Defendant Haskins answered. He denied that his possessory interest in the property was based upon the four lode mining claims and two millsites. He admitted that the claims and millsites had been declared null and void by the Interior Board of Land Appeals. He denied that that decision was final and binding, stating that a reasonable time had not elapsed in which to obtain judicial review of the decision.

Defendant also filed a counterclaim in which he makes it clear that his present claim to the possession of the property must be determined on the basis of his assertion of valid placer mining claim locations of the same property which had been encompassed by the lode mining claim locations and millsites. He alleged that his patent application to obtain a patent to the Haskins Quarries Placer Mining Claim was filed on May 27, 1968, and that the processing of that application had been frustrated by the decision of the Bureau of Land Management that the then pending litigation before the Interior Board of Land Appeals, in effect, involved the same property.

The plaintiff moved for summary judgment. In opposition to the motion, defendant filed, among other things, an affidavit of E. Rowland Tragitt, a graduate of the Missouri School of Mines and Metallurgy in 1923 and a registered professional engineer in Missouri and Arizona. In addition to sixteen years of experience working for mining companies, Mr. Tragitt was employed by the Bureau of Land Management as a Field Examiner and later Supervising Engineer and Lands and Minerals Officer from 1939 until 1957. From 1957 until 1968, Mr. Tragitt was Chief Mining Engineer for Region 3 of the Forest Service, United States Department of Agriculture, Albuquerque, New Mexico. The affidavit states that in March of 1972, he made a thorough examination of the Haskins Quarries Placer Mining Claim and determined that there is a minimum of 900,000 tons of dolomite on the claims and that the use of dolomite in the Los Angeles area included the following: Flux in iron and steel foundries, filler in paints, asphalt and rubber, the manufacture of glass, paper, refractories, insulation and fertilizer, and as a supplement in animal feed. Mr. Tragitt also stated: "That in addition to the dolomite, there are a minimum of 100,000 tons of decorative stone marketable for use as roofing granules, terrazzo chips, and decorative stone in walls, rock gardens, fire places, and patios."

The District Court heard the motion for summary judgment and filed a memorandum opinion denying the motion. The following quotation summarizes the basis for the decision:

"In moving for a summary judgment of dismissal of defendant's counterclaim, the Government urges that since the land embraced within the lode claims was held to be without commercial value in the contest proceedings, the issue is res adjudicata in the patent application proceedings relating to the placer claim. But this is not necessarily so. There is after all a difference between a lode claim and a placer claim. The former relates to a vein of quartz or other rock in place, whereas a placer claim covers all forms of deposit except a vein of quartz or other rock in place, and what might be an insufficient showing of commercial value in support of a lode claim might well be sufficient to establish a valid placer mining claim. Both types of claims can, of course, be made upon the same property and can co-exist, even though in different ownership."

The Court determined that the application for patent to the placer claims should be remanded to the Department of the Interior for administrative determination. The Court also certified the case as one appropriate for interlocutory appeal under 28 U.S.C. § 1292(b), and the appeal was accepted by this Court. The District Court stated the following as the controlling questions of law involved in its decision:

"1. Can the defendant pursue his application for patent of the Haskins' Placer Mining Claim pursuant to Title 30 U.S.C. § 38 where his lode claims under which he had previously worked the property have been declared invalid for lack of discovery?

"2. Does defendant's possession of the property which antedates the effective date of the Watershed Withdrawal Act of 1928 by more than five years, entitle him to proceed with his patent application notwithstanding the fact that his notice of intention to hold as a placer mining claim was not filed until subsequent to the effective date of the Watershed Withdrawl Act?

"3. If the defendant is entitled to proceed with his patent application and since the Government has chosen this Court as a forum, does this Court nave jurisdiction over the patent application proceeding to the extent that it may make an order declaring the defendant entitled to a patent, or should these proceedings be remanded to the Department of the Interior to process defendant's application adminstratively?"

The instant controversy has a long history. The Haskins family has occupied this land within Angeles National Forest since the turn of the century. Between 1894 and 1908, Haskins' mother located lode mining claims for gold, silver, vanadium and uranium. In 1929, she filed a patent application for the lode claims known as Lone Jack, Lap Wing and for the Lap Wing Millsite. The Forest Service filed a protest. In the meantime, on May 29, 1928, Congress had enacted 45 Stat. 956 which withdrew these lands, among others, within Angeles National Forest from location and entry under the mining laws. The Withdrawal Act declared that it would not defeat or affect any lawful right which had already attached under the mining laws. Mrs. Haskins' patent applications were processed between 1929 and 1936 and the final decision was that the applications were rejected. In the course of these proceedings, a Forest Service Minerals Examiner had rendered a report in which he observed that the Lady Helen Claim, lying west of the Lone Jack, was "unquestionably patentable." It should be noted that in the administrative hearings in the 1930's, testimony was received from Mrs. Haskins and Bartholomew J. Haskins, who were then living, and that the proceedings resulted in the rejection of patents for the Lone Jack and Lap Wing claims.

The Haskins remained in possession.

In about June of 1962, Richard P. Haskins filed a verified statement specifying the exact nature of his mining claims. He claimed the four lode mining claims known as Lone Jack, Lap Wing, Roger Williams and Lady Helen and the Lap Wing Millsite and Lady Helen Millsite. In 1964, the Government initiated contest proceedings against these claims. In the administrative hearings, Haskins testified that while his predecessors had originally been looking for gold and silver, he was now interested only in dolomite. The decision of the Examiner was to the effect that there is not now a valuable mineral deposit on any of the four lode claims that the two millsites are not being used for mining or milling processes. He declared the lode claims null and void for lack of a presently valuable mineral deposit and the millsites null and void for lack of use. This is the decision which became final on July 30, 1971 by virtue of the decision of the Interior Board of Land Appeals.

In the meantime, Haskins had filed an application for patent to the ground in question as the "Haskins Quarries Mining Claim" under 30 U.S.C. § 38 (based on adverse possession under state law), and under 30 U.S.C. § 161 authorizing entry on lands chiefly valuable for building stone under the provisions of the law in relation to placer mineral claims.

The record before the Court shows that limestone is calcium carbonate and dolomite is a combination of calcium carbonate and magnesium carbonate. A 1937 report of the California State Minerologist shows that the Haskins dolomite deposit consists of a series of lenses of dolomite in the gneissoid granite from thirty to forty feet thick and from one hundred to two hundred feet in length. An analysis of one sample showed approximately 36% magnesium carbonate and 58% calcium carbonate and of another approximately 12% magnesium carbonate and 87% calcium carbonate.

1. APPLICABILITY OF 30 U.S.C. § 38.

Section 38, Title 30, United States Code, provides as follows:

"Where such person or association, they and their grantors, have held and worked their claims for a period equal to the time prescribed by the statute of limitations for mining claims of the State or Territory where the same may be situated, evidence of such possession and working of the claims for such period shall be sufficient to establish a right to a patent thereto under this chapter * * *."

This savings clause has been part of the general mining law since 1870 (16 Stat. 217). Its purpose is to obviate the necessity of proving formal compliance with requirements for locating a claim but not to dispense with proof of discovery. Cole v. Ralph, 252 U.S. 286, 40 S.Ct. 321, 64 L.Ed. 567 (1920).

We agree with the district court that the section is applicable to this case. The evidence unequivocally shows that Haskins and predecessors have been in possession of the ground and have worked the claims for over half a century and for much longer than five years prior to the enactment of the Watershed Withdrawal Act of May 29, 1928. Section 38 permits them to assert valid placer locations for the ground in question without proof of posting, recording notices of location and the like. Springer v. Southern Pac. Co., 67 Utah 590, 248 P. 819 (Utah 1926); Newport Mining Co. v. Bead Lake G. C. M. Co., 110 Wash. 120, 188 P. 27 (Wash. 1920); Humphreys v. Idaho Gold Mines, etc. Co., 21 Idaho 126, 120 P. 823 (Ida. 1912).

The Government criticizes these authorities because they involved a contest between private adverse claimants and contends that the statute does not apply against the United States, pointing to *dicta* in United States v. Consolidated Mines & Smelting Co., Inc., 455 F.2d 432 (9th Cir. 1971). We think, however, that the Supreme Court, in Cole v. Ralph, *supra,* has made it plain that the statute was intended to apply in claims for patent against the United States, saying:

"The only real divergence of opinion respecting the section has been as to whether it is available in an adverse suit, such as these are, or is addressed merely to the land department. Some of the courts have held it available only in proceedings in the department, McCowan v. Maclay, 16 Mont. 234, [40 Pac. 602] and others in greater number have held it available in adverse suits. Upton v. Santa Rita Mining Co., [14 N.M. 96, 89 Pac. 275] supra, and cases cited. The latter view has received the approval of this court. Reavis v. Fianza, [215 U.S. 16, 30 S.Ct. 1, 54 L.Ed. 72] supra; Belk v. Meagher, [104 U.S. 279, 26 L.Ed. 735] supra."

Haskins having occupied and worked the ground for more than five years may assert placer locations without proof of recording and posting. He must, nevertheless, prove discovery of a valuable mineral because the statute has no application to a trespasser on public lands, title to which cannot be acquired by entry under the mining laws of the United States. Cole v. Ralph, *supra;* Chanslor-Canfield Midway Oil Co. v. United States, 266 F. 145 (9th Cir. 1920). . . .

. . . .

The order of the District Court is affirmed and the case remanded for further proceedings consistent with this Opinion.

B. Posting the Notice of Location

ANACONDA CO. V. WHITTAKER
610 P.2d 1177 (Mont. 1980)

. . . .

SHEEHY, Justice.

This is an action involving the conflicting mining claims of Morton K. Whittaker and the Anaconda Company. Whittaker appeals from a judgment entered in the District Court, Sixth Judicial District, Sweet Grass County, in favor of Anaconda. Under the judgment, Anaconda is entitled to the possession and enjoyment of the area covered by its Eve 62 and Eve 69 mining claims which conflict with Whittaker's Pine mining claim. Whittaker also appeals from a denial of his motion for a judgment notwithstanding the verdict.

Whittaker located the Pine claim on October 1, 1950. Anaconda, on the other hand, is a successor in interest to the Eve 62 and Eve 69 claims which were located on June 10, 1968, by R. Davidson Piper. Piper was employed by Anaconda to supervise engineering crews in locating and staking approximately 79 mining claims generally known as the Eve group claims. These claims were located in an area about four to five miles in length beginning on the Boulder River and moving up the slope of Chrome Mountain. Piper signed the certificates of location for Eve 62 and Eve 69 verifying he was the locator of the two mining claims and had complied with the legal requirements for locating and recording mining claims. Section 50-701, et seq., R.C.M.1947. Piper's certificates were based upon information provided to him by the engineers and geologists of Anaconda. Under an agreement with Anaconda, Piper was to transfer to Anaconda any mining claim Piper located in Montana.

In June 1976, Whittaker applied to the Bureau of Land Management for a patent to the Pine claim. Anaconda filed an adverse claim with that agency and brought this cause to determine its right of possession to the area covered by its Eve 62 and Eve 69 mining claims.

The jury trial of this cause began on February 26, 1979. Following Anaconda's case-in-chief, Whittaker moved for a directed verdict on the grounds that Anaconda had failed to establish a valid mining location for Eve 62 and Eve 69 and therefore, lacked standing to challenge Whittaker's patent application. The motion was taken under advisement, and Whittaker was required to present evidence regarding the validity of the Pine claim.

The cause was submitted to the jury on special interrogatories, and the jury returned a verdict in favor of Anaconda. Under the verdict, the jury found Whittaker had not abandoned the Pine claim but had subjected the claim to forfeiture. The jury further found that Whittaker had in fact forfeited the Pine claim when Anaconda validly located the Eve 62 and Eve 69 claims in 1968. Accordingly, judgment was entered in favor of Anaconda.

Whittaker moved for a judgment notwithstanding the verdict, alleging the same grounds as were alleged for his motion for a directed verdict. The District Court did not rule on the motion, resulting in the motion being deemed denied. Rules 50(b) and 59(d), M.R.Civ.P. Whittaker now appeals.

The sole issue upon appeal is whether sufficient evidence supports the jury's verdict that Anaconda validly located the Eve 62 and Eve 69 mining claims. Having carefully examined the briefs of the parties and the record in this cause, we hold there is insufficient evidence to support the jury verdict.

At the outset, we note that the validity of mining locations must be judged by the law in effect at the time of the attempted location. Therefore, we judge the validity of Anaconda's attempts to locate its Eve 62 and Eve 69 mining claims under section 50-701, R.C.M.1947, as it existed prior to the 1971 amendments.

Our function in reviewing the issue presented is to determine whether substantial credible evidence in the record supports the jury's verdict. We must view the evidence in a light most favorable to Anaconda, the prevailing party below, and where the record presents conflicting evidence, resolved by the jury, this Court is precluded from disturbing the verdict. *Strong v. Williams* (1969), 154 Mont. 65, 68-69, 460 P.2d 90, 92. Here, however, there is insufficient evidence to support the jury's findings that Anaconda validly (1) discovered a vein, lode, or ledge of rock in place bearing valuable mineral deposits or (2) posted a notice of location at the point of discovery. Accordingly, the judgment entered by the District Court must be reversed. Section 50-701, R.C.M.1947.

An attempted location of a mining claim fails unless there is substantial compliance with the statutory requirements. *Ferris v. McNally* (1912), 45 Mont. 20, 25, 121 P. 889, 892. Moreover, the acts required by the statute are independent of each other, and all must be performed before a valid location exists. The last act to be performed does not relate back to the first act performed. *Thornton v. Kaufman* (1910), 40 Mont. 282, 286, 106 P. 361, 362.

The actual discovery of a vein, lode, or ledge of rock in place bearing a valuable mineral deposit is a condition precedent to a grant from the government to the exclusive possession and enjoyment of the ground located. *Upton v. Larkin* (1885), 5 Mont. 600, 603, 6 P. 66, 68. There is insufficient evidence in the record to support a finding that such an actual discovery was made on the Eve 62 and Eve 69 claims. Richard N. Miller, Anaconda's project geologist for the Stillwater complex, testified that in his opinion the legal requirements for a valid discovery had been met. However, on cross-examination, Miller admitted that no one, to his knowledge, had actually found minerals in place on the Eve 62 and Eve 69 claims. The testimony of the other Anaconda witnesses was to the same effect.

According to Anaconda, the type of discovery necessary in a controversy between rival locators has been treated much more liberally than that required in a controversy involving the federal government, and therefore, an attempted discovery based on geological studies for potential mineralization is valid. The liberality, however, which exists in a contest between rival claimants is in the consideration and application of the evidence admitted at trial and does not involve a liberal construction of the statutory requirements. 1 American Law Of Mining, § 4.46, at 650-51.

There also is not sufficient evidence in the record to support the jury's finding that Anaconda posted a notice of location at the point of discovery on the Eve 62 and Eve 69 claims. *Butte Northern Copper Co. v. Radmilovich* (1909), 39 Mont. 157, 163, 101 P. 1078, 1080. Granted, it may often times be impossible to post notice squarely on the point of discovery. Yet, the record here shows that notice was not posted near any discovery point. Dean E. Yongue, the surveyor who staked out the Eve group claims, testified regarding the method used to stake out those claims. According to Yongue, a U.S. geological map was used to stake out the corners of each claim, and once this was accomplished, previously prepared notices of location were then posted in the center of each claim, generally 50 feet from one end line and 300 feet from the corners. Yongue testified further that he never saw any mineralization at the point where the notice of location was posted. The testimony of Anaconda's other witnesses was to the same effect.

Having found no evidence whatsoever in the record to support the jury's findings that Anaconda validly (1) discovered a vein, lode or ledge of rock in place bearing a valuable mineral deposit or (2) posted a notice of location at or near the point of discovery, the judgment of the District Court is reversed. The cause is remanded to the District Court with directions to vacate the judgment entered in favor of Anaconda.

HASWELL, C. J., and DALY, SHEA and HARRISON, JJ., concur.

NOTES

1. Compare *Brewer v. Heine,* 106 P.2d 495 (Ariz. 1940) with the principal case. In *Brewer* a location was attacked on the ground that the notice of location was posted over 100 feet from the point of discovery and, thus, not "at or contiguous to the point of discovery." In upholding the validity of the claim the court found that since the notice was posted on the claim near the vein and since the monument on which it was posted was so conspicuous that it was visible for over a mile that, in fact, the location notice was posted contiguous to the point of discovery.

2. Just as the stakes that mark the boundaries of a claim need not be maintained, see *Book v. Justice Mining Co., infra,* neither is the miner obligated to maintain the notice of location. In *Bender v. Lamb,* 24 P.2d 208 (Cal. 1933) the court stated:

> Appellants urge that defendant has lost title to his mining claim . . . for the reason that he did not preserve and restore monuments, keep the boundaries well marked, and that he did not notify plaintiffs of his claim. He

was under no duty to keep the monuments in place and location notices posted so long as they were not obliterated or destroyed by his fault while he continued to perform the necessary work on the claims. *Id.* at 209.

3. "In regulating matters of posting and recording location notices and certificates, the states have generally adopted one of two systems. Under one system, which for convenience may be called the "Notice-Certificate System," a relatively simple form of notice is posted, and after the location work has been completed, a location certificate containing more detailed information must be recorded. In Colorado, Washington, and Wyoming, a very simple form of lode claim notice, containing only the name of the claim, the name of the locator, and the date, will suffice. Since such a brief notice will protect the locator, in each direction from the point of discovery, only to the extent of one-half of the total length claimed, it is prudent to add a brief indication of the extent of the ground claimed. On the other hand, where the statute does not require that the course of the vein be specified in the posted notice, it is inadvisable to do so unless the course is known with relative certainty. Silence on this point will allow the locator greater opportunity to ascertain the strike of the vein before committing himself to a specific orientation of the claim.

Under the other system, which for convenience may be called the "Recorded Notice System," the recorded location notice is a copy of the posted notice, and both the recorded notice and the posted notice are required to contain detailed information regarding the location. The Oregon statute prescribing the contents of the posted location notice includes the phrase "together with a description, either by legal subdivisions, if practicable, or if not, then by reference to some natural object or permanent monument in the vicinity of the claim, which will identify the claim located." The phrase is obviously misplaced, as it is not a statement of what the notice should contain, but rather the specification of a second act of location, and as such it should be in parallel with the phrase "by posting a notice thereon," as it was in the statute as originally enacted." 1 American Law of Mining § 5.51 (1982)

4. Typically, state statutes dealing with location of mining claims provide that all the required acts of location must be completed within a certain number of days after the discovery of valuable mineral. " 'It seems useless to add that, if [the acts of location] are not completed within the legal time, it is mere folly to pull down the old notice and put up another of a later date.' . . . If [a locator] could make a discovery and post his discovery notice on the 1st of January, and without performing any labor erase the former date and redate the notice in March, and, again, without performing any labor do the same act in May, to the exclusion of those who desire to claim a location upon the same property and develop it, there is no reason why he might not continue to do so indefinitely until he found some person who was able and willing to buy him off."

What would be the effect of changing a date on the location notice in the absence of intervening rights? See, generally, *Rummell v. Bailey*, 320 P.2d 653 (Utah 1958).

C. Discovery Workings

GLOBE MINING CO. V. ANDERSON
318 P.2d 373 (Wyo. 1959)

[The facts of this case are set forth at page 165, *supra.*]

. . . .

Adverting then to Phil Nos. 5, 6 and 8 on which the court has found discovery of mineral, the evidence showing it to be in *rock in place,* we next consider the findings of the court on the subject of discovery workings on the three claims. Some of the statements made are worthy of quotation:

"The pit on Phil 5 Claim is cut across the south shoulder of a steep hill or slope immediately adjacent to the discovery stake at which an actual original discovery was made. The pit is shown on Plaintiff's Exhibit 3 to be only 8½ feet deep, and the Court places the original depth at nine feet, allowing for one-half foot of silt washed into the deepest part of the cut, which was determined by digging down to solid rock by the writer at the deepest point of the cut. There is at least one foot of dirt or overburden at the top of the cut, making a total exposed vein or rock in place of only eight feet in height. In the words of the witness Hand, the top six feet of this formation is a rusty brown sandstone with two feet of conglomerate lens at the bottom. This last strata is apparently the only true vein matter to be found in the cut.

*   *   *

"***pit P-6B was apparently dug by the A.E.C. This pit is deep enough and long enough to meet the statutory requirements and exposes a vein of mineralized material, but it is not located on the center line of the claim.

"The pit on Phil 8 is about 145 feet south and west of the discovery stake. The surrounding terrain is relatively flat and should be classified as a shaft rather than an open cut. It is eleven feet deep with about one foot of dirt on top. A vein of light, brown sandstone with stakes of medium and coarse gravel is exposed for a depth of ten feet in height and over ten feet in length. Again, this pit is not located on the center line of the claim as staked.

"In conclusion, the Court finds that none of the discovery work relied upon by the plaintiff was performed in substantial compliance with the Wyoming statute, either because no vein at all was cut or the vein exposed was not cut for the required ten feet in length and ten feet in height or the work was not performed on the center line of the claim."

In analyzing the statement that plaintiff's discovery work on these three claims failed of substantial compliance with the Wyoming statutes, we consider first the evidence regarding the depth of the three pits. Jenkins and Brown testified positively that the pit on each of the claims was dug to a depth of at least ten feet in November 1953. There was no testimony to the contrary and apparently the court was convinced on the point because the findings do not list insufficient depth as a defect.

Whether the trial court meant to find that a vein was not exposed for the length of ten feet on Phil Nos. 5 and 6 is not fully apparent from a perusal of the conclusion reached. (The findings classified the "pit on Phil 8*** as a shaft rather than an open cut"; and, therefore, the ten-foot length requirement is inapplicable.)The findings show that the pit on Phil No. 6 was "long enough." As to Phil No. 5, they are ambiguous but reasonably interpreted indicate a substantial compliance with § 57-917, W.C.S. 1945, as to length.

We turn then to the alleged implication in the findings that a vein must be exposed for ten feet in height. Any such interpretation is in conflict with §§ 57-916 and 57-917, W.C.S. 1945, which provide respectively that the shaft be sunk to the "depth of ten [10] feet from the lowest part of the rim of such shaft at the surface" and "any open cut*** with face ten [10] feet in height." The references are clearly to the depth of the "shaft" (or "cut") and not to the height of the vein.

The statement that "pit P-6B was apparently dug by the A.E.C.," though not traceable to the court's conclusion, merits some comment. There is no testimony to support this finding and no contention that it made any difference. In fact, defendants in their brief said "the court did not find that this pit was dug by the A.E.C., but merely commented that it may have been dug by the AEC."

The court's last-mentioned reason for holding that plaintiff had not substantially complied with the statutes as to discovery work was that the work was not performed on the center line of the claim. Surprisingly, defendants fail to concur with the trial court on this point and in their brief state that:

> "***the court did not hold that such a failure invalidates a claim in Wyoming, but merely pointed out that such failure was just one more instance in which the appellant had failed to substantially comply with the mining laws of Wyoming.***"

The difficulty seems to stem from the fact that plaintiff disregarded the first paragraph of § 57-916 (requiring the discovery shaft or cut to be dug before the filing of a location certificate), recorded the location notices with the county clerk, and thereafter performed the discovery work at points some distance from the discovery monuments. The statute on its face seems positive in the requirement that the discovery work be done prior to the filing of the location certificate, but this view has long since been tempered by judicial decision. In Dean v. Omaha-Wyoming Oil Co., 21 Wyo. 133, 129 P. 881, 883, 128 P. 1023, the court stated:

> "***while it may be said that discovery should chronologically precede the acts of location it may follow, instead of preceding, such acts, and will be held good as against all who have not acquired intervening rights (Costigan on Min. Law, p. 160; Beals v. Cone, 27 Colo. 473, 62 P. 948, 83 Am.St.Rep. 92; Erwin v. Perego [8 Cir.], 93 F. 608, 35 C.C.A. 482; Lindley on Mines, § 330)."

In the instant case, plaintiff's placing the cart before the horse by posting the location notices and recording same before sinking a shaft or making a cut failed of strict complaince with the statute. But under accepted interpretation a challenger who insists on such acts being done in the proper order cannot be heard to complain if discovery occurs before his rights intervene. The trial court found that there had been discovery workings on these three claims long before defendants appeared on the scene, and they could not validly question plaintiff's delayed compliance with the statute. Nevertheless, defendants may take advantage of plaintiff's failure to place the discovery shaft at a point other than midway between the designated side lines since such moving of the discovery shaft inevitably limits the width of the claim to which a locator is entitled. Section 57-913, W.C.S. 1945, states:

> "The width of any lode claim located within Wyoming shall not exceed three hundred [300] feet on each side of the discovery shaft, the discovery shaft being always equally distant from the side lines of the claims.***"

As we interpret this definitive statute, it means that in no instance may a claim extend to more than 300 feet from the center point between the side lines. A deviation of the discovery shaft from the original center point cannot alter the position of the side line closest thereto, but automatically delimits the position of the other side line to a point "equally distant" from the discovery shaft. We find no litigation of identical problems, probably because the Wyoming statute is unique; but in the past there has arisen the question of a locator including within his claim an area in excess of the statutory limit by reason of some error in measurement. 2 Lindley on Mines, 3d ed., p. 827, states:

> "The courts uniformly hold that such a location, where it injures no one at the time it is made, is not unreasonably excessive, and where it has been made in good faith, is voidable only to the extent of the excess."

To the same effect is the case of Hawley v. Romney, 42 Idaho 645, 247 P. 1069, 1071, in which the court said:

> "***The fact that the discovery points are not in the center of the claims would not invalidate them. Where the locators extend their claims too far, it would seem that they do not on that account lose their right to the ground they were entitled to take. Flynn Group Mining Co. v. Murphy, 18 Idaho 226, 109 P. 851, 138 Am.St.Rep. 201; 2 Lindley on Mines (3d Ed.) § 362.***"

Such philosophy would seem to govern in the present situation. Plaintiff must lose that part of his claim which is in excess of the amount allowed by the statute.

To summarize this phase of the case, our analysis of the record shows that by undisputed evidence plaintiff complied substantially with the requirements of the statutes as to discovery workings on Phil Nos. 5, 6, and 8; and the trial court's findings to the contrary were, therefore, in error.

NOTES

1. The requirement of discovery workings has nothing to do with the requirement that there be a discovery of a valuable mineral deposit. The state law discovery work requirement is complied with if a hole of the requisite dimensions is dug whether or not any mineral is actually discovered or exposed.

Completion of discovery workings has absolutely no bearing on the question of whether a discovery has been made within the meaning of the mining law. "The fact of discovery is a fact of itself totally disconnected with the idea of a discovery shaft, the discovery shaft being a process of location subsequent to discovery. . . . A locator may have a [valid location under the mining law], although technically he had no discovery shaft." *United States v. Arizona Manganese Corp.*, 57 I.D. 558 (1942).

2. The courts are stricter in compelling compliance with discovery work requirements than with the other state law location requirements. The following statement is typical:

> We recognize that the statutory requirements relating to mining locations are to be liberally construed, and that only when the locator fails to comply substantially with the law must his mining locations be held invalid; however, failure to perform the statutorily required discovery work will not constitute substantial compliance.

White v. Ames Mining Co., 349 P.2d 550, 555 (Idaho 1960).

Thus, in states where discovery work is required, one cannot have a valid location unless the discovery is actually performed. However, if the discovery work is actually undertaken, only substantial compliance with the requirements of the statute is required. *Hedrick v. Lee*, 227 P. 27 (Idaho 1924).

3. The purpose of the discovery work requirement is to demonstrate that the locator intends in good faith to develop his claim. At one time, every state had a discovery work requirement. While the details varied, each state required that a shaft or pit be drilled or excavated on every claim. The depth of the shaft or pit, typically ten feet, was unrelated to the depth at which minerals were likely to be found. The state law discovery work requirement thus led to the ridiculous spectacle of shallow pits being dug on claims that contained mineral, if at all, at depths many hundreds of times that of the discovery pits. In *Adams v. Benedict*, 64 N.M. 234, 327 P. 2d 308 (1958), for example, state law mandated a ten foot discovery shaft. The uranium for which the claim was located, however, was found at a depth of 2000 feet. The recognition of the futility of the requirement and its irrelevance to meaningful exploration, combined with the substantial harm it caused the environment, has resulted in the repeal of the requirement in every state.

D. Marking the Claim on the Ground

PARKER V. JONES
572 P.2d 1034 (Ore. 1978)

. . . .

Plaintiffs filed this suit to quiet title to three quartz mining claims, Summit #1, Summit #2, and Summit #3, located in Baker County [footnote omitted]. The defendant claims ownership as a prior locator and contends the plaintiff "jumped" his claims. Plaintiff contends the defendant's claims are void for failure to post proper location notices on the claims, failure to mark the boundaries of the claims, and failure to perform the annual assessment work. The trial court found for the plaintiff on the grounds defendant failed to mark the boundaries of the claims. Defendant appeals. Since we agree with the trial court on the second issue, it is unnecessary to consider the other alleged deficiencies.

An overview of the Oregon statutes relating to filings on quartz claims is necessary.

ORS 517.010 requires one locating a vein or lode to post a notice on the claim. The notice must contain the name of the claim; the name of the locator; the date of location; the number of linear feet claimed along the vein or lode each way from the point of discovery, with the width on each side; and the general course of the vein or lode. Also, within 30 days after posting the notice the locator must mark the boundaries "by six substantial posts, projecting not less than three feet above the surface of the ground, and not less than four inches square or in diameter, or by substantial mounds of stone, or earth and stone, at least two feet in height, to wit: one such post or mound of rock at each corner and at the center ends of such claims." ORS 517.010(2).

Thereafter, the locator shall file a copy of the posted notice with the county clerk. ORS 517.030.

ORS 517.065 provides that all locations filed after December 31, 1898, that do not comply with ORS 517.010 or 517.030 "are void."

While federal statutes require that the locations must be distinctly marked so that boundaries can be readily traced, state statutes "may particularize" further the character of the marking. Also, the requirement of distinctly marking the boundaries "is an imperative and indisputable condition precedent to a valid location * * *." 2 Lindley on Mines 871, 872, § 371 (3d ed 1941).[2]

In the instant case, the defendant staked the three claims in 1973 [footnote omitted]. As partial boundary markers for one claim, he used three posts that had been previously placed by a former owner who abandoned the claim. The defendant, who appeared without counsel at the trial, testified that he did not place any boundary stakes on any of the claims and that he considered red strips placed on trees to be sufficient. When the trial court and the parties viewed the claims, the defendant had difficulty pointing out the trees which he claimed marked the boundaries, and he could not find any of the flagged or blazed trees. In fact, defendant admitted that he became "lost" while trying to find the boundaries.

The defendant made no attempt to comply with ORS 517.010 regarding marking the boundaries of his attempted locations and, under the statute, his locations are void. The obvious purpose of marking the boundaries is to give notice to others that that area has been appropriated. Plastic strips on trees not only fail to comply with the statutes but also are not permanent and, more importantly, they fail to point out the boundaries to anyone, as was demonstrated to the trial court when the parties viewed the claims. We agree with the

---

[2] In Wright v. Lyons, 45 Or. 167, 77 p. 81 (1904), the locator failed to mark the boundaries as required by the statue by omitting the two middle stakes and also failed to file an affidavit in proof of work. We held that such omissions were fatal and the claim invalid.

trial court that defendant's attempted location of the three claims must fail.

. . . .

Affirmed.

NOTES

1. The locator is not required to maintain the boundary markers of the claim on the ground. In *Book v. Justice Mining Co.,* 58 F. 106, 113 (1893), the court stated that "[i]t is not to be expected that all of the stakes and monuments would have remained in place, exposed as they were to the winds and rough weather, and liabilities of being torn down and destroyed by either innocent or evil-disposed people, for a period of four years. . . . Could it be claimed that a location is invalid on that account? Certainly not."

2. Many state location statutes provide that a claim is to be marked on the ground with substantial posts. The statutes, however, do not define what is a post. A post need not be made of wood. But, "[a] stake is not a post. The latter signifies more permanence, and to sink it in the ground requires more effort and outlay than to drive a stake. It suggests larger proportions, is more readily seen than a stake." *United States v. Sherman,* 288 F. 497 (8th Cir. 1923). Other courts have apparently treated stakes and posts as equivalents. See the quotation from *Book v. Justice Mining Co.* that follows.

3. What is a sufficient marking of a claim on the ground depends in part on the topography of the area in which the claim is located. "A location on a hill covered by a dense forest might require more definite marking than a location on a bald mountain, where the stakes, wherever placed, could be readily seen." *Book v. Justice Mining Co.,* 58 F.106, 113 (1893).

E. Filing the Location Certificate

LOMBARDO TURQUOISE MILLING & MINING V. HEMANES
430 F. Supp. 429 (Nev. 1977)

OPINION

. . . .

BRUCE R. THOMPSON, District Judge.

This action was commenced on December 31, 1975. Plaintiff alleges ownership of the Windy 1, 3, 4, 5 through 16, and New Imperial 1 and 2 unpatented mining claims (hereafter the Windy Group). Plaintiff alleges the illegal location and possession by defendants of the following unpatented claims: Marie, Blue Mary, Blue Mary Extension, Darlene, Silver Bell No. 1, and Silver Bell No. 2, which conflict with his claims. Plaintiff prays for a temporary restraining order, a preliminary and final injunction, ejectment and damages. Plaintiff has waived a jury trial.

. . . .

In 1971, the Nevada Legislature drastically revised the Nevada mining laws.

. . . .

The instant case is a prime example of the imposition on federal district courts created by diversity of citizenship as a basis of jurisdiction. The new Nevada mining law has not been construed by the Nevada Supreme Court, except to hold it constitutional. *Barton v. DeRousse,* 91 Nev. 347, 535 P.2d 1289 (1975).

Before 1971, the Nevada law required the locator of a lode mining claim to perform location work on the claim within 90 days after location. NRS 517.040; NCL 4121. The primary effects of the 1971 amendments were twofold: (1) to eliminate the requirement of the performance of location work; (2) to require the preparation and recordation of a map which would more accurately fix the location of the claim than under the previous statutory requirements. The principal issues of statutory interpretation here involved are: Is a mining claim absolutely void if the map prepared and recorded fails accurately to designate the township and range and section where the mining claim is located? (2) Does the recorded map control over the monumentation on the ground with respect to the true location and dimensions of the mining claim?

The hub of this entire case is the Marie claim. It is the claim which was occupied and worked by defendants. This activity of defendants instigated the commencement of this action by plaintiff.

. . . .

Defendants' first claim, the Marie claim, was first located by Nadler and Hammon in August, 1972. The recorded certificate of location and map place the claim in Section 21, T 20 N R 46 E (Exs. 34 and 35). The claim was monumented. The recorded information about the claim was grossly in error. The claim as located on the ground was situated mosty in Section 22, with a tip in Section 27, T 20 N R 47 E. Thus, the County Surveyor's map and the recorded information in the County Recorder's office placed no one on notice of existence of the Marie claim at the place where it was situated. Plaintiff relies on other errors in the recorded descriptions of the location of the Marie claim, which are immaterial in the light of the gross errors already noted.

On October 23, 1973, defendant Hemanes entered into an agreement to purchase the Marie claim from the original locators, made a down payment, and the final down payment, and took possession in April, 1974. He moved equipment on and started mining. Late in 1974, Hemanes located buffer claims, adjacent to the Marie claim, named the Blue Bell, Blue Mary, Blue Mary Extension, Silver Bell No. 1, Silver Bell No. 2, and Darlene. These claims are not important to the resolution of the disputes now before the Court, for reasons which will be hereinafter noted, so no detailed findings will be made respecting their monumentation and recordation. In the fall of 1974, Hemanes discovered that the Marie claim and buffer claims had been recorded in the wrong section and township, and in December, 1974, with the assistance of an engineer, Chilton, prepared and recorded amended certificates of location and an amended map, as authorized by law (NRS 517.200).

There is no disagreement between the parties with respect to the correct location on the ground of the Marie claim. The professional surveyors for both parties agree. Defendants' surveyor, Mr Alan Means, prepared a map (Ex. 64). It shows the Marie claim and associated claims situated in Sections 21, 22, 27 and 28 T 20 N R 47 E, . . .

. . . .

The dispute in this case arises because of plaintiff's contention that the Windy claims—four claims laid contiguously end to end and tied to a government survey marker, the quarter section marker between Sections 27 and 28, each location claiming a length of 1,500 feet and a width of 600 feet for each claim, if resurveyed do in fact encompass the area occupied by the Marie claim. The claimed conflict is between Windy No.4 and the Marie claim, and is demonstrated by plats prepared by plaintiff's engineers.

. . . .

The location of the Marie claim by Nadler and Hammon was not absolutely void because of the gross errors in description.

The principal touchstone on this legal issue is *Claybaugh v. Gancarz*, 81 Nev. 64, 398 P.2d 695 (1965). That was a quiet title action by the senior locator against the junior locator of an unpatented mining claim. The statute then in effect required a miner to record a certificate of location within 90 days that met statutory requirements, else the mining claim location would be void. The certificate of location recorded by the plaintiff was found to be defective. Nevertheless, the Nevada Supreme Court reversed the trial court and held that the good faith of the senior locator and the bad faith of the junior locator justified a liberal construction of substantial compliance with the statutory requirements for recording a certificate of location. The Court said:

"However, with or without such statute, jurisdiction after jurisdiction has considered this question and has decided mining conflicts on the basis of the presence or absence of good faith. The purpose of the certificate is to impart constructive notice to subsequent locators of the existence of the claim, its location and extent, just as the markings upon the ground are intended to impart actual notice of the same facts. As to parties having actual notice, as respondent did in this instance, the defects in the certificate, whatever they may be, are to be deemed immaterial. *Heilman v. Loughrin*, 57 Mont. 380, 188 P. 370, citing the Montana statute and 2 Lindley on Mines § 379 (3rd ed. 1914).

"In view of the increasing emphasis placed by the courts in recent years on the question of the good faith of the conflicting junior claimant and to excuse defects in the senior location if this is not shown, we hold that the existence of good faith in behalf of Claybaugh in the location of the Nine-oh claim and the bad faith of Gancarz in the relocation of said claim preclude Gancarz from challenging the title of the good faith senior locator. The good or bad faith of the senior and junior locators was a real and important issue to be determined by the trial court.

"It was error for the trial court to grant respondent's motion to strike appellant's location notice and his location certificate. They were important items in support of his good faith. It was also error for the court to refuse to hear evidence concerning the lease to respondent in existence at the time respondent relocated over appellant's claim. Such evidence was relevant and material with reference to the asserted bad faith of respondent.

The trial court's explanation of its rulings that Claybaugh 'had nothing to lease' simply begged the question—whether Claybaugh's Nine-oh was or was not a valid subsisting claim.

As the record contains ample evidence of the good faith of appellant in the location of the Nine-oh and bad faith of the respondent in relocating the claim as the Gancarz, no purpose will be served in remanding the case for new trial.

The foregoing is without intent to indicate that this court would not, in the absence of such element of the junior locator's bad faith, hold the senior locator to a substantial compliance with the requirements of the statute as amended in 1941." . . .

Cf. *Columbia Standard Corp. v. Ranchers Explor. & Dev. Inc.,* 468 F.2d 547 (10th Cir. 1972).

The point is of importance because even if it should be held that the Windy No. 4 claim did not in fact occupy the area of the Marie claim, the other claims for which plaintiff filed certificates of location in February, 1973, do. If the Marie location is void because of the misdescriptions in the certificate of location, that ground was open to entry by a subsequent locator. *Gustin v. Nevada-Pacific Development Corp.,* 125 F.Supp. 811 (D.C.Nev.1954).

The plaintiff's bad faith in locating the additional mining claims is evident from the facts hereinabove reported in support of the findings on adverse possession.

Was it the intention of the Nevada Legislature when it enacted the 1971 amendments to the mining laws to overrule the good faith principles of the *Claybaugh* case? We think not. The 1971 Legislature reenacted N.R.S. 517.050 requiring recordation of a certificate of location in substantially the same form, including the specific language construed in Claybaugh declaring the location of a mining claim "absolutely void" for substantial non-compliance. The amendments made to N.R.S. 517.050 were those required by the substitution of the mapping requirement for the location work. (1971 Sts. of Nev. 2199-30.) We infer that the *Claybaugh* interpretation was intended to apply to the amended statutes, that is, that equitable principles will be applicable in a contest between a claim jumper and a senior locator claiming under a defective location, and the demonstrated bad faith of the junior locator will preclude recognition of his claim to the property. Further, we observe that the 1971 amendments do not contemplate accuracy in mapping as a substitute for monumentation on the ground. The requirements of pre-existing law with respect to defining the boundaries of the claim (N.R.S. 517.030) were retained. The amendments to this section pertain to the substitution of a map for the location work. The amendments provide that where an official corner of the public land survey cannot be found after due diligence, the prospector may build a "claim location marker", a rock pillar four feet high or a steel post five feet high, and that only one mineral claim marker is required for each contiguous group of claims. The statute also says: "The locator need not employ a professional surveyor or engineer, but each locator shall prepare a map which is in accordance with his abilities to map and properly set forth the boundaries and location of his claim." From these provisions it is apparent that basic reliance was still to be placed on the monumentation of the claim and that the recorded map would not necessarily be sufficient to give constructive notice of the place of its location. Thus the quoted language from *Claybaugh,* supra, is still applicable: "The purpose of the certificate is to impart constructive notice to subsequent locators of the existence of the claim, its location and extent, just as the markings upon the ground are intended to impart actual notice of the same facts. As to parties having actual notice, as respondent did in this instance, *the defects in the certificate, whatever they may be, are to be deemed immaterial.*" (Emphasis added.)

On July 1, 1971, the Nevada Bureau of Mines and Geology issued a printed pamphlet containing questions and answers respecting the new mining law. The answers were reviewed and approved by the Attorney General of Nevada. This is persuasive authority in the absence of more controlling precedent. Question and Answer 19 are as follows:

"Q. If I make a mistake in plotting my claim(s) on the map or in tying to the land corner or claim location marker, does this invalidate my claim?

"A. No, the claim monuments on the ground always mark the legal position of the claim. However, if a mistake is discovered, a new, correct map must be filed, in order to comply with the law."

Each case of this character must be decided on its facts. In the usual case every senior locator will be held "to a substantial compliance with the requirements of the statute" (*Claybaugh,* supra, 81 Nev. at p. 81, 398 P. 2d at p. 705).

The correct dimensions and locations of an unpatented mining claim are fixed by the monumentation on the ground, not by the recorded map.

The Court has found that the Windy No. 4 claim, as located on the ground, did not encroach on the Marie claim, as located on the ground. It is probable that a resurvey of the Windy claims and the Marie claim extending them to the full length claimed for each location (1,500 feet), would prove some encroachment irrespective of whether the claims are platted along the ridge line, an adjustment for magnetic declination having been made, or are platted as shown on the Hendrix and Hodges recorded map (Ex. 5). See also Ex. 66. Thus, we must decide whether the claims as monumented and located on the ground prevail over the recorded descriptions.

The Nevada law is clearly stated in *Gray, et al. v. Cuykendall, et al.,* 53 Nev. 466, 6 P.2d 442 (1931). The court said:

"It was said in *Treadwell v. Marrs,* 9 Ariz. 333, 83 P. 350, 355, on an issue as to the location of a mining claim, 'that, where the monuments are found upon the ground, or *their position or location can be determined with certainty,* the monuments govern, rather than the location certificate; but where the course and distances are not with certainty defined by monuments or stakes, the calls in the location notice must govern and control.

This is a salutary and well-settled rule *calculated to require the best evidence of the true boundaries* of a claim, and *to prevent the swinging or floating of claims to the detriment of subsequent locators.* Or course inaccuracies or mistakes in a mining location will not invalidate the location, and in such cases monuments originally erected on the ground control the courses and distances. *Book v. Justice Min. Co.* (C.C.) 58 F. 106; *Gibson v. Hjul,* 32 Nev. 360, 108 P. 759. It is by such means that mistakes may be made known. But this applies only where the monuments or stakes can be clearly ascertained, otherwise the description in the location notice controls. *Swanson v. Koeninger,* 25 Idaho 361, 137 P. 891; *Tiggeman v. Mrzlak,* 40 Mont. 19, 105 P. 77; *Flynn Group Min. Co. v. Murphy,* 18 Idaho 266, 109 P. 851, 138 Am.St.Rep. 201; *Thallman v. Thomas* (C.C.) 102 F. 935; Lindley on Mines (3d ed.), sec. 375; 40 C.J. 807." (Emphasis supplied.)

See also: *Cardoner v. Stanley Consol. Min. & Mill Co.,* 193 F. 517 at 519 (D.Idahl 1911). The authorities on this point were fully collated and discussed in the dissenting opinion of Justice Harnsberger in *Masek v. Ostlund,* 358 P.2d 100 (Wyo. 1960). No useful purpose would be served by repeating them here.

The problem in application of the law to the facts of this case is one of the sufficiency of the proof. With respect to the location on the ground of the original Windy Claims, about the only points of reference which everyone found were the government survey section marker between sections 28 and 27 and the location monument for Windy No. 1. Hendrix and Hodges testified that they had fully monumented the claims. Lombardo testified that he had fully reconstructed and reestablished all corners and center posts and location monuments after he purchased the claims. Yet, few of these could be found and none clearly identified by disinterested witnesses who carefully examined the claims early in 1976. The suspicion is that monuments were destroyed. In the light of Lombardo's testimony, the testimony of James J. Owens, Engineer, is incredible; not that he didn't find what he said he found, but his identification and characterization of his findings are unbelievable. The only boundary of the Windy claims here in contention is the north end line of Windy No. 4. The best evidence of the true location of that end line, well south of the Marie claim, is the testimony of Hendrix, Hodges, Hammon, and Nadler. The testimony of other witnesses that Lombardo disavowed any encroachment on the Marie claim is also credited. Lombardo's acquiescence in the mining activity on the Marie claim is corroborative. In sum, overwhelming evidence establishes with certainty the location on the ground of the north end line of Windy No. 4. That evidence controls.

All the prospectors involved in this lawsuit were experienced miners. It is common knowledge that a miner, locating a claim, almost uniformly claims by written description the full distances authorized by federal and state law, that is, 1,500 feet in length and 600 feet in width. That is the case here. The monumentation on the ground did not encompass the full area authorized. It controls. Thus the locators of the Marie claim are the senior locators and the locators of the Windy claims and Imperial claims are the junior locators.

Plaintiff cites *Allen v. Laudahn,* 59 Idaho 207, 81 P.2d 734, for the proposition, in substance, that the locator of a mining claim is incompetent to testify in impeachment of his recorded title. The opinion is inapposite. It pertains to testimony by the original locator that he had not made a discovery of valuable mineral. The reported decisions are replete with testimony respecting the situation of the claim on the ground vis-a-vis the recorded description, most of which are discussed in *Masek v. Ostlund, supra.* Lombardo did not rely on the Hodges and Hendrix map when he bought the Windy claims. Hodges told him that the claim down below was the Ralph King property. While it may well be that a locator cannot deny that he made a discovery to invalidate a recorded title which he conveyed, the law is clear that satisfactory proof of the actual location of a mining claim will prevail over the calls and distances of the recorded description.

. . . .

Our conclusions from the foregoing are that defendants are the owners of the Marie claim and are entitled to a decree quieting title and enjoining plaintiff from any use or occupancy of the property. . . .

. . . .

ATHERLEY V. BULLION MONARCH URANIUM CO.
335 P.2d 71 (Utah 1959).

. . . .

COWLEY, District Judge.

This is an action brought by the plaintiff-appellant, hereinafter referred to as plaintiff, to quiet title to an unpatented mining claim known as the Poison Fraction. Defendant-respondent, hereinafter referred to as defendant, in its answer denied the validity of such claim and sought by counterclaim to quiet its title to an unpatented mining claim known as Farmer John No. 3. The alleged Poison Fraction claim of plaintiff overlaps the southeastern portion of the alleged Farmer John No. 3 claim. This overlapping constitutes the area of dispute in this case.

In the trial court defendant filed a motion for summary judgment based upon the pleadings and the deposition of plaintiff. The trial court granted this motion, holding that there was no triable issue of fact, and as a matter of law defendant was entitled to have its Farmer John No. 3 claim quieted to the exclusion of the disputed overlapping portion of plaintiff's Poison Fraction claim. Plaintiff appeals.

The Farmer John No. 3 claim was located in 1943 by one James M. Sargent who subsequently conveyed his interest therein to defendant. The mining of uranium from said claim was the first uranium mining conducted in the state of Utah and is located near Marysvale, Piute County.

The side lines of the Farmer John No. 3 claim as originally located by James M. Sargent in 1943 ran in a northeast-southwest direction, having a strike of North 50 east, and running parallel to a fluorspar vein. This original notice of location was properly filed of record as required under section 40-1-4, U.C.A. 1953. A few years later, but at least by 1952, defendant shifted its corner stakes so that the side lines on the ground of the relocation run due east and west and crossed the fluorspar vein rather than paralleling it. This relocation took in new unoccupied ground east and south of the old northeast-southwest boundary line. Defendant did not file of record the 1952 amended location notice.

Plaintiff located his Poison Fraction claim in May of 1955, and because he discovered that defendant had not filed of record in Piute County an amended location notice, he staked over and overlapped the southeast portion of Farmer John No. 3 as amended. Plaintiff knew that the boundary lines of Farmer John No. 3 as amended had been in their present location at least since 1952 at the time he located his Poison Fraction claim. Plaintiff also knew at the time he located his claim that defendant was in possession of the area in dispute through its lessee and was and had been conducting mining operations thereon for a few years previously.

Nearly all of the mining operation of Farmer John No. 3 has been conducted on this conflict area. Between 1949 and 1952 plaintiff under contract with defendant removed some ten thousand tons of ore from the area now in dispute, and the claim was leased in 1954 to Vanadium Corporation of America, which company has since worked and developed the mine. Plaintiff estimates in his deposition that $300,000 has been expended by defendant or its lessees and contractors in developing the conflict area.

It is conceded that defendant or its predecessors in interest have complied with all requirements under the mining laws of the United States, Title 30 U.S.C.A. § 22 et seq.; and the Utah mining laws, Title 40, Chapter 1, U.C.A. 1953, except as to the provision, section 4 of the Utah law, requiring the recording of a "copy of location notice" as it applies to the 1952 amended location notice of the Farmer John No. 3.

The only issue on this appeal is whether or not a mining locator, with full knowledge of the claim of a prior claimant, may deliberately stake over the boundaries of said prior claimant while the latter is in possession and mining the property claimed, and assert the invalidity of the prior claim, on the sole ground that a few years before the prior claimant had relocated his claim without filing of record an amended location certificate.

Plaintiff contends that since no amended notice of location was filed he had a right to rely on the *original recorded* notice of location, thereby claiming that the area in dispute in this case falls outside of the Farmer John No. 3 claim, and that defendant therefore cannot assert a prior right to the conflict area against this plaintiff. In this plaintiff is in error for reasons hereinafter stated.

Under federal law the only requirements imposed upon a locator of a mining claim is the discovery of mineral within the limits of the claim, and the segregation of the claim from the public domain by distinctly marking the corners of the ground so that its boundaries can be readily traced. There is no requirement of recording a location notice under federal law. The Utah law relating to the location of mining claims on the public domain provides no additional requirements insofar as the location itself, as distinguished from the record of the claim is concerned. Said law does provide, however, that a copy of the location notice should be filed of record in the office of the county recorder of the county in which the claim is located within 30 days after the location of the claim. The recording of a notice of location is not requisite to the initiation of title under the mining laws, and the failure to record does not forfeit a title properly initiated. The locator's title to a mining claim under the mining laws is initiated by the discovery of mineral coupled with the segregation of the claim from the public domain by the marking of the boundaries thereof. . . .

The title to a mining claim is therefore initiated by discovery and segregation both of which requirements were performed in this case. An estate immediately vested and the Utah law does not provide for a forfeiture for failure to record. Other cases holding that the right to a mining claim will not be forfeited by a failure to record a notice of location, in the absence of a state statute expressly providing for a forfeiture on that ground are Jupiter Mining Co. v. Bodie Consolidated Mining Co., C.C., 11 F. 666; Dripps v. Allison's Mines Co., 45 Cal. App. 95, 187 P. 448; Indiana Nevada Mining Co. v. Gold Hills Min. & Mill Co., 35 Nev. 158, 126 P. 965; Johnson v. Ryan, 43 N.M. 127, 86 P.2d 1040.

Plaintiff had actual knowledge in this case of defendant's amended claim and exclusive possession at the time he located his Poison Fraction claim. The actual notice which plaintiff had is equivalent to valid record notice, Flynn v. Velvestad, D.C., 119 F.Supp. 93, affirmed, 9 Cir., 230 F.2d 695. . . .

It is well established law that a locator, with full knowledge that a particular tract of land is claimed by another, may not enter such land for the purpose of establishing a mining claim thereon while such other person is in possession and working the claim.

It should be noted that the rule is applied only in possessory actions between mining claimants, such as the instant case, and not in those cases where the rights of United States or those of persons claiming under nonmineral laws are involved. As was stated in Houck v. Jose, D.C., 72 F.Supp. 6, 10, affirmed, 9 Cir., 171 F.2d 211:

"No presumptions are indulged in favor of a claimant, even in possession, against the United States but as between a locator in possession and a subsequent intruding locator, the law favors the locator who, in good faith, occupies mineral lands and does improvement work on them against the intruder who goes on the land which he knows has been located, claimed and occupied by another and tries to oust him."

In Eilers v. Boatman, 3 Utah 159, 167, 2 P. 66, 72, the territorial court of Utah held that one cannot locate ground on which another is in the actual possession under claim and color of right, because such ground is not vacant and unoccupied, in the following language:

"It is conceded by the respondents, and it is doubtless true, that, as between two locators, and as affecting their rights only, one cannot locate ground of which the other is in actual possession under claim or color of right, because such ground would not be vacant and unoccupied."

Affirmed, 111 U.S. 356, 357, 4 S.Ct. 432, 28 L.Ed. 454.

The contention of the subsequent locator in the Eilers case was that the prior locator had not properly stated his claim so as to segregate the same from the public domain.

In a fairly recent Idaho case, Gerber v. Wheeler, 1941, 62 Idaho 673, 115 P.2d 100, 103, the court, after noting that the subsequent locator had actual knowlege of the boundaries of the prior claim, said:

"We recently passed upon a somewhat similar question in the case of Independence Placer Mining Co. v. Hellman, 62 Idaho 180, 109 P.2d 1038, 1042, and said: 'One who had actual notice, that a prior locator is claiming a tract of mining ground and has done location work thereon and continued to do prospecting and assessment work on the property, is not in a position to make a valid location on such property. In such case he has notice that the ground is claimed by another and that so much of it as is claimed and occupied is no longer public domain subject to location; and he may not question the sufficiency of the original location or the character of the original occupant's title.' " [Citing cases]—

Plaintiff's contention that defendant's priority of location to the conflict area cannot be maintained because of its failure to record the 1952 amended location notice is only correct where there are intervening rights in third parties at the time the amendment is made taking in the new ground. But where, as here, there were no intervening rights in third parties or this plaintiff in the conflict area at the time of the amendment, there can be no question as to defendant's right to amend its claim so as to take in new territory not originally claimed. Shoshone Min. Co. v. Rutter, 9 Cir., 87 F. 801. As said in Lindley, Volume 2, Third Edition, Section 396:

"There is no statute, law, rule or regulation which prevents a locator of a mining claim from amending his location and including additional vacant ground unclaimed by other parties, * * *"

* * *

NOTES

1. As the principal case states, "[t]here is no requirement of recording a location notice under federal law." Section 28 of the federal mining law does provide, however, "[a]ll records of mining claims . . . shall contain the name or names of the locators, the date of the location, and such a description of the claim or claims located by reference to some natural object or permanent monument as will identify the claim." This provision has been construed not as requiring the filing of a location certificate, but only as specifying the minimum contents of the certificate if one is required by state law. *Haws v. Victoria Copper Mining Co.,* 160 U.S. 303 (1895).

2. The courts strongly disfavor "paper" or "office" locations, that is locations that are made without ever entering onto the land. Such purported locations involve filing certificates of location without performing any of the other acts of location. Thus, in *Vevelstad v. Flynn,* 230 F.2d 695, 704 (9th Cir. 1956), the court held that "a locator may not acquire a claim merely by walking into the recorders office and filing a location certificate. . . ." See also, *United States v. Zweifel,* 508 F. 2d 1150 (10th Cir. 1975).

3. Many state statutes dealing with location procedures require that the certificate of location contain a description of the claim. It is well settled that the description contained in the certificate of location is not required to meet the same standard that would be applied to a deed or to most other legal documents. The test for mining claims is not whether the description describes one and only one parcel of ground, but the much more liberal standard of whether a reasonable person "who was making an honest attempt to find the boundary lines of [the] claim could determine [what] was meant." *Steele v. Preble,* 77 P.2d 418 (Ore. 1938).

This rule of construction is based in part on the "natural inclination" of the courts to favor the senior locator. *Book v. Justice Mining Co.,* 58 F. 106 (1893). It is also based on the practical recognition that "locations are often made without any accurate knowledge of the true course and directions which a compass would readily give, and mistakes in the notice as to the direction and course of the ground located often occur. But such mistakes do not invalidate the location. Positive exactness in such matters should never be required. It is the marking of the location by posts and monuments that determines the particular ground located." *Id.* at 115.

Notwithstanding the liberality which the courts display, not every description will be upheld. In *J.E. Riley Inv. Co. v. Sakow,* 98 F.2d 18, 10 (9th Cir. 1938) a claim was described as being on "the right limit of Otter Creek." Since Otter Creek was 8 or 9 miles long, the court found the description inadequate to identify the claim. *Id.* at 11. On the other hand, in *Dennis v. Barnett,* 85 P.2d 916 (Cal App 1938) the court found a claim described simply as "on the north side of the Mojave river about 400 yards from the Union Pacific track and in Cave Canyon Mining District" to be adequately described. *Id.* at 918.

Moreover, the description must be sufficiently definite to prevent the miner from "floating" the claim to cover after-discovered ore to the prejudice of the rights of intervening locators.

4. The certificate of location is required to be recorded mainly to give constructive notice to third persons. "If those facts are already known to would-be locators, neither the failure to record nor the recording of a notice containing an insufficient description should affect the rights initiated by the prior claimant." *Bradshaw v. Miller,* 377 P.2d 781 (Utah 1963).

HENRY D. FRIEDMAN
49 IBLA 97 (1980)

. . . .

On January 15, 1980, the Alaska State Office, Bureau of Land Management (BLM), received by mail a copy of a location notice for the Wickersham Below Discovery placer mining claim from Henry D. Friedman, the locator of this claim, which notice stated that it was located on October 12, 1979. On February 15, 1980, BLM issued a decision rejecting this proof and declaring the claim abandoned and void under 43 CFR 3833.4(a) for failure to comply with the requirement set out at 43 CFR 3833.1-2(b) that Friedman, as the owner of an unpatented mining claim located on Federal land after October 21, 1976, file a copy of the offical record of the notice or certificate of location of his claim within 90 days of the date of location. [Authors note: 43 C.F.R. § 3833.0-1 et seq. contains the regulations promulgated by the Interior Department to implement the filing provisions of the Federal Land Policy and Management Act, 43 U.S.C. § 1701.] Friedman (appellant) appealed this decision.

As BLM held, appellant was required by 43 CFR 3833.1-2(b) to "file" a copy of the official record of the notice or certificate of location of the claim with BLM within 90 days of the date of location, in this case, on or before January 10, 1980. This section expressly notes that "file shall mean being received and date stamped by the proper BLM office." Appellant's documents were not received and date stamped by the Alaska State Office, Anchorage, which is the " proper BLM office," until January 15, 1980, 5 days late.

Under 43 CFR 3833.4(a), the failure to file the instrument required by 43 CFR 3833.1-2(b) within the time period prescribed therein is deemed conclusively to constitute an abandonment of the mining claim and to void it. We have consistently applied the statutory requirement for strict enforcement of the 90-day deadline for filing in these circumstances. *Arthur W. Schmidt,* 47 IBLA 143 (1980); *Eric Murray,* 47 IBLA 112 (1980); *George Toole,* 47 IBLA 89 (1980); *Jim Spicer,* 42 IBLA 288 (1978); and cases cited therein. Accordingly, BLM properly rejected appellant's untimely tendered notice of location and declared the claim abandoned and void.

Appellant notes that he mailed the required papers to BLM from McKinley Park, Alaska, on January 5, 1980, and that the mailing must have been delayed due to circumstances beyond his control. The mailing envelope is in the record and is postmarked as of the morning of January 6, 1980. Thus, it apparently took 9 days for the letter to reach BLM.

However, this fact is of no benefit to appellant, as merely mailing the notice of location within the 90-day period is not timely "filing" where it does not arrive at BLM prior to the deadline. *M.J. Reeves,* 41 IBLA 92, 93 (1979). It is established that a claimant must bear the consequences of mishandling of mailed instruments by the postal service where he selects that method of transmitting them. *Everett Yount,* 46 IBLA 74 (1980); *James E. Yates,* 42 IBLA 391 (1979); *Amanda Mining and Manufacturing Ass'n,* 42 IBLA 144 (1979).

Appellant also asserts that the fact that they were mailed 9 days before they were date stamped suggests that BLM received these papers timely but delayed date stamping them until after the deadline. Absent any evidence to support this speculation, it is pure conjecture. There is nothing in the record to support such a conjecture. Where a mining claimant merely raises the possibility that BLM officials mishandled notices of location submitted in attempted compliance with the requirements of 43 CFR 3833.1-2(b), causing them to be date stamped as untimely, he has not met the burden of rebutting the presumption that BLM officials have properly discharged their duties in receiving and promptly date stamping all such notices tendered to them. *E.M. Koppen,* 36 IBLA 379 (1978); see *A.G. Golden,* 22 IBLA 261 (1975); *Amoco Production Co.,* 16 IBLA 215 (1974). Therefore, pursuant to the authority delegated to the Board of Land

Appeals by the Secretary of the Interior, 43 CFR 4.1, the decision appealed from is affirmed.

NOTES

1. As the present case demonstrates, the Interior Department strictly construes and enforces the filing provisions of FLPMA. These provisions are regarded by the Interior in much the same way that the courts regard statutes of limitations, i.e., they are enforced mechanically and without much concern for the equities that might be present in a particular situation. Like statutes of limitations, FLPMA may prove to be a fertile ground for attorney malpractice. The filing requirements of FLPMA are also applicable with regard to the performance of assessment work, and they are considered in much more detail in the next chapter.

F. Special Considerations in the Location of Placer Claims

SNOW FLAKE FRACTION PLACER
37 L.D. 250 (1908)

This is an appeal by Otto W. Carlson et al. from the action of your office of July 25, 1907, citing them to show cause why their entry (No. 63, Juneau, Alaska) for the Snow Flake Fraction placer mining claim, survey No. 596, should not be canceled because of the non-conformity of the claim to the system of the public land surveys and the rectangular subdivision thereof.

The claim was located July 17, 1900, upon land not embraced by the public surveys. The United States mining laws had been theretofore expressly extended to the District of Alaska by the acts of May 17, 1884 (23 Stat., 24, 26), and June 6, 1900 (31 Stat., 321, 329). According to the field notes and plat of the mineral survey the claim, which is designated as a "bench" placer, has an area of 16,178 acres, and is bounded by six courses. One of the boundary lines runs nearly east and west, but the other five are laid at diagonals to the courses of public survey lines. For the most part the claim represents a diamond-shaped figure with the greatest traverse dimension from east to west. . . .

This case involves the proper construction of sections 2329 to 2331, inclusive, of the revised statutes. . . .

On January 5, 1884, Secretary Teller in a decision reversing the Commissioner of the General Land Office employed this language in the case of William Rablin (2 L.D., 764):

> It appears that the location was made since 1872, and after official survey of the adjacent territory, that it covers the bed of Bear River for some 12,000 feet and a small quantity of surface-ground along, its banks, and that it does not conform to the system of surveys. From the evidence on file it appears that the "Bear River" is a very small unnavigable stream,

winding through a canyon with precipitous, non-mineral and uncultivable banks, wherein have accumulated extensive placer deposits, which are embraced in said location.

Your decision is grounded on the alleged fact that the location does not conform "as near as practicable" to the system of public surveys, for the reason that the law requires "that placer locations upon the surveyed lands shall conform to the public surveys in all cases, except where this is rendered impossible by the previous appropriation or reservation of a portion of the legal subdivision of ten acres upon which the claim is situated." I think that sections 2329 to 2331, Rev. Stat. should not receive so narrow a construction. While they provide for ten-acre subdivisional surveys, they also contemplate cases where it is not practicable to conform the location to such subdivisional lines. They do not limit such cases to those where there has been a prior appropriation of a part of the subdivision, but extend it to every case where it may be impracticable to so locate the claim. The expression "as near as practicable," is therefore to be read "as near as reasonably practicable," and in each case presenting itself a sound discretion must be exercised in determining the question of practicability.

On October 14, 1887, Acting Secretary Muldrow, in the case of Pearsall (6 L.D., 227, 231) decided that—

The proper construction of sections 2329 to 2331 Revised Statutes, was carefully considered by this Department in the case of William Rablin (2 L.D.764), wherein it is held that the requirement of the statute that the claim upon surveyed land must conform to the legal subdivisions thereof "as near as practicable," must be construed to mean that the claim must conform only "as near as reasonably practicable"; that it is the intention of the mining laws generally, to permit persons to take a certain quantity of land fit for mining and not compel them to take such a quantity irrespective of its fitness for mining; that the act of July 9, 1870 (16 Stat., 217) was modified by the act of May 10, 1872 (17 Stat., 91), so as to provide for exceptional cases.

The question of the conformity of placer claims to the United States system of public land surveys and the rectangular subdivisions of such surveys, had long lain in abeyance in the Department until it was again presented and passed upon in the case of Miller Placer Claim (30 L. D., 225). Relying upon the decisions quoted (2 L. D., 764, and 6 L. D., 227) placer miners located claims of every conceivable form. The practice in the various mining districts had in the meantime produced some incongruous results. Placer claims of all shapes and forms were presented and approved for patent. The only restriction seems to have been that the placer location should not exceed the amount of land allowed by law. Little or no attention was given to the conformity provision of the statute. The survey of the Miller placer was remarkable in shape. It was composed of two large tracts of land over three miles apart. The southernmost tract embraced in its limits and followed the general course of the south fork of the South Platte River, while the northernmost tract had running through it for its entire length a stream known as Lost Park Creek. The two tracts were connected by a narrow strip of land over three miles long, apparently from thirty to fifty feet wide, which formed a portion of the claim as a whole. The Department disallowed the claim because it not only failed to approximately conform to the United States system of public land surveys and the rectangular subdivisons thereof but appeared to be totally at variance with such system, holding that the law affords no warrant for cutting the public lands into lengthy strips of such narrow width and such great length, whether the claim be located on surveyed or unsurveyed lands. The Department hereby especially approves the decision in the Miller Placer Claim case. Such a fantastically shaped claim is unwarranted.

. . .

The foregoing, together with many unreported decisions to the same general effect, have resulted from the incongruous forms and extravagant dimensions of numbers of placer locations which have of late years come before the land department for adjudication. Upon the theory that the conformity provisions had no relation to locations upon unsurveyed lands, and that the only limitation imposed by the law was that of area, it was considered that such locations could be elongated in proportion as they were narrowed, so as to secure the maximum area available under the law. For example, upon that theory, a location by eight persons to embrace one hundred and sixty acres, confined to an average of fifty feet in width, could be extended to a length of twenty-six miles; and this conception of flexibility of outline, which has often manifested itself in locations of curious shapes, has in numbers of cases been employed in the appropriation of water-courses, ravines, etc., for inordinate distances. A case decided by the Department October 6, 1900 (not reported), involved a single location over sixteen miles in length, with an average width of about fifty-one feet, containing 102.974 acres. Concrete instances could be multiplied.

In the correction of what the Department regards as clearly subversive of the law, the lines have been so tightly drawn as practically to impose a strict conformity, with few exceptional cases, to legal subdivisions if upon surveyed lands, or in accordance with the system of east-and-west and north-and-south bounding lines and of dimensions corresponding to appropriate legal subdivisions if made upon unsurveyed lands. In the light of the pending case, however, considered in connection with certain others of similar import now pending here on appeal and with the several accompanying briefs, without receding from the view that the limitations imposed by the law were designed to keep such locations within reasonable bounds, the Department is persuaded that it has observed a more rigid interpretation of the letter of the statute than is warranted by a just regard for the mining conditions and customs and the interests in harmony therewith which must have been within the legislative contemplation.

Sections 2329 and 2330 are taken from the placer act of July 9, 1870 (16 Stat., 217), which amended the original lode law of July 26, 1866. The provisions of the act of 1870 carried into section 2329 permitted placer claims to be located both upon surveyed and unsurveyed lands, and contained the positive requirements, however, that locations on surveyed lands should strictly conform to the legal subdivisions of the public lands. The provisions of the same act which appear in section 2330, on the other hand, dealt with locations upon surveyed lands; authorized the further subdivision of established 40-acre legal subdivisions into 10-acre tracts; permitted joint entry of contiguous claims of any size, although less than 10 acres each, which might result from the division or partial appropriation of fractional subdivisions, and fixed the maximum area of a placer location at 160 acres with a requirement that it conform to the United States surveys.

The law of 1870, now appearing in sections 2329 and 2330, was too harsh and inflexible when actually put in operation. It was so unsatisfactory and so widely at variance with the methods theretofore prevailing in locating placers that Congress was speedily prevailed upon to change the law. It was made more elastic by the act of 1872, found in section 2331. This section plainly supplements and modifies the act of 1870, sections 2329 and 2330, as the Department has already held in Wood Placer Mining Company, supra. It is obvious from its opening clause that this section relates to locations both upon surveyed and unsurveyed lands. It not only waives further survey and plat when locations upon surveyed lands conform to legal subdivisions but impliedly contemplates cases of non-conformity. The act also by necessary implication recognizes locations upon unsurveyed lands. Then follows the broad provision that "All placer mining claims located after the tenth day of May, eighteen hundred and seventy-two, shall conform as near as practicable with the United States system of public land surveys and the rectangular subdivisions of such surveys;" clearly meaning that these limitations shall apply whether the locations be upon surveyed or unsurveyed land. It also has the further provision that 'No such location shall include more than twenty acres for each individual claimant." The Department holds that this section 2331 applies to placer locations upon both surveyed and unsurveyed lands. The words in section 2331 "system of public land surveys and the rectangular subdivisions of such surveys" when applied to unsurveyed lands simply means that claims should, if practicable, have east-and-west and north-and-south bounding lines, and that the claim should be rectangular, if practicable, and in compact form so that when the adjacent land is surveyed by the Government it will not find it cut into all conceivable shapes.

In 1 Lindley on Mines, 2nd ed., sec. 448, it is said: "As to whether it is practicable to make a location or survey conform to legal subdivisions is a matter which rests entirely within the land department. . . .

Whether placer claims conform sufficiently is a question of fact to be determined by the Department. Each case must be decided upon its own facts. It is the policy of the Government to have entries, whether they be for agricultural or mining lands, in compact form. Congress has repeatedly announced this principle, and the Department has always and does now insist upon it. The public domain must not be cut into long and narrow strips. No shoe-string claims should ever receive the sanction of the Department.

The Department is informed that most of the placer claims in Alaska are 1320 feet in length by 660 feet in width; also that in most cases the lines do not correspond to the rectangular subdivisions of our system of public surveys, that is to say, the bounding lines do not run on due north-and-sourth or east-and-west courses but usually follow the lines of old creek beds. The placer claim in this case is in Alaska. The public surveys have been extended very little there. It is entirely probable that the public lands in Alaska will not be surveyed to any great extent for years to come. The Director of the Geological Survey reports that he has given careful attention to mining conditions in Alaska; that there are thousands upon thousands of placer mining claims there; that practically none of them conform to the east-and-west or north-and-south lines of our system of public survey; but that the claims are compact in form for the most part; that to attempt now to require conformity would involve the claimants in thousands of law-suits. It is a matter of public history that the late rulings of this Department upon the question of conformity have deterred most of the placer claimants in Alaska from making application for patents. The owners prefer to hold their claims without securing patents and to work out the placer deposits and then abandon them. It is also true that with the very strict construction heretofore placed upon the law by this Department the placer claimants are unable to sell or dispose of their claims to advantage. Investors do not readily purchase unpatented lode or placer claims. They must be assured that no conflicts or law-suits can arise over the titles which they purchase. With a more liberal construction of the conformity provision of our placer act a large number of placer claimants in Alaska would apply for patents, and thereby enrich the Government to the extent of many thousands, perhaps millions of dollars. The interests of the Territory of Alaska demand a more favorable construction of the place act. The Alaska miners are for the most part in the undisturbed and quiet possession of their respective placer claims. Our decisions on the conformity provision of the statute ought to encourage this harmony if possible rather than to precipitate lawsuits and strife and retard mining development. Placer claims in Alaska in reasonably compact form, containing the proper area, and located according to the rules, regulations and customs of miners, ought to be approved for patent.

The Department would now be unwilling to approve such long and irregular-shaped claims as were allowed in the case of William Rablin (2 L. D., 764) and in the case of Pearsall (6 L. D., 227), although the law in those cases is clearly and correctly stated. The Department also holds that it is unreasonable, impracticable and not in harmony with the conformity provision of the statute to require a claimant to conform to legal subdivisions of the public surveys and the rectangular subdivisions thereof when such requirement would compel a claimant to place his lines on other prior located claims or when his claim is surrounded by prior locations, and therefore disapproves the doctrine announced in Rialto No. 2 Placer Mining Claim (34 L. D., 44), and in stating this no distinction should be made whether the claim be on surveyed or unsurveyed lands.

* * * *

Each case presented must be considered and decided on its own facts. Conformity is required if practicable. In the interest of wise administration and under the power which we think Congress has vested in this Department in the phrase "shall conform as near as practicable," taken from section 2331, supra, and in order to keep claims in compact form and not split the public domain into narrow, long and irregular strips, and to provide for a less harsh rule than that which has been followed recently, and to cover cases where strict conformity is impracticable, it is the view of this Department that a claim hereafter located by one or two persons which can be entirely included within a square forty-acre tract, and a claim located by three or four persons which can be entirely included in two square forty-acre tracts placed end to end, and a claim located by five or six persons which can be entirely included in three square forty-acre tracts, and a claim located by seven or eight persons which can be entirely included in four square forty-acre tracts, should be approved. In stating this rule it is necessary to say that we do not intend that the forties which are made the unit of measure should necessarily have north-and-south and east-and-west boundary lines. Thus, no inordinately long and narrow claim could be patented, and no locator would be compelled to include non-placer ground unless he so desired, as was permitted in the case of Hogan and Idaho Placer Mining Claim, supra. Each claim heretofore located, as it comes up for patent, must be adjudged and decided upon its own facts.

The case is reversed and the claim will be passed to patent in the absence of other objection.

NOTES

1. The rule of Snow Flake Fracture has been codified at 43 C.F.R. § 3842.1-5 (1983) as follows:

Conformity of placer claims to the public land surveys.

(a) All placer-mining claims located after May 10, 1872, shall conform as near as practicable with the United States system of public-land surveys and the rectangular subdivisions of such surveys, whether the locations are upon surveyed or unsurveyed lands.

(b) Conformity to the public-land surveys and the rectangular subdivisions thereof will not be required where compliance with such requirement would necessitate the placing of the lines thereof upon other prior located claims or where the claim is surrounded by prior locations.

(c) Where a placer location by one or two persons can be entirely included within a square 40-acre tract, by three or four persons within two square 40-acre tracts placed end to end, by five or six persons within three square 40-acre tracts, and by seven or eight persons within four square 40-acre tracts, such locations will be regarded as within the requirements where strict conformity is impracticable.

(d) Whether a placer location conforms reasonably with the legal subdivisions of the public survey is a question of fact to be determined in each case, and no location will be passed to patent without satisfactory evidence in this regard. Claimants should bear in mind that it is the policy of the Government to have all entries whether of agricultural or mineral lands as compact and regular in form as reasonably practicable, and that it will not permit or sanction entries or locations which cut the public domain into long narrow strips or grossly irregular or fantastically shaped tracts. (Snow Flake Fraction Placer, 37 L.D. 250.)

2. A placer claim located by one individual cannot exceed 20 acres. Even though the mining claimant may have made an actual discovery on such a 20 acre claim, the mining claimant is not necessarily entitled to a patent to the whole 20 acres. In addition to proving the discovery, the mining claimant must also establish that the majority of the 20 acres is mineral in character. If less than 10 acres is mineral in character, then the claimant will receive a patent to 10 acres only. If more than 10 acres is mineral in character, then the claimant will receive a patent to the entire 20 acres. This is for the reason that the smallest legal subdivision on the federal lands is 10 acres, i.e., plots smaller than 10 acres will not be approved.

UNITED STATES, EX REL. UNITED STATES BORAX CO. V. ICKES
98 F.2d 271 (D.C. Cir. 1938)

[footnotes omitted]

STEPHENS, A.J.:

This is an appeal from a decree of the District Court of the United States for the District of Columbia dismissing the petition of the United States Borax Company, relator-appellant, hereafter referred to as appellant, for a writ of mandamus directing the appellee, Harold L. Ickes, Secretary of the Interior, to cause to be issued and delivered to the appellant a patent of the United States for 80 acres of land in California. The appellant asserted, under the mining laws of the United States, a right of patent to this land as a placer mining location. It appears that a rule was issued by the District Court against the appellee to show cause why a writ of mandamus should not issue, and that the appellee filed a return to the rule and an answer to the petition for mandamus. To this return and answer the appellant demurred. After a hearing upon the demurrer, the same was overruled. The appellant elected to stand upon the demurrer, whereupon the petition was dismissed and this appeal taken.

*   *   *   *

. . . [O]ne Widdess and seven others, as an association of persons, took steps, commencing in May, 1925, to locate in California a 160 acre tract of land referred to as the Big Keen No. 2 placer claim. To this end Widdess drilled a well, referred to as Well No. 47, in May and June of 1925, and found what was described as "seams of blue shale containing a trace of boric acid." On January 7, 1927, Widdess and his associates deeded such rights as they had in respect of this tract to the appellant. On March 8 of the same year, the appellant made an admittedly valid discovery of borax on the tract in a well referred to as Well No. 62; on July 13, it filed an application in the United States Land Office at Los

Angeles, California, for a patent to the entire tract of 160 acres. Omitting reference to intermediate proceedings not here material, this application was ultimately disallowed by the appellee, except as to 20 acres immediately surrounding the discovery in Well No. 62. This disallowance was upon the three grounds that: four of Widdess' associates were not *bona fide* so that the area available for location and patent was in any event not greater than 80 acres; the "trace of boric acid'" assertedly found in Well No. 47 did not fulfil the legal requirements for discovery, so that at the time of the conveyance to the appellant on January 7, 1927, there had been no perfected location; when the valid discovery of March 8, 1927, was made, in Well No. 62, there was but one individual claimant, the corporation appellant, and that it was as such entitled to but 20 acres. The question whether four of Widdess' associates were *bona fide* is out of the case; there is now no contention on the part of the appellant that it is entitled to more than 80 acres. Also—and properly—there is no serious contention that the discovery in Well No. 47 was valid. There remains as the sole substantive question that of the correctness of the third ground upon which the appellee based his disallowance, except in respect of 20 acres, of the application. That question may be otherwise stated as follows: Is the transferee of an association placer claim of more than 20 acres, who, after the transfer, makes a discovery, entitled to a patent to more than the 20 acres immediately surrounding the discovery?

* * * *

We conclude that the points made and authorities urged by the appellant do not operate to make the decision of the appellee disallowing the patent, except as to 20 acres, and the decision of the trial court refusing to issue a writ of mandamus, wrong.

We think moreover that certain further considerations demonstrate the decision of the appellee and of the trial court to have been right.

One such consideration is that the construction which the appellant puts upon the statutory provisions primarily involved would permit the accomplishment indirectly through the device of an association transfer, of what cannot be accomplished directly. It is clear that if a non-association claimant, either individual or corporate, were to locate eight contiguous 20 acre tracts, it must make a discovery on each of such tracts, this because Rev. Stat. § 2331, 30 U.S.C.A. § 35, which was enacted in 1872, provides that "no such [placer] location shall include more than twenty acres for each individual claimant," and because under the provisions of Rev. Stat. § 2329 and § 2320, 30 U.S.C.A. §§ 35, 36, above set forth, no location of a mining claim shall be made until there has been a discovery within the limits of the claim located, whether lode or placer. It is true that the language of Rev. Stat. § 2330, 30 U.S.C.A. § 36, "no location of a placer-claim . . . shall exceed one hundred and sixty acres for any one person or association of persons," would, standing alone, seem to warrant the location of a 160 acre placer claim by one person. But this provision was enacted in 1870, and we think that the words "person or" therein were impliedly repealed by Rev. Stat. § 2331, 30 U.S.C.A. § 35. This apparently was the view of the Supreme Court in St. Louis Smelting Co. v. Kemp, 104 U.S. 636, 26 L. Ed. 875 (1881). The Circuit

Court of the United States for the District of Colorado had instructed the jury substantially as follows:

> "That a patent for a mining claim, since the passage of the act of Congress of 1870, could not embrace more than one hundred and sixty acres; that individuals and associations were, by that act, put upon the same footing and that either might take that amount, but that by the mining act of Congress of 1872 an individual claimant was limited to twenty acres, whilst an association of persons could still take one hundred and sixty, as before. . . ."

[104 U.S. at 638, 639]

The trial court was reversed upon another point but apparently without disagreement with the proposition set forth in that portion of the instruction above quoted—because the Supreme Court in its opinion commented upon the sequence of the statutes as follows:

> "Placer claims first became the subject of regulation by the mining act of July 9, 1870, c. 235 (16 Stat. 217), which provided that patents for them might be issued under like circumstances and conditions as for vein or lode claims, and that persons having contiguous [sic] claims of *any size* might make joint entry thereof. But it also provided that no location of a placer claim thereafter made should exceed one hundred and sixty acres for one person or an association of persons. The mining act of May 10, 1872, c. 152 (17 id. 91), declared that a location of a placer claim subsequently made should not include more than twenty acres for each individual claimant. . . ."

[104 U.S. at 650, 651]

To the effect that the courts will discountenance the accomplishment indirectly of what cannot be accomplished directly under the mining laws, see Nome & Sinook Co. v. Snyder, 187 F. 385 (9 Cir. 1911). In that case five individuals attempted to locate as an association upon 100 acres. By agreement between them, two were to have but a nominal interest in the claim, one less than one-fifth, one largely more than one-fifth, and one more than one-half. After discussing the very statutory provisions involved in the instant case, the court held that the scheme was illegal and the location void because of the attempt to obtain for an individual more than 20 acres. And see Cook v. Klonos, 164 F. 529 (9 Cir. 1908). Such rulings are in accord with the general policy of the mining laws of the United States. This has been to promote widespread development of mineral deposits and to afford mining opportunities to as many persons as possible. See Costigan, Mining Law (1908) § 2, pp. 6-7. To permit an individual prediscovery transferee to validate by a single discovery, subsequent to transfer, the location of an entire 160 acre tract would result in the development of minerals within a small portion of the tract only, and would be also to foreclose mining opportunity upon the balance to other individuals.

A further and final and perhaps the most cogent consideration supporting the decision of the appellee and the trial court upon the substantive question under discussion is the following: In H.H. Yard, 38 L.D. 59 (1909), the Secretary of the Interior had ruled that a gold placer location of 160 acres made by eight persons, who subsequently conveyed to a single individual before discovery, could not be perfected by the transferee through discovery after the transfer, and in this case Chrisman v. Miller was cited, although apparently only upon the question of what constitutes a valid discovery. Subsequently in Bakersfield Fuel & Oil Co., 39 L.D. 460 (1911), the Secretary made a similar ruling in respect of an oil placer location, and in that decision Miller v. Chrisman, as decided in the Supreme Court of California, was referred to as a state court decision clearly adverse to the doctrine of the H.H. Yard Case, and Chrisman v. Miller, as decided in the Supreme Court of the United States, was described as not adopting the doctrine laid down by the Supreme Court of California. It appears also in Bakersfield Fuel & Oil Co. that it had been called to the attention of the Secretary that the rule of the H.H. Yard Case would, as applied to oil placer locations, work hardship, because it had for many years been a common practice in California in the development of oil lands for an association of eight persons to locate upon 160 acres as a single placer mining claim and then prior to discovery to convey to a corporation. This practice had been sanctioned by the Department of the Interior and patents issued under it until the H.H. Yard decision. But the Secretary commented that if the interpretation of the law in the H.H. Yard Case in respect of gold placer locations, and reiterated in Bakersfield Fuel & Oil Co. in respect of oil placer locations, was inequitable, relief could be secured through Congress, and he noted that remedial legislation had been recommended to Congress in respect of *bona fide* locators who, relying upon the practice in existence prior to the H.H. Yard Case, had diligently prosecuted their work to fruition. As the apparent result of this recommendation Congress passed the Act of March 2, 1911, 36 Stat. 1015, c. 201, 30 U.S.C.A. § 103, reading as follows:

"An act to protect the locators in good faith of oil and gas lands who shall have effected an actual discovery of oil or gas on the public lands of the United States, or their successors in interest."

"*Be it enacted by the Senate and House of Representatives of the United States of America in Congress assembled,* That in no case shall patent be denied to or for any lands heretofore located or claimed under the mining laws of the United States containing petroleum, mineral oil, or gas solely because of any transfer or assignment thereof or of any interest or interests therein by the original locator or locators, or any of them, to any qualified persons or person, or corporation, prior to discovery of oil or gas therein, but if such claim is in all other respects valid and regular, patent therefor not exceeding one hundred and sixty acres in any one claim shall issue to the older or holders thereof, as in other cases: *Provided, however,* That such lands were not at the time of inception of development on or under such claim withdrawn from mineral entry."

The Senate and House Committee Reports, which recommend the passage of this legislation and which include correspondence with the Secretary of the Interior on the subject of the legislation, show that Congress, in passing the Act, was fully advised of Miller v. Chrisman and Chrisman v. Miller and of the H.H. Yard and Bakersfield Fuel & Oil Co. decisions. Therefore with full knowledge of the departmental ruling and of the consequence thereof, Congress nevertheless modified that ruling part only. That is to say, by virtue of the Act of March 2, 1911, Congress made the ruling of the Secretary of the Interior in the H.H. Yard and Bakersfield Fuel & Oil Co. Cases inapplicable to lands containing petroleum, mineral oil or gas, and located prior to the date of the Act, but it left the Secretary's ruling unmodified in respect of lands containing other kinds of mineral and in respect of all lands located under the mining laws after the date of the Act. Thus it left the ruling of the Secretary unmodified in respect of such claims as the borax claim of the appellants in the instant case. If it cannot be said that by thus passing the Act of March 2, 1911, Congress finally determined the law, at least it must be said that Congress gave strong evidence of approval of the Secretary's ruling to the extent that it omitted to modify the same. The failure of Congress to amend a statute, after administrative rulings have been made construing or applying it, has been recognized as evidence of Congressional approval of such rulings. Costanzo v. Tillinghast, 287 U.S. 341, 53 S.Ct. 152, 77 L.Ed. 350 (1932); Corning Glass Works v. Robertson, 62 App. D.C. 130, 65 F.2d 476 (1933), certiorari denied 290 U.S. 645, 54 S.Ct. 63, 78 L.Ed. 559 (1933). Even more cogent evidence of Congressional approval of an administrative ruling must be affirmative action on the part of Congress modifying the ruling in part and leaving it otherwise standing.

We conclude on the merits of the substantive question in the instant case that the ruling of the appellee and of the trial court were correct.

. . . .

NOTES

1. Would the result have been the same in the principal case if prior to the transfer to Borax a valid discovery had been made?

2. The main advantages of an association claim are that a large amount of land can be claimed and the entire claim will be valid even though supported by only one discovery. Of less significance, perhaps, $100 worth of assessment work need not be done on each 20 acre tract. It is sufficient if $100 worth of work is done on the claim as a whole. *McDonald v. Montana Wood Co.,* 35 P. 668 (Mont. 1894); *Hall v. McKinnon,* 193 F. 572 (9th Cir. 1911).

3. The danger of an association claim, of course, is that it is always vulnerable to attack on the ground that one or more of the locators were "dummies." In *United States v. Toole,* 224 F. Supp. 440 (D. Mont. 1963) eight individuals located an association claim of 160 acres. After locating the claim, the individuals all transferred their interests to a corporation. One of the locators, Toole, was the majority stockholder of the corporation. When the validity of the association claim was attacked, the court held that it was invalid for the use of dummy locators, stating that "any scheme or device entered into whereby one individual is to acquire more than that amount or proportion in area [i.e., 20 acres] constitutes a fraud upon the law, and consequently a fraud upon the government, . . . and any location made in pursuance of such a scheme or device is without legal support and void." The court went on to hold that since the corporation could not itself have filed the 160 acre claim "[i]t would appear from all the evidence that dummy locators were used in acquiring the property for the corporation and its principal shareholders." Would you expect the same result if each of the eight locators owned a 12½% interest in the corporation to which the association claim were transferred? Cf. *Nome & Sinook Co. v. Snyder,* 187 F. 385 (9th Cir. 1911).

6 THE REQUIREMENT OF ANNUAL FILINGS AND ASSESSMENT WORK

A. The Federal Land Policy Management Act

RECORDATION OF MINING CLAIMS
43 U.S.C. 1744

(a) Filing requirements. The owner of an unpatented lode or placer mining claim located prior to October 21, 1976 shall, within the three-year period following October 21, 1976 and prior to December 31 of each year thereafter, file the instruments required by paragraphs (1) and (2) of this subsection. The owner of an unpatented lode or placer mining claim located after October 21, 1976 shall, prior to December 31 of each year following the calendar year in which the said claim was located, file the instruments required by paragraphs (1) and (2) of this subsection:

(1) File for record in the office where the location notice or certificate is recorded either a notice of intention to hold the mining claim (including but not limited to such notices as are provided by law to be filed when there has been a suspension or deferment of annual asssessment work), an affidavit of assessment work performed thereon, on [sic] a detailed report provided by section 28-1 of Title 30, relating thereto.

(2) File in the office of the Bureau designated by the Secretary a copy of the official record of the instrument filed or recorded pursuant to paragraph (1) of this subsection, including a description of the location of the mining claim sufficient to locate the claimed lands on the ground.

(b) Additional filing requirements. The owner of an unpatented lode or placer mining claim or mill or tunnel site located prior to October 21, 1976 shall, within the three-year period following October 21, 1976, file in the office of the Bureau designated by the Secretary a copy of the official record of the notice of location or certificate of location, including a description of the location of the mining claim or mill or tunnel site sufficient to locate the claimed lands on the ground. The owner of an unpatented lode or placer mining claim or mill or tunnel site located after October 21, 1976 shall, within ninety days after the date of location of such claim, file in the office of the Bureau designated by the Secretary a copy of the official record of the notice of location or certificate of location, including a description of the location of the mining claim or mill or tunnel site sufficient to locate the claimed lands on the ground.

(c) Failure to file as constituting abandonment; defective or untimely filing. The failure to file such instruments as required by subsections (a) and (b) of this section shall be deemed conclusively to constitute an abandonment of the mining claim or mill or tunnel site by the owner; but it shall not be considered a failure to file if the instrument is defective or not timely filed for record under other Federal laws permitting filing or recording thereof, or if the instrument is filed for record by or on behalf of some but not all of the owners of the mining claim or mill or tunnel site.

(d) Validity of claims, waiver of assessment, etc., as unaffected. Such recordation or application by itself shall not render valid any claim which would not be otherwise valid under applicable law. Nothing in this section shall be construed as a waiver of the assessment and other requirements of such law. (Pub. L. 94-579, title III § 314, Oct. 21, 1976, 90 Stat. 2769.)

NOTES

1. FLPMA requires that the affidavit of assessment work be filed prior to December 31 of each calendar year following the calendar year in which the claim is located. 30 U.S.C. § 28, however, does not "require the performance of assessment work until the end of the assessment year commencing on the first day of September succeeding the date of location of the claim." Thus, if a claim were located on November 1, 1981, assessment work would not be due until

September 1, 1983. In such a case, when would the first FLPMA filing be due? Of the three alternative FLPMA filings, which one would be most appropriate in this case? See *Dilday,* 88 I.D. 682 (1981).

2. The presumption of abandonment contained in § 314 is conclusive. Unlike common law abandonment, it does not depend for its operation on any actual intention of the mining claimant. "Extraneous evidence indicating an intention not to abandon a claim, including recordation of the claim with the county and the BLM [other than timely recordation of the original and annual FLPMA filings] cannot be considered in light of the statutory conclusive presumption of abandonment which results from the failure to file an instrument required by 43 U.S.C. § 1744 (1976). The matter is governed by statute and not by common law." *Robert E. Fennell,* 58 I.B.L.A. 43, GFS (Min.) 192 (1981).

3. FLPMA requires that the owner of an unpatented mining claim located prior to October 21, 1976, shall file with the BLM a copy of the official record of the notice of location or certificate of location. It is possible that a claim could be perfectly valid without a certificate of location ever being filed. 30 U.S.C. § 38 provides that "working of the claims for [the period prescribed by the local statute of limitations for mining claims] shall be sufficient to establish a right to a patent . . . under this chapter." The purpose of section 38 "is to obviate the necessity of proving compliance with requirements for locating a claim" including the requirement of filing a location certificate. *United States v. Haskins,* 505 F. 2d 246 (9th Cir. 1974). What should a mining claimant who relies on section 38 to validate his claim do to comply with FLPMA and prevent his claim from being deemed abandoned and void? In *Phillip M. Sayer,* 42 IBLA 296, 1979 GFS (Min) 69, the IBLA referred to this problem as a "gap" in the law, and directed the BLM to be flexible in working with the claimant and determining what type of evidence it would accept in satisfaction of the FLPMA filing requirement.

EFFECT OF FAILURE TO RECORD TIMELY UNDER SEC. 314(b)
Federal Land Policy And Management Act Of 1976
84 I.D. 188 (1977)

Subject: Effect of Failure to Record Timely Under Sec. 314(b), Federal Land Policy And Management Act Of 1976

Question

The Bureau of Land Management has requested this office to determine whether, under sec. 314 of the Federal Land Policy and Management Act, the Secretary of the Interior has the authority to accept a notice of recordation of a mining claim located after Oct. 21, 1976, if the notice of recordation is filed more than 90 days after the date of location of the claim.

Conclusion

A mining claim located after Oct. 21, 1976, for which a notice of recordation required to be filed by sec. 314(b) of the Federal Land Policy and Management Act of 1976, has not been filed within 90 days from the date of location is void, and the Department may not accept or give force to a notice of recordation filed after the 90-day period.

Background

On Oct. 21, 1976, the Federal Land Policy and Management Act became law. Federal Land Policy and Management Act of 1976, 90 Stat.2743 (referred to as FLPMA) Sec. 314 of the FLPMA says, in part:

(b) * * * The owner of an unpatented lode or placer mining claim or mill or tunnel site located after the date of approval of this Act *shall, within ninety days after the date of location* of such claim file in the office of the Bureau designated by the Secretary a copy of the official record of the notice of location or certificate of location, including a description of the location of the mining claim or mill or tunnel site sufficient to locate the claimed lands on the ground.

(c) *The failure to file such instruments as required by subsections (a) and (b) shall be deemed conclusively to constitute an abandonment of the mining claim* or mill or tunnel site by the owner; but it shall not be considered a failure to file if the instrument is defective or not timely filed for record under other Federal laws permitting filing or recording thereof, or if the instrument is filed for record by or on behalf of some but not all of the owners of the mining claim or mill or tunnel site (Italics added).

Sec. 314(b)-(c), FLPMA.

Prior to the enactment of the FLPMA, the Department of the Interior did not require a mining claimant, in general, to file a record of his claim with the Federal government. A state or a mining district usually required this information. *See* 30 U.S.C. § 28 (1970).

The Bureau of Land Management has informed us that several claimants filed their recordation notices more than 90 days after they located their claims. The Bureau requests our advice whether the late filing of a notice of recordation has any effect, or whether a person who fails to file within the 90-day period must make a new location of the claim, and subsequently record that location with the appropriate office in 90 days.

Discussion

The first question which must be asked is whether the FLPMA imposes a mandatory requirement on the locator to file a notice of recordation within 90 days from the date of location. If so, the second question which must be asked is what are the effects of a failure to record on time. A cardinal rule of statutory construction is that the interpretation of a statute should be consistent with Congress' intentions. *FTC v. Fred Meyer, Inc.* 390 U.S. 341, 349 (1968). "The starting point in a search for legislative intent is of course the pertinent statutory language." *DuPuy v. DuPuy*, 511 F.2d 641 (5th Cir. 1975).

Sec. 314(b) of the FLPMA says, "The owner of an unpatented lode or placer mining claim or mill or tunnel site located after the approval of the date of this Act *shall,* within ninety days from the date of location of such claim, file in the office of the Bureau designated by the Secretary a copy of the official record of the notice of location or certificate of location. * * * " Unless the context requires otherwise the use of the word "shall" in a statute indicates the "language of command." *Anderson v. Yungkau,* 329 U.S. 482, 485 (1946); *Richbourg Motor Co. v. United States,* 281 U.S. 528, 534 (1930). Examination of the legislative history shows that Congress intended *"shall"* to be used in its normal meaning sense.

. . .

The legislative history of the Act gives no indication that "shall" was not intended to be given its normal meaning. The purpose of the recordation provision, prompt notice to the Federal Government of new claims, would also be frustrated if filing was not mandatory. I hold that the duty to file a notice of recordation within 90 days from the date of location is mandatory and cannot be waived. *Compare* sec. 314(b) of FLPMA *with* 43 U.S.C. § 687(a)-(1) (1970), which requires applicants for trade and manufacturing sites to record their claims within 90 days, but which specifically permits late filings.

Since the requirement to file is mandatory, it is necessary to determine what consequences attach to the failure to file. Sec. 314(c) of FLPMA says, "The failure to file such instruments as required by subsections (a) and (b) shall be deemed conclusively to constitute the abandonment of the mining claim." Although the determination whether real property, including a mining claim, has been abandoned normally depends on the intention of the owner, *eg. Lakin v. Sierra Buttes Gold Mining Co.,* 25 F. 337 (C.C.D.). Cal. (1885); *Hurkander v. Carrol,* 76 F. 474 (D. Alaska 1896), Congress here has explicitly provided that failure to record is to be "deemed" to be an abandonment. By using the word "deem," Congress established a substantive rule of law that a failure to record, in time is an abandonment without regard to the locator's intent. See *Bowers v. United States,* 226 F.2d 424, 428-29 (5th Cir. 1955). *Kohn v. Myers,* 266 F.2d 353, 357 (2d Cir. 1959). I hold that regardless of the intent of a locator, for the purposes of section 314 of FLPMA, a claim not recorded timely is abandoned. The consequence of abandonment is clear: an abandoned claim reverts to the status of the public domain and is void.

NOTES

1. What exactly was the issue before the Solicitor? What exactly did he hold? Was it necessary to hold that a late filing rendered a claim void, or only void as against the United States?

2. If, as the Solicitor indicates, the purpose of § 314 was to enable the Department of Interior to engage in meaningful land use planning, should the failure to make a required FLPMA filing have any effect as between rival claimants? For example, assume that Sr. has located and perfected a mining claim supported by a valid discovery. Should Jr. be permitted to jump Sr.'s claim if Sr. fails to make a required FLMPA filing? What public policy is served by deciding in favor of Jr.?

3. Assume that an otherwise valid mining claim is conclusively deemed abandoned as a result of the claimant's failure to make a required filing. Will a timely filing in subsequent years cure this defect? What course of action would you advise this claimant to take?

TOPAZ BERYLLIUM CO. V. UNITED STATES
649 F.2d 775 (10th Cir. 1981)

Before McWILLIAMS, DOYLE and McKAY, Circuit Judges.
McKAY, Circuit Judge.

Appellants seek a declaration that the provisions of 43 C.F.R. §§ 3833.3, 3833.4(a) (and certain regulations allegedly related thereto), and 3833.5(d) are "in excess of statutory jurisdiction, authority, or limitations, or short of statutory right" and thus unlawful under 5 U.S.C. § 706(2)(C). Appellants also seek injunctive relief. This appeal follows the district court's grant of the Secretary of Interior's cross-motion for summary judgment.

I.

The Mining Act of 1872, 17 Stat. 91, set out procedures by which any person could locate, perfect, or claim valuable mineral deposits on public lands. From 1872 until 1976, these unpatented mining claims were governed largely by state statutory schemes. The federal government did not exercise any significant authority over unpatented claims and was not even entitled to notice of such claims until the patent process was begun.

The increased use of public lands following World War II resulted in a concomitant burden on public lands administrators. The Public Land Law Review Commission (PLLRC) was created by Congress in 1964 to review existing laws and to suggest revisions. PLLRC, *One Third the Nation's Land* (1970). The PLLRC issued a wide ranging report that included a specific proposal regarding the filing of unpatented mining claims. *See id.* at 130. The resulting legislation, the Federal Land Policy and Management Act of 1976, Pub.L.No. 94-579, 90 Stat. 2743 (codified at 43 U.S.C. §§ 1701-82) (FLPMA), repealed several outdated statutes, provided the Bureau of Land Management with land use planning authority, revised the laws governing sales, exchanges, and rights of way, established improved range management authority, and provided for the recordation of unpatented mining claims. Section 1744 provides for the recordation with the federal government of unpatented mining claims:

[The text of section 1744 is reproduced at the beginning of this Chapter and is, *therefore, omitted here.*]

In keeping with its general policy of vesting in the Secretary broad authority to promulgate rules and regulations to aid him in his administration of the public lands [footnote omitted], Congress declared part of its policy in FLPMA to be that "in administering public land statutes and exercising discretionary authority granted by them, the Secretary be required to establish comprehensive rules and regulations. . . ." 43 U.S.C. § 1701(a)(5). Congress also commanded in FLPMA that "[t]he Secretary, with respect to the public lands, shall promulgate rules and regulations to carry out the purposes of this Act and of other laws applicable to the public lands. . . ." *Id.* § 1740. Finally, it is pertinent here to note Congress' declaration that "the national interest will be best realized if the public lands and their resources are periodically and systematically inventoried and their present and future use is projected through a land use planning process coordinated with other Federal and State planning efforts." *Id.* at 1701(a)(2).

II.

Appellants American Mining Congress and Colorado Mining Association, but not Topaz Beryllium Company, urge that 43 C.F.R. § 3833.4(a) is invalid because it deems conclusively that an unpatented claim is abandoned and void if its owner fails to file documents that are not specifically required by 43 U.S.C. § 1744's recordation system. Appellants argue that since § 1744 is relatively specific, the Secretary is limited by its terms when he promulgates the regulations necessary to its implementation.

It is true that certain subparts of 43 C.F.R. § 3833 demand more of a holder of an unpatented claim than does § 1744.[1] However, 43 C.F.R. § 3833.4(a) does not deem a claim abandoned and void if such supplemental filings are not made. Section 3833.4(a) authorizes such a result only if "an instrument required by §§ 3833.1-2(a), (b), and 3833.2-1" is not filed, and appellants do not allege that §§ 3833.1-2(a), (b), and 3833.2-1 require any more than does § 1744. We conclude that the Secretary has not ignored § 1744(c) which assumes that even defective filings put the Secretary on *notice* of a claim, and we hold that once on notice, the Secretary cannot deem a claim abandoned merely because the supplemental filings required only by § 3833—and not by the statute—are not made. This is also the Secretary's view: failure to file the supplemental information is treated by the Secretary as a *curable* defect. A claimant who fails to file the supplemental information is notified and given thirty days in which to cure the defect. If the defect is not cured, "the filing will be rejected by an appealable decision."[2] The Secretary does not contemplate any automatic extinguishment of a claim for faulty filing.

Placed in their proper perspective, the challenged supplemental filings represent the Secretary's effort to "fill in" the broad outlines of FLPMA. Names, addresses, and the other information that the challenged regulations required of those making filings pursuant to § 1744 do not constitute the regulatory horrible that appellants attempt to vivify. Rather, the supplementary information enables the Secretary to integrate § 1744's information with other data pertaining to land use planning. As the district court noted,

---

[1] Appellants challenge . . . [the regulations requiring them] to identify themselves to the BLM, to give their address and to give notice of a change of address, to state the legal description assigned to each claim by the BLM, to file amended instruments which change or alter the description of a claim, and to comply with certain standards when submitting a notice of intention to hold a mining claim. None of these "extra" filings are specifically called for by 43 U.S.C. § 1744.

[2] Appellants allege that the . . . IBLA is . . . deeming claims abandoned unless the supplemental information is supplied. Such erroneous decisions . . . can be appealed to federal district court where the intrepretation given § 3833.4(a) by this court will be controlling at least in this circuit.

Congress could not foresee and did not attempt to foresee all of the information that might be needed to efficiently administer 43 U.S.C. § 1744 and to coordinate its operation with the rest of the FLPMA and with other public land laws. These reasons were among those Congress had for delegating broad authority to the Secretary in 43 U.S.C. § 1740.

Topaz Beryllium Co. v. United States, 479 F.Supp. 309, 314-15 (D.Utah 1979). The Supreme Court has consistently held that similar grants of general rule-making authority sustain the validity of detailed regulations which are designed to achieve with reasonable effectiveness the purposes for which Congress has acted, *E. I. du Pont de Nemours & Co. v. Train*, 430 U.S. 112, 132, 97 S.Ct. 965, 977, 51 L.Ed.2d 204 (1977), or which are reasonably related to the purposes of the enabling legislation, *Mourning v. Family Publications Service, Inc.*, 411 U.S. 356, 369, 93 S.Ct. 1652, 1660, 36 L.Ed.2d 318 (1973). *See In re Permanent Surface Mining Regulation Litigation*, No. 79-1144 (D.C.Cir. Apr. 1, 1981).

III.

All appellants challenge 43 C.F.R. § 3833.5(d) which provides that notice of an action or contest affecting an unpatented mining claim need be given only to those owners who have recorded their claim or site pursuant to § 3833.1-2 or have filed a notice of transfer of interest pursuant to § 3833.3. Appellants allege that this provision would allow parties other than the government to initiate contests and win default judgments contrary to the intent of Congress, and further that, even where the government brings an action, the provision creates a substantial risk of loss of valuable mining claims that was not authorized by Congress in 43 U.S.C. § 1744.

We do not find these contentions persuasive. First, we agree with the district court that § 3833.5(d) speaks only to government-initiated contests. In a contest initiated by a third party, that party cannot rely on § 3833.5(d) and ignore local records—the official repositories—when determining to whom he must send notice. Appellants' fear that § 3833.5(d) will be read more broadly should be assuaged by this opinion. Any such broad reading will be appealable and this interpretation given § 3833.5(d) will be controlling at least in this circuit.

Second, appellants err in attempting to shackle these regulations to § 1744; 43 C.F.R. § 3833.5(d) simply does not operate as an automatic forfeiture provision as 43 U.S.C. § 1744 does. As noted above, FLPMA contains numerous provisions evidencing Congress' intent to grant the Secretary broad regulatory authority over public lands. Part of that authority is expressed in the Secretary's ability to initiate a proceeding contesting or clarifying a party's interest in a particular parcel of public land. 43 C.F.R. § 4.451-1. See *Davis v. Nelson*, 329 F.2d 840 (9th Cir. 1964). The notice of transfer provisions merely provide a procedure by which the Secretary can more efficiently satisfy his due process obligation to give notice to affected parties when he initiates a contest. It does not by itself work a forfeiture; it merely facilitates the giving of notice of a government challenge under § 4.451-1. As the district court stated, "It is easier and more efficient to require millions of claim holders to say to the government early on, 'tell me' if you intend to challenge my interest, than to require the government to ferret out millions of interested persons from local records scattered in thousands of locations." 479 F.Supp. at 316.

As we interpret the notice-of-transfer regulations, a transferee who fails to file a notice of transfer is in danger of going without notice in a government-initiated contest only until he files his first annual filing required by 43 U.S.C. § 1744. The regulations require

> the government, in a government-initiated contest proceeding, to search all of the records filed with it pursuant to 43 C.F.R. Subpart 3833, not just notices of transfer. The Secretary concedes that if a new owner is identified as such on one of the required annual filings, his failure to file a notice of transfer would not authorize the government to forego giving him notice of a contest.

479 F.Supp. at 316. We hold that this notice procedure is reasonably related to the broad concerns for the management of public lands set forth in FLPMA, as well as to the Secretary's unchallenged authority to initiate contests concerning public lands, and that the procedure wholly comports with due process of law.

AFFIRMED.

NOTES

1. The BLM's procedure for handling "curable defects" is specified in Organic Act Directive No. 80-5 (October 31, 1979), which provides:

> The claimant will be issued a decision specifically listing the information required, and giving him at least 30 days in which to cure the defects. Upon a reasonable showing an extension of time should be allowed. If the called for information is not submitted, the filing will be rejected by an appealable decision.

When a filing is rejected, it is as though the original defective filing was not timely made, and the claim is deemed abandoned and void. *Park City Chief Mining Co.,* 57 I.B.L.A. 342, 1981 GFS (Min) 301. Is OAD 80-5 consistent with the requirements of the principle case?

2. FLPMA requires that the claimant file with the BLM a copy of the official record of the notice of location. In *W.C. Miles,* 48 I.B.L.A. 214, 1980 GFS (Min) 157, the issue was whether a hand written copy was sufficient. The Board held that a "handwritten copy of a notice or certificate of location which has or will be recorded in the local jurisdiction meets the regulatory requirement." The key is not the method of reproduction but whether the copy accurately reflects the contents of the original notice.

UNITED STATES V. LOCKE
Argued Nov. 6, 1984.
Decided April 1, 1985.
471 U.S. 84 (1985)

Justice MARSHALL delivered the opinion of the Court.

The primary question presented by this appeal is whether the Constitution prevents Congress from providing that holders of unpatented mining claims who fail to comply with the annual filing requirements of the Federal Land Policy and Management Act of 1976 (FLPMA), 43 U.S.C. § 1744, shall forfeit their claims.

I

From the enactment of the general mining laws in the nineteenth century until 1976, those who sought to make their living by locating and developing minerals on federal lands were virtually unconstrained by the fetters of federal control. The general mining laws, 30 U.S.C. § 22 *et seq.,* still in effect today, allow United States citizens to go onto unappropriated, unreserved public land to prospect for and develop certain minerals. "Discovery" of a mineral deposit, followed by the minimal procedures required to formally "locate" the deposit, gives an individual the right of exclusive possession of the land for mining purposes, 30 U.S.C. § 26; as long as $100 of assessment work is performed annually, the individual may continue to extract and sell minerals from the claim without paying any royalty to the United States, 30 U.S.C. § 28. For a nominal sum, and after certain statutory conditions are fulfilled, an individual may patent the claim, thereby purchasing from the federal government the land and minerals and obtaining ultimate title to them. Patenting, however, is not required, and an unpatented mining claim remains a fully recognized possessory interest. *Best v. Humboldt Placer Mining Co.,* 371 U.S. 334, 335, 83 S.Ct. 379, 381, 9 L.Ed.2d 350 (1963).

By the 1960s, it had become clear that this nineteenth century laissez faire regime had created virtual chaos with respect to the public lands. In 1975, it was estimated that more than six million unpatented mining claims existed on public lands other than the national forests; in addition, more than half the land in the National Forest System was thought to be covered by such claims. S.Rep. No.94-583, p. 65 (1975). Many of these claims had been dormant for decades, and many were invalid for other reasons, but in the absence of a federal recording system, no simple way existed for determining which public lands were subject to mining locations, and whether those locations were valid or invalid. *Ibid.* As a result, federal land managers had to proceed slowly and cautiously in taking any action affecting federal land lest the federal property rights of claimants be unlawfully disturbed. Each time the Bureau of Land Management (BLM) proposed a sale or other conveyance of federal land, a title search in the county recorder's office was necessary; if an outstanding mining claim was found, no matter how stale or apparently abandoned, formal administrative adjudication was required to determine the validity of the claim.[1]

After more than a decade of studying this problem in the context of a broader inquiry into the proper management of the public lands in the modern era, Congress in 1976 enacted the Federal Land Policy and Management Act, Pub.L. 94-579, 90 Stat. 2743 (codified at 43 U.S.C. § 1701 *et. seq.*). Section 314 of the Act establishes a federal recording system that is designed both to rid federal lands of stale mining claims and to provide federal land managers with up-to-date information that allows them to make informed land management decisions. For claims located before FLPMA's enactment,[3] the federal recording system imposes two general requirements. First, the claims must initially be registered with the BLM by filing, within three years of FLPMA's enactment, a copy of the official record of the notice or certificate of location. 90 Stat. 2743, § 314(b); 43 U.S.C. § 1744(b). Second, in the year of the initial recording, and "prior to December 31" of every year after that, the claimant must file with state officials and with BLM a notice of intention to hold the claim, an affidavit of assessment work performed on the claim, or a detailed reporting form. 90 Stat. 2743, § 314(c); 43 U.S.C. § 1744(a). Section 314(c) of the Act provides that failure to comply with either of these requirements "shall be deemed conclusively to constitute an abandonment of the mining claim . . . by the owner." 43 U.S.C. § 1744 (c).

The second of these requirements—the annual filing obligation—has created the dispute underlying this appeal. Appellees, four individuals engaged "in the business of operating mining properties in Nevada,"[4] purchased in 1960 and 1966 ten unpatented mining claims on public lands near Ely, Nevada, These claims were major sources of gravel and building material: the claims are valued at several million dollars,[5] and, in the 1979-1980 assessment year alone, appellees' gross income totalled more than one million dollars.[6] Throughout the period during which they owned the claims, appellees complied with annual state law filing and assessment work requirements. In addition, appellees satisfied FLPMA's initial recording requirement by properly filing with BLM a notice of location, thereby putting their claims on record for purposes of FLPMA.

At the end of 1980, however, appellees failed to meet on time their first annual obligation to file with the Federal Government. After allegedly receiving

---

[1] See generally Strauss, *Mining Claims on Public Lands: A study of Interior Department Procedures,* 1974 Utah L. Rev. 185, 193, 215-219.

[3] A somewhat different scheme applies to claims located after October 21, 1976, the date the Act took effect.

[4] Complaint ¶ 2.

[5] *Id.,* ¶ 15.

[6] *Locke v. United States,* 573 F.Supp. 472, 474 (1983). From 1960 to 1980, total gross income from the claims exceeded four million dollars. *Ibid.*

misleading information from a BLM employee,[7] appellees waited until December 31 to submit to BLM the annual notice of intent to hold or proof of assessment work performed required under section 314(a) of FLPMA, 43 U.S.C. § 1744(a). As noted above, that section requires these documents to be filed annually "prior to December 31." Had appellees checked, they further would have discovered that BLM regulations made quite clear that claimants were required to make the annual filings in the proper BLM office "on or before December 30 of each calendar year." 43 CFR § 3833.2-1(a) (1980) (current version at 43 CFR 3833.2-1(b)(1) (1984). Thus, appellees' filing was one day too late.

This fact was brought painfully home to appellees when they received a letter from the BLM Nevada State Office informing them that their claims had been declared abandoned and void due to their tardy filing. In many cases, loss of a claim in this way would have minimal practical effect; the claimant could simply locate the same claim again and then rerecord it with BLM. In this case, however, relocation of appellees' claims, which were initially located by appellees' predecessors in 1952 and 1954, was prohibited by the Common Varieties Act of 1955, 30 U.S.C. § 611; that Act prospectively barred location of the sort of minerals yielded by appellees' claims. Appellees' mineral deposits thus escheated to the Government.

After losing an administrative appeal, appellees filed the present action in the United States District Court for the District of Nevada. Their complaint alleged, *inter alia,* that § 314(c) effected an unconstitutional taking of their property without just compensation and denied them due process. On summary judgment, the District Court held that § 314(c) did indeed deprive appellees of the process to which they were constitutionally due. The District Court reasoned that § 314(c) created an impermissible irrebuttable presumption that claimants who failed to make a timely filing intended to abandon their claims. Rather than relying on this presumption, the Government was obliged, in the District Court's view, to provide individualized notice to claimants that their

---

[7] An affidavit submitted to the District Court by one of appellees' employees stated that BLM officials in Ely had told the employee that the filing could be made at the BLM Reno office "on or before December 31, 1980." Affidavit of Laura C. Locke ¶ 3. The 1978 version of a BLM Question and Answer pamphlet erroneously stated that the annual filings had to be made "on or before December 31" of each year. Staking a Claim on Federal Lands 9-10 (1978). Later versions have corrected this error to bring the pamphlet into accord with the BLM regulations that require the filings to be made "on or before December 30."

Justice STEVENS and Justice POWELL seek to make much of this pamphlet and of the uncontroverted evidence that appellees were told a December 31 filing would comply with the statute. See *post,* at 1791, 1793, 1794. However, at the time appellees filed in 1980, BLM regulations and the then-current pamphlets made clear that the filing was required "on or before December 30." Thus, the dissenters' reliance on this pamphlet would seem better directed to the claim that the United States was equitably estopped from forfeiting appellees' claims, given the advice of the BLM agent and the objective basis the 1978 pamphlet provides for crediting the claim that such advice was given. The District Court did not consider this estoppel claim. Without expressing any view as to whether, as a matter of law, appellees could prevail on such a theory, see *Heckler v. Community Health Services of Crawford County, Inc.,* 467 U.S. ——, 104 S.Ct. 2218, 81 L.Ed.2d 42 (1984), we leave any further treatment of this issue, including fuller development of the record, to the District Court on remand.

claims were in danger of being lost, followed by a post-filing-deadline hearing at which the claimants could demonstrate that they had not, in fact, abandoned a claim. Alternatively, the District Court held that the one-day late filing "substantially complied" with the Act and regulations.

Because a District Court had held an Act of Congress unconstitutional in a civil suit to which the United States was a party, we noted probable jurisdiction under 28 U.S.C. § 1252, 467 U.S. 1225, 104 S.Ct. 2218, 81 L.Ed.2d 42 (1984).[8] We now reverse.

II

Appeal under 28 U.S.C. § 1252 brings before this Court not merely the constitutional question decided below, but the entire case. *McLucas v. DeChamplain,* 421 U.S. 21, 31, 95 S.Ct. 1365, 1371, 43 L.Ed.2d 699 (1975); *United States v. Raines,* 362 U.S. 17, 27 n. 7, 80 S.Ct. 519, 526, n. 7, 4 L.Ed.2d 524 (1960). The entire case includes nonconstitutional questions actually decided by the lower court as well as nonconstitutional grounds presented to, but not passed on, by the lower court. *United States v. Clark,* 445 U.S. 23, 27-28, 100 S.Ct. 895, 899-900, 63 L.Ed.2d 171 (1980).[9] These principles are important aids in the prudential exercise of our appellate jurisdiction, for when a case arrives here by appeal under 28 U.S.C. § 1252, this Court will not pass on the constitutionality of an Act of Congress if a construction of the Act is fairly possible, or some other nonconstitutional ground fairly available, by which the constitutional question can be avoided. See *Heckler v. Mathews,* 465 U.S.728, 741-44, 104 S. Ct. 1387, 79 L.Ed.2d 646 (1984); *Johnson v. Robison,* 415 U.S. 361, 366-367, 94 S.Ct. 1160, 1165, 39 L.Ed.2d 389 (1974); cf. *United States v. Congress of Industrial Organizations,* 355 U.S. 106, 110, 68 S.Ct. 1349, 1351, 92 L.Ed. 1849 (1948) (appeals under former Criminal Appeals Act); see generally *Ashwander v. TVA,* 297 U.S. 288, 347, 56 S.Ct. 466, 483, 80 L.Ed. 688 (Brandeis, J., concurring) (1936). Thus, we turn first to the nonconstitutional questions pressed below.

III
A

Before the District Court, appellees asserted that the section 314(a) requirement of a filing "prior to December 31 of each year" should be construed

---

[8] That the District Court decided the case on both constitutional and statutory grounds does not affect this Court's obligation under 28 U.S.C. § 1252 to take jurisdiction over the case; as long as the unconstitutionality of an Act of Congress is one of the grounds of decision below in a civil suit to which the United States is a party, appeal lies directly to this Court. *United States v. Rock Royal Co-operative, Inc.,* 307 U.S. 533, 541, 59 S.Ct. 993, 997, 83 L.Ed. 1446 (1939).

Another District Court in the West similarly has declared § 314(c) unconstitutional with respect to invalidation of claims based on failure to meet the initial recordation requirements of § 314(a) in timely fashion. *Rogers v. United States,* 575 F.Supp. 4 (Mont.1982).

[9] When the nonconstitutional questions have not been passed on by the lower court, we may vacate the decision below and remand with instructions that those questions be decided, see *Youakin v. Miller,* 425 U.S. 231, 96 S.Ct. 1399, 47 L.Ed.2d 701 (1976), or we may choose to decide those questions ourselves without benefit of lower court analysis, *see United States v. Clark,* 445 U.S. 23, 100 S.Ct. 895, 63 L.Ed.2d 171 (1980). The choice between these options depends on the extent to which lower court fact-finding and analysis of the nonconstitutional questions will be necessary or useful to our disposition of those questions.

to require a filing "on or before December 31." Thus, appellees argued, their December 31 filing had in fact complied with the statute, and the BLM had acted ultra vires in voiding their claims.

Although the District Court did not address this argument, the argument raises a question sufficiently legal in nature that we choose to address it even in the absence of lower court analysis. See, *e.g., United States v. Clark, supra.* It is clear to us that the plain language of the statute simply cannot sustain the gloss appellees would put on it. As even appellees conceded at oral argument, § 314(a) "is a statement that Congress wanted it filed by December 30th. I think that is a clear statement . . ." Tr. of Oral Arg. 27; see also *id.,* 445 U.S., at 37, 100 S.Ct., at 904 ("A literal reading of the statute would require a December 30th filing. . . ."). While we will not allow a literal reading of a statute to produce a result "demonstrably at odds with the intentions of its drafters," *Griffin v. Oceanic Contractors, Inc.* 458 U.S. 564, 571, 102 S.Ct. 3245, 3250, 73 L.Ed.2d 973 (1982), with respect to filing deadlines a literal reading of Congress' words is generally the only proper reading of those words. To attempt to decide whether some date other than the one set out in the statute is the date actually "intended" by Congress is to set sail on an aimless journey, for the purpose of a filing deadline would be just as well served by nearly any date a court might choose as by the date Congress has in fact set out in the statute. "Actual purpose is sometimes unknown," *U.S. Railroad Retirement Board v. Fritz,* 449 U.S. 166, 180, 101 S.Ct. 453, 462, 66 L.Ed.2d 368 (1980)(STEVENS, J., concurring), and such is the case with filing deadlines; as might be expected, nothing in the legislative history suggests why Congress chose December 30 over December 31, or over September 1 (the end of the assessment year for mining claims, 30 U.S.C. § 28), as the last day on which the required filings could be made. But "[d]eadlines are inherently arbitrary," while fixed dates "are often essential to accomplish necessary results." *United States v. Boyle,* 469 U.S. 241, 249, 105 S.Ct. 687, 692, 83 L.Ed.2d 622 (1984). Faced with the inherent arbitrariness of filing deadlines, we must, at least in a civil case, apply by its terms the date fixed by the statute. Cf. *United States Railroad Retirement Board v. Fritz,* 449 U.S., at 179, 101 S.Ct., at 461.[10]

Moreover, BLM regulations have made absolutely clear since the enactment of FLPMA that "prior to December 31" means what it says. As the current version of the filing regulations states:

"The owner of an unpatented mining claim located on Federal lands

---

[10] Statutory filing deadlines are generally subject to the defenses of waiver, estoppel, and equitable tolling. See *Zipes v. Trans World Airlines, Inc.,* 455 U.S. 385, 392-398, 102 S.Ct. 1127, 1131-1135, 71 L.Ed.2d 234 (1982). Whether this general principle applies to the deadlines that run in favor of the Government is a question on which we express no opinion today. In addition, no showing has been made that appellees were in any way "*unable* to excercise the usual care and diligence" that would have allowed them to meet the filing deadline or to learn of its existence. See *United States v. Boyle,* 469 U.S. 241, 254, 105 S.Ct. 687, ——, 83 L.Ed.2d 622 (1985) (BRENNAN, J., concurring). Of course, at issue in *Boyle* was an explicit provision in the Internal Revenue Code that provided a reasonable cause exception to the Code's filing deadlines, while FLPMA contains no analogous provision.

. . . shall have filed or caused to have been filed *on or before December 30* of each calendar year . . . evidence of annual assessment work performed during the previous assessment year or a notice of intention to hold the mining claim." 43 CFR § 3833.2-1(b)(1)(1984)(emphasis added).

See also 43 CFR § 3833.2-1(a) (1982) (same); 43 CFR 3833.2-1(a) (1981)(same); 43 CFR 3833.2-1(a) (1980)(same); 43 CFR 3833.2-1(a) (1979)(same); 43 CFR 3833.2-1(a)(1)(1978) ("prior to" Dec. 31); 43 CFR 3833.2-1(a)(1) (1977) ("prior to" Dec. 31). Leading mining treatises similarly inform claimants that "[i]t is important to note that the filing of a notice of intention or evidence of assessment work must be done *prior* to December 31 of each year, *i.e.,* on or before December 30." 2 American Law of Mining § 7.23D, p. 150.2 (Supp.1983) (emphasis in original); see also 23 Rocky Mountain Mineral Law Institute 25 (1977) (same). If appellees, who were businessmen involved in the running of a major mining operation for more than 20 years, had any questions about whether a December 31 filing complied with the statute, it was incumbent upon them, as it is upon other businessmen, see *United States v. Boyle, supra,* to have checked the regulations or to have consulted an attorney for legal advice. Pursuit of either of these courses, rather than the submission of a last-minute filing, would surely have led appellees to the conclusion that December 30 was the last day on which they could file safely.

In so saying, we are not insensitive to the problems posed by congressional reliance on the words "prior to December 31." See *post,* p. 117 (STEVENS, J., dissenting). But the fact that Congress might have acted with greater clarity or foresight does not give courts a *carte blanche* to redraft statutes in an effort to achieve that which Congress is perceived to have failed to do. "There is a basic difference between filling a gap left by Congress' silence and rewriting rules that Congress has affirmatively and specifically enacted." *Mobil Oil Corp. v. Higginbotham,* 436 U.S. 618, 625, 98 S.Ct. 2010, 2015, 56 L.Ed.2d 581 (1978). Nor is the judiciary licensed to attempt to soften the clear import of Congress' chosen words whenever a court believes those words lead to a harsh result. See *Northwest Airlines, Inc., v. Transport Workers,* 451 U.S. 77, 98, 101 S.Ct. 1571, 1584, 67 L.Ed.2d 750 (1981). On the contrary, deference to the supremacy of the legislature, as well as recognition that congressmen typically vote on the language of a bill, generally require us to assume that "the legislative purpose is expressed by the ordinary meaning of the words used." *Richards v. United States,* 369 U.S. 1, 9, 82 S.Ct. 585, 591, 7 L.Ed.2d 492 (1962). "Going behind the plain language of a statute in search of a possibly contrary congressional intent is 'a step to be taken cautiously' even under the best of circumstances." *American Tobacco Co. v. Patterson,* 456 U.S. 63, 75, 102 S.Ct. 1534, 1540, 71 L.Ed.2d 748 (1982)(quoting *Piper v. Chris-Craft Industries, Inc.,* 430 U.S. 1, 26, 97 S.Ct. 926, 941, 51 L.Ed.2d 124 (1977)). When even after taking this step nothing in the legislative history remotely suggests a congressional intent contrary to Congress' chosen words, and neither appellees nor the dissenters have pointed to anything that so suggests, any further steps take the courts out of the realm of interpretation and place them in the domain of legislation. The phrase "prior to" may be clumsy, but its meaning is clear.[11] Under these circumstances, we are obligated to apply the "prior to December 31" language by its terms. See, *e.g., American Tobacco Co. v. Patterson, supra,* 456 U.S., at 68, 102 S.Ct., at 1537; *Consumer Product Safety Comm'n v. GTE Sylvania, Inc.,* 447 U.S. 102, 108, 100 S.Ct. 2051, 2056, 64 L.Ed.2d 766 (1980).

The agency's regulations clarify and confirm the import of the statutory language by making clear that the annual filings must be made on or before December 30. These regulations provide a conclusive answer to appellees' claim, for where the language of a filing deadline is plain and the agency's construction completely consistent with that language, the Agency's construction simply cannot be found "sufficiently unreasonable" as to be unacceptable. *FEC v. Democratic Senatorial Campaign Committee,* 454 U.S. 27, 39, 102 S.Ct. 38, 46, 70 L.Ed.2d 23 (1981).

We cannot press statutory construction "to the point of disingenuous evasion" even to avoid a constitutional question. *Moore Ice Cream Co. v. Rose,* 289 U.S. 373, 379, 53 S.Ct. 620, 622, 77 L.Ed. 1265 (1933) (Cardozo, J.)[12] We therefore hold that BLM did not act ultra vires in concluding that appellees' filing was untimely.

B

Section 314(c) states that failure to comply with the filing requirements of §§ 314(a) and 314(b) "shall be deemed conclusively to constitute an abandonment of the mining claim." We must next consider whether this provision expresses a congressional intent to extinguish all claims for which filings have not been made, or only those claims for which filings have not been made *and* for which the claimants have a specific intent to abandon the claim. The District Court adopted the latter interpretation, and on that basis conluded that § 314(c)

---

[11] Legislative drafting books are filled with suggestions that the phrase "prior to" be replaced with the word "before," *see, e.g.,* R. Dickerson, Materials on Legal Drafting 293 (1981), but we have seen no suggestion that "prior to" be replaced with "on or before"—a phrase with obviously different substantive content.

[12] We note that the United States Code is sprinkled with provisions that require action "prior to" some date, including at least 14 provisions that contemplate action "prior to December 31." See 7 U.S.C. § 609(b)(5); 12 U.S.C. §1709(o)(1)(E); 12 U.S.C. § 1823(g); 12 U.S.C. § 1841(a)(5)(A); 22 U.S.C. § 3784(c); 26 U.S.C. § 503(d)(1); 33 U.S.C. § 1319(a)(5)(B); 42 U.S.C.A. § 415(a)(7)(E)(ii) (1983); 42 U.S.C. § 1962(d)-17(b); 42 U.S.C. § 5614(b)(5); 42 U.S.C. § 7502(a)(2); 42 U.S.C. § 7521(b)(2); 43 U.S.C. § 1744(a); 50 U.S.C.App. § 1741(b)(1). Dozens of state statutes and local ordinances undoubtedly incorporate similar "prior to December 31" deadlines. In addition, legislatures know how to make explicit an intent to allow action on December 31 when they employ a December 31 date in a statute. See, *e.g.,* 7 U.S.C. § 609(b)(2); 22 U.S.C. §§ 3303(b)(3)(B) and (c); 43 U.S.C. § 256a.
    It is unclear whether the arguments advanced by the dissenters are meant to apply to all of these provisions, or only to some of them; if the latter, we are given little guidance as to how a court is to go about the rather eclectic task of choosing which "prior to December 31" deadlines it can interrupt "flexibly." Understandably enough, the dissenters seek to disavow any intent to call all these "prior to December 31" deadlines into question and assure us that *this* is a "unique case," *post,* at 1084 n.3 (POWELL, J., dissenting); involving a unique factual matrix," *post,* at ——(STEVENS, J., dissenting). The only thing we can find unique about this particular December 31 deadline is that the dissenters are willing to go through such tortured reasoning to evade it.

created a constitutionally impermissible irrebuttable presumption of abandonment. The District Court reasoned that, once Congress had chosen to make loss of a claim turn on the specific intent of the claimant, a prior hearing and findings on the claimant's intent were constitutionally required before the claim of a non-filing claimant could be extinguished.

In concluding that Congress was concerned with the specific intent of the claimant even when the claimant had failed to make the required filings, the District Court began from the fact that neither § 314(c) nor the Act itself defines the term "abandonment" as that term appears in § 314(c). The District Court then noted correctly that the common law of mining traditionally has drawn a distinction between "abandonment" of a claim, which occurs only upon a showing of the claimant's intent to relinquish the claim, and "forfeiture" of a claim, for which only noncompliance with the requirements of law must be shown. See, *e.g.*, 2 American Law of Mining § 8.2, pp. 195-196 (1983)(relied upon by the District Court). Given that Congress had not expressly stated in the statute any intent to depart from the term-of-art meaning of "abandonment" at common law, the District Court concluded that § 314(c) was intended to incorporate the traditional common-law distinction between abandonment and forfeiture. Thus, reasoned the District Court, Congress did not intend to cause a forfeiture of claims for which the required filings had not been made, but rather to focus on the claimant's actual intent. As a corollary, the District Court understood the failure to file to have been intended to be merely one piece of evidence in a factual inquiry into whether a claimant had a specific intent to abandon his property.

This construction of the statutory scheme cannot withstand analysis. While reference to common-law conceptions is often a helpful guide to interpreting open-ended or undefined statutory terms, see, *e.g., NLRB v. Amax Coal Co.,* 453 U.S. 322, 329, 101 S.Ct. 2789, 2794, 69 L.Ed.2d 672(1981); *Standard Oil Co. v. United States,* 221 U.S. 1, 59, 31 S.Ct. 502, 515, 55 L.Ed. 619 (1911), this principle is a guide to legislative intent, not a talisman of it, and the principle is not to be applied in defiance of a statute's overriding purposes and logic. Although § 314(c) is couched in terms of a conclusive presumption of "abandonment," there can be little doubt that Congress intended § 314(c) to cause a forfeiture of all claims for which the filing requirements of §§ 314(a) and 314(b) had not been met.

To begin with, the Senate version of § 314(c) provided that any claim not properly recorded "shall be conclusively presumed to be abandoned and shall be void." S. 507, 94th Cong., 1st Sess. § 311.[13] The Committee Report accompanying S. 507 repeatedly indicated that failure to comply with the filing requirements would make a claim "void." See S.Rep. No. 94-583, p. 65, 66 (1975). The House legislation and reports merely repeat the statutory language

---

[13] The Senate bill required only initial recordings, not annual filings, but this factor is not significant in light of the actions of the Conference Committee; the clear structure of the Senate bill was to impose the sanction of claim extinguishment on those who failed to make whatever filings federal law required.

without offering any explanation of it, but it is clear from the Conference Committee Report that the undisputed intent of the Senate—to make "void" those claims for which proper filings were not timely made—was the intent of both chambers. The Report stated: "Both the Senate bill and House amendments provided for recordation of mining claims and for *extinguishment* of abandoned claims." H.R.Rep. No. 94-1724, 94th Cong., 2nd Sess. 62 (1976), U.S.Code Cong. & Admin. News 1976, pp. 6175, 6233 (emphasis added).

In addition, the District Court's construction fails to give effect to the "deemed conclusively" language of § 314(c). If the failure to file merely shifts the burden to the claimant to prove that he intends to keep the claim, nothing "conclusive" is achieved by § 314(c). The District Court sought to avoid this conclusion by holding that § 314(c) does extinguish automatically those claims for which *initial* recordings, as opposed to annual filings, have not been made; the District Court attempted to justify its distinction between initial recordings and annual filings on the ground that the dominant purpose of § 314(c) was to avoid forcing BLM to the "awesome task of searching every local title record" to establish initially a federal recording system. 573 F.Supp. 472, 477 (Nev. 1983). Once this purpose had been satisfied by an initial recording, the primary purposes of the "deemed conclusively" language in the District Court's view, had been met. But the clear language of § 314(c) admits of no distinction between initial recordings and annual filings: failure to do either "shall be deemed conclusively to constitute an abandonment." And the District Court's analysis of the purposes of § 314(c) is also misguided, for the annual filing requirements serve a purpose similar to that of the initial recording requirements; millions of claims undoubtedly have now been recorded, and the presence of an annual filing obligation allows BLM to keep the system established in § 314 up to date on a yearly basis. To put the burden on BLM to keep this system current through its own inquiry into the status of recorded claims would lead to a situation similar to that which led Congress initially to make the federal recording system self-executing. The purposes of a self-executing recording system are implicated similarly, if somewhat less substantially, by the annual filing obligation as by the initial recording requirement, and the District Court was not empowered to thwart these purposes or the clear language of § 314(c) by concluding that § 314(c) was actually concerned with only initial recordings.

For these reasons, we find that Congress intended in § 314(c) to extinguish those claims for which timely filings were not made. Specific evidence of intent to abandon is simply made irrelevant by § 314(c); the failure to file on time, in and of itself, causes a claim to be lost. See *Western Mining Council v. Watt,* 643 F.2d 619, 628 (CA9 1981).

C

A final stautory question must be resolved before we turn to the constitutional holding of the District Court. Relying primarily on *Hickel v. Shale Oil Corp.,* 400 U.S. 48, 91 S.Ct. 196, 27 L.Ed.2d 193 (1970), the District Court held that, even if the statute required a filing on or before December 30, appellees had "substantially complied" by filing on December 31. We cannot accept this view of the statute.

The notion that a filing deadline can be complied with by filing sometime after the deadline falls due is, to say the least, a surprising notion, and it is a notion without limiting principle. If 1-day late filings are acceptable, 10-day late filings might be equally acceptable, and so on in a cascade of exceptions that would engulf the rule erected by the filing deadline; yet regardless of where the cutoff line is set, some individuals will always fall just on the other side of it. Filing deadlines, like statutes of limitations, necessarily operate harshly and arbitrarily with respect to individuals who fall just on the other side of them, but if the concept of a filing deadline is to have any content, the deadline must be enforced. "Any less rigid standard would risk encouraging a lax attitude toward filing dates." *United States v. Boyle,* 469 U.S., at 249, 105 S.Ct., at 692. A filing deadline cannot be complied with, substantially or otherwise, by filing late— even by one day.

Hickel v. Shale Oil Co., supra, does not support a contrary conclusion. *Hickel* suggested, although it did not hold, that failure to meet the annual assessment work requirements of the general mining laws, 30 U.S.C § 28, which require that "not less than $100 worth of labor shall be performed or improvements made during each year," would not render a claim automatically void. Instead, if an individual complied substantially but not fully with the requirement, he might under some circumstances be able to retain possession of his claim.

These suggestions in *Hickel* do not afford a safe haven to mine owners who fail to meet their filing obligations under any federal mining law. Failure to comply fully with the physical requirement that a certain amount of work be performed each year is significantly different from the complete failure to file on time documents that federal law commands be filed. In addition, the general mining laws at issue in *Hickel* do not clearly provide that a claim will be lost for failure to meet the assessment work requirements. Thus, it was open to the Court to conclude in *Hickel* that Congress had intended to make the assessment work requirement merely an indicia of a claimant's specific intent to retain a claim. Full compliance with the assessment work requirements would establish conclusively an intent to keep the claim, but less than full compliance would not by force of law operate to deprive the claimant of his claim. Instead, less than full compliance would subject the mine owner to a case-by-case determination of whether he nonetheless intended to keep his claim. See *Hickel, supra,* 400 U.S., at 56-57, 91 S.Ct., at 200-201.

In this case, the statute explicitly provides that failure to comply with the applicable filing requirements leads automatically to loss of the claim. See Part II-B, *supra.* Thus, Congress has made it unnecessary to ascertain whether the individual in fact intends to abandon the claim, and there is no room to inquire whether substantial compliance is indicative of the claimant's intent—intent is simply irrelevant if the required filings are not made. *Hickel's* discussion of substantial compliance is therefore inapposite to the statutory scheme at issue here. As a result, *Hickel* gives miners no greater latitude with filing deadlines than have other individuals.[14]

IV

Much of the District Court's constitutional discussion necessarily falls with our conclusion that § 314(c) automatically deems forfeited those claims for which the required filings are not timely made. The District Court's invalidation of the statute rested heavily on the view that § 314(c) creates an "irrebuttable presumption that mining claims are abandoned if the miner fails to timely file" the required documents—that the statute presumes a failure to file to signify a specific intent to abandon the claim. But, as we have just held, § 314(c) presumes nothing about a claimant's actual intent; the statute simply and conclusively deems such claims to be forfeited. As a forfeiture provision, § 314(c) is not subject to the individualized hearing requirement of such irrebuttable presumption cases as *Vlandis v. Kline,* 412 U.S. 441, 93 S.Ct. 2330, 37 L.Ed.2d 63 (1973) or *Cleveland Bd. of Education v. LaFleur,* 414 U.S. 632, 94 S.Ct. 791, 39 L.Ed.2d 52 (1974), for there is nothing to suggest that, in enacting § 314(c), Congress was in any way concerned with whether a particular claimant's tardy filing or failure to file indicated an actual intent to abandon the claim.

There are suggestions in the District Court's opinion that, even understood as a forfeiture provision, § 314(c) might be unconstitutional. We therefore go on to consider whether automatic forfeiture of a claim for failure to make annual filings is constitutionally permissible. The framework for analysis of this question, in both its substantive and procedural dimensions, is set forth by our recent decision in *Texaco, Inc. v. Short,* 454 U.S. 516, 102 S.Ct. 781, 70 L.Ed.2d 738 (1982). There we upheld a state statute pursuant to which a severed mineral interest that had not been used for a period of 20 years automatically lapsed and reverted to the current surface owner of the property, unless the mineral owner filed a statement of claim in the county recorder's office within two years of the statute's passage.

---

[14] Since 1982, BLM regulations have provided that filings due on or before December 30 will be considered timely if postmarked on or before December 30 and received by BLM by the close of business on the following January 19th. 43 CFR 3833.0-5(m) (1983). Appellees and the dissenters attempt to transform this regulation into a blank check generally authorizing "substantial compliance" with the filing requirements. We disagree for two reasons. First, the regulation was not in effect when appellees filed in 1980; it therefore cannot now be relied on to validate a purported "substantial compliance" in 1980. Second, that an agency has decided to take account of holiday mail delays by treating as timely filed a document postmarked on the statutory filing date does not require the agency to accept all documents hand delivered any time before January 19th. The agency rationally could decide that either of the options in this sort of situation—requiring mailings to be received by the same date that hand deliveries must be made or requiring mailings to be postmarked by that date—is a sound way of administering the statute.

Justice STEVENS further suggests that BLM would have been well within its authority to promulgate regulations construing the statute to allow for December 31st filings. Assuming the correctness of this suggestion, the fact that two interpretations of a statute are equally reasonable suggests to us that the agency's interpretation is sufficiently reasonable as to be acceptable. See *FEC v. Democratic Senatorial Campaign Committee,* 454 U.S., at 39, 102 S.Ct., at 46.

A

Under *Texaco,* we must first address the question of affirmative legislative power: whether Congress is authorized to "provide that property
rights of this character shall be extinguished if their owners do not take the
affirmative action required by the" statute. *Id.,* at 525, 102 S.Ct., at 790. Even with
respect to vested property rights, a legislature generally has the power to impose
new regulatory constraints on the way in which those rights are used, or to
condition their continued retention on performance of certain affirmative
duties. As long as the constraint or duty imposed is a reasonable restriction
designed to further legitimate legislative objectives, the legislature acts within its
powers in imposing such new constraints or duties. See, *e.g., Village of Euclid v.
Ambler Realty, Co.,* 272 U.S. 365, 47 S.Ct. 114, 71 L.Ed. 303 (1926); *Turner v.
New York,* 168 U.S. 90, 94, 18 S.Ct. 38, 40, 42 L.Ed. 392 (1879); *Vance v. Vance,*
108 U.S. 514, 517, 2 S.Ct. 854, 856, 27 L.Ed. 808 (1883); *Terry v. Anderson,* 5
Otto 628, 95 U.S. 628, 24 L.Ed. 365 (1877). "[L]egislation readjusting rights and
burdens is not unlawful solely because it upsets otherwise settled expectations."
Usery v. Turner Elkhorn Mining Co., 428 U.S. 1, 16, 96 S.Ct. 2882, 2893, 49
L.Ed.2d 752 (1976) (citations omitted).

This power to qualify existing property rights is particularly broad with
respect to the "character" of the property rights at issue here. Although owners
of unpatented mining claims hold fully recognized possessory interests in their
claims, see *Best v. Humboldt Placer Mining Co.,* 371 U.S. 334, 335, 83 S.Ct. 379,
381, 9 L.Ed.2d 350 (1963), we have recognized that these interests are a "unique
form of property." *Id.,* 371 U.S., at 335, 83 S.Ct., at 382. The United States, as
owner of the underlying fee title to the public domain, maintains broad powers
over the terms and conditions upon which the public lands can be used, leased,
and acquired. See, *e.g., Kleppe v. New Mexico,* 426 U.S. 529, 539, 96 S.Ct. 2285,
2291, 49 L.Ed.2d 34 (1976).

> "A mining location which has not gone to patent is of no higher quality
> and no more immune from attack and investigation than are unpatented
> claims under the homestead and kindred laws. If valid, it gives to the
> claimant certain exclusive possessory rights, and so do homestead and
> desert claims. But no right arises from an invalid claim of any kind. All must
> conform to the law under which they are initiated; otherwise they work an
> unlawful private appropriation in derogation of the rights of the public."
> *Cameron v. United States,* 252 U.S. 450, 460, 40 S.Ct. 410, 412, 64 L.Ed.
> 659 (1920).

Claimants thus must take their mineral interests with the knowledge that the
Government retains substantial regulatory power over those interests. Cf. *Energy
Reserves Group, Inc. v. Kansas Power & Light Co.,* 459 U.S. 400, 413, 103 S.Ct.
697, 706, 74 L.Ed.2d 569 (1983). In addition, the property right here is the right
to a flow of income from production of the claim. Similar vested economic rights
are held subject to the Government's substantial power to regulate for the public
good the conditions under which business is carried out and to redistribute the
benefits and burdens of economic life. See, *e.g., National Railroad Passenger*

Corp. v. Atchison, T., & S.F.R. Co., 470 U.S. 451, 105 S.Ct. 1441, 84 L.Ed.2d 432 (1985); *Usery v. Turner Elkhorn Mining Co., supra;* see generally *Walls v. Midland Carbon Co.,* 254 U.S. 300, 315, 41 S.Ct. 118, 121, 65 L.Ed. 276 (1920) ("in the interest of the community, [government may] limit one [right] that others may be enjoyed").

Against this background, there can be no doubt that Congress could condition initial receipt of an unpatented mining claim upon an agreement to perform annual assessment work and make annual filings. That this requirement was applied to claims already located by the time FLPMA was enacted and thus applies to vested claims does not alter the analysis, for any "retroactive application of [FLPMA] is supported by a legitimate legislative purpose furthered by rational means. . . . " *PBSC v. R.A. Gray & Co.,* 467 U.S. 717, 104 S.Ct. 2709, 81 L.Ed.2d 601 (1984). The purposes of applying FLPMA's filing provisions to claims located before the Act was passed—to rid federal lands of stale mining claims and to provide for centralized collection by federal land managers of comprehensive and up-to-date information on the status of recorded but unpatented mining claims—are clearly legitimate. In addition, § 314(c) is a reasonable, if severe, means of furthering these goals; sanctioning with loss of their claims those claimants who fail to file provides a powerful motivation to comply with the filing requirements, while automatic invalidation for noncompliance enables federal land managers to know with certainty and ease whether a claim is currently valid. Finally, the restriction attached to the continued retention of a mining claim imposes the most minimal of burdens on claimants; they must simply file a paper once a year indicating that the required assessment work has been performed or that they intend to hold the claim.[15] Indeed, appellees could have fully protected their interests against the effect of the statute by taking the

---

[15] Appellees suggest that *Texaco* further requires that the restriction imposed be substantively reasonable in the sense that it adequately relate to some common law conception of the nature of the property right involved. Thus, appellees point to the fact that, in *Texaco,* failure to file could produce a forfeiture only if, in addition, the mineral interest had lain dormant for 20 years; according to appellees, conjunction of a 20-year dormancy period with failure to file a statement of claim sufficiently indicated abandonment, as that term is understood at common law, to justify the statute.

Common-law principles do not, however, entitle an individual to retain his property until the common-law would recognize it as abandoned. Legislatures can enact substantive rules of law that treat property as forfeited under conditions that the common-law would not consider sufficient to indicate abandonment. See *Hawkins v. Barney's Lessee,* 5 Pet. 456, 467, 8 L.Ed. 190 (1831). ("What is the evidence of an individual having abandoned his rights or property? It is clear that the subject is one over which every community is at liberty to make a rule for itself"). As long as proper notice of these rules exists, and the burdens they impose are not so wholly disproportionate to the burdens other individuals face in a highly regulated society that some people are being forced "alone to bear public burdens which, in all fairness and justice, must be borne by the public as a whole," *Armstrong v. United States,* 364 U.S. 40, 49, 80 S.Ct. 1563, 1569, 4 L.Ed.2d 1554 (1960), the burden imposed is a reasonable restriction on the property right. Here Congress has chosen to redefine the way in which an unpatented mining claim can be lost through imposition of a filing requirement that serves valid public objectives, imposes the most minimal of burdens on property holders, and takes effect only after appellees have had sufficient notice of their need to comply and a reasonable opportunity to do so. That the filing requirement meets these standards is sufficient, under *Texaco,* to make it a reasonable restriction on the continued retention of the property right.

minimal additional step of patenting the claims. As a result, Congress was well within its affirmative powers in enacting the filing requirements, in imposing the penalty of extinguishment set forth in § 314(c), and in applying the requirements and sanction to claims located before FLPMA was passed.

B

We look next to the substantive effect of § 314(c) to determine whether Congress is nonetheless barred from enacting it because it works an impermissible intrusion on constitutionally protected rights. With respect to the regulation of private property, any such protection must come from the Fifth Amendment's proscription against the taking of private property without just compensation. On this point, however, *Texaco* is controlling: "this Court has never required [Congress] to compensate the owner for the consequences of his own neglect." 454 U.S., at 530, 102 S.Ct., at 792. Appellees failed to inform themselves of the proper filing deadline and failed to file in timely fashion the documents required by federal law. Their property loss was one appellees could have avoided with minimal burden; it was their failure to file on time—not the action of Congress—that caused the property right to be extinguished. Regulation of property rights does not "take" private property when an individual's reasonable, investment-backed expectations can continue to be realized as long as he complies with reasonable regulatory restrictions the legislature has imposed. See, *e.g., Miller v. Schoene,* 276 U.S. 272, 279-280, 48 S.Ct. 246, 247, 72 L.Ed. 568 (1928); *Terry v. Anderson,* 5 Otto, at 632-633, 95 U.S. at 632-633; cf. *Hawkins v. Barney's Lessee,* 5 Pet., at, 465, 8 L.Ed. 190 ("What right has any one to complain, when a reasonable time has been given him, if he has not been vigilant in asserting his rights?").

C

Finally, the Act provides appellees with all the process that is their constitutional due. In altering substantive rights through enactment of rules of general applicability, a legislature generally provides constitutionally adequate process simply by enacting the statute, publishing it, and, to the extent the statute regulates private conduct, affording those within the statute's reach a reasonable opportunity both to familiarize themselves with the general requirements imposed and to comply with those requirements. *Texaco,* 454 U.S., at 532, 102 S.Ct., at 793; see also *Anderson National Bank v. Luckett,* 321 U.S. 233, 243, 64 S.Ct. 599, 604, 88 L.Ed. 692 (1944); *North Laramie Land Co. v. Hoffman,* 268 U.S. 276, 283, 45 S.Ct. 491, 494, 69 L.Ed. 953 (1925). Here there can be no doubt that the Act's recording provisions meet these minimal requirements. Although FLPMA was enacted in 1976, owners of existing claims, such as appellees, were not required to make an initial recording until October 1979. This three-year period, during which individuals could become familiar with the requirements of the new law, surpasses the two-year grace period we upheld in the context of a similar regulation of mineral interests in *Texaco.* Moreover, the specific annual filing obligation at issue in this case is not triggered until the year after which the claim is recorded initially; thus, every claimant in appellees' position already has filed once before the annual filing obgliations come due.

That these claimants already have made one filing under the Act indicates that they know, or must be presumed to know, of the existence of the Act and of their need to inquire into its demands.[16] The requirement of an annual filing thus was not so unlikely to come to the attention of those in the position of appellees as to render unconstitutional the notice provided by the 3-year grace period.[17]

Despite the fact that FLPMA meets the three standards laid down in *Texaco* for the imposition of new regulatory restraints on existing property rights, the District Court seemed to believe that individualized notice of the filing deadlines was nonetheless constitutionally required. The District Court felt that such a requirement would not be "overly burdensome" to the Government and would be of great benefit to mining claimants. The District Court may well be right that such an individualized notice scheme would be a sound means of administering the Act.[18] But in the regulation of private property rights, the Constitution offers the courts no warrant to inquire into whether some other scheme might be more rational or desirable than the one chosen by Congress; as long as the legislative scheme is a rational way of reaching Congress' objectives, the efficacy of alternative routes is for Congress alone to consider. "It is enough to say that the Act approaches the problem of [developing a national recording system] rationally; whether a [different notice scheme] would have been wiser or more practical under the circumstances is not a question of constitutional dimension." *Usery v. Turner Elkhorn Mining,* 428 U..S at 19, 96 S.Ct., at 2894. Because we deal here with purely economic legislation, Congress was entitled to conclude that it was preferable to place a substantial portion of the burden on claimants to make the national recording system work. See *Ibid; Weinberger v. Salfi,* 422 U.S. 749, 95 S.Ct. 2457, 45 L.Ed.2d 522 (1975); *Mourning v. Family Publications Service, Inc.,* 411 U.S. 356, 93 S.Ct. 1652, 36 L.Ed.2d 318 (1973). The District Court therefore erred in invoking the Constitution to supplant the valid administrative scheme established by Congress. The judgment below is reversed, and the case remanded for further proceedings consistent with this opinion.

It is so ordered.

---

[16] As a result, this is not a case in which individual notice of a statutory change must be given because a statute is "sufficiently unusual in character, and triggered in circumstances so commonplace, that an average citizen would have no reason to regard the triggering event as calling for a heightened awareness of one's legal obligations." *Texaco,* 454 U.S., at 547, 102 S.Ct., at 801 (BRENNAN, J., dissenting).

[17] BLM does provide for notice and a hearing on the adjudicative fact of whether the required filings were actually made, and appellees availed themselves of this process by appealing, to the Department of Interior Board of Land Appeals, the BLM order that extinguished their claims for failure to make a timely filing.

[18] In the excercise of its administrative discretion, BLM for the last several years has chosen to mail annual reminder notices to claimants several months before the end of the year; according to the Government, these notices state that "you must file on or before 12/30 [of the relevant year.] Failure to file timely with the proper BLM office will render your claim abandoned." Brief for Appellants 31-32, n. 22.

NOTES

1. The concurring and dissenting opinions to the decision in the principal case are omitted.These opinions are described in *TOSCO Corp. v. Hodel*, 611 F. Supp. 1130, 1193 (D. Colo. 1985) as follows (citations to the *Locke* case are omitted):

"Although Justice O'Connor joined the majority opinion, she also wrote a concurring opinion to emphasize that this might be an appropriate case to assert equitable estoppel against the government. Justice O'Connor noted that the regulations of the BLM and the actions of its employees were partly responsible for the late filing of the assessment notices.

"Justice Powell filed a dissenting opinion. He concluded that § 314(c) was too uncertain to have given the Lockes proper notice of what they should have done to protect their interests. As such, he would have found a forfeiture imposed for filing one day late to have been invalid. Justice Powell also agreed with Justice Steven's [sic] conclusion that the parties have substantially complied with the requirements of the statute.

"Justice Stevens filed a separate dissenting opinion, in which he was joined by Justice Brennan. According to Justice Stevens, the language of the statute was ambiguous as to when the Lockes were to file their assessment notices. He was of the opinion that Congress intended the filing date to be at anytime prior to the end of the year. Relying on *Hickel v. The Oil Shale Co.*, 400 U.S. 48 (1970), Justice Stevens noted that the Lockes had filed their documents only one day late and long before the BLM extinguished their claims. As such, he concluded that they had substantially complied with the requirements of the statute."

2. In *Park City Chief Mining Co.*, 57 I.B.L.A. 342, 1981 GFS (Min) 301, the claimant made its FLPMA filing timely, but omitted from the filing the date on which its claim had been located. The BLM sent the claimant a deficiency notice stating that "all claims must show the date of location" and that failure to cure within 30 days would "result in the claim(s) being considered abandoned." The claimant did not cure within 30 days, and the BLM, in accordance with 43 C.F.R. 3833.1-2(c) rejected the original filing, rendering the claim void. The mining claimant appealed and the IBLA reinstated the claim, finding that the failure to cure was justified by the temporary incapacity of Richard S. Johnson, the person in the BLM charged with handling such matters. Apparently, in Mr. Johnson's absence, no one was available to attend to normal business matters of this type. The Board wrote that "[w]hile allegations of the disability would not excuse a late filing, E.M. Koppen, 36 I.B.L.A. 379, 1978 GFS (Min) 94, this case does not present a question of a late filing but, rather, a question of a curable deficiency. In the latter regard, we believe that Johnson's disability was sufficient to excuse the failure to respond timely, especially, when appellant promptly cured the defect upon learning that Johnson had not."

Why should curable defects be treated any differently from a failure to file altogether? One as much as the other interferes with the BLM's ability to make land use plans for the public lands. Does *Topaz Beryllium* shed any light on this question?

3. Janie Nelson's mining claim was declared void for failure to make timely filings pursuant to FLPMA. Nelson filed timely, but in the wrong office of the BLM. By the time the mistake was discovered and the filing made in the proper office, the deadline for filing had passed. Nelson's claim was located near the dividing line between "Northern" and "Southern" Alaska, and because of the poor quality of the map used by the BLM it was "virtually impossible" for Nelson to determine in which district the claim was situated, and with which office of the BLM the filing should be made (Alaska is the only state with two offices having jurisdiction to receive FLPMA filings). The Board concluded in these circumstances that a timely filing in one BLM office will constitute a timely filing in the proper office. Janie S. Nelson, 55 I.B.L.A. 289, 1981 GFS (Min) 180.

4. The *Locke* decision is noted at 21 LAND & WATER L. REV. 485 (1986)

B. What Constitutes Assessment Work

UNITED STATES V. 9,947.71 ACRES OF LAND, MORE OR LESS
220 F.Supp. 328 (Nev. 1963)

[footnotes omitted]

. . . .

PEIRSON M. HALL, District Judge.

The question to be resolved is whether or not defendants, Fibreboard Paper Products Corporation (Fibreboard), and Stauffer Chemical Co. (Stauffer) had a compensable property interest in a certain road at the time the United States filed its suit in condemnation and secured an order for possession, which was October 12 and 13, 1952, hereafter referred to as the date of "taking." The land taken in condemnation is and has been known as "Lake Mead Base," a military installation.

This memorandum is based on a stipulation of facts, and a supplemental stipulation of facts, as they were clarified by statements of counsel on argument. A map showing the road, the mining claims which it served, and the area taken by the United States in this case was attached to the stipulation, and from it was extracted certain information hereinafter set forth.

Many years prior to the taking, predecessors in interest of both Stauffer and Fibreboard located and maintained valid mining claims for gypsum and other nonmetallic substances, under the mining laws of the United States. Some were lode and some were placer. Some of the claims were patented before the "taking," and some since, and there is no question raised in these proceedings as to the validity of the mining claims involved. The Stauffer group claims were known as the Anniversary claims and the Fibreboard claims, as the Lovell claims.

All claims were completely surrounded by the Public Domain, and no surface access, either ingress or egress, could be had, except over and across public lands of the United States. The Anniversary claims are 10 to 15 miles farther from a public highway and railroad than the Lovell claims and were located and worked upon prior, in point of time, to the Lovell claims. In 1921 Stauffer's predecessors built a road about 20 to 25 miles in length across public lands from the Union Pacific Railroad at a point near the S.W. corner of Sec. 15, T. 19, S.R. 62 E., M.D.B.M. southeasterly, through what are now the Lovell claims, to the Anniversary claims in sections 10, 11, 14, 15, and 23, T., 20 S *** R. 65 E., M.D.B. & M., which is about 6 miles south and 20 miles east from the railroad. This road was constructed through a mountain pass and was meanderingly laid out so as to require a minimum length of haul over the lowest possible grade in the rough mountainous country. The road crossed what is now U.S. Highway 91-93, about 3 miles from the railroad, thus giving access to both the railroad and said Highway. Beginning at said Highway, the road passed through the land taken in this case for Lake Mead Base for a distance of about 7 miles, which is the only portion of the road we are concerned with here.

The Anniversary group (Stauffer) used the entire road in connection with active mining operations on the claims from 1921 to 1928, and thereafter, until the date of "taking" in 1952, used it in connection with annual assessment work, a watchman, intermittent visits by engineers, and the transportation of men, materials, supplies, equipment, machinery and ore incident to such operations.

The Lovell group (Fibreboard) used the portion of the road between its claims and the railroad in connection with active mining operation on the claims from 1939 to 1949, and thereafter, until the date of "taking" in 1952, used it for inspection and maintenance of the mine and annual assessment work, and the transportation of men, materials, supplies, equipment, machinery, and ore incident to such operations.

Such use by both groups involved the use of the portion of the road passing through the area which was taken in the within action.

Stauffer's predecessor in 1924 filed a certificate under the Nevada Statutes (Act of Mar. 8, 1865; NCL Sec. 5448; Sec. 406.020 NRS) for a toll road covering a portion of the road, and in 1939 sold its rights thereunder to Fibreboard's predecessor, who thereupon (1939), filed an eminent domain action to condemn, and secured a judgment of condemnation in the Nevada State Court covering not only all of the road involved in the instant proceedings, but an additional stretch of road beyond the land taken herein sufficient to reach the Lovell claims, but not any portion of the road beyond the Lovell claims which led to the Anniversary claims. The defendants were the County of Clark and several owners of mining claims, all of whom disclaimed. The United States was not a party. It could have appeared. (1911 C.P.A. Sec. 671; NCL, Sec. 9160; NRS sec. 37.080). Mining was declared to be a public use by the Nevada Statutes of 1887 (NCL, Sec. 4154, NRS 516.010), and miners were authorized to condemn roads for all mining purposes by Nevada Civil Practice Act of 1911, Sec. 664 (NCL, Sec. 9153; NRS 37.010), as were those who complied with the Nevada Statutes for toll roads (NCL, Sec. 5450; NRS 406.040).

The area taken by the United States in these proceedings is about 12 square miles, and, as above noted, within the perimeter thereof is included approximately the first seven miles of the road which lies easterly from U.S. Highway 91-93. None of the mining claims are included in the instant "taking," nor is any of the road easterly of the "taking" to the mines. Since the date of "taking" the use of the portion of the road within the present "taking" has been denied to both Stauffer and Fibreboard by the United States as well as the public generally. This being the only vehicular surface access to defendants' mining claims such denial has effectively prevented both Stauffer and Fibreboard from having access to their claims, unless they built new roads over other public lands.

The position of counsel for the government briefly stated is that neither defendant had any right in and to the road which constituted "private property" for which either of them is entitled to "just compensation" under the Fifth Amendment to the Constitution of the United States, for two reasons: (1) the fee title to the land over which the road traversed has always been in the United States and the United States has done nothing, by statutory grant or otherwise to vest a property interest in the road in either defendant, and (2) that any interest which might be adverse to the United States was an interest which constituted the road a *public highway*, and that all *public highways* are specifically excluded from the "taking."

The defendants do not claim they had any right to the fee title of the land, but do assert that the Acts of Congress relating to mining coupled with the acts of the actual construction of the road and its use in the operation of their mining claims, buttressed by their compliance with the Nevada Statutes relating to toll roads and eminent domain proceedings for the road, gave them such right to the use of the road as to amount to a private property right for which they are entitled to just compensation.

Counsel for the parties state that there is a paucity of case authority on the precise question involved.

It is not difficult to perceive that such lack of case authority arises from the sheer logic of the proposition that, when the government granted mining rights on the vast mountainous, and often impassable, areas of the West which were in public domain, accessible only by passing over the public domain, it granted, as a necessary corollary to mining rights, the right not only to pass over the public domain but also a property right to the continued use of such roadway or trail, once it was established and used for that purpose. To realize the force of the proposition just stated, one need but to raise their eyes, when traveling through the West to see the innumerable roads and trails that lead off, and on, through the public domain, into the wilderness, where some prospector has found a stake (or broke his heart) or a homesteader has found the valley of his dreams and laboriously and sometimes at very great expense built a road to conform to the terrain, and which in many instances is the only possible surface access to the property by vehicles required to haul heavy equipment, supplies and machinery.

If the builders of such roads to property surrounded by the public domain had only a right thereto revocable at the will of the government, and had no property right to maintain and use them after the roads were once built, then the rights granted for the development and settlement of the public domain, whether for mining, homesteading, townsite, mill sites, lumbering, or other uses, would have been a delusion and a cruel and empty vision, inasmuch as the claim would be lost by loss of access, as well as the investment therein, which in many cases of mines required large sums of money, before a return could be had.

Congress did not leave the rights of miners and others to such chance, but passed the Act of July 26, 1866, (14 Stat. 251) which declared in Section 1 thereof (30 U.S.C. § 22) that the mineral lands of the public domain were open to exploration and occupation, subject to regulations as may be prescribed by law and subject also to local customs and rules of miners so far as such may not be in conflict with the laws of the United States. Other sections provided for perfecting title to claims and for sale or patent thereof to the claimant. Section 5 (30 U.S.C. § 43) provided one of the conditions of sale that, "in the absence of necessary legislation by Congress, the local legislature of any State or Territory may provide rules for working mines, involving easements, drainage, and other necessary means to their complete development." Section 8 of the Act (43 U.S.C. § 932) provided that "the right-of-way for the construction of highways over public lands, not reserved for public uses, is hereby granted."

Counsel have not cited, and the Court has not been able to find on independent research, a case involving the right of the holder of the right-of-way to such a highway or road over the public domain to compensation in a condemnation suit by the United States. There is nevertheless a respectable body of authority which supports the position of the defendants.

Two of the authorities should command the respect of the plaintiff, the United States of America, as they are the product of the governmental agency having charge of Public Lands and Mines and mining locations.

The first is 43 C.F.R. 244.57 and 244.58, which read as follows in their pertinent parts:

"Sec. 244.57 *Statutory authority* R.S. 2477 (43 U.S.C. 932), grants rights-of-way for the construction of highways over public lands, not reserved for public uses."

"Sec. 244.58 *Effective date and extent of grant.* (a) Grants of rights-of-way referred to in the preceding section become effective upon the construction or establishment of highways, in accordance with the State laws, over public lands, not reserved for public uses. No application should be filed under R.S. 2477, as no action on the part of the Government is necessary ***." This principle is in accord with long established case law, as will be seen directly.

The second authority, which should command the respect of the government here is the decision by the Department of the Interior of the United States of America (Plaintiff here) set forth in the opinion of its acting solicitor on

October 20, 1959, (66 I.D. 361) wherein, after reviewing the decisions of the United States General Land Office relating thereto, he pointed out that the United States could not charge a miner for a right-of-way which gave access to his mine inasmuch as having built the road "his right to use it for mining purposes is as evident as his right to mine." The decision also noted that the United States had long ago adopted the policy that work done in the construction of roads for ingress and egress to the mining claims for the purpose of operating such claims was creditable as legitimate annual assessment work required to obtain a patent.

The Land Office decisions cited in the opinion of the solicitor were in conformity with Court opinions which uniformly held that work done on roads for necessary mining purposes were credited towards annual assessment work for the patent.

Doherty v. Morris, (1891) 17 Colo. 105, 28 P. 85, is a case in point. There the court said, (28 P., at p. 86):

"We do not hesitate to assert that labor performed by the owner of a mine in constructing a wagon road thereto for the purpose of better developing and operating the same may be treated as a compliance with the law relating to annual assessment work thereon. This view, besides being correct on principle, is also, we think, in accord with the rule laid down in the following cases: St. Louis, etc., Co. v. Kemp, 104 U.S. 636, 11 Morr.Min. Rep. 673 [26 L.Ed. 875]; Mount Diablo Mill, etc., Co. v. Callison, 5 Sawy. 439, 9 Morr.Min.Rep. 616 (Fed. Case No. 9886, Nev. 1879). The opinion in St. Louis, etc., Co. v. Kemp, supra, uses this language [at (104 U.S. p. 655)]: 'Labor and improvements, within the meaning of the statute, are deemed to have been had on a mining claim * * * when the labor is performed or the improvements are made for its development,—that is, to facilitate the extraction of the metals it may contain,—though in fact such labor and improvements may * * * be at a distance from the claim itself.' And in Mt. Diablo Mill, etc., Co. v. Callison, supra, it is declared that 'work done outside of the claim, * * * if done for the purpose and as a means of prospecting or developing the claim, * * * is as available for holding the claim as if done within the boundaries of the claim itself.' "

The same principle was applied by the Supreme Court of the State of Washington, in Sexton v. Washington Min. & Mill Co. (1909), 55 Wash. 380, 104 P. 614, in connection with the building of a road. The Court cited with approval Doherty v. Morris, supra, in support of the proposition that independent of the State Statute, "there could be little doubt but that the performance of this labor in the construction of a road aiding in the general development of the combined properties would be a full compliance with the statutory requirement as to assessment work." The Court also held that even though the parties did not comply with a Washington Statute permitting road building in accordance with rules adopted by an "organized" mining district that, "* * * the building and construction of roads which can and are intended to be used in the general development of the mining property is a doing of assessment and improvement work within the meaning of the law." (104 P. p. 616). The Court further stated (104 P. p. 615) "the courts have uniformly held that any work done upon a claim, or outside of any claim, if done for the purpose of furthering the development of such claim, is permissible and available as assessment work, as if done within the boundaries of the claim itself. St. Louis, etc., Co. v. Kemp, 104 U.S. 636, 26 L.Ed. 875; Mt. Diablo, etc., Co. v. Callison, 5 Sawy. 439, Fed.Cas.No.9, 886 (U.S.C.C.D. of Nev.1879); Book v. Justice Mining Co. [(C.C.D.Nev.1893)] 58 Fed. 106."

The rule that *road work* to the claims was sufficient to satisfy the requirement of annual assessment work is followed in California. Ring v. United States Gypsum (1923) 62 Cal.App. 87, 216 P. 409; Lind v. Baker (1939) 31 Cal.App.2d 631, 88 P.2d 777; Pepperdine et al. v. Keys et al., (1961) 198 Cal. App.2d 25, 17 Cal.Rptr. 709.

The same rule is followed in New Mexico; Pinkerton v. Moore (1959) 66 N.M. 11, 340 P.2d 844-846.

In Hall v. Kearny (1893) 18 Colo. 505, 33 P. 373, the Colorado Supreme Court on the authority of Doherty v. Morris, supra, and St. Louis, etc., Co. v. Kemp (1881) 104 U.S. 636, 26 L.Ed. 875 sustained the proposition that work done on a tunnel outside a mining claim was sufficient to satisfy the requirements of the United States laws for annual assessment work. The Court further held that it was immaterial whether or not such tunnel work was done on patented (private) property or unpatented (public) property. To the same effect in Sherlock v. Leighton (1901) 9 Wyo. 297, 63 P. 580-581, 63 P. 934.

The opinion in neither case mentions the Act of February 11, 1875, 18 Stat. 315, (now the last paragraph of 30 U.S.C. § 28), which permitted work done on tunnels to count as work done on mining claims if done for the purpose of developing the mine. That statute is silent as to whether or not the tunnel work on other than mining claims could be credited on the statutory assessment work, thus leaving the determination of that question to the courts, which have uniformly followed the rule that such work off the claims would satisfy the annual assessment work.

Nevada Expl. & Min. Co. v. Spriggs (1912) 41 Utah 171, 124 P. 770, involved the sinking of a shaft for mining purposes which, it was contended "was too far distant" from the mining claims involved to count as assessment work toward holding the claims or obtaining a patent. Here again the Court rested its conclusion on Doherty v. Morris, supra, and held that if the location of the ore bodies in place was known, work done other than upon the claims would be counted as annual assessment work if the purpose of the work was to facilitate the extraction of the ores and minerals. The Court construed the statement in Chambers v. Harrington (1884) 111 U.S. 350, at 353, 4 S.Ct. 428, at 430, 28 L.Ed. 452, that such work off the claims must be in accordance with a "general system" to mean that the work "as it is commenced on the ground, is such that, if continued, will lead to a discovery and development of the veins or ore bodies that are supposed to be in the claims," and that the term did not mean any fixed plan or specification as to how the work should be done.

Numerous other cases throughout the West have applied and followed the principles set forth in the above case and it would be a work of supererogation to burden this memorandum with their citations and analysis. No cases to the contrary have been found or cited.

By Sections 5 and 6 of the Act of May 10, 1872, 17 Stats. 92 (now 30 U.S.C. §§ 28 and 29), a minimum of one hundred dollars worth of work was required to be done each year and a minimum of five hundred dollars was required to secure a patent to a mining claim.

It follows by simple logic that, if the work done on making a roadway to a mining claim could be allowed as annual assessment work to the value of at least one hundred dollars, or a total of five hundred dollars on the mining claim, then the road or right-of-way had some value, and was property.

. . . .

NOTES

1. If a friend of the locator assists in performing the assessment work and does not charge for his labor, can the value of his labor nevertheless be included in calculating whether the requisite $100 of assessment work has been performed? See *Pasco v. Richards,* 20 Cal. Rptr. 416 (Cal. App. 1962) holding that work performed gratuitously by a stranger was properly attributable to the required assessment work of the claim holder.

2. Conversely, if a contractor is hired to do the annual assessment work, and the contractor does the required work but the mining claimant wrongfully refuses to pay for the work, is the location subject to forfeiture for failure to perform the required assessment work? See *Eveleigh v. Darneille,* 81 Cal. Rptr. 301 (Cal. App. 1969). What if the contractor is paid to do the work, but the contractor either does not perform the work or performs the work so poorly that its value is less than $100?

GREAT EASTERN MINES, INC. V. METALS CORPORATION OF AMERICA
527 P.2d 112 (N.M. 1974)

OPINION

McMANUS, Chief Justice.

Plaintiff brought suit against defendants claiming valid and subsisting ownership of certain unpatented mining claims described as the Wall Street Claims Numbers I through VII, inclusive. Plaintiffs also sought damages for alleged slander of title. All damage claims were later withdrawn and the issue was submitted to the court and jury on the question of ownership only. All of said claims were in Sierra County, New Mexico. As the trial progressed all parties stipulated that the only claims in dispute were the Wall Street Claims 2, 3 and 5. The jury returned a verdict for the plaintiffs and the trial court entered judgment thereon.

The evidence disclosed that in 1951 plaintiffs filed notice of location on the claims in question. The defendants located their claims in January 1967, resulting in the conflict before us. Plaintiffs' work on the claims for fiscal year 1966 (September 1, 1965 to August 31, 1966) consisted of mapping and survey and the taking of ore samples, including bulk and channel samples. Bulldozer work to obtain samples and expose older material was also accomplished and jackhammer, drilling and blasting samples were forwarded to a mill in Colorado for evaluation by a geologist. Evidence as to the value of the work showed it was in excess of $1,000. Plaintiffs failed to file a proof of labor for that year.

The defendants first contend that:

"In taking of ore samples by a geologist for testing, mapping or survey work does not constitute valid assessment work when the requirements of 30 U.S.C.A. Sec. 28-1 and 2 have not been met."

Those sections of 30 U.S.C.A. provide:

§ 28-1 "The term 'labor', as used in the third sentence of section 28 of this title, shall include, without being limited to, geological, geochemical and geophysical surveys conducted by qualified experts and verified by a detailed report filed in the county office in which the claim is located which sets forth fully (a) the location of the work performed in relation to the point of discovery and boundaries of the claim, (b) the nature, extent, and cost thereof, (c) the basic findings therefrom, and (d) the name, address, and professional background of the person or persons conducting the work. Such surveys, however, may not be applied as labor for more than two consecutive years or for more than a total of five years on any one mining claim, and each such survey shall be nonrepetitive of any previous survey on the same claim."

§ 28-2. As used in section 28-1 of this title,

"(a) The term 'geological surveys' means surveys on the ground for mineral deposits by the proper application of the principles and techniques of the science of geology as they relate to the search for and discovery of mineral deposits;

"* * *

"(c) The term 'geophysical surveys' means surveys on the ground for mineral deposits through the employment of generally recognized equipment and methods for measuring physical differences between rock types or discontinuities in geological formations;

"(d) The term 'qualified expert' means an individual qualified by education or experience to conduct geological, geochemical or geophysical surveys, as the case may be."

Was the work done on the claims in question for the year 1966 valid assessment work? The record discloses that discovery of minerals had been made prior to 1966, thus the work done during that year was not for exploratory purposes. The sampling made during this period was quite extensive, including extraction of bulk and channel samples, accomplished by bulldozing, blasting and drilling, with well over one thousand pounds of samples being extracted at a cost to appellees of over $1,000. Evidence of such sampling would clearly be visible on the ground. The testimony shows that the work was done for the purpose of determining the milling characteristics of the ore located on the subject claims to facilitate mineral development of the area.

Appellants rely on Pinkerton v. Moore, 66 N.M. 11, 340 P.2d 844 (1959), which held that reconnaissance and counter-reconnaissance do not constitute valid assessment work, and Bishop v. Baisley, 28 Or. 119, 41 P. 936 (1895), which held that taking samples from the walls of the shaft or outcroppings in small quantities and making tests could not be credited as annual labor. These two cases are clearly distinguishable from the facts of the instant case.

In Pinkerton, supra, the surveys were not of a character that would enure to the benefit of the claim. Bishop, supra, is also distinguishable in that sampling from the walls of the shaft, et cetera, was done to determine if there was a "pay chute," with that court differentiating between survey work done for the purpose of discovering a "pay chute" and that done for the purpose of developing it, as in this case. Here it is evident that the work performed benefitted a claim and was not done to ascertain whether there was a "pay chute" in the mine, but rather to determine the milling characteristics of the ore already known to exist.

The general rule in regard to the character of ground work is that the work must be of such a character as directly tends to develop and protect the claim and to facilitate the extraction of minerals. Eveleigh v. Darneille, 276 Cal. App.2d 638, 81 Cal.Rptr. 301 (1965).

Guidelines for the determination we must make regarding the work done by plaintiffs are set out in Schlegel v. Hough, 182 Or. 441, 186 P.2d 516, reh. denied, 182 Or. 449, 188 P.2d 158 (1947), as follows:

"* * * The question to be considered is whether or not the work was done in good faith 'for the purpose of working, prospecting or developing the mining ground embraced in the location, or for the purpose of facilitating the extraction or removal of the ore therefrom.' [Citations omitted.]"

2 American Law of Mining § 7.6, at 108 (The Rocky Mountain Mineral Law Foundation, ed. 1973), addresses itself to the "good faith" requirement mentioned by the court in Schlegel, supra. In addition to the good faith requirement, it is well settled that the work must tend to develop the claim and facilitate the extraction of ore therefrom. However, if the work is performed in good faith, the court will not substitute its own judgment for that of the miner. The work need not be performed openly and notoriously.

Dale Carlson, a geologist, and a witness at the trial on the significance of the work done during the period in question, testified as follows:

"Q. Mr. Carlson, then in regard to this work that was done, can you tell us whether or not there was work done in all of the seven Wall Street claims in the period from September 1st, 1965 through the end of the year?

"A. From the samples there was work done. If you will give me this exhibit over here, I can tell you which. There was work done on Wall Street 1, Wall Street 2, Wall Street 3, Wall Street 4 and Wall Street 5.

"Q. Would that work have been beneficial to all of the claims?

"A. There are two major veins on the property.

"Q. Let's back up, I just want first an answer to the question, yes or no?

"A. Yes, I believe it was.

"Q. Will you explain that, please?

"A. Well, there are two veins on the property that we work on, and all the claims are located on these two veins. And development of any part of the vein and knowledge gained on any part of the vein, of course, benefits development of the entire claims."

This would indicate that the work was done after discovery of the mineral in place and for the purpose of development of the claim in question.

The work done by plaintiffs was not accomplished for the discovery of mineral deposits nor for the purpose of measuring physical differences between rock types or discontinuities in geological formation. It was done to determine the milling characteristics of the mineral deposit already known to exist. Because of these facts, these samples were outside the definitions contained in § 28-2, supra, and outside the labor requirements of § 28-1, supra. However, this was labor for the purpose of developing rather than discovering, and complied with assessment work requirements on mining claims regardless of §§ 28-1 and 28-2, supra. See and compare Bishop v. Baisley, supra; Schlegel v. Hough, supra; Eveleigh v. Darnielle, supra; Simmons v. Muir, 75 Wyo. 44, 291 P.2d 810 (1955); Sampson v. Page, 129 Cal.App.2d 356, 276 P.2d 871 (1954).

Appellants' second point, claiming error on the part of the trial court for not instructing the jury that §§ 28-1 and 28-2, supra, had to be complied with, is found to be without merit for the above stated reasons.

Affirmed. It is so ordered.

OMAN and STEPHENSON, JJ., concur.

NOTES

1. Would placing a watchman on a mining claim constitute assessment work? In *James v. Krook,* 25 P.2d 1026, 1027-28 (Ariz. 1933), the court said that "the expense of a watchman or keeper has been allowed as annual assessment [where] he has actually resided on the property and guarded it against intruders or wrongdoers who might steal or destroy it."

2. In order to obtain a patent to a mining claim, it must be shown that "five hundred dollars worth of labor has been expended or improvements made upon the claim." 30 U.S.C. § 29. As a general proposition, labor or improvements that satisfy the annual assessment requirement of § 28 will also satisfy the "five hundred dollar" requirement of § 29. *See Re Copper Glance Lode,* 29 L.D. 542 (1900).

C. Effect of Failure to Perform the Annual Assessment Work

1. As Against the United States

HICKEL V. THE OIL SHALE CO.
400 U.S. 48 (1970)

Mr. Justice DOUGLAS delivered the opinion of the Court.

This case involves six groups of claims to oil shale located in Colorado and asserted under the General Mining Act of 1872, 17 Stat. 91, now 30 U.S.C. §§ 22, 26, 28, and 29. Section 28 provides that until a patent issued "not less than $100 worth of labor shall be performed or improvements made during each year."[1]

And § 29 provides that a patent to the claim could issue on a showing that the claimant had expended $500 worth of labor or improvements on the claim. These claims are not patented and were canceled in the early 1930's on the ground that the amount of labor or improvement specified in § 28 had not been made "during each year."[2]

Some of the claimants in this case applied for patents between 1955 and 1962. The General Land Office rejected the patent applications because the claims had been canceled. On appeal, the Secretary of the Interior, acting through the Solicitor, ruled that these cancellations were effective, later judicial determinations of the invalidity of the grounds for cancellation notwithstanding. *Union Oil Co.,* 71 I.D. 169.[3] These claimants then sought an order to compel the Department to issue the patents. They argued that the Land Office was without authority to cancel the claims when it did and that then Secretary of the Interior had nullified all the contest proceedings in 1935. In the alternative, they sought judicial review of those contest rulings. Respondent Oil Shale Corp. commenced this action in the District Court, not to require the Secretary to issue a patent, but to expunge the rulings of the Secretary canceling the claims and to

---

[1] Section 28 reads in part:
"On each claim located after the 10th day of May 1872, and until a patent has been issued therefor, not less than $100 worth of labor shall be performed or improvements made during each year. . . . [U]pon a failure to comply with these conditions, the claim or mine upon which such failure occurred shall be open to relocation in the same manner as if no location of the same had ever been made, provided that the original locators, their heirs, assigns, or legal representatives, have not resumed work upon the claim after failure and before such location. . . ."

Section 29 reads in part:
"The claimant at the time of filing this application, or at any time thereafter, within the sixty days of publication, shall file with the Manager a certificate of the United States Chief Cadastral Engineer that $500 worth of labor has been expended or improvements made upon the claim by himself or grantors. . . ."

[2] For a description of the claims involved in this case see the Appendix to this opinion.

[3] It was admitted that the cancellations may have been erroneous. He declared, however, that the Commissioner of the General Land Office had jurisdiction to make the determinations. Therefore, since the rulings were not appealed from, they were *res judicata,* not subject to attack in 1962.

enjoin him from enforcing them. All the cases were consolidated for trial in the District Court. The District Court granted the relief, 261 F.Supp. 954, and the Court of Appeals affirmed, 406 F.2d 759, both holding that cancellations for lack of assessment work were void because the Department did not have jurisdiction over the subject matter. The case is here on petition for certiorari, which we granted to consider whether *Wilbur v. Krushnic*, 280 U.S. 306, and *Ickes v. Virginia-Colorado Development Corp.*, 295 U.S. 639, had been correctly construed and applied to invalidate the Secretary's action in protection of the public domain.

Before we come to a consideration of the *Krushnic* and *Virginia-Colorado* cases it should be noted that in 1920, Congress by enacting § 21 of the Mineral Lands Leasing Act, 41 Stat. 445, 30 U.S.C. § 241(a), completely changed the national policy over the disposition of oil shale lands. Thereafter such lands were no longer open to location and acquisition of title but only to lease. But § 37 contained a Saving Clause which covered "valid claims existent on February 25, 1920, and thereafter maintained in compliance with the laws under which initiated, which claims may be perfected under such laws, including discovery." 30 U.S.C. § 193. Respondents contend that their claims fall within that exception.

Respondents assert that a like claim was recognized and approved in the *Krushnic* case. In that case, however, labor in the statutory amount had been performed, including the aggregate amount of $500. The only default was in the failure to perform labor for one year during the period. Mandamus for the issuance of a patent was directed, the Court saying:

> "Prior to the passage of the Leasing Act, annual performance of labor was not necessary to preserve the possessory right, with all the incidents of ownership . . . , as against the United States, but only as against subsequent relocators. So far as the government was concerned, failure to do assessment work for any year was without effect. Whenever $500 worth of labor in the aggregate had been performed, other requirements aside, the owner became entitled to a patent, even though in some years annual assessment labor had been omitted." 280 U.S., at 317.

The Court further held that the claims were "maintained" within the Saving Clause of the Leasing Act by a resumption of the assessment work before a challenge of the claim by the United States had intervened.

Virginia-Colorado also involved claims on which labor had been expended except for one year. It was alleged, however, that the claimant had planned to resume the assessment work but for the Secretary's adverse action and that the claims had not been abandoned. The Court held that the claims had been "maintained" within the meaning of the Saving Clause of the Leasing Act of 1920.

Those two cases reflect a judicial attitude of fair treatment for claimants who have substantially completed the assessment work required by 30 U.S.C. § 28. There are, however, dicta both in *Virginia-Colorado* and in *Krushnic* that the failure to do assessment work gives the Government no ground for forfeiture but inures only to the benefit of relocators.

Indeed 30 U.S.C. § 28, which derives from the 1872 Act, as already noted,[4] provides that upon the failure to do the assessment work, "the claim or mine upon which such failure occurred shall be open to relocation in the same manner as if no location of the same had ever been made," provided the assessment work has not been "resumed" upon the claim "after failure and before such location." It is therefore argued that so far as the 1872 Act is concerned the failure to do the assessment work concerns not the Government but only "rival or adverse claimants."[5]

The problem in those two cases and the present one concerns the Saving Clause in the Leasing Act which, as noted, makes available for patent "valid claims existent on February 25, 1920, and thereafter maintained in compliance with the laws under which initiated." Concededly, failure to maintain a claim made it "subject to disposition only" by leasing by the United States. See § 37 of the 1920 Act, 30 U.S.C. § 193. Hence if we assume, *arguendo*, that failure to do assessment work as provided in the 1872 Act concerned at the time only the claimant and any subsequent relocator, the United States, speaking through the Secretary of the Interior, became a vitally interested party by reason of the 1920 Act. For it was by that Act that Congress reclaimed portions of the public domain so that land might be disposed of by a different procedure (leasing) to the same end (oil shale production[6]) or devoted to wholly different purposes[7] within the purview of public policy as determined by Congress.

It appears that shortly before 1920 oil shale claims were affected by a speculative fever. Then came a period of calm. By the late forties and continuing into the sixties speculators sought out the original locators or their heirs, obtained quitclaim deeds from them, and thereupon eliminated all other record titleholders by performing assessment work for one year.[8] It appears that 94 of the 98 claims involved in the present litigation were of that character. There is nothing reprehensible in the practice, if the procedure is one which Congress has approved. But the command of the 1872 Act is that assessment work of $100

---

[4] See n. 1, supra. For a recent account of the operation of the 1872 Act and the Leasing Act of 1920 see One Third of the Nation's Land, Report by the Public Land Law Review Commission 124-138.

[5] The regulations provide:
"The annual expenditure of $100 in labor or improvements on a mining claim, required by section 2324 of the Revised Statutes (30 U.S.C. 28), is . . . solely a matter between rival or adverse claimants to the same mineral land, and goes only to the right of possession, the determination of which is committed exclusively to the courts." 43 CFR § 3420.4.

[6] The value to the Government of the Leasing Act is shown by the magnitude of the interests at stake. We are told that respondent Oil Shale Corp. bid for a lease of 5,120 acres of federal oil shale land in Colorado. 33 Fed.Reg. 16154. The projected operations were estimated to yield 40 gallons of oil per ton, the royalty being 24 cents per ton. *Id.,* at 16156. The projected mining rate of 66,000 tons per day for 330 days a year would produce an annual royalty of close to $5,230,000 the project life was 20 years.

[7] The lands containing oil shale became open to agricultural and other nonmineral entries including, *inter alia,* those under the Stock-Raising Homestead Act of 1916, 39 Stat. 862, 43 U.S.C. § 291 *et seq.,* to oil and gas and sodium leasing under the 1920 Act, to Indian tribal lands in Utah, and to grazing districts under the Taylor Grazing Act, 48 Stat. 1269. 43 U.S.C. § 315 *et seq.*

[8] See n. 3, Appendix, *infra.*

be done "during each year" and the Saving Clause of § 37 of the 1920 Act requires that for lands to escape the leasing requirement the claims must be "maintained in compliance with the laws under which initiated."

The legislative history of the 1872 Act does not throw much light on the problem. Senator Cole, proponent of that Act, explained, however, that the requirement of assessment work was made to adopt the Spanish law which granted mining titles but subjected them "to what they term denouncement of the title or defeasance of the title upon failure to work the mine after a certain time." Cong. Globe, 42d Cong., 2d Sess., 2459 (1872). While the objective of the 1872 Act was to open the lands "to a beneficial use by some other party," once the original claimant defaulted, the defeasance inevitably accrued to the United States, owner of the fee. On that premise it would seem that the dicta in *Krushnic* and in *Virginia-Colorado* are not valid.

The history of the 1920 Act throws little light on the problem. In the Senate there was considerable debate over the addition of the words "including discovery" at the end of § 37, which contains the Saving Clause.

"Mr. JONES of New Mexico. Suppose we use the words 'including discovery.'

"Mr. SMOOT. Very well; if the Senator desires to insert the words 'including discovery' I shall offer no objection.

"Mr. WALSH of Montana. Mr. President, I was going to say to Senators that to my mind discovery does not necessarily perfect the claim, because the claimant would not be entitled to a patent unless he had performed $500 worth of work, and in a just sense his claim would not be protected.

"Mr. SMOOT. The words 'under such laws' cover everything—the $500 worth of work, discovery, and everything else.

"Mr. WALSH of Montana. But the words 'including discovery,' now proposed, it seems to me, will make it plain.

"Mr. SMOOT. I have no objection to those words going in the bill." 58 Cong.Rec. 4584.[9]

The "perfection" of the claims "under such laws" thus seemingly meant compliance with "everything" under 30 U.S.C. § 28 which, taken literally would mean assessment work of $100 "during each year."

If we were to hold to the contrary that enforcement of the assessment work of § 28 was solely at the private initiative of relocators, the "maintenance" provision of § 37 becomes largely illusory, because relocation of oil shale claims became impossible after the 1920 Act. So if enforcement of the assessment work requirement of § 28 were dependent solely on the activities and energies of oil shale relocators, there was no effective enforcement device. While the area covered by the claims might possibly be relocated for wholly different purposes, the likelihood was so remote that the Court of Appeals concluded that: "The old claims were thus sheltered by the [1920] Act." 406 F.2d at 763. That meant that a

---

[9] The amendment was thereupon agreed to. There was no change made in the House in this respect. H. Rep. No. 398, 66th Cong., 1st Sess., 11. And see the Conference Report, H.R.Rep. No. 600, 66th Cong., 2d Sess., 16.

claim could remain immune from challenge by anyone with or without any assessment work, in complete defiance of the 1872 Act.

The Court concluded in *Virginia-Colorado* that the lapse in assessment work was no basis for a charge of abandonment. 295 U.S., at 645-646. We construe that statement to mean that on the facts of that case failure to do the assessment work was not sufficient to establish abandonment. But it was well established that the failure to do assessment work was evidence of abandonment. *Union Oil Co. v. Smith,* 249 U.S. 337, 349; *Donnelly v. United States,* 228 U.S. 243, 267. If, in fact, a claim had been abandoned, then the relocators were not the only ones interested. The United States had an interest in retrieving the lands. See G. Widman, T. Brightwell, & J. Haggard, Legal Study of Oil Shale on Public Lands 189-193 (1969). The policy of leasing oil shale lands under the 1920 Act gave the United States a keen interest in recapturing those which had not been "maintained" within the meaning of § 37 of that Act. We agree with the Court in *Krushnic* and *Virginia-Colorado* that every default in assessment work does not cause the claim to be lost. Defaults, however, might be the equivalent of abandonment; and we now hold that token asssessment work, or assessment work that does not substantially satisfy the requirements of 30 U.S.C. § 28, is not adequate to "maintain" the claims within the meaning of § 37 of the Leasing Act. To hold otherwise would help defeat the policy that made the United States, as the prospective recipient of royalties, a beneficiary of these oil shale claims. We cannot support *Krushnic* and *Virginia-Colorado* on so broad a ground. Rather, their dicta to the contrary, we conclude that they must be confined to situations where there had been substantial compliance with the assessment work requirements of the 1872 Act, so that the "possessory title" of the claimant, granted by the 30 U.S.C. § 26, will not be disturbed on flimsy or insubstantial grounds.

Unlike the claims in *Krushnic* and *Virginia-Colorado,* the Land Commissioner's findings indicate that the present claims had not substantially met the conditions of § 28 respecting assessment work. Therefore we cannot say that *Krushnic* and *Virginia-Colorado* control this litigation. We disagree with the dicta in these opinions that default in doing the assessment work inures only to the benefit of relocators, as we are of the view that § 37 of the 1920 Act makes the United States the beneficiary of all claims invalid for lack of assessment work or otherwise. It follows that the Department of the Interior had, and has, subject matter jurisdiction over contests involving the performance of assessment work. We conclude therefore that the judgments below must be reversed.

Respondents rely upon the response of the Department of the Interior to the *Virginia-Colorado* case in which the Secretary declared the contest in that case to be "void." He also declared that "other Departmental decisions in conflict with this decision are hereby overruled." *Shale Oil Co.,* 55 I.D. 287, 290. This decision, they argue, nullified the previous contest proceedings in which their claims were voided. Moreover, they contend that this administrative rule of 35 years, upon which the Department itself has relied, may not now be retroactively changed. In addition, they claim that these contest decisions, if still valid, are subject to direct judicial review at this time, testing both substantive and procedural errors, such as lack of notice.[10]

These contentions present questions not decided below. Therefore, on remand all issues relevant to the current validity of those contest proceedings will be open, including the availability of judicial review at this time. To the extent that they are found void, not controlling, or subject to review, all issues relevant to the invalidity of the claims will be open, including inadequate assessment work, abandonment, fraud, and the like. Likewise all issues concerning the time, amount, and nature of the assessment work will be open so that the claimants will have an opportunity to bring their claims within the narrow ambit of *Krushnic* and *Virginia-Colorado,* as we have construed and limited these opinions.

Reversed and remanded.

Mr. Justice HARLAN, Mr. Justice WHITE, and Mr. Justice MARSHALL took no part in the consideration or decision of this case.

---

[10] The Secretary has held that the old default proceedings are subject to reopening as to any locator for whom receipt of service is not adequately shown. *Union Oil Co. of Calif.,* 72 I.D. 313.

NOTES

1. The principal case is commonly referred to by the acronym *TOSCO* formed from the first letters of the claimant corporation's name.

2. Does the *TOSCO* case hold that the United States can rely on the failure to perform assessment work in all cases, or only in cases involving Leasing Act minerals? Is the court's rationale applicable to non-Leasing Act minerals?

3. Under *TOSCO* does the failure to do the annual assessment work result in automatic forfeiture of the claims involved? Consider 43 C.F.R. § 3851.3(a) which provides as follows:

Failure of a mining claimant to comply substantially with the requirement of an annual expenditure of $100 in labor or improvements on a claim imposed by section 2324 of the Revised Statutes (30 U.S.C. § 28) will render the claim subject to cancellation.

The quoted regulation, like the *TOSCO* decision, requires only substantial, and not strict compliance with the assessment work requirement. What is substantial compliance? In *Tosco Corp. v. Hodel,* 611 F. Supp. 1130, 1183 (D. Colo. 1985) the court held that the "[s]ubstantial compliance called for in 30 U.S.C. § 28 and in those cases interpreting it [*e.g. TOSCO*] demands primarily a good faith effort on the part of the locator to develop the claim and facilitate the eventual extraction of mineral from the earth."

4. On remand of the *TOSCO* litigation, the District Court held that *TOSCO* had substantially complied with the assessment work requirement of the mining law, and hence that its claims were valid. *Tosco Corporation v. Hodel,* 611 F.

Supp. 1130 (D. Colo. 1985). The court also held that the Interior Department was estopped from asserting the invalidity of the claims based on its "affirmative" misconduct in misleading the claimants with regard to the assessment work requirement. A summary of the court's opinion (the total opinion is 90 pages long) dealing with the substantial compliance issue is set forth below:

G. SUMMARY—SUBSTANTIAL COMPLIANCE

As we discussed earlier, the Supreme Court in *Hickel v. Oil Shale Corp.,* 400 U.S. 48, 91 S.Ct. 196, 27 L.Ed.2d 193 (1970), "h[e]ld that token assessment work, or assessment work that does not substantially satisfy the requirements of 30 U.S.C. § 28 [was] not adequate to 'maintain' the claims within the meaning of § 37 of the Leasing Act." *Id.* at 57, 91 S.Ct. at 201. We have interpreted "token assessment work" to mean minimal, nominal or slight work. The work performed by these claimants was certainly more than minimal or nominal. Substantial sums of money were expended by the claimants before they applied for patents to their claims.

We are aware that there are years for which there is no evidence of assessment work. However, such a default in the assessment work requirement is insufficient to deprive a claimant of his claim. See *United States v. Locke,* 471 U.S. 84, 105 S.Ct. 1785, 1796, 85 L.Ed.2d 64 (1985). Rather, it subjects the mine owner to a case-by-case determination of whether he intended to keep his claim. *Id.* It must be noted that the claimants in *Ickes v. Virginia-Colorado Development Corp.,* 295 U.S. 639, 55 S.Ct. 888, 79 L.Ed. 1627 (1935) and *Wilbur v. Krushnic,* 280 U.S. 306, 50 S.Ct. 103, 74 L.Ed. 445 (1930) had not performed the annual assessment work each year. Yet, their claims were not extinguished. In order to determine if less than full compliance with the assessment work requirement evidences an intent to abandon or relinquish these claims, we must look to the amount of work done, as well as the circumstances under which that work was performed.

These claims have existed for over 65 years. They have been maintained during a time when there has been a constant ebb and flow of changes in BLM regulations. Additionally, the history of mining law was such that performance of annual assessment work was important only between rival claimants. There was never a requirement that an affidavit be filed to show that assessment work had been completed in order to maintain a claim. As long as work was resumed before the claim was relocated, a failure to do assessment work was of no consequence to the claimant. The assessment work requirement was disregarded during much of this time, by individuals within the industry, as well as the BLM. Significantly, patents were issued for other claims where claimants had not performed annual assessment work. To further add to the confusion, the 1935 decision by Interior in *Shale Oil Company* reversed prior decisions which had invalidated claims for nonperformance of assessment work.

Under these circumstances, it would be very difficult and arbitrary to establish a bright line and then determine whether the assessment work the claimants performed fell within or beyond that bright line. Furthermore, it would be unfair to establish such a line and then ask these claimants to reconstruct year-by-year, over fifty years worth of work. Since it was not necessary to file an affidavit to show that the work had been done, the absence of an affidavit does little to prove that the work was not done. Many of the witnesses to the assessment work have fading memories or have since died. In 1929, a Commissioner of the General Land Office was unable to locate physical evidence of work only a short time after the work had been completed. It is therefore not unreasonable to assume that after more than fifty years, few if any, physical signs of assessment work would remain.

Given a half of a century of confusing and oftentimes contradictory statements regarding the need to perform annual assessment work, we cannot conclude that the work performed by these claimants was merely token, minimal or nominal. As such, we have determined that they have substantially satisfied the requirements of 30 U.S.C. § 28. We are not saying that in other circumstances the lapses of time in performance of assessment work present here would be sufficient to substantially comply with the statute. We also recognize that our conclusion is opposite of that reached by the Commissioner of the General Land Office and Judge Sweitzer (with regard to the Elizabeth and Carbon claims). *See Hickel v. Oil Shale Corp.,* 400 U.S. 49, 57, 91 S.Ct. 196, 201, 27 L.Ed.2d 193 (1970); *United States v. Bohme,* 48 I.B.L.A. 267, 320-322 (1980); *United States v. Bohme,* No. 658, 659, 660 (ALJ Decision, July 17, 1979). However, under the circumstances present before this Court, we are of the opinion that our decision is in keeping with the spirit of the mining laws and the intent of Congress, which was to insure that mining claims did not lay dormant.

---

2. As Against Rival Claimants

PUBLIC SERVICE COMPANY OF OKLAHOMA V. BLEAK
656 P.2d 600 (Ariz. 1982)

[footnotes omitted]

FELDMAN, Justice.

Plaintiffs, Getty Oil Company (Getty). Public Service Company of Oklahoma (Public Service) and Beall J. Masterson, brought this action to establish their possessory rights to a number of unpatented mining claims. Following a jury trial, a verdict was returned in favor of plaintiffs and judgment was entered that plaintiffs were entitled to exclusive possession of the claims as against the defendants, Floyd and Clyda Bleak (Bleak), Berthel and Joyce Trent, Leo and Mary Ellen Crowley, and Leo F. Childs. Defendants appeal from the judgment and the denial of their motion for a new trial. We have jurisdiction pursuant to Ariz. Const. art. 6, § 5(3), and Ariz.R.Civ.App.P. 19(e), 17A A.R.S. We affirm.

FACTS

The unpatented mining claims in question are located in Mohave County near Artillery Peak. The area was first recognized as having potential for uranium mineralization in 1955. Beall J. Masterson and his family located ten claims in July, 1955. Later that same year, James Saunders and his wife entered the area and began staking unpatented mining claims to the south and east of Masterson claim group. In February, 1956, Tejano Mines, a limited partnership, through Beura Childs, one of the partners, began locating claims to the south of the Masterson claims. In March, 1956, Saunders and Tejano Mines entered into a written agreement by which they agreed to work together on their group of claims, all of which were located south and east of the Masterson claims. The parties stipulated that these original claims were made on unappropriated ground.

Eventualy there was a falling out between the Saunders and Tejano groups, and there is conflicting evidence on the question of whether any work was done on the joint Saunders-Tejano claims for a period of approximately thirteen years from 1958 through 1971. In the midst of this period, in May, 1968, Hecla Mining Company entered the area, inspected the ground and the records, and eventually located 59 claims, known as the J.L. claims. These claims overlaid a substantial portion of the claims filed by the Saunders and Tejano groups in 1955 and 1956. At trial, the parties stipulated that Hecla's locations were made in good faith. There was testimony that Hecla's employees never observed any indication of active conflicting claims. Hecla did not perform the annual assessment work for the assessment year ending September 1, 1972.

In 1971, Floyd Bleak appeared on the scene and purportedly entered into an agreement with Saunders whereby Bleak was to relocate part of the Saunders-Tejano claims and take over the assessment work on all the claims. Bleak was to pay Saunders a percentage of the net proceeds from the sale or operation of the claims. On May 1, 1971, Bleak attempted to locate (in the name of Berthel Trent) the Big Sandys #1 through #15 and #18 through #51. The physical location of these claims was in dispute.

Between July of 1973 and September of 1974, Getty and Public Service entered the area. Getty leased the Masterson claims. It also staked lode-mining claims called Hots #1 through #46. Public Service located claims known as A.P.s #1 through #44. This work was done as part of a joint venture between Getty and Public Service. The Getty-Public Service claims completely overlay the area and are in direct conflict with the Saunders-Tejano claims. They also overlay, in part at least, Bleak's Big Sandy claims.

The chief factual issue in the case revolves around the question of whether Bleak had actually done the work necessary to perfect valid locations of the Big Sandy claims, and, if he had, whether he had done the annual assessment work required to retain his possessory rights to all of the claims, including the Saunders-Tejano group. Bleak testified to having done the necessary work, while representatives of both Getty and Public Service testified that they had searched the area prior to location and found no evidence of conflicting claims or recent assessment work. They testified that the Getty and Public Service claims were located in good faith without knowledge of any conflicting claims. To bolster this position, they testified that Getty and Public Service employees had checked with people in the area and found that none of the local residents had knowledge of any conflicting claims and that none had seen any recent work in the area. A search of the public records had also failed to show any evidence of active conflicting claims.

In May, 1977, Getty and Public Service first became aware of Bleak's claim of a possessory right to both the Saunders-Tejano claims and the Big Sandy claims. As a result of Bleak's claims, plaintiffs brought this possessory action to establish their exclusive right of possession to the Masterson claims, the Hots #1 through #46 and the A.P.s #1 through #44. The defendants sought judgment that the Saunders-Tejano and Big Sandy claims entitled them to a prior right of possession wherever there were conflicts with the plaintiffs' group of claims.

At trial, the parties stipulated that a valid discovery of minerals was made on all claims and that all acts necessary for valid locations were performed on all claims except the 1971 Big Sandys.

Defendants raise several assignments of error dealing with instructions and evidentiary rulings and also allege that the verdict was contrary to the weight of the evidence. Further facts will be given where appropriate in discussion of the legal issues raised by this appeal.

INSTRUCTIONS
Effect of Forfeiture

The primary legal issue raised by this appeal is whether the Saunders-Tejano possessory right was revived when, and if, Bleak resumed assessment work on those claims following the forfeiture resulting from the failure of Saunders and Childs to do the assessment work and the subsequent location and abandonment of the claims by Hecla. Plaintiffs claimed that when Childs and Saunders failed to perform their assessment work, their claims became subject to location by a new locator. This is a correct statement of the law. 30 U.S.C. § 28 (1976). Plaintiffs next claim that Hecla's location therefore terminated the Saunders-Childs possessory rights. This, too, is a correct statement of the law. *Id.* Plaintiffs then argue that when Hecla abandoned the claims which it had located over the Saunders-Tejano claims, the mineral deposits became subject to new location, even though Bleak may have reentered on behalf of Saunders and Childs and resumed the assessment work. Under plaintiffs' theory, Bleak could reacquire exclusive possession only by making a new location. Defendants claim, however, that when Hecla abandoned the claims Bleak's resumption of assessment work reinstated his exclusive possessory rights and prevented valid locations by any of the plaintiffs.

This legal dispute was resolved in plaintiff's favor by the trial court, which put the principle to the jury in the following intruction:

Where the senior locator of a mining claim has failed to do the required assessment work and the claim is relocated by a second locator who later abandons the claim or fails to do the assessment work, the senior locator may not resume assessment work and prevent the relocation of the claim by a third locator.

Defendants argue on appeal that this instruction is an incorrect statement of the law. There are conflicting views on this issue.

The right created by the valid location of an unpatented mining claim is a right of exclusive possession. *Malone v. Jackson,* 137 F. 878 (9th Cir.1905). The right is merely a possessory right because title to the property remains in the United States until the claim is patented. *Bagg v. New Jersey Loan Co.,* 88 Ariz. 182, 188-89, 354 P.2d 40, 44 (1960). To maintain the right of exclusive possession, the locator of a claim must perform annual labor or "assessment work" on the claim. 30 U.S.C. § 28 (1976).

The failure to perform annual assessment work does not in itself work a forfeiture of a locator's possessory right, but the statute provides that:

[U]pon a failure to comply with these conditions, the claim or mine upon which such failure occurred shall be open to relocation in the same manner as if no location of the same had ever been made, provided that the original locators, their heirs, assigns, or legal representatives, have not resumed work upon the claim after failure and before such location. *Id.*

Thus the statute allows an original locator who has "defaulted" in his annual labor to retain his possessory right by resuming that labor before a subsequent location is made. If a subsequent relocation is made before the assessment work is resumed, the land is open and unappropriated and is subject to relocation "in the same manner as if no location of the same had ever been made."

The statute is silent with regard to what occurs when a valid subsequent relocation is made, but abandoned, and the original locator then resumes assessment work. Three cases hold that in such a situation the original relocator revives his right to exclusive possession by resuming assessment work. *Justice Mining Co. v. Barclay,* 82 F. 554 (D.Nev. 1897); *Richen v. Davis,* 76 Or. 311, 148 P. 1130 (1915); *Klopenstine v. Hays,* 20 Utah 45, 57 P. 712 (1899). Two cases hold that when the claim was validly relocated because of the original locator's failure to do the assessment work, the possessory right of the original locator cannot be revived by resumption of assessment work, despite the fact that the intervening locator abandoned the claim or failed to do the assessment work. *Florence-Rae Copper Co. v. Kimbel,* 85 Wash. 162, 147 P. 881 (1915); *Knutson v. Fredlund,* 56 Wash. 634, 106 P. 200 (1910).

The latter view has been adopted by the Rocky Mountain Mineral Foundation. 2 *American Law of Mining* § 8.7H (1960). The leading authority on mining law also supports this view:

In the case of *Justice Mining Co. v. Barclay,* Judge Hawley expressed the view that where relocations have been made after the owner of the original location has failed beyond the statutory time to do the necessary assessment work, but such relocations are afterward abandoned, and thereafter the owner of the original location performs assessment work *which revives his rights,* the fact of such intermediate relocations cannot aid one who [like plaintiffs in the case at bench] subsequently attempts to relocate the same ground. These views were quoted with approval by the Supreme Court of Utah. This is not altogether consistent with the theory that after a valid relocation has once been made the rights of the original locator have been completely lost. Yet the effect given to the relocation under the statute is that of an original location,—the same "as if no location of the same had ever been made." If after intervening valid relocations are made, and become subject to forfeiture, the original owner may, by simply resuming work, reinstate his original *status,* his original estate must simply have been in suspense during the period when the ground was covered by valid relocations. It seems to us that the new entry of the relocator terminates the estate of the original locator, and in turn the estate of the relocator can only be divested by a new entry and a new location.

2 C. Lindley, *Lindley on Mines* § 651, at 1632-33 (3d ed. 1914) (emphasis in original; footnotes omitted).

Lindley also states that when there has been a valid relocation because of the failure of the original locator to perform his assessment work, the relocation effects a forfeiture of the estate of the original locator and that "estate . . . is hopelessly lost, and there is no possibility of its being restored" absent a new location by the original locator. *Id.* at 1631.

We believe that the position of the Washington cases, the Rocky Mountain Mineral Foundation, and Lindley is the better rule. It is in accord with the plain language and objectives of the statute. We recognize that the law abhors forfeiture, but once a forfeiture occurs—here by the words of the statute—the requirement of certainty, necessary for the orderly development of mineral resources, prevails. The rule that an original locator could revive his exclusive right to possession without making a relocation would place unrealistic demands on third parties attempting to determine whether mineral land is open to location. We therefore adopt as our rule the principle that upon relocation for failure of the original locator to do his assessment work, the possessory right of the original locator is forfeited and cannot be revived by resumption of assessment work. Upon location and subsequent abandonment by an intervening locator, the ground is open and available for location. The trial court did not err, therefore, in giving the instruction.

Resumption of Assessment Work

Some of the Saunders-Tejano claims were not covered by Hecla's intervening location, but were covered by later locations of Getty and Public Service. Defendants claim that Bleak had resumed assessment work on behalf of Saunders and Childs on these claims prior to the location by plaintiffs. Plaintiffs contend, on the other hand, that Bleak did not resume assessment work and that if he did any work, it was not sufficient or proper to qualify as "annual labor." The trial court instructed the jury that:

The one resuming the work must intend such work to be a resumption of the assessment work on such claims and the work performed must constitute an outward manifestation to resume such work and the person must in fact perform such work on or for the benefit of such claims and the work performed must be proper assessment work.

Defendants objected to the portion of the instruction which stated that the work "must constitute an outward manifestation to resume such work." Defendants argue that any work which would qualify as assessment work is sufficient, even if there is no physical manifestation of the work. The defendants argue that, for example, taking samples and performing assay analyses of the samples qualifies as a resumption of assessment work. Defendant is correct that taking samples and performing assay analyses can qualify as assessment work. 43 C.F.R. § 3851.2 (1981). The instruction, however, did not indicate to the contrary and did not require a *physical* manifestation of the work on the land. It did require "an outward manifestation," and this is a correct statement of the law. Assessment work means the *performance of some act,* rather than the mere intention or preparation to act. See 2 Lindley, *supra* §§ 652-654.

The instructions correctly informed the jury that proper assessment work could consist of "the performance of labor or the making of improvements on *or for the benefit of* a mining claim." (Emphasis supplied.) Clearly, the instruction did not restrict assessment work to that which results in a physical manifestation *on* the land. Viewing the instruction in question as a whole, we find that the rules of law applicable to this case were correctly stated and the instruction was not erroneous.

. . . .

The judgment below and denial of defendant's motion for a new trial are affirmed.

NOTES

1. If a locator fails to do the annual assessment work, is he free to relocate that same claim, or does the failure to do the assessment work serve as a bar to the relocation. In *Judson v. Herrington,* 162 P.2d 931, 933 (Cal. App. 1945) the court held "It [section 2324] expressly declares that, if the work required is not done within the year specified, the claim or mine 'shall be open to relocation as if no location of the same had ever been made.' In other words, it is then to be considered as vacant public land of the United States, subject to entry by any qualified person, . . . If the original locator is a qualified person, he is eligible to make a location under this language as a stranger would be." Is the *Judson* holding still good law in light of section 314 of FLPMA?

2. Assume that a locator fails to perform assessment work during the year required, but that thereafter, and prior to any intervening rights, the assessment work is resumed. Is the claim nevertheless open to relocation? Must the claim be relocated, or is the mere resumption of assessment work enough to protect the locator's rights? See, *Belk v. Meagher,* 104 U.S. 279 (1881).

D. Group Assessment Work

CHAMBERS V. HARRINGTON
111 U.S. 350 (1884)

. . .

Mr. JUSTICE MILLER delivered the opinion of the court. This is an appeal from the Supreme Court of the Territory of Utah.

. . .

The only question on the merits of the case requiring much attention arises out of the requirement of § 2324 of the Revised Statutes, that some work should be done on every claim, in every year, from the date of the discovery until the issue of the patent. The language of the statute on the subject is this:

"On each claim located after the tenth day of May, 1872, and until a patent has been issued therefor, not less than one hundred dollars' worth of labor shall be performed or improvements made during each year. On all claims located prior to the tenth of May, 1872, ten dollars' worth of labor shall be performed or improvements made by the 10th day of June, 1874, and each year thereafter for each one hundred feet in length along the vein until a patent has been issued therefor; but when such claims are held in common such expenditures may be made upon any one claim."

It then provides for proceedings in favor of co-owners who do their work or pay for it, against those who do not, to forfeit their interest in the claim.

This latter clause clearly shows that one meaning of the phrase "held in common" is where there are more owners of the claim than one, while the use of the word *claims* held in common, on which work done on one of such claims shall be sufficient, shows that there must be more than one claim so held, in order to make the case where work on one of them shall answer the statute as to all of them.

It is not difficult, in looking at the policy of the government in regard to its mineral lands, to understand the purpose of this provision. For many years after the discovery of the rich deposits of gold and silver in the public lands of the United States, millions of dollars' worth of these metals were taken out by industrious miners without any notice or attention on the part of the government. The earliest legislation by Congress simply recognized the obligatory force of the local rules of each mining locality in regard to obtaining, transferring, and identifying the possession of these parties.

Later, provision was made for acquiring title to the land where these deposits were found, and prescribing rules for the location and identification of claims, securing their possession against trespass by others than their discoverers.

But in all this legislation to the present time, though by appropriate proceedings and the payment of a very small sum, a legal title in the form of a patent may be obtained for such mines, the possession under a claim established according to law is fully recognized by the acts of Congress, and the patent adds little to the security of the party in continuous possession of a mine he has discovered or bought.

These mineral lands being thus open to the occupation of all discoverers, one of the first necessities of a mining neighborhood was to make rules by which this right of occupation should be governed as among themselves; and it was soon discovered that the same person would mark out many claims of discovery and then leave them for an indefinite length of time without further development, and without actual possession, and seek in this manner to exclude others from availing themselves of the abandoned mine. To remedy this evil a mining regulation was adopted that some work should be done on each claim in every year, or it would be treated as abandoned.

In the statute we are considering, Congress, when it came to regulate these matters and provide for granting a title to claimants, adopted the prevalent rule as to claims asserted prior to the statute, and as to those made afterwards it required one hundred dollars' worth of labor or improvement to be made in each year on every claim. Clearly the purpose was the same as in the matter of similar regulations by the miners, namely to require every person who asserted an exclusive right to his discovery or claim to expend something of labor or value on it as evidence of his good faith, and to show that he was not acting on the principle of the dog in the manger.

When several claims are held in common, it is in the line of this policy to allow the necessary work to keep them all alive, to be done on one of them. But obviously on this one the expenditure of money or labor must equal in value that which would be required on all the claims if they were separate or independent. It is equally clear that in such case the claims must be contiguous, so that each claim thus associated may in some way be benefited by the work done on one of them.

The principle is well stated by Judge Sawyer in the case of *Mount Diabolo M. & M. Company v. Callison,* 5 Sawyer, 439.

"Work done," he says, "outside of the claim, or outside of any claim, if done for the purpose and as a means of prospecting or developing the claim, as in cases of tunnels, drifts, &c., is as available for holding the claim, as if done within the boundaries of the claim itself. One general system may be formed well adapted and intended to work several contiguous claims or lodes, and where such is the case work in furtherance of the system is work on the claims intended to developed." In the case of *Jackson v. Roby,* decided at the present term, 109 U.S. 440, similar language is used. "It often happens that for the development of a mine upon which several claims have been located, expenditures are required exceeding the value of a single claim, and yet without such expenditures the claim could not be successfully worked. In such cases it has always been the practice for the owners of the different locations to combine and work them as one general claim; and expenditures which may be necessary for the development of all the claims may then be made on one of them. . . . In other words, the law permits a general system to be adopted for adjoining claims held in common, and in such case, the expenditures required may be made or the labor be performed, upon any one of them." That was a case of placer mining in which the tailings from one claim were carried by a flume and deposited on another which was contiguous, and it was held this latter claim was not aided, but its development rather injured, by this work. This claim was not, therefore, kept valid by such work, and some remarks were made in the opinion which would not, perhaps, be strictly applicable to discoveries and works done in developing lodes or veins.

In the case before us the appellees became successively owners of three claims contiguous to each other, supposed to be located on the same lode. These were, first, the Parley's Park claim; second, the Central; and third, the Lady of the Lake. They continued their work on the Parley's Park claim from 1872 until July 19th, 1878, when they transferred it to the Lady of the Lake claim, and did no more work on the other until September 13th, 1879, when one Cassidy, claiming that the Parley's Park claim was forfeited for want of work on it for more than a year, located a mining claim called the Accidental, which embraces the premises in dispute, and which is part of the Parley's Park claim.

This claim of Cassidy—the Accidental—is the one on which appellants, who became its owners, now rely, and if the work done on the Lady of the Lake is not work done in common on the three claims of appellees, within the meaning of the statute, the claim of the appellant must prevail.

The finding of facts by the court below on that point is as follows:

"5th. That during the year beginning on the 19th of July, 1878, the owners of the Parley's Park claim were also the owners of two certain claims, called respectively the 'Central' and 'Lady of the Lake'—the Central adjoining the Parley's Park and Lady of the Lake adjoining the Central mining claim—and that, with a view to the future working and development of all three of said claims, the owners thereof located what is called the 'Main Shaft' in the Lady of the Lake surface ground. That said shaft is in such proximity to said Parley's Park mining claim that work in it has a tendency to develop said claim, and said shaft was located and intended for the purpose of developing all of said claims.

"I find that during said last named year work was prosecuted in said shaft, and by improvements made thereat exceeding in value $300, and of not less than two thousand dollars in value. No work was done in said year after July 19th, 1878, and prior to the 15th day of September, 1879, in Parley's Park surface ground, or within its limits, by the owners thereof."

We are of opinion that this brings the case clearly within the principles we have laid down, and the work was effectual to protect the Parley's Park claim against an intruder.

By the act of February 11th, 1875, 18 Stat. 315, § 2324 was so amended that work on a tunnel in a mine should be held to dispense with work on the surface and taken and considered as work expended on the lode, whether located prior to or since the passage of that act.

We are not able to see that this affects the character of other work to be done or improvements to be made according to the law as it stood before, except as it gives a special value to making a tunnel.

NOTES

1. According to *Chambers v. Herrington,* assessment work can only be applied to a group of claims if the claims are contiguous. Are claims which only touch at the corners contiguous? What if two claims are located opposite each other on either side of a narrow stream? In either of these cases, if you conclude that the claims are not contiguous, must you then also conclude that assessment work done on one of the claims, assuming that all other requirements are met, cannot be used to satisfy the assessment work requirement on the other of the claims? See *Powell v. Atlas,* 615 P.2d 1225 (Utah 1980).

2. The central requirement for group assessment work is an intent to benefit not just the claim on which the work is done, but all of the claims in the group. The reason for the contiguity requirement is that it provides evidence of intent, the presumption being that the further claims are from each other, the less likely a locator in doing work on one intended to benefit all. A second requirement for group assessment work is that there be "a community of interest" in each location claimed to be benefited by the group assessment work. The reason for the requirement is clear; otherwise, an idle locator could claim the benefit of a road or ditch, for example, constructed by his industrious neighbor. Just what constitutes the requisite community of interest is not so clear. The "interest need not be of strictly legal nature, and different owners of adjoining claims can undoubtedly join in a legal agreement whereby a single shaft may be sunk or a tunnel driven on one of the claims for the joint benefit of the respective claims, even though not owned in common, and this will count as assessment work on all claims actually benefited, as being a part of a general scheme or development." LINDLEY ON MINES, § 630 at 1552 (3d ed.). In *New Mercur Mining Co. v. South Mercur Mining Co.,* 128 P.2d 269 (Utah 1942) the court found that where one person held a lease with an option to purchase on two separately owned claims, a sufficient community of interest existed so that work done by the lessee on one claim could be counted as assessment work on the other.

3. Silliman was the owner of 84 mining claims located in Grand County, Utah. During the period 1974 to 1978, Powell located 97 claims, which conflicted with all but twelve of the Silliman claims. Powell claimed that the Silliman claims were subject to relocation for failure to perform the annual assessment work. The trial court found for Powell. The Supreme Court of Utah reversed in *Silliman v. Powell,* 642 P.2d 388, 391 (1982), for the following reason, among others:

> There is another problem with the indefiniteness of the findings [of the trial court]. Finding No. 18 states that ". . . the assessment work claimed by the plaintiffs to satisfy the annual assessment work requirement is not of such character or amount to benefit the entire group of plaintiff's claims to the extent of $100.00 for each claim." This finding contemplated too high a requirement. Plaintiff must only do $100.00 worth of work on those claims which were located over by the defendants in the following year. For example, in the first year involved here defendants Powells [sic] located 20

claims. It would only be on plaintiffs' eight claims underlying these 20 claims that the required assessment work would have to be done in the preceding year in order to defeat the relocated claims of defendants—not $100.00 worth of work on all 84 claims of plaintiffs.

4. When assessment work is done on a group basis, a problem of allocation may arise. If one locator owns 10 claims, he is required to do a minimum of $1000 of assessment work annually. A problem arises if he does less than $1000 worth of work. Assume, for example, that he spends $900 constructing a tunnel on one claim that benefits all the claims. Are any of the claims then subject to forfeiture and relocation? The courts have split on this issue. In *James v. Krook,* 25 P.2d 1026 (Ariz. 1933) the court held that since the average spent on each claim was less than $100 (in the example it would be $90) all of the claims were subject to relocation. See also, *Duncan v. Eagle Rock Gold Mining and Reduction Co.,* 111 P. 588 (Colo. 1910) to the same effect. On rehearing *James v. Krook,* the Arizona Supreme Court adopted a second position, and held that if the locator could prove on which claims a $100 or more worth of work had actually been done, then those claims, at least, would not be subject to relocation. *James v. Krook,* 27 P.2d 519 (Ariz. 1933). A third alternative would be to allow the locator to decide which of the claims the work should be allocated to, and which of the claims should be subject to relocation. This approach was adopted by the court in *McKirahan v. Gold King Mining Co.,* 165 N.W. 542 (S.D. 1917).

E. Forfeiture of a Co-Locator's Interest

JORDIN V. VAUTHIERS

575 P.2d 709 (Wash. 1978)

HICKS, Associate Justice.

Respondents Jordin and Lancaster, and appellant Vauthiers, were co-owners of two unpatented mining claims in the Swauk Mining District in Kittitas County. The claims, described as Nelson Hill No. 1 and Nelson Hill No. 2, were discovered in 1968 and location notice of each was recorded in the office of the Kittitas County Auditor. Following a disagreement among the co-owners, Jordin and Lancaster brought this action against Vauthiers for partition of the property. Vauthiers, appearing pro se, appeals from the trial court's judgment partitioning by sale the above mining claims. We affirm.

These mining claims are located within public lands of the United States open to mineral entry pursuant to the mining laws of the United States. 30 U.S.C. § 22, *et seq.* In order to hold a mining claim, following discovery and location and prior to issuance of a patent thereon, federal law requires that not less than $100 worth of labor be performed or improvements made on the claim during each year. 30 U.S.C. § 28. In the case of co-owners, the law requires contribution from those who did not participate in the assessment work to those who did, provided certain notices are given; failure to contribute may result in a loss of the noncontributor's interest in the claim. 30 U.S.C. § 28. To establish of record that assessment work has been done, an affidavit of labor reciting that fact may be recorded in the office of the county auditor where the claim is located—in this case, Kittitas County.

Over the years, disputes concerning contributions for assessment work occurred among these parties. Vauthiers, on one occasion, acquiesced in a demand upon him for contribution and paid $555 to Jordin. Thereafter, Vauthiers prepared a notice of delinquent assessment contribution demanding $466.66 for discovery and location work on Nelson Hill Nos. 1 and 2, and $266.66 for assessment work on the two claims for the years 1969, 1970, 1972 and 1974. This notice was served upon Jordin and recorded in the office of the Kittitas County Auditor. Jordin promptly recorded an affidavit denying Vauthiers' claim and alleging the notice to be void.

Following unsuccessful negotiations among the co-owners, Jordin and Lancaster commenced this action against Vauthiers seeking to partition the mining claims and to enjoin him from attempting to terminate their rights in the mining claims through use of the notice previously recorded by him. Vauthiers answered the complaint by asserting that Jordin and Lancaster had no interest in the mining claims, as such interest as they may have possessed had been forfeited to him under 30 U.S.C. § 28.

In this posture the case came to trial before the court sitting without a jury. It appears from the record before us that during opening remarks to the trial court the parties agreed that affidavits of labor had been recorded in the auditor's office by Jordin and Lancaster in each year from the time of discovery to the time of trial. Consequently, the trial court preliminarily ruled that the issue of forfeiture of the interests of Jordin and Lancaster in the mining claims was foreclosed, absent a showing by Vauthiers that one or more of the affidavits were fallacious and that the assessment work had not been done. Vauthiers contended that the affidavits filed were false and the trial proceeded on the forfeiture issue.

After hearing numerous witnesses, the court ruled that there was no forfeiture and ordered the partition by sale of the claims. Vauthiers appeals solely from the determination that respondents' interests had not been forfeited.

Included in the court's findings of facts are Nos. 5 and 9 which state:

5. Reference hereafter to the mining claims involved in this action refers only to the Nelson Hill #1 and Nelson Hill #2 unpatented lode claims. It is acknowledged that said claims were properly discovered and located and that all of the required annual assessment work and discovery work has been completed to date and the claims are in good standing.

9. With respect to the assessment years and assessment work questioned in the defendant Vauthiers' answer, 1969, 1970, 1972 and 1974, the Court finds that plaintiffs Ollie Jordin and William Lancaster performed annual assessment work in at least the minimum value required by law, personally and by agents or employees of theirs, including but not limited to the following persons: Ollie Jordin, William Lancaster, Vernon A. Summers, Mr. Bula, Ernest Cochrun, Tom West, Larry Karr, Dorothy Lancaster and

Dale Lewis. As a result, the Court further finds that the allegation of defendant Vauthiers that, pursuant to his claim for contribution for said years the rights of the plaintiffs in and to said claims have been adjudicated and the plaintiffs have no interest therein, is not supported by the facts and the evidence, and there is no forfeiture of plaintiffs' right, title and interest in and to said claims.

No challenge was taken to either of these findings and they become the established facts in this case. ROA I-43; *Goodman v. Bethel School Dist. 403,* 84 Wash. 2d 120, 124, 524 P.2d 918 (1974). Our review, therefore, is limited to determining whether those facts support the conclusion that there was no forfeiture. *Goodman,* at page 124, 524 P.2d 918.

The relevant statute, 30 U.S.C. § 28, being one of forfeiture, must be strictly construed. *Turner v. Sawyer,* 150 U.S. 578, 585, 14 S.Ct. 192, 37 L.Ed. 1189 (1893). After establishing the requirement that labor and improvements be made annually on every mining claim, 30 U.S.C. § 28 provides in part:

> Upon the failure of any one of several co-owners to contribute his proportion of the expenditures required hereby, the co-owners who have performed the labor or made the improvements may, at the expiration of the year, give such delinquent co-owner personal notice in writing or notice by publication in the newspaper published nearest the claim, for at least once a week for ninety days, and if at the expiration of ninety days after such notice in writing or by publication such delinquent should fail or refuse to contribute his proportion of the expenditure required by this section, his interest in the claim shall become the property of his co-owners who have made the required expenditures.

For a forfeiture to be effectuated, the owner claiming contribution must have performed all the necessary work (*Pack v. Thompson,* 223 F. 635 (9th Cir. 1915), and the allegedly forfeiting owner must have failed to contribute his share of the expenditure required. *Brundy v. Mayfield,* 15 Mont. 201, 38 P. 1067 (1895). The court's conclusion here that there was no forfeiture is, therefore, clearly and sufficiently supported by its finding that Jordin and Lancaster had performed the necessary work in each of the years in question.

The trial court's determination that ownership of the mining claims is in all parties as co-owners and that partition of the claims shall be accomplished by sale is affirmed.

WRIGHT, C. J., and ROSELLINI, HAMILTON, STAFFORD, UTTER, BRACHTENBACH, HOROWITZ and DOLLIVER, JJ., concur.

NOTES

1. The forfeiture provision of § 28 provides a convenient and effective way of clearing title to mining claims by cutting off the interests of unknown and unknowable claimants. In *Hamilton v. Ertl,* 360 P.2d 660 (Colo. 1961), for example, Ertl acquired a 1/12th interest in a mining claim by virtue of a quitclaim deed. Ertl thereafter performed the assessment work and, pursuant to 30 U.S.C. § 28 forfeited the interests of the other co-owners (who owned 11/12th of the claim).

2. In *Evalina Gold Mining Co. v. Yoseminite Gold Mining and Milling Co.* 115 P. 946 (Cal. 1911), a co-owner's interest was declared forfeit under § 28. The co-owner appealed on the ground that he had done more than his proportion of the assessment work for the year in question. That work consisted of "unwatering" the mine so that it could be shown to prospective purchasers. The court held that this work could not be counted as assessment work and, hence, that the forfeiture of the interest was proper. The court reasoned that "the work done . . . was not done for the development or improvement of the mine, nor was it done to enable the [owners] to perform work on the mine. They testified that it was not done as assessment work nor was it intended to be so considered. Under such circumstances, we are satisfied that the work was not such as is contemplated by the United States statute."

7 CHANGING THE LOCATION

A. **Changing during the period allowed for completing the Acts of Location**
   Sierra Blanca Mining & Reduction Co. v. Winchell
   Sanders v. Noble
B. **Changes accomplished through amendment and relocation**
   Zerres v. Vanina
   R. Gail Tibbetts

A. Changes During the Period Allowed for Completing the Acts of Location

SIERRA BLANCA MINING & REDUCTION CO. V. WINCHELL
83 P. 628 (Colo. 1905)

GABBERT, C.J.

. . . The controversy is thus narrowed to a determination of the rights of the parties in the conflict between the Jessie Mac and Cripple Creek. The judgment must be reversed, because of the refusal to give an instruction requested by plaintiff. This instruction was to the effect that if it appeared from the testimony that the locators of the Jessie Mac discovered mineral and posted notice of discovery, and that the location of the Cripple Creek was based upon a discovery and location within the ground claimed by the Jessie Mac according to its notice of discovery, made within 60 days from the date such notice was posted, then the location of the Cripple Creek lode was invalid.

. . . There was testimony on the part of the plaintiff (which does not appear to have been contradicted) to the effect that the discovery notice of the Jessie Mac was posted on the 30th day of June, 1899. The testimony on behalf of the defendant was to the effect that the discovery notice of the Cripple Creek was posted on August 28th following. The ground claimed by the latter was within the boundaries of the Jessie Mac, as indicated by the notice of discovery thereon. According to the stipulation of the parties, mineral in place was discovered in what was claimed to be the respective discovery cuts of the two claims. The other acts necessary to perfect a mineral location were contested, especially the sufficiency of the discovery work on the Jessie Mac lode. Whether or not, however, this work was performed was not controlling. If the discovery and location of the Cripple Creek was within the boundaries of the Jessie Mac, as evidenced by its discovery notice, and such discovery and location was made within 60 days of the date the Jessie Mac notice of discovery was posted, then the Cripple Creek location was invalid, and this invalidity would not be cured by the failure of the claimant of the Jessie Mac to perform the necessary discovery work.

A location based upon a discovery within the limits of an existing and valid location is void. Sullivan v. Sharp, (Colo. Sup.) 80 Pac. 1054. A location notice properly made and posted upon a valid discovery of mineral is an appropriation of the territory therein specified for the period of 60 days. During this period, no one can initiate title thereto which would be rendered valid by the mere failure of the first appropriator to perform the necessary discovery work within the time prescribed by law. Omar v. Soper, 11 Colo. 380, 18 Pac. 443, 7 Am. St. Rep. 246.

Judgment reversed.

NOTES

1. As in the principal case, most states have enacted statutes specifying the period of time during which the acts of location may be completed, and giving the locator protection from rival claimants during that period. Even in the absence of such a statute, the locator has a reasonable time to complete the acts of location. *Doe v. Waterloo Mining Co.,* 70 F. 455, 459 (9th Cir. 1895).

2. Assume that Nelson posted a notice of location for a mining claim on January 1 in a jurisdiction that allowed 60 days within which to complete the acts of location. Assume further that Nelson did no work on the claim until July 13, but that on May 31 he erased the original date on the notice of location posted on the claim, January 1, and substituted May 31 as the date of location. On July 13, Nelson completed the acts of location, but sometime prior to that date, but after May 31, one Coffey entered the area, staked his own claim and completed the acts of location within the 60 days allowed by statute. If Nelson sues Coffey to quiet title alleging that he, Nelson, had the exclusive right to possession for the 60 days allowed by law following the "amended" location of his claim on May 31, what result would you expect? In *Ingemarson v. Coffey,* 92 P. 908 (Colo. 1907) the court rejected a similar argument on the ground that "If Nelson could make a discovery and post his discovery notice on the 1st of January, and without performing labor erase the former date and redate the notice in . . . May, to the exclusion of those who desire to make a location upon the same property and develop it, there is no reason why he might not continue to do so indefinitely. . . ." Id. at 911.

SANDERS V. NOBLE
22 Mont.110; 55 P.1037 (1899)

HUNT, J. Plaintiffs (appellants here) sued the defendants (who are the respondents) to enjoin certain trespasses upon the Never Sweat lode claim, and to enjoin them from asserting title to any portion of said claim, the ownership and possession of which plaintiffs allege to be in themselves. Defendants denied the ownership and possession of plaintiffs, and the validity of the Never Sweat location, set up their own title to the Yukon lode claim, and prayed that the same be quieted in themselves. The trial was had before a jury, and testimony was heard on both sides. At the conclusion of the plaintiffs' rebuttal testimony, the defendants moved the court to instruct the jury to find in defendants' favor. The court granted the motion. Verdict and judgment were rendered in defendants' favor. Plaintiffs appeal from the judgment and an order overruling a motion for a new trial.

The ground of the defendants' motion to direct a verdict was that the plaintiffs had failed to make any proof of a compliance with the statute in respect to disclosing a well-defined crevice at the point of discovery of the Never Sweat claim for the depth of 10 feet. The court, however, did not sustain the motion upon the ground included therein, but held that defendants were entitled to a verdict because the plaintiffs were bound strictly by their location notice, and that, the plaintiffs having infringed upon the defendants' claim, they must be held to the lines of their location notice, and could not "get off onto some adjoining claimant's claim," and that, if they made a mistake, the prejudice lies at their door, and not at the door of the other parties upon whose rights they have infringed. To make the ruling of the court intelligible, and state the case on its merits, it is necessary to briefly recite what the evidence tended to show.

In August, 1897, W. H. Sanders, Henry Knight, and J. W. Knight, three of the plaintiffs, were working and prospecting in the vicinity of the ground in controversy. They were co-owners in the Copper Crown lode claim, which lies in a southwesterly direction, and adjacent to the Never Sweat. In a northeasterly direction from the Copper Crown there was an unappropriated triangular tract, approximately 600 by 900 feet. Plaintiffs, after endeavoring to trace float rock, finally succeeded, and followed the same up the hillside, where they commenced to dig, and found what appears to be the apex of the Never Sweat lode. On August 7th they made their discovery. They dug down about 2 feet, and on the surface cut a hole about 2½ by 3 feet, finding in the hole what one of the plaintiffs says was a ledge of quartz, in a northerly and southerly direction, as near as he could tell. This ledge was traced by the float on the surface, but there was no out-cropping on either side of the hole. On August 7th, Sanders and Knight, for themselves and the other plaintiffs, posted a notice of location at the point of discovery. It was in the usual form of location notices. It named the quartz claim as the "Never Sweat," and continued as follows:

"Extending along said vein or lode five hundred feet in a southerly direction and one thousand feet in a northerly direction, from the center of the discovery shaft (at which shaft this notice and statement is posted), and three hundred feet on each side from the middle or center of said lode vein at the surface; comprising in all fifteen hundred feet in length along said vein or lode, and six hundred feet in width."

Plaintiffs testified that, when they made this discovery, they intended to take the fraction above referred to, and supposed that their claim was running pretty near north and south. After putting up this notice of location of the Never Sweat, plaintiffs left that vicinity entirely, to fulfill a contract elsewhere, and were gone about 30 days. During their absence, the defendants, in August, went upon the ground involved in this controversy, and located the Yukon mining claim. One of the locators testified that he found some rich float upon August 28th; that they saw the notice which was posted at the Never Sweat, and read it. Desirous of avoiding the locating of any ground unless it was vacant, the defendants started from the location of the Never Sweat, and went due north, determining where due north was by the shadow of the sun about noon of the day they made their location. After measuring due north about 350 feet, they measured 300 feet down the hill, and concluded that they had about reached the side line of the Never Sweat. Then they measured 50 feet more, to allow the Never Sweat locators room "to swing their claim a little; we thought 50 feet was enough." They measured 150 feet from their discovery, and located the Yukon claim easterly and westerly. Defendants ran a tunnel to the vein disclosing the same at depth of 10 feet or more. They explored and concluded their staking within a period of 30 days after the posting of the Yukon notice. They filed a declaratory statement with the county recorder of Madison county within 90 days, but the date of filing such statement was subsequent to the filing of the plaintiffs' declaratory statement. When the plaintiffs got back to the Never Sweat, the defendants had completed the work of locating the Yukon, and had gone. Plaintiffs sunk a 10-foot shaft, established corner monuments, and recorded their declaratory statement of their location of the Never Sweat, all within 90 days after the posting of their notice as aforesaid. When they staked their claim, they located parallel to the Copper Crown, and included the discovery cut of the Yukon, which was 700 feet from the discovery point of the Never Sweat. The plaintiffs and the defendants had some conversation in relation to the conflicts, but it never resulted in any agreement between them. Plaintiffs also commenced to run a tunnel some 27 feet north of the mouth of the defendants' tunnel, and prosecuted this work until they tapped the vein claimed by defendants as the Yukon, about 12 feet at the head of the defendants' workings. This work was done after they had staked their claim so as to include the point referred to. Then plaintiffs notified the defendants to keep off the ground. The defendants refused, and both plaintiffs and defendants continued to work until suit was brought. The accompanying diagram illustrates the ground in question.

The respondents contend that there was no sufficient discovery made of any mineral, lode, or vein at the time the Never Sweat was located, and for that reason the Never Sweat location was void. We are advised, however, upon argument in this court, that the learned judge of the district court did not pass upon this question raised by the motion of the respondents. It is here conceded that his decision was based solely upon the right of the locator of a mining claim to swing his claim within the statutory period of 90 days after the date of his discovery and notice thereof, and that he passed upon no other point.

Under the circumstances, therefore, we do not feel called upon to positively decide whether the location of the Never Sweat was absolutely void or not, for lack of sufficient discovery.

. . . .

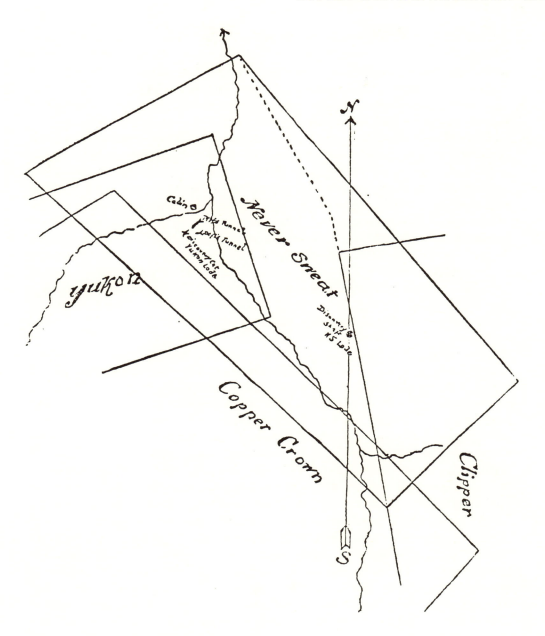

Passing, then, the question of a sufficient discovery, we address ourselves to the requirements concerning the marking of mining claims so that the boundaries can be readily traced, and to a consideration of the demands of the federal statutes bearing upon the possessory rights to mining locations.

Section 2324, Rev.St.U.S., provides: "The location must be distinctly marked on the ground so that its boundaries can be readily traced. All records of mining claims hereafter made shall contain the name or names of the locator or locators, the date of the location, and such a description of the claim or claims located by reference to some natural object or permanent monument, as will identify the claim." This statute does not require a description of the claim to be included in the notice of location; nor does the United States demand more than that the claim shall be distinctly marked upon the ground, so that its boundaries can be readily traced. The simple requirements of the laws of the United States have led courts to regard the mining laws as beneficial,—to be literally, not technically, construed; to be expounded with as little differentiation as may be between former known actual customs of miners and the formulated expressions of congress based upon those customs in present positive law. Justice Bach in Upton v. Larkin, 7 Mont. 449, 17 Pac. 728, said: "What are the two chief requirements of the statutes as far as the possessory right is concerned? (1) Discovery; (2) the marking of the claim upon the ground so that the boundaries can be readily traced. The first requirement is made for the benefit of the United States, so that the land cannot be acquired under this law until its character is first ascertained to be mineral. The second is made in order that those going upon the ground may know that others have acquired and claim title thereto. Certainly, these steps are very simple. The intricacies are those found by the courts of the states and territories wherein mineral lands are situated."

. . . .

Appellants' position is that, under these state statutes a claimant has 90 days after posting notice of location within which to define the boundaries of his claim, and that the course of the lead as given in the posted notice is but preliminary, and not binding upon the locator. Respondents, on the other hand, insist that, although a locator has 90 days within which to complete his location, nevertheless the statute does not and could not extend the time within which a locator must mark the ground so that its boundaries can be readily traced, as required by the United States statute; in other words, a distinction is sought to be drawn between the federal statute as to marking the ground so that the boundaries of the claim can be traced, and the state statute allowing 90 days within which to stake the claim, record the notice, and perfect the location.

. . . [T]o initiate and complete a mining location, five acts must be performed: (1) There must be a discovery; (2) there must be a definition of boundaries, . . . (3) there must be a posting of notice at the point of discovery; (4) there must be development within 90 days from the date of posting the required notice; (5) there must be a declaratory statement filed in the office of the county clerk. The first essential was performed so far as the case here presents itself; and, it having been complied with, by immediately thereafter placing at the point of discovery a notice as required by statute, we believe that, until the expiration of 90 days thereafter, the plaintiffs' claim was valid and subsisting. All persons were warned of the claim of the Never Sweat lode, and, by the law, prospectors or others going within the limits included within the notice, to locate another claim, were tresspassers. Coming after the discovery made, it was an appropriation of the land specified therein; and the two acts—discovery and posting the notice—constituted the origin of a good title to the Never Sweat mining claim. The condition of a continued ownership was development and a definition of boundaries, by marking a tree or rock in place, or by setting a post or stone at each corner or angle of the claim, as set forth in section 3611, supra.

In the interpretation of statutes substantially like ours, we have the repeated adjudications of both federal and state courts, the more important of which we here collate.

Erhardt v. Boaro . . . was determined by the Supreme Court of the United States on appeal (113 U.S. 527, 5 Sup. Ct. 560), in 1885, and the views that had been expressed by Justice Miller from the circuit court were affirmed through Justice Field. The Hawk Lode, involved in that case, was claimed by the following notice, posted at the point of discovery: "Hawk Lode. We, the undersigned, claim 1,500 feet on this mineral-bearing lode, vein, or deposit. Dated June 17, 1880. Joel B. Erhardt, 4/5ths; Thomas Carroll, 1/5th." After holding that the notice on the stake, placed at the point of discovery, contained a sufficient specification or description of the ground claimed by the locators, the court expressly held that the statute of the United States allows a discoverer to locate a claim upon a lode or vein to the extent of 1,500 feet, and the Erhardt's notice informed all persons subsequently seeking to excavate and open the lode or vein that the locators claimed all that the law permitted them to take. The notice was regarded as indefinite, simply, however, in not stating the number of feet claimed on each side of the discovery point, but that, as a notice of discovery and original location, it was sufficient. The court goes on to say: "Greater particularity of description of a location of a mining claim on a lode or vein could seldom be given until subsequent excavations have disclosed the course of the latter. These excavations are to be made within sixty days after the discovery. Then the location must be distinctly marked on the ground, so that its boundaries can be readily traced, and, within one month thereafter,—that is, within three months from the discovery,—a certificate of the location must be filed for record in the county in which the lode is situated, containing the designation of the lode, the names of the locators, the date of the location, the number of feet claimed on each side of the center of the discovery shaft, the general course of the lode, and such a description of the claim, by reference to some natural object or permanent monument, as will identify it with reasonable certainty. Rev. St. U.S. § 2324; Gen. Laws Colo. §§ 1813, 1814. But during the intermediate period, from the discovery of the lode or vein and its excavation, a general designation of the claim by notice, posted on a stake placed at the point of discovery, such as was posted by Carroll, stating the date of the location, the extent of the ground claimed, the designation of the lode, and the names of the locators, will entitle them to such possession as will enable them to make the necessary excavations and prepare the proper certificate for record. The statute of Colorado requries that the discoverer, before a certificate of location is filed for record, shall, in addition to posting the notice mentioned at the point of discovery, sink a shaft upon the lode to the depth of at least ten feet from the lowest part of such shaft under the surface, or deeper, if necessary, to show a defined crevice, and to mark the surface boundaries of the claim. Before this work could be done by the plaintiff and his co-locator, the ground claimed by them was taken possession of by the defendants; the stake at the point of discovery, upon which the notice was posted, was removed; and Carroll was thereby, and by threats of violence, prevented from re-entering upon the premises and completing the work required to perfect the location and prepare a certificate for record,—at least, the evidence tended to establish these facts. If they existed,—and this was a question for the jury,—the plaintiff was entitled to recover possession of the premises. To the extent of seven hundred and fifty feet on the course of the lode on each side from the point of discovery, he and his co-locator were entitled to protection in the possession of their claim. They did not lose their right to perfect their location, and perform the necessary work for that purpose, by the wrongful intrusion upon the premises, and by threats of violence if they should attempt to resume possession. As against the defendants, they were entitled to be reinstated into the possession of their claim. They could not be deprived of their inchoate rights by the tortious acts of others; nor could the intruders and tresspassers intitiate any rights which would defeat those of the prior discoverers." Further on in the opinion it is laid down that, whenever preliminary work is required to define and describe the claim located, the first discoverer must be protected in the possession of the claim until sufficient excavations and development can be made so as to disclose whether a vein or deposit of such richness exists as to justify work to extract the metal. "Otherwise," say the court, "the whole purpose of allowing the free exploration of the public lands for the precious metals would in such cases be defeated, and force and violence in the struggle for possession, instead of previous discovery, would determine the rights of claimants." And, as meeting the argument of the responents' counsel in the case under consideration, that the laws of the United States require the excavations necessary to enable the locator to prepare and record a certificate to be made directly after his discovery, the court certainly held that the federal laws do not prescribe any time in which such excavations and record shall be made, but say that that is left to the legislation of the state, which in Colorado prescribed at that time 60 days for the excavations upon the vein from the date of discovery, and 30 days afterwards for the preparation of the certificate and filing. Again, this case of Erhardt v. Boaro refutes that portion of the respondents' argument wherein it is said that the plaintiffs' location of the Never Sweat was for speculative purposes, and made without discovery, with a view to profit by the explorations and discoveries of the defendants. Justice Field said that if there is a discovery of the presence of the precious metals in the location, or in such proximity to it as to justify a reasonable belief in their existence, "then protection will be afforded to the locator to make the excavations and prepare the proper certificate for record."

In Iron Silver Mining Co. v. Elgin Mining & Smelting Co., 118 U.S. 196, 6 Sup. Ct. 1177, the Supreme Court considered the federal statute requiring the location of a claim to be distinctly marked on the ground, so that its boundaries may be readily traced, and used the following language: "Such location often precedes any extended explorations, and is therefore made without accurate knowledge of the course and direction of the vein. When a vein has been discovered, the rules of miners, and the legislative regulations of mining states and territories, generally allow some specified time for exploration before the location is definitely marked. But miners discovering a lode are sometimes in such haste to locate their claim, and mark its extent and boundaries on the surface, that they omit to make sufficient explorations to guide them aright in measuring the ground and fixing its end lines. Hence efforts are not infrequently made to change those lines when the true course and direction of the vein are ascertained by subsequent developments." After discussing the difficulty in applying the statutes of the United States providing for the extent of the right of the possession and enjoyment of all the surface included within the lines of mining locations, it was remarked: "The remedy must be found, until the statute is changed, in carefully marking the location, and in postponing the marking of its boundaries until explorations can be made to ascertain, as near as possible, the course and direction of the vein. In Colorado the statute allows for this purpose sixty days after notice of the discovery of the lode. Then the location must be distinctly marked on the ground, and thirty days thereafter are given for the preparation of the proper certificate of location to be recorded. Erhardt v. Boaro, 113 U.S. 527, 5 Sup. Ct. 560." This case thoroughly affirms so much of the Erhardt v. Boaro decision as implied the allowance of 60 days given by the state statute for the marking of the boundaries until explorations could be made to ascertain, as near as possible, the course and direction of the vein, before distinctly marking the location on the ground.

In Omar v. Soper (decided in 1888) 11 Colo. 380, 18 Pac. 443, it was said: "To hold that the miner, as soon as he discovers a lode, must immediately stake the territory which he is entitled to claim thereon, in order to protect it from the invasion and claims of other persons learning of his find, would be an unreasonable, if not an impossible requirement. An attempt to do so would result, in many cases, in leaving the main portion of the lode outside the staked boundaries. The object of the statute in giving sixty days for sinking the discovery shaft was evidently to afford the miner time to sink his shaft, and to ascertain the true course of his lode, when he would be qualified to mark its boundaries on the surface. When the legislative intent is clear, or can be reasonably inferred, it is held to be the duty of the courts to so construe the statute as to render it effective, if possible to do so under the rules of statutory construction. Simmons v. Powder Works, 7 Colo. 285-289, 3 Pac. 420. To hold that the claim is protected throughout its whole extent, during this period, from invasion and adverse claims, by a notice which, in addition to the statutory requirements, shall specify the extent of territory claimed along the vein or both sides of the point of discovery, is both reasonable and equitable. It is likewise consistent with the spirit and policy of the statute, and a construction which renders it effective. Such a notice, properly made and posted, is an appropriation of the territory specified therein for the period of sixty days. It has been repeatedly held that only the unappropriated mineral lands of the United States are open to exploration and location. No one can therefore lawfully enter upon the territory so claimed, during the period named, for the purpose of initiating a claim thereto; and it necessarily and logically follows, from an application of the same rules and principles, that no one, during this period, can stand outside such appropriated territory, and in any manner initiate a claim thereto capable of being rendered valid in the future by the happening of fortuitous circumstances."

The statutes of South Dakota (Pol. Code, Comp. Laws Dak. § 1997 et seq.) require a discoverer of a lode to record his claim within 60 days from the date of the discovery, by a location certificate containing much the same information required by the laws of Montana, and that before filing such certificate the discoverer shall do certain development work, and post a notice, and mark the surface boundaries. These statutes were construed in Marshall v. Manufacturing Co. (decided in 1890) 1 S.D. 350, 47 N.W. 290. As particulary appropriate to the facts of the present case, we quote from that decision: "The testimony of the plaintiffs shows that they did make the discovery, uncovered and disclosed the lode, and placed at the point of discovery a notice as required by the statute and, until the expiration of sixty days, their claim was a valid, subsisting mining claim, by reason of this discovery. The notice posted notified any one coming within the limits described by that notice, for the purpose of making another location, that there had been a previous location; and, if they attempted to occupy any portion or all of that ground described within the limits of the notice, they would be trespassers. In all legislation, whether by congress or the state or territory, and by all mining regulations and rules, discovery and appropriation are recognized as the sources of title to mining claims, and development, by working, as the condition of continued ownership, until it is obtained. Whenever preliminary work is required to define and describe the claim located, the first discoverer must be protected in the possession of the claim until sufficient excavations and developments can be made so as to disclose whether a vein or deposit of such richness exists as to justify work to extract the metal. The notice of plaintiffs of July, 1884, constituted an appropriation of the territory specified for the period of sixty days; and if the location of Coates was a portion of that territory, or all of it, and was made before the sixty days had expired, it was not a valid location, and he could acquire no right by reason of it. . . ."

. . . .

Lindley, in his valuable and highly approved work on Mines, . . . says: "To hold that the miner, as soon as he discovers a lode, must immediately stake the territory which he is entitled to claim, in order to protect it from invasion and claims of other persons, would be an unreasonable, if not impossible requirement." Section 339. He also lays it down that, where the statutes require preliminary work in order to define and describe the claim located, the first discoverer "must be protected in the possession of the claim until sufficient excavations and development can be made so as to disclose whether a vein or deposit of such richness exists as to justify the work to extract the metal." He sums up the logical consequence of the rules established by the case of Erhardt v. Boaro, and the later federal decisions which have followed that decision, in the following language: "The effect of this rule is practically to reserve, after the discovery and during the statutory period allowed for perfecting the claim, a surface area circular in form, the radius of which may be the length claimed on the discovered lode, within which area the location may be ultimately made.

Such is the manifest intent of the rule. This was the custom under the act of 1866. The miner posted his notice, claiming so many linear feet on the vein; and under the law as then interpreted, prior to fixing the situs of his lode, by filing a diagram for patent purposes, he might follow the vein wheresoever it ran, to the length claimed. When he filed his diagram, and inclosed his lode within surface boundaries, his right to pursue the vein on its course ceased, when it passed out of his surface lines. Under the existing state of the law, the location must be marked within a certain period of time, whereupon the locator's rights become definitely fixed and confined, except as to the extralateral right, to his marked boundaries. Until this is done, however, and within the prescribed periods, his right to be protected to the extent heretofore stated is well settled." Section 339.

The decisions of the supreme court of the territory and of the state rendered prior to the enactment of the statutes which require development work before boundaries are to be defined cannot control the present condition of the law. It is true, we think, that one of the objects in requiring a location to be marked upon the ground is to fix the claim, and to prevent floating or swinging, so that those who are in good faith looking for unoccupied ground may know exactly what has been appropriated; and we thoroughly agree with the principle announced in Hauswirth v. Butcher, 4 Mont. 299, 1 Pac. 714, that the provisions of the law designed for the attainment of this object are very important, and ought not to be frittered away by construction; but, on the other hand, it is of equal importance that the miner have ample opportunity to perfect his mining location, in order that he may be protected in the full enjoyment of the rights accorded to him by the federal statutes. And it was for the purpose of affording the full enjoyment of these rights that the state statutes were passed, merely postponing the necessity for definition by marking the boundaries of his claim until he may have full opportunity to ascertain the strike or course of the vein or lode which he has discovered. The law has said that he must do all this within 90 days. Thereafter there can be no floating or swinging. But up to the expiration of that time, under the decisions quoted, we are forced to conclude that, if in good faith, he may use his discovery post as a pivot, and move his lines, at least in the general course of his vein given in his notice, so as to secure the full benefit of his discovery.

The distinction between the notice of discovery or notice of location required to be posted on the claim by section 3610, and the declaratory statement required to be filed for record by section 3612, is a substantial one, easily understood when the purpose of each is kept in mind. The notice of discovery should be, and usually is, posted immediately at the discovery hole, and often before the discoverer can possibly survey or even measure his ground. It is often done before even specific bearings are known. It is a simple announcement, and meant only to be a simple notice of a discovery, and of an intention to claim the vein discovered, and, by posting it, the discoverer finds an easy and quick way of announcing his claim. Afterwards, though, when an opportunity is had to follow the vein on its strike, then the boundaries must be marked, and the claim must be described by reference to natural objects or permanent monuments. Then it is, too, but not before, that the evidence of the location must be preserved, by recording the declaratory statement containing such description of the location with reference to some natural object or permanent monument as will identify the claim. The notice of location is a protection to the discoverer during the process of location. "The record of a mining claim," says Judge Ross in Gird v. Oil Co., 60 Fed. 531, "when one is required, is intended to contain a more exact and specific description of the claim than the notice posted upon it." Gleeson v. Mining Co., 13 Nev. 465.

But respondents' counsel say, even if this be the law generally, yet in this case, plaintiffs have described their location by their notice as extending along the Never Sweat lode claim in a southerly and northerly direction from the center of the discovery shaft, they cannot now object to the acts of defendants in running the lines of the Never Sweat due north and due south, . . . This argument, of course, involves the proposition that the statute which requires a notice to be posted at the point of discovery, in which must be contained the general course of the vein or lode "as near as may be," demands an accurate description of the course of the vein by the points of the compass. We cannot adopt such a construction of the law without frittering away the underlying purpose of the statute to give to the discoverer 90 days in which to define the boundaries of his claim; for, if he must accurately state the general course of the vein in his notice posted at the point of his discovery; and at the time thereof, and is to be held to such course literally, the development work that he is required to do to demonstrate whether he has a claim worth further exploitation would be of no avail to him if it should demonstrate that the course of his vein varies even to the slightest extent from the general course given in his discovery notice. The statute requires only that he give the general course "as near as may be"; and where, as in this case, the course is given as southerly and northerly, and it subsequently appears by the surveyor's plats that the course of the vein is not due north and south, in the absence of proof of a lack of good faith we hold that such a notice is sufficient and valid.

. . . .

NOTES

1. A less extravagant view of the right to swing was adopted by the court in *Wiltsee v. King of Arizona Min. & Mill. Co.,* 7 Ariz. 95, 60 P. 896 (1900). There, the court held that "A notice of location, therefore, which gives the course of the location as running westerly so many feet and easterly so many feet from a discovery shaft or point of discovery, until boundaries are definitely located by the erection of monuments, must be held to reserve from entry by subsequent locators the surface area which might be included within any location so made that, were a line drawn lengthwise through the center of said claim from the west center end through the point of discovery to the east center end of said claim, said line would lie at some point between east 45', north, and east 45', south, from the point of discovery." *Id.* at 898.

B. Changes Accomplished Through Amendment and Relocation

Review *Atherley v. Bullion Monarch Uranium Co.,* 335 P.2d 71 (Utah 1959), Chapter 5, *supra.*

NOTES

1. In *Atherley v. Bullion Monarch Uranium Co.* the court held that the failure to file an amended certificate of location did not work a forfeiture of the claim and that a subsequent locator with knowledge of the claim as amended could not take advantage of the failure. In *R. Gail Tibbets,* 43 IBLA 210, 1979 GFS (Min) 92, the Interior Board of Land Appeals held that this rule was applicable to rival claimants, but not to the United States. "In conformity with this interpretation," the Board wrote, "we hold that while the failure to record a mining claim as required by . . . State law does not, in and of itself, render the claim invalid, the withdrawal of the premises by the United States, prior to any corrective action by the claimant, would serve to nullify the claim." Id. at 225. 43 U.S.C. § 314(b).

ZERRES V. VANINA
150 F. 564 (9th Cir. 1907)

GILBERT, Circuit Judge. The plaintiffs in error brought ejectment to recover the possession of a certain mining claim. The claim had been located as the "Eddy Claim" on February 9, 1902, by the grantors of the defendant in error. On that date notice of the location of the claim was posted on the claim by the locator, and on March 20, 1902, it was recorded in the office of the district recorder of Searchlight mining district, Nev., in which district the claim is situate. The ground was marked with monuments and staked. Soon after the location was made a shaft was sunk on the ground, disclosing mineral at a depth of about 14 feet. In compliance with the laws of the state of Nevada (Cutt. Comp. Laws, § 209), during the year 1903 labor was expended upon the claim to the extent of over $100. The plaintiffs in error claimed title under a relocation made on January 1, 1904. It was the contention of the plaintiffs in error that the prior location was void by reason of defects in the notice and a failure to record the certificate of location within 90 days after posting the notice of location. A jury trial was waived, and the case was tried before the court. Thereupon a general finding was made for the defendant in error, and judgment was rendered in his favor. The plaintiffs in error have assigned as error that the court admitted in evidence the notice of location of the Eddy claim an amended certificate of location thereof, and an amended additional certificate; also that the court erred in finding the issues in favor of the defendant in error and against the plaintiffs in error.

One may make an original location of a mining claim upon land marked and occupied under an attempted prior location if such prior location is void by reason of failure to comply with the law as to location notice or recording the same, but he cannot make a relocation of such a claim. Such land, if mineral, is, notwithstanding the prior proceedings, unappropriated public land subject to location. Relocation is authorized only for forfeiture or abandonment of a prior location. By making a relocation the locator makes admission of the validity of the prior location and precludes himself from contesting it. Belk v. Meagher, 104 U.S. 284, 26 L. Ed. 735. . . . In the leading case of Belk v. Meagher, Humphries and Allison were the original locators of a mining claim. Thereafter Belk made a location on the same ground for failure of the original locators to perform the requisite annual labor. He described his claim as a relocation of the original Humphries and Allison lode. More than a year thereafter Meagher attempted to locate the same mining claim, posted his notice, and performed the acts required by law. Belk brought ejectment against Meagher to recover possession. Meagher defended on the ground that Belk had been premature in making his location, in that the time of the original locators to perform their annual labor had not then expired. Upon these issues it became important to determine the validity of the original location and the right of Belk, who had declared himself to be a relocator. The court said:

"Mining claims are not open to relocation until the rights of a former locator have come to an end. A relocator seeks to avail himself of mineral in the public lands which another has discovered. This he cannot do until the discoverer has in law abandoned his claim and left the property open for another to take it up."

In Wills v. Blaim, 4 N.M. 378, 20 Pac. 798, the court said:

"The relocator, when he so describes himself in the notice, solemnly admits in an instrument which is made a matter of record that he is not a discoverer of mineral, but an appropriator thereof on the ground that the original discoverer had perfected his right. The notice becomes in some sense an instrument of title—a record. It is the equivalent of an admission of record to the original locator that the relocator claims a forfeiture by reason of a failure on the part of the first locator to make his annual expenditure. This we believe to be the doctrine of Belk v. Meagher."

In the present case the notice posted on the ground by the plaintiffs in error is headed, "Notice of relocation Eddy Quartz Claim," and at the end of the notice it is recited, "This claim was previously known as the Eddy." These recitals under the doctrine of the authorities above cited are an admission of record of the validity of the proceedings and steps taken to locate the Eddy claim. Their force as an admission of record is not impaired by the fact that the defendant in error on the trial introduced in evidence the documentary proofs of the Eddy location. Such proofs were unnecessary, and are to be disregarded. The plaintiffs in error could only recover, if at all, on the strength of their own title. They had elected to acquire title by relocating the claim, and they were obliged to abide by the record which they had made. This also is the doctrine of the decision in Belk v. Meagher. In that case, in considering the effect of the recitals in Belk's relocation notice, the court said, concerning the admission of the books from the office of the recorder of Deer Lodge county to prove the record of the location of the original lode claim by Humphries and Allison:

"As Belk sets up title only as a relocator of part of the original lode claim, he impliedly admits the validity of the prior location. There can be no relocation unless there has been a prior valid location, or something equivalent, of the same property. It is nowhere disputed that Humphries and Allison were the locators and owners of the claim originally. The proof by the record was therefore probably unnecessary."

The foregoing considerations dispose of all the questions presented on the writ of error, and necessarily result in an affirmance of the judgment of the court below.

NOTES

1. The Black Queen mining claim overlapped the Excelsior mining claim. The Excelsior claim was senior. During the year 1884 the owners of the Excelsior claim did not perform the annual assessment work. The Black Queen claimed and the lower court held "that, as the owners of the Black Queen continued in possession and at work on their claim during and after the year 1884, while operations on the Excelsior had been suspended, and that as the two claims overlapped, . . . the failure of the owners of the Excelsior claim to do any work during the year 1884 was an abandonment of their superior right to the space where the claims overlapped, and that as to such territory the title of the Black Queen became paramount. . . ." On appeal the decision was reversed. The Eighth Circuit held for the owners of the Excelsior claim. "The necessary conclusion seems to be that neither the failure of the owner to occupy or to work his claim during a given year will operate to divest him of his title, and to confer it upon another. A failure to work a claim to the extent required by statute simply entitles a third party to relocate it in the mode pointed out by the existing laws, and . . . if the statutes in that respect are not pursued, the status of all persons remains unaltered, barring the possible effect of limitations or laches; and if at any time the original owner re-enters, and resumes the work, the right of relocation is lost." *Oscamp v. Crystal River Mining Co.,* 58 Fed. 293, 296 (8th Cir. 1893).

2. When a claim is relocated, it is not necessary for the relocator to restake the boundaries of the claim if the original stakes are still in place. Instead, the original stakes or markers may be adopted by the relocator. *Hagan v. Dutton,* 181 P. 578 (Ariz. 1919).

3. In *Brothers v. United States,* 594 F.2d 740 (9th Cir. 1979), the original claimant constructed two cabins on her claim. After the original claimant abandoned the claim, the Brothers relocated it. They claimed that by virtue of the relocation they acquired title to the claim and the cabins. The government contended that it owned the cabins. In a suit to establish the title to the cabins, what result would you expect?

R. GAIL TIBBETTS
43 I.B.L.A. 210, 1979 GFS (Min.) 92

R. Gail Tibbetts appeals from three decisions of the Utah State Office, Bureau of Land Management (BLM), each dated August 28, 1978, declaring various lode mining claims null and void ab initio. Ray Tibbetts appeals from one of these decisions, AD-51-78. The State Office decisions recited that the various groups of claims had been located on March 3, 1974, May 20, 1974, and February 1, 1975. The decisions noted, however, that the claims were located upon land which had been included in the Glen Canyon National Recreation Area by the Act of October 27, 1972, P.L. 92-593, 86 Stat. 1311, and had been placed under the administration of the National Park Service. The decisions also noted that the Act had withdrawn the land from location, entry, and patent under the mining laws.

The State Office held that since the claims were located after the passage of the Act withdrawing the land, the claims were null and void ab initio. The decisions recognized appellants' assertion that the locations were meant to be amended locations of earlier claims, but pointed out that nothing on the various location notices indicated that they were amendatory to prior locations.

While a number of departmental, federal, and state court decisions have attempted to draw a distinction between relocation of a former claim and an amended location of such a claim, it is clear that nothing approaching uniformity has resulted. This confusion is understandable since it finds its germination in the 1872 Mining Act, itself. Section 5 of the Mining Act, *as amended,* 30 U.S.C. § 28 (1976) contains the only reference to relocation:

> On each claim located after the 10th day of May 1872, and until a patent has issued therefor, not less than $100 worth of labor shall be performed or improvements made during each year. * * * [A]nd upon a failure to comply with these conditions, the claim or mine upon which such failure occurred shall be open to *relocation* in the same manner as if no location of the same had ever been made, provided that the original locators, their heirs, assigns, or legal representatives, have not resumed work upon the claim after failure and before such location. [Emphasis added.]

There was *no* reference in the original mining law of the United States to an "amended" location. The term " amended notice of location" was used in section 1 of the Act of August 12, 1953, 30 U.S.C. § 501(a) (1976) and in section 1 of the Act of August 13, 1954, 30 U.S.C. § 521(a) (1976) relating to mining claims originally located on lands which were embraced by either a mineral lease or a mineral lease application. The term, however, was not defined. It is in no small part due to this omission that the subsequent history of mining law adjudication has been mired in a seemingly endless sea of contradictory statements.

The difficulty arose virtually immediately as a number of states passed laws which permitted amended and additional certificates of location. *See Tonopah & Salt Lake Mining Co. v. Tonopah Mining Co.,* 125 F. 389 (C.C.D. Nev. 1903). This was necessitated by the fact that it was not unusual for the original notice of location to contain various minor defects, particularly as regards the actual physical location of the claim. Thus as early as 1885 the Federal courts recognized the right of the mineral locator to amend his location. *See McEvoy v. Hyman,* 25 F. 596 (C.C.D. Colo. 1885). It is interesting to note that at this early date, the court recognized, in interpreting the Colorado statute authorizing amended locations, that "[i]t is perhaps unfortunate that the question of amending a certificate and of changing the boundaries of claim, which amounts to a relocation, should be expressed in general terms relating to both subjects, and in one section of the law." *Id.* at 599-600. The court continued noting that the right of correction of the certificate of location had been recognized independently of statutes expressly authorizing amendments to certificates. *See also Fred B. Ortman,* 52 L.D. 467, 471, (1928). Moreover, the court opined that the provision of the statute limiting its relation back to those situations in which no intervening rights had been initiated referred to the situation where the boundaries of the claim were changed, *i.e.,* a relocation, and not to the amendment of a certificate of location. *Accord, Hagerman v. Thompson,* 68 Wyo. 515, 235 P.2d 750, 756 (1951); *Nichols v. Ora Tahoma Mining Co.,* 62 Nev. 343, 151, P.2d 615, 625 (1944). *See also Brattain Contractors, Inc.,* 37 IBLA 233 (1978).[a]

Similarly, in a case styled *John C. Teller,* 26 L.D. 484 (1898), the Department held that an amended location, permitted by Colorado State law was "made in furtherence of the original location and for the purpose of giving additional strength or territorial effect thereto, while [a relocation] is a new and independent location which can only be made where the original location and all rights thereunder have been lost by failure to make the necessary annual expenditure." *Id.* at 486.

A relocation is, by the terms of the statute, adverse to the original location, being permissible only where there has been a failure by the original locator to perform assessment work. *See Burke v. Southern Pacific R.R. Co.,* 234 U.S. 669, 693 (1914); *Belk v. Meagher,* 104 U.S. (14 Otto) 279, 284 (1881); *State of South Dakota v. Madill,* 53 I.D. 195, 200 (1930). Thus, unlike an amended location for which credit may be obtained for expenditures made on behalf of the original location (*see Tam v. Story,* 21 L.D. 440, 443-44 (1895)), moneys spent in the development of an original claim may not be applied to a relocated claim to fulfill the statutory requirement that $500 be expended on development prior to the issuance of patent. *See Tough Nut No. 2 and Other Lode Mining Claims,* 36 L.D. 9 (1907); *Yankee Lode Claims,* 30 L.D. 289, (1900). A critical question, and one crucial to this case, is whether and in what circumstances an amended location relates back to the date of the original location.

For the purposes of this decision, we will define an "amended" location as a location which is made in furtherance of an earlier valid location and which may or may not take in different or additional ground. The term "relocation" will be limited to those situations in which the subsequent location is adverse to the original location.[1]

---

[a] GFS (MIN) 110 (1978).

[1] No attempt will be made to reconcile the terminology used herein with all prior Departmental decisions for the simple reason that they are virtually irreconcilable. *See generally* G. Reeves, *Amendment v. Relocation,* 14 Rocky Mt. Min. Law Inst. 207 (1968).

It will be seen that generally an amended location relates back, *where no adverse rights have intervened,* to the date of the original location. *See* Morrison, *Mining Rights,* 16th ed. (1936), at 159-163. Thus, in *Bunker Hill & Sullivan Mining & Concentrating Co. v. Empire State-Idaho Mining & Development Co.,* 134 F. 268 (1903), the Circuit Court for the District of Idaho noted: "It has long been held that a mining location may be amended without the forfeiture of any rights acquired by the original location, *except such as are inconsistent with the amendment, but new rights cannot be added which are inconsistent with those acquired by other locations made between the dates of the original and the amended location.*" *Id.* at 270. Additionally, there are certain circumstances in which an amended location notice will relate back to the date of the original notice even in the face of intervening adverse claims. Thus, it has been held that if the amended notice is made to cure obvious defects in the original notice without including any new ground, it will relate back to the original notwithstanding intervening locations. *McEvoy v. Hyman, supra; Gobert v. Butterfield,* 23 Cal. App. 1, 136 P. 516 (1913); *Berquist v. West Virginia-Wyoming Copper Co.,* 18 Wyo. 270, 106 P. 673, 677-78 (1910).

While the *Bunker Hill* case notes that the amended location relates back to the extent it is not inconsistent with the intervening *rights* of others, it must be remembered that if the original claim was valid and was maintained in conformance with the law, the land embraced by the claim would not be open to the initiation of adverse *rights (Farrell v. Lockhart,* 210 U.S. 142 (1908)), and thus an amendment would of necessity relate back, provided no new land was included in the amendment. *See generally Waskey v. Hammer,* 223 U.S. 85 (1912); *Atherley v. Bullion Monarch Uranium Co.,* 8 Utah 2d 362, 335 P.2d 71 (1959). No amended location is possible, however, if the original location was void. *See Brown v. Gurney,* 201 U.S. 184, 191 (1906). A void claim would be one in which a locator has failed to comply with a material statutory requirement. *Flynn v. Vevelstad,* 119 F. Supp. 93 (D. Alaska 1954), *aff'd,* 230 F.2d 695 (9th Cir. 1956).

There is no doubt that withdrawal of land from mineral entry constitutes such an appropriation of the land as to prevent the initiation of new rights. *See Mark W. Boone,* 33 IBLA 32 (1977); *Lyman B. Crunk,* 68 I.D. 190, 194 (1961); *James M. Wells,* A-28549 (February 10, 1961); *United States Phosphate Co.,* 43 L.D. 232 (1914). But to the extent that the amended location merely furthers rights acquired by a valid subsisting location, withdrawal of land subject to existing rights will not prevent the amended location. It should be emphasized, however, that the original claim must have been valid, and not voidable, in this situation. While it is true that a legal presumption arises in favor of a mineral claimant in possession and working the claim against the attempts of another claimant to enter upon the land and make a discovery, such presumption does not arise against the United States. *Brattain Contractors, Inc., supra* at 238 and cases cited. *See Houck v. Jose,* 72 F. Supp. 6, 10, (S.D. Cal. 1947), *aff'd,* 171 F.2d 211 (9th Cir. 1948). By withdrawing the land, the United States has prohibited the initiation of new claims and also prevented the curing of substantive defects in other claims.[2]

Thus, we hold that to the extent that an amended location, *i.e.,* once made in furtherance of an original location, merely changes a notice of location without attempting to enlarge the rights appurtenant to the original location, such amended location relates back to the original. Examples of such amended locations would be a change in the name of the claim (*Butte Consolidated Mining Co. v. Barker,* 35 Mont. 327, 89 P. 302, *aff'd on rehearing,* 90 P. 177 (1907); *Seymour v. Fisher,* 16 Colo. 188, 27 P. 240 (1891)), the exclusion of excess acreage so long as the original discovery point is preserved (*see Waskey v. Hammer, supra*), and a change in the record owners of a claim where such change is reflective of an existing fact *(United States v. Consolidated Mines & Smelting Co.,* 455 F.2d 432, 441 (9th Cir. 1971); *Thompson v. Spray,* 72 Cal. 528, 14 P. 182 (1887)).

Finally, we would point out that if an amended claim had been filed, the recording of such amended claim under section 8 of the Mining in the Parks Act, 90 Stat. 1342, 1343, 16 U.S.C. § 1907 (1976), or under section 314 of the Federal Land Policy and Management Act of 1976, 90 Stat. 2744, 2769, 43 U.S.C. § 1744 (1976), together with such other information as is required by the applicable regulations, would constitute compliance with the Federal recording requirements since the two notices must be construed together. *Hagerman v. Thompson, supra; Bergquist v. West Virginia-Wyoming Copper Co., supra; Giverson v. Tuolumne Copper Mining Co.,* 41 Mont. 396, 109 P. 974 (1910); *Duncan v. Fulton,* 15 Colo. 140, 61 P. 244 (1900).

Turning to the facts of the appeal before us, we note that the State of Utah, unlike many other Western States, does not have a specific statute permitting or regulating amended locations. The Supreme Court of Utah, however, has recognized the right of locators to amend. *See Cranford v. Gibbs,* 123 Utah 447, 260 P.2d 870 (1953).

The three State Office decisions involved separate groups of claims. . . . [These are the Copperspur claims, the Jean Group and the RG claimants.] Appellants aver that all of these were amended locations of prior existing claims; we will examine each group separately.

* * * *

Thus, we reach the question which is essential to this appeal: were the actions variously taken in 1974 and 1975 in the nature of "amended" notices of location, or were they relocations made after the land had been withdrawn?

The decision of the State Office noted that nothing on the face of the notices for the Copperspur, Jean, and RG claims indicated that these were

---

[2] We are aware that placer claimants have, in certain instances, been required both to obtain new land and relinquish land originally claimed in order to conform the claim to an official survey. Inasmuch as that fact situation is not presented herein, we need not determine whether, in these circumstances, the inclusion of new land operates as an exception to the general rule.

amended notices or even relocations. This is true. There is no absolute requirement, however, that an amended location or a relocation state that this is its purpose on its face.

The general rule is that an "amended" certificate need not state the specific purpose of the amendement. *See Tonopah & Salt Lake Mining Co. v. Tonopah Mining Co., supra* at 397; *Johnson v. Young,* 18 Colo. 625, 34 P. 173 (1893); *Lindley on Mines* (1897) at § 398. We have been unable, however, to discover any court case dealing with an alleged amended certificate of location in which the documents do not, on their face, indicate that they are amended or additional location notices. We feel that while this omission does not inevitably lead to the conclusion that no amended location was intended, it does properly give rise to an inference that such was not the intent. *See The Heirs of M. K. Harris,* 42 IBLA 44 (1979).

In *United States v. Consolidated Mines & Smelting Co., supra,* the Ninth Circuit Court of Appeals noted that the appellant:

[C]laimed that some of its location notices were actually relocation notices. This contention was dismissed by the Department with the observation that relocation is necessarily adverse to the interests of prior locators. Thus, the Department concluded, Consolidated's rights in its mining claims must date from the "relocation" notices filed after the withdrawal. This generalization is correct only if the relocator claims against, rather than through, the prior locator. *If a relocator claims through the prior locator, ordinarily the relocation notice relates back.* * * * The evidence before the Department did not indicate whether Consolidated claimed through or against its predecessors. Thus the Department's generalization is supported only by an unjustifiable assumption of fact. Accepting arguendo Consolidated's status as a relocator, hearings would have been desirable to ascertain the relationship between Consolidated's relocations and prior location made by persons through whom Consolidated claimed.

Given a disputed issue of fact, hearings were required before the Department could declare Consolidated's claims null and void. [Emphasis supplied.]

We believe that this precedent is applicable herein. A number of problems have been delineated above. First, there is a question whether appellants obtained title to the mining claims prior to the 1974 locations. Second, there is a question whether the 1974 actions were intended to be amendments of the prior location, relocations, or new locations. These matters are best determined at a hearing.

We also note that the appellants contend that they relied on the advice of a National Park Service employee, one Harold Ellingson, in their actions, particularly in the recordation of the claims. It is axiomatic that regardless of the validity of the 1974 locations, nothing in the decision below adversely affected the prior locations. However, since these prior locations were not recorded, they would now be void under section 8 of the Mining in the Parks Act, 90 Stat. 1343, 16 U.S.C. § 1907 (1976).

The circumstances in which estoppel will lie against the Government are of a very limited nature. We do not now decide whether, if it could be proved that appellants were misled as to which claims should be recorded, estoppel would lie herein. It is sufficient to note that inasmuch as we are referring the matter to the Hearings Division for the assignment of an Administrative Law Judge, the hearing should include an inquiry into this question, so that we may resolve any future question without substantial factual uncertainties. Insofar as the testimony of Ellingson would be critical to such determinations, we request that provision be made for his appearance.

Accordingly, pursuant to the authority delegated to the Board of Land Appeals by the Secretary of the Interior, 43 CFR 4.1, the decisions appealed from are affirmed as regards the RG Nos. 131-152, and set aside as to all other claims, and the case files for such claims as hereby referred to the Hearings Division for the assignment of an Administrative Law Judge who will conduct a hearing inquiring into the matters set out in the text. The appellants will have the burden of showing that the 1974 and 1975 location notices were amended locations rather than new locations or relocations. The Judge will issue an initial decision which may be appealed by any party adversely affected.

ADMINISTRATIVE JUDGE GOSS CONCURRING:

I concur in the majority analysis, except in two respects.

I submit that the inference to be drawn from failure to designate an alleged amended location notice as "amended" should be more limited. The inference that there was no intent to "relocate" rather than to amend should apply only (1) where the locators on the new document are not the same or successors to those on the prior document, or (2) where there has been a lapse in required assessment work. If the parties are not in privity, an adversary relationship can be presumed, at least to the extent of the differences. If assessment work is not performed, an abandonment by the locator and a "relocation" is a possibility.

While I concur that the specified BLM decision should be set aside, I would remand to BLM, rather than to the Hearings Division, for further proceedings. The contemplated hearing could prove costly, time-consuming, and possibly unnecessary. Appellants have not applied for the 261 patents and application may never be made. BLM is burdened with the implementation of the Federal Land Policy and Management Act of 1976, 43 U.S.C. §§ 1701-82 (1976) and other matters. Therefore, in the interest of administrative convenience and economy, BLM should be given authority to chart its course. The Board should rule that the claims are not to be declared void ab initio without the hearing specified. Among the options available to BLM would be the following: (1) the scheduling of the withdrawal hearing; (2) recognition of the later locations as amended locations of claims prior to the withdrawal; (3) reservation of the question of validity of the later locations as amendments until a later time or until the question is precipitated as to a particular claim by an application for patent; and (4) review of the claims to determine whether any content [sic] should be brought and to determine whether such a contest could be any less burdensome than the hearing on the withdrawal.

NOTES

1. How significant is the relation back that accompanies an amendment?

2. You represent a client who has just purchased over 1000 lode claims. Your client intends to commence extensive development work. She advises you that the original claims were laid out sloppily, so that some of the claims overlap, and some of them are not contiguous, with the result that there are gaps between them. Your client wants to clean up this mess before she commences development of the claims. What procedure should you recommend to your client, amendment or relocation?

8 RIGHTS OF SURFACE USE APPURTENANT TO A VALID MINING LOCATION

United States v. Curtis-Nevada Mines, Inc.
United States v. Etcheverry
United States v. Cruthers

There is no requirement of the mining law that a locator seek a patent and thereby attempt to obtain fee title from the United States. After a valid discovery has been made and all the acts of location complied with, the locator is said to have a possessory title. In traditional property terms, this title would be classified as an equitable title on a condition subsequent. The legal title is still in the United States since it is the owner of record. The conditions subsequent which will cause the involuntary divestiture of the equitable title are, primarily, failure to perform the annual assessment work and failure to timely make the required FLPMA filings. An abandonment will also result in divestiture of title.

While this title is often called a possessory title, actual possession by the locator is not required to maintain it. The word "possessory" has reference to the right of the miner to the exclusive possession of the claim, and not to any obligation of the miner to stay in actual possession of the claim. In *Belk v. Meagher,* 104 U.S. 279, 283 the court expressed this relationship as follows:

> There is nothing in the act of Congress which makes actual possession any more necessary for the protection of the title acquired to such a claim by a valid location, than it is for any other grant from the United States. The language of the act is that the locators "shall have the exclusive right of possession and enjoyment of all the surface included within the lines of their locations" [sec. 2332], which is to continue until there shall be a failure to do the requisite amount of work within the prescribed time.

In the oft quoted words of *Cole v. Ralph,* 252 U.S. 286, 295 (1919), this possessory title is property in the "fullest sense of the word." Thus, at least in theory, the rights of the locator prior to patent are substantially identical to the rights of the locator after patent. The qualifying parenthetical in the preceding sentence is an important one. It will be observed, that prior to patent there has been no judicial or administrative determination that the location is in fact a valid one. Thus, while in theory the location may confer a valid possessory title, in practice it is always subject to contest. Can you think of additional reasons why a patented title is superior to a possessory one? The cases that follow illustrate some considerations relevant to this question.

UNITED STATES V. CURTIS-NEVADA MINES, INC.
611 F.2d 1277 (9th Cir. 1980)

Before TRASK and HUG, Circuit Judges, and ORRICK, District Judge.
HUG, Circuit Judge:
This case concerns the right of the general public to use the surface of land upon which unpatented mining claims have been located, when that use does not interfere with mining activities. The principal issue is whether the owner of unpatented mining claims has the right to exclude members of the general public from such use of the surface of the land for recreational purposes or access to other public lands unless they have obtained a specific governmental permit or license for such use. To resolve this issue, we are called upon to construe the provisions of the Surface Resources and Multiple Use Act of 1955 ("Multiple Use Act"), Pub.L.No.84-167, 69 Stat. 367 (codified at 30 U.S.C. §§ 611-612).

The United States brought this action to enjoin Curtis-Nevada Mines, Inc. and its president, Robert Curtis, from prohibiting members of the public from using the surface of appellees' unpatented mining claims for recreational purposes or for entrance to adjacent National Forest lands. Since 1970, appellees located approximately 203 mining claims on public lands administered by the Bureau of Land Management under the Department of the Interior and on lands within the Toiyabe National Forest administered by the Forest Service under the Department of Agriculture. These claims cover approximately 13 square miles; 21 of the claims are in Nevada and the remainder in California. This action arose after appellees prevented members of the public from entering their unpatented mining claims and barred access to several roads which crossed their claims. Jurisdiction is based upon 28 U.S.C. §§ 1291 and 1345.

The District Court, ruling on cross motions for summary judgment, held that under section 4 (b) of the Multiple Use Act, 30 U.S.C. § 612(b), the public is entitled to use the surface of unpatented mining claims for recreational purposes and for access to adjoining lands, but that this use and access is available only to those members of the public who hold specific recreation licenses or permits from a state or federal agency. *United States v. Curtis-Nevada Mines, Inc.,* 415 F.Supp. 1373 (E.D.Cal.1976). The United States appeals from the portion of the judgment that allows access to the mining claims only to those persons having specific written licenses or permits from a state or federal agency. We reverse that portion of the judgment and affirm the remainder of the judgment.

I

Curtis states that he located and filed the 203 claims after stumbling upon an outcropping of valuable minerals while on a deer hunting trip. He states that, within the 13-mile area, he has located gold, platinum, copper, silver, tungsten, pitchblend, palladium, triduim, asmium, rhodium, ruthenium, scanduim, vanduim, ytterbuim, yttrium, europium, and "all the rare earths." These minerals he maintains have a value in the trillions. The mining activity of the appellees was very limited. At the time this litigation was instituted there was only one employee, who performed chiefly caretaking duties such as watching after equipment and preventing the public from entering the claims.

Hunters, hikers, campers and other persons who had customarily used the area for recreation were excluded by the appellees. Curtis posted "no trespassing" signs on the claims and constructed barricades on the Blackwell Canyon Road and the Rickey Canyon Road, which lead up into the mountains and provide access to the Toiyabe National Forest. After receiving numerous complaints, the United States filed this action asserting the rights of the general public to the use of the surface of the mining claims. The district court heard the matter on cross motions for summary judgment and held:

> [A]ny member of the public, who possesses a license or permit from any state or federal agency which allows that person to engage in any form of recreation on public land, including National Forests, can enter onto the surface of unpatented mining claims in order to engage in that recreation, or to gain access to another area to engage in that recreation, so long as there is no interference with ongoing mining operations.

415 F.Supp. at 1378. The court denied the request of the United States that Curtis be enjoined from using guards or manned gates. The court held that Curtis can use gates or barricades if personnel are available to remove the barricades for persons requesting admittance with a proper permit.

II

Section 4 (b) of the Multiple Use Act provides in pertinent part:

> Rights under any mining claim hereafter located under the mining laws of the United States shall be subject, prior to issuance of patent therefor, to the right of the United States to manage and dispose of the vegetative surface resources thereof and to manage other surface resources thereof (except mineral deposits subject to location under the mining laws of the United States). Any such mining claim shall also be subject, prior to issuance of patent therefor, to the right of the United States, its permittees, and licensees, to use so much of the surface thereof as may be necessary for such purposes or for access to adjacent land: *Provided, however,* That any use of the surface of any such mining claim by the United States, its permittees or licensees, shall be such as not to endanger or materially interfere with prospecting, mining or processing operations or uses reasonably incident thereto . . . .

30 U.S.C. § 612(b).

As noted by the district court, the meaning of "other surface resources" and of "permittees and licensees" is somewhat ambiguous. The principal issues in this case are whether recreational use is embodied within the meaning of "other surface resources" and whether the phrase "permittees and licensees" includes only those members of the public who have specific written permits or licenses. We agree with the district court that administrative interpretation of the language by the Solicitor's Office in theDepartment of Interior does not provide any clear direction in the construction of this section of the statute, 415 F.Supp. at 1378.

We look first to the legislative history of the Act. As this court has previously noted, Congress did not intend to change the basic principles of the mining laws when it enacted the Multiple Use Act. *Converse v. Udall*, 399 F.2d 616, 617 (9th Cir. 1968), *cert. denied,* 393 U.S. 1025, 89 S.Ct. 635, 21 L.Ed.2d 569 (1969). The Multiple Use Act was corrective legislation, which attempted to clarify the law and to alleviate abuses that had occurred under the mining laws. H.R.Rep.No. 730, 84th Cong., 1st Sess. 7-8, *reprinted in* [1955] 2 U.S. Code Cong. & Admin. News, pp. 2474, 2480 (hereinafter House Report 730); *Converse,* 399 F.2d at 617. The statute was designed to provide for "multiple use of the surface of the same tracts of public lands, compatible with unhampered subsurface resource development." H.R.Rep.No.730 at 8, U.S.Code Cong. & Admin.News, p. 2480; 101 Cong.Rec. 8743 (1955). The purpose of the Multiple Use Act as stated broadly in House Report 730 is:

> to permit more efficient management and administration of the surface resources of the public lands by providing for multiple use of the same tracts of such lands.
>
> . . . to prohibit the use of any hereafter located unpatented mining claim for any purpose other than prospecting, mining, processing, and related activities.
>
> . . . to limit the rights of a holder of an unpatented mining claim hereafter located to the use of the surface and surface resources.

H.R.Rep.No.730 at 2, U.S.Code Cong. & Admin.News, pp. 2474-75 [footnote omitted].

This concept of multiple use of surface resources of a mining claim was not intended, however, to interfere with the historical relationship between the possessor of a mining claim and the United States.

> This language, carefully developed, emphasizes the committee's insistence that this legislation not have the effect of modifying long-standing essential rights springing from location of a mining claim. Dominant and primary use of the locations hereafter made, as in the past, would be vested first in the locator; the United States would be authorized to manage and dispose of surface resources, or to use the surface for access to adjacent lands, so long as and to the extent that these activities do not endanger or materially interfere with mining, or related operations or activities on the mining claim.

Id. at 10, U.S. Code Cong. & Admin.News, p. 2483.

Under the general mining law enacted in 1872 [footnote omitted], individuals were encouraged to prospect, explore and develop the mineral resources of the public domain through an assurance of ultimate private ownership of the minerals and the lands so developed. The system envisaged by the mining law was that the prospector could go out into the public domain, search for minerals and upon discovery establish a claim to the lands upon which the discovery was made. This required location of the claim, which involved staking the corners of the claim, posting a notice of location thereon and complying with the state laws concerning the filing or recording of the claim in the appropriate office. A placer mining claim cannot exceed 20 acres and a lode claim cannot be larger than 1500 feet by 600 feet (which is slightly over 20 acres). The locator thus obtained "the exclusive right of possession and enjoyment of all the surface included within the lines of their locations." 30 U.S.C. § 26.

Before the 1955 Act this exclusive possession and use was recognized so long as the use was incident to prospecting and mining. *United States v. Richardson,* 599 F.2d 290, 292-93 (9th Cir. 1979); *United States v. Nogueira,* 403 F.2d 816, 824-25 (9th Cir. 1968). The claimant thus had the present and exclusive possession for the purpose of mining, but the federal government retained fee title and could protect the land and the surface resources from trespass, waste or from uses other than those associated with mining. *Richardson,* 599 F.2d at 293. The claimant could apply for a patent to the land under 30 U.S.C. § 29, and, upon meeting the statutory requirements, would be granted a patent which usually conveyed the full fee title to the land [footnote omitted].

In order to obtain the patent the claimant would have to establish that there was a legitimate discovery of a valuable mineral deposit on the land which a prudent man would be justified in developing [footnote omitted]. In many instances an investigation and hearing would be required prior to granting a patent. However, claimants could continue mining activities on the claims, without ever obtaining a patent. As a practical matter, mining claimants could remain in exclusive possession of the claim without ever proving a valid discovery or actually conducting mining operations. This led to abuses of the mining laws when mining claims were located with no real intent to prospect or mine but rather to gain possession of the surface resources. Furthermore, even persons who did have the legitimate intent to utilize the claim for the development of the mineral content at the time of the location often did not proceed to do so, and thus large areas of the public domain were withdrawn, and as a result these surface resources could not be utilized by the general public for other purposes.

It was to correct this deficiency in the mining law that Congress in 1955 enacted the Multiple Use Act. Some of the abuses and problems that the legislation was designed to correct are detailed in House Report 730:

> The mining laws are sometimes used to obtain claim or title to valuable timber actually located within the claim boundaries. Frequently, whether or not the locator so intends, such claims have the effect of blocking access-road development to adjacent tracts of merchantable Federal timber, or to generally increase costs of administration and management of adjacent lands. The fraudulent locator in national forests, in addition to obstructing orderly management and the competitive sale of timber, obtains for himself high-value, publicly owned, surface resources bearing no relationship to legitimate mining activity.

> Mining locations made under existing law may, and do, whether by accident or design, frequently block access: to water needed in grazing use of the national forests or other public lands; to valuable recreational areas;

to agents of the Federal Government desiring to reach adjacent lands for purposes of managing wild-game habitat or improving fishing streams so as to thwart the public harvest and proper management of fish and game resources on the public lands generally, both on the located lands and on adjacent lands.

. . . .

Under existing law, fishing and mining have sometimes been combined in another form of nonconforming use of the public lands: a group of fisherman-prospectors wil locate a good stream, stake out successive mining claims flanking the stream, post their mining claims with "No trespassing" signs, and proceed to enjoy their own private fishing camp. So too, with hunter-prospectors, except that their blocked-out "mining claims" embrace wildlife habitats; posted, they constitute excellent hunting camps.

The effect of nonmining activity under color of existing mining law should be clear to all: a waste of valuable resources of the surface on lands embraced within claims which might satisfy the basic requirement of mineral discovery, but which were, in fact, made for a purpose other than mining; for lands adjacent to such locations, timber, water, forage, fish and wildlife, and recreational values wasted or destroyed because of increased cost of management, difficulty of administratrion, or inaccessibility; the activities of a relatively few pseudominers reflecting unfairly on the legitimate mining industry.

H.R.Rep.No. 730 at 6, U.S.Code Cong. & Admin.News, pp. 2478-79. House Report 730 further points out that one of the ways to combat these abuses would be to step up federal government action to contest location of claims:

If fraudulent locations are made, under present law the United States has the right to refuse patents (if application is made), or to attack such locations in court.

Modification of presently authorized administrative action alone does not appear the answer. Presently available remedies are time-consuming, are costly, and, in the end, not conclusive. Where a location is based on discovery, it is extremely difficult to establish invalidity on an assertion by the United States that the location was, in fact, made for a purpose other than mining.

If locations must be proven fraudulent in court before dispossession, the mining laws must be so drawn or so framed as to make clear to locators what can and what cannot be done. On the other hand, continual interference by Federal agencies in an effort to overcome this difficulty would hamper and discourage the development of our mineral resources, development which has been encouraged and promoted by Federal mining law since shortly after 1800.

Id. at 7, U.S.Code Cong. & Admin.News, p. 2479.

The alternative chosen by Congress was to limit the exclusive possession of mining claimants so as to permit the multiple use of the surface resources of the claims prior to the patenting of the claims, so long as that use did not materially interfere with prospecting or mining operations.

In the district court proceedings Curtis asserted that recreational uses are not encompassed within the meaning of "other surface resources" in § 612(b). However, as the district court properly held, the phrase "other surface resources" was clearly intended to include recreational uses. It is apparent from the previously quoted portions of House Report 730 at 6, as well as committee hearings cited by the district court, 415 F.Supp. at 1378, that recreation was one of the "other surface resources" to which 30 U.S.C. § 612(b) refers. This conclusion is further buttressed by the Bureau of Land Management regulations implementing the Multiple Use Act [footnote omitted]. It is therefore a surface resource that the United States has a right to manage and that the United States and its permittees and licensees have a right to use so long as the use does not "endanger or materially interfere with prospecting, mining or processing operations or uses reasonably incident thereto." 30 U.S.C. § 612(b).

The remaining question that the district court addressed concerns the identification of the "permittees and licensees" of the United States entitled to use the surface resources. The district court held that the "permittees and licensees" are only those who have specific written permits or licenses from any state or federal agency allowing those persons to engage in any form of recreation on public land. The court mentions hunting, fishing or camping permits as illustrative of the required permits. It is at this point that we disagree with the district court.

Historically the United States has managed the lands within the public domain as fee owner and trustee for the people of the United States. *Light v. United States,* 220 U.S. 523, 527, 31 S.Ct. 485, 55 L.Ed. 570 (1911); *Camfield v. United States,* 167 U.S. 518, 524, 17 S.Ct. 864, 42 L.Ed. 260 (1897). Also, in the management of public lands, the United States has historically allowed the general public to use the public domain for recreation and other purposes, and often without a specific, formal permit. Such access has been described as an implied license.

. . . .

One of the clear purposes of the 1955 legislation was to prevent the withdrawal of surface resources from other public use merely by locating a mining claim. The inertia of the situation was previously with the mining claimant who retained exclusive possession of the surface of the claim until the location was invalidated by affirmative action. As to claims located after the 1955 legislation, however, the inertia works the other way. Essentially, the surface resources remain in the public domain for use as before with the exception that the mining claimant is entitled to use the surface resources for prospecting and mining purposes and that the other uses by the general public cannot materially interfere with the prospecting and mining operation. Thus, the vast acreage upon which mining claims have been located since 1955 or claims which, by operation of the statute, have become subject to the provisions of section 612(b),

remain open for public use except for the restrictions imposed where actual mining or prospecting operations are taking place.[1]
. . . .

It should be noted that mining claimants have at least two remedies in the event that public use interferes with prospecting or mining activities. Section 612(b) provides that "any use of the surface . . . shall be such as not to endanger or materially interefere with prospecting, mining or processing operations or uses reasonably incident thereto." The mining claimant can protest to the managing federal agency about public use which results in material interference and, if unsatisfied, can bring suit to enjoin the activity. Secondly, a claimant with a valid claim can apply for a patent which, when granted, would convey fee title to the property.

In the present case, appellees have not presented any evidence that the public use of land included within their unpatented mining claim has "materially interfered" with any mining activity. Absent such evidence, section 612(b) applies in this case to afford the general public a right of free access to the land on which the mining claims have been located for recreational use of the surface resources and for access to adjoining property. Therefore, we reverse the portion of the judgment that requires specific written permits or licenses for entry onto the mining claims, and we remand this case to the district court for entry of an injunction consistent with the views expressed in this opinion.

NOTES

1. The Surface Resources Act is applicable only in the period prior to patent. It does not restrict the use to which the surface can be put after a patent is obtained. 30 U.S.C. § 615 provides that "nothing in this Act shall be construed in any manner to authorize inclusion in any patent hereafter issued by the United States for any mining claim hereafter or heretofore located, of any reservation, limitation, or restriction not otherwise authorized by law."

2. Unlike the Surface Resources Act, the Wilderness Act applies in the period after patent. The Wilderness Act provides that mineral prospecting and exploration are permitted uses in wilderness areas until midnight December 31, 1983. If a valid discovery is made, the locator is entitled to a patent. The patent, however, that is issued pursuant to the Wilderness Act conveys a much more limited title than does the patent ordinarily issued pursuant to the mining law. 16

---

[1] Section 5 of the Multiple Use Act, 30 U.S.C. § 613 provides an in rem procedure to identify which patented claims will be subject to the provisions of § 612, briefly stated § 613 provides that the federal agency having responsibility for administering the surface resources may publish a notice requiring claimants to file within 150 days a verified statement concerning their mining claims. Failure to file the statement constitutes a waiver of any rights in the claims that are contrary to the limitations of § 612. The failure to file does not, however, affect the validity of the claim itself but only subjects the claim to the limitations of § 612.

U.S.C. § 1133(d) (2) provides that "Mining locations lying within the boundaries of such wilderness areas shall be held and used solely for mining or processing operations and uses reasonably incident thereto; and hereafter, subject to valid existing rights, all patents issued under the mining laws of the United States affecting . . . lands designated by this Act as wilderness areas shall convey title to the mineral deposit within the claim . . . but each such patent shall reserve to the United States all title in or to the surface of the lands and products thereof. . . ." This provision of the Wilderness Act is incorporated by reference into FLPMA. 43 U.S.C. § 1782(c).

UNITED STATES V. ETCHEVERRY
230 F. 2d 193 (10th Cir. 1956)

PICKETT, Circuit Judge.

The United States brought this action against the defendants, Paul Etcheverry and John Etcheverry, to recover damages for alleged trespass on certain lands of the public domain in Colorado, and to enjoin further trespass. The Kerogen Oil Company, a corporation, was in possession of the lands by virtue of valid placer mining claims. The defendants leased the lands from the Kerogen Oil Company for grazing purposes and grazed cattle and sheep thereon during the years 1951 and 1952. On July 1, 1953, the Kerogen Oil Company made application for a patent to the mining claims, which was allowed upon payment of the required purchase price, and a final certificate was issued January 8, 1954, showing it to be entitled to a patent. The United States concedes that after the issuance of the final certificate, it was not entitled to a restraining order. This appeal is from a judgment denying the recovery of damages for trespass prior to the issuance of the final certificate.

Two questions are presented: (1) Does the owner of a valid mining claim have the right to lease or to use the surface of the claim for the grazing of livestock not incident to the mining operations; and (2) After the United States accepts payment and issues a final certificate or a patent to mining claims, may it recover damages for trespass committed prior to the issuance of the final certificate or patent but during the time the land was held under a valid mining location?

30 U.S.C.A. § 22 provides that "all valuable mineral deposits in lands belonging to the United States, both surveyed and unsurveyed, shall be free and open to exploration and purchase, and the lands in which they are found to occupation and purchase, by citizens of the United States * * * under regulations prescribed by law, and according to the local customs or rules of miners in the several mining districts, so far as the same are applicable and not inconsistent with the laws of the United States."

After a valid mining location is made, 30 U.S.C.A. § 26 gives to the locator "the exclusive right of possession and enjoyment of all the surface included within the lines of their locations, and of all veins, lodes, and ledges throughout their entire depth, * * *."

The law is well settled by innumerable decisions that when a mining claim has been perfected under the law, it is in effect a grant from the United States of the exclusive right of possession to the same. It constitutes property to its fullest extent, and is real property subject to be sold, transferred, mortgaged, taxed, and inherited without infringing any right or title of the United States. Ickes v. Virginia-Colorado Development Corp., 295 U.S. 639, 55 S.Ct. 888, 79 L.Ed. 1627; Wilbur v. U.S. ex rel. Krushnic, 280 U.S. 306, 50 S.Ct. 103, 74 L.Ed. 445; Clipper Mining Co. v. Eli Mining & Land Co., 194 U.S. 220, 24 S.Ct. 632, 48 L.Ed. 944; St. Louis Mining & Mill Co. v. Montana Mining Co., 171 U.S. 650, 19 S.Ct. 61, 43 L.Ed. 320; Belk v. Meagher, 104 U.S. 279, 26 L.Ed. 735.

Although Section 22 declares that all valuable mineral deposits belonging to the United States shall be free and open to exploration and purchase, there is no specific provision in the statute which gives to a locator the right to use the lands for purposes of profit or to lease lands for purposes other than for exploration and production of minerals. In all the cases above cited, where broad language was used in connection with the exclusive right of possession by the locator, the controversy arose over the legality of mining claims or the right of possession of the claim for mining purposes. The right of the locator to use the surface for purposes other than for mining, or the right to dispose of timber, grass or other materials on or under the surface of the lands was not under consideration. We construe these cases to hold that the exclusive possession of the surface of the land to which the locator is entitled is limited to use for mining purposes.

We are satisfied that under the statute the mere location of a mining claim gives to the locator only the right to explore for and mine minerals, and to purchase the land if there has been a compliance with the provisions of the statute. As against third parties, the locator or his assigns have exclusive right to use the surface of this land, but as against the United States, his right is conditional and inchoate. Shiver v. United States, 159 U.S. 491, 16 S.Ct. 54, 40 L.Ed. 231. The land is no longer a part of the public domain so far as the minerals are concerned, and it is not open to relocation until the rights of a former locator have terminated.

In Teller v. United States, 8 Cir., 113 F. 273, 280, the facts as to the mining claim and the alleged trespass were the same as those in the instant case except that timber, not grass, was sold by the locator. The court recognized the public policy of making gratuitous grants to citizens of the possessory right of mineral claims, but it was stated that the United States "has not seen fit to give away the land containing the minerals, but, on the contrary, has adopted the policy of selling the same to the locator, if he desires to purchase, on terms fixed by the acts of congress." It held that the location segregated and withdrew the land from the public domain to the extent that a rival claimant could not locate on the same lands for mining purposes. It was said that the location gave no more than the present and exclusive possession of the land for the purpose of mining and did not divest the legal title of the United States or impair its right to protect the land from trespass or waste. It was held that the locator's right of possession did not segregate the land from the public domain for all purposes and appropriate it to the locator's private use. The court said that the land did not cease to be part of the public domain until absolute title was acquired in the manner provided by statute. United States v. Rizzinelli, D.C.N.D. Idaho, 182 F. 675, is to the same effect. We think the reasoning of the Teller and Rizzinelli cases is sound and we hold that under the statute, general grazing rights of the public domain are not included in the possessory rights of a mining claim. To hold otherwise would permit the owner of a valid mining claim, with no intention of purchasing the fee, to strip the surface of the land of all the valuable property and materials thereon to his own profit, and then to abandon the claim.

The trial court, applying the doctrine of relation back, denied recovery of damages for trespass on the public domain because upon the issuance of final certificates, which entitled the owner of a mining location to a patent, the United States relinquished all of its interest in the property in question and could not maintain an action for trespass committed on the lands prior to the issuance of the final certificates. The authorities sustain this conclusion. In United States v. Freyberg, 7 Cir., 32 F. 195, a homestead entryman sold timber from the entry prior to the issuance of a final certificate or patent. The court denied recovery by the United States upon the ground that after the timber was taken, the entryman was issued a patent. It was held that upon the issuance of the patent, the title related back to the date of the original entry. The same question arose in United States v. Ellis, 9 Cir., 122 F. 1016, and the decision was the same as in the Freyberg case. Teller v. United States, 8 Cir., 117 F. 577, is to the same effect except that it was held there that when the final certificate issued, it related back to the date of the application for patent. In Reed v. Munn, 8 Cir., 148 F. 737, 757, certiorari denied 207 U.S. 588, 28 S.Ct. 255, 52 L.Ed. 353, it was said: "So long as the locator or his assignee performs the required amount of work, his right of possession is exclusive against every person and against the United States. He may never obtain the patent, but when it does issue, it has relation back to the location." In United States v. Detroit Timber & Lumber Co., 200 U.S. 321, 26 S.Ct. 282, 286, 50 L.Ed. 499, the lumber company purchased timber from the entrymen on timber land before the patents had issued. In speaking of the doctrine of relation, the court said:

"* * * If it be contended, that, by virtue of the contracts for the sale of timber, it had acquired some interest in the lands prior to the issue of patents, it is sufficient to say that, by the doctrine of relation, the patents, when issued, became operative as of the dates of the entries. It is true that this doctrine is but a fiction of the law, but it is a fiction resorted to whenever justice requires. It is that principle by which an act done at one time is considered to have been done at some antecedent time. It is a doctrine of frequent application, designed to promote justice. Thus, a sheriff's deed takes effect not of its date, but of the time when the lien of the judgment attached. The ordinary railroad land grants have been grants in praesenti, and under them the title has been adjudged to pass, not at the completion of the road, but at the date of the grant. Leavenworth, Lawrence & Galveston Railroad v. United States, 92 U.S. 733, 23 L.Ed. 634; St. Paul, M. & M. Railway Co. v. Phelps, 137 U.S. 528, 11 S.Ct. 168, 34 L.Ed. 767; St. Paul &

Pacific R. Co. v. Northern Pacific R. Co., 139 U.S. 1, 11 S.Ct. 389, 35 L.Ed. 77; United States v. Southern Pacific Railroad, 146 U.S. 570, 13 S.Ct. 152, 36 L.Ed. 1091. A patent from the United States operates to transfer the title, not merely from the date of the patent, but from the inception of the equitable right upon which it is based. Shepley v. Cowan, 91 U.S. 330, 23 L.Ed. 424. Indeed, this is generally true in case of the merging of an equitable right into a legal title. Although the patents in this case were not issued until after the sales of the timber, yet, when issued, they became operative as of the date of the original entries. This doctrine has frequently been recognized by this and other courts. * * *"

See also Knapp v. Alexander-Edgar Lumber Co., 237 U.S. 162, 35 S.Ct. 515, 59 L.Ed. 894; Hussman v. Durham, 165 U.S. 144, 17 S.Ct. 253, 41 L.Ed. 664; United States v. Bagnell Timber Co., 8 Cir., 178 F. 795. All of these decisions on relation back presuppose that the United States has paramount title to the land and the right to protect it from trespass and waste.

When a mining location is perfected and there has been compliance with the statute, the owner has an absolute right to purchase the fee title to the land at any time thereafter. Under the facts of this case, it would not serve the purpose of justice to permit the United States to recover damages for the grazing of grass on lands which the owner of a valid claim had an unquestioned right to purchase, where he has later exercised his right and received the fee title. The United States has suffered no damage.

Affirmed.

UNITED STATES V. CRUTHERS
523 F.2d 1306 (9th Cir. 1975)

OPINION

Before BROWNING and WALLACE, Circuit Judges, and WILLIAMS, District Judge.

PER CURIAM:

Appellant, Charles R. Cruthers, was convicted of theft of government property. 18 U.S.C. § 641. Appellant's alleged theft consisted of cutting 70 pole size Ponderosa Pines from the surface of his unpatented mining claim and using the timber to construct a residential cabin on private property—his adjacent patented claim.

The issue on appeal is whether the district court erred in instructing the jury that "a claimant to an unpatented claim may not cut or remove trees or logs for use for any purpose on private property." Appellant's proffered instruction, rejected by the trial court, would have required acquittal if the jury found that "the cabin was to be used for purposes of operating the unpatented mining claim."

Timber on an unpatented mining claim cannot be cut or removed "[e]xcept to the extent required for the mining claimant's prospecting, mining or processing operations and uses reasonably incident thereto, or for the construction of buildings or structures in connection therewith. . . ." 30 U.S.C. § 612(c). Rather than limiting the place where timber from an unpatented claim may be used, the statute allows use of such timber, including use for the construction of buildings, "to the extent required" for uses "reasonably incident to" or "in connection" with legitimate mining operations related to the unpatented claim. Thus, nothing in the statute prohibits use of timber cut from the surface of an unpatented claim on private property if such timber is required for a use reasonably incident to legitimate mining operations in connection with the unpatented claim. Timber may be cut on a mining claim only if it is required for use in development of that claim, but it need not be used within the physical limits of the claim. An interpretation of the statute unconditionally barring use, on any other land under any circumstances, of timber cut on an unpatented claim would place an arbitrary obstacle in the way of orderly mining operations on unpatented claims and would thwart the statute's purpose of promoting proper development of mining claims on public lands without abuse of the surface resources.

The instruction given was therefore erroneous. The error was clearly prejudicial. The conviction must be set aside.

Reversed and remanded.

NOTES

1. An unpatented mining claim may only be used for prospecting, mining or processing operations together with uses reasonably incident thereto. While it is not possible to enumerate all of the uses that might, depending on circumstances, be reasonably incident, it is possible to enumerate some that clearly are not. Thus, the miner is forbidden to use his claim for "filling stations, curio shops, cafes, tourist or fishing and hunting camps." 43 C.F.R. § 3712.1 (b) (1983).

2. If a use is clearly incident to mining or prospecting, does the Surface Resources Act validate that use no matter the destructive impact it may have on the environment? In *United States v. Richardson*, 599 F.2d 290 (9th Cir. 1979), the locator was engaged in prospecting, a use explicitly approved by the Surface Resources Act. There was no question that the locator "was engaged in genuine prospecting activities conducted at considerable expense (some $40,000) for the purpose of developing a mine." *Id.* at 291. The method of prospecting employed by the locator, however, was extremely damaging to the national forest in which the claim was located, and involved the extensive use of a bulldozer, backhoe and dynamite. The forest service brought suit to enjoin further damage to the environment. The locator defended on the ground that since his use was a permitted one under the Surface Resources Act, it could not be enjoined. The court enjoined the locator holding that the Surface Resources Act required a balancing of the value of the intended use against the destruction that use caused to the public lands. In the instant case the court found that the locator's "methods of exploration were unnecessary and unreasonably destructive of surface resources and damaging to the environment." *Id.* at 295. The premise for this finding was that the exploration could have been conducted much less destructively, albeit more expensively, by drilling. Would the Surface Resources Act permit even destructive exploration methods to be enjoined in a case where there was no other feasible exploration method available? Would the *Richardson* case have been decided differently if the land involved had been BLM land?

9 EXTRALATERAL RIGHTS

Silver Surprize, Inc. v. Sunshine Mining Co.

SILVER SURPRIZE, INC. V. SUNSHINE MINING CO.
15 Wash. App. 1, 547 P.2d 1240 (Wash. App. 1976)

GREEN, Judge.

This is a contract action . . . brought by the plaintiff, Silver Surprize, Inc., against the defendant, Sunshine Mining Co., to require defendant to account for ore removed from the "Yankee Girl Vein" (YGV) within plaintiff's mining claim or, alternatively, for cancellation of the contract. In defense, Sunshine asserts that, because it owns the extralateral rights to the YGV, that vein is not covered by the contract and, therefore, an accounting is not required. Alternatively, Sunshine contends the action is barred by statutes of limitation and laches. While the trial court refused to find that Sunshine owned extralateral rights in the YGV, it did find that the YGV was not subject to the contract and, even if it were, Sunshine acquired title to the ore removed by ouster of its cotenant, Silver Surprize, through adverse possession. Further, the court held the action was barred by statutes of limitation and laches and denied Silver Surprize's request to cancel the contract. Both parties appeal from a judgment of dismissal.

The factual background is as follows: Silver Surprize owns a mining claim in the Coeur d'Alene Mining District near Kellogg, Idaho. This claim is located near claims owned by Sunshine and borders other mining claims in which Sunshine has contractual interests [footnote omitted]. . . .

In 1946, Silver Surprize and Sunshine entered into an exploration agreement. Under that agreement, Sunshine conveyed to Silver Surprize its interest in three small claims located in the upper section of the Silver Surprize group, reserving

> . . . any *extralateral rights* within the exterior boundaries of said claims which Sunshine may have owned, in whole or in part, prior to the location of said claims.

(Italics ours.) In return, Silver Surprize conveyed an undivided one-half interest in the Surprize group to Sunshine, together with an unlimited right of surface and underground ingress and egress. Under this agreement Sunshine was to explore and develop the Surprize group as "in Sunshine's judgment is warranted as a sound mining venture." Gross receipts were to be shared equally between them after deductions for Sunshine's expenses. Sunshine was required to:

> . . . furnish Surprize, either monthly or quarterly, statements of production and costs, together with general information as to the amount, location and character of the work performed.

Silver Surprize was given the right to inspect the underground work being performed.

Sunshine has never rendered an accounting to Silver Surprize, although it removed in excess of $2 million worth of ore from that part of the YGV located within the Surprize group of claims. When an accounting was demanded just prior to commencement of this action in 1965, Sunshine refused.

The assigned errors present four major issues:

(1) Does Sunshine own extralateral rights in the YGV, thereby rendering the 1946 agreement inapplicable to that vein?

(2) If Sunshine does not own extralateral rights in the YGV, was that vein nevertheless excluded from the agreement?

(3) If the YGV is covered by the agreement, did Sunshine acquire title to the ore removed through the ouster of its cotenant, Silver Surprize, by adverse possession?

(4) Is the claim of Silver Surprize barred by statutes of limitation or laches?

I. DOES SUNSHINE OWN EXTRALATERAL RIGHTS TO THE YGV?

The rights of possession and enjoyment running to the locator of a mining claim are governed by the Act of May 10, 1872.[1] The act provides:

> The locators of all mining locations made on any mineral vein, lode, or ledge . . . shall have the exclusive right of possession and enjoyment of all the surface included within the lines of their locations, and of all veins, lodes, and ledges throughout their entire depth, the top or apex of which lies inside of such surface lines extended downward vertically, although such veins, lodes, or ledges may so far depart from a perpendicular in their course downward as to extend outside the vertical side lines of such surface locations. But their right of possession to such outside parts of such veins or ledges shall be confined to such portions thereof as lie between vertical planes drawn downward as above described, through the end lines of their locations, so continued in their own direction that such panes [sic] will intersect such exterior parts of such veins or ledges.

30 U.S.C. § 26 (1971). The right to follow a vein outside the boundaries of one's own claim has come to be called "extralateral rights." *See* 2C. Lindley, *Mines, American Law Relating to Mines and Mineral Lands* § 566 at 1252 (3d ed. 1914). Extralateral rights attach only to those veins which have their apex within the boundaries of a claim. The concept of extralateral rights is illustrated as follows:

---

[1] 30 U.S.C. § 26 (1971).

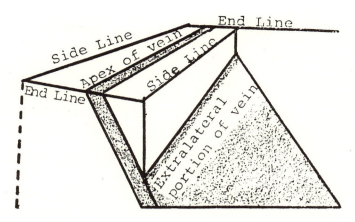

In other words, once a claimant establishes the apex of a vein within the boundaries of his claim, he may follow that vein on its downward course (dip) outside the claim so long as he remains within the extension of the end lines of his claim.

A locator of a mining claim is presumed to own all ore within the boundaries of his claim extended downward vertically. *St. Louis Mining & Milling Co. v. Montana Mining Co.* 194 U.S. 235, 239, 24 S.Ct. 654, 48 L.Ed. 953 (1904); *Calhoun Gold Mining Co. v. Ajax Gold Mining Co.,* 182 U.S. 499, 508, 21 S.Ct. 885, 45 L.Ed. 1200 (1901). Thus, one who asserts extralateral rights to a vein penetrating another's claim has the burden of proving that the vein has its apex within the boundaries of his claim. *Heinze v. Boston & M. Consol. Copper & Silver Mining Co.,* 30 Mont. 484, 77 P. 421 (1904); *Barker v. Condon,* 53 Mont. 585, 165 P. 909, 912 (1917); *Collins v. Bailey,* 22 Colo.App. 149, 125 P. 543, 548 (1912). This rule is firmly stated in *Consolidated Wyoming Gold Mining Co. v. Champion Mining Co.,* 63 F. 540, 550-51 (N.D.Cal. 1894):

> The respondent [surface owner] has the undoubted right to say to complainant [extralateral claimant], "Hands off of any and everything within my surface lines extending vertically downward, until you prove that you are working upon and following a vein which has its apex within your surface claim, of which you are the owner!"

Here, the trial court held that Sunshine failed to meet the substantial burden of proof required of an extralateral rights claimant.[2]

First, Sunshine contends that its extralateral right to the YGV was established by evidence sufficient to prove a surface apex in the Thin Claim and that entry of findings and conclusions to the contrary was error. We disagree.

The trial court found that Sunshine demonstrated the apex of some vein which courses throughout the length of the Thin Claim.

. . . but Sunshine has failed to prove continuity of the vein mineraliza-

---

[2] Although for purposes of this opinion we need not determine whether the YGV is a "vein, lode or ledge" to which extralateral rights attach, the trial court's findings based upon geological data, testimony of the experts, and prior judicial interpretation support the conclusion that the YGV between the 2700- and 3700-foot levels is a vein, lode or ledge as understood by the "practical miner." [citations omitted]

tion or gangue between that apex on the Thin Claim and the Yankee Girl Vein seen between the 2700 and 3700-foot levels. [Challenged finding of fact No. 33] Sunshine attempted to prove continuity and identity between the claimed surface apex on its Thin Claim and the YGV between the 2700-and 3700-foot level by mineral samples taken from drill holes along the projected downward course of the YGV between the surface and the 2700-foot level. The trial court characterized this evidence as "not too revealing," specifically finding that:

From reading the drill logs covering drilling above 2700 it is impossible to determine the configuration of the Yankee Girl Vein between the Yankee Girl adit and the 2700-foot level. Commencing with Hole 27—011 at the 2400-foot level to the surface, it is apparent that the vein is irregular and very narrow. It likewise does not possess those characteristics which distinguish it and give it its identity between the 3700 and 2700-foot levels. There is no concentration of mineralized stringers that interlace, converge, or weave in and out. There are many isolated stringers in the area, so it is imperative that in showing continuity Sunshine clearly demonstrate a concentration of mineralized stringers or a continuous single fissure. Apparently at the higher levels we are dealing with one vein with precise boundaries. Whether it is continuous over this vast distance of nearly half a mile cannot be established by the interceptions of diamond drill holes, some of which are 800 feet apart. It requires a large amount of geological speculation to tie this extremely narrow band of mineralized rock for over a half a mile with an apex on the basis of these drill hole intercepts. There is no way of telling whether the drill holes intercept the same narrow vein or band of mineralization at the various levels as they could be discontinued at any number of horizons. The drill holes certainly do not show a vein configuration similar to that between the 3700 and 2700-foot levels, and without that showing it seems extremely difficult to tie a single fissure or very narrow band existing in the St. Regis rock between the 2700-foot level and the surface with the Yankee Girl Vein at depth. [Challenged finding of fact No. 34]

There is no established degree of continuity or identity which an extralateral rights claimant must show between an apex within the boundaries of his claim and the vein he is pursuing into an adjoining claim. The required showing of continuity and identity is dependent upon the facts of each case. *Gold, Silver & Tungsten, Inc. v. Wallace,* 104 Colo. 273, 91 P.2d 975, 979 (1939). Here, the trial court was presented with mineral samples recovered from narrow drill holes often hundreds of feet apart between the surface and the 2700-foot level. The recovered samples contain material common, not only to the YGV between the 2700- and 3700-foot levels, but throughout the Coeur d'Alene Mining District. The trial court summed up the difficulty of establishing an apex without further demonstrative evidence:

Nor has Sunshine mined down dip from the surface on the Yankee Girl Vein to reveal for certain its angle of dip and configuration. It is that fact which makes the case somewhat unusual as compared to the reported cases. In all of the latter cases there has been extensive work at or near the surface of the claim demonstrating the strike and dip of the vein. In addition, what geological projections were made weren't over such extensive distances as involved in this case. This case is very unusual in that Sunshine has mined the ore at the lower levels and projected up-dip for nearly half a mile in an attempt to tie their mining in with a surface apex in claims under its control. [Unchallenged finding of fact No. 35]

Continuity and identity have been found to exist between a vein at depth and its surface apex based upon actual workings of the mine between those positions. In *Alameda Mining Co. v. Success Mining Co.,* 29 Idaho 618, 161 P. 862 (1916), the court observed, at page 867:

> In the case at bar, it is proper to consider that the proof of the *actual working of the mine,* the way it was worked, what was found therein, and the condition of the many open stopes and veins . . . *is certainly better evidence of the course,* dip, angles, spurs, and character of the vein *than any expert testimony* that could be given.

(Italics ours.) On the other hand, continuity and identity will not be presumed over substantial unexposed distances. For example, in *Collins v. Bailey, supra,* the court refused to find continuity between an apex and a vein over an unexposed distance of 550 feet. Again, in *Heinze v. Boston & M. Consol. Copper & Silver Mining Co., supra,* 77 P. at 423, the court said:

> . . . the plaintiffs have not by their operations so developed their own workings from the apex of their vein down to the disputed territory as to furnish substantial evidence that their claim is probably well founded. Indeed, while they concede that there is a vein in the defendant's ground dipping to the south, *their own contention is based exclusively upon the opinion of their engineers* that, if the vein having its apex in the Minnie Healy ground continues to dip at the same angle from certain points where it is exposed in the upper levels in their workings, it will reach the point where the defendant is conducting its operations. *This is not sufficient to overcome the presumption that the defendant owns the ores found beneath its own surface. This presumption may not be overturned by speculative conjecture or even intelligent guess.*

(Italics ours.)

Here, the area between the surface and the 2700-foot level is unworked and unexposed. The only physical evidence of continuity and identity over this distance are the drillhole samples taken at intervals of up to 800 feet. These samples show a pattern of mineralization common to the entire mining district, and not unique to the YGV. Consequently, the trial court properly found that Sunshine failed to meet its burden of proving a surface apex to the YGV.

Second, Sunshine contends that the trial court's unchallenged finding that the apex of the YGV "undoubtedly lies somewhere" on property owned or controlled by Sunshine is sufficient to establish its extralateral right to the vein. We disagree.

In support of this contention, Sunshine analogizes its position to that of a claimant of extralateral rights under a "blind apex." A "blind apex" is one that does not outcrop, but lies below the surface. However, such an apex must be proved with the same degree of certainty as a surface apex. *Flagstaff Silver Mining Co. of Utah, Ltd. v. Tarbet*, 8 Otto 463-470, 98 U.S. 463, 25 L.Ed. 253 (1879); *Calhoun Gold Mining Co. v. Ajax Gold Mining Co.*, 182 U.S. 499, 21 S.Ct. 885, 45 L.Ed. 1200 (1901); *Jim Butler Tonopah Mining Co. v. West End Consol. Mining Co.*, 247 U.S. 450, 38 S.Ct. 574, 62 L.Ed. 1207 (1918); *Iron Silver Mining Co. v. Murphy*, 3 F. 368 (D.Nev.1880); 1 Lindley, *Mines, A Treatise on the American Law Relating to Mines and Mineral Lands*, § 309 at 685 (3d ed. 1914). Thus, Sunshine's analogy to a "blind apex" is of little value.

The reason for requiring a greater showing of specificity as to the location of an apex than is present here is clear from the inherent limitation contained in the Act:

> But their right of possession to such outside parts of such veins . . . shall be confined to such portions thereof as lie between vertical planes drawn downward . . . *through the end lines of their locations . . .*

(Italics ours.) The following diagrams of the surface area of a claim illustrate some possible locations of an apex in relation to end lines and the effect that such location has upon the extent of extralateral rights granted under the Act:

1. In the ideal case the apex of a vein crosses both end lines of the claim entitling the locator to exercise his extralateral rights to the greatest extent allowable under the Act. *See* 1 Lindley on *Mines, American Law Relating to Mines and Mineral Lands*, § 309 at 684 (3d ed. 1914).

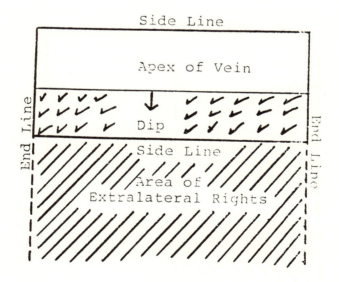

2. Where the apex of a vein crosses an end line of a claim and then passes out through a side line, the courts locate an imaginary end line at the point where the apex crosses the side line. *Del Monte Mining & Milling Co. v. Last Chance Mining & Milling Co.*, 171 U.S. 55, 18 S.Ct. 895, 43 L.Ed. 72 (1898); *Parrot Silver & Copper Co. v. Heinze*, 25 Mont. 139, 64 P. 326 (1901).

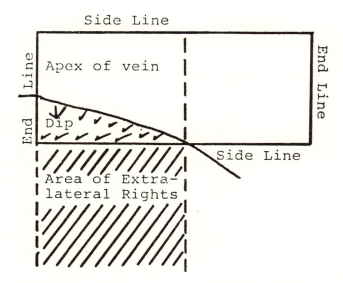

3. Where the apex of a vein crosses one end line and terminates at some point within the claim without crossing any other lines, an imaginary end line is drawn at the point where the vein terminates. *(See Republican Mining Co. v. Tyler Mining Co., 79 F. 733 (9th Cir.), cert. denied, 166 U.S. 720, 17 S.Ct. 998, 41 L.Ed. 1187 (1897)).*

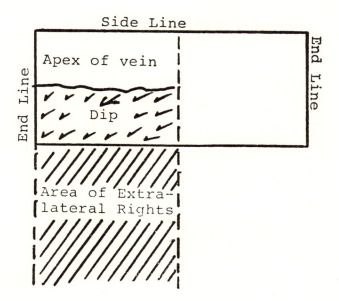

4. Where the apex of a vein crosses both side lines of a claim, the end lines become the side lines and the side lines become the end lines for purposes of extralateral rights. *See Flagstaff Silver Mining Co. of Utah, Ltd. v. Tarbet,* 8 Otto 463-470, 98 U.S. 463, 25 L.Ed. 253 (1879); *King v. Amy & Silversmith Consol. Mining Co.,* 152 U.S. 222, 14 S.Ct. 510, 38 L.Ed. 419 (1894); *Northport Smelting*

& Refining Co. v. Lone Pine Surprize Consol. Mines Co., 271 F. 105
(E.D.Wash.1920), *aff'd,* 278 F. 719 (9th Cir. 1922).

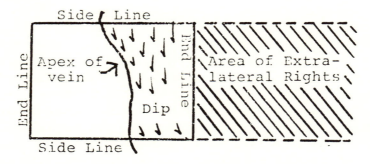

It is apparent from these illustrations that the location of an apex in relation
to the end lines of a claim determines the sweep of extralateral rights. Hence, the
apex must be located with some precision.

Sunshine virtually admits that it cannot precisely locate the apex of the YGV
in relation to the end lines of its claim or those claims under its control. The
intriguing argument that wherever the apex is located on such properties, it will
entitle Sunshine to extralateral rights to the YGV on the Silver Surprize claims is
illustrated as follows:

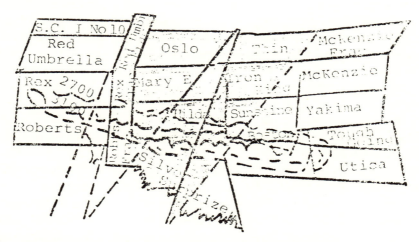

In effect, Sunshine is arguing for a "floating apex" concept.

To adopt Sunshine's "floating apex" concept would require this court to
ignore the express limitation contained in the Act of 1872, *i.e.,* an extralateral
rights claimant must prove the location of an apex of a vein in relation to the end
lines of his claim before he will be permitted to follow that vein into another's
property.[3] No authority is cited that would allow deviation from this long

---

[3] Arguably, a 1945 preliminary draft of the 1946 agreement proposed by Sunshine would have
eliminated its burden of establishing the exact location of the apex. The proposal was that
Sunshine reserve "any existing rights it may have, in whole or in part, to any veins or ore bodies
within the conveyed area which *apex north* thereof [Surprize Group] . . ." (Italics ours.) (Ex.
298) This provision was rejected by Silver Surprize.

established statutory limitation and our research discloses none. Curtis H. Lindley, the foremost authority on mining law, describes the spirit in which courts should approach statutes on this subject by quoting Justice Brewer in *Del Monte Mining & Milling Co. v. Last Chance Mining & Milling Co., supra,* 18 S.Ct. at 899:

> And it must be borne in mind in considering the questions presented that we are dealing simply with statutory rights. There is no showing of any local customs or rules affecting the rights defined in and prescribed by the statute, *and beyond the terms of the statute courts may not go. They have no power of legislation. They cannot assume the existence of any natural equity, and rule that by reason of such equity a party may follow a vein into the territory of his neighbor, and appropriate it to his own use. If cases arise for which congress has made no provision, the courts cannot supply the defect. Congress having prescribed the conditions upon which extralateral rights may be acquired, a party must bring himself within those conditions, or else be content with simply the mineral beneath the surface of his territory.* It is undoubtedly true that the primary thought of the statute is the disposal of the mines and minerals, and in the interpretation of the statute this primary purpose must be recognized, and given effect. Hence, whenever a party has acquired the title to ground within whose surface area is the apex of a vein with a few or many feet along its course or strike, a right to follow that vein on its dip for the same length ought to be awarded to him if it can be done, and only if it can be done, under any fair and natural construction of the language of the statute. If the surface of the ground was everywhere level, and veins constantly pursued a straight line, there would be little difficulty in legislation to provide for all contingencies; but mineral is apt to be found in mountainous regions where great irregularity of surface exists, and the course or strike of the veins is as irregular as the surface, so that many cases may arise in which statutory provisions will fail to secure to a discoverer of a vein such an amount thereof as equitably it would seem he ought to receive.

(Italics ours.) 2 Lindley, Mines, *American Law Relating to Mines and Mineral Lands* § 581 at 1295 (3d ed. 1914). Justice Brewer further said:

> We make these observations because we find in some of the opinions assertions by the writers that they have devised rules which will work out equitable solutions of all difficulties. Perhaps those rules may have all the virtues which are claimed for them, and, if so, it were well if congress could be pursuaded to enact them into statute; but, be that as it may , the question in the courts is not what is equity, but what saith the statute.

This approach to the act was recognized in *Quilp Gold Mining Co. v. Republic Mines Corp.,* 96 Wash. 439, 450-51, 165 P. 57, 61 (1917):

> [W]e must keep in view that we are dealing with contractual rights of the parties, and also that the parties in contracting with reference to the matter had in view their statutory rights as provided by the mining statutes of the United States. Congress prescribed the conditions upon which extralateral rights might be acquired; and a party dealing with mining locations neces-

sarily must bring himself within those conditions, or else be content with simply the mineral beneath the surface of his own territory.

The "floating apex" concept was not contemplated by the act of 1872. That act was written for the day when locators of claims ordinarily discovered the apex of veins at the surface of the ground. To encourage the discovery of minerals, the locator was granted the right to pursue that vein on dip outside the sidelines of his claim but within the extension of the end lines of his claim. The instant case is evidence of the fact that times have changed. Here, Sunshine has a network of tunnels radiating from its Jewell Shaft intersecting veins many thousands of feet underground. One of these tunnels intersected the YGV at a depth of about 3100 feet. Under these circumstances, a substantial burden is placed upon an extralateral claimant to overcome the presumption that an owner of a claim owns all of the ore within the boundaries of his claim. Mining up-dip to establish an apex at or near surface is often not economically justifiable. To avoid this burden, parties frequently enter into exploration agreements, as the parties attempted to do in this case. This practice may account for the lack of recent case authority on apex law.

Modern mining practice seems to require amendment of the act of 1872 to deal specifically with the problems that arise from deep underground discoveries. However, this court may not so legislate. Under existing law, the trial court, based on substantial evidence, properly concluded that because Sunshine did not prove the location of an apex to the YGV in relation to the end lines of any of its claims, it failed to prove its right to remove ore from beneath the Surprize group of claims by virtue of its extralateral rights to the YGV.

NOTES

1. Section 26 of the mining law is in derogation of two well established principles of the common law of property. First, it conflicts with the maxim "first in time, first in right." Thus, the senior locator who does not locate on the apex will find that his rights are subordinate to the junior locator who does so locate. Second, it conflicts with the maxim *"Cujus est solum ejus est usque ad coelum et ad infernos"* i.e., to whomsoever the soil belongs, he owns also to the sky and to the depths. In light of this conflict, it is not surprising that section 26 has been strictly construed, and that the courts have insisted upon literal compliance with its terms before extralateral rights will be awarded.

2. The apex of a vein is the leading or highest edge of the vein. This is not necessarily the portion of the vein closest to the surface. Thus, a portion of vein may be exposed at the surface due to errosion, and yet, if the vein goes underground and rises above the exposed portion within a mountain, the exposed portion would not be the highest edge and would not be the apex.

3. If a vein does not outcrop at the surface, it is said to have a blind apex. If a vein outcrops on land that is not open to entry, for example because it has already been disposed of pursuant to some other public land law, then it is possible to establish a theoretical apex. The "theoretical apex" is that portion of the vein that would constitute the apex if the vein had no actual existence in the land disposed of. *See* 1 AMERICAN LAW OF MINING § 5.14 (1982).

4. One of the essential requisites to the successful assertion of extralateral rights is continuity of the vein in question. "For the exercise of [extralateral rights] it must appear that the vein outside is identical with and a continuation of the one inside those lines. But if the mineral disappears or the fissure with its walls of the same rock disappears, so that its identity can no longer be traced, the right to pursue it outside of the perpendicular lines of claimant's survey is gone [Syllabus]." *Iron Silver Min. Co. v. Chessman,* 116 U.S. 529 (1885). The one asserting extralateral rights has the burden of proving continuity. *Collins v. Bailey,* 22 Colo. App. 149, 125 P. 543 (1912). Continuity is a question of fact, and it must be established by tracing the fissure itself. Speculation, conjecture or mathematical projection is not sufficient. *Id.* at 161-162, 125 P. at 548.

5. The reason for the requirement of parallel end lines is not difficult to discern. Were it not for the requirement, diverging endlines would eventually encompass the globe. The intent of the congress was to permit the exercise of extralateral right for no more than 1500 feet along the vein. If the end lines converged rather than diverged, would it be appropriate to allow extralateral rights notwithstanding the non-parallelism of the end lines? *See Grant v. Pilgrim,* 95 F.2d 562 (9th Cir. 1938).

6. Extralateral rights permit the miner to follow the dip or downward course of the vein outside of the sidelines of his claim. In order to assert extralateral rights, therefore, it must be shown that the vein has a downward course. A perfectly horizontal vein would, presumably, not carry with it any extralateral rights.

10 PATENT PROCEDURES

A. In general
   State of South Dakota v. Andrus
B. Patent procedures
   Freese v. United States
   California Coastal Commission v. Granite Rock Company
C. Protests, contents and adverse suits
   In Re Pacific Coast Molybdenum Co.
   United States v. Carlile

A. In General

STATE OF SOUTH DAKOTA V. ANDRUS
614 F.2d 1190 (8th Cir. 1980)

Before BRIGHT and HENLEY, Circuit Judges, and REGAN, Senior District Judge.

HENLEY, Circuit Judge.

This is an appeal from a judgment entered by The Honorable Andrew W. Bogue of the United States District Court for the District of South Dakota dismissing the State of South Dakota's suit in which the State sought declaratory and injunctive relief to compel the United States Department of Interior to prepare an Environmental Impact Statement (EIS) prior to its issuance of a mineral patent to the Pittsburgh Pacific Company (Pittsburgh). On appeal the State contends that the district court erred and asks us to reverse and remand this case for a trial on the merits. After careful review of the district court's judgment, we affirm.

I

Pittsburgh filed an application under the General Mining Act of 1872, 30 U.S.C. § 21 et seq., for a mineral patent to twelve contiguous twenty acre mining claims located within the Black Hills National Forest in Lawrence County, South Dakota. Pittsburgh claimed discovery of some 160 million tons of relatively low grade iron ore and sought a mineral patent covering the discovery lands. Pittsburgh proposed to mine 96 million tons of the ore through open pit mining at an annual rate of approximately seven million long tons a year. The general plan of operation also included processing the best of this ore into hard pellets as well as loading these pellets into railroad cars for shipping.

In 1971, however, Pittsburgh's application for a mineral patent was contested, at the request of the United States Forest Service, by the Bureau of Land Management. The Bureau contended that Pittsburgh had not discovered a valuable mineral deposit under the 1872 Mining Act. The Administrative Law Judge nonetheless dismissed the complaint and approved the mineral patent.

The Bureau then appealed the decision to the Interior Board of Land Appeals alleging that the Administrative Law Judge erred in his geological and economic analysis in determining whether Pittsburgh had discovered a "valuable" deposit. In addition, the State of South Dakota petitioned to intervene and was permitted to file an amicus brief in which the State argued, *inter alia,* that the Administrative Law Judge had not given proper consideration to the cost of compliance with environmental quality statutes. Recognizing that Pittsburgh's proposed mining project would take 240 to 1,140 acres from a national forest and discard approximately 2.3 million tons of waste annually, the State argued that the Secretary must prepare an EIS before a mineral patent could issue. The Board determined that an EIS need not be prepared prior to the issuance of a mineral patent for these claims. *United States v. Pittsburgh,* 30 IBLA 388 (1977). The Board, however, set aside the decision of the Administrative Law Judge on other grounds and remanded the case for further hearings with respect to the expense of complying with environmental laws as well as any other issue which might arise.

Subsequently, the State filed an original action in federal district court seeking to compel preparation of an EIS prior to the issuance of a mineral patent naming as defendants the United States Department of the Interior and Pittsburgh. Both defendants moved to dismiss contending the issuance of a mineral patent is not a major federal action which requires an EIS, and Judge Bogue granted the motion. *South Dakota v. Andrus,* 462 F.Supp. 905 (D.S.D. 1978).

II

The issue on this appeal is whether the United States Department of the Interior is required by § 102(2)(C) of the National Environmental Policy Act, 42 U.S.C. § 4332(C) to file an EIS prior to the issuance of a mineral patent [footnote omitted].

Our starting point is, of course, the statutory language. Section 102(2)(C) provides in part that an EIS is required for "major Federal actions significantly affecting the quality of the human environment [footnote omitted]." Applied to this case, § 102(2)(C) mandates the filing of an EIS if (1) the issuance of a mineral patent is an "action" within the meaning of the provision, and (2) the alleged federal action is "major" in the sense that it significantly affects the quality of the human environment.

A

We turn first to the question whether the granting of a mineral patent constitutes an "action" within the meaning of NEPA. As the district court noted, it is well established that the issuance of a mineral patent is a ministerial act. Both the Supreme Court, in a series of decisions in the early part of this century,

Wilbur v. United States ex rel. Krushnic, 280 U.S. 306, 318-19, 50 S.Ct. 103, 105, 74 L.Ed. 445 (1929); *Cameron v. United States,* 252 U.S. 450, 454, 40 S.Ct. 410, 64 L.Ed. 659 (1920); *Roberts v. United States,* 176 U.S. 221, 231, 20 S.Ct. 376, 379, 44 L.Ed. 443 (1900), and, more recently, the Interior Board of Land Appeals, *United States v. Kosanke Sand Corp.,* 12 IBLA 282, 290-91 (1973); *United States v. O'Leary,* 63 ID 341 (1956),[1] have so concluded.

Ministerial acts, however, have generally been held outside the ambit of NEPA's EIS requirement. Reasoning that the primary purpose of the impact statement is to aid agency decisionmaking, courts have indicated that nondiscretionary acts should be exempt from the requirement. *N.A.A.C.P. v. Medical Center, Inc.,* 584 F.2d 619, 634 (2d Cir. 1978); *Monroe County Conservation Council, Inc. v. Volpe,* 472 F.2d 693, 697 (2d Cir. 1972); *Environmental Defense Fund, Inc. v. Corps of Engineers of United States Army,* 470 F.2d 289, 294 (8th Cir. 1972), *cert denied,* 412 U.S. 931, 93 S.Ct. 2749, 37 L.Ed.2d 160 (1973); *Calvert Cliffs' Coordinating Committee, Inc. v. A.E.C.,* 146 U.S.App.D.C. 33, 38, 449 F.2d 1109, 1114 (D.C.Cir.1971).

In light of these decisions, it is at least doubtful that the Secretary's nondiscretionary approval of a mineral patent constitutes an "action" under § 102(2)(C).[2]

B

But even if a ministerial act may in some circumstances fall within § 102(2)(C), we still cannot say that the issuance of a mineral patent is a "major" federal action under the statute. This conclusion does not stem from the court's belief that an agency itself must propose to build a facility and directly affect the environment in order to constitute a "major" federal action within the meaning of NEPA. We fully recognize that NEPA's impact statement procedure has been held to apply where the federal government grants a lease, *Cady v. Morton,* 527 F.2d 786 (9th Cir. 1975); *Davis v. Morton,* 469 F.2d 593 (10th Cir. 1972); issues a permit or license, *Greene County Planning Board v. F.P.C.,* 455 F.2d 412 (2d Cir.), *cert. denied,* 409 U.S. 849, 93 S.Ct. 56, 34 L.Ed.2d 90 (1972); or approves

---

[1] As the district court observed, *South Dakota v. Andrus, supra,* 462 F.Supp. at 907, the Board, in *United States v. Kosanke Sand Corp., supra,* concluded:
Upon satisfaction of the requirements of the statute, the holder of a valid mining claim has an absolute right to a patent from the United States conveying fee title to the land within the claim, and the actions taken by the Secretary of the Interior in processing an application for patent by such claimant are not discretionary; issuance of a patent can be compelled by court order. [Citations omitted.] The patent may contain no conditions not authorized by law. [Citation omitted.] The claimant need not, however, apply for patent to preserve his property right in the claim, but may if he chooses continue to extract and freely dispose of the locatable minerals until the claim is exhausted, without ever having acquired full legal title to the land. [Citations omitted.] The patent, if issued, conveys fee simple title to the land within the claim, but does nothing to enlarge or diminish the claimant's right to its locatable mineral resources. 30 U.S.C. § 26 (1971).

[2] The Supreme Court has not yet resolved the issue of whether nondiscretionary actions fall within the scope of NEPA's EIS requirement. Although the Tenth Circuit in its 1975 decision, *Scenic Rivers Ass'n v. Lynn,* 520 F.2d 240, 245 (10th Cir. 1975), *rev'd on other grounds sub nom. Flint Ridge Development Co. v. Scenic Rivers Ass'n,* 426 U.S. 776, 96 S.Ct. 2430, 49 L.Ed.2d 205 (1976), held that ministerial acts constitute "major federal actions" under NEPA, the Supreme Court in reversing did not discuss this issue.

or funds state highway projects, *Iowa Citizens for Environmental Quality, Inc. v. Volpe,* 487 F.2d 849 (8th Cir. 1973); *Lathan v. Volpe,* 455 F.2d 1111 (9th Cir. 1971).

In each of these cases, however, an agency took a "major" federal action because it enabled a private party to act so as to significantly affect the environment. Such enablements have consistently been held subject to N.E.P.A. *See National Forest Preservation v. Butz,* 485 F.2d 408, 412 (9th Cir. 1973), and authorities cited therein. But in the instant case, the granting of a mineral patent does not enable the private party, Pittsburgh, to do anything. Unlike the case where a lease, permit or license is required before the particular project can begin, the issuance of a mineral patent is not a precondition which enables a party to begin mining operations. 30 U.S.C. § 26.

As the Supreme Court noted in *Union Oil Co. v. Smith,* 249 U.S. 337, 39 S.Ct. 308, 63 L.Ed. 635 (1919), if a qualified locator of a mining claim locates, marks and records his claim to unappropriated public lands in accordance with federal and local law, he has an "exclusive right of possession to the extent of his claim as located, with the right to extract the minerals, even to exhaustion, without paying any royalty to the United States as owner, and without ever applying for a patent. . . ." *Id.* at 348-49, 39 S.Ct. at 311. Furthermore, in *Wilbur v. United States ex rel. Krushnic, supra,* 280 U.S. at 316-17, 50 S.Ct. at 104, the Court revealed:

> The rule is established by innumerable decisions of this Court, and of state and lower federal courts, that, when the location of a mining claim is perfected under the law, it has the effect of a grant by the United States of the right of present and exclusive possession . . . so long as he complies with the provisions of the mining laws, his possessory right, for all practical purposes of ownership, is as good as though secured by patent.

In recent years the mining laws governing the locating of mineral claims have remained unchanged, 30 U.S.C. §§ 22, 26, and modern decisions have continued to allow locators of mining claims to extract minerals without a patent provided they have met the statutory prerequisites. *See, e.g., Lombardo Turquoise Milling & Mining Co. v. Hemanes,* 430 F.Supp. 429 (D.Nev. 1977).

In light of the fact that a mineral patent in actuality is not a federal determination which enables the party to mine, we conclude in present context that the granting of such a patent is not a "major" federal action within the meaning of § 102(2)(C).

III

In reaching this conclusion, we do not decide the question whether an EIS should be required at some point after the mineral patent has issued. While a federal agency need not prepare an EIS during the "germination process of a potential proposal," *Kleppe v. Sierra Club,* 427 U.S. 390, 401 n.12, 406, 96 S.Ct. 2718, 2728, 49 L.Ed.2d 576 (1976), this is not to say that at some later date an EIS will not be required. We note that Pittsburgh's proposed mining project is substantial and that if Pittsburgh decides to build the mine many actions may be necessary. For example, the claims at issue will presumedly need permits from the Forest Service for roads, water pipelines and railroad rights of way. 43 U.S.C.

§ 1761(a)(1) and (a)(6). Moreover, the company may possibly seek to make land exchanges with the Forest Service. We leave to another day the question whether an EIS would be required in connection with any one or more such actions.

It is sufficient for the moment to conclude that in the present case an EIS need not be filed prior to the issuance of a mineral patent. Accordingly, the judgment of the district court is affirmed.

NOTES

1. Issuance of the patent does not mean that all mining activity can take place without the purview of NEPA. To the extent that BLM or Forest Service approvals are required for the conduct of mining operations (such as the approval of access routes either before or after the issuance of a patent) major federal action may be involved and compliance with NEPA required.

2. Does it follow that because the locator can mine a deposit without the necessity of obtaining a patent that the issuance of a patent is not major federal action? Does this argument overlook the fact that while obtaining a patent may not be a legal necessity it is often a practical one?

3. As a general proposition, no permission is required from the BLM to prospect or explore for minerals on the public domain. If, however, the exploratory work is to take place in lands under wilderness review, and if the activity is one listed in 43 C.F.R. § 3802.1-1, i.e., the type of activity that might impair the area's suitability for inclusion in the wilderness system, then the miner's plan of operations must be approved by the BLM. Such approval, in appropriate circumstances, would constitute major federal action.

Similarly, the Forest Service has promulgated regulations requiring that the locator, "to the extent possible, harmonize operations with scenic values." The Forest Service regulations are more detailed than the BLM's and apply to all Forest Service lands, not just lands slated for wilderness review. 36 C.F.R. § 252.8(d).

B. Patent Procedures

FREESE V. UNITED STATES
639 F.2d 754 (Ct. Cl. 1981)

Before FRIEDMAN, Chief Judge, and KUNZIG and BENNETT, Judges.
ON CROSS-MOTIONS FOR PARTIAL SUMMARY JUDGMENT
KUNZIG, Judge:
This taking case comes before the court on the parties cross-motions for partial summary judgment on Count I of plaintiff's petition. Plaintiff is the owner of five unpatented mining claims located on federal lands. In 1972, Congress incorporated these lands into the newly established Sawtooth National Recrea-

tion Area (Sawtooth). The law creating Sawtooth expressly terminated the ability of existing claimholders to proceed to patent upon claims located in the recreation area, i.e., to obtain fee title to the lands in which the claims are located. This case concerns the question whether Congress' action amounts to an unconstitutional taking by inverse condemnation. We hold for the Government. While plaintiff's opportunities have been somewhat narrowed, plaintiff has not suffered a deprivation of "private property" within the meaning of the fifth amendment.

Mining claims upon lands owned by the United States are "initiated by prospecting for minerals thereon, and, upon the discovery of minerals, by locating the lands upon which such discovery has been made. A location is made by (a) staking the corners of the claim . . . (b) posting notice of location thereon, and (c) complying with the State laws, regarding the recording of the location in the county recorder's office. . . ." 43 C.F.R. § 3831.1 (1979). In order to hold the claim, "not less than $100 worth of labor must be performed or improvements made thereon annually." 43 C.F.R. § 3851.1 (1979). The owner of the mining claim "shall have the exclusive right of possession and enjoyment" of the claim. 30 U.S.C. § 26 (1976). Ownership of a mining claim does not confer fee title to the lands within which the claim is located. Fee title passes only upon the issuance of a patent therefor. See Best v. Humboldt Placer Mining Co., 371 U.S. 334, 336, 83 S.Ct. 379, 382, 9 L.Ed.2d 350 (1963); Benson Mining and Smelting Co. v. Alta Mining and Smelting Co., 145 U.S. 428, 430, 12 S.Ct. 877, 878, 36 L.Ed. 762 (1892).

A patent for any land claimed and located for valuable deposits may be obtained in the following manner: Any person . . . or corporation authorized to locate a claim under . . . this title [Mineral Lands and Regulations in General] . . . having claimed and located a piece of land for such purposes, who has . . . complied with the terms of this title . . . may file in the proper land office an application for a patent, under oath, showing such compliance, together with a plat and field notes of the claim . . . made by or under the direction of the Director of the Bureau of Land Management, showing accurately the boundaries of the claim . . . which shall be distinctly marked by monuments on the ground, and shall post a copy of such plat, together with a notice of such application for a patent, in a conspicuous place on the land embraced in such plat previous to the filing of the application for a patent, and shall file an affidavit of at least two persons that such notice has been duly posted, and shall file a copy of the notice in such land office, and shall thereupon be entitled to a patent for the land, in the manner following: The register of the land office, upon the filing of such application, plat, field notes, notices, and affidavits, shall publish a notice that such application has been made, for the period of sixty days, in a newspaper to be by him designated as published nearest to such claim; and he shall also post such notice in his office for the same period. The claimant at the time of filing this application, or at any time thereafter, within the sixty days of publication, shall file with the register a certificate of the Director of the Bureau of Land Management that $500 worth of labor has been expended or improvements made upon the claim by himself or grantors; that the plat is correct, with such further description by such reference to natural objects or permanent monuments as shall identify the claim, and furnish an accurate description, to be incorporated in the patent. At the expiration of the sixty days of publication the claimant shall file his affidavit, showing that the plat and notice have been posted in a conspicuous place on the claim during such period of publication. If no adverse claim shall have been filed with the register of the proper land office at the expiration of the sixty days of publication, it shall be assumed that the applicant is entitled to a patent, upon the payment to the proper officer of $5 per acre, and that no adverse claim exists; and thereafter no objection from third parties to the issuance of a patent shall be heard, except it be shown that the appellant has failed to comply with the terms of . . . this title . . . .

30 U.S.C. § 29 (1976). *See generally* 43 C.F.R.§§ 3861.1-3864.1-4 (1979).

Between the years 1955 and 1970, plaintiff acquired five unpatented mining claims upon federal lands located in Idaho.[3] In 1972 Congress established the Sawtooth National Recreation Area, including within its boundaries the lands containing plaintiff's claims. Pub.L.No. 92-400, August 22, 1972, 86 Stat. 612, 16 U.S.C. §§ 460aa-460aa-14 (1976) (Sawtooth Act). The Sawtooth Act expressly provides that, "Subject to valid existing rights, all Federal lands located in the recreation area are hereby withdrawn from all forms of location, entry, and patent under the mining laws of the United States." 16 U.S.C. § 460aa-9 (1976). The Act further provides that, "Patents shall not hereafter be issued for locations and claims heretofore made in the recreation area under the mining laws of the United States." 16 U.S.C. § 460aa-11 (1976). The impact of these provisions is that, while the right of possession and enjoyment attaching to valid claims existing upon the effective date of the Act is expressly recognized and preserved, the ability to obtain patents upon these claims is expressly denied. *See* Conf. Rep.No. 92-1276, 92d Cong. 2d Sess., *reprinted in* [1972] U.S.Code Cong. & Ad.News 3013, 3047. *See generally* 36 C.F.R. §§ 292.14-292.18 (1979). Plaintiff now contends that he has suffered an unconstitutional taking by virtue of the denial of his ability to obtain patents upon the five unpatented mining claims which he held upon the effective date of the Act.[4] Plaintiff's contention has no merit. There is no maintainable legal theory in support of his view that he has suffered a deprivation of "private property" as that term is used in the fifth amendment.

As Professor Tribe aptly observes: "[N]othing could be clearer, even today, than that a sufficiently unambiguous governmental seizure of private property

---

[3] The United States has the power under the mining laws to initiate a contest of the validity of unpatented mining locations. *See United States v. Springer,* 491 F.2d 239, 241 (9th Cir.) *cert. denied,* 419 U.S. 834, 95 S. Ct. 60, 42 L.Ed. 2d 60 (1974). Heretofore, the Government has failed to initiate any such contest against plaintiff's claims. Solely for the purpose of disposing of the pending motions, the Government requests this court to assume *arguendo* the validity of plaintiff's claims.

[4] For purposes of these cross-motions, plaintiff makes no contention that he has actually been hindered in any way in his ability to exploit his mining claims. His argument relates solely to the denial of his ability to obtain patents, i.e., fee title to the lands.

for public use—a sufficiently clear laying-on of official hands followed by a transfer of possession and title to the general public—is unconstitutional unless followed by payment to the former owner of the fair market value of what was taken." L. Tribe, *American Constitutional Law* § 9-2, at 459 (1978). " 'Property', as used in the constitutional provision mandating that property shall not be taken for public use without just compensation, is treated as a word of most general import and liberally construed." J. Sackman, 2 *Nichols on Eminent Domain* § 5.1[1] (Rev. 3d ed. 1979).

> [T]he corporeal object, (although the subject of property), is, when coupled with possession, merely the indicia—the visible manifestation—of invisible rights. Property in a specified object . . . is composed of the rights of use, enjoyment and disposition of such object, to the exclusion of all others.

Id.[5]

It is a matter beyond dispute that federal mining claims are "private property" enjoying the protection of the fifth amendment. Judge Finesilver of the federal district court has nicely summarized the applicable concepts:

> A mining claim is an interest in land which cannot be unreasonably or unfairly dissolved at the whim of the Interior Department. Once there is a valid discovery and proper location, a mining claim, in the language of the Supreme Court, is "real property in the highest sense." Legal title to the land remains in the United States, but the claimant enjoys a valid, equitable, possessory title, subject to taxation, transferable by deed or devise, and otherwise possessing the incidents of real property."

Oil Shale Corp. v. Morton, 370 F.Supp. 108, 124 (D.Colo. 1973). Had plaintiff suffered an uncompensated divestment of his federal mining claims, we would have a clear constitutional violation. *See North American Transportation & Trading Co. v. United States,* 53 Ct.Cl. 424 (1918), aff'd, 253 U.S. 330, 40 S.Ct. 518, 64 L.Ed. 935 (1920). The case before us, however, does not present such facts. Instead, all of plaintiff's "valid existing rights" in his mining claims are expressly recognized and preserved by the Sawtooth Act. His rights of use, enjoyment and disposition in his unpatented mining claims remain undiminished.

Plaintiff's argument rests upon the two following propositions: 1) that his

---

[5] In *United States v. General Motors Corp.,* 323 U.S. 373, 377-378, 65 S.Ct. 357, 359, 89 L.Ed. 311 (1945), the Supreme Court wrote:

> The critical terms [in the just compensation clause] are "property," "taken" and "just compensation." It is conceivable that the first [term] was used in its vulgar and untechnical sense of the physical thing with respect to which the citizen exercises rights recognized by law. On the other hand, it may have been employed in a more accurate sense to denote the group of rights inhering in the citizen's relation to the physical thing, as the right to possess, use and dispose of it. In point of fact, the construction given the phrase has been the latter. When the sovereign exercises the power of eminent domain it substitutes itself in relation to the physical thing in question in place of him who formerly bore the relation to that thing, which we denominate ownership. In other words, it deals with what lawyers term the individual's "interest" in the thing in question. That interest may comprise the group of rights for which the shorthand term is "a fee simple" or it may be the interest known as an "estate or tenancy for years," as in the present instance. The constitutional provision is addressed to every sort of interest the citizen may possess.

right to the issuance of a patent upon each of his mining claims vested as soon as he completed the discovery and location of each claim, and 2) that, as a consequence, he has suffered an unconstitutional divestment of his vested rights through the denial of his ability to obtain patents upon his claims. Plaintiff is correct in his assumption that the divestment of a vested right to a patent is tantamount to divestment of the patent itself, i.e., a divestment of "property". *See Benson Mining and Smelting Co. v. Alta Mining and Smelting Co.,* 145 U.S. 428, 431, 433, 12 S.Ct. 877, 878, 879, 36 L.Ed.762 (1892); *Global Exploration and Development Corp. v. United States,* Ct.Cl. No. 135-78 (Order entered Sept. 29, 1978). The flaw in plaintiff's argument, however, inheres in his view that he has a vested right to the issuance of patents. The law is well-settled that this vested right does not arise until there has been full compliance with the extensive procedures set forth in the federal mining laws for the obtaining of a patent. *See Wyoming v. United States,* 255 U.S. 489, 497, 41 S.Ct. 393, 395, 65 L.Ed. 742 (1921); *Benson Mining and Smelting Co. v. Alta Mining and Smelting Co.,* 145 U.S. 428, 433, 12 S.Ct. 877, 879, 36 L.Ed. 762 (1892); *Willcoxson v. United States,* 313 F.2d 884, 888 (D.C.Cir.), *cert. denied,* 373 U.S. 932, 83 S.Ct. 1538, 10 L.Ed.2d 690 (1963); *cf. Andrus v. Utah,* 446 U.S. 500, 100 S.Ct. 1803, 64 L.Ed.2d 458 (1980) (Taylor Grazing Act reserves discretion on the part of Interior Secretary to classify lands within a federal grazing district as proper for school indemnity selection). In this case, plaintiff had not yet taken the first step towards obtaining patents upon any of his mining claims when the Sawtooth Act intervened on August 22, 1972.

The case before us thus ultimately reduces to the question whether plaintiff has suffered an unconstitutional divestment solely by virtue of the fact that he no longer has the option *to apply for* patents upon his claims. Common sense dictates a negative response. At best, plaintiff has suffered a denial of the opportunity to obtain greater property than that which he owned upon the effective date of the Sawtooth Act. This cannot fairly be deemed the divestment of a property interest, save by the most overt bootstrapping.

All other arguments raised by plaintiff, although not directly addressed by this opinion, have been considered and found to be without merit.

Accordingly, after consideration of the submissions of the parties, without oral argument of counsel, plaintiff's motion for partial summary judgment is denied. Defendant's motion for partial summary judgment is granted. Count I of the plaintiff's petition is dismissed.

NOTES

1. Regulations of the department require that all patent applications be accompanied by either a certificate of title or an abstract of title showing "full title" in the applicant. 43 C.F.R. § 3862.1-3 (1982). This requirement does not mean that the applicant is required to address the existence of actual or potential conflicting claims. "It does not require that the applicant demonstrate that his title is legally superior to all other existing claims, but merely that he is successor to possessory title dating back to the original location of the claim which he seeks to patent, and that he presently has full legal possessory title of record." *John R. Meadows,* 43 I.B.L.A. 35, 38 (1979).

2. In addition to the adverse claim, any interested party may file a protest to the issuance of a patent. See section C, *infra.*

3. The Interior Department regulations covering patents and patent procedures are found at 43 C.F.R. Part 3860. A detailed description of patent procedures and the patent application is contained in T. MALLEY, MINING LAW FROM LOCATION TO PATENT (1985) at 461-90. For a scholarly, but slightly outdated critique of BLM patent procedures, *see* Strauss, *Mining Claims on Public Lands: A Study of Interior Department Procedures,* 1974 UTAH L. REV. 185 (1974). *See also* Erisman and Williams, *Watts up for Patenting,* 29 ROCKY MOUNTAIN MINERAL LAW INSTITUTE 321 (1983).

The advantages of obtaining a patent are obvious. One acquires an indefeasible fee title to land for only a token charge. There are disadvantages as well, however. Consider the following opinion.

CALIFORNIA COASTAL COMMISSION v. GRANITE ROCK COMPANY
_____ U.S. _____, 107 S.Ct. 1419 (1987)

Justice O'CONNOR delivered the opinion of the Court.

This case presents the question whether Forest Service regulations, federal land use statutes and regulations, or the Coastal Zone Management Act (CZMA), 16 U.S.C. § 1451 *et seq.* (1982 ed. and Supp. III), pre-empt the California Coastal Commission's imposition of a permit requirement on operation of an unpatented mining claim in a national forest.

I

Granite Rock Company is a privately owned firm that mines chemical and pharmaceutical grade white limestone. Under the Mining Act of 1872, 17 Stat. 91, codified, as amended, at 30 U.S.C. § 22 *et seq.,* a private citizen may enter federal lands to explore for mineral deposits. If a person locates a valuable mineral deposit on federal land, and perfects the claim by properly staking it and complying with other statutory requirements, the claimant "shall have the exclusive right of possession and enjoyment of all the surface included within the lines of their locations," 30 U.S.C. § 26, although the United States retains title to the land. The holder of a perfected mining claim may secure a patent to the land by complying with the requirements of the Mining Act and regulations promulgated thereunder, see 43 CFR § 3861.1 *et seq.* (1986), and, upon issuance of the patent, legal title to the land passes to the patentholder. Granite Rock holds unpatented mining claims on federally owned lands on and around Mount Pico Blanco in the Big Sur region of Los Padres National Forest.

From 1959 to 1980, Granite Rock removed small samples of limestone from this area for mineral analysis. In 1980, in accordance with federal regulations, see 36 CFR § 228.1 *et seq.* (1986), Granite Rock submitted to the Forest Service a 5-year plan of operations for the removal of substantial amounts of limestone.

The plan discussed the location and appearance of the mining operation, including the size and shape of excavations, the location of all access roads and the storage of any overburden. App. 27-34. The Forest Service prepared an Environmental Assessment of the plan. *Id.,* at 38-53. The Assessment recommended modifications of the plan, and the responsible Forest Service Acting District Ranger approved the plan with the recommended modifications in 1981. *Id.,* at 54. Shortly after Forest Service approval of the modified plan of operations, Granite Rock began to mine.

Under the California Coastal Act (CCA), Cal.Pub.Res.Code Ann. § 30000 *et seq.,* any person undertaking any development, including mining, in the State's coastal zone must secure a permit from the California Coastal Commission. §§ 30106, 30600. According to the CCA, the Coastal Commission exercises the State's police power and constitutes the State's coastal zone management program for purposes of the federal CZMA, described *infra,* at _____. In 1983 the Coastal Commission instructed Granite Rock to apply for a coastal development permit for any mining undertaken after the date of the Commission's letter.[1]

Granite Rock immediately filed an action in the United States District Court for the Northern District of California seeking to enjoin officials of the Coastal Commission from compelling Granite Rock to comply with the Coastal Commission permit requirement and for declaratory relief under 28 U.S.C. § 2201 (1982 ed., Supp. III). Granite Rock alleged that the Coastal Commission permit requirement was pre-empted by Forest Service regulations, by the Mining Act of 1872, and by the CZMA. Both sides agreed that there were no material facts in dispute. The District Court denied Granite Rock's motion for summary judgment and dismissed the action. 590 F.Supp. 1361 (1984). The Court of Appeals for the Ninth Circuit reversed. 768 F.2d 1077 (1985). The Court of Appeals held that the Coastal Commission permit requirement was pre-empted by the Mining Act of 1872 and Forest Service regulations. The Court of Appeals acknowledged that the statute and regulations do not "go so far as to occupy the field of establishing environmental standards," specifically noting that Forest Service regulations "recognize that a state may enact environmental regulations in addition to those established by federal agencies," and that the Forest Service "will apply [the state standards] in exercising its permit authority." 768 F.2d at 1083. However, the Court of Appeals held that "an independent state permit system to enforce state environmental standards would undermine the Forest Service's own permit authority and thus is pre-empted." *Ibid.*

The Coastal Commission appealed to this Court under 28 U.S.C. § 1254(2). We postponed consideration of the question of jurisdiction to the hearing of the case on the merits, 475 U.S. _____, 106 S.Ct. 1489, 89 L.Ed.2d 891 (1986).

---

[1] The Coastal Commission also instructed Granite Rock to submit a certification of consistency pursuant to the consistency review process of CZMA, 16 U.S.C. § 1456(c)(3)(A), described *infra,* at ——-——. The Commission subsequently admitted that it had waived its right to review the 1981-1986 plan of operation under the CZMA consistency provision by failing to raise its right to review in a timely manner. App. 17.

II

First we address two jurisdictional issues. In the course of this litigation, Granite Rock's 5-year plan of operations expired. The controversy between Granite Rock and the Coastal Commission remains a live one, however, for two reasons. First, the Coastal Commission's 1983 letter instructed Granite Rock that a Coastal Commission permit was required for work undertaken after the date of the letter. App. 22-24. Granite Rock admitted that is has done work after that date. *Id.,* at 83. Because the Coastal Commission asserts that Granite Rock needed a Coastal Commission permit for the work undertaken after the date of the Commission's letter, the Commission may require "reclamation for the mining that [has] occurred, measures to prevent pollution into the Little Sur River." Tr. of Or.Arg. 8. Granite Rock disputes the Coastal Commission's authority to require reclamation efforts. Second, Granite Rock stated in answer to interrogatories that its "investments and activities regarding its valid and unpatented mining claims require continuing operation beyond the present Plan of Operations," and that it intended to conduct mining operations on the claim at issue "as long as [Granite Rock] can mine an economically viable and valuable mining deposit under applicable federal laws." App. 83-84. Therefore it is likely that Granite Rock will submit new plans of operations in the future. Even if future participation by California in the CZMA consistency review process, see *infra,* at _____, or requirements placed on Granite Rock by the Forest Service called for compliance with the conditions of the Coastal Commission's permit, dispute would continue over whether the Coastal Commission itself, rather than the Federal Government, could *enforce* the conditions placed on the permit. This controversy is one capable of repetition yet evading review. See *Wisconsin Dept. of Industry v. Gould, Inc.,* 475 U.S. ___, ___, n. 3, 106 S.Ct. 1057, 1060, n. 3, 89 L.Ed.2d 223 (1986); *Dunn v. Blumstein,* 405 U.S. 330, 333 n. 2, 92 S.Ct. 995, 998, n.2, 31 L.Ed.2d 274 (1972). Accordingly, this case is not moot.

The second jurisdictional issue we must consider is whether this case is properly within our authority, under 28 U.S.C. § 1254(2), to review the decision of a federal court of appeals by appeal if a state statute is "held by a court of appeals to be invalid as repugnant to the Constitution, treaties or laws of the United States. . . ." Statutes authorizing appeals are to be strictly construed. *Silkwood v. Kerr-McGee Corp.,* 464 U.S. 238, 247, 104 S.Ct. 615, 620, 78 L.Ed.2d 443 (1984); *Perry Education Assn. v. Perry Local Educators' Assn.,* 460 U.S. 37, 43, 103 S.Ct. 948, 953, 74 L.Ed.2d 794 (1983). As noted in *Silkwood, supra,* at 247, 104 S.Ct., at 620, "we have consistently distinguished between those cases in which a state statute is expressly struck down" as repugnant to the Constitution, treaties or laws of the United States, and those cases in which "an exercise of authority under state law is invalidated without reference to the state statute." This latter group of cases do not fall within this Court's appellate jurisdiction.

In the present case, the Court of Appeals held that the particular exercise of the Coastal Commission permit requirement over Granite Rock's operation in a national forest was pre-empted by federal law. The Court of Appeals did not invalidate any portion of the California Coastal Act. In fact, it did not discuss whether the CCA itself actually authorized the imposition of a permit require-ment over Granite Rock. See Cal.Pub.Res.Code Ann. § 30008 (West) (1986) (limiting jurisdiction over federal lands to that which is "consistent with applica-ble federal . . . laws"). Accordingly this case is one in which "an exercise of authority under state law is invalidated without reference to the state statute," *Silkwood, supra,* at 247, 104 S.Ct., at 620, and not within our § 1254(2) appellate jurisdiction. We therefore treat the jurisdictional statement as a petition for certiorari, 28 U.S.C. § 2103, and having done so, grant the peition and reverse the judgment of the Court of Appeals.

III

Granite Rock does not argue that the Coastal Commission has placed any particular conditions on the issuance of a permit that conflict with federal statutes or regulations. Indeed, the record does not disclose what conditions the Coastal Commission will place on the issuance of a permit. Rather, Granite Rock argues, as it must given the posture of the case, that there is no possible set of conditions the Coastal Commission could place on its permit that would not conflict with federal law—that any state permit requirement is *per se* pre-empted. The only issue in this case is this purely facial challenge to the Coastal Commission permit requirement.

The Property Clause provides that "Congress shall have Power to dispose of and make all needful Rules and Regulations respecting the Territory or other Property belonging to the United States." U.S. Const., Art. IV, § 3, cl. 2. This Court has "repeatedly observed" that " '[t]he power over the public land thus entrusted to Congress is without limitations.' " *Kleppe v. New Mexico,* 426 U.S. 529, 539, 96 S.Ct. 2285, 2291, 49 L.Ed.2d 34 (1976), quoting *United States v. San Francisco,* 310 U.S. 16, 29, 60 S.Ct. 749, 756, 84 L.Ed. 1050 (1940). Granite Rock suggests that the Property Clause not only invests unlimited power in Congress over the use of federally owned lands, but also exempts federal lands from state regulation whether or not those regulations conflict with federal law. In *Kleppe, supra,* 426 U.S., at 543, 96 S.Ct., at 2293, we considered "totally unfounded" the assertion that the Secretary of Interior had even proposed such an interpretation of the Property Clause. We made clear that "the State is free to enforce its criminal and civil laws" on federal land so long as those laws do not conflict with federal law. *Ibid.* The Property Clause itself does not automatically conflict with all state regulation of federal land. Rather, as we explained in *Kleppe,*

"Absent consent or cession a State undoubtedly retains jurisdiction over federal lands within its territory, but Congress equally surely retains the power *to enact legislation* respecting those lands pursuant to the Property Clause. *And when Congress so acts,* the federal legislation necessarily overrides conflicting state laws under the Supremacy Clause." *Ibid.* (cita-tions omitted) (emphasis supplied).

We agree with Granite Rock that the Property Clause gives Congress plenary power to legislate the use of the federal land on which Granite Rock holds its unpatented mining claim. The question in this case, however, is whether Con-gress has enacted legislation respecting this federal land that would pre-empt any requirement that Granite Rock obtain a California Coastal Commission permit. To answer this question we follow the pre-emption analysis by which the Court has been guided on numerous occasions:

"[S]tate law can be pre-empted in either of two general ways. If Congress evidences an intent to occupy a given field, any state law falling within that field is pre-empted. [*Pacific Gas & Electric Co. v. State Energy Resources Conservation & Development Comm'n,* 461 U.S. 190, 203-204, 103 S.Ct. 1713, 1721-1722, 75 L.Ed.2d 752 (1983)]; *Fidelity Federal Savings & Loan Assn. v. De la Cuesta,* 458 U.S. 141, 153 [102 S.Ct. 3014, 3022, 73 L.Ed.2d 664] (1982); *Rice v. Santa Fe Elevator Corp.,* 331 U.S. 218, 230 [67 S.Ct. 1146, 1152, 91 L.Ed 1447] (1947). If Congress has not entirely displaced state regulation over the matter in question, state law is still pre-empted to the extent it actually conflicts with federal law, that is, when it is impossible to comply with both state and federal law, *Florida Lime & Avocado Growers, Inc. v. Paul,* 373 U.S. 132, 142-143 [83 S.Ct. 1210, 1217-1218, 10 L.Ed.2d 248] (1963), or where the state law stands as an obstacle to the accomplishment of the full purposes and objectives of Congress, *Hines v. Davidowitz,* 312 U.S. 52, 67 [61 S.Ct. 399, 404, 85 L.Ed. 581] (1941)." *Silkwood v. Kerr-McGee Corp., supra,* 464 U.S., at 248, 104 S.Ct., at 621.

A

Granite Rock and the Solicitor General as *amicus* have made basically three arguments in support of a finding that any possible state permit requirement would be pre-empted. First, Granite Rock alleges that the Federal Government's environmental regulation of unpatented mining claims in national forests demonstrates an intent to pre-empt any state regulation. Second, Granite Rock and the Solicitor General assert that indications that state land use planning over unpatented mining claims in national forests is pre-empted should lead to the conclusion that the Coastal Commission permit requirement is pre-empted. Finally, Granite Rock and the Solicitor General assert that the CZMA, by excluding federal lands from its definition of the coastal zone, declared a legislative intent that federal lands be excluded from all state coastal zone regulation. We conclude that these federal statutes and regulations do not, either independently or in combination, justify a facial challenge to the Coastal Commission permit requirement.

Granite Rock concedes that the Mining Act of 1872, as originally passed, expressed no legislative intent on the as yet rarely contemplated subject of environmental regulation. Brief for Appellee 31-32. In 1955, however, Congress passed the Multiple Use Mining Act, 69 Stat. 367, 30 U.S.C. § 601 *et seq.,* which provided that the Federal Government would retain and manage the surface resources of subsequently located unpatented mining claims. 30 U.S.C. § 612(b). Congress has delegated to the Secretary of Argiculture the authority to make "rules and regulations" to "regulate [the] occupancy and use" of national forests. 16 U.S.C. § 551. Through this delegation of authority, the Department of Argiculture's Forest Service has promulgated regulations so that "use of the surface of National Forest System lands" by those such as Granite Rock, who have unpatented mining claims authorized by the Mining Act of 1872, "shall be conducted so as to minimize adverse environmental impacts on National Forest System surface resources." 36 CFR § 228.1, § 228.3(d) (1986). It was pursuant to these regulations that the Forest Service approved the Plan of Operations submitted by Granite Rock. If, as Granite Rock claims, it is the federal intent that Granite Rock conduct its mining unhindered by any state environmental regulation, one would expect to find the expression of this intent in these Forest Service regulations. As we explained in *Hillsborough County v. Automated Medical Laboratories, Inc.* 471 U.S. 707, 718, 105 S.Ct. 2371, 2377, 85 L.Ed.2d 714 (1985), it is appropriate to expect an administrative regulation to declare any intention to pre-empt state law with some specificity:

"[B]ecause agencies normally address problems in a detailed manner and can speak through a variety of means, . . . we can expect that they will make their intentions clear if they intend for their regulations to be exclusive. Thus, if an agency does not speak to the question of pre-emption, we will pause before saying that the mere volume and complexity of its regulations indicate that the agency did in fact intend to pre-empt."

Upon examination, however, the Forest Service regulations that Granite Rock alleges pre-empt any state permit requirement not only are devoid of any expression of intent to pre-empt state law, but rather appear to assume that those submitting plans of operations will comply with state laws. The regulations explicitly require all operators within the National Forests to comply with state air quality standards, 36 CFR § 228.8(a) (1986), state water quality standards, § 228.8(b), and state standards for the disposal and treatment of solid wastes, § 228.8(c). The regulations also provide that, pending final approval of the plan of operations, the Forest Service officer with authority to approve plans of operation "will approve such operations as may be necessary for timely compliance with the requirements of Federal and *State laws. . . .*" § 228.5(b) (emphasis added). Finally, the final subsection of § 228.8, "[r]equirements for environmental protection," provides:

"(h) Certification or other approval issued by *State agencies* or other Federal agencies of compliance with laws and regulations relating to mining operations will be accepted as compliance with similar or parallel requirements of these regulations" (emphasis supplied).

It is impossible to divine from these regulations, which expressly contemplate coincident compliance with state law as well as with federal law, an intention to pre-empt all state regulation of unpatented mining claims in national forests. Neither Granite Rock nor the Solicitor General contends that these Forest Service regulations are inconsistent with their authorizing statutes.

Given these Forest Service regulations, it is not surprising that the Forest Service team that prepared the Environmental Assessment of Granite Rock's plan of operation, as well as the Forest Service officer that approved the plan of operation, expected compliance with state as well as federal law. The Los Padres National Forest Environmental Assessment of the Granite Rock plan stated that "Granite Rock is responsible for obtaining any necessary permits which may be required by the California Coastal Commission." App. 46. The Decision Notice and Finding of No Significant Impact issued by the Acting District Ranger accepted Granite Rock's plan of operation with modifications, stating:

> "The claimant, in exercising his rights granted by the Mining Law of 1872, shall comply with the regulations of the Departments of Agriculture and Interior. The claimant is further responsible for obtaining any necessary permits required by State and/or county laws, regulations and/or ordinance." *Id.,* at 54.

B

The second argument proposed by Granite Rock is that federal land management statutes demonstrate a legislative intent to limit States to a purely advisory role in federal land management decisions, and that the Coastal Commission permit requirement is therefore pre-empted as an impermissible state land use regulation.

In 1976 two pieces of legislation were passed that called for the development of federal land use management plans affecting unpatented mining claims in national forests. Under the Federal Land Policy and Management Act (FLPMA), 90 Stat. 2744, 43 U.S.C. § 1701 *et seq.,* (1982 ed. and Supp. III), the Department of Interior's Bureau of Land Mangement is responsible for managing the mineral resources on federal forest lands; under the National Forest Management Act (NFMA), 90 Stat. 2949, 16 U.S.C. §§ 1600-1614 (1982 ed. and Supp. III), the Forest Service under the Secretary of Agriculture is responsible for the management of the surface impacts of mining on federal forest lands. Granite Rock, as well as the Solicitor General, point to aspects of these statutes indicating a legislative intent to limit States to an advisory role in federal land management decisions. For example, the NFMA directs the Secretary of Agriculture to "develop, maintain, and, as appropriate, revise land and resource management plans for units of the National Forest System, coordinated with the land and resource management planning processes of State and local governments and other Federal agencies," 16 U.S.C. § 1604(a). The FLPMA directs that land use plans developed by the Secretary of the Interior "shall be consistent with State and local plans to the maximum extent [the Secretary] finds consistent with Federal law," and calls for the Secretary, "to the extent he finds practical," to keep apprised of state land use plans, and to "assist in resolving, to the extent practical, inconsistencies between Federal and non-Federal Government plans." 43 U.S.C. § 1712(c)(9).

For purposes of this discussion and without deciding this issue, we may assume that the combination of the NFMA and the FLPMA preempt the extension of state land use plans onto unpatented mining claims in national forest lands. The Coastal Commission[2] asserts that it will use permit conditions to impose

---

[2] Although the California Coastal Act requires local governments to adopt Local Coastal Programs, which include a land use plan and zoning ordinance, see Cal.Pub.Res.Code Ann. §§ 30500, 30512, 30513, no Local Coastal Program permit requirement is involved in this case. The permit at issue in this litigation is issued by the Coastal Commission directly. § 30600(a), (c); Tr.Or.Arg. 52 ("We're dealing with the second type of permitting, which is by the Coastal Commission itself, not a local government. . . . [T]he Coastal Commission issues permits based upon compliance with the environmental criteria in the Coastal Act itself.")

environmental regulation. See Cal.P᠁b.Res.Code Ann. § 30233 (West) (1986) (quality of coastal waters); § 30253(2) (erosion); § 30253(3) (air pollution); § 30240(b) (impact on environmentally sensitive habitat areas).

While the CCA gives land use as well as environmental regulatory authority to the Coastal Commission, the state statute also gives the Coastal Commission the ability to limit the requirements it will place on the permit. The CCA declares that the Coastal Commission will "provide maximum state involvement in federal activities allowable under federal law or regulations. . . ." Cal.Pub.Res. Code Ann. § 30004 (West). Since the state statute does not detail exactly what state standards will and will not apply in connection with various federal activities, the statute must be understood to allow the Coastal Commission to limit the regulations it will impose in those circumstances. In the present case, the Coastal Commission has consistently maintained that it does not seek to prohibit mining of the unpatented claim on national forest land. See 768 F.2d at 1080 ("The Coastal Commission also argues that the Mining Act does not preempt state environmental regulation of federal land *unless the regulation prohibits mining altogether. . . .'*) (emphasis supplied); 590 F.Supp. at 1373 ("The [Coastal Commission] seeks not to prohibit or 'veto,' but to regulate [Granite Rock's] mining activity in accordance with the detailed requirements of the CCA. . . . There is no reason to find that the [Coastal Commission] will apply the CCA's regulations so as to deprive [Granite Rock] of its rights under the Mining Act. . . ."); Defendants' Memorandum of Points and Authorities in Opposition to Plaintiff's Motion for Summary Judgment 41-42, *California Coastal Commission v. Granite Rock Co.,* No. C-83-5137 (N.D.Cal.1983) ("Despite Granite Rock's characterization of Coastal Act regulation as a 'veto' or ban of mining, Granite Rock has not applied for any coastal permit, and the State . . . has not indicated that it would in fact ban such activity. . . . [T]he question presented is merely whether the state can *regulate* uses rather than *prohibit* them. Put another way, the state is not seeking to *determine* basic uses of federal land: rather it is seeking to *regulate* a given mining use so that it is carried out in a more environmentally sensitive and resource-protective fashion.")

The line between environmental regulation and land use planning will not always be bright; for example, one may hypothesize a state environmental regulation so severe that a particular land use would become commercially impracticable. However, the core activity described by each phrase is undoubtedly different. Land use planning in essence chooses particular uses for the land; environmental regulation, at its core, does not mandate particular uses of the land but requires only that, however the land is used, damage to the environment is kept within prescribed limits. Congress has indicated its understanding of land use planning and environmental regulation as distinct activities. As noted above, 43 U.S.C. § 1712(c)(9) requires that the Secretary of Interior's land use plans be consistent with state plans only "to the extent he finds practical." The immediately preceding subsection, however, requires that the Secretary's land use plans "provide for compliance with applicable pollution control laws, including State and Federal air, water, noise, or other pollution standards or implementation plans." § 1712(c)(8). Congress has also illustrated its understanding of land use planning and environmental regulation as distinct activities by delegating the authority to regulate these activities to different agencies. The stated purpose of Part 228, subpart A of the Forest Service regulations, 36 CFR § 228.1, is to "set forth rules and procedures" through which mining on unpatented claims in national forests "shall be conducted so as to minimize adverse environmental impacts on National Forest System surface resources." The next sentence of the subsection, however, declares that "[i]t is not the purpose of these regulations to provide for the management of mineral resources; the responsibility for managing such resources is in the Secretary of the Interior." Congress clearly envisioned that although environmental regulation and land use planning may hypothetically overlap in some instances, these two types of activity would in most cases be capable of differentiation. Considering the legislative understanding of environmental regulation and land use planning as distinct activities, it would be anomalous to maintain that Congress intended any state environmental regulation of unpatented mining claims in national forests to be *per se* pre-empted as an impermissible exercise of state land use planning. Congress' treatment of environmental regulation and land use planning as generally distinguishable calls for this Court to treat them as distinct, until an actual overlap between the two is demonstrated in a particular case.

Granite Rock suggests that the Coastal Commission's true purpose in enforcing a permit requirement is to prohibit Granite Rock's mining entirely. By choosing to seek injunctive and declaratory relief against the permit requirement before discovering what conditions the Coastal Commission would have placed on the permit, Granite Rock has lost the possibility of making this argument in this litigation. Granite Rock's case must stand or fall on the question whether *any possible* set of conditions attached to the Coastal Commission's permit requirement would be pre-empted. As noted in the previous section, the Forest Service regulations do not indicate a federal intent to pre-empt all state environmental regulation of unpatented mining claims in national forests. Whether or not state land use planning over unpatented mining claims in national forets is pre-empted, the Coastal Commission insists that its permit requirement is an exercise of environmental regulation rather than land use planning. In the present posture of this litigation, the Coastal Commission's identification of a possible set of permit conditions not pre-empted by federal law is sufficient to rebuff Granite Rock's facial challenge to the permit requirement. This analysis is not altered by the fact that the Coastal Commission chooses to impose its environmental regulation by means of a permit requirement. If the Federal Government occupied the field of environmental regulation of unpatented mining claims in national forests—concededly not the case—then state environmental regulation of Granite Rock's mining activity would be pre-empted, whether or not the regulation was implemented through a permit requirement. Conversely, if reasonable state environmental regulation is not pre-empted, then the use of a permit requirement to impose the state regulation does not create a conflict with federal law where none previously existed. The permit requirement itself is not talismanic.

C

Granite Rock's final argument involves the CZMA, 16 U.S.C. § 1451 *et seq.*, through which financial assistance is provided to States for the development of coastal zone management programs. Section 304(a) of the CZMA, 16 U.S.C. § 1453(1), defines the coastal zone of a State, and specifically excludes from the coastal zone "lands the use of which is by law subject solely to the discretion of or which is held in trust by the Federal Government, its officers or agents." The Department of Commerce, which administers the CZMA, has interpreted § 1453(1) to exclude all federally-owned land from the CZMA definition of a state's coastal zone. 15 CFR § 923.33(a) (1986).

Granite Rock argues that the exclusion of "lands the use of which is by law subject solely to the discretion of or which is held in trust by the Federal Government, its officers or agents" excludes all federally-owned land from the CZMA definition of a State's coastal zone, and demonstrates a congressional intent to pre-empt any possible Coastal Commission permit requirement as applied to the mining of Granite Rock's unpatented claim in the national forest land.

According to Granite Rock, because Granite Rock mines land owned by the Federal Government, the Coastal Commission's regulation of Granite Rock's mining operation must be limited to participation in a consistency review process detailed in the CZMA. Under the CZMA, once a state coastal zone management program has been approved by the Secretary of Commerce for federal administrative grants, "any applicant for a required Federal license or permit to conduct an activity affecting land or water uses in the coastal zone of that state shall provide in the application . . . a certification that the proposed activity complies with the state's approved program and that such activity will be conducted in a manner consistent with the [state] program." 16 U.S.C. § 1456(c)(3)(A). At the same time, the applicant must provide the State a copy of the certification. The State, after public notice and appropriate hearings, is to notify the federal agency concerned that the State concurs or objects to the certification. If the State fails to notify the federal agency within six months of receiving notification, it is presumed that the State concurs. If the State neither concurs nor is presumed to concur, the federal agency must reject the application, unless the Secretary of Commerce finds that the application is consistent with the objectives of the CZMA or is "otherwise necessary in the interest of national security." *Ibid.*

In order for an activity to be subject to CZMA consistency review, the activity must be on a list that the State provides federal agencies, which describes the type of federal permit and license applications the State wishes to review. 15 CFR § 930.53 (1986). If the activity is unlisted, the State must within 30 days of receiving notice of the federal permit application inform the federal agency and federal permit applicant that the proposed activity requires CZMA consistency review. § 930.54. If the State does not provide timely notification, it waives the right to review the unlisted activity. In the present case, it appears that Granite Rock's proposed mining operations were not listed pursuant to § 930.53, and that the Coastal Commisson did not timely notify the Forest Service or Granite Rock that Granite Rock's plan of operations required consistency review. App. 17. Therefore, the Coastal Commission waived its right to consistency review of the 1981-1986 plan of operations.

Absent any other expression of congressional intent regarding the pre-emptive effect of the CZMA, we would be required to decide, first, whether unpatented mining claims in national forests were meant to be excluded from the § 1453(1) definition of a State's coastal zone, and second, whether this exclusion from the coastal zone definition was intended to pre-empt state regulations that were not pre-empted by any other federal statutes or regulations. Congress has provided several clear statements of its intent regarding the pre-emptive effect of the CZMA; those statements, which indicate that Congress clearly intended the CZMA *not* to be an independent cause of pre-emption except in cases of actual conflict, end our inquiry.

16 U.S.C. § 1456(e)(1) provides:

"Nothing in this chapter shall be construed—

"(1) to diminish either Federal or state jurisdiction, responsibility, or rights in the field of planning, development, or control of water resources, submerged lands, or navigable waters; nor to displace, supersede, limit, or modify any interstate compact or the jurisdiction or responsibility of any legally established joint or common agency of two or more states or of two or more states and the Federal Government; nor to limit the authority of Congress to authorize and fund projects. . . ."

The Senate Report describes the above section as "a standard clause disclaiming intent to diminsh Federal or State authority in the fields affected by the Act," or "to change interstate agreements." S.Rep. No. 753, 92d Cong., 2d Sess., 20 (1972). The Conference Report stated, "[t]he Conferees also adopted language which would make certain that there is no intent in this legislation to change Federal or state jurisdiction or rights in specified fields, including submerged lands." H.R.Conf.Rep. No. 1544, 92d Cong., 2d Sess., 14 (1972), U.S. Code Cong. & Admin.News 172, pp. 4776, 4794, 4824. While the land at issue here does not appear to fall under the categories listed in 16 U.S.C. § 1456(e)(1), the section and its legislative history demonstrate Congress' refusal to use the CZMA to alter the balance between state and federal jurisdiction.

The clearest statement of congressional intent as to the pre-emptive effect of the CZMA appears in the "Purpose" section of the Senate Report, quoted in full:

"[The CZMA] has as its main purpose the encouragement and assistance of States in preparing and implementing management programs to preserve, protect, develop and whenever possible restore the resources of the coastal zone of the United States. The bill authorizes Federal grants-in-aid to coastal states to develop coastal zone management programs. Additionally, it authorizes grants to help coastal states implement these management programs once approved, and States would be aided in the acquisition and operation of estuarine sanctuaries. Through the system of providing grants-in-aid, the States are provided financial incentives to undertake the responsibility for setting up management programs in the coastal zone. *There is no attempt to diminish state authority through federal preemption.* The intent of this legislation is to enhance state authority by encouraging and assisting the states to assume planning and regulatory powers over their coastal zones." S.Rep. No. 753, *supra,* at 1, U.S.Code Cong. & Admin. News 1972, p. 4776 (emphasis supplied.)

Because Congress specifically disclaimed any intention to pre-empt pre-existing state authority in the CZMA, we conclude that even if all federal lands are excluded from the CZMA definition of "coastal zone," the CZMA does not automatically pre-empt all state regulation of activities on federal lands.

IV

Granite Rock's challenge to the California Coastal Commission's permit requirement was broad and absolute; our rejection of that challenge is correspondingly narrow. Granite Rock argued that any state permit requirement, whatever its conditions, was *per se* pre-empted by federal law. To defeat Granite Rock's facial challenge, the Coastal Commission needed merely to identify a possible set of permit conditions not in conflict with federal law. The Coastal Commission alleges that it will use its permit requirement to impose reasonable environmental regulation. Rather than evidencing an intent to pre-empt such state regulation, the Forest Service regulations appear to assume compliance with state laws. Federal land use statutes and regulations, while arguably expressing an intent to pre-empt state land use planning, distinguish environmental regulation from land use planning. Finally, the language and legislative history of the CZMA expressly disclaim an intent to pre-empt state regulation.

Following an examination of the "almost impenetrable maze of arguably relevant legislation," *post,* at 1438, Justice POWELL concludes that "[i]n view of the Property Clause . . ., as well as common sense, federal authority must control. . . ." *Post,* at 1438. As noted above, the Property Clause gives Congress plenary power over the federal land at issue; however, even within the sphere of the Property Clause, state law is preempted only when it conflicts with the operation or objectives of federal law, or when Congress "evidences an intent to occupy a given field," *Silkwood v. Kerr-McGee Corp.,* 464 U.S., at 248, 104 S.Ct., at 621. The suggestion that traditional pre-emption analysis is inapt in this context can be justified, if at all, only by the assertion that the state regulation in this case would be "duplicative." The description of the regulation as duplicative, of course, is based on the conclusions of the dissent that land use regulation and environmental regulation are indistinguishable, *post,* at ___, and that any state permit requirement, by virtue of being a permit requirement rather than some other form of regulation, would duplicate federal permit requirements, *post,* at ___. Because we disagree with these assertions, see *supra* at ___, ___, we apply the traditional pre-emption analysis which requires an actual conflict between state and federal law, or a congressional expression of intent to preempt, before we will conclude that state regulation is preempted.

Contrary to the assertion of Justice POWELL that the Court today gives States power to impose regulations that "conflict with the views of the Forest

Service," *post,* at 1438, we hold only that the barren record of this facial challenge has not demonstrated any conflict. We do not, of course, approve any future application of the Coastal Commission permit requirement that in fact conflicts with federal law. Neither do we take the course of condemning the permit requirement on the basis of as yet unidentifiable conflicts with the federal scheme.

The judgment of the Court of Appeals is reversed and the case is remanded for further proceedings consistent with this opinion.

It is so ordered.

Justice POWELL, with whom Justice STEVENS joins, concurring in part and dissenting in part.

Because I agree that this case is properly before us, I join Parts I and II of the Court's opinion. In Part III, the court considers the Forest Service's approval of Granite Rock's plan to operate its mine in a national forest. Because I canot agree with the Court's conclusion that Congress intended to allow California to require a state permit, I dissent from Part III.

I
A

To understand Part III of the Court's opinion, one must have some knowledge of two groups of statutes and regulations. The first group of provisions regulates mining. As the Court explains, the basic source of federal mining law is the Mining Act of 1872, ch. 152, 17 Stat. 91 (codified, as amended, at 30 U.S.C. § 22 *et seq.*). In general, that law opens the public lands to exploration. If one discovers valuable mineral deposits, the statute grants him the right to extract and sell the minerals without paying a royalty to the United States, as well as the right—subject to certain statutory requirements—to obtain fee title to the land. See Mining Act § 1, 30 U.S.C. § 22; *United States v. Locke,* 471 U.S. 84, 86, 105 S.Ct. 1785, 1788, 85 L.Ed.2d 64 (1985). As the demand for minerals has increased during the past century, Congress has emphasized that an "economically sound and stable domestic mining . . . industr[y]" is important to the economy, and to our Nation's security. See Mining and Minerals Policy Act of 1970, § 2, 30 U.S.C. § 21a.[1]

B

The second area of federal law important to this case concerns the management of federal lands. In response to the increasing commercial importance of federal lands, as well as the awareness of the environmental values of these lands, Congress passed the Federal Land Policy and Management Act of 1976 (FLPMA), 43 U.S.C. § 1701 *et seq.* (1982 ed. and Supp. III). That statute promotes

---

[1] See also National Materials and Minerals Policy, Research and Development Act of 1980, § 2(a)(1), 30 U.S.C. § 1601(a)(1) (congressional finding that the availability of minerals "is essential for national security, economic well-being, and industrial production"); § 2(a)(3), 30 U.S.C. § 1601(a)(3) (Congressional finding that the extraction of minerals is "closely linked with national concerns for energy and the environment"); § 3, 30 U.S.C. § 1602 ("[I]t is the continuing policy of the United States to promote an adequate and stable supply of materials necessary to maintain national security, economic well-being and industrial production with appropriate attention to a long-term balance between resource production, energy use, a healthy environment, natural resources conservation, and social needs").

the effective development of federal lands in two ways pertinent to this case. First, it directs the Secretary of the Interior to inventory the resources located on federal lands and to develop comprehensive plans for future development. §§ 1701(a)(2), 1711, 1712. Second, it ensures that the States' interests in these resources will not be ignored:

"[T]he Secretary shall . . . coordinate [his plans] with the land use planning and management programs of . . . the States and local goverments within which the lands are located. . . . Land use plans of the Secretary . . . shall be consistent with State and local plans to the maximum extent he finds consistent with Federal law and the purposes of this Act." § 1712(c)(9).

Significantly, the FLPMA only requires the Secretary to listen to the States, not obey them. As the Conference Report explained: "[T]he ultimate decision as to determining the extent of feasible consistency between [the Secretary's] plans and [State or local] plans rests with the Secretary of the Interior." H.R.Conf.Rep. No. 94-1724, p. 58 (1976), U.S.Code Cong. & Admin.News 1976, pp. 6175, 6229.

The surface management provisions of the FLPMA do not apply to national forest lands. 43 CFR § 3809.0-5(c) (1985). Congress first provided for management of these lands in the Organic Administration Act of 1897. The current version of that statute delegates to the Secretary of Agriculture the authority to "regulate [the] occupancy and use" of national forests. 16 U.S.C. § 551. The Forest Service, as the Secretary's delegate, has promulgated regulations to control the "use" of national forests. 36 CFR § 228.1 *et seq.* (1986). Persons wishing to mine in the National Forests submit plans of operation detailing their anticipated activities. If the Forest Service determines that the plans comply with the regulations, it approves them and authorizes the mining operation. The Court, by focusing on the Forest Service's concern for preservation of the national forests, characterizes these regulations as "environmental" regulations, in its view something entirely different from "land use" regulations. *Ante,* at 1427-1428.

In fact, the regulation of land use is more complicated than the Court suggests. First, as is true with respect to the Secretary of the Interior, the Secretary of Agriculture has been directed to develop comprehensive plans for the use of resources located in national forests. See Forest and Rangeland Renewable Resources Planning Act of 1974 (Forest Planning Act) § 3(a), as amended, 16 U.S.C. § 1601. The Forest Planning Act initially did not require the Forest Service to consider the views of state regulators. But when Congress passed the FLPMA in 1976, it also passed the National Forest Management Act (NFMA), that amended the Forest Planning Act. Of special importance, § 6(a) of the NFMA requires the Secretary of Agriculture to coordinate his land management plans "with the land and resource management planning processes of State and local governments." 16 U.S.C. § 1604(a). Section 14 specifically requires the Secretary of Agriculture to give state governments "adequate notice and an opportunity to comment upon the formulation of standards, criteria, and guidelines applicable to Forest Service programs." § 1612(a). Thus, it is clear that the Secretary of Agriculture has the final authority to determine the best use for federal lands, and that he must consider the views of state regulators before making a decision. There is no suggestion in the statute or the legislative history that state regulators should have the final authority in determining how particular federal lands should be used.

The Forest Service also has a role in implementing the Nation's mineral development policy. The Court shrugs off the importance of this obligation, noting that "the responsibility for managing [mineral] resources is in the Secretary of the Interior." *Ante,* at 1429 (quoting 36 CFR § 228.1 (1986)). This statement erroneously equates mineral resources management with land use management. Title 43 of the Code of Federal Regulations details the activities of the Bureau of Land Management (BLM) in this context. Generally, BLM manages the process by which rights to minerals are obtained from the United States and protected against others, the payment of royalties to the Federal Government, and the conservation of the minerals themselves. In some cases—like oil, gas, and coal—BLM supervises leasing of the right to extract the materials. But this case involves "hardrock" minerals governed by the Mining Act of 1872. With respect to those minerals, the BLM's actions are limited to determining whether the land is subject to location under the mining laws; whether a mining claim is properly located and recorded; whether assessment work is properly performed; and whether the requirements for patenting a claim have been complied with. See 43 CFR Parts 3800-3870 (1985). None of these determinations is a "land use" determination in the sense of balancing mineral development against environmental hazard to surface resources. The Forest Service makes these determinations through its review of a mining plan of operation.

The Organic Administration Act of 1897 makes clear that the Forest Service must act consistently with the federal policy of promoting mineral development. Section 1 of that Act precludes the Secretary of Agriculture from taking any action that would "prohibit any person from entering upon such national forests for all proper and lawful purposes, including that of prospecting, locating, and developing the mineral resources thereof." 16 U.S.C. § 478.[2] Forest Service materials confirm its duty to balance "[t]he demand for mineral development . . . against the demand for renewable resources and the land management agency's responsibility to reasonably protect the environment." United States Dept. of Agriculture, Forest Service Minerals Program handbook preface (1983). See also Forest Service Manual § 2802 (Dec. 1986) (stating that the Forest Service's policy is to "ensure that exploration, development, and production of mineral and energy resources are conducted in an environmentally sound manner and that these activities are integrated with planning and management of other national forest resources"); 30 U.S.C. § 1602. In sum, although the Secretary of the Interior has a substantial responsibility for managing mineral resources, Congress has entrusted the task of balancing mineral development and envi-

---

[2] More recently, congressional solicitude for development of federal mineral resources led Congress to order the President to "coordinate the responsible departments and agencies to, among other measures . . . encourage Federal agencies to facilitate availability and development of domestic resources to meet critical materials needs." 30 U.S.C. § 1602(7).

ronmental protection in the national forests to the Department of Agriculture, and its delegate the Forest Service.

II

The Court's analysis of this case focuses on selected provisions of the federal statutes and regulations, to the exclusion of other relevant provisions and the larger regulatory context. First, it examines the Forest Service regulations themselves, apart from the statutes that authorize them. Because these regulations explicitly require the federal permits to comply with specified state environmental standards, the Court assumes that Congress intended to allow state enforcement of any and all state environmental standards. Careful comparison of the regulations with the authorizing statutes casts serious doubt on this conclusion. The regulations specifically require compliance with only three types of state regulation: air quality, see 36 CFR § 228.8(a) (1986); water quality, see § 228.8(b); and solid waste disposal, see § 228.8(c). But the Court fails to mention that the types of state regulation preserved by § 228.8 already are preserved by specific nonpre-emption clauses in other federal statutes. See 42 U.S.C. § 7418(a) (Clean Air Act requires federal agencies to comply with analogous state regulations); 33 U.S.C. § 1323(a) (similar provision of the Clean Water Act); 42 U.S.C. § 6961 (similar provision of the Solid Waste Disposal Act). The Forest Service's specific preservation of certain types of state regulation— already preserved by federal law—hardly suggests an implicit intent to allow the States to apply other types of regulation to activities on federal lands. Indeed the maxim *expressio unius est exclusio alterius* suggests the contrary.[3]

The second part of the Court's analysis considers both the NFMA and the FLPMA. The Court assumes, *ante,* at 1427, that these statutes "pre-empt the extension of state land use plans onto unpatented mining claims in national forest lands." But the Court nevertheless holds that the Coastal Commission can require Granite Rock to secure a state permit before conducting mining operations in a national forest. This conclusion rests on a distinction between "land use planning" and "environmental regulation." In the Court's view, the NFMA and the FLPMA indicate a congressional intent to pre-empt state land use regulations, but not state environmental regulations. I find this analysis unsup-

---

[3] The Court rests this part of its pre-emption analysis on *Hillsborough County v. Automated Medical Laboratories, Inc.,* 471 U.S. 707, 105 S.Ct. 2371, 85 L.Ed.2d 714 (1985). In that case, the Court stated: "[W]e will pause before saying that the mere volume and complexity of [an agency's] regulations indicate that the agency did in fact intend to pre-empt." *Id.* at 718, 105 S.Ct., at 2377 *Hillsborough,* however, is quite different from this case. First, the state regulations were designed to ensure the health of plasma donors, an aim entirely separate from the aim of the federal regulations, to ensure the purity of the donated plasma. In this case, by contrast, federal authorities already have considered the environmental effects of Granite Rock's mine. The California Coastal Commission seeks only to reconsider the decision of the federal authorities. In any event, the argument for pre-emption in this case does not rest on the Forest Service regulations alone, but also on the comprehensive regulatory system enacted by Congress. The Court cannot make *Hillsborough* controlling simply by considering the regulations separately from their statutory source. As I explain, *infra,* at 1436-1438, the complex of applicable statutes and regulations, considered as a whole, pre-empts the Coastal Commission's permit requirement.

portable, either as an interpretation of the governing statutes or as a matter of logic.

The basis for the alleged distinction is that Congress has understood land use planning and environmental regulation to be distinct activities. The only statute cited for this proposition is § 202(c)(8) of the FLPMA, 43 U.S.C. § 1712(c)(8), that requires the Secretary of the Interior's land use plans to "provide for compliance with applicable pollution control laws, including State and Federal air, water, noise, or other pollution standards or implementation plans." But this statute provides little support for the majority's analysis. A section mandating consideration of environmental standards in the formulation of land use plans does not demonstrate a general separation between "land use planning" and "environmental regulation." Rather, § 202(c)(8) recognizes that the Secretary's land use planning will affect the environment, and thus directs the Secretary to comply with certain pollution standards.

Nor does this section support the Court's ultimate conclusion, that Congress intended the Secretary's plans to comply with all state environmental regulations. As I have explained *supra,* at 6, other federal statutes require compliance with the listed standards.[4] Also, because the FLPMA requires compliance only with "applicable" standards, it is difficult to treat this one section as an independent and controlling command that the Secretary comply with all state environmental standards. Rather, viewing the complex of statutes and regulations as a whole, it is reasonable to view § 202(c)(8) simply as a recognition that the Secretary's plans must comply with standards made applicable to federal activities by other federal laws.

The only other authority cited by the Court for the distinction between environmental regulation and land use planning is a Forest Service regulation stating that the Forest Service's rules do not "provide for the management of mineral resources," 36 CFR § 228.1 (1986). From this, the Court concludes that the Forest Service enforces environmental regulation but does not engage in land use planning. This conclusion misunderstands the division of authority between the BLM and the Forest Service. As explained *supra,* at 1433-1434, the BLM's management of minerals does not entail management of surface resources or the evaluation of surface impacts. Indeed, the Court acknowledges that the Forest Service is "responsible for the management of the surface impacts of mining on federal forest lands." *Ante,* at 1427. The Forest Planning Act and the NFMA direct the Secretary of Agriculture and the Forest Service to develop comprehensive plans for the use of forest resources. Similarly, the Organic Administration Act commands the Secretary of Agriculture to promulgate regu-

---

[4] The Forest Service regulations discussed above mention a slightly different set of environmental standards than does the FLPMA. Both provisions specifically preserve air and water standards. The Forest Service regulations also mention solid waste disposal standards; the Land Management Act also mentions noise control standards. Cf. 42 U.S.C. § 4901(a)(3) (Noise Control Act provisions stating that the "primary responsibility for control of noise rests with State and local governments"). The slight difference between the two lists of pollution standards, however, is insignificant. The feature that *all* the listed standards have in common is that other federal statutes specifically preserve a place for state regulation. See *supra,* 1434-1435.

lations governing the "occupancy and use" of national forests, 16 U.S.C. § 551. These regulations are integral to the Forest Service's management of national forests. To view them as limited to environmental concerns ignores both the Forest Service's broader responsibility to manage the use of forest resources and the federal policy of making mineral resources accessible to development.[5] The Coastal Commission has no interest in the matters within the jurisdiction of the BLM; the regulations that it seeks to impose concern matters wholly within the control of the Forest Service. Thus, this regulation does not support the Court's distinction between environmental regulation and land use planning.

The most troubling feature of the Court's analysis is that it is divorced from the realities of its holding. The Court cautions that its decision allows only "reasonable" environmental regulation and that is does not give the Coastal Commission a veto over Granite Rock's mining activities. But if the Coastal Commission can require Granite Rock to secure a permit before allowing mining operations to proceed, it necessarily can forbid Granite Rock from conducting these operations. It may be that reasonable environmental regulations would not force Granite Rock to close its mine. This misses the point. The troubling fact is that the Court has given a state authority—here the Coastal Commission—the power to prohibit Granite Rock from exercising the rights granted by its Forest Service permit. This abdication of federal control over the use of federal land is unprecedented.[6]

III

Apart from my disagreement with the Court's characterization of the governing statutes, its pre-emption analysis accords little or no weight to both the location of the mine in a national forest, and the comprehensive nature of the federal statutes that authorized Granite Rock's federal permit.

One important factor in pre-emption analysis is the relative weight of the state and federal interests in regulating a particular matter. Cf. *Hines v. Davidowitz,* 312 U.S. 52, 66-69, 61 S.Ct. 399, 403-405, 85 L.Ed. 581 (1941). The Court recognizes that the mine in this case is located in a national forest, but curiously attaches no significance to that fact. The Property Clause specifically grants

---

[5] The lack of statutory support for the Court's distinction is not surprising, because—with all respect—it seems to me that the distinction is one without a rational difference. As the Court puts it: "Land use planning in essence chooses particular uses for the land; environmental regulation, at its core, does not mandate particular uses of the land but requires only that, however the land is used, damage to the environment is kept within prescribed limits." *Ante,* at 1428. This explanation separates one of the reasons for Forest Service decisions from the decisions themselves. In considering a proposed use of a parcel of land in the national forest, the Forest Service regulations consider the damage the use will cause to the environment as well as the federal interest in making resources on public lands accessible to development. The Forest Service may decide that the proposed use is appropriate, that it is inappropriate, or that it would be appropriate only if further steps are taken to protect the environment. The Court divides this decision into two distinct types of regulation and holds that Congress intended to pre-empt duplicative state regulation of one part but not the other. Common sense suggests that it would be best for one expert federal agency, the Forest Service, to consider all these factors and decide what use best furthers the relevant federal policies.

[6] I express no view as to the Court's conclusion that the Coastal Zone Management Act of 1972 (CZMA), 16 U.S.C. § 1451 *et seq.* (1982 ed, and Supp. III), does not pre-empt the state regulation in this case. See *ante,* at 1429-1431.

Congress "Power to dispose of and make all needful Rules and Regulations respecting the Territory or other Property belonging to the United States." U.S. Const., Art. IV, § 3, cl. 2. See *Utah Power & Light Co. v. United States,* 243 U.S. 389, 404, 37 S.Ct. 387, 389, 61 L.Ed. 791 (1917). This provision may not of its own force pre-empt the authority of a State to regulate activities on federal land, but it clearly empowers Congress to limit the extent to which a State may regulate in this area. In light of this clear constitutional allocation of power, the location of the mine in a national forest should make us less reluctant to find pre-emption than we are in other contexts.

The state regulation in this case is particularly intrusive because it takes the form of a separate, and duplicative, permit system. As the Court has recognized, state permit requirements are especially likely to intrude on parallel federal authority, because they effectively give the State the power to veto the federal project. See *International Paper Co. v. Ouellette,* 479 U.S. _____, _____, 107 S.Ct. 805, _____, 93 L.Ed.2d 883 (1987); *First Iowa Hydro-Electric Cooperative v. FPC,* 328 U.S. 152, 164, 66 S.Ct. 906, 911, 90 L.Ed. 1143 (1946). Although the intrusive effect of duplicate state permit systems may not lead to a finding of pre-emption in all cases, it certainly is relevant to a careful pre-emption analysis.

The dangers of duplicative permit requirements are evident in this case. The federal permit system reflects a careful balance between two important federal interests: the interest in developing mineral resources on federal land, and the interest in protecting our national forests from environmental harm. The Forest Service's issuance of a permit to Granite Rock reflects its conclusion that environmental concerns associated with Granite Rock's mine do not justify restricting mineral development on this portion of a federal forest. Allowing the Coastal Commission to strike a different balance necessarily conflicts with the federal system.

Furthermore, as discussed *supra,* at 1433-1434, Congress already has provided that affected States must be afforded an opportunity to communicate their concerns to the federal regulators charged with deciding how federal lands should be used.[7] Because Congress has ensured that any federal decision will

---

[7] The discussion in Part I deals primarily with the FLPMA and the NFMA. In this case, the Coastal Commission actually had yet another statutory basis for influencing the federal decisionmaking process. Because Granite Rock's mine is near the California Coast, the Coastal Commission has a right to consistency review under the CZMA. Thus, if the Coastal Commission had voiced its concerns, the Secretary could not have approved this permit unless he determined, after a hearing, "that the activity is consistent with the objectives of [the CZMA] or is otherwise necessary in the interest of national security." 16 U.S.C. § 1456(c)(3)(A). Although the Coastal Commission had notice of Granite Rock's application to the Forest Service, it did not object to Granite Rock's activities until two years after the application was approved and Granite Rock began mining pursuant to the federal permit. Because the Coastal Commission failed to make a timely complaint to the Forest Service, it forfeited its right to consistency review under the CZMA.

By noting the provision for consistency review, I do not imply that the CZMA itself pre-empts the Coastal Commission's permit requirement. See n. 6, *supra.* I believe, however, that the provision for consistency review, considered with the other specific provisions for state participation in the federal regulatory process, indicates that Congress did not believe the States could have imposed separate permit requirements, even before passage of the CZMA.

reflect the environmental concerns of affected States, a duplicative system of permits would serve no purpose. Indeed, the potential for conflict between state and federal decisions has obvious disadvantages.

IV

In summary, it is fair to say that, commencing in 1872, Congress has created an almost impenetrable maze of arguably relevant legislation in no less than a half-dozen statutes, augmented by the regulations of two Departments of the Executive. There is little cause for wonder that the language of these statutes and regulations has generated considerable confusion. There is an evident need for Congress to enact a single, comprehensive statute for the regulation of federal lands.

Having said this, it is at least clear that duplicative federal and state permit requirements create an intolerable conflict in decisionmaking.[8] In view of the Property Clause of the Constitution, as well as common sense, federal authority must control with respect to land "belonging to the United States." Yet, the Court's opinion today approves a system of twofold authority with respect to enviromental matters. The result of this holding is that state regulators, whose views on environmental and mineral policy may conflict with the views of the Forest Service, have the power, with respect to federal lands, to forbid activity expressly authorized by the Forest Service. I dissent.

Justice SCALIA, with whom Justice WHITE joins, dissenting.

I agree with the Court that this case is live because of continuing dispute over California's ability to assert a reclamation claim, *ante,* at 1424[1] In my view, however, the merits of this case must be decided on simpler and narrower grounds than those addressed by the Court's opinion. It seems to me ultimately irrelevant whether state environmental regulation has been pre-empted with respect to federal lands, since the exercise of state power at issue here is not environmental regulation but land use control. The Court errs in entertaining the Coastal Commission's contention "that its permit requirement is an exercise of environmental regulation," *ante,* at 1429; and mischaracterizes the issue when it describes it to be whether "any state permit requirement, whatever its conditions, [is] *per se* pre-empted by federal law," *ante,* at 1431. We need not

---

[8] The Court concludes that Granite Rock has failed to demonstrate a conflict because it rejects my conclusion that land use regulation and environmental regulation are indistinguishable and because it sees no harm in allowing state permit requirements to supersede the decisions of federal officials. *Ante,* at 1431-1432.

[1] I would not rely upon the alternative ground that the dispute between these parties is "capable of repetition yet evading review." *Ante,* at 1424. Assuming that Granite Rock submits a new five-year plan to the Forest Service and that California again seeks to require it to comply with the coastal permitting requirements, I see no reason why that action would evade our review. See *Weinstein v. Bradford,* 423 U.S. 147, 149, 96 S.Ct. 347, 348, 46 L.Ed.2d 350 (1975). Moreover, for a dispute to be "capable of repetition," there must be a "reasonable expectation that the same complaining party [will] be subjected to the same action again." *Ibid.* The Court may be correct that it is *possible* that California will seek to enforce its permit requirement directly again, *ante,* at 1424; but since California may well be able to accomplish what it wants through the Coastal Zone Management Act's consistency review procedures, 16 U.S.C. § 1456(c)(3)(A), I do not think it likely that it will do so.

speculate as to what the nature of this permit requirement was. We are not dealing with permits in the abstract, but with a specific permit, purporting to require application of particular criteria, mandated by a numbered section of a known California law. That law is plainly a land use statute, and the permit that statute requires Granite Rock to obtain is a land use control device. Its character as such is not altered by the fact that the State may now be agreeable to issuing it so long as environmental concerns are satisfied. Since, as the Court's opinion quite correctly assumes, *ante,* at 1427, state exercise of land use authority over federal lands is pre-empted by federal law, California's permit requirement must be invalid.

The permit at issue here is a "coastal development permit," required by the California Coastal Act, Cal.Pub.Res.Code Ann. § 30000 *et seq.* (West 1986). It is provided for by § 30600 of chapter 7 of that Act (entitled "Development Controls"), which states that a person wishing to undertake any "development" in the coastal zone—a term defined to include construction, mining, and "change in the density or intensity of use of land," § 30106—must obtain a coastal development permit from a local government or the California Coastal Commission. The permit is to be granted if the proposed development is in conformity with a state-approved local coastal program or, where no such program yet exists, if the proposed development "is in conformity with the provisions of Chapter 3 . . . and . . . will not prejudice the ability of the local government to prepare a local coastal program that is in conformity with Chapter 3." § 30604. The "local coastal programs" to which these provisions refer consist of two parts: (1) a land use plan, and (2) zoning ordinances, zoning maps and other implementing actions. §§ 30511(b), 30512, 30513. Chapter 3 of the Act, with which these local coastal programs must comply, consists largely of land use prescriptions—for example, that developments providing public recreational opportunities shall be preferred, § 30213; that oceanfront land suitable for recreational use shall be protected for recreational use and development, § 30221; that commercial recreational facilities shall have priority over private residential, general industrial, or general commercial development, but not over agriculture or coastal-dependent industry, § 30222; that oceanfront land suitable for coastal dependent aquaculture shall be protected for that use, § 30222.5; that facilities serving the commercial fishing and recreational boating industries shall be protected and, where feasible, upgraded, § 30234; that the maximum amount of prime agricultural land shall be maintained in agricultural production, § 30241; that all other lands suitable for agricultural use shall not be converted to nonagricultural use except in specified circumstances, § 30242; that conversions of coastal commercial timberlands in units of commercial size to other uses shall be limited to providing for necessary timber processing and related facilities, § 30243; that the location and amount of new development should maintain and enhance public access to the coast, § 30252; that coastal-dependent developments shall have priority over other developments on or near the shoreline, § 30255; and that coastal-dependent industrial facilities shall be encouraged to locate or expand within existing sites, § 30260.[2]

It could hardly be clearer that the California Coastal Act is land use regulation. To compound the certainty, California has designated its Coastal Act as the State's coastal management program for purposes of the Coastal Zone Management Act (CZMA), 16 U.S.C. § 1451 *et seq.* Cal.Pub.Res.Code Ann. § 30008 (West 1986). The requirements for such a program include "[a] definition of what shall constitute permissible land uses and water uses within the coastal zone," 16 U.S.C. § 1454(b)(2), and "[a]n identification of the means by which the state proposes to exert control over [those] land uses and water uses." § 1454(b)(4).

The § 30600 permit requirement, of course, is one of those means of control—and whenever a permit application is evaluated pursuant to the statutory standards, land (or water) use management is afoot. Even if, as the State has argued before us and as the Court has been willing to postulate, California intended to employ the land use permit in this case only as a device for exacting environmental assurances, the power to demand *that permit* nevertheless hinges upon the State's power to do what the statutory permitting requirements authorize: to control land use. The legal status of the matter is that Granite Rock, having received land use approval from the Federal Government, has been requested to obtain land use approval from the State of California. If state land use regulation is in fact pre-empted in this location, there is no justification for requiring Granite Rock to go through the motions of complying with that *ultra vires* request on the chance that permission will be granted with no more than environmental limitations. It is inconceivable that, if a labor union federally certified as an authorized bargaining agent sought injunctive or declaratory relief

---

[2] The state Coastal Commission is responsible for issuing coastal development permits until the Commission has certified a local land use plan, Cal.Pub.Res.Code Ann. § 30600.5(b) (West 1986), at which time the responsibility devolves on the local government, *ibid.* Regardless of which governmental entity has the authority to issue the permit, the requirements for its issuance are those set forth in Chapter 3 of the California Coastal Act discussed *supra*. These apply directly if a local coastal program has not been certified, § 30604(a), or by enforcement of the requirements of the local coastal program, § 30604(b), whose land use plan must conform with that chapter in order to be certified, §§ 30512(c), 30512.1(c), 30512.2. Because local coastal programs consist of such classic land use regulation tools as a land use plan, zoning maps, zoning ordinances and other implementing devices, §§ 30511(b), 30512, permits issued upon a showing of consistency with a local coastal program may be even more obviously land use control devices than permits issued upon a showing of consistency with the provisions of Chapter 3. But under the plain terms of the statute, the latter no less than the former are permits for land use. To establish the contrary proposition, which is essential to its holding, the majority relies upon nothing more substantial than the statement of counsel for the Commission, in oral argument before us, that "[T]he Coastal Commission issues permits based upon compliance with the environmental criteria in the Coastal Act itself." Tr.Or.Arg. 52, quoted *ante,* at 1427, n. 2. Read literally (*i.e.* without inferring the adverb "exclusively"), the statement is true (the Act does contain some environmental criteria) but unhelpful to the majority's case. If, however, counsel meant to imply that the Commission's permits could not be conditioned upon compliance with the land use criteria, the statement would not only contradict the plain language of the Act, but would also be inconsistent with the litigating position taken by the Commission in the previous stages of this lawsuit, see *infra,* at 1440-1441.

against a requirement that it submit to state certification for the same purpose, we would say that "[b]y choosing to seek . . . relief against the . . . requirement before discovering what conditions the [State] would have placed on the [certification], [the union] has lost the possibility" of prevailing. *Ante*, at 14. I see no basis for making the equivalent statement here. In the one case as in the other, the demand for state approval is in and of itself invalid. As the Ninth Circuit said in a similar case that we summarily affirmed:

> "The issue is whether [the State] has the power of ultimate control over the Government's lessee, and this issue persists whether or not a use permit would eventually be granted." *Ventura County v. Gulf Oil Corp.,* 601 F.2d 1080, 1085 (1979), aff'd mem., 445 U.S. 947 [100 S.Ct. 1593, 63 L.Ed.2d 782] (1980).

Even on the assumption, therefore, that California was only using its land use permit requirement as a means of enforcing its environmental laws, Granite Rock was within its rights to ignore that requirement—*unless* California has land use authority over the federal lands in question.

In fact, however, this case is even more straightforward than that, for there is not reason to believe that California was seeking anything less than what the Coastal Act requires: land use regulation. The Commission's letter to Granite Rock demanding permit application read as follows:

> "Because of the significant control and authority enjoyed by Granite Rock Company over the land subject to its mining claims at Pico Blanco and the concommitant [*sic*] significant diminution of federal discretionary control, this land cannot be included among the federal lands excluded from the coastal zone by the CZMA. . . . Consequently, because the land is located seaward of the coastal zone boundary established by the state legislature effective January 1, 1977, it is subject to the permit requirements of the California Coastal Act.
>
> "This letter will serve to notify Granite Rock of its obligation to apply to the Coastal Commission for a coastal development permit for any development, as defined in Section 30106 of the Coastal Act, at the site undertaken after the date of this letter." App.22.

This letter contains no hint that only environmental constraints are at issue, as opposed to compliance with all of the requirements of the State's coastal management program. Even in the litigation stage—both in the District Court and in the Court of Appeals—the argument that California was (or might be) seeking to enforce only environmental controls was merely an alternate position. The Commission's more sweeping contention was that the land in question is not excluded from the CZMA, and that the CZMA permits designated state coastal management programs to override the Mining Act. See App. to Juris. Statement A-4, A-12, A-24. That argument has not been pressed here, having been rejected by both lower courts. *Granite Rock Co. v. California Coastal Commission,* 768 F.2d 1077, 1080-1081 (CA9 1985); *California Coastal Commission v. Granite Rock,* 590 F.Supp. 1361, 1370-1371 (N.D.Cal.1984). It is perfectly clear, however, that the assertion that the State is only enforcing its environmental laws is purely a litigating position—and a late-asserted one at that.

On any analysis, therefore, the validity of California's demand for permit application, and the lawfulness of Granite Rock's refusal, depend entirely upon whether California has authority to regulate land use at Pico Blanco. The Court is willing to assume that California lacks such authority on account of the National Forest Management Act of 1976 (NFMA), 16 U.S.C. § 1600 *et seq.* (1982 ed. and Supp. III), and the Federal Land Policy and Management Act of 1976 (FLPMA), 43 U.S.C. § 1701 *et seq.* (1982 ed. and Supp. III). *Ante,* at 1437. I believe that assumption is correct. Those statutes, as well as the CZMA, require federal officials to coordinate and consult with the States regarding use of federal lands in order to assure consistency with state land use plans to the maximum extent compatible with federal law and objectives. 16 U.S.C. §§ 1456(c)(3)(A), 1604(a), 43 U.S.C. § 1712(c). Those requirements would be superfluous, and the limitation upon federal accommodation meaningless, if the States were meant to have independent land use authority over federal lands. The Court is quite correct that the CZMA did not purport to change the status quo with regard to state authority over the use of federal lands. *Ante,* at 15-19. But as the CZMA's federal lands exclusion, 16 U.S.C. § 1453(1), and consistency review provisions, 16 U.S.C. § 1456(c)(3)(A), clearly demonstrate, that status quo was assumed to be exclusive federal regulation.

Finally, any lingering doubt that exercise of Coastal Act authority over federal lands is an exercise of land use authority pre-empted by federal laws is removed by the fact that that is not only the view of the federal agencies in charge of administering those laws, see Brief for United States as *Amicus Curiae,* but also was the original view of California, which until 1978 excluded from the Coastal Act, in language exactly mirroring that of the federal lands exclusion from the CZMA, 16 U.S.C. § 1453(1), "lands the use of which is by law subject solely to the discretion of or which is held in trust by the federal government, its officers or agents." 1976 Cal.Stats., ch. 1331, § 1, amended by 1978 Cal.Stats., ch. 1075, § 2, codified at Cal.Pub.Res.Code Ann. § 30008.

Any competent lawyer, faced with a demand from the California Coastal Commission that Granite Rock obtain a § 30600 coastal development permit for its Pico Blanco operations, would have responded precisely as Granite Rock's lawyers essentially did: Our use of federal land has been approved by the Federal Government, thank you, and does not require the approval of the State. We should not allow California to claim, in the teeth of the plain language of its legislation, and in violation of the assurance it gave to the Federal Government by designating its Coastal Act as a coastal management program under the CZMA, that it would use the permitting requirement to achieve, not land use management, but only environmental controls. We should particularly not give ear to that claim since it was not the representation made to Granite Rock when application for the permit was demanded. If environmental control is, as California now assures us, its limited objective in this case, then it must simply achieve that objective by means other than a land use control scheme. If and when it does so, we may have occassion to decide (as we need not today) whether state environmental controls are also pre-empted. More likely, however, the question will not arise in the future, as it has not arisen in the past, because of the Federal Government's voluntary accommodation of state environmental concerns—an accommodation that could not occur here only because California neglected to participate in the proceedings. *Ante,* at 1423, n. 1,1430.

I would affirm the court below on the ground that the California Coastal Act permit requirement constitutes a regulation of the use of federal land, and is therefore pre-empted by federal law.

C. Protests, Contests and Adverse Suits

IN RE PACIFIC COAST MOLYBDENUM CO.
68 I.B.L.A. 325, 1982 GFS (MIN.) 329

OPINION BY ADMINISTRATIVE JUDGE BURSKI

This decision is solely concerned with the question of the standing of the Sierra Club (Alaska Chapter), the United Southeast Alaska Gillnetters (USAG), and the Southeast Alaska Conservation Council (SEACC), to appeal from a denial of protests rejecting to Pacific Coast Molybdenum Company's mineral patent application, AA-11319, or to independently initiate a private contest, under the provisions of 43 CFR 4.450-1, to determine the validity of various mining claims. In order to put these questions in perspective, it is necessary to set forth some of the procedural history which has transpired to date.

On April 19, 1979, Pacific Coast Molybdenum Company (PCM), a wholly-owned subsidiary of Quartz Hill Holding Company, which, in turn, was a wholly-owned subsidiary of Pacific Coast Mines, Inc., filed mineral patent application AA-11319.

While the lands embraced by PCM's claims had been open to mineral entry at the time PCM's claims were located, the lands were set apart and reserved as part of the Misty Fiords National Monument on December 1, 1978, by Presidential Proclamation No. 4623 (93 Stat. 1466), pursuant to section 2 of the Antiquities Act, Act of June 8, 1906, 34 Stat. 225, 16 U.S.C. § 431 (1976). On December 5, 1978, notice was published in the *Federal Register* of an application, AA-23139, filed by the United States Department of Agriculture, on November 28, 1978, seeking a withdrawal of various lands, including those embraced by PCM's claims, from location and entry under the general mining laws. 43 FR 57134 (Dec. 5, 1978). Under the provisions of section 204(b)(1) of the Federal Land Policy and Management Act of 1976 (FLPMA), 90 Stat. 2751, 43 U.S.C. § 1714(b)(1) (1976), the publication of this notice served to segregate the lands involved for a period of 2 years or until such time as the application was either approved or disapproved, whichever came first. *See generally James R. Robinson,* 68 IBLA 84 (1982).

Notice of PCM's mineral patent application was duly published, as required by 30 U.S.C. § 29 (1976), on October 19, 1979. Subsequent thereto, various groups filed "protests" or "protest-contests" alleging an adverse interest in the lands embraced by the claims and further arguing that the claims were invalid and that the patent application was deficient for numerous reasons. Of importance herein, the USAG filed a notice of intent to protest on Decemer 7, 1979, and a formal protest on January 2, 1980. SEACC filed both a contest and a protest on December 10, 1979. Sierra Club (Alaska Chapter) filed neither a protest nor a contest.

By various orders dated April 11, 1980, BLM informed the protestants, including USAG, that the protests were being held in abeyance pending a field examination by the United States Forest Service. In addition, SEACC was informed by BLM that its contest complaint was deemed to be a protest and was further notified that its protest was being held in abeyance pending the Forest Service field examination. On September 9, 1980, SEACC submitted a memorandum in support of its patent contest and protest, incorporating by reference a memorandum of points and authorities filed by the National Marine Fisheries Service on August 6, 1980.

The report of the Forest Service field examination was submitted on November 28, 1980. The mineral examiners concluded that "each of the previously listed 49 lode mining claims of the U.S. Borax and Chemical Corporation contain a valuable mineral deposit within its boundaries."

On August 3, 1981, the Chief, Branch of Lands and Mineral Operations, Alaska State Office, denied the various protests. On September 4, 1981, an attorney for the Sierra Club Legal Defense Fund filed a notice of appeal on behalf of USAG, SEACC, and the Sierra Club (Alaska Chapter). On November 3, 1981, a statement of reasons in support of the appeal was filed with the Board. The next day, however, counsel for PCM filed a motion to dismiss the appeal alleging that the appellants lacked standing to prosecute the appeal. On December 2, 1981, PCM filed an answer to appellant's statement of reasons for appeal; on December 3, 1981, appellants filed a memorandum in opposition to the motion to dismiss the appeal, and on December 29, 1981, filed a request for a fact-finding hearing.

Subsequently, PCM filed a reply brief reiterating its request that the appeal be dismissed. On January 18, 1982, the Office of the Regional Solicitor filed a memorandum opposing a fact-finding hearing. On January 25, 1982, PCM also objected to granting appellants a fact-finding hearing. On February 1, 1982, the Office of the Regional Solicitor filed an answer.

On February 22, 1982, this Board notified the parties that it would issue a separate decision on the motion to dismiss filed by PCM, and afforded all parties the opportunity to file additional briefs on the standing questions. On April 1, 1982, appellants filed an additional brief supporting their standing both to appeal from the denial of the protest and to initiate a private contest. While the Solicitor's Office had not earlier taken a position on whether appellants had standing to appeal from a denial of their protests, by a document submitted on April 6, 1982, the Solicitor joined in PCM's motion to dismiss.

PCM's motion to dismiss is grounded on the following analysis. First, it notes that:

The Mining Law of 1872 articulates a comprehensive scheme for processing mineral patents. An essential component of that scheme is a carefully crafted process for resolving any conflict raised by third parties. Holders of conflicting interests in the land, if any, are required to initiate an adverse claim proceeding during a 60-day publication period or their interests are deemed to be waived. 30 U.S.C. § 29 (1976), * * *.

Motion to Dismiss at 6 (citation omitted). PCM then cites the last portion of section 29, "[T]hereafter no objection from third parties to the issuance of a patent shall be heard, except it be shown that the applicant has failed to comply with the terms of this chapter," and argues that this provides the sole statutory basis for even entertaining protests.

PCM places particular emphasis on early Departmental and judicial pronouncements examining the status of protestants as amici curiae. *See, e.g., Wight v. Dubois,* 21 F. 693 (C.C. Colo. 1884); *Bright v. Elkhorn Mining Co.,* 8 L.D. 122 (1889). Thus, Secretary Vilas noted in *Elkhorn Mining:*

A person protesting against the issuance of patent upon a mineral claim, who stands solely in the relation of amicus curiae, and who alleges no interest in the result of the application, can not question the judgment of the land office in passing upon said application and protest, and is not entitled to the right of appeal from such decision. And this is so whether the mineral claimant has or has not complied with the terms of the statute, because if the protestant claims no interest in the suit, the right of the mineral claimant will be considered solely as between the claimant and the government.

Id. at 122-23. PCM argues that only an individual claiming an interest in the subject lands is authorized to appeal from a denial of a protest to a patent application, that appellants claim no such interest in the land, and, thus, appellants have no standing to appeal herein. While these statements may be generally correct, we disagree that appellants USAG and SEACC lack the necessary interest to prosecute this appeal.

Initially, we note that PCM puts more store on the "comprehensive nature" of section 29 than is warranted. First, the "adverse claim" language found in section 29, as well as in section 30, applies only to "adverse claims" by *mining claimants. See, e.g., John R. Meadows,* 43 IBLA 35, 37 (1979). Thus, in *Wright v. Town of Hartville,* 81 P. 649 (Wyo. 1905), *rehearing denied* 82 P. 450 (1905), the Supreme Court of Wyoming expressly held that an individual, or, as in *Wright,* a town, claiming a right to the land under the public land laws, could not file an adverse claim under 30 U.S.C. §§ 29 and 30 (1976).

It will be observed that * * * [30 U.S.C. § 30 (1976)] provides a method by which a court of competent jurisdiction is to determine the right of possession between two or more mining claimants, and not to determine the character of the lands involved as to whether they are mineral or nonmineral. This statute only gives the court jurisdiction of suits when the parties are all mining claimants and when the land embraced in the claim is unpatented government land. It follows, therefore, that the court would not have jurisdiction in a suit in support of an adverse claim, where the parties were all mining claimants, and a patent had already been issued to one of the claimants; or where one of the parties is a mining claimant and the other a town site claimant, whether patent had been issued or not; or, stating the proposition more generally, where one of the parties is an applicant for a patent to mineral land and the other party claims the same or any part of the land embraced in the mining claim under any of the laws providing for the disposal of nonmineral lands. *In other words, the court has jurisdiction only where the suit is between adverse mining claimants to the same unpatented mineral land.* (Emphasis supplied.)

81 P. at 650. *See also Iron Silver Mining Co. v. Campbell,* 135 U.S. 286 (1890).

These judicial determinations were in accord with Departmental decisions. Thus, in *Ryan v. Granite Hill Mining and Development Co.,* 29 L.D. 522 (1900), then Assistant Attorney-General Van Devanter, writing for Secretary Hitchcock, expressly held "the provisions of [30 U.S.C. §§ 29 and 30 (1976)] relative to adverse claims contemplate proceedings to determine only the right of possession as between claimants of the same unpatented mineral lands; and not to decide controversies respecting the character of the public lands, that is, whether they are mineral or nonmineral lands." *Id.* at 524.[6] Under this analysis, the Department held that a millsite claimant was not required to adverse a rival mining claimant. *Helena etc. Co. v. Dailey,* 36 L.D. 144 (1907).[7] Similarly, an agricultural claimant did not hold an adverse claim within the meaning of section 29. *See Powell v. Ferguson,* 23 L.D. 173 (1896).

The language of section 29 which PCM cites relating to objections by third parties merely has the effect of prohibiting anyone who may adverse, but fails to timely do so, from asserting *priority of possession* as a bar to the patent application. It does not serve to limit the rights of those whose claim or interest is not premised on a mineral entry from objecting to the patent application on the grounds that the applicant has not complied with the general mining laws.

The distinction made in cases such as *Bright v. Elkhorn Mining Co., supra,* between the rights of protestants who have an "interest" in the subject of the patent application and the rights of a protestant who does not have such an "interest" is not based on either section 29 or 30. Rather, it proceeds on the simple analysis that anyone can protest, but only one who has an interest

---

[6] It should be noted that while the interpretation of sections 29 and 30 set forth in *Granite Hill* is now universally accepted *(see, e.g., American Law of Mining* § 9.13A), a few early judicial and Departmental decisions did not follow the analysis and permitted nonmineral claimants to utilize the "adverse claim" procedures. *See Young v. Goldstein,* 97 F. 303 (D. Alaska 1899); *Bonnie v. Meikle,* 82 F. 697 (C.C. Nev. 1897); *Northern Pacific R. Co. v. Cannon,* 54 F. 252, 257 (1893); *McGarrahan v. New Idria Mining Co.,* 3 L.D. 422 (1885). A number of these decisions were adverted to in *Grand Canyon Ry. Co. v. Cameron,* 35 L.D. 495 (1907), and expressly rejected.

[7] Paradoxically, it has also been held that where a millsite claimant has a claim conflicting with a patent application for another millsite claim, the adverse procedures of 30 U.S.C. §§ 29 and 30 (1976) are mandatory, since in such a case it is the right of possession rather than the character of the land that is at issue. *See Ebner Gold Mining Co. v. i. C. Hallum,* 47 L.D. 32 (1919).

adversely affected by the denial of a protest has standing to appeal.[8] It is, indeed, the exact standard which the Board presently applies in reviewing appeals from denials of any protest. *Compare* 43 CFR 4.450-2 *with* 43 CFR 4.410. The questions to be decided by this Board under 43 CFR 4.410 are whether appellants are parties to a case whose interests were adversely affected by the denial of their protests. Assuming the answer is in the affirmative, the question then becomes, under 43 CFR 4.450-1, whether appellants possess the necessary interest "in the land" to permit them to initiate a private contest.

PCM contends that appellants are not parties to a case nor were they adversely affected by the decision denying their protests since they lacked an "interest" in the subject matter of the action. Insofar as USAG and SEACC are concerned, we disagree.

The leading Board decision on what constitutes a "party to the case" is *California Association of Four Wheel Drive Clubs,* 30 IBLA 383 (1977). Therein, we quoted from an order of Judge Conti rendered in *Citizens' Committee to Save Our Public Lands v. Kleppe,* C 76-32 SC (Jan. 23, 1976):

> [W]here an individual or group such as the Citizens' Committee uses the Federal land in question and is recognized by the Federal Land Management as a bona fide representative of the community and is provided with notice of all proceedings and actions by the Bureau of Land Management regarding the land in question, and actively and extensively participates in formulating land use plans for the land in question, and takes the position in a dispute concerning the use of the land in question contrary to another individual or group, that individual or group is a party within the meaning of 43 C.F.R. 4.410.

30 IBLA at 386.

In the instant case both USAG and SEACC filed protests alleging that PCM's patent application should be denied for various reasons relating to compliance with the general mining laws. These protests were duly denied. We think it clear that both USAG and SEACC are parties to the case.

The same, however, cannot be said of Sierra Club (Alaska Chapter). Sierra Club filed no protest. In the absence of a protest, Sierra Club was not a party to the decisions relating to the patent application. *See Elaine Mikels,* 41 IBLA 305 (1979). Nor could it become a party to the case by appealing from the denial of a protest filed by someone else. *Conoco, Inc.,* 61 IBLA 23, 25, n.1 (1981), *C&K Petroleum Co.,* 59 IBLA 301, 302, n.1 (1981). Thus, insofar as Sierra Club (Alaska Chapter) is concerned, the purported appeal must be dismissed.

PCM suggests that USAG and SEACC are not parties to the case since they

---

[8] In this regard, Judge Brewer's oft-quoted statement in *Wight* v. *Dubois, supra,* relating to the rights of protestants is relevant only to those protestants who do not have an "interest" in the subject of the patent application. This is obvious when one remembers that a townsite or agriciultural entryman who, indeed, was attempting to acquire title adverse to a mining claimant was denominated a "protestant." *See, e.g., Powell* v. *Ferguson, supra.* There was never any question that such a protestant could appeal to Federal court, though the deference then given to determinations of the Land Department as to the character of the land made the likelihood of success minimal.

lack any interest which is adversely affected. This argument, however, obscures the fact that there are two separate and discrete prerequisites to prosecution of the appeal: (1) that the appellant be a "party to the case;" and (2) that the appellant be "adversely affected" by the decision below. As we have indicated above, denial of a protest makes an individual a party to a case. Such a denial, however, does not necessarily establish that an individual is adversely affected. *See Elaine Mikels, supra* at 307, n.1; *United States v. United States Pumice Corp.*, 37 IBLA 153, 158-59 (1977). Rather, an unsuccessful protestant must show that a legally recognizable "interest" has been adversely affected by denial of the protest. We turn, therefore, to the question whether appellants USAG and SEACC have alleged a sufficient interest, adversely affected, to maintain this appeal.

As we read PCM's arguments, the basic thrust of the motion to dismiss is that only someone who claims a legal interest in the specific land involved has standing to appeal from denial of a protest. So restrictive an interpretation is impossible to sustain.

We note, initially, that there is no necessary congruity between the standing requirements which control the availability of judicial review and those which animate the arena of administrative practice. *Koniag, Inc. v. Andrus,* 580 F.2d 601, 606 (D.C. Cir. 1978). As Judge Bazelon has shown in his concurring opinion in *Koniag,* the underpinnings of judicial standing are functionally discrete from those which buttress standing requirements in an administrative agency. Rather than being based on other constitutional or prudential factors, administrative standing is more properly determined by an analysis embracing "the nature of the asserted interest, the relationship of [this] interest to the functions of the agency, and whether an award of standing would contribute to the attainment of these functions." *Id.* at 615 (Bazelon, J., concurring).

This is not, of course, to say that determinations of judicial standing are irrelevant. On the contrary, they provide a useful guide as to the types of interests which have been deemed relevant and the concerns which are properly considered in adjudicating administrative appeals. We will, to that extent, be guided by judicial determinations on such matters.

In its initial protest, USAG stated that its members fish for salmon stock bound for Keta and Wilson-Blossom rivers and that important tributaries of those rivers are located in the patent area. They contended that mining the deposit as proposed "could have significant adverse environmental impact to the fishery resource and habitat." For its part, SEACC, in its protest complaint, alleged that it was an organization designed to promote the conservation and appreciation of the scenic, wilderness, fish, wildlife, recreation, and other natural resources of southeast Alaska. It specifically alleged that individual members of SEACC have used the areas within the Misty Fiords Monument for a variety of purposes and further claimed that "many members make a substantial portion of their livelihood from the commercial fishery and wilderness values which may be impaired by the proposed mining activities of [PCM]."

It is clear to us that the nature of the asserted interest is such as has been recognized in a number of judicial pronouncements as sufficient to confer standing in a general sense, that is, when such a showing is coupled with a showing of causality between the objected action and the complained injury in a specific case, standing will lie. *See United States* v. *Students Challenging Regulatory Agency Procedures (SCRAP),* 412 U.S. 669 (1973); *Save the Bay, Inc.* v. *United States Corps of Engineers,* 610 F.2d 322 (5th Cir. 1980), *cert. denied,* 444 U.S. 900 (1980); *Animal Welfare League* v. *Kreps,* 561 F.2d 1002 (D.C. Cir. 1977), *cert. denied,* 434 U.S. 1013 (1978). We will discuss the casuality aspect below.

PCM also suggests that appellants lack standing to appeal from a denial of their protest because of the nature of the patent application process. Thus, it argues, "where transfer of title is required by law, the subject matter at issue is limited to rights in land determinable in statutory adverse proceedings, and qualifications of patentees determinable by BLM adjudicators by provisions and limitations of law." We reject this contention for a number of reasons.

In the first place, the premise of the argument, namely, "where transfer of title is required by law," falsely assumes the ultimate conclusion—that transfer of title *is* required by law. Appellants' basic contention on appeal is that the mining claims in issue are not now, and were not on December 1, 1978, supported by a discovery. If appellants could prove their allegations, not only would transfer of title not be required by law, it would be prohibited.

Second, as we have shown above, the statutory "adverse claims" language relates only to adverse mineral claims. PCM's argument would, in effect, prohibit those claiming an interest in the land under the agricultural laws from even appealing within the Department. Such has never been the practice of the Department.

Third, it implicitly assumes that only an interest "in the land" is sufficient to grant a protestant status of a "party aggrieved." While such a standard is, indeed, relevant in determining the standing of a party to initiate a private contest (*see* discussion *infra*), it is not relevant to determining standing to appeal. *See e.g., Elaine Mikels, supra; Alaska* v. *Sarakovikoff,* 50 IBLA 284, 288 (1980); *Crooks Creek Commune,* 10 IBLA 243 (1973).

We recognize, of course, that ultimately it is the Department's responsibility to determine whether a patent applicant has complied with the mining laws. In this sense, it could be argued that *any* protest or even private contest of a patent application is made as an amicus curiae, since the ultimate purpose is to assist the Department in its affirmative obligation to safeguard the public domain "to the end that valid claims may be recognized, invalid ones eliminated, and the rights of the public preserved." *Cameron* v. *United State,* 252 U.S. 450, 460 (1920). This fact, however, does not serve to deprive a protestant, who possesses a cognizable interest adverse to the mineral claimant, from appealing the denial of its protest within the Department.

It is true, as we have recognized in various contexts, that a patent is not necessary to afford a mineral claimant the right to extract and dispose of the locatable minerals until they are exhausted. *See, e.g., United States* v. *Kosanke Sand Corp. (On Reconsideration),* 12 IBLA 282, 80 I.D. 538 (1973). *See also South Dakota* v. *Andrus,* 614 F.2d 1190, 1194 (8th Cir. 1980), *aff'g* 462 F. Supp.

905, 907 (D.S.D. 1978). Thus, it is certainly arguable that the real injury of which appellants complain is unrelated to the patent proceeding, since its cause is the mining of the deposit which could be accomplished in the absence of any patent application. It could be further contended that, in order to be consistent, the Board must either permit protests in the absence of a patent application or deny them when a patent application is involved since in both circumstances it is the actual mining and not the patent proceedings which cause the alleged injury.

While there is a certain logic to the above argument, it ignores the fact that absent a patent application there is no "action" by BLM which can be subject to a protest under 43 CFR 4.450-2. A mining claim is located and operated solely by the claimant without any affirmative action by BLM whatsoever. Nor does the location or mining of a claim in anyway [sic] initiate a "proceeding" before BLM. A patent, however, can only be granted in furtherance of the Department's expressed duty to recognize valid claims, under procedures duly established by statute and regulation. Such recognition is clearly "action proposed to be taken in a proceeding before the Bureau," and, as such, is properly the subject of a protest and, where an adverse interest is shown, appeal. We hold, therefore, that appellants SEACC and USAG have established that they are parties to the case and have alleged interests which were adversely affected by the denial of their protests within the meaning of 43 CFR 4.410, and, thus, can maintain the instant appeal.

The last question to be examined is the contention of appellants that they possess the requisite interest to initiate a private contest under 43 CFR 4.450-1. That regulation reads:

> Any person who claims title to or an interest in land adverse to any other person claiming title to or an interest in such land * * * may initiate proceedings to have the claim of title or interest adverse to this claim invalidated for any reason not shown by the records of the Bureau of Land Management. Such a proceeding will constitute a private contest and will be governed by the regulations herein.

This provision was extensively analyzed in *United States* v. *United States Pumice Corp., supra.* In that decision we quoted the Ninth Circuit's decision in *Duguid* v. *Best,* 291 F.2d 235 (9th Cir. 1961), *cert. denied,* 372 U.S. 906 (1963), which had held that the purpose of the private contest regulation is:

> To *assist* the Secretary of the Interior in carrying out his duties to protect the interest of the government and the public in public lands, in that by such method there may be called to the attention of the Bureau of Land Management invalid claims to title or interest in public lands, the invalidity of which does not appear on the records of the Bureau of Land Management and of which the Bureau may be without knowledge. [Emphasis supplied.]

Id. at 241-42. In *Pumice,* while noting that the effect of this regulation was to broaden the rights of certain individuals "as an administrative mechanism to supplement Departmental activities," we pointed out that only those who could show "an interest in the land" could avail themselves of this provision. And we expressly held that "the 'interest in the land' to which the regulation refers is an interest which must be grounded on a specific statutory grant."

United States v. *United States Pumice Corp., supra,* at 159, n.4. *Accord, Alaska* v. *Sarakovikoff, supra,* at 287.

We reject appellants' attempt to fit their "interest" under this standard. Appellants do not purport to be seeking title to the land under any statute. Contrary to their argument, no property rights to Federal land can be acquired by the mere use of the land. Nor are we aware of anything in either the Alaska National Interest Lands Conservation Act, 94 Stat. 2371, 16 U.S.C. § 3101 (Supp. 1980) or the Alaska Constitution that provides them with such a property right. Lacking such an "interest in the land" appellants may not initiate a private contest of the patent application. We affirm the State Office's determination in this regard.

Appellants SEACC and USAG are hereby afforded a period of 60 days in which to file a reply to the answers filed by PCM and the Office of the Solicitor, on the substance of their appeal. Should any party wish to file additional pleadings, such party should first seek permission of this Board.

Therefore, pursuant to the authority delegated to the Board of Land Appeals by the Secretary of the Interior, 43 CFR 4.1, the motion to dismiss is granted as to Sierra Club (Alaska Chapter) and denied as to SEACC and USAG.

UNITED STATES V. CARLILE
67 I.D. 417 (1960)

[footnotes omitted]

Appeal From the Bureau of Land Management

On January 28, 1954, the Forest Service, Department of Agriculture, protested the application, Oregon 02133, of Kenneth F. and George A. Carlile for patent covering eight lode mining claims situated within the Umpqua National Forest, Oregon. A contest against the claims was initiated on February 1, 1954, and on May 6, 1954, a hearing was held on the charges brought by the Forest Service. In a decision dated October 24, 1955, the hearings officer found that the contestant had not sustained the charge brought against one of the claims (the Maine), that the land is nonmineral in character, but that, as to the seven other claims, it had sustained its charge that minerals had not been found within the limits of the claims in sufficient quantities to constitute a discovery under the mining laws (30 U.S.C., 1958 ed., sec. 21 *et seq.*) The Carliles appealed to the Director of the Bureau of Land Management.

Thereafter, by agreement, a further examination of four of the claims was made. As the result of this examination, made in 1956, the Forest Service agreed that a discovery had been made on two of the claims, the Albany and the Faber, but it contended that the supplemental examination had failed to reveal a discovery on the Dirigo and the Golden Curry claims.

By decision dated November 14, 1958, the Acting Director, Bureau of Land Management, held that the evidence presented at the hearing with respect to the seven claims had been correctly appraised by the hearings officer but that the supplemental evidence submitted thereafter showed that there have been sufficient discoveries on the Albany, the Faber, and the Dirigo claims to support the issuance of patents. He held that although the Teddy, Harris, Fairview, and Golden Curry claims contain veins and fissures which give mineral indications, there has not been such a discovery of valuable mineral deposits on any of them as will support the issuance of a patent. The Acting Director denied the application for patent covering those claims but, apparently because the protest made by the Forest Service went only to the issuance of the patent, he stated that the Carliles "may continue in possession of these claims so long as the lands remain unappropriated for other purposes and there is persistent and diligent prosecution of work leading to the discovery of valuable mineral deposits."

The Forest Service has appealed to the Secretary of the Interior from the decision of the Acting Director insofar as that decision held, on the basis of the new evidence presented after the hearing, that patent should be allowed on the Dirigo claim. It also requests clarification of the decision insofar as it permits the claimants to remain in possession of the other claims.

. . .

We turn now to a consideration of the request of the Forest Service for a clarification of the portion of the Acting Director's decision which reads as follows:

"It is evident from the complete record that although the Teddy, Harris, Fairview and Golden Curry lode claims contain veins and fissures which give mineral indications, there has not been such a discovery of valuable mineral deposits on them as will support the issuance of a patent. The charges against the claims by the Forest Service representing a protest to the application for patent, are considered as having a bearing only with respect to the issuance of mineral patent for the claims. Therefore, although the evidence of mineralization on the Teddy, Harris, Fairview and Golden Curry lode claims is insufficient to sustain the issuance of patent, the contestees may continue in possession of these claims so long as the lands remain unappropriated for other purposes and there is persistent and diligent prosecution of work leading to the discovery of valuable mineral deposits."

The Forest Service states that this wording makes it difficult to determine whether or not the claims as to which patent has been refused are subject to the act of July 23, 1955 (30 U.S.C., 1958 ed., sec. 601 *et seq.*).

Section 4 of that act (30 U.S.C., 1958 ed., sec. 612) provides that any mining claim "hereafter located" shall not be used, prior to issuance of patent, for other than mining purposes and reserves as to such claims the right of the United States to manage and dispose of the surface resources. Section 5 of the act (30 U.S.C., 1958 ed., sec. 613) provides, as to claims located prior to the date of the act, a procedure whereby the right of the claimants to the use of surface resources may be determined. Since the claims involved in this proceeding were located prior to the date of the act, the question of the Forest Service is whether a further proceeding under section 5 must be brought against the claims as to which patent has been refused before the United States may make use of the surface resources.

. . . .

It is clear . . . that even though a location has been made a mining claimant acquires no rights as against the United States until he makes a discovery. Until that time, he is a mere licensee or tenant at will. Upon discovery, and only upon discovery, he acquires as against the United States and all the world an exclusive right of possession to the claim which is property in the fullest sense of the word. See also *Cole v. Ralph, supra,* at p. 295. The property right that the holder of a valid claim has does not depend upon issuance of a patent to him. He need never apply for a patent.

. . . We next consider the procedure that must be followed where the United States believes that a valid discovery has not been made on a mining claim. In *Cameron v. United States,* 252 U.S. 450 (1920), the Court said:

A mining location which has not gone to patent is of no higher quality and no more immune from attack and investigation than are unpatented claims under the homestead and kindred laws. If valid, it gives to the claimant certain exclusive possessory rights, and so do homestead and desert claims. But no right arises from an invalid claim of any kind. All must conform to the law under which they are initiated; otherwise they work an unlawful private appropriation in derogation of the rights of the public.

Of course, the land department has no power to strike down any claim arbitrarily, but so long as the legal title remains in the Government it does have power, after proper notice and upon adequate hearing, to determine whether the claim is valid and, if it be found invalid, to declare it null and void. * * * (p. 460)

In line with this ruling, the established procedure of the Department, where it is thought that a valid discovery has not been made on a claim, has been to institute adverse proceedings against the claim and to hold a hearing for the purpose of receiving evidence on this issue. *The Dredge Corporation,* 65 I.D. 336 (1958). Upon the basis of such evidence, a determination is made as to whether or not a discovery has been made.

If it is determined that a valid discovery has not been made, the mining claim is declared invalid, or null and void. As was said in the Cameron case, supra, the Government has power, if a claim if found invalid, "to declare it null and void."

. . . .

What is the effect of the declaration of invalidity? It is that the mining claimant has acquired no rights against the United States; he has no exclusive right of possession to the land in his claim which is property in the fullest sense of the word. If the United States wishes to withdraw the land in the invalidated claim or otherwise dispose of it under the public land laws, it can do so. If the land has already been included in a withdrawal or some other form of disposition, the withdrawal will attach to the land or the prior disposal will remain unimpaired. No further notice to the claimant or further proceedings against the claim are necessary to achieve these results.

If, however, at the time of invalidation of the claim for lack of discovery the land has not been withdrawn or otherwise disposed of, the claimant may resume occupation of the land, or remain in occupation, and so long as he is engaged in persistent and diligent prosecution of work looking to a discovery have *pedis possessio*. But until he makes a discovery, he has no rights against the United States and the United States can withdraw or otherwise dispose of the land without giving him further notice. In other words, he has the same status as anyone seeking to make a mining location on land open to mining.

What has just been said is true with respect to a mining claim for which no application for patent has been filed. Is it equally true as to claim for which a patent application has been filed?

The Acting Director found that there had not been such a discovery of a valuable mineral deposit on the claims in issue "as will support the issuance of a patent." He concluded that although the evidence was insufficient "to sustain the issuance of patent, the contestees may continue in possession of these claims so long as the lands remain unappropriated for other purposes and there is persistent and diligent prosecution of work leading to the discovery of valuable mineral deposits."

On its face, this language comports with the views just expressed as to the effect of the invalidation of a claim for lack of discovery. Doubt, however, is cast upon this view of the Acting Director's decision by the fact that he refrained from declaring the claims invalid, adverted to testimony by the Forest Service mineral examiner that the validity of the claims was not being challenged except with respect to their eligibility for patent, and said that the Forest Service charges "are considered as having a bearing only with respect to the issuance of mineral patent." The Acting Director cited *United States v. Josephine Lode Mining and Development Company,* A-27090 (May 11, 1955), and *United States v. Margherita Logomarcini,* 60 L.D. 371 (1949).

An examination of these cases and of other cases shows that over a period of years the Department has followed the practice in some mining contests involving application for patents, where the issue of discovery was raised, of simply rejecting the applications for patent and not declaring the claims to be invalid. . . . The customary statement in most of those cases is the same as in the Acting Director's decision here, that is, that the claimant may remain in possession so long as he is looking for a discovery. . . .

A mining claimant has the ultimate burden of establishing by a preponderance of the evidence that his claim is valid. *Foster v. Seaton,* 271 F2d. 836 (D.C. Cir. 1959). If upon application for patent he is unable to prove that he has made a valid discovery, there seems to be no logical basis for holding that, although he must be refused a patent because of lack of discovery, nevertheless his claim will still be considered to be a valid claim.

. . .

It should be understood that this discussion has been concerned solely with the situation where discovery is the issue in the patent proceedings. If the issue is one that does not necessarily go to the validity of the claim, rejection of the patent application would not invalidate the claim. For example, if a discovery has been made but the necessary $500 worth of labor and improvements has not been made, the patent application must be rejected but the validity of the claim would not be impaired. See *United States v. C. F. Smith,* 66 I.D. 169 (1959).

To summarize up to this point, it is my opinion that where in a contest against a mining claim it is found that a valid discovery has not been made, it necessarily follows that the claim is invalid, or null and void, without regard to whether the contest was brought as the result of an application for patent or in the absence of an application for patent. The consequences of the invalidation are as described earlier.

Turning finally to the specific question of the Forest Service—whether the act of July 23, 1955, *supra,* is applicable to the claims for which no valid discovery has been found—the answer becomes clear. The claimants having been found to have no rights against the United States, section 4 of the act, which describes the extent of the rights of the United States in claims located after the date of the act, is applicable. Section 5 of the act, which provides a procedure for determining the rights to the use of surface resources of holders of claims located prior to the date of the act, is inapplicable.

This conclusion affects the Dirigo, Teddy, Harris, Fairview, and Golden Curry claims. So long as the land in those claims remains available for mining location, the claimants, like anyone else, are free to attempt to make a discovery on the land. Until discovery, they have no more than the right of *pedis possessio.* . . . Any claims perfected by discovery made after July 23, 1955, will be subject to section 4 of the act of that date.

Therefore, pursuant to the authority delegated to the Solicitor by the Secretary of the Interior (sec. 210.1.1A(4) (a), Departmental Manual; 24 F.R. 1348), the decision of the Acting Director is reversed in part and modified in accordance with this decision.

NOTES

1. One commentator has argued that the result of *Carlile* is to permit the Government to "mindlessly void . . . claims which fail to gain approval for patent. . . . The *Carlile* rule hinders the purposes of the mineral policies act of 1970, 30 U.S.C. § 21a, by which Congress declared it is the continuing policy of the federal government, in the national interest, to foster and encourage private mineral development of the public lands. *Carlile* impedes this national policy without good reason." Do you agree? If a patent application results in a claim being declared "null and void" under *Carlile,* is the locator any worse off than he was before the application? With respect to the Government? With respect to rival claimants? How are the purposes of the Minerals Policy Act furthered by validating claims which are not supported by a valid discovery?

2. The Administrative Procedure Act, 5 U.S.C. § 556(d), provides: "Except as otherwise provided by statute, the proponent of a rule or order has the burden of proof." When the United States contests the validity of claim, it is at least arguably the proponent of a "rule or order," namely, the order that the claim is

invalid. Nevertheless, the United States does not have the burden of proof in a contest. The United States need only present a prima facie case, and then the mining claimant must bear the burden of proving that he has satisfied all the requirements of the mining laws for establishing a valid claim. In *United States v. Springer,* 491 F.2d 239, 242 (9th Cir. 1974) the Ninth Circuit harmonized this apparent inconsistency as follows:

> "Many public land laws, including the mining laws, give a person a right to initiate a claim to public lands by his ex parte act of entry. If he thereafter complies with all the requirements of the law, his initial entry may ripen into an enforceable claim to title as against the United States. The entryman is the true proponent of the rule or order within the meaning of the . . . Administrative Procedure Act."

BOWEN V. CHEMI-COTE PERLITE CORPORATION
432 P.2d 435 (Az. 1967)

[At this point you should review the *Bowen* case, chapter 2, *supra.*]

NOTES

1. The adverse suit may be used only to litigate matters of possession between rival mineral claimants. It may not be used to determine other issues, such as the rights of co-tenants or the existence or extent of extralateral rights. In the adverse suit, the plaintiff is always the adverse claimant and never the patent applicant. The defendant is always the patent applicant. The proper venue is the state court of general jurisdiction located in the judicial district in which the claim is situated. Since the adverse suit relates only to matters of possession, no federal question is involved, and the federal courts do not have federal question jurisdiction. The federal courts may exercise jurisdiction in the adverse suit based on diversity of citizenship.

2. The failure to adverse a patent application is conclusive on the rights of the adverse claimant as to all matters that could have been raised in the adverse suit. The only exception is that the adverse claimant is not deprived of those remedies "which a court of equity might allow to be urged against a judgment of law." *Golden Reward Mining Co. v. Buxton Mining Co.,* 79 Fed. 868, 874 (S.D. 1897).

3. As the principal case states, the adverse suit is unique in that three verdicts are possible: for the plaintiff, for the defendant, and for neither. In the typical case, the plaintiff must prove his case by a preponderance of the evidence, and if he fails to do so the defendant is entitled to a verdict in his favor. Not so in the adverse suit. In that type of action "each party is practically a plaintiff, and must show his title; . . . there can be no non-suit, but . . . , if neither shows his title, the verdict must be special, and the title, of course remains in the United States

. . . . *IBA v. Central Association of Wyoming,* 5 Wyo. 355, 360, 40 P. 527, 528 (1895).

"The defendant must introduce evidence directly and affirmatively establishing his claim, and an instruction in such a case that the plaintiff must prove his case by a fair preponderance of the evidence, and, if the evidence was equally balanced, the defendant must recover, was held erroneous. . . . The reasons for these distinctions between this class of actions and others is obvious. The whole proceeding in the government land office is stayed upon the filing of the adverse claim to the application for the patent, until the rights of the parties and those of the government are judicially determined. If one of the parties litigant establishes his claim, it must be so found; if neither, that finding must be made." *IBA v. Central Association of Wyoming* at 364, 40 P. at 530.

4. The state court's decision in the adverse suit is binding on the BLM, and the department cannot issue a patent to the party or parties against whom judgment was rendered in that suit. The judgment is not affirmatively binding on the Department, however, and just because a judgment is rendered in favor of a party in the adverse suit does not mean that that party is entitled to a patent. To obtain the patent, compliance with all necessary requirements, including a valid discovery good against the United States, must be shown.

APPENDIX

Selected Sections from Title 30, United States Code,
Mineral Lands and Mining

§ 21. Mineral lands reserved [R.S. § 2318]

In all cases lands valuable for minerals shall be reserved from sale, except as otherwise expressly directed by law.

§ 21a. National mining and minerals policy; definition of minerals; execution of policy under other authorized programs; report to Congress

The Congress declares that it is the continuing policy of the Federal Government in the national interest to foster and encourage private enterprise in (1) the development of economically sound and stable domestic mining, minerals, metal and mineral reclamation industries, (2) the orderly and economic development of domestic mineral resources, reserves, and reclamation of metals and minerals to help assure satisfaction of industrial, security and environmental needs, (3) mining, mineral, and metallurgical research, including the use and recycling of scrap to promote the wise and efficient use of our natural and reclaimable mineral resources, and (4) the study and development of methods for the disposal, control, and reclamation of mineral waste products, and the reclamation of mined land, so as to lessen any adverse impact of mineral extraction and processing upon the physical environment that may result from mining or mineral activities.

For the purpose of this section "minerals" shall include all minerals and mineral fuels including oil, gas, coal, oil shale and uranium.

It shall be the responsibility of the Secretary of the Interior to carry out this policy when exercising his authority under such programs as may be authorized by law other than this section. For this purpose the Secretary of the Interior shall include in his annual report to the Congress a report on the state of the domestic mining, minerals, and mineral reclamation industries, including a statement of the trend in utilization and depletion of these resources, together with such recommendations for legislative programs as may be necessary to implement the policy of this section.

§ 22. Lands open to purchase by citizens [R.S. § 2319]

Except as otherwise provided, all valuable mineral deposits in lands belonging to the United States, both surveyed and unsurveyed, shall be free and open to exploration and purchase, and the lands in which they are found to occupation and purchase, by citizens of the United States and those who have declared their intention to become such, under regulations prescribed by law, and according to the local customs or rules of miners in the several mining districts, so far as the same are applicable and not inconsistent with the laws of the United States.

§ 23. Length of claims on veins or lodes [R.S. § 2320]

Mining claims upon veins or lodes of quartz or other rock in place bearing gold, silver, cinnabar, lead, tin, copper, or other valuable deposits, located prior to May 10, 1872, shall be governed as to length along the vein or lode by the customs, regulations, and laws in force at the date of their location. A mining claim located after the 10th day of May 1872, whether located by one or more persons, may equal, but shall not exceed, one thousand five hundred feet in length along the vein or lode; but no location of a mining claim shall be made until the discovery of the vein or lode within the limits of the claim located. No claim shall extend more than three hundred feet on each side of the middle of the vein at the surface, nor shall any claim be limited by any mining regulation to less than twenty-five feet on each side of the middle of the vein at the surface, except where adverse rights existing on the 10th day of May 1872 render such limitation necessary. The end lines of each claim shall be parallel to each other.

§ 24. Proof of citizenship [R.S. § 2321]

Proof of citizenship, under sections 21, 22 to 24, 26 to 28, 29, 30, 33 to 48, 50 to 52, 71 to 76 of this title and section 661 of title 43, may consist, in the case of an individual, of his own affidavit thereof; in the case of an association of persons unincorporated, of the affidavit of their authorized agent, made on his own knowledge, or upon information and belief; and in the case of a corporation organized under the laws of the United States, or of any State or Territory thereof, by the filing of a certified copy of their charter or certificate of incorporation.

§ 25. Affidavit of citizenship

Applicants for mineral patents, if residing beyond the limits of the district wherein the claim is situated, may make any oath or affidavit required for proof of citizenship before the clerk of any court of record or before any notary public of any State or Territory.

§ 26. Locators' rights of possession and enjoyment [R.S. § 2322]

The locators of all mining locations made on any mineral vein, lode, or ledge, situated on the public domain, their heirs and assigns, where no adverse claim existed on the 10th day of May 1872 so long as they comply with the laws of the United States, and with State, territorial, and local regulations not in conflict with the laws of the United States governing their possessory title, shall have the exclusive right of possession and enjoyment of all the surface included within the lines of their locations, and of all veins, lodes, and ledges throughout their entire depth, the top or apex of which lies inside of such surface lines extended downward vertically, although such veins, lodes, or ledges may so far depart from a perpendicular in their course downward as to extend outside the vertical side lines of such surface locations. But their right of possession to such outside parts of such veins or ledges shall be confined to such portions thereof as lie between vertical planes drawn downward as above described, through the end lines of their locations, so continued in their own direction that such planes will intersect such exterior parts of such veins or ledges. Nothing in this section shall authorize the locator or possessor of a vein or lode which extends in its downward course beyond the vertical lines of his claim to enter upon the surface of a claim owned or possessed by another.

§ 27. Mining tunnels; right to possession of veins on line with; abandonment of right [R.S. § 2323]

Where a tunnel is run for the development of a vein or lode, or for the discovery of mines, the owners of such tunnel shall have the right of possession of all veins or lodes within three thousand feet from the face of such tunnel on the line thereof, not previously known to exist, discovered in such tunnel, to the same extent as if discovered from the surface; and locations on the line of such tunnel of veins or lodes not appearing on the surface, made by other parties after the commencement of the tunnel, and while the same is being prosecuted with reasonable diligence, shall be invalid; but failure to prosecute the work on the tunnel for six months shall be considered as an abandonment of the right to all undiscovered veins on the line of such tunnel.

§ 28. Mining district regulations by miners: location, recordation, and amount of work; marking of location on ground; records; annual labor or improvements on claims pending issue of patent; co-owner's succession in interest upon delinquency in contributing proportion of expenditures; tunnel as lode expenditure [R.S. § 2324]

The miners of each mining district may

make regulations not in conflict with the laws of the United States, or with the laws of the State or Territory in which the district is situated, governing the location, manner of recording, amount of work necessary to hold possession of a mining claim, subject to the following requirements: The location must be distinctly marked on the ground so that its boundaries can be readily traced. All records of mining claims made after May 10, 1872, shall contain the name or names of the locators, the date of the location, and such a description of the claim or claims located by reference to some natural object or permanent monument as will identify the claim. On each claim located after the 10th day of May 1872, and until a patent has been issued therefor, not less than $100 worth of labor shall be performed or improvements made during each year. On all claims located prior to the 10th day of May 1872, $10 worth of labor shall be performed or improvements made each year, for each one hundred feet in length along the vein until a patent has been issued therefor; but where such claims are held in common, such expenditure may be made upon any one claim; and upon a failure to comply with these conditions, the claim or mine upon which such failure occurred shall be open to relocation in the same manner as if no location of the same had ever been made, provided that the original locators, their heirs, assigns, or legal representatives, have not resumed work upon the claim after failure and before such location. Upon the failure of any one of several coowners to contribute his proportion of the expenditures required hereby, the coowners who have performed the labor or made the improvements may, at the expiration of the year, give such delinquent co-owner personal notice in writing or notice by publication in the newspaper published nearest the claim, for at least once a week for ninety days, and if at the expiration of ninety days after such notice in writing or by publication such delinquent should fail or refuse to contribute his proportion of the expenditure required by this section, his interest in the claim shall become the property of his co-owners who have made the required expenditures. The period within which the work required to be done annually on all unpatented mineral claims located since May 10, 1872, including such claims in the Territory of Alaska, shall commence at 12 o'clock meridian on the 1st day of September succeeding the date of location of such claim.

Where a person or company has or may run a tunnel for the purposes of developing a lode or lodes, owned by said person or company, the money so expended in said tunnel shall be taken and considered as expended on said lode or lodes, whether located prior to or since May 10, 1872; and such person or company shall not be required to perform work on the surface of said lode or lodes in order to hold the same as required by this section. On all such valid claims the annual period ending December 31, 1921, shall continue to 12 o'clock meridian July 1, 1922.

§ 28-1. Inclusion of certain surveys in labor requirements of mining claims; conditions and restrictions

The term "labor", as used in the third sentence of section 28 of this title, shall include, without being limited to, geological, geochemical and geophysical surveys conducted by qualified experts and verified by a detailed report filed in the county office in which the claim is located which sets forth fully (a) the location of the work performed in relation to the point of discovery and boundaries of the claim, (b) the nature, extent, and cost thereof, (c) the basic findings therefrom, and (d) the name, address, and professional background of the person or persons conducting the work. Such surveys, however, may not be applied as labor for more than two consecutive years or for more than a total of five years on any one mining claim, and each such survey shall be nonrepetitive of any previous survey on the same claim.

§ 28-2. Definitions

As used in section 28-1 of this title,

(a) The term "geological surveys" means surveys on the ground for mineral deposits by the proper application of the principles and techniques of the science of geology as they relate to the search for and discovery of mineral deposits;

(b) The term "geochemical surveys" means surveys on the ground for mineral deposits by the proper application of the principles and techniques of the science of chemistry as they relate to the search for and discovery of mineral deposits;

(c) The term "geophysical surveys" means surveys on the ground for mineral deposits through the employment of generally recognized equipment and methods for measuring physical differences between rock types or discontinuities in geological formations;

(d) The term "qualified expert" means an individual qualified by education or experience to conduct geological, geochemical or geophysical surveys, as the case may be.

§ 28b. Annual assessment work on mining claims; temporary deferment; conditions

The performance of not less than $100 worth of labor or the making of improvements aggregating such amount, which labor or improvements are required under the provisions of section 28 of this title to be made during each year, may be deferred by the Secretary of the Interior as to any mining claim or group of claims in the United States upon the submission by the claimant of evidence satisfactory to the Secretary that such mining claim or group of claims is surrounded by lands over which a right-of-way for the performance of such assessment work has been denied or is in litigation or is in the process of acquisition under State law or that other legal impediments exist which affect the right of the claimant to enter upon the surface of such claim or group of claims or to gain access to the boundaries thereof.

§ 28c. Length and termination of deferment

The period for which said deferment may be granted shall end when the conditions justifying deferment have been removed: *Provided,* That the initial period shall not exceed

one year but may be renewed for a further period of one year if justifiable conditions exist: *Provided further,* That the relief available under sections 28b to 28e of this title is in addition to any relief available under any other Act of Congress with respect to mining claims.

§ 28d. Performance of deferred work

All deferred assessment work shall be performed not later than the end of the assessment year next subsequent to the removal or cessation of the causes for deferment or the expiration of any deferments granted under sections 28b to 28e of this title and shall be in addition to the annual assessment work required by law in such year.

§ 28e. Recordation of deferment

Claimant shall file or record or cause to be filed or recorded in the office where the notice or certificate of location of such claim or group of claims is filed or recorded, a notice to the public of claimant's petition to the Secretary of the Interior for deferment under sections 28b to 28e of this title, and of the order or decision disposing of such petition.

§ 29. Patents; procurement procedure; filing: applications under oath, plat and field notes, notices, and affidavits; posting plat and notice on claim; publication and posting notice in office; certificate; adverse claims; payment per acre; objections; nonresident claimant's agent for execution of application and affidavits [R.S. § 2325]

A patent for any land claimed and located for valuable deposits may be obtained in the following manner: Any person, association, or corporation authorized to locate a claim under sections 21, 22 to 24, 26 to 28, 29, 30, 33 to 48, 50 to 52, 71 to 76 of this title and section 661 of title 43, having claimed and located a piece of land for such purposes, who has, or have, complied with the terms of sections 21, 22 to 24, 26 to 28, 29, 30, 33 to 48, 50 to 52, 71 to 76 of this title, and section 661 of title 43, may file in the proper land office an application for a patent, under oath, showing such compliance, together with a plat and field notes of the claim or claims in common, made by or under the direction of the Director of the Bureau of Land Management, showing accurately the boundaries of the claim or claims, which shall be distinctly marked by monuments on the ground, and shall post a copy of such plat, together with a notice of such application for a patent, in a conspicuous place on the land embraced in such plat previous to the filing of the application for the patent, and shall file an affidavit of at least two persons that such notice has been duly posted, and shall file a copy of the notice in such land office, and shall thereupon be entitled to a patent for the land, in the manner following: The register of the land office, upon the filing of such application, plat, field notes, notices, and affidavits, shall publish a notice that such application has been made, for the period of sixty days, in a newspaper to be by him designated as published nearest to such claim; and he shall also post such notice in his office for the same period. The claimant at the time of filing this application, or at any time thereafter, within the sixty days of publication, shall file with the register a certificate of the Director of the Bureau of Land Management that $500 worth of labor has been expended or improvements made upon the claim by himself or grantors; that the plat is correct, with such further description by such reference to natural objects or permanent monuments as shall identify the claim, and furnish an accurate description, to be incorporated in the patent. At the expiration of the sixty days of publication the claimant shall file his affidavit, showing that the plat and notice have been posted in a conspicuous place on the claim during such period of publication. If no adverse claim shall have been filed with the register of the proper land office at the expiration of the sixty days of publication, it shall be assumed that the applicant is entitled to a patent, upon the payment to the proper officer of $5 per acre, and that no adverse claim exists; and thereafter no objection from third parties to the issuance of a patent shall be heard, except it be shown that the applicant has failed to comply with

the terms of sections 21, 22 to 24, 26 to 28, 29, 30, 33 to 48, 50 to 52, 71 to 76 of this title and section 661 of title 43. Where the claimant for a patent is not a resident of or within the land district wherein the vein, lode, ledge, or deposit sought to be patented is located, the application for patent and the affidavits required to be made in this section by the claimant for such patent may be made by his, her, or its authorized agent, where said agent is conversant with the facts sought to be established by said affidavits.

§ 30. **Adverse claims; oath of claimants; requisites; waiver; stay of land office proceedings; judicial determination of right of possession; successful claimants' filing of judgment roll, certificate of labor, and description of claim in land office, and acreage and fee payments; issuance of patents for entire or partial claims upon certification of land office proceedings and judgment roll; alienation of patent title [R.S. § 2326]**

Where an adverse claim is filed during the period of publication, it shall be upon oath of the person or persons making the same, and shall show the nature, boundaries, and extent of such adverse claim, and all proceedings, except the publication of notice and making and filing of the affidavit thereof, shall be stayed until the controversy shall have been settled or decided by a court of competent jurisdiction, or the adverse claim waived. It shall be the duty of the adverse claimant, within thirty days after filing his claim, to commence proceedings in a court of competent jurisdiction, to determine the question of the right of possession, and prosecute the same with reasonable diligence to final judgment; and a failure so to do shall be a waiver of his adverse claim. After such judgment shall have been rendered, the party entitled to the possession of the claim, or any portion thereof, may, without giving further notice, file a certified copy of the judgment roll with the register of the land office, together with the certificate of the Director of the Bureau of Land Management that the requisite amount of labor has been expended or improvements made thereon, and the description required in other cases, and shall pay to the register $5 per acre for his claim, together with the proper fees, whereupon the whole proceedings and the judgment roll shall be certified by the register to the Director of the Bureau of Land Management, and a patent shall issue thereon for the claim, or such portion thereof as the applicant shall appear, from the decision of the court, to rightly possess. If it appears from the decision of the court that several parties are entitled to separate and different portions of the claim, each party may pay for his portion of the claim, with the proper fees, and file the certificate and description by the Director of the Bureau of Land Management whereupon the register shall certify the proceedings and judgment roll to the Director of the Bureau of Land Management, as in the preceding case, and patents shall issue to the several parties according to their respective rights. Nothing herein contained shall be construed to prevent the alienation of the title conveyed by a patent for a mining claim to any person whatever.

§ 31. Oath: agent or attorney in fact, beyond district of claim

The adverse claim required by section 30 of this title may be verified by the oath of any duly authorized agent or attorney in fact of the adverse claimant cognizant of the facts stated; and the adverse claimant, if residing or at the time being beyond the limits of the district wherein the claim is situated, may make oath to the adverse claim before the clerk of any court of record of the United States or of the State or Territory where the adverse claimant may then be, or before any notary public of such State or Territory.

§ 32. Findings by jury; costs

If, in any action brought pursuant to section 30 of this title, title to the ground in controversy shall not be established by either party, the jury shall so find, and judgment shall be entered according to the verdict. In such case costs shall not be allowed to either

party, and the claimant shall not proceed in the land office or be entitled to a patent for the ground in controversy until he shall have perfected his title.

§ 33. Existing rights [R.S. § 2328]

All patents for mining claims upon veins or lodes issued prior to May 10, 1872, shall convey all the rights and privileges conferred by sections 21, 22 to 24, 26 to 28, 29, 30, 33 to 48, 50 to 52, 71 to 76 of this title and section 661 of title 43 where no adverse rights existed on the 10th day of May, 1872.

§ 34. Description of vein claims on surveyed and unsurveyed lands; monuments on ground to govern conflicting calls [R.S. § 2327]

The description of vein or lode claims upon surveyed lands shall designate the location of the claims with reference to the lines of the public survey, but need not conform therewith; but where patents have been or shall be issued for claims upon unsurveyed lands, the Director of the Bureau of Land Management in extending the public survey, shall adjust the same to the boundaries of said patented claims so as in no case to interfere with or change the true location of such claims as they are officially established upon the ground. Where patents have issued for mineral lands, those lands only shall be segregated and shall be deemed to be patented which are bounded by the lines actually marked, defined, and established upon the ground by the monuments of the official survey upon which the patent grant is based, and the Director of the Bureau of Land Management in executing subsequent patent surveys, whether upon surveyed or unsurveyed lands, shall be governed accordingly. The said monuments shall at all times constitute the highest authority as to what land is patented, and in case of any conflict between the said monuments of such patented claims and the descriptions of said claims in the patents issued therefor the monuments on the ground shall govern, and erroneous or inconsistent descriptions or calls in the patent descriptions shall give way thereto.

§ 35. **Placer claims; entry and proceedings for patent under provisions applicable to vein or lode claims; conforming entry to legal subdivisions and surveys; limitation of claims; homestead entry of segregated agricultural land [R.S. §§ 2329, 2331]**

Claims usually called "placers," including all forms of deposit, excepting veins of quartz, or other rock in place, shall be subject to entry and patent, under like circumstances and conditions, and upon similar proceedings, as are provided for vein or lode claims; but where the lands have been previously surveyed by the United States, the entry in its exterior limits shall conform to the legal subdivisions of the public lands. And where placer claims are upon surveyed lands, and conform to legal subdivisions, no further survey or plat shall be required, and all placer-mining claims located after the 10th day of May 1872, shall conform as near as practicable with the United States system of public-land surveys, and the rectangular subdivisions of such surveys, and no such location shall include more than twenty acres for each individual claimant; but where placer claims cannot be conformed to legal subdivisions, survey and plat shall be made as on unsurveyed lands; and where by the segregation of mineral land in any legal subdivision a quantity of agricultural land less than forty acres remains, such fractional portion of agricultural land may be entered by any party qualified by law, for homestead purposes.

§ 36. **Subdivisions of 10-acre tracts; maximum of placer locations; homestead claims of agricultural lands; sale of improvements [R.S. § 2330]**

Legal subdivisions of forty acres may be subdivided into ten-acre tracts; and two or more persons, or associations of persons, having contiguous claims of any size, although such claims may be less than ten acres each, may make joint entry thereof; but no location of a placer claim, made after the 9th day of July 1870, shall exceed one hundred and sixty acres for any one person or association of persons, which location shall conform to the United States surveys; and nothing in this section contained shall defeat or impair any bona fide homestead claim upon agricultural lands, or authorize the sale of the improvements of any bona fide settler to any purchaser.

§ 37. **Proceedings for patent where boundaries contain vein or lode; application; statement including vein or lode; issuance of patent: acreage payments for vein or lode and placer claim; costs of proceedings; knowledge affecting construction of application and scope of patent [R.S. § 2333]**

Where the same person, association, or corporation is in possession of a placer claim, and also a vein or lode included within the boundaries thereof, application shall be made for a patent for the placer claim, with the statement that it includes such vein or lode, and in such case a patent shall issue for the placer claim, subject to the provisions of sections 21, 22 to 24, 26 to 28, 29, 30, 33 to 48, 50 to 52, 71 to 76 of this title and section 661 of title 43, including such vein or lode, upon the payment of $5 per acre for such vein or lode claim, and twenty-five feet of surface on each side thereof. The remainder of the placer claim, or any placer claim not embracing any vein or lode claim, shall be paid for at the rate of $2.50 per acre, together with all costs of proceedings; and where a vein or lode, such as is described in section 23 of this title, is known to exist within the boundaries of a placer claim, an application for a patent for such placer claim which does not include an application for the vein or lode claim shall be construed as a conclusive declaration that the claimant of the placer claim has no right of possession of the vein or lode claim; but where the existence of a vein or lode in a placer claim is not known, a patent for the placer claim shall convey all valuable mineral and other deposits within the boundaries thereof.

§ 38. Evidence of possession and work to establish right to patent [R.S. § 2332]

Where such person or association, they and their grantors, have held and worked their claims for a period equal to the time prescribed by the statute of limitations for mining claims of the State or Territory where the same may be situated, evidence of such possession and working of the claims for such period shall be sufficient to establish a right to a patent thereto under sections 21, 22 to 24, 26 to 28, 29, 30, 33 to 48, 50 to 52, 71 to 76 of this title and section 661 of title 43, in the absence of any adverse claim; but nothing in such sections shall be deemed to impair any lien which may have attached in any way whatever to any mining claim or property thereto attached prior to the issuance of a patent.

§ 39. Surveyors of mining claims [R.S. § 2334]

The Director of the Bureau of Land Management may appoint in each land district containing mineral lands as many competent surveyors as shall apply for appointment to survey mining claims. The expenses of the survey of vein or lode claims, and the survey and subdivision of placer claims into smaller quantities than one hundred and sixty acres, together with the cost of publication of notices, shall be paid by the applicants, and they shall be at liberty to obtain the same at the most reasonable rates, and they shall also be at liberty to employ any United States deputy surveyor to make the survey. The Director of the Bureau of Land Management shall also have power to establish the maximum charges for surveys and publication of notices under sections 21, 22 to 24, 26 to 28, 29, 30, 33 to 48, 50 to 52, 71 to 76 of this title and section 661 of title 43; and, in case of excessive charges for publication, he may designate any newspaper published in a land district where mines are situated for the publication of mining notices in such district, and fix the rates to be charged by such paper; and, to the end

that the Director may be fully informed on the subject, each applicant shall file with the register a sworn statement of all charges and fees paid by such applicant for publication and surveys, together with all fees and money paid the register of the land office, which statement shall be transmitted, with the other papers in the case, to the Director of the Bureau of Land Management.

§ 40. Verification of affidavits [R.S. § 2335]

All affidavits required to be made under sections 21, 22 to 24, 26 to 28, 29, 30, 33 to 48, 50 to 52, 71 to 76 of this title, and section 661 of title 43 may be verified before any officer authorized to administer oaths within the land district where the claims may be situated, and all testimony and proofs may be taken before any such officer, and, when duly certified by the officer taking the same, shall have the same force and effect as if taken before the register of the land office. In cases of contest as to the mineral or agricultural character of land, the testimony and proofs may be taken as herein provided on personal notice of at least ten days to the opposing party; or if such party cannot be found, then by publication of at least once a week for thirty days in a newspaper, to be designated by the register of the land office as published nearest to the location of such land; and the register shall require proof that such notice has been given.

§ 41. Intersecting or crossing veins [R.S. § 2336]

Where two or more veins intersect or cross each other, priority of title shall govern, and such prior location shall be entitled to all ore or mineral contained within the space of intersection; but the subsequent location shall have the right-of-way through the space of intersection for the purposes of the convenient working of the mine. And where two or more veins unite, the oldest or prior location shall take the vein below the point of union, including all the space of intersection.

§ 42. Patents for nonmineral lands: application, survey, notice, acreage limitation, payment [R.S. § 2337]

(a) Vein or lode and mill site owners eligible

Where nonmineral land not contiguous to the vein or lode is used or occupied by the proprietor of such vein or lode for mining or milling purposes, such nonadjacent surface ground may be embraced and included in an application for a patent for such vein or lode, and the same may be patented therewith, subject to the same preliminary requirements as to survey and notice as are applicable to veins or lodes; but no location made on and after May 10, 1972 of such nonadjacent land shall exceed five acres, and payment for the same must be made at the same rate as fixed by sections 21, 22 to 24, 26 to 28, 29, 30, 33 to 48, 50 to 52, 71 to 76 of this title and section 661 of title 43 for the superficies of the lode. The owner of a quartz mill or reduction works, not owning a mine in connection therewith, may also receive a patent for his mill site, as provided in this section.

(b) Placer claim owners eligible

Where nonmineral land is needed by the proprietor of a placer claim for mining, milling, processing, beneficiation, or other operations in connection with such claim, and is used or occupied by the proprietor for such purposes, such land may be included in an application for a patent for such claim, and may be patented therewith subject to the same requirements as to survey and notice as are applicable to placers. No location made of such nonmineral land shall exceed five acres and payment for the same shall be made at the rate applicable to placer claims which do not include a vein or lode.

§ 43. Conditions of sale by local legislature [R.S. § 2338]

As a condition of sale, in the absence of necessary legislation by Congress, the local legislature of any State or Territory may provide rules for working mines, involving easements, drainage, and other necessary means to their complete development; and those conditions shall be fully expressed in the patent.

§ 49a. Mining laws of United States extended to Alaska; exploration and mining for precious metals; regulations; conflict of laws; permits; dumping tailings; pumping from sea; reservation of roadway; title to land below line of high tide or high-water mark; transfer of title to future State

The laws of the United States relating to mining claims, mineral locations, and rights incident thereto are extended to the Territory of Alaska: *Provided,* That, subject only to the laws enacted by Congress for the protection and preservation of the navigable waters of the United States, and to the laws for the protection of fish and game, and subject also to such general rules and regulations as the Secretary of the Interior may prescribe for the preservation of order and the prevention of injury to the fish and game, all land below the line of ordinary high tide on tidal waters and all land below the line of ordinary high-water mark on nontidal water navigable in fact, within the jurisdiction of the United States, shall be subject to exploration and mining for gold and other precious metals, and in the Chilkat River, and its tributaries, within two and three-tenths miles of United States survey numbered 991 for all metals, by citizens of the United States, or persons who have legally declared their intentions to become such, under such reasonable rules and regulations as the miners in organized mining districts may have heretofore made or may hereafter make governing the temporary possession thereof for exploration and mining purposes until otherwise provided by law: *Provided further,* That the rules and regulations established by the miners shall not be in conflict with the mining laws of the United States; and no exclusive permit shall be granted by the Secretary of the Interior authorizing any person or persons, corporation, or company to excavate or mine under any of said waters, and if such exclusive permit has been granted it is revoked and declared null and void. The rules and regulations prescribed by the Secretary of the Interior under this section shall not, however, deprive miners on the beach of the right given to dump tailings into or pump from the sea opposite their claims, except where such dumping would actually obstruct navigation or impair the fish and game, and the reservation of a roadway sixty feet wide under section 687a-2 of title 43, shall not apply to mineral lands or town sites. No person shall acquire by virtue of this section any title to any land below the line of ordinary high tide or the line of ordinary high-water mark, as the case may be, of the waters described in this section. Any rights or privileges acquired hereunder with respect to mining operations in land, title to which is transferred to a future State upon its admission to the Union and which is situated within its boundaries, shall be terminable by such State, and the said mining operations shall be subject to the laws of such State.

§ 49b. Mining laws relating to placer claims extended to Alaska

The general mining laws of the United States so far as they are applicable to placer-mining claims, as prior to May 4, 1934, extended to the Territory of Alaska, are declared to be in full force and effect in said Territory: *Provided,* That nothing herein shall be held to change or affect the rights acquired by locators or owners of placer-mining claims prior to May 4, 1934, located in said Territory under act August 1, 1912 (37 Stat. 242, 243) and amendatory act March 3, 1925 (43 Stat. 1118).

§ 49c. Recording notices of location of Alaskan mining claims

Notices of location of mining claims shall be filed for record within ninety days from the date of the discovery of the claim described in the notice, and all instruments shall be recorded in the recording district in which the property or subject matter affected by the instrument is situated, and where the property

or subject matter is not situated in any established recording district the instrument affecting the same shall be recorded in the office of the clerk of the division of the court having supervision over the recording division in which such property or subject matter is situated.

§ 49d. Miners' regulations for recording notices in Alaska; certain records legalized

Miners in any organized mining district may make rules and regulations governing the recording of notices of location of mining claims, water rights, flumes and ditches, mill sites and affidavits of labor, not in conflict with this Act or the general laws of the United States; and nothing in this Act shall be construed so as to prevent the miners in any regularly organized mining district not within any recording district established by the court from electing their own mining recorder to act as such until a recorder therefor is appointed by the court: *Provided further,* All records regularly made by the United States commissioner prior to June 6, 1900, at Dyea, Skagway, and the recorder at Douglas City, not in conflict with any records regularly made with the United States commissioner at Juneau, are legalized. And all records made in good faith prior to June 6, 1900, in any regularly organized mining district are made public records.

§ 49e. Annual labor or improvements on Alaskan mining claims; affidavits; burden of proof; forfeitures; location anew of claims; perjury

During each year and until patent has been issued therefor, at least $100 worth of labor shall be performed or improvements made on, or for the benefit or development of, in accordance with existing law, each mining claim in Alaska heretofore or hereafter located. And the locator or owner of such claim or some other person having knowledge of the facts may also make and file with the said recorder of the district in which the claims shall be situated an affidavit showing the performance of labor or making of improvements to the amount of $100 as aforesaid and specifying the character and extent of such work. Such affidavits shall set forth the following: First, the name or number of the mining claims and where situated; second, the number of days' work done and the character and value of the improvements placed thereon; third, the date of the performance of such labor and of making improvements; fourth, at whose instance the work was done or the improvements made; fifth, the actual amount paid for work and improvement, and by whom paid when the same was not done by the owner. Such affidavit shall be prima facie evidence of the performance of such work or making of such improvements, but if such affidavits be not filed within the time fixed by this section the burden of proof shall be upon the claimant to establish the performance of such annual work and improvements. And upon failure of the locator or owner of any such claim to comply with the provisions of this section, as to performance of work and improvements, such claim shall become forfeited and open to location by others as if no location of the same had ever been made. The affidavits required may be made before any officer authorized to administer oaths, and the provisions of sections 1621 and 1622 of title 18, are extended to such affidavits. Said affidavits shall be filed not later than ninety days after the close of the year in which such work is performed.

§ 50. Grants to States or corporations not to include mineral lands [R.S. § 2346]

No act passed at the first session of the Thirty-eighth Congress, granting lands to States or corporations to aid in the construction of roads or for other purposes, or to extend the time of grants made prior to the 30th day of January 1865 shall be so construed as to embrace mineral lands, which in all cases are reserved exclusively to the United States, unless otherwise specially provided in the act or acts making the grant.

§ 51. Water users' vested and accrued rights; enumeration of uses; protection of interest; rights-of-way for canals and ditches; liability for injury or damage to settlers' possession [R.S. § 2339]

Whenever, by priority of possession, rights to the use of water for mining, agricultural, manufacturing, or other purposes have vested and accrued, and the same are recognized and acknowledged by the local customs, laws, and the decisions of courts, the possessors and owners of such vested rights shall be maintained and protected in the same; and the right-of-way for the construction of ditches and canals for the purposes herein sepcified is acknowledged and confirmed; but whenever any person, in the construction of any ditch or canal, injures or damages the possession of any settler on the public domain, the party committing such injury or damage shall be liable to the party injured for such injury or damage.

§ 52. Patents or homesteads subject to vested and accrued water rights [R.S. § 2340]

All patents granted, or homesteads allowed, shall be subject to any vested and accrued water rights, or rights to ditches and reservoirs used in connection with such water rights, as may have been acquired under or recognized by section 51 of this title.

§ 54. Liability for damages to stock raising and homestead entries by mining activities

Notwithstanding the provisions of any Act of Congress to the contrary, any person who on and after June 21, 1949 prospects for, mines, or removes by strip or open pit mining methods, any minerals from any land included in a stock raising or other homestead entry or patent, and who had been liable under such an existing Act only for damages caused thereby to the crops or improvements of the entryman or patentee, shall also be liable for any damage that may be caused to the value of the land for grazing by such prospecting for, mining, or removal of minerals. Nothing in this section shall be considered to impair any vested right in existence on June 21, 1949.

§ 601. Rules and regulations governing disposal of materials; payment; removal without charge; lands excluded

The Secretary, under such rules and regulations as he may prescribe, may dispose of mineral materials (including but not limited to common varieties of the following: sand, stone, gravel, pumice, pumicite, cinders, and clay) and vegetative materials (including but not limited to yucca, manzanita, mesquite, cactus, and timber or other forest products) on public lands of the United States, including, for the purposes of this subchapter, land described in subchapter V of chapter 28 of title 43, if the disposal of such mineral or vegetative materials (1) is not otherwise expressly authorized by law, including, but not limited to, subchapter I of chapter 8A of title 43, and the United States mining laws, and (2) is not expressly prohibited by laws of the United States, and (3) would not be detrimental to the public interest. Such materials may be disposed of only in accordance with the provisions of this subchapter and upon the payment of adequate compensation therefor, to be determined by the Secretary: *Provided, however,* That, to the extent not otherwise authorized by law, the Secretary is authorized in his discretion to permit any Federal, State, or Territorial agency, unit or subdivision, including municipalities, or any association or corporation not organized for profit, to take and remove, without charge, materials and resources subject to this subchapter, for use other than for commercial or industrial purposes or resale. Where the lands have been withdrawn in aid of a function of a Federal department or agency other than the department headed by the Secretary or of a State, Territory, county, municipality, water district or other local governmental subdivision or agency, the Secretary may make disposals under this subchapter only with the consent of

such other Federal department or agency or of such State, Territory, or local governmental unit. Nothing in this subchapter shall be construed to apply to lands in any national park, or national monument or to any Indian lands, or lands set aside or held for the use or benefit of Indians, including lands over which jurisdiction has been transferred to the department of the Interior by Executive order for the use of Indians. As used in this subchapter, the word "Secretary" means the Secretary of the Interior except that it means the Secretary of Agriculture where the lands involved are administered by him for national forest purposes or for the purposes of title III of the Bankhead-Jones Farm Tenant Act [7 U.S.C. 1010 et seq.] or where withdrawn for the purpose of any other function of the Department of Agriculture.

§ 602. Bidding; advertising and other notice; conditions for negotiation of contract

(a) The Secretary shall dispose of materials under this subchapter to the highest responsible qualified bidder after formal advertising and such other public notice as he deems appropriate: *Provided, however,* That the Secretary may authorize negotiation of a contract for the disposal of materials if—

(1) the contract is for the sale of less than two hundred fifty thousand board-feet of timber; or, if

(2) the contract is for the disposal of materials to be used in connection with a public works improvement program on behalf of a Federal, State or local governmental agency and the public exigency will not permit the delay incident to advertising; or, if

(3) the contract is for the disposal of property for which it is impracticable to obtain competition.

(b) Repealed. Pub. L. 96-470, title I, § 102(a), Oct. 19, 1980, 94 Stat. 2237.

§ 604. Disposal of sand, peat moss, etc., in Alaska; contracts

Subject to the provisions of this subchapter, the Secretary may dispose of sand, stone, gravel, and vegetative materials located below highwater mark of navigable waters of the Territory of Alaska. Any contract, unexecuted in whole or in part, for the disposal under this subchapter of materials from land, title to which is transferred to a future State upon its admission to the Union, and which is situated within its boundaries, may be terminated or adopted by such State.

§ 611. Common varieties of sand, stone, gravel, pumice, pumicite, or cinders, and petrified wood

No deposit of common varieties of sand, stone, gravel, pumice, pumicite, or cinders and no deposit of petrified wood shall be deemed a valuable mineral deposit within the meaning of the mining laws of the United States so as to give effective validity to any mining claim hereafter located under such mining laws: *Provided, however,* That nothing herein shall affect the validity of any mining location based upon discovery of some other mineral occurring in or in association with such a deposit. "Common varieties" as used in this subchapter and sections 601 and 603 of this title does not include deposits of such materials which are valuable because the deposit has some property giving it distinct and special value and does not include so-called "block pumice" which occurs in nature in pieces having one dimension of two inches or more. "Petrified wood" as used in this subchapter and sections 601 and 603 of this title means agatized, opalized, petrified, or silicified wood, or any material formed by the replacement of wood by silica or other matter.

§ 612. Unpatented mining claims

(a) Prospecting, mining or processing operations

Any mining claim hereafter located under the mining laws of the United States shall not be used, prior to issuance of patent therefor, for any purposes other than prospecting, mining or processing operations and uses reasonably incident thereto.

(b) Reservations in the United States to use of the surface and surface resources

Rights under any mining claim hereafter located under the mining laws of the United States shall be subject, prior to issuance of patent therefor, to the right of the United States to manage and dispose of the vegetative surface resources thereof and to manage other surface resources thereof (except mineral deposits subject to location under the mining laws of the United States). Any such mining claim shall also be subject, prior to issuance of patent therefor, to the right of the United States, its permittees, and licensees, to use so much of the surface thereof as may be necessary for such purposes or for access to adjacent land: *Provided, however,* That any use of the surface of any such mining claim by the United States, its permittees or licensees, shall be such as not to endanger or materially interfere with prospecting, mining or processing operations or uses reasonably incident thereto: *Provided further,* That if at any time the locator requires more timber for his mining operations than is available to him from the claim after disposition of timber therefrom by the United States, subsequent to the location of the claim, he shall be entitled, free of charge, to be supplied with timber for such requirements from the nearest timber administered by the disposing agency which is ready for harvesting under the rules and regulations of that agency and which is substantially equivalent in kind and quantity to the timber estimated by the disposing agency to have been disposed of from the claim: *Provided further,* That nothing in this subchapter and sections 601 and 603 of this title shall be construed as affecting or intended to affect or in any way interfere with or modify the laws of the States which lie wholly or in part westward of the ninety-eighth meridian relating to the ownership, control, appropriation, use, and distribution of ground or surface waters within any unpatented mining claim.

(c) Severance or removal of timber

Except to the extent required for the mining claimant's prospecting, mining or processing operations and uses reasonably incident thereto, or for the construction of buildings or structures in connection therewith, or to provide clearance for such operations or uses, or to the extent authorized by the United States, no claimant of any mining claim hereafter located under the mining laws of the United States shall, prior to issuance of patent therefor, sever, remove, or use any vegetative or other surface resources thereof which are subject to management or disposition by the United States under subsection (b) of this section. Any severance or removal of timber which is permitted under the exceptions of the preceding sentence, other than severance or removal to provide clearance, shall be in accordance with sound principles of forest management.

§ 613. Procedure for determining title uncertainties

(a) Notice to mining claimants; request; publication; service

The head of a Federal department or agency which has the responsibility for administering surface resources of any lands belonging to the United States may file as to such lands in the office of the Secretary of the Interior, or in such office as the Secretary of the Interior may designate, a request for publication of notice to mining claimants, for determination of surface rights, which request shall contain a description of the lands covered thereby, showing the section or sections of the public land surveys which embrace the lands covered by such request, or if such lands are unsurveyed, either the section or sections which would probably embrace such lands when the public land surveys are extended to such lands or a tie by courses and distances to an approved United States mineral monument.

The filing of such request for publication shall be accompanied by an affidavit or affidavits of a person or persons over twenty-one years of age setting forth that the affiant or affiants have examined the lands involved in a reasonable effort to ascertain whether any person or persons were in actual possession of or engaged in the working of such lands or any part thereof, and, if no person or persons were found to be in actual possession of or engaged in the working of said lands or any part thereof on the date of such examination, setting forth such fact, or, if any person or persons were so found to be in actual possession or engaged in such working on the date of such examination, setting forth the name and address of each such person, unless affiant shall have been unable through reasonable inquiry to obtain information as to the name and address of any such person, in which event the affidavit shall set forth fully the nature and results of such inquiry.

The filing of such request for publication shall also be accompanied by the certificate of a title or abstract company, or of a title abstractor, or of an attorney, based upon such company's abstractor's, or attorney's examination of those instruments which are shown by the tract indexes in the county office of record as affecting the lands described in said request, setting forth the name of any person disclosed by said instruments to have an interest in said lands under any unpatented mining claim heretofore located, together with the address of such person if such address is disclosed by such instruments of record. "Tract indexes" as used herein shall mean those indexes, if any, as to surveyed lands identifying instruments as affecting a particular legal subdivision of the public land surveys, and as to unsurveyed lands identifying instruments as affecting a particular probable legal subdivision according to a projected extension of the public land surveys.

Thereupon the Secretary of the Interior, at the expense of the requesting department or agency, shall cause notice to mining claimants to be published in a newspaper having general circulation in the county in which the lands involved are situate.

Such notice shall describe the lands covered by such request, as provided heretofore, and shall notify whomever it may concern that if any person claiming or asserting under, or by virtue of, any unpatented mining claim heretofore located, rights as to such lands or any part thereof, shall fail to file in the office where such request for publication was filed (which office shall be specified in such notice) and within one hundred and fifty days from the date of the first publication of such notice (which date shall be specified in such notice), a verified statement which shall set forth, as to such unpatented mining claim—

(1) the date of location;

(2) the book and page of recordation of the notice or certificate of location;

(3) the section or sections of the public land surveys which embrace such mining claims; or if such lands are unsurveyed, either the section or sections which would probably embrace such mining claim when the public land surveys are extended to such lands or a tie by courses and distances to an approved United States mineral monument;

(4) whether such claimant is a locator or purchaser under such location; and

(5) the name and address of such claimant and names and addresses so far as known to the claimant of any other person or persons claiming any interest or interests in or under such unpatented mining claim;

such failure shall be conclusively deemed (i) to constitute a waiver and relinquishment by such mining claimant of any right, title, or interest under such mining claim contrary to or in conflict with the limitations or restrictions specified in section 612 of this title as to hereafter located unpatented mining claims, and (ii) to constitute a consent by such mining claimant that such mining claim, prior to issuance of patent therefor, shall be subject to the limitations and restrictions specified in section 612 of this title as to hereafter located unpatented mining claims, and (iii) to preclude thereafter, prior to issuance of patent, any assertion by such mining claimant of any right or title to or interest in or under such mining claim contrary to or in conflict with the limitations or restrictions specified in sec-

tion 612 of this title as to hereafter located unpatented mining claims.

If such notice is published in a daily paper, it shall be published in the Wednesday issue for nine consecutive weeks, or, if in a weekly paper, in nine consecutive issues, or if in a semiweekly or triweekly paper, in the issue of the same day of each week for nine consecutive weeks.

Within fifteen days after the date of first publication of such notice, the department or agency requesting such publication (1) shall cause a copy of such notice to be personally delivered to or to be mailed by registered mail or by certified mail addressed to each person in possession or engaged in the working of the land whose name and address is shown by an affidavit filed as aforesaid, and to each person who may have filed, as to any lands described in said notice, a request for notices, as provided in subsection (d) of this section, and shall cause a copy of such notice to be mailed by registered mail or by certified mail to each person whose name and address is set forth in the title or abstract company's or title abstractor's or attorney's certificate filed as aforesaid, as having an interest in the lands described in said notice under any unpatented mining claim heretofore located, such notice to be directed to such person's address as set forth in such certificate; and (2) shall file in the office where said request for publication was filed an affidavit showing that copies have been so delivered or mailed.

(b) Failure to file verified statement

If any claimant under any unpatented mining claim heretofore located which embraces any of the lands described in any notice published in accordance with the provisions of subsection (a) of this section, shall fail to file a verified statement, as provided in such subsection (a), within one hundred and fifty days from the date of the first publication of such notice, such failure shall be conclusively deemed, except as otherwise provided in subsection (e) of this section, (i) to constitute a waiver and relinquishment by such mining claimant of any right, title, or interest under such mining claim contrary to or in conflict with the limitations or restrictions specified in section 612 of this title as to hereafter located unpatented mining claims, and (ii) to constitute a consent by such mining claimant that such mining claim, prior to issuance of patent therefor, shall be subject to the limitations and restrictions specified in section 612 of this title as to hereafter located unpatented mining claims, and (iii) to preclude thereafter, prior to issuance of patent, any assertion by such mining claimant of any right or title to or interest in or under such mining claim contrary to or in conflict with the limitations or restrictions specified in section 612 of this title as to hereafter located unpatented mining claims.

(c) Hearings

If any verified statement shall be filed by a mining claimant as provided in subsection (a) of this section, then the Secretary of Interior shall fix a time and place for a hearing to determine the validity and effectiveness of any right or title to, or interest in or under such mining claim, which the mining claimant may assert contrary to or in conflict with the limitations and restrictions specified in section 612 of this title as to hereafter located unpatented mining claims, which place of hearing shall be in the county where the lands in question or parts thereof are located, unless the mining claimant agrees otherwise. Where verified statements are filed asserting rights to an aggregate of more than twenty mining claims, any single hearing shall be limited to a maximum of twenty mining claims unless the parties affected shall otherwise stipulate and as many separate hearing[s] shall be set as shall be necessary to comply with this provision. The procedures with respect to notice of such a hearing and the conduct thereof, and in respect to appeals shall follow the then established general procedures and rules of practice of the Department of the Interior in respect to contests or protests affecting public lands of the United States. If, pursuant to such a hearing the final decision rendered in the matter shall affirm the validity and effectiveness of any mining claimant's so asserted right or interest under

the mining claim, then no subsequent proceedings under this section shall have any force or effect upon the so-affirmed right or interest of such mining claimant under such mining claim. If at any time prior to a hearing the department or agency requesting publication of notice and any person filing a verified statement pursuant to such notice shall so stipulate, then to the extent so stipulated, but only to such extent, no hearing shall be held with the respect to rights asserted under that verified statement, and to the extent defined by the stipulation the rights asserted under that verified statement shall be deemed to be unaffected by that particular published notice.

(d) Request for copy of notice

Any person claiming any right under or by virtue of any unpatented mining claim heretofore located and desiring to receive a copy of any notice to mining claimants which may be published as provided in subsection (a) of this section, and which may affect lands embraced in such mining claim, may cause to be filed for record in the county office of record where the notice or certificate of location of such mining claim shall have been recorded, a duly acknowledged request for a copy of any such notice. Such request for copies shall set forth the name and address of the person requesting copies and shall also set forth, as to each heretofore located unpatented mining claim under which such person asserts rights—

(1) the date of location;

(2) the book and page of the recordation of the notice or certificate of location; and

(3) the section or sections of the public land surveys which embrace such mining claim; or if such lands are unsurveyed, either the section or sections which would probably embrace such mining claim when the public land surveys are extended to such lands or a tie by courses and distances to an approved United States mineral monument.

Other than in respect to the requirements of

subsection (a) of this section as to personal delivery or mailing of copies of notices and in respect to the provisions of subsection (e) of this section, no such request for copies of published notices and no statement or allegation in such request and no recordation thereof shall affect title to any mining claim or to any land or be deemed to constitute constructive notice to any person that the person requesting copies has, or claims, any right, title, or interest in or under any mining claim referred to in such request.

(e) Failure to deliver or mail copy of notice

If any department or agency requesting publication shall fail to comply with the requirements of subsection (a) of this section as to the personal delivery or mailing of a copy of notice to any person, the publication of such notice shall be deemed wholly ineffectual as to that person or as to the rights asserted by that person and the failure of that person to file a verified statement, as provided in such notice, shall in no manner affect, diminish, prejudice or bar any rights of that person.

§ 614. Waiver of rights

The owner or owners of any unpatented mining claim heretofore located may waive and relinquish all rights thereunder which are contrary to or in conflict with the limitations or restrictions specified in section 612 of this title as to hereafter located unpatented mining claims. The execution and acknowledgment of such a wiaver and relinquishment by such owner or owners and the recordation thereof in the office where the notice or certificate of location of such mining claim is of

record shall render such mining claim thereafter and prior to issuance of patent subject to the limitations and restrictions in section 612 of this title in all respects as if said mining claim had been located after July 23, 1955, but no such waiver or relinquishment shall be deemed in any manner to constitute any concession as to the date of priority of rights under said mining claim or as to the validity thereof.

§ 615. Limitation of existing rights

Nothing in this subchapter and sections 601 and 603 of this title shall be construed in any manner to limit or restrict or to authorize the limitation or restriction of any existing rights of any claimant under any valid mining claim heretofore located, except as such rights may be limited or restricted as a result of a proceeding pursuant to section 613 of this title, or as a result of a waiver and relinquishment pursuant to section 614 of this title; and nothing in this subchapter and sections 601 and 603 of this title shall be construed in any manner to authorized inclusion in any patent hereafter issued under the mining laws of the United States for any mining claim heretofore or hereafter located, of any reservation, limitation, or restriction not otherwise authorized by law, or to limit or repeal any existing authority to include any reservation, limitation, or restriction in any such patent, or to limit or restrict any use of the lands covered by any patented or unpatented mining claim by the United States, its lessees, permittees, and licensees which is otherwise authorized by law.